DICTIONARY
OF LANGUAGES

DICTIONARY
OF LANGUAGES

The Definitive Reference to more than 400 Languages

Andrew Dalby

BLOOMSBURY

First published in 1998 by
Bloomsbury Publishing plc
38 Soho Square
London W1V 5DF

A copy of the CIP entry for this book
is available from the British Library

ISBN 07475 3117 X

3 5 7 9 10 8 6 4 2

Typeset by Hewer Text Ltd, Edinburgh
Printed by Clays Ltd, St Ives plc

PREFACE

The language and language family headings in this book are in alphabetical order from Abkhaz to Zulu. Cross-references are given in SMALL CAPITALS. Maps, and sometimes boxes listing numerals or other examples, often bring together information on two or three related languages: the cross-references always serve as a guide.

It has usually been possible to give at least the numerals, 1 to 10, as an example of the way a language looks and sounds. Other information often displayed adjacent to the text includes foreign scripts and their equivalents in the familiar Latin alphabet. A surprising number of these scripts can now be found as TrueType fonts on the World Wide Web (see acknowledgements on p. 734).

This book is not designed as a bibliography or reading list. Often, however, information and examples in the language entries are drawn from sources to which an interested reader could go to find out more. Thus, wherever it may be useful, full references to sources have been given.

Putting sounds on paper

No ordinarily used writing system is adequate for recording all the sounds of any and all human languages. Alphabets as short as the Greek (24 letters) or the familiar Latin alphabet (26 letters) are not fully adequate even for most single languages. English, for example, by the usual count has about 40 'phonemes' or structurally distinct sounds.

Linguists therefore use special extended alphabets to record pronunciation precisely. The commonest is the International Phonetic Alphabet (IPA). Specialists in some language families have their own conventional alphabets and signs (see box at MORDVIN for an example).

Since the IPA has to be learnt, and this book is intended for non-specialists, the IPA has not been used here.

Languages that are usually written in the Latin alphabet are written here according to their usual spelling. For Chinese the official Pinyin transliteration is given, and for the languages of India I have kept close to the standard agreed at an Orientalist Congress a century ago. Languages usually written in other alphabets have been transliterated into Latin, giving the consonants the sounds they usually have in English, and the vowels the following sounds:

a   like *a* in English *father*
i   like *i* in English *machine*
u   like *oo* in English *boot*
e   midway between *ea* of *bear* and *i* of *machine*
o   midway between *oa* of *boar* and *oo* of *boot*

An additional consonant is familiar from non-standard English:

'   this apostrophe is often used for a glottal stop, the consonant that replaces *t* as the third sound in the London colloquial pronunciation of *butter*.

Three symbols have been borrowed from the IPA for sounds that are not easily distinguished otherwise:

ə   Often called by its Hebrew name *schwa*, this is the second vowel of English *father*
ɛ   The open *e* sound of English *bear*
ɔ   The open *o* sound of English *boar*

Three additional symbols, familiar in German and Turkish, have been used frequently in this book for sounds not found in English but common in many other languages:

ɪ   The vowel of Russian мы 'we'. To imitate it, say 'ugh' while gritting your teeth
ö   The vowel of French *coeur* 'heart' and German *hör* 'listen!' Make the 'uhh' sound of hesitation while rounding your lips
ü   The vowel of French *mur* 'wall' and German *für* 'for'. Say 'ee' while pursing your lips tightly

A dot below a consonant usually makes it a *retroflex consonant*, one that is formed with the tongue turned back towards the roof of the mouth – these are the sounds that help to typify an 'Indian accent' in speaking English, and they are indeed found in most Indian languages.

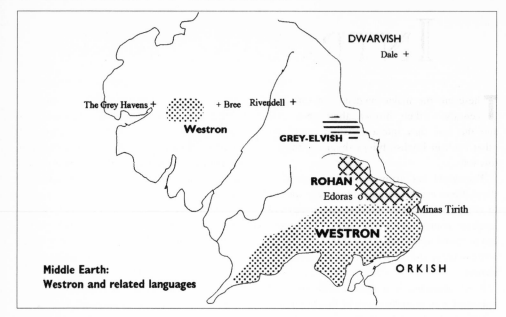

Middle Earth:
Westron and related languages

A line above a vowel makes it long. An acute accent on a vowel means that stress falls on that syllable. In tonal languages, however, these and similar signs have sometimes been used to mark tones: ˉ for high level, ´ for rising, ` for falling, and an underline for low level tone.

In general, to make easier reading, words usually written with a forest of accents are accented only on the first occasion that they are used.

The statistics

Unless otherwise stated, the figures in this book give the number of 'native' or 'mother tongue' speakers for each language. Some, from English and French to Amharic and Tagalog, are spoken by many millions more as second languages. This is one reason why statistics in different reference books may seem to conflict (see also 'Facts, real facts and statistics', p. xiii).

The maps

Language boundaries are not like national boundaries: languages spread, and overlap, in a way that only very detailed statistical maps can show accurately. The two hundred maps in this book show simply and clearly where each language is spoken and, if possible, its nearest neighbours. Nearly all the maps are drawn to a standard scale – 320 miles to the inch. Just as the statistics allow a comparison of native speakers for each language, so the maps show what area of the earth each language covers.

Each map deals with a language or language group, and these are named in bold face. Shading indicates the main areas where these languages are spoken. Isolated places where the same languages can be heard are marked with a cross. Other neighbouring languages, not closely related to these, are named in lighter type. Major cities are marked by a circle. As an example, this map of J. R. R. Tolkien's Middle Earth shades the areas where Westron, Grey-Elvish and the language of Rohan are spoken.

There are a few smaller scale maps (for example, the map of 'Language families of the world' on pp. xii–xiii). All these are at the scale of 1,000 miles to the inch. Italic face is used in lettering these maps as an eye-catching reminder of the difference in scale.

INTRODUCTION

These are the major languages of the 20th century – their history, their geography and the way they interact. Astonishingly, no other book in English brings them together in this way.

The world has many more languages than these. From over five thousand that are spoken in 1997, a selected four hundred languages and language groups have entries here. Many more can be found in the index, but they are still only a minority of the total number of living languages.

Every language is a unique and uniquely important way to make sense of the world; but a choice had to be made. The languages selected here are those spoken by the great majority of the people of the world. These are the languages that the 20th century needs to know about *first*: national languages of independent countries, languages of important minorities that will make news, classical languages of the past. Most entries are for languages with more than a million speakers. Some, such as English, Spanish, Arabic, Russian and Chinese, are spoken by hundreds of millions.

All the languages that have *not* been given entries in this book have fewer than a million speakers. Some have only one or two speakers, and many that were until recently spoken by thriving communities are now extinct. This is an accelerating trend. It is easy to foresee a time, perhaps a hundred years ahead or less, when most of the languages left out of this book will not be spoken at all, and when many of those included will – so to speak – be struggling for speakers.

As a language falls out of use, one of those unique ways of making sense of the world is lost.

Why languages grow apart

All 'living languages' or 'mother tongues' – all the languages that children learn when they first learn to speak – are continually changing. The change happens in at least two ways: for language change comes from the very nature of childhood learning, and also from the demands that we make, throughout life, on the astonishingly flexible medium of communication that language is.

Look first at the way children learn to speak.

Language is a palette of sounds, a dictionary of words made up of those sounds, and a grammar of rules for combining the words meaningfully. Usually we are unaware of the making of sounds, the choosing of words and the applying of rules, yet this is how we speak and this is how we understand what others say. Every child that learns to speak practises sounds, builds up a dictionary, and works out a set of rules. Every child does all this largely unconsciously, with incomplete help and unreliable guidance from parents and friends and teachers who, themselves, are only half conscious of the rules. Every child does this *afresh*. The range of people from whom each child learns is different. And children are not clones of one another.

Thus everyone's sound patterns, everyone's dictionary and everyone's language rules are original and slightly different from everyone else's. This is how change and originality are built into the nature of human language learning. And this, incidentally, is why the 'grammar of a language', as opposed to the grammar of a single person's speech, is an abstract formulation – a highly useful one that we simply cannot do without when we want a standard language, or a foreign language, to be taught.

Since those living in a community interact most with others in the same community, everyday speech in any one community tends, over time, to diverge from that in others. We notice the differences: we talk of the 'accent' or of the 'dialect' of those whose speech uses identifiably different sound patterns, different words or different grammatical rules – though still so close to our own that we can understand it easily. Aus-tralian English and British English have grown apart, quite distinctly, in little over a hundred years.

When most people lived all their lives in a single community, travelling little and seldom meeting outsiders, the language of a region – which might once have been 'the same' lan-guage – steadily differentiated into distinct local dialects. As the process continued, the dialects eventually became so different that speakers of one could not understand speakers of another. When this point is reached, then – by one often-used definition – we are not dealing with sep-arate dialects any longer but with separate lan-guages.

This is the single overriding reason for the great number of languages in the world today, and the effect is well demonstrated by the fact that a great many very different languages, each with small numbers of speakers, tend to be found in mountainous regions where communi-cations are difficult, such as the Caucasus and the southern valleys of the Himalayas.

Why languages converge

But there are influences in the opposite direction too. If those who travel for study or work, and those who pay attention to press, radio and television, begin to make up a large proportion of the population, they will limit the tendency for community dialects to diverge. And those who want to make a good impression – as ex-amination candidates or job applicants or em-ployees or traders or politicians or preachers –

have to limit the extent to which their own accent or dialect or choice of words will distract others from their message.

Thus the second process of language change takes effect – in which older children and adults continually adjust their speech to their hearers' expectations, in order to get a message across. Speakers pick up new words, new phrases and new tones of voice from those around them. They imitate not only others who are speaking 'the same' language, but also those speaking a different dialect (perhaps a more prestigious one, the dialect of a capital city or a university), or indeed a completely different language (per-haps the language used in government or in an army or in business). We can, of course, learn several languages and keep them apart. But in practice we also need to mix them. The English that is standard in India has always differed in vocabulary from British English: the special vocabulary is naturally used, just as it was under British rule, in speaking of concepts that belong to the politics and way of life of the subconti-nent.

How many dialects, how many dialect speak-ers make up a language? There is no answer to this question. The hundreds of millions of speakers of English speak it in very different ways, but all recognise what is in practical terms the same standard for writing and formal speech. Some African standard languages, such as TSONGA and Ronga, or EWE and Fon, differ from one another far less than do the local dialects of English: yet, given no overall literary or political unity, those who first devised their written forms had no basis on which to develop a standard language covering several dialects, while the speakers of any one dialect had no reason to attend to, or to respect, those who used an unfamiliar dialect.

Tracing language history

Every language displays, to the practised eye or ear, some of its own history: words clearly bor-rowed from other languages; voice inflections, and turns of phrase, that seem to be shared by two adjacent but otherwise very different languages. These are among the phenomena of language convergence.

The more pervasive, more regular phenomena of language change – those of divergence – can also be traced and reconstructed.

Historical linguistics uses three forms of evidence. Comparisons are pursued between two or more known languages that appear to share a range of vocabulary and a set of grammatical rules. Written texts, preserved from an earlier period, are explored to reconstruct the sounds and patterns of the spoken language that lay behind them. The recorded history of peoples and their migrations is searched for possibilities as to when languages diverged and how they reached their known locations on the map. If all three forms of evidence are available, all three will be used and they will all act as controls on one another.

One result of this kind of interactive research is that it gives a clearer understanding of human history – of the way that people have 'constructed' their own 'identity' (as we might say now), linguistic, cultural, tribal, national, ethnic, racial. Where did they think that they belonged? What was their view of those who did not belong? What was the upshot – between cultural mergers and wars of extermination?

There are other results. The older written texts will be better understood, or understood for the first time. The recorded history will be reinterpreted, and something will be learnt of the silent majority whose lives and travels do not get into recorded history. A language history will be built up, tracing the two or more known languages back to the 'ancestral' language from which they diverged.

The next step seems to follow naturally. Even if the ancestral language was never recorded – no written texts – it now becomes conceivable to reconstruct it. This means building up a sound system, a grammatical system and a list of words and meanings which, after language change and divergence, would have resulted in the forms that actually exist in the two or more languages from which the investigation began.

In scholarly work, by convention, reconstructed words from unrecorded forms of language are marked with a *. The box at INDO-EUROPEAN gives some examples.

The reconstruction is a 'formula'. It may explain the known forms; it may do so in the neatest possible way; it may be open to confirmation or disproof when a third or fourth related language is brought into the comparison. Still, if there are no written records, nothing can prove that it represents a real language that was actually spoken at some time. The controls on the reconstruction process are weak (we can ask whether the processes of change that have been hypothesised can be shown ever to have occurred in recorded language change; whether the sound system and grammatical system that are hypothesised fit the pattern of known languages; and, finally, whether the reconstruction will fit in to more ambitious reconstructions of even earlier ancestral languages).

What do proto-languages mean in historical terms?

Hypothetical as they are, such reconstructions are used to build even shakier structures. Beyond the reach of recorded history, language relationships are compared with archaeology to retrace the prehistoric movements of languages – on the twin assumptions that these must relate to migrations of peoples, and that those in turn must relate to ceramic styles or burial customs or food choices or other human habits that happen to leave buried evidence. Wordlists are used to rebuild the environment of speakers of ancestral languages – and to evaluate their 'cultural level' and technological prowess.

At a conference on the BANTU LANGUAGES, a teasing question by an archaeologist led two linguists to pin down their view of linguistic reconstruction:

PIERRE DE MARET: Is proto-Bantu a theoretical construct, or is it a language that was spoken at a certain time, at a certain place? If the linguists tell us that it's that, we can go and dig for it.

A.-E. MEEUSSEN: It seems a bit bold to say 'both'; but that's roughly the right answer. There's more than one way of looking at the question, but, when you come down to it, there must have been a more or less unified language, during some shorter or longer period, which is the origin of the Bantu languages of today.

But the most certain facts in all this are the ones that are least useful to you. There was certainly a root -*di* 'eat' and almost certainly an infinitive *kuda* 'to eat' and so on. Around this nucleus there are further details that are far less certain: vocabulary dealing with technology, with the minutiae of everyday life. We know much less about these. And there must have been further features of the language that we know nothing at all about . . .

CLAIRE GRÉGOIRE: Like M. Meeussen, I think that there must have been a single, relatively unified language, spoken somewhere. I don't see that it matters all that much to you archaeologists whether it was exactly the same as what we reconstruct in the abstract and call 'proto-Bantu', or whether it was something a little different.

P. DE MARET: You see, if it turns out that proto-Bantu has a time depth, if what you're giving us is a telescoped proto-Bantu but we're supposed to understand that the language was actually evolving, for half a millennium, somewhere in the Grassfields [of Cameroun], this may make a big difference to where we locate proto-Bantu vis-à-vis other known languages.

C. GRÉGOIRE: No, we certainly mustn't imagine that proto-Bantu just sprang into view somewhere. Proto-Bantu itself was evolving from something earlier, and so on and so on. The time depth is there. We haven't got it measured, but it's there. People didn't suddenly start out speaking a new language.

L'expansion bantoue: Viviers (France) 4–16 avril 1977 ed. Larry M. Hyman, Jan Voorhoeve, Luc Bouquiaux (Paris: SELAF, 1980) p. 730

How to use languages

In a sense, there is no such thing as a 'flair for languages' – or, if there is, we all have it. If you have learned to speak your mother tongue, you have proved that you have the ability to learn languages.

But you spent a long time learning it. If you

were lucky enough to grow up bilingual, you have spent a long time learning both languages. Not necessarily a long time in the classroom – not necessarily any time at all in formal language learning – but a long time, several solid years by any count, listening and speaking, sometimes being corrected, more often correcting yourself.

Mithradates: father of multilingualism

In 1784 Catherine the Great, Empress of Russia, initiated a research project to collect lists of about 225 common words from the languages of the world, and especially from the Russian Empire. The lists were eventually published in Adelung and Vater's compilation *Mithridates oder allgemeine Sprachkunde*.

Any classically educated nineteenth-century reader would have known why the book was called *Mithradates*. King Mithradates Eupator of Pontus (132–63 BC), who fought against the Romans and was defeated by Pompey, spoke twenty-two languages. He is the first historical figure famous for multilingual skills.

The way to retain the ability to learn languages is to go on using it. The younger that children are when they learn a second language, the more easily they will learn it, and the third language will come easier still. Unfortunately, youth isn't everything. They also have to *need* to learn the new language, and to *need* to practise it. In learning languages we are harnessing a skill that is inborn in human beings – but laziness, the least effort for the most reward, is also inborn in us, and if we can get by with one language, we will. In many countries in the world children are now growing up trilingual: they learn a local mother tongue, then a national language, then English. They are not three times as intelligent as children whose mother tongue is English: but they *need* to use these languages, in successive stages of education, and they *need* to practise their linguistic skills when reading and watching television, when going about a city, and when dealing with businesses and government offices. Most English-speaking children, in Britain and

North America and some other countries, can get by entirely with English: so most of them do, and relatively few of them ever learn a second language really well.

When learning a language, as a child or an adult, we need to know why we are learning it – and we need to practise it.

That the country needs linguists, and that a school curriculum demands a foreign language, are both good reasons for learning a foreign language – but they may not be quite good enough to overcome the laziness. Learning a language is hard work. That one needs to use the language in everyday life is the best reason, and the best opportunity, for learning it. Children, or college students, from a monolingual country have the best opportunity to learn a foreign language if they live abroad. And it is only a minority of British or North American children who do this.

So far we have talked of 'learning a language' – meaning, I suppose, learning to speak it, to understand it when spoken, to write it, to read it and to know something of the culture that underlies the written word. The learning process may continue until one speaks the language 'like a native'. It is a process that never ends: in a foreign language, as in one's own, there are always new words, and whole new sub-cultures, just about to be invented or patiently waiting to be discovered.

But apart from 'learning a language' whole, we also have the ability to learn a language selectively, and this ability is worth cultivating. It is used, most obviously, by those who learn a classical language. Many people, in many countries, learn Latin or classical Greek or Pali or Sanskrit. They learn to read the literature of those languages. Very few of them learn to speak the languages fluently: for most, that would be a useless skill.

Many develop this kind of knowledge of modern languages too. 'Language for special purposes' is now a recognised field of teaching – for business purposes, or for the ability to assimilate a technical text in one's own specialised field, or simply to understand essentials and make oneself understood when travelling.

But a good many linguists will agree that there is a threshold beyond which the learning of a language seems to develop a momentum of its own. Even after one has begun to learn a language for a very simple or specialised reason, the fascination of understanding more and more of a foreign way of life, its culture and its literature, takes hold.

The names of languages

Most people who speak English can happily call it 'English'. Though England is the name of a geographical region, it is not the name of a nation state, and speakers do not feel excluded or politicised by the term 'English'.

Language and political theory

The old Soviet Union was in some ways relatively enlightened in its handling of minority languages and their statistics. But the concept of *Language of the USSR* caused serious anomalies. German, spoken by millions in the USSR, was excluded from lists and from privileges because it was the national language of another sovereign state. The language of Moldavia had to be called 'Moldavian' to make it a separate language from Romanian. Tajik had to be similarly classed as a separate language from Persian-Dari. On the other hand Yiddish, Romani, Kurdish and Aramaic were allowed the all-important status of Language of the USSR because, even if the majority of their speakers lived in other countries, they had not the status of national languages in those countries.

The European Union has a similar ideological problem. Its Office of Minority Languages has to call Albanian *Arbëresh* when it is spoken in Italy and *Arvanitika* when it is spoken in Greece.

With many other languages it is not so simple. Until the 1940s the lingua franca of the southeast Asian archipelago was called 'Malay' by nearly everybody. For newly independent Indonesia the term had been found unsuitable because of its connection with Malaya, still Brit-

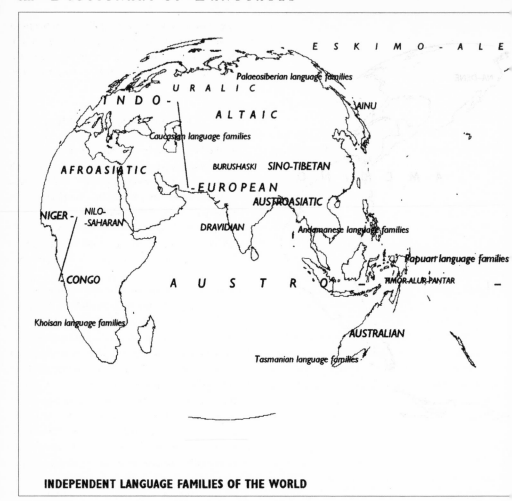

INDEPENDENT LANGUAGE FAMILIES OF THE WORLD

ish-ruled. So the form of Malay that became the national language of Indonesia had to be called 'Indonesian' – and independent Malaysia, incorporating Malaya and three other British territories, had to follow suit and call its language 'Malaysian'. It is still 'Malay' in Singapore and Brunei.

Thus language names often carry a political charge. In this book the headings chosen will not please everybody. I have tried, however, to be uncontroversial. For national or minority languages of a single state I have usually chosen the current official name used in that state, or an obvious English equivalent. For languages that are more widely spoken I have preferred a neutral term if any exists, and I have always

tried to explain, and index, the different names that are in use. Sometimes a language will have a different name in each of the different countries in which it is used.

Linguists (like other social scientists) love to invent words. Sometimes they have done so to solve this very problem: see MANDEKAN for an example. More often, linguists have invented names for language groups and families – and they have felt free to change the names whenever their view of a language relationship changes. So we have Semito-Hamitic, Hamito-Semitic, AFROASIATIC, Afrasian and Erythraic, all as alternative names for the same language family. The headings chosen here for language families are not intended to promote any parti-

specifically, but I have generally called the most inclusive, generally recognised language groupings 'families': I have not used the terms 'stock' and 'phylum' that some linguists prefer for designating very large groupings.

Facts, real facts and statistics

At the head of each entry an estimate of number of speakers appears. This is intended as a rough estimate of the number of people for whom this is the mother tongue or first language. The figures must be treated with suspicion.

Some of them come from national censuses. Are they accurate? That depends on what question was asked, how it was understood, and, besides, on a whole range of more emotive issues. In some countries there may be a cachet in claiming to adhere to a minority language which is actually falling out of use. In Ireland the IRISH language is a national symbol. Of the 1,000,000 who say they know it, how many can or do use it regularly? In many countries where nationalism is to the fore it may be safest to claim to speak the majority language even when one uses another mother tongue nearly all the time. This will swell the figures for languages like GREEK and TURKISH. In others again, minority areas may not be reached by any census.

Other figures – especially in countries where minority statistics are not officially published, or where certain minorities are not officially admitted to exist – come from non-official social and linguistic research. Usually these figures are extrapolated from sample surveys or from localised fieldwork. Sometimes they will turn out to go back to nothing more than hearsay. See AZERI (language of Azerbaijan, also spoken by a minority of unknown size in Iran) for an example of the resulting variation.

There will certainly be inaccuracies in the statistics in this book. What matters more than the statistics is the fact that language does not correspond with national frontiers, in spite of the increasing barbarism with which, over the last two centuries, human beings have fought and killed with the aim of making the two coincide.

cular view, but are in general the most widely used.

In some schools of linguistic research there is a custom of designing the names of proposed language groups to match a hierarchy – just like the different Latin terminations used by botanists and zoologists to distinguish sub-families, families and orders. Evidently such hierarchies are a useful tool for botanists and zoologists. For linguists they are more misleading, because language relationships do not work like that. I have not always bothered to mention such designer terms as *Hellenic* for GREEK and *Bodic* and *Bodish* for TIBETAN and its relatives (ugly names, these). I have used the terms 'family', 'branch' and 'group' without trying to pin them down too

Let's hope that the aim will never be achieved: for minorities and multilingualism are essential to human relations, on a community scale and on a world scale.

Language families of the world

If humans are genetically endowed with language, then, logically, all languages are related. This doesn't mean the relationship can be traced. This listing and the map on pp. xii–xiii show the families, and the single languages, mentioned in this book which have not yet been convincingly shown to be related to one another. When all languages have been shown to be related, a revised version of this map and list will have only one entry.

Single languages which have not been proved to be related to any others are known as 'linguistic isolates'. Several are included here. But in the present state of our knowledge it is not sensible to try to draw a complete map of linguistic isolates. In addition to the few that are well known in linguistic literature (Ainu, Basque, Burushaski, Ket, etc.) there are many little-studied languages in Asia, Africa, New Guinea and the Americas for which no linguistic relationships have been discovered. Only a few of these will really be isolates. Most of them will eventually be shown to belong to one or other known family – if ever they are fully recorded and investigated before they cease to be spoken.

AFROASIATIC LANGUAGES

Ainu (see JAPANESE)

ALTAIC LANGUAGES, probably including TURKIC, MONGOLIAN and Tungusic languages (see MANCHU) and perhaps KOREAN and JAPANESE

AMERIND LANGUAGES, a family grouping that remains highly controversial, may perhaps include ALGONQUIAN LANGUAGES, ARAUCANIAN, AYMARA, Iroquoian languages (see CHEROKEE), MAYAN LANGUAGES, QUECHUA, Uto-Aztecan languages (see NAHUATL) and many others

Angan languages (see PAPUAN LANGUAGES)

AUSTRALIAN LANGUAGES

AUSTROASIATIC LANGUAGES

AUSTRO-TAI LANGUAGES, probably including AUSTRONESIAN LANGUAGES, Miao-Yao languages (see MIAO and YAO) and KADAI LANGUAGES

Burushaski (see DRAVIDIAN LANGUAGES)

Central and South New Guinean languages (see PAPUAN LANGUAGES)

Chukotko-Kamchatkan languages (see PALAEOSIBERIAN LANGUAGES)

Dani-Kwerba languages (see PAPUAN LANGUAGES)

DRAVIDIAN LANGUAGES

East New Guinea Highlands languages (see PAPUAN LANGUAGES)

ESKIMO-ALEUT LANGUAGES

Great Andamanese languages (see AUSTROASIATIC LANGUAGES)

Hadza (see KHOISAN LANGUAGES)

Huon-Finisterre languages (see PAPUAN LANGUAGES)

INDO-EUROPEAN LANGUAGES

Kartvelian or South Caucasian languages (see GEORGIAN and MINGRELIAN)

Ket (see PALAEOSIBERIAN LANGUAGES)

Khwe languages (see KHOISAN LANGUAGES)

Little Andamanese languages (see AUSTROASIATIC LANGUAGES)

NA-DENÉ LANGUAGES

Nakh or North Central Caucasian languages (see CHECHEN)

NIGER-CONGO LANGUAGES

Nihali (see AUSTROASIATIC LANGUAGES)

NILO-SAHARAN LANGUAGES

Nivkh or Gilyak (see PALAEOSIBERIAN LANGUAGES)

North East CAUCASIAN LANGUAGES

Northern San languages (see KHOISAN LANGUAGES)

North West Caucasian languages (see ABKHAZ and CIRCASSIAN)

Sepik-Ramu languages (see PAPUAN LANGUAGES)

SINO-TIBETAN LANGUAGES

Southern San languages (see KHOISAN LANGUAGES)

Tasmanian languages (see AUSTRALIAN LANGUAGES)

Timor-Alur-Pantar languages (see MALAY)

URALIC LANGUAGES

West Papuan languages (see TERNATE)
Wissel Lakes-Kemandoga languages (see PA-
PUAN LANGUAGES)
Yukaghir (see PALAEOSIBERIAN LANGUAGES)

Questions and answers

Most of the time, our use of language is
unconscious: we say what we mean, and understand what others mean, without concentrating
on the sounds or the individual words or their
grammar – and we learnt to do most of this
unconsciously, 'instinctively'. This leaves a
surprisingly wide field for misunderstandings
and misstatements about the way language
works.

Is language change wrong? You're entitled to
your moral views. But change is built into language, into the way we learn it and the way we
use it. It cannot be prevented.

Do some people speak ungrammatically?
'Grammar' is the sequence of rules through
which human speech is produced. So the answer is no. We all have a built-in grammar, or
several grammars, for the different languages
and speech registers that we use. But when you
are beginning a new language, your grammar
may at first be so different from the one you
are aiming at that no one can understand
you . . .

Should parents correct children's speech? Yes:
by example. Children have to learn to interact
with others effectively.

**Should parents teach children a different way of
speaking from their own?** Probably not, unless
the parents can speak it fluently.

Should teachers correct children's speech? In
every country children need to know at least
one standard language if they are to succeed in
everyday adult life. Schools that do not teach a
standard language are failing in a crucial part of
their job. Schools that punish children for using
the language they learnt at home – whether
Welsh, Black English, a Sign Language (just
three examples from recent history) or any other
– are also failing them. Human beings are naturally multilingual. No one needs to speak the
same language in a job interview as when chat-
ting with friends or family. A school's primary
linguistic task is to *add* the standard language of
their country to children's developing linguistic
skills.

Should schools teach grammar? Yes. We *can* learn
to speak without learning any grammar formally.
But to learn to speak and write our standard
language, or a foreign language, effectively, we
need a basic understanding of grammar.

**Are some languages unable to deal with modern
civilisation?** People use the languages they need.
If a new skill, such as car maintenance or abstract
mathematics or spice cookery, is demanded of
the speakers of a language which has no technical terms for such things, they will learn and
use the necessary words.

Are some languages more difficult than others?
In the abstract, no. Whatever language they learn
from those around them, whether it is English or
Chinese or Nahuatl, by the age of about seven
children have learnt it pretty well. Writing systems, which are conscious inventions, differ from
natural language. Chinese script really is much
more difficult to learn than alphabets like Latin
or Arabic.

When we learn a new language in later life, it
will be easier if it is close in structure and
vocabulary to one we already know. There are
some languages that even practised linguists
have found unusually difficult – BASQUE and
KHOISAN LANGUAGES among them.

Should we speak the way we write? Historically,
speech comes first and is the most natural use of
language. We need to speak to inform, interest
and persuade others. Doing this effectively often
means using a style that is different from our
written language.

Is it difficult for children to grow up bilingual? In
most communities it is necessary and natural. In
some, notably among English speakers in Britain
and the United States, bilingualism is very rare
and quite difficult to achieve, not because children are less intelligent or less gifted linguistically, but because the environment they grow up
in is not naturally bilingual.

Does our language affect the way we think? Yes.
But anyone can learn another language.

The survival of ancient language

A language is no less of a language if it is unwritten, and a literature is no less of a literature if it is transmitted by speech rather than in books. But many alphabets, syllabaries and ideographic scripts are illustrated in this book.

Different peoples have found very different reasons for their first use of writing. No simple generalisation holds. Apparently, some written cultures (Linear A, Mycenaean Greek) began with a need for accounting systems, some (Latin) for the fixing of laws, some (Persian, Thai, Turkic) for the recording of royal achievements, some (Classical Greek, according to one theory) for epics or genealogies, some (Pali) for scriptures. In many cases, though, we cannot be sure what was the first impulse. Texts may be intended to serve a single occasion or to last for a month, a year, a generation or a lifetime. Of the more ephemeral of older writings, only a small sample now survives.

Ancient literature survives in some languages because writing material was chosen that has happened to last, like the baked clay tablets of the Near East, the papyrus of Egypt and the paper of central Asia; in others, it survives only because the literature was valued for a long time and later copies replaced the older ones. This is the case with nearly all of Greek, Latin, Hebrew, Avestan, Sanskrit, Pali and Chinese literature. In all of these, we know that masses of early writings are lost and will surely never be rediscovered. Stone inscriptions last well, but even they are subject to erosion and to the reuse of the stone. It took a bold author to feel so confident of the power of his work as to write, on a papyrus roll many of which he had seen erased or destroyed:

Exegi monumentum aere perennius	I have built a monument more lasting than bronze
regalique situ pyramidum altius,	And taller than the pyramids' royal skyline –
quod non imber edax, non Aquilo impotens	One that no hungry rain, no thin North Wind
possit diruere aut innumerabilis	Shall destroy, nor the uncountable
annorum series et fuga temporum.	Succession of years and the flight of time.

Q. Horatius Flaccus ('Horace', Latin poet of the 1st century BC), *Odes* iii.30

DICTIONARY
OF LANGUAGES

ABKHAZ AND ABAZA

300,000 SPEAKERS

Georgia, Turkey, Russia

A group of five dialects, belonging to the family of North West CAUCASIAN LANGUAGES, is spoken in the north-western extremity of Georgia, among mountains that slope steeply down to the Black Sea coast, and across the Caucasian watershed in the Cherkess republic of Russia. There may be 100,000 or more Abkhaz speakers in Turkey, and others in Syria, whose ancestors had fled to the Ottoman Empire to escape Christian rule when Russia conquered this part of the Caucasus in 1864. Since Georgia became independent from the Soviet Union, Abkhaz speakers (though a minority in the administrative district of Abkhazia) have been fighting the Georgians for their own independence, with military support from Russia.

The dialects of Georgia are conventionally classed as 'Abkhaz', and many speakers are bilingual in Georgian, which is now the national language. Speakers of the southern Abzhui dialect are frequently trilingual, able to converse in MINGRELIAN as well. The dialects in Cherkessia are 'Abaza': speakers here are bilingual in the related CIRCASSIAN.

Literary Abkhaz is based on the Abzhui dialect spoken at the capital, Sukhumi. It has fewer consonant phonemes than Bzyp' and is thus said to be slightly easier for non-natives to learn. The literary form of Abaza is based on the Tapanta dialect.

Abkhaz was occasionally written in Cyrillic script before the Russian Revolution: Latin, Georgian, a revised Cyrillic and (since the end of the Soviet Union) a revised Georgian script have been used in succession. To cope with its great number of consonants, 14 extra consonant letters were added to the Abkhaz variant of the Cyrillic alphabet.

For a table of numerals see CIRCASSIAN.

North West Caucasian languages on the map

Abkhaz and *Abaza* together make up four dialects: Bzyp', Abzhui or Abzhuwa, Ashkhar or Ashkharwa and Tapanta, the last being rather different from the rest. The dialects spoken in Georgia are grouped as Abkhaz and have about 90,000 speakers. The dialects in Cherkessia (Ashkharwa and Tapanta) are counted as Abaza and have about 60,000 speakers.

Adyge and *Kabardian* or Kabardo-Cherkess are the languages of Cherkessia and neighbouring districts, though most speakers are to be found in Turkey: together these languages are called CIRCASSIAN. There are four Adyge dialects, Bzhedugh, Shapsugh, Abzakh and Temirgoi – but Shapsugh and Abzakh have almost disappeared from Russia through emigration.

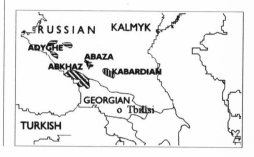

ACHEHNESE

2,000,000 SPEAKERS

Indonesia

A chehnese is spoken in northern Sumatra, where Banda Aceh was once the capital of an independent Muslim kingdom and a major port of call in the eastern Indian Ocean (see map at CHAM).

The closest relatives of Achehnese – far closer than the other languages of the big island of Sumatra – are the AUSTRONESIAN LANGUAGES of Vietnam, notably Cham, which also was once the 'national' language of an independent kingdom. But *why* are Achehnese and Cham closely related? When and by what route did an original single language split into these two that are spoken so far apart? That is as yet a mystery. Clues will come from the borrowings from Austroasiatic languages that occur in both Achehnese and Cham: further work may show which Austroasiatic language is responsible, whether Khmer, Mon or one of the Aslian languages of Malaya.

Achehnese also has borrowings from Sanskrit, some of them shared with Cham, Khmer and Mon. There are Malay loanwords, too, for Malay was used officially in Aceh even during its independence and (as Indonesian) remains the national language today. Dutch, language of the former colonial power, has influenced modern Achehnese heavily.

Formerly written in Arabic script, Achehnese now has a standard orthography in the Latin alphabet, agreed in 1979.

Numerals in Achehnese and Cham		
Achehnese		**Cham**
sa	1	tha
duwa	2	dwa
lhɛə	3	klŏw
pɪət	4	pa
limɔng	5	limu
nam	6	năm
tujoh	7	tadjuh
lapan	8	talipăn
si-kurɪəng	9	thalipăn
si-ploh	10	tha pluh

 Afar

PERHAPS 500,000 SPEAKERS

Eritrea, Djibouti, Ethiopia

Afar, one of the Lowland East CUSHITIC LANGUAGES, is spoken in the desert region of southern Eritrea, in Djibouti (once the 'French Territory of the *Afars* and Issas') and in neighbouring parts of Ethiopia.

The speakers call themselves '*A'far* and their language '*A'far af* 'mouth of the Afar'. In Arabic they are *Danakil* (singular *Dankali*), while in Ethiopia they are officially called *Adal*, the name of the old sultanate that once ruled this region.

Henry Salt's *Voyage to Abyssinia* (1814) contained the first published word list of Afar, which has been studied by many linguists since his time. Some textbooks and religious texts have appeared in Afar; both Latin and Ethiopic scripts have been used.

Speakers are Muslims and the region has long been under strong Arabic influence. Arabic is a national language of Djibouti and of Eritrea, and Arabic is the everyday language of the two major towns in Afar territory, Djibouti and Massawa. Yet the basic vocabulary of Afar contains relatively few Arabic loanwords.

The first ten numerals in Afar are: *enek, nammay, sidoh, ferey, konoy, lehey, malhin, bahar, sagal, taban*.

Afar, Saho and BEJA on the map

Afar has three main dialects, *Southern* (including Bādu and Aussa subdialects), *Central* in Djibouti, *Northern* in Eritrea.

Saho or Shaho, the northern extension of the Afar dialect continuum, is a language of Muslim pastoralists on the seaward-facing mountains of northern Eritrea, with about 120,000 speakers. The three dialects of Saho are *Hadu, Miniferi* and *Assaorta*. The *Irob* people are Christians who are bilingual in Saho and Tigrinya.

BEJA, only distantly related to Afar and Saho, is the Northern Cushitic language of the nomadic 'Bedouin' of north-eastern Sudan and northern Eritrea.

Northeast Africa: Afar, Saho and Beja

AFRIKAANS

6,000,000 SPEAKERS

South Africa

Afrikaans ('African') is a daughter language of Dutch: thus it belongs to the GERMANIC group of INDO-EUROPEAN LANGUAGES. It was one of the two national languages of white-ruled South Africa; it is still one of the eleven official languages of the country, spoken by the third largest linguistic community, after Zulu and Xhosa. There are Afrikaans-speaking minorities in Namibia and Zimbabwe.

The white speakers of Afrikaans were called, in Afrikaans and South African English, *Boers*, literally 'farmers'. The word is the same in origin as German *Bauern* 'peasants'.

A local variety of Dutch had begun to develop not long after the foundation of Cape Town by the Dutch East India Company in 1652. Landmarks in the establishment of Afrikaans as a separate language are: the expansion of the Dutch-speaking settler population across South Africa in the 18th and 19th centuries; the development of a linguistically and racially mixed community, with intermarriage and the immigration of Malay and Indian language speakers; the annexation of the Cape by Britain in 1806, and the establishment of the self-governing Union of South Africa in 1910. Under the new democratic constitution of South Africa the formerly pre-eminent position of Afrikaans is likely to decay: English, less closely identified with racial exclusivity, is more generally acceptable in the role of lingua franca.

The local language was initially called *Cape Dutch* (or *Taal Dutch, Cape Coloured Dutch, Baby-Hollands*). It was slow to gain recognition as a real language, partly because it served at first mostly as an argot spoken within the sub-cultures of separate ethnic communities, and as a household jargon for communication with and among servants. The first printed book in Afrikaans was an Islamic religious text in Arabic script, in the *Cape Malay* or *Cape Afrikaans* variety of the language; it appeared in 1856.

Afrikaans has served as the basis for other, more ephemeral, mixed languages in South Africa. *Orange River Afrikaans* or *Kleurling-Afrikaans* was a creolised Afrikaans adopted by mixed populations called Griqua and Koranna, the majority of them former speakers of KHOISAN LANGUAGES, Nama and others. The Rehoboth Basters ('bastards'), a rural population descending from Dutch men and Khoi women, spoke a similar creolised variety.

Ironically, then, in view of its recent position as the ruling language of a racially exclusive community, Afrikaans has complex origins – which it demonstrates in a rich variety of loanwords from Portuguese, Malay, Bantu languages and Khoisan languages. It has also borrowed from English, and has in turn influenced the regional English of South Africa. The sound patterns of the two languages have naturally tended to converge.

Flytaal or *Flaaitaal*, now better known as *Tsotsitaal*, is an Afrikaans-based jargon of black youths around Johannesburg and Pretoria: for its Zulu- and Sotho-based equivalent, *Iscamtho*, see SOTHO. It developed among criminal gangs west of the big city. In the 1940s and after, criminal gangs were the preferred role models for urban black South African youngsters: their language spread rapidly.

By contrast with Dutch, Afrikaans has no noun gender: *die man* 'the man', *die vrou* 'the woman'. A double negative, comparable to French *ne . . . pas*, is the usual rule: *hy staan **nie** op **nie*** 'he does not stand up'.

Afrikaans has contributed numerous loan-words to English, including the notorious *apartheid*, literally 'separateness'. *Kraal* 'enclosure' is in origin an Afrikaans loan from Portuguese *curral* 'farmyard', which is also the origin of American English *corral*. For a table of numerals see DUTCH.

AFROASIATIC LANGUAGES

Theodor Benfy demonstrated the relationship between Egyptian and the Semitic languages in 1844, and named the family *Semito-Hamitic* in 1869. These are key dates in the gradual recognition by scholars that the SEMITIC LANGUAGES so well known from Biblical and Orientalist study were part of a much wider family that also included BERBER LANGUAGES, CHADIC LANGUAGES, CUSHITIC LANGUAGES, OMOTIC LANGUAGES and Ancient EGYPTIAN.

Scholars who have looked at Afroasiatic linguistic relationships have no doubt of them. There once was a language something like the 'proto-Afroasiatic' that is now being reconstructed. But some of those who work on Semitic languages, on the Ancient Near East and on European prehistory have not yet thought through this century-old discovery. Even more strikingly than the Uralic and Indo-European families, the Afroasiatic language family cuts across usually perceived racial boundaries. It is an exciting challenge for archaeologists, anthropologists and linguists to trace its origin and the steps by which the individual groups diverged and spread.

Among present-day scholars of Afroasiatic languages, Christopher Ehret has been the most productive and successful: see his *Reconstructing Proto-Afroasiatic* (Berkeley: University of California Press, 1995). Ehret has postulated a series of divisions in which first the Omotic languages, then Cushitic, then Chadic, separated off as early dialects. This leaves a 'Boreafrasian' group, out of which emerged Berber, Egyptian and Semitic.

This is the language side of the story. In human terms, it goes with a hypothesis that proto-Afroasiatic was spoken, perhaps 18,000 years ago, in the Horn of Africa. Omotic, Cushitic and Chadic languages remain as the traces of a very early westward expansion: later, speakers of the earliest Boreafrasian dialects spread northwards across what is now the Sahara (but was a less arid environment then) and expanded both westwards and eastwards, eventually occupying the vast area that stretches from Morocco to Arabia.

As a result of this expansion, the Berber and ancient Egyptian cultures developed in North Africa itself, while across the Red Sea, the earliest Semitic dialects spread northwards from the Arabian peninsula to the Fertile Crescent, first emerging into history when speakers of the Semitic language AKKADIAN seized power in southern Iraq, where previously the quite unrelated SUMERIAN language had been pre-eminent.

It is because of the great length of time involved here that proto-Afroasiatic has been more difficult to work on than proto-Indo-European. There is another difficulty. All the Afroasiatic languages are built on word roots consisting of consonants, between which vowels are inserted to create various verb and noun forms. The Semitic languages have three-consonant roots. The others have mainly two-consonant roots, and it has not been clear how the Semitic forms could in practice have developed out of these. Ehret has presented persuasive evidence that single-consonant suffixes, with various fixed meanings, still found in some of the other Afroasiatic languages, became attached invariably to word roots in 'pre-proto-Semitic', thus resulting in the well-known three-consonant roots of modern Semitic languages.

Most Afroasiatic languages have two series of forms for nouns, 'independent' and 'construct': for example, Hebrew *dəbarīm* 'words' but *dibrē 'emet* 'words of truth'. Most languages of the family have a masculine/feminine gender distinction, feminine forms being marked with a *-t*:

in Berber, *imishshu* 'male cat', *timishshut* 'female cat'; in Ethiopic, *bəˀasi* 'man', *bəˀasit* 'woman'.

The names of Afroasiatic

The name *Hamitic* or *Chamitic* was already used in very early scholarship to cover some of the groups now combined in 'Afroasiatic'. It comes from Ham, one of the Biblical sons of Noah. Benfy used *Semito-Hamitic* to make clear his view that the already recognised Semitic group was a co-ordinate half of the same family. Later Benfy's term was inverted, to make *Hamito-Semitic*, because scholars recognised that Semitic, though it belonged to the group, was just one of several divisions of it, while 'Hamitic' covered all the rest.

Afroasiatic is now a more popular term. It is less culture-specific: 'Hamito-Semitic' makes sense only to those who remember the Biblical story of Noah and his sons. But geographically, the term 'Afroasiatic' is a little too all-embracing, because there are many languages of Africa and Asia that do not belong to this family. *Erythraic* (after the Classical Greek name for the Red Sea), *Afrasian* and *Lisramic* (an invented compound of two Hamito-Semitic roots) have also been tried.

These terms are 'part of the dialect geography of linguistic terminology: roughly Semito-Hamitic for Eastern Europe; Hamito-Semitic for the rest of Europe; Erythraic in the focal area of the School of Oriental and African Studies, London; Afroasiatic in the U.S. generally; Lisramic and Afrasian still on the doorstep waiting to be adopted. Lisramic is the only one based on roots from the languages themselves (**lis* "tongue, language"; Egyptian *rāmač* "people").'

After Carleton T. Hodge in *The non-Semitic languages of Ethiopia* ed. M. L. Bender
(East Lansing: African Studies Center, Michigan State University, 1976) p. 43

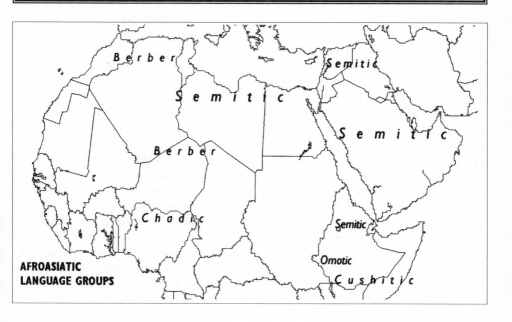

**AFROASIATIC
LANGUAGE GROUPS**

AHOM

EXTINCT LANGUAGE OF INDIA

A hom is one of the TAI LANGUAGES (see map at SHAN). It was spoken by a conquering band who ruled the lower Brahmaputra valley, modern Assam, for six hundred years from their capital at Sibsagar.

> The Ahoms' own name for themselves was *Tai*. In ASSAMESE they were called *Asam* (nowadays pronounced *Ohom*), a word related to *Shan* and to *Siamese*, both of them designations for Tai peoples. The state of *Assam* is named after them.

The Ahoms invaded Assam in the 13th century and established a kingdom. In the 18th century their power began to fade: the accession of King Lakshmi Singha in 1769 was followed by rebellions, Burmese invasions and civil wars. British rule, imposed after the treaty of Yandabu in 1826, allowed the Ahom kings to retain Upper Assam. But the local Indo-Aryan tongue, Assamese, had long since become their court language.

Ahom has had rather little linguistic influence on Assamese. But the Ahom kings encouraged a kind of literature almost unique in India. This was the prose chronicle, *buranji*, at first written in Ahom but destined in the 17th century to become one of the glories of Assamese literature.

The Ahom alphabet had 41 characters. Ahom was almost certainly a tonal language, like its Tai relatives, but the tones were not recorded in the script so they are now unknown.

The first ten numerals in Ahom are: *it, chang, chām, chi, hā, ruk, cit, pet, kāo, chip.*

The twelve months in Ahom script

After B. Barua, N. N. Deodhai Phukan, *Ahom lexicons* (Gauhati: Department of Historical and Antiquarian Studies in Assam, 1964)

 AKAN

5,000,000 SPEAKERS

Ghana, Ivory Coast

Akan, often called Twi, is one of the Kwa group of NIGER-CONGO LANGUAGES. It was the ruling language of the Ashanti Empire and is now the most important African language of Ghana. Even among some who use other languages in daily life, Akan is the language of the priesthood and of liturgical texts in the Ashanti religion, still widely practised.

> Since the 1950s *Akan* has been the preferred term for the language as a whole. *Twi* is an alternative, often used for the Asante dialect in particular. There are three standard forms of Akan, all mutually intelligible: Twi or *Asante* (of the region of Kumasi, centre of the *Ashanti* Empire), *Fante* and *Akuapem* (of southern Ghana).

Long before the rise of the Ashanti Empire, an Akan-speaking kingdom had its capital at Bono-Mansu, whose ruins are a hundred miles north of Kumasi. It was founded around 1300 and its gold mines made it a city of legendary wealth. In 1740, after defeat by Ashanti, it was destroyed. The Brong dialect, the most north-westerly of the Akan group, remains to show the former reach of the Bono kingdom.

The founder of the Ashanti Empire was Osei Tutu (ruled 1695–1731). By the early 19th century his successors controlled much of modern Ghana from their capital at Kumasi, and wherever their rule spread, so did their Asante language. Meanwhile Fante, the language of the coastal districts west of Accra, and Akuapem, of the hills north of Accra, had both achieved importance as inland trade from coastal ports increased – and both had been adopted as written languages for religious publications. A grammar of Fante had been published in Danish as early as 1764, a reminder that this was once the Danish Gold Coast; it was preceded by a glossary of Asante published in German in 1673.

When the British captured Kumasi in 1874, Akan in its three forms remained the single most useful African language on the Gold Coast and in its newly conquered hinterland, continuing to spread with roads, schools and missions. Religious and secular publications in Fante and Twi multiplied.

To replace the three standard orthographies for Asante, Fante and Akuapem – and so to make publishing in Akan a more rewarding activity – a new Akan orthography was promoted in the 1980s.

Although English, the official national language and the language of broadcasting, is still in many situations the most useful lingua franca, Akan has a growing role as the language of markets and transport across much of modern Ghana: in the north-east, where Hausa may be a second language for men, Akan is more likely to be the market language for women.

To the west of the Akan-speaking area, where Anyi and Sehwi (see BAULE) are the local languages, Akan is used in church, in trade and in most schools. To the south and east the situation is similar. In these districts, therefore, many people are bilingual in Akan. Akan has had a strong influence on GĀ (the local language of Accra) and EWE, both of which have borrowed Akan terms relating to food (including sea fishing) and statecraft.

Akan personal names have also been fashionable in these languages – names such as Kofi and Kwame, which relate to the days of the week (see table at BAULE). This is an important detail of Akan traditional belief, since each of the eight or nine paternal lineages, *ntoro*, in Akan society sets aside a specific day of the week for ritual washing: hence the common conversational gambit, 'Which *ntoro* do you wash?'

Akan has two tones – high and low. It also has a 'vowel harmony' rule based on the position of the root of the tongue: a word may contain either 'advanced' or 'unadvanced' vowels but not both. In the Fante dialect (as in the neighbouring Baule which, like Akan, belongs to the Tano or Volta-Comoe subgroup of Kwa languages), vowel harmony is more complex, depending also on the position of the lips: rounded and un-rounded vowels may not be mixed in the same word.

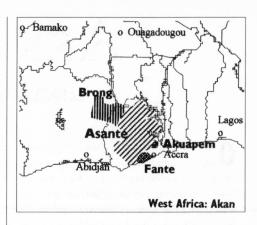

West Africa: Akan

When not to trust

Kontromfí sè: Áfei ne ampã – 'Monkey says: Now I am going to tell the truth!'

The dialects of Akan

In the 1960 census, when Ghana had a total population of 6.7 million, first-language speakers of the eight main dialects of Akan were enumerated separately:

Asante or Twi	913,270
Fante	708,470
Brong or Abron	320,240
Akuapem or Akwapim	144,790
Akyem	203,820
Agona	49,080
Kwahu	131,970
Wasa	94,260

Brong (which some consider a separate language) has an additional 75,000 speakers in neighbouring districts of the Ivory Coast.

From *The languages of Ghana*
ed. M. A. Kropp Dakubu
(London: Kegan Paul, 1988)

Numerals in Akan		
	Twi	**Brong**
1	biakõ	ekõ
2	abieng	enyõ
3	abiesã	esã
4	anang	enã
5	anum	enũ
6	asĩa	ensyĩ
7	asong	ensõ
8	awotwe	moqie
9	akrong	enkunõ
10	edu	edu

AKKADIAN

EXTINCT LANGUAGE OF IRAQ

One of the SEMITIC LANGUAGES, Akkadian was once a ruling language in Iraq and Syria. Some of the oldest literature in the world comes to us on clay tablets in Akkadian cuneiform script – including the *Epic of Gilgamesh*, and myths of the Creation and the Flood which have pervasive similarities with the HEBREW Biblical texts.

After it was supplanted by Aramaic and Greek (see below) Akkadian fell from use. For nearly two thousand years it was a forgotten language. Stone inscriptions and clay tablets in the strange wedge-shaped script were first encountered by modern travellers in the 17th century, and the painstaking work of decipherment began. It is because of these texts – literature, chronicles, business accounts, school exercises, even recipes – that knowledge of Akkadian exists today. Through deciphering Akkadian, the recorded history of the Middle East has been gradually extended thousands of years into the past.

> Akkadian is named after Akkad, capital city of the empire ruled by Sargon (2350–2294 BC according to one chronology). The terms Assyrian and Babylonian are also found, usually as the names of the two dialects of Akkadian that became standard languages of the later empires of Assyria and Babylon.

The cuneiform writing system was not a new invention when it was first applied to Akkadian about 2350 BC. Until then it had been used for SUMERIAN, the ancient and unrelated language of the oldest kingdoms of southern Iraq. Speakers of Akkadian, advancing northwards from the Arabian peninsula, had occupied the region and their language had begun to replace Sumerian in everyday use around 2500.

In this process Akkadian borrowed heavily from Sumerian – but it did not borrow verbs. Sumerian verb forms were built up by adding affixes. Akkadian verbs, like those in other Semitic languages, are modified by means of internal changes, mainly of vowels. Sumerian verbs were not made to fit the pattern. However, when compared with other Semitic languages, Akkadian is seen to have a great number of Sumerian noun loanwords.

The Akkadian script also borrowed Sumerian word forms directly – using them as ready-made logograms for Akkadian words that had the same meaning but sounded quite different. In addition, whole long texts of Sumerian literature were recopied and preserved in Akkadian libraries, sometimes in bilingual versions meant to help in the understanding of the old classical language of Sumer.

By 2000, a distinction can be observed between the dialects of northern Iraq (Assyria and places linked with Assyria) and southern Iraq (the Sumerian cities, later Babylonia).

> Eblaite is the language of the once-important city of Ebla, whose ruins were excavated at Tell Mardikh, forty miles south of Aleppo, in 1975. Far away from southern Iraq, this kingdom also had a writing system based on Sumerian cuneiform. Tens of thousands of tablets were recovered and are being deciphered. Eblaite was surprisingly similar to Akkadian, though not identical with it. It also seems to have many Sumerian loanwords.

Akkadian was at its most important in the second millennium BC. A great range of literature was written down in Old Babylonian, to be preserved in libraries or archives. Meanwhile, Akkadian was becoming the first truly international language of business and diplomacy in the Middle East. Akkadian texts of this period are to be found in Egypt and in Anatolia, far away from the regions where Akkadian was an everyday language. Special forms of the language, such as the 'Amarna Akkadian', mixed with Canaanite, of the Tell el-Amarna tablets, were written by people who perhaps seldom spoke the language, using it simply as a recording medium. Akkadian was – for a while – at the centre of a multilingual culture, in which linguistic influences flowed in all directions. The spread of the cuneiform script mirrors these influences: after passing from Sumerian to Akkadian, it was afterwards used in different forms for Hurrian and Urartian (see CAUCASIAN LANGUAGES), Hittite, Ugaritic, Elamite (see DRAVIDIAN LANGUAGES), Old Persian and several other languages. All of these languages borrowed words from Akkadian.

New Assyrian, and late New Babylonian texts, show that by their time both dialects were strongly influenced by Aramaic, which must eventually have become the everyday speech of almost all of Iraq and was to be the administrative language of the Persian Empire. Assyrian, as far as can be seen from surviving tablets, ceased to be written altogether about 600, while Babylonian texts continue as late as the 1st century BC.

Periods of Akkadian

Northern Iraq	Dates BC	Southern Iraq
Old Akkadian	2500–2000	Old Akkadian
Old Assyrian	2000–1500	Old Babylonian
Middle Assyrian	1500–1000	Middle Babylonian
New Assyrian	1000–600	New Babylonian
–	600–1	Late New Babylonian

The Akkadian writing system

The characters in which Akkadian was written are called *cuneiform* 'made of wedge-shaped strokes'. They were usually formed with a pointed stylus on a wet clay surface which was then dried and sometimes baked. Huge libraries and archives of these clay tablets have been found in the excavation of big Assyrian and Babylonian cities. There are also monumental stone inscriptions: on these, engravers imitated the same style of writing.

There were over a thousand characters, some syllabic, some representing a whole word or concept. Many come originally from characters used for the quite unrelated Sumerian language. Scribes had to learn hundreds of characters, and might come to know the whole range, but businessmen were able to write letters and keep accounts with a knowledge of no more than 150 signs.

Some of the latest Akkadian inscriptions, erected by Persian emperors in the 5th century BC, were trilingual. These were the keys to decipherment – names, in particular, could be recognised in all three languages, and the signs so recognised made a beginning in the reading of other words. The Danish schoolteacher G. F. Grotefend took this first step in 1802. Decipherment was closer to completion by 1857, when the Royal Asiatic Society sponsored a competition in deciphering Akkadian. The result was that four similar – and essentially correct – translations of the same text were submitted.

Akkadian numerals

Masculine		Feminine
ishtēn	1	ishtiat
shina	2	shitta
shalāsh	3	shalāshat
erba	4	erbet
ḫamish	5	ḫamshat
?	6	sheshshet
sebe	7	sebet
samāne	8	?
tishe	9	tishīt
esher	10	esheret

In Akkadian texts, numerals are usually written in figures rather than in words – so the pronunciation of some numerals is still unknown. As in many Semitic languages, a feminine numeral goes with a masculine noun and vice versa.

For large numbers, bases of 60 and 100 were used together: 60 *shūshum*, 100 *mētum*, 120 *shina shūshi*, 200 *shitta mētim*, 240 *erbet shūshi*, 300 *shalash me'āt*, 600 *nēr*, 1000 *lim* . . .

ALBANIAN

5,000,000 SPEAKERS

Albania, Yugoslavia, Italy, Greece

Albanian forms a separate branch of the INDO-EUROPEAN LANGUAGES, quite distinct in its development from Greek and its other modern neighbours. It is the official language of Albania, also spoken by the majority in the Kosovo Metohija province of Serbia and by long-established minorities in Italy and Greece.

> The local name of Albania is *Shqipëria* and of the language *Shqip*. An ancient term for a tribe from this region, classical Latin *Albani*, still survives in the name that the Albanian speakers of Italy give to themselves, *Arbëresh*; in the Greek name, *Arvanítis*; and in the Balkan names, such as Romanian *Arnăut*. As *Albania* it has become the English and international name for the country and its language.

Where, exactly, were the speakers of Albanian during the thousands of years that have passed since the proto-Indo-European dialects began to grow apart? Names and a few other words from languages of the ancient Balkans had been noted down by Latin and Greek authors. Some of these languages, such as Illyrian, are reminiscent of Albanian, but none has been identified as the exact precursor of the modern language.

Albanian itself was not recorded in writing until early modern times. Apart from single words, the first certain record of the language is a formula for baptism, written down in 1462 for occasions when no priest was available. One line of Albanian is given to the hero of a Latin play published in Venice in 1483, Thomas Medius's *Epirota* 'The Man from Albania'. In 1555 a prayer book in Albanian was printed. Composed by Gjon Buzuku, bishop of Shkodra, this is the oldest known book from Albania itself. The first Albanian publication from Sicily,

also a religious text, appeared in 1592.

The greatest Albanian literature is poetry. There are oral epics, comparable to those in SERBIAN from neighbouring Bosnia. These and shorter folk poems were the inspiration for the poetry that was printed in Albania and Italy in the 17th, 18th and 19th centuries. A national renaissance (*Relindja*) in the late 19th century saw political independence, and the development of a unified literary language and of a new alphabet.

A Latin–Albanian dictionary, by Blanchus (Bardhi), appeared in 1635. J. H. Xylander, who published a grammar in 1835, showed that Albanian was an Indo-European language. He noticed regular patterns such as the correspondence of Albanian *gj-*, Latin *s-*, Ancient Greek *h-*. An example is the word for 'snake': Albanian *gjarpër*, Latin *serpens*, cf. Greek *hérpyllos* 'creeping thyme'.

The basic vocabulary of Albanian is Indo-European: *ne*, Latin *nos*, 'we'; *krimb*, Old Irish *cruim*, 'worm'; *ëndër*, Greek *óneiros*, 'dream'; *darkë*, Greek *dórpon*, 'supper'; *i parë*, Sanskrit *pūrvaḥ*, 'first'. With Albania belonging first to the Roman Empire, then to Byzantium, and then for five hundred years to the Turkish (Ottoman) Empire, the Albanian language has borrowed many words from Latin, Greek and Turkish: *djallë*, Greek *diábolos*, 'devil'; *këndoj*, Latin *canto*, 'sing'. The majority of Albanian speakers are Muslims; numerous words and names are borrowed from Arabic, language of the Qur'ān.

> A striking feature of Albanian is the use of periphrastic expressions to avoid a tabu word: thus for 'wolf' one says *mbyllizogojën* (from *mbylli Zot gojën* 'may God close his mouth!') and for 'fairy' *shtozovalle* (from *shtoju Zot vallet* 'may God increase their round-dances!').

The Balkans: language convergence? language substrate?

Albanian has striking similarities with other Balkan languages, BULGARIAN, SERBIAN, GREEK and ROMANIAN: Albanian *treg*, Serbian *trg*, Romanian *tîrg*, 'market'; Albanian *shtrungë*, Romanian *strungă*, Bulgarian *strâga*, 'milking-place at entrance to a sheep-fold'; Albanian *i shtrëmbër*, Romanian *strîmb*, 'crooked', Greek *strabós* 'cross-eyed'; Albanian *mëz*, Romanian *mînz*, 'foal'. Often the same Latin word is used in these languages with the same special meaning: Latin *paludem* 'marsh', Rumanian *pădure* 'woodland', Albanian *pyll* 'woodland'. Some features are shared more widely, with TURKISH, HUNGARIAN or ROMANI.

Languages which share a culture, and are often used side by side, do grow together in the course of time. This is why English, since the Norman conquest, came to have many more similarities to French than its relative German has.

Like English and French, Balkan languages are only distantly related in the usual linguistic sense of the word. Yet the resemblances among them are so striking as to demand some special explanation. They are seen not only in individual words but in basic features such as the definite article – this has different forms in the different languages, but in all of them it forms a suffix to the noun: Romanian *zi* 'day', *ziua* 'the day'; Bulgarian *tsaritsa* 'queen', *tsaritsata* 'the queen'.

Many linguists consider that a linguistic 'substrate' is at work – an older language, once spoken all over the region, which, before it died, influenced all the surviving languages in the same ways. Some consider the main substrate language of the Balkans to be Latin, which in the last centuries of the Roman Empire, and until the Slavonic invasions, was certainly spoken widely all over the Balkans.

Others would argue that travel, migration, seasonal transhumance and bilingualism among Balkan peoples, lasting over a very long period (at least from the Roman Empire to the present day), brought all the languages closer to one another. Romanians (especially Aromunians), Albanians and Romani, in particular, were forever on the move.

Albanian alphabets

The only surviving copy of Buzuku's 1555 prayer book, with some missing pages, is in the Vatican Library. 'This is the first book in our language, and was very difficult to make.' Buzuku and some other pre-19th-century Geg writers used the Roman alphabet with extra characters for some unfamiliar sounds. Early texts in Tosk are sometimes in the Greek alphabet. But literature from both north and south was often written and printed in the same Arabic alphabet that was used for Turkish, the ruling language of pre-20th-century Albania.

The modern alphabet, adopted in 1908 at the Monastir (Bitolj) Congress after fierce debate, counts 36 letters. The Turkish government fiercely opposed its introduction. The dispute contributed to Albania's declaration of independence from Turkey on 28 December 1912.

The Albanian alphabet

a b c ç d dh e ë f g gj h i j k l ll m n nj o p q r rr s sh t th u v x xh y z zh

---

The map of Albanian

The two big dialect groups, Geg and Tosk, are quite different from each other, so different that some consider them separate languages. Geg has many more vowel sounds than Tosk: not only the seven that are recorded directly in the Albanian alphabet, but also five nasals, which can be written *â, ê, î, ô, ŷ*, and in Geg all twelve of these vowels may be either long or short. Geg (specifically the South Geg of Elbasan) was the literary standard of the early 20th century, but since 1945 Tosk has taken its place.

Geg is the language of northern Albania and the 1,750,000 Albanian speakers of Kosovo Metohija in Serbia. Tosk is spoken in southern

Counting down in Albanian

Dymbdhet muj na i ka vjeti,	**Twelve** months has the year,
Njimbdhet muj pela mazin,	**Eleven** months the mare a foal,
Dhet muej lopa viqin,	**Ten** months the cow a calf,
Nand muej gruej djalin,	**Nine** months the woman a boy,
Tet cica na i ka dosa,	**Eight** teats has the sow,
Shtat sy na i ka naleti,	**Seven** eyes has the devil,
Gjasht muej bajn gjys vjeti,	**Six** months make half a year,
Pes gishta na i ka dora,	**Five** fingers has the hand,
Kater kamb' na i ka dhija,	**Four** legs has the goat,
Tri kamb' terezija,	**Three** legs has the scale,
Dy lula na i ka vasha,	**Two** flowers has the girl,
Vasha ka bylbylin-o,	The girl's taken by the nightingale,
Vasha po këndon malit-o,	The girl sings on the mountain
Sall per hater djalit-o!	Naked beside her lover!

This counting song is recorded in several versions from different villages. Some say 'The tenth month the army takes' and some say 'Two apples has the girl'.

After Max Lambertz, *Lehrgang des Albanischen* part 3 (Halle: Niemeyer, 1959) pp. 219–25; Eric P. Hamp, 'Albanian' in *Indo-European numerals* ed. Jadranka Gvozdanovic (Berlin: Mouton De Gruyter, 1992) pp. 835–927

Southern Europe: Albanian

Albania, in parts of central Greece, and in scattered districts in Italy. The Tosk dialects of Sicily and southern Italy are known as *Arbëresh*, those of Greece as *Arvanitika*. There are Tosk-speaking villages in Bulgaria and in Ukraine (near Melitopol), and a Geg-speaking community, Arbanasi, near Zadar on the Dalmatian coast.

Albanian communities in Greece and southern Italy have been there for many centuries, their numbers regularly refreshed by continuing migration.

ALGONQUIAN LANGUAGES

LANGUAGE FAMILY OF NORTH AMERICA

From the 15th century onwards, explorers and settlers of the eastern seaboard of North America received their first impressions of New World natives from speakers of Algonquian languages. This group of AMERIND LAN-GUAGES has about fifteen living members, stretching from Labrador to Alberta and Wyoming; there were once many more, as far south as Carolina, but intensive European settlement in what is now the eastern United

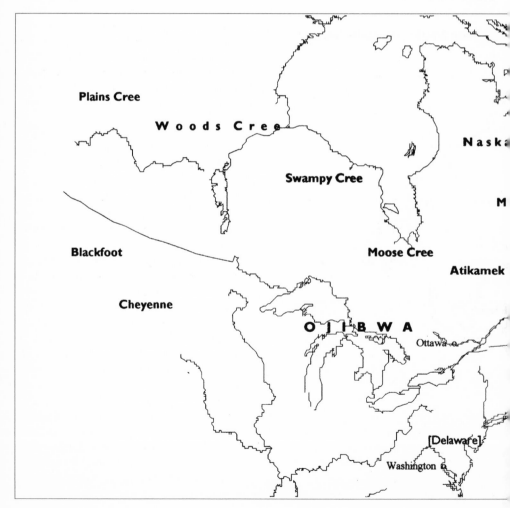

Plains Cree

Woods Cree

Naska

Swampy Cree

M

Blackfoot

Moose Cree

Atikamek

Cheyenne

O J I B W A

Ottawa o

[Delaware]

Washington o

States drove out and eradicated many Algonquian peoples.

Two trade languages have had an Algonquian basis. Mitchif or French Cree was spoken in North Dakota and in the Great Plains of Canada. The Atlantic Jargon of New Jersey was used between English and Dutch traders and New Jersey Indians. It was influenced by English grammar, but its vocabulary was largely Algonquian.

Algonquian languages have contributed a mass of place names to the map of North America. Massachusett, Narragansett, Connecticut, Cheyenne and Illinois are all names of extinct Algonquian peoples and languages. Delaware and Ottawa are names of languages that are still spoken, though the few living speakers of Delaware live a thousand miles away from the state that is named after their ancestral tribe.

English has numerous Algonquian loanwords. *Squash*, with the meaning of 'pumpkin', comes from Narragansett, a now-extinct New England Algonquian language; so does *moose*. Others, such as *toboggan*, come from Abenaki, once an important language in Maine and Quebec, now with fewer than twenty speakers.

Algonquian languages on the map

The Algonquian or Algonkian group includes several languages with some thousands of remaining speakers: CREE, OJIBWA, Blackfoot (9,000 speakers), Cheyenne (2,000 speakers), Micmac (8,000 speakers) and Montagnais (7,000 speakers). Further Algonquian languages, still spoken but by very small numbers, are Abenaki, Algonquin, Arapaho, Atsina, Fox, Kickapoo, Maliseet and Passamaquoddy, Menominee, Munsee, Potawatomi, Shawnee and Unami (or Delaware).

Algonquian languages seem to be distantly related to the extinct *Wiyot* and the dying *Yurok* of north-western California, as was first suggested by Edward Sapir in 1913.

There are five main dialects of Cree. The Montagnais dialects in Quebec and Naskapi in Labrador (few remaining speakers) may, like Atikamek, be considered part of a dialect continuum with Cree.

Plains Cree is spoken in central Saskatchewan and Alberta. *Woods Cree* is spoken in northern Saskatchewan and north-western Manitoba. *Swampy Cree* is spoken in the remainder of Manitoba and most of Ontario. *Moose Cree* is spoken near Moose Factory, on the west coast of James Bay. *Atikamek* (3,000 speakers), sometimes regarded as a separate language, is spoken north of Trois-Rivières.

Ojibwa is now spoken in Indian reservations in Ontario, Manitoba, Saskatchewan, Michigan, Wisconsin, Minnesota, Montana and North Dakota. There are 50,000 speakers in Canada and 30,000 in the United States.

Ottawa and *Odawa* are alternative names for Eastern Ojibwa.

North America: Algonquian languages

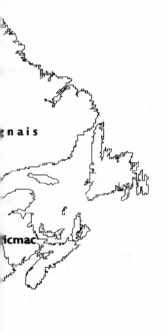

ALTAIC LANGUAGES

A family of languages of northern and central Asia. Most research on them still centres on the individual groups that make up the family, TURKIC LANGUAGES, MONGOLIAN LANGUAGES and TUNGUSIC LANGUAGES.

The name *Altaic* is taken (paralleling *Uralic*) from the Altai mountain range of Asiatic Russia which seems to lie close to the point of origin from which Altaic languages must, many millennia ago, have begun to spread.

Language typology and the Ural-Altaic theory

Many linguists once believed that two well-known language families, Finno-Ugric and Turkic, were historically related. They were well known because both had representatives in Europe – and there was a temptation to link them because, although the individual word forms in these languages looked wholly different, the way that words were formed was almost identical. They were *agglutinative* languages, in which nouns and verbs were built of individual identifiable units: a verb might have, in addition to its basic 'root', a plural suffix and suffixes to identify the subject ('person'), the time past or present, the 'mood' factual or hypothetical, and perhaps others, all added in sequence, all separately audible (or at least visible when the word was written down).

This seemed wholly different from the other two families best known to European linguists, the Indo-European and Semitic languages. In typical *fusional* languages of both of these groups, words are indeed modified to reflect such features as plurality, person, time and mood, but the modifications appear to form an unanalysable whole – and sometimes appear inseparable from the root. A further contrast could be seen with *isolating* languages such as Chinese, in which all these ideas that need to be expressed take the form of separate words.

The postulated grouping was called Ural-Altaic – because both Finno-Ugric and Turkic languages had already recognised links with less-known groups. But scholars who worked on proving the wider relationship had little success. The actual words of the languages could scarcely ever be related to one another. And it became obvious that language *typology*, though relevant, was not in itself a firm guide to the *genetic* relationships between languages. Few now work on the Ural-Altaic link, which must lie very far back in prehistory.

A reaction followed. Linguists began to doubt even the lower-level relationships that had been assumed among the URALIC LANGUAGES (Finno-Ugric and Samoyedic) and among the Altaic languages.

Some now feel that the Turkic, Mongolian and Tungusic languages should be regarded as quite separate families. But this goes too far. Individual word histories do come together to show regular patterns of sound change, linking the three groups. Their grammars, too, are clearly related. The Altaic family is here to stay. Many linguists would include KOREAN in the family, but that link, also, must lie far back in prehistory. Some now add JAPANESE.

AMERIND LANGUAGES

The American continent was discovered, and began to be inhabited, perhaps twenty thousand years ago. It seems likely that early inhabitants spread gradually across the continent from the north-west, the first arrivals having reached it by crossing the Bering Strait.

Whether the oldest stratum of languages of the Americas consists of a single all-inclusive language family – the Amerind languages – is a question charged with controversy. If a single family, it is the most diverse of all those dealt with in this book, with about 300 languages in Canada and the United States; about 70 in Central America; about 600 in South America. Hundreds more, probably, have become extinct in the last two centuries. The total number of speakers of these languages is relatively small: 300,000 in the north; six million in Mexico and the other countries of Central America; eleven million south of the Isthmus of Panama.

The 15th-century European explorers thought at first that they had reached the East Indies, so they called the inhabitants of this new continent *Indians*. *Red Indian*, *American Indian*, *Amerindian* are attempts at clarification of the earlier misleading name. *America* is named after the discoverer of mainland Brazil, Amerigo Vespucci. His fellow-Italian Christophoro Colombo (in Spanish *Cristóbal Colón*) is commemorated in the name of *Colombia*, and in the term *pre-Columbian* for American peoples, cultures and languages as they existed before the European discoveries.

The study of American Indian languages began with Spanish missionaries in Central and South America in the 16th century. Some relationships have been known for a long time. Andrés Pérez Ribas, in 1645, suggested that the languages of Sinaloa were linked to Nahuatl. The group is now called Uto-Aztecan, and the relationship was worked on by the great American linguist Edward Sapir in the early 20th century.

In 20th-century work on the languages of 'Native America' over a hundred language families were identified, along with numerous 'isolates' – single languages apparently lacking any relatives. Some of the isolates were necessarily listed as such because the languages became extinct before they had been properly recorded. The Summer Institute of Linguistics (the Wycliffe Bible Translators) has recently been at the forefront of research, with grammars, dictionaries, Bible translations, and comparative studies.

In the abstract, most of these families and isolates might plausibly turn out to be related. Siberia and Alaska are fairly inhospitable places in themselves, and the number of separate times that people would independently determine on migration in this direction is unlikely to be large. So in arguing for just three migrations and presenting linguistic evidence for just three language families – ESKIMO-ALEUT LANGUAGES, now found on both sides of the Bering Strait; NA-DENÉ LANGUAGES, a family comprising a few languages of the north-west and Navaho; and Amerind languages, all the remainder – the linguist Joseph Greenberg was not doing anything surprising. But high-level classification in this area had always been controversial, and Greenberg's, the most ambitious of all, is no exception: see his *Language in the Americas* (Stanford: Stanford University Press, 1987).

He has not really demonstrated his thesis for all the small families and all the language isolates. For many languages now extinct, never fully recorded, it will probably be impossible to demonstrate. But Greenberg has changed the agenda. As evidence assembles that the major language families are distantly linked, it becomes necessary in the case of the remainder to explain why they should not be linked with the rest.

Tukano multilingualism

Among the Tukano of the north-west Amazon it is incest if a man has a wife who speaks his language. Tukano villages have a language of men, languages of women, and a shared regional trade language.

After B. B. Kachru, 'Bilingualism' in *International encyclopedia of linguistics* (New York: Oxford University Press, 1992)

Many Amerind languages must always have had small numbers of speakers. Communication has, for centuries and perhaps millennia, demanded the use of second languages, lingua francas of various kinds, and pidgins. With Inca rule Quechua spread rapidly along the Andes in the last few centuries before the Spanish conquest. Tupí, now dying, was once the *lingua geral* of Portuguese-ruled Brazil. There was much bilingualism, notably in Nahuatl and Yucatec, in pre-Columbian Mexico. Amerind-European contact languages of North America have included Chinook Jargon of the north-west, Mobilian of the Mississippi valley, and Mitchif or French Cree. Plains Indian Sign Language, now kept alive by Boy Scouts, was once essential among Amerindian traders and travellers in the Midwest. Spanish, French and English came to fill a role as long distance languages among 'Native Americans' as well as among newly dominant peoples.

The north-western United States, a region of mountains and valleys, was the home of many small language communities. Soon after 1800 English sailors at the mouth of the Columbia River found that local people were speaking to travellers in a mixed trade language or 'jargon'. In the course of the 19th century it spread across much of Oregon, Washington State and British Columbia; in the 20th century it has died away as English has spread. This *Chinook Jargon* was clearly of Amerindian origin – its sound patterns were those of local languages including Chinook and Nootka – but it included French, English and Chehalis words as well as many of unknown origin. Whether it originated for local trade, or to deal with Europeans, is not known.

Mexico is a linguistic maze, clearly of long standing. There has been plant cultivation here from 5000 BC, sizeable villages from 2000 BC, ceremonial centres from about 1000 BC – always with a variety of cultures. NAHUATL was the language of government in the Valley of Mexico, and so it became the lingua franca in early Spanish times. But many neighbouring languages, in the Valley and bordering on it, are to all appearance not related to Nahuatl (Tarascan, QUICHÉ, Tzutuhil, MIXTEC) – and each major town tended to have its own well-marked dialect. They developed in parallel, without much travel and contact. So dialects diverged into languages, and there was rather little borrowing among them except for the names of obvious trade goods. There was no widespread literacy – even where it did exist, scripts were not fully linked to the sounds of words – and so little need for the emergence and maintenance of standard literary languages.

Amerind languages: what the dispute means

The squabble among scholars of American Indian languages – between the lumpers and the splitters – is not one of first principles. All natural human languages are related. It is about the use of scientific evidence. It matters because the evidence used and highlighted by linguists becomes an ingredient in the work of anthropologists and archaeologists – and thus, eventually, in people's understanding of their own cultural origins.

Consider two hypotheses. One is that, twenty thousand years ago or so, the early people who crossed to Alaska already spoke two or more very different languages – not unlikely, considering the linguistic diversity of Siberia now and the symbioses that occur among linguistically diverse cultures there. If that were so, the time depth separating some 'Amerind languages' from others might be far more than twenty thousand years, and they might be less closely related to one another than they are to some languages of the Old World.

The second hypothesis is that all the people who crossed the Bering Strait in that early migration spoke the same language, and that the 'Amerind languages' have diversified from that one. We know nothing of the migration, but in the abstract this seems an equally likely hypothesis. If it were so, the time depth separating some Amerind languages from others would be about twenty thousand years: rather greater, probably, but not vastly greater, than that separating the branches of the Afroasiatic family. They would be more closely related to one another than they are to any of the languages of the Old World.

To decide between these hypotheses, linguists would have to be able to trace language relationships, by way of phonetic and lexical reconstruction, at least twenty thousand years back. Some (such as Eric P. Hamp) doubt that they will ever be able to do this, and argue that hypothetical family groupings implying such a timescale are useless because unprovable. Others (such as Joseph Greenberg) prefer to set out a hypothesis on the basis of initially weak evidence, and then get down to attempting a proof.

Greenberg has all the history of science on his side. This is how progress is made. But it has pitfalls, illustrated by the big world classifications of languages that are published from time to time – and illustrated by the headings AMERIND LANGUAGES, AUSTRO-TAI LANGUAGES and ALTAIC LANGUAGES in this book. These family groupings are still in the waiting room between inspired guesswork and established fact. Because classifiers like to classify, some languages firmly pinned down in reference books may turn out to belong somewhere quite different when the real work gets under way.

Major language families of the Americas

This book cannot deal fully with the immense variety of Amerind languages, most of which are spoken now by small and shrinking communities. The map gives a location to some families and linguistic isolates of historical importance. Cross-references (the small capitals in this list) point to larger-scale maps.

ALGONQUIAN, including Cree and Ojibwa
ARAUCANIAN
Arawakan, a family of vast range, extending from Belize to Paraguay, and including Black Carib or Garifuna (perhaps 100,000 speakers in Central American countries) and Guajiro (125,000 in Colombia and Venezuela)
Chibchan, including Guaymí and Cuna
Ge-Pano-Cariban, including Carib
Hokan
Iroquoian, including CHEROKEE
Jivaroan, including Shuar and Aguaruna
MAYAN LANGUAGES, including Cakchiquel, Quiché and Yucatec
Misumalpan, including Miskito (perhaps 100,000 speakers or more)
Mixe-Zoque languages, including Mixe, Zoque, and Popoluca
Muskogean, including Mobilian
Otomanguean, a large family including MIXTEC and ZAPOTEC
Paezan, spoken from Panama to Ecuador and including Páez
Penutian, including Chinook Jargon
QUECHUA and AYMARA, sometimes said to be related but regarded as isolates by others
Tarascan, a linguistic isolate of Michoacán, Mexico
Totonacan languages, including Totonac (250,000 speakers)
Tukanoan, including Tucano, an important lingua franca of the upper Amazon
Tupian, including Chiriguano, GUARANÍ and TUPÍ
Uto-Aztecan, including NAHUATL
Yanomami
Zuñi, a linguistic isolate of New Mexico

SOME AMERIND LANGUAGE GROUPS

AMHARIC

14,000,000 SPEAKERS

Ethiopia

About two thousand years ago a gathering, *habashat*, of speakers of an early Arabic or South Arabian dialect crossed the Red Sea and founded a kingdom in modern Eritrea and Ethiopia. Their language was ETHIOPIC. Splintered by the very difficult communications in this mountainous country, the earliest Ethiopic has divided into several daughter languages, of which Amharic is the most important – it is the national language of modern Ethiopia.

The country used to be called by outsiders *Abyssinia* (from *habashat*): Christian Tigrinya speakers are still called *habesh* in Eritrea (Muslim Tigrinya speakers reject the name 'habesh' and may be called *Jabarta*). *Amharic* is called by its own speakers *Amərinnya*, a name derived from the district of *Amhara*, apparently the historic centre of the language. *Tigriñya* (sometimes written *Tigriña*, or with the Italian spelling *Tigrigna*) is similarly in origin the language of *Tigre* province.

Thus Amharic is one of the SEMITIC LANGUAGES like Arabic and Hebrew. Originally a minor dialect of a region south of Axum, Amharic could claim to be the 'Language of the King' since the accession of the Solomonid dynasty in the 13th century, a crucial lifting of its status.

By the 17th century Amharic was a language of everyday communication, and particularly of the army, throughout the Christian empire of Ethiopia. Its spread was accelerated by the considerable use of and trade in slaves in traditional Ethiopia: the slaves were drawn from peoples of southern Ethiopia of various mother tongues, so slaves and owners necessarily used Amharic as a lingua franca. Thus it was the language in which the Jesuits made their short-lived attempt to convert the Ethiopians to Roman Catholicism. This was a calculated break with tradition, for classical Ethiopic was (and to some extent still is) the language of the established Ethiopian Christian church.

Amharic literature goes back to the royal praise poetry of the 14th century. Ethiopic, however, remained the language of literature and education until the 19th century. Even nowadays, educated speakers of Amharic use a form of speech which is much influenced by the classical language.

As the language of the modern central government, Amharic continues to gain ground as the everyday language of the capital, Addis Ababa, though the native language in the country round about is OROMO. Amharic also serves as a lingua franca in Ethiopia generally. The total of speakers who use the language regularly may be as high as 30,000,000.

Amharic still has a mainly Semitic vocabulary. As with Arabic, Amharic word structure is largely based on consonant-only roots, with inserted vowels marking number, tense and other grammatical features. Naturally there are loanwords from Cushitic languages, such as *wəshsha* 'dog', *səga* 'meat', and from modern European languages, *bolis* 'police' from French, *tayp* 'typewriter' from English, *fabriqa* 'factory' from Italian. Ethiopia was under Italian rule from 1935 to 1941.

Amharic is written in Ethiopic script, which, like Indian scripts, combines a consonant with a following vowel in a single complex symbol. The first box contains one-seventh of the full Amharic alphabet table, showing the consonant letters combined with the vowel *ä*. For a table of numerals see TIGRINYA.

Based partly on works by M. L. Bender, including *Language in Ethiopia* ed. M. L. Bender and others (London: Oxford University Press, 1976)

The Amharic alphabet: the 'first order'

ሀለሐመሠረሰሸቀበተቸኀነኘአከኸወዐዘዠየደጀ
ገጠጨጰጸፀፈፐ

h l h m s r s sh k' b t ch h n ny ä k h w ä z zh y d j g
t' ch' p' c c f p

**The Amharic alphabet:
'h' with the seven vowels**

ሀ ሁ ሂ ሃ ሄ ህ ሆ
hä hu hi ha he hə ho

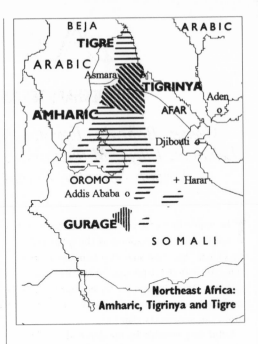

**Northeast Africa:
Amharic, Tigrinya and Tigre**

Amharic, TIGRINYA and Tigre on the map

The modern Semitic languages of Ethiopia are AMHARIC, Harari (13,000 speakers in the city of Harar), East Gurage (200,000 speakers), West Gurage (500,000 speakers), Soddo or Aymellel or Northern Gurage (100,000 speakers), Tigre and TIGRINYA.

There is relatively little dialect division in Amharic, though dialects of Shoa and Gojjam provinces are distinguished. The dialects of the old capital, Gondar, and the new capital, Addis Ababa, are both prestigious.

The heartland of *Tigrinya* speech is the highlands of southern Eritrea, and Tigre province across the Ethiopian border. Tigrinya is also dominant, serving as the national lingua franca, in the cities and towns of the Eritrean coast.

There are two dialects of *Tigre*, which may have about 100,000 speakers. The *Southern* or Highland dialect is spoken by the Mensa, Ad Timaryam and Ad Tekla tribes and most of the Red Marya. The *Northern* or Lowland dialect is spoken by the Habaab and Black Marya. This is the dialect in which the *Beni Amir* of Eritrea and Sudan are now bilingual (see BEJA).

ARABIC

PERHAPS 165,000,000 SPEAKERS

Algeria, Bahrain, Egypt, Eritrea, Iraq, Jordan, Kuwait, Lebanon, Libya, Mauritania, Morocco, Oman, Qatar, Saudi Arabia, Somalia, Sudan, Syria, Tunisia, Yemen

The importance of Arabic in the modern world goes back to its position as the language of the Qur'ān, the language of a conquering religion. As national language of nearly twenty countries, Arabic is now by far the most important of the SEMITIC LANGUAGES, which are a group within the AFROASIATIC family.

Arabic may possibly be the descendant of the language of the 'proto-Sinaitic' inscriptions of Mount Sinai, dated to about 1500 BC, but they are not fully deciphered. The first certain record of Arabic is in inscriptions from various parts of northern and central Arabia in the last few centuries BC. This is 'pre-classical' Arabic. Already several regional dialects existed.

Classical Arabic originates in the 7th century AD, when the masterpieces of pre-Qur'ānic poetry were composed (though written down only later) and when the Qur'ān itself was compiled. It immediately became the sacred text of the new religion of Islam – and, as Islam was spread by conquest, the Arabic language (in which the Qur'ān must be recited) spread with it.

The outreach of Arabic

So Arabic was from the beginning the literary and religious language of the rapidly spreading Islamic states of medieval North Africa and Asia. ARAMAIC of the Near East, COPTIC of Egypt, and BERBER LANGUAGES of North Africa retreated as Arabic advanced. Westwards, by the end of the 7th century, the Muslims held the whole north African coast. From here they advanced northwards across the Straits of Gibraltar (in 711) and on into Spain and southern France; southwards to the edge of the Sahara, and eventually across the desert to the plains of the western Sudan.

At this period Arabic must have spread very rapidly among people with different mother tongues, and there are signs – in the shape of Arabic loanwords in Spanish, for example – that pidgin and creole forms of the language existed. At least one Arabic text of the 11th century attempts to reproduce the pidgin Arabic of medieval Mauritania, with the remark: 'the blacks have mutilated our beautiful language and spoilt its eloquence with their twisted tongues' (quoted by S. G. Thomason and A. Elgibali).

In large parts of the conquered regions, Arabic eventually advanced from being the language of government, education and religion to become the language of everyday life. In most of these countries Arabic is now the national and majority language – but the Islamic countries were never entirely unified politically, and it is not surprising that over this great geographical range the language of the conquerors has split into dialects that are so different as to be mutually unintelligible.

In the Arabian Peninsula itself the dialects of Arabic have a history that goes back beyond Islamic times. They remain vigorous – even beyond the confines of the peninsula, for in northern Somalia the Yemeni and Hadhramaut dialects of Arabic are used as second languages, especially by traders.

Elsewhere, probably, a common language grew up among widely recruited armies, among

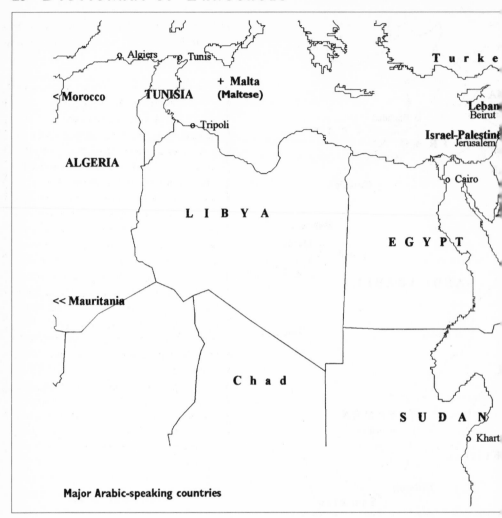

Major Arabic-speaking countries

Loanwords from Arabic

Italian *dogana*, French and international *douane* 'customs house'	*diwān* 'office'
Italian *fondaco* 'warehouse', Spanish *alóndiga* 'cornmarket'	*funduq* 'inn'
French *alchimie*, English *alchemy*; French *chimie*, English *chemistry*	*kīmīā* 'alchemy' (originally from Greek *khēmeíā*)
French *chiffre* 'figure', English *cypher*; Spanish *cero* 'zero', English *zero*	*sifr* 'zero'
French *sucre*, English *sugar*, Spanish *azucar*	*sukkar* 'sugar' (originally from Sanskrit *śarkarā*)
Shona *ndarama* 'money', Tswana *talama* 'button'	*darāhim* 'money' (plural of *dirham* 'coin', borrowed from ancient Greek *drakhma*)

of Malta (MALTESE) has noticeable Italian features. In Egypt, COPTIC survived alongside Arabic down to modern times.

Arabic and the transmission of cultural loanwords

'In many ways the Arabs did not create the culture they brought to Africa. They . . . handed on what they had previously acquired from other peoples, mainly the peoples of antiquity. That is why we find today in African languages words of such diverse origin as the words for pen, money, army and shirt from LATIN; for philosophy, paper, diamond and list from GREEK; for lead, temple, poor man and sulphur from Babylonian [AKKADIAN]; for offering, angel, praise and prayer from Syriac [ARAMAIC]; for soap, sugar, banana and musk from SANSKRIT. Most of the words they brought are genuinely Arabic, however, such as *zabīb* "grape", *sufūr* "copper", *katan* "cotton", *dawāt* "ink", *ibrīq* "kettle" and *dhahab* "gold".'

Jan Knappert, 'Contribution from the study of loanwords to the cultural history of Africa' in D. Dalby and others, *Language and history in Africa* (London: Cass, 1970) pp. 78–88

The further reaches

Eastwards, too, Islam spread rapidly – to Iran and central Asia, to large areas of northern India, to the Malay Archipelago, and many coastal kingdoms and provinces from Mozambique all the way to central Vietnam. Although Arabic did not become the everyday language of the majority in these areas, it became and remains a crucial influence. Wherever Islam is the religion, Arabic must be the language of religious education and traditional culture (map 2). Islamic fundamentalists, for example in Algeria and Turkey, tend to promote the sacred language and to depreciate local languages. And 'just as Latin and Greek supply the European language community with scientific terms and an educated vocabulary, Arabic performs that function within the Islamic

governments and the governed, and it is from this medieval Arabic common language or *koiné* that the modern dialects (map 1) descend.

Their differences come partly from the different later cultural history of their homelands. Thus in Morocco, Algeria and Tunisia Latin and Berber were native, and Berber languages are still spoken; French became a ruling language in the 19th century and is still widely known. The Arabic of Spain (long extinct) was also influenced by Berber because the armies that conquered Spain were recruited in north Africa. The Arabic of modern north Africa contains many local terms, such as plant names, which are of Berber origin. The Arabic dialect

world; thus lexical items like *jāmi ʿ* "mosque", *madrasa* "school", *qāʿida* "rule" exist in nearly all languages of Muslim peoples' (W. Fischer).

In parts of the Islamic world, religion remained the main field in which Arabic was used. But this can amount to a big slice of daily life. Arabic is the common language of those who undertake the pilgrimage to Mecca, and is used for communication in all the towns and cities on the usual pilgrimage routes. Arabic came to be essential in some everyday fields, such as trade. On the edges of the Arabic-speaking world, strongly marked dialects, shading into pidgins and creoles, have developed. Alongside the dialectal Arabic of Mauritania, Chad, Sudan and lowland Eritrea, there are Arabic pidgins and creoles in Nigeria, Chad, Sudan and upland Eritrea.

Well beyond the Arabic language zone some isolated Arabic-speaking communities were established: some survive. There are still a few Arabic speakers in Afghanistan, claiming to be descendants of the Arabian nomads who once formed the armies of Islam.

Although so closely associated with Islam, Arabic is also the language of some Christian communities, notably the Maronites of Lebanon and Cyprus. Arabic in Syriac script, called *Karshuni*, is used in some religious texts of the Syrian Orthodox Church (whose everyday language is ARAMAIC). The first Arabic printed book was in Christian-Arabic Karshuni, though medieval block prints from Egypt take the history of printed Arabic further back – well before the introduction of printing into Europe.

Distinctive forms of Arabic, sometimes called *Yahudi*, are spoken by Jews of Morocco, Tunisia, south-eastern Turkey and other countries.

> Although persecuted for centuries, the Yezidi religion is maintained in some Kurdish villages in Iraq, Iran, Syria and south-western Turkey by up to 150,000 believers. Originating from an early heretical Islamic sect, and with some Jewish, Christian and pagan elements, its religious rites are carried out in Arabic. Each believer has a special bond with a brother or sister in the next world.

Classical and modern

While regional dialects have continued to differentiate across the Arabic-speaking world, classical Arabic has – for 1,300 years – remained alive and vigorous. It is the official language of Arabic-speaking governments, the written language of literature, and the spoken language of inter-regional communication and trade. Without the Arabic tradition of education, centred on the Islamic religion and the Qur'ān, this position could not possibly have been maintained.

In the last two centuries, with the spread of modern education and communications, the position of classical Arabic has strengthened even further. It is the natural medium, in all Arabic-speaking countries, for the press, broadcasting and films.

Naturally 'modern standard Arabic' has its own regional accents and shows some dialect variation, reflected more or less noticeably in individuals' speech. But it is now so different from the various colloquial spoken forms of Arabic that these are often studied quite separately from the classical written language.

In the centuries after Muhammad, Arabic had become the vehicle of one of the great literary cultures of the world. Beside original writings, translations from Greek and Syriac contributed to the flourishing of Arabic science, medicine and philosophy. Many of these texts were afterwards translated into Latin for European scholars, helping to create an early renaissance – preceding the real Renaissance – in Western scholarship. After some centuries of stagnation, Arabic literature is flourishing once more in the 20th century.

Arabic in the world

The dialects of Arabic group as follows: Central Asian, Iraqi, Arabian, Syro-Lebano-Palestinian, Egyptian, North African (Maghrebi), MALTESE, West African (Hassaniya), Chadic (Shua), Sudanese. The Arabian dialects show the greatest differentiation.

Turku is a name (no longer used locally) for an

Arabic pidgin spoken east of Lake Chad and in the Bodélé depression.

Sudanese Creole Arabic (or Juba Arabic or Mongallese or Bimbashi Arabic) is an important lingua franca of the southern Sudan, a first language for some people, also used by many whose first languages are Nilo-Saharan.

Nubi is an Arabic creole that grew out of this, now spoken in Kenya (notably in the Kibera suburb of Nairobi) and Uganda (notably at Bombo near Kampala) by the descendants of slave troops who were recruited from various Sudanese peoples into the Egyptian army during the Egyptian conquest of the Sudan in the 19th century. Most of them transferred to the British Army in East Africa in the 1890s.

Well beyond the countries in which it has become the language of everyday life, Islamic conquests and religious proselytism have spread the knowledge of the language as a means of communication. Here Arabic remains necessary as the language of the Qur'ān and of education, but other languages are used outside these contexts: TEMNE, SUSU, SONINKE, MANDEKAN, BERBER LANGUAGES, SONGHAY, YORUBA, HAUSA, FULANI, KANURI, MABA, TIGRINYA, OROMO, SOMALI, SWAHILI, AZERI, CHECHEN, PERSIAN, TURKISH, URDU, BENGALI, MALAY, CHAM. All these have been strongly influenced by Arabic in their role as languages of Islamic states and peoples.

A second map looks at the South Arabian

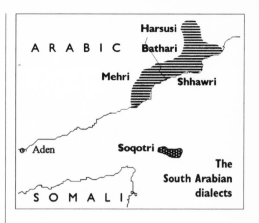

The South Arabian dialects

languages. Epigraphic South Arabian is a language known from inscriptions of the early city states of south-west Arabia, possibly beginning as early as the 8th century BC and continuing to the 6th century AD. There are five dialects, Sabaean, Minaean, Qatabanian, Ḥaḍramī and Awsanian. The scripts used in early South Arabian inscriptions are closely related to early Arabic scripts and to the writing system used for Ethiopic. Some modern dialects of southern Arabia, not closely related to Arabic, seem likely to represent a modern form of the same language (though the ancient inscriptions have not been deciphered fully enough to be quite certain). The best known of the modern South Arabian languages are Mehrī, Shhawrī and Soqotrī (of the island of Socotra).

Arabic numerals			
	Standard Arabic: masculine	**Standard Arabic: feminine**	**Hassaniya dialect**	**Nubi Arabic creole**
1	aḥad	iḥdā	wahad	wai
2	ithnāni	ithnatāni	azenein	tinin
3	thalātha	thalāth	tlata	talata
4	arba'a	arba'	arba	arba
5	khamsa	khams	khamsa	khamsa
6	sitta	sitt	sitta	sita
7	sab'a	sab'	saba	saba
8	thamāniya	thamānin	esmania	tamanya
9	tis'a	tis'	tissa	tisa
10	'ashara	'ashr	ashra	ashara

Arabic script

Arabic script developed in the 6th century AD. It originates from an early Aramaic alphabet, which in turn was derived from Phoenician.

The Arabic alphabet

ن م ل ى ق ف غ ع ظ ط ض ص ش س ز ر ذ د خ ح ج ث ت ب ا

ي و ه

a b t t j ḥ kh d ḍ r z s š ṣ ḍ ṭ ẓ ' gh f q k l m n h w y

In the box the full form of each individual letter is shown, arranged from left to right to match the transliterations in the second row. But Arabic is written and read from right to left, and much-simplified forms of some letters are used in normal writing and printing when they are joined into words.

Thus *al-Qur'ān* 'the Qur'ān' is written الفرآن.

Arabic is the fastest and most cursive of all scripts: but short vowels are in general not written and the reader must supply them from a knowledge of the language and its structure. Vowels can, if necessary, be fully marked in Arabic writing by the use of signs above and below the line, but these are generally used only in texts of the Qur'ān itself, where correct pronunciation is essential for religious reasons.

Arabic script has been carried to many parts of the world with Islamic culture and religion. In slightly varying forms it is used for a number of other languages quite unrelated to Arabic, notably Persian and Urdu. It is no longer the usual script for Turkish, Malay, Swahili and Hausa, as it was until early in the 20th century.

ARAMAIC AND SYRIAC

200,000 SPEAKERS

United States, Georgia, Iraq, Turkey, Iran, Syria

One of the SEMITIC LANGUAGES, Aramaic was an international language of the Near East from the 7th century BC and was the ruling language of the great Persian Empire from the 6th to the 4th centuries. Syriac, a later form of Aramaic, was the principal language of the borderland between the Roman and Parthian empires. Both Aramaic and Syriac have been important languages of religion. Tenuously, Aramaic still survives as a living language today.

In the Bible, Aram was one of the sons of Shem. The Aramaeans, whose ancestor he was supposed to be, first appear in Biblical and other Near Eastern texts as a nomadic people of the desert east of Palestine and south-east of Syria, threatening, and eventually conquering, Damascus and other cities in Syria and northern Iraq.

Old Aramaic inscriptions, the first direct evidence of the language, are found in all these regions and are dated to the 10th century BC onwards.

Classical (or Imperial) Aramaic was the form of the language that was used in the Assyrian, Babylonian and Persian empires and in the period that followed. It was under Persian rule that Aramaic spread most widely. In the last few centuries BC, inscriptions in Aramaic were erected all the way from the Greek-speaking Hellespont to the Prakrit-speaking plains of the lower Indus valley. Aramaic was a world language.

Yet, with the destruction of the Persian Empire by Alexander the Great and his successors, Aramaic was now no longer the national language of a major state. It remained in very widespread use in the Greek and other kingdoms that supplanted Persia, but it now gradually split into dialects, usually grouped into 'West Aramaic' and 'East Aramaic'.

In the course of the Jewish migrations recorded in the Old Testament, Aramaic had become the everyday language of the Jews. It was the language of some of the Dead Sea Scrolls, and it was certainly the daily language spoken by Jesus Christ. Although nearly all of the Old Testament itself was composed in Hebrew, there are Aramaic passages in the Biblical books of Ezra (iv.8 to vi.18, vii.12 to 26) and Daniel (ii.4 to vii.28). Later Jewish religious texts, notably the vast collection known as the *Jerusalem Talmud*, are in Aramaic throughout. In due course, with continued Jewish migrations, Aramaic too fell out of everyday use: but a Jewish religious education still embraces both Hebrew and Aramaic. This *Jewish Palestinian Aramaic* is normally written in Hebrew script.

Jewish Palestinian Aramaic is the best-known representative of 'West Aramaic'. To the same dialect group belong the languages, as recorded in many inscriptions, of two important states on the border of the Roman Empire – Palmyra (once called Tadmor) and Nabataea, whose capital was at Petra. The spoken language of Petra was apparently Arabic: its inscriptions are in a dialect of Aramaic that is clearly mixed with early Arabic forms. Samaritan, language of a separate Jewish community of Roman and early medieval Palestine, was a fourth dialect of 'West Aramaic'.

The surviving Samaritans of Nablus in Israel now speak Arabic, but their religious texts and ceremonies are in Samaritan Aramaic, which they continued to use as a literary language till the 19th century.

Centring in the originally independent kingdom of Edessa (now Urfa), to the north-east of Palestine and Roman Syria, *Syriac* became the vehicle of a flourishing Christian culture. The New Testament and many other Greek religious texts were translated into Syriac. An original literature of hymns, sermons and theological and historical works grew up in this form of Aramaic, with its distinctive alphabet (see box). Syriac was the medium through which early Christian writings reached Armenia and Arabia and were re-translated into those languages. Syriac literature is dated to the 3rd to 13th centuries AD.

East Aramaic includes Syriac, and also Mandaean and *Babylonian Aramaic*. The latter was the language of the Jews of the Parthian and later Persian Empire: it is the language, therefore, of the *Babylonian Talmud* and of many magical texts of the 4th to 6th centuries. *Mandaean* or Mandaic is the distinctive written language of the Gnostic Christians of Iraq, whose literature dates from the 3rd to 8th centuries.

Much further east, the Nestorian Christians took their Syriac language across central Asia, where Syriac inscriptions near Bishkek and Tokmak in Kyrgyzstan date back to the 14th century. For nearly two thousand years there was a Syriac-speaking Christian community, the 'St Thomas Christians', in south India. Their Bibles and other religious manuscripts in Syriac were rediscovered with astonishment by Western scholars in the 19th century, though by that time few if any of the congregations were able to understand the language.

Modern dialects of Aramaic are still spoken by small minorities in Iraq, Turkey, Iran and Syria (see map). Numbers are difficult to determine. The majority of speakers, it is said, are in émigré communities in Armenia and Georgia (where they migrated after the Russo-Persian War of 1827) and in the United States. It is a mark of the cohesion of these émigré communities that Aramaic was recognised as a 'national language of the USSR', with a new Cyrillic orthography. The major modern dialect, *Sūriṯ* or 'Assyrian', has 15 vowels, in three sets of five: each word shows vowel harmony, with all its vowels belonging to one set.

Periods of recorded Aramaic		
Palestine, Jordan and western Syria		**Eastern Syria and Iraq**
Old Aramaic	1000–700 BC	Old Aramaic
Classical Aramaic	700–100 BC	Classical Aramaic
Palestinian, Samaritan, Palmyrene, Nabataean	100 BC–AD 700	Babylonian Aramaic, Mandaean
	AD 200–1300	Syriac
Modern West Aramaic	AD 1800 to date	Modern East Aramaic ('Modern Assyrian') émigrés

Modern Aramaic on the map

An East Aramaic dialect, *Ṭūroyo* (sometimes called 'modern Assyrian' or 'Neo-Syriac') is spoken by Christian communities of the Syrian Orthodox Church whose traditional homes are on the Ṭūr 'Abdīn plateau in Turkey. Their religious texts are in Syriac and Arabic, in the western Syriac script. Most of the 30,000 remaining Turkish speakers of Turoyo now live in Istanbul.

A second East Aramaic dialect, *Sūriṯ*, is spoken by 'Chaldaean' Christians in Iraq and in a few villages in eastern Turkey. Some Nestorian or 'Assyrian' Christian communities remain in Iran (the plateau of Urmiā), Iraq (near Mosul) and Turkey: they also speak Surit and they have a written form of their language for daily use. Both

Nestorians and Chaldaeans use classical Syriac, in eastern Syriac script, for worship. The majority of the Christian communities no longer live in these country districts. Most of those who have not emigrated now cluster in the big cities, Tehran and Baghdad. There were also Jewish communities speaking Surit, but they have migrated en masse to Israel, and may already have ceased to use their language.

Numerals in Aramaic		
Biblical		
Aramaic		**Sūrit**
hadh	1	kha
tərēn	2	tre
təlāthā	3	ṭlå
'arbə'ā	4	årpå
hamshā	5	khamsha
shittā	6	ishtæ
sibh'ā	7	shåvå
təmanyā	8	tmænyæ
tish'ā	9	ïchå
ashrā	10	ïsrå

David Cohen, *Les langues chamito-sémitiques*
(Les langues dans le monde ancien et moderne
ed. Jean Perrot, pt 3) (Paris: CNRS, 1988)

The third East Aramaic dialect is *Modern Mandaean*, spoken near Akhwaz and Khorramshahr in Iran. In three villages near Damascus –

Ma'lūla, Jubb'adīn and Bah'a – a West Aramaic dialect is still spoken. It is sometimes called Ma'lūla.

Aramaic writing systems

Aramaic in writing

ℸ ℷ ℸ ℸ ℸ ℸ ℷ ℷ ⨀ ℨ ℸ ℓ ℷ ℷ ℸ ○ ℷ ℸ ℘ ℸ Ш ✕
'bgdhwzḥṭyklmns'pṣqršt

The oldest known Aramaic alphabets (an example is shown in the top line of the first box) were developed from an early Phoenician script. These Aramaic alphabets had many local variants, such as the Nabataean shown in the third line of the box. They were the parents from which were developed the Syriac, Arabic and Hebrew scripts of medieval and modern times.

Still sometimes seen in print is the Syriac alphabet, which is essentially that of the Christian Syriac literature of Roman times and after. Syriac script, like the Arabic from which it derives, is able to indicate vowels by using diacritical marks. The second alphabet box shows the consonant signs of the East Syriac (above) and West Syriac (below) alphabets as now printed.

The Syriac alphabet

'bgdhwzḥṭyklmns'pṣqršt

Fonts from *Gamma Unitype* (Gamma Productions)

ARAUCANIAN

PERHAPS 300,000 SPEAKERS

Chile, Argentina

One of the AMERIND LANGUAGES, Araucanian is still spoken by one of the larger linguistic communities of the southern half of South America (see map at QUECHUA). It has no close relatives.

> Its speakers call themselves Mapuche, 'people of the earth [*mapu*]', and their name for their language is *Mapudungun*. In Spanish it is *Araucano*: this word comes from the name of the town *Arauco* 'limestone', as does the botanical name of the monkey puzzle tree, *Araucaria imbricata*.

Araucanian was once spoken over most of central Chile, from Copiapo, five hundred kilometres north of Santiago, southwards to the island of Chiloe, and all the way across Argentina to the bay of Comodoro Rivadavia. The warlike Mapuche did not submit easily to Spanish-speaking suzerains, and suffered repeated military defeats and massacres. Nowadays Araucanian speakers have almost disappeared from Argentina, while even in Chile Araucanian-speaking country now begins several hundred kilometres south of Santiago, around Temuco, the town that used to be called *Mapuchu cara*, 'city of the Mapuche'. Few speakers are now monolingual in Araucanian; most, if not bilingual, are at least accustomed to using Spanish as well as their mother tongue.

Araucanian has contributed to Spanish – and thus to English – the word *gaucho* (Araucanian *cauchu* 'nomad, adventurer'), which became the name for the mixed Araucanian and Spanish nomadic population of the pampas. Many Chilean place names are of Araucanian origin, such as *Caramavida* from *carü mahuida* 'green mountain'.

The first ten numerals in Araucanian are: *kiñe, epu, küla, meli, kechu, kayu, relke, pura, ailla, mari*.

Based on M. Malherbe, *Les langues de l'humanité* (Paris: Laffont, 1995) pp. 1196–200, and other sources

ARDHAMAGADHI

CLASSICAL LANGUAGE OF INDIA

One of the INDO-ARYAN LANGUAGES, Ardhamagadhi is the language of the canonical Jain scriptures. It is known in two forms. One, found in the earliest sutras, is roughly contemporary with Pali. The other, dating from around the 6th century AD, may be based on the spoken language of what is now eastern Uttar Pradesh; an almost identical dialect was also used for Buddhist dramas.

The Jains (Sanskrit *Jaina*, 'follower of a *jina* or victor') hold to a strongly ascetic religion that arose in northern India around the same time as Buddhism. It has never been a mass movement. Its believers are to be found mostly in Gujarat and Rajasthan. Most Jains have the surname *Shah*.

Ardhamagadhī is 'half-Magadhī', a name that links the language to the Prakrit dialect of north-eastern India, which was also claimed to be the closest relative of Pali, the language of Buddhism.

There is no single Jain holy book: the canonical scriptures as known today are incomplete and the two sects (*Dīgambara*, 'sky-clothed', whose ascetics go naked; *Svētāmbara*, 'white-clothed') disagree over their authenticity. Jains (including émigré communities, such as those in East Africa) still use Ardhamagadhi in religious ritual, though most have not learnt the language and do not understand what is said.

The first ten numerals in Ardhamagadhi are: *ege, do, tao, cattaro, paṃca, cha, satta, aṭṭha, nava, dasa.*

ARMENIAN

2,000,000 SPEAKERS

Armenia, Iran

For more than 1,500 years Armenia was ruled by Persia, or by kings who owed allegiance to Persia. As a result, Armenian is so heavily influenced by Persian that scholars once counted it as an Iranian language. It is now certain that Armenian forms a separate branch of the INDO-EUROPEAN LANGUAGES. It is spoken in the Republic of Armenia, in north-western Iran, and by several large and well-established Armenian communities in other parts of the world.

The Armenians call themselves *Hai*. The name of *Armenia* is found in Persian and Greek texts from the 6th century BC onwards.

Most Indo-European scholars think that early Armenian speakers reached eastern Asia Minor, perhaps as late as the first millennium BC, after migrating across Asia Minor from the west. No clear archaeological evidence has been found to support this, but Armenian seems to have similarities with Greek and with the extinct Indo-European dialects of the early Balkans. The language is spoken approximately where the Urartians, whose language was Caucasian and not Indo-European, reigned in the 9th to 6th centuries BC.

The history of Armenia becomes clearer after the first Persian conquest, around 500 BC. There was, from this time onwards, Greek cultural influence: Greek plays were performed, and even written, at the Armenian court. The overlordship of Armenia was to be a long-running dispute between the Roman and Sassanian (Persian) empires. Armenia was in classical times a far larger state than it is now, and the language was spoken across eastern Turkey as far south as Edessa, capital of the state of Osroene, which was bilingual in Syriac (see ARAMAIC) and Armenian.

Christianity in Armenia may be dated to the conversion of King Trdat by St Gregory the Illuminator in AD 314. Armenian literature began in the 5th century with literal translations of Christian texts: for the Armenian Orthodox church, though eventually independent, was at first heavily dependent on Greek teaching. Words coined by the translators, anxious to find a precise match for Greek and Syriac religious terminology, still survive in modern Armenian. Persian political dominance, meanwhile, gave rise to numerous loanwords. Words of Iranian and Persian origin actually form a majority of the entries in Armenian dictionaries.

Classical Armenian, the *grabar*, essentially the language of the translations and the earliest Armenian literature, is still taught. It is now a very different language from the modern spoken dialects. These, in the 19th century, formed the basis of two essentially new literary languages or dialects, Eastern Armenian of the present Republic of Armenia (which became independent from the Soviet Union in 1991), and Western Armenian of Turkey and the diaspora.

Rich in consonants like the CAUCASIAN LANGUAGES that surround it, full of foreign loanwords from its dramatic history, Armenian still has a clearly Indo-European structure. Nouns have seven cases, singular and plural. As in ancient Greek, classical Armenian verbs have an *e-* prefix to mark the past tense, though this is now only added to monosyllabic forms: *berē* 'he bears', *eber* 'he bore'.

South-west
Asia:
Armenian

Armenians across the world

Both in their own homeland and in their migrations, Armenians have long lived in a multilingual environment. Persian, Russian and Turkish have been necessary not only politically but also to communicate with near neighbours. There is a fine body of oral epic poetry in Armenia and eastern Asia Minor. It is not surprising that oral poets in recent centuries often had bilingual skills, in Armenian and Turkish, or even trilingual, able to entertain Persian-speaking audiences as well.

The *Hemsinli* are Armenians of Asia Minor who converted to Islam in the 15th and 16th centuries: they remain settled in valleys of Artvin province in Turkey, where many work in the transport business. *Posha* or *Boşa*, a variety of Armenian with many Indo-Aryan words, is spoken by a Gypsy-like nomadic group, the Lomavren, of Azerbaijan, Armenia and the Lake Van region of Turkey.

A considerable population of Armenians settled in the Crimea, under Genoese rule, in the 14th and 15th centuries. They eventually moved on to Poland and Transylvania in the 17th century, by which time they spoke not Armenian but a Kipchak Turkic dialect (which they wrote in Armenian script) and they had converted to Roman Catholicism.

Other Armenian colonies are also long-established. The first Armenian daily newspaper was published in Constantinople in 1832. The Armenian Mekhitarist monastery on the Venetian island of San Lazaro has printed Armenian literature and religious texts since its foundation by Mekhitar in 1717 – but Armenians had settled in Venice ever since the 13th century. Gherla (German *Armenierstadt*) and Dumbrăveni (German *Elisabethstadt*) in Romania were once Armenian towns. There have been large Armenian communities in Smyrna, Vienna, Lwów, Moscow, Cairo and Aleppo. Beirut, Paris, Montreal and Los Angeles are important Armenian centres today.

The Armenian dialects

The lands where Armenian was spoken have been politically divided for many centuries. In medieval times the south-western half, 'Cilician Armenia' or 'Little Armenia', makes frequent appearances in the history of the Crusades. 'Greater Armenia' to the north-east was approximately where the Republic of Armenia is now. As a result, already in the 10th century there were two dialects of spoken Armenian. One was the ancestor of the Eastern Armenian still spoken in the Republic of Armenia and in Iran. The independence of Armenia (the medieval 'Greater Armenia'), asserted at the Russian Revolution, was crushed by Turkish and then Russian troops. Independence was again declared in 1991.

The other dialect, Western Armenian, was the language of Cilician Armenia and was still spoken in that region until the genocide of 1913, when most of the Armenian Christians living within the borders of what is now Turkey (the majority Turkish speakers, the minority retaining their ancestral Armenian) were killed. Western Armenian is still spoken by the 75,000 Armenians of Istanbul and is the dominant dialect in the worldwide Armenian diaspora.

Nagorno-Karabakh (Mountain Karabakh, half of the old Khanate of Karabakh) is an Armenian-speaking enclave within the borders of Azerbaijan. The latest Armenian attempt to annex Nagorno-Karabakh, in 1988, has led to war and the expulsion of hundreds of thousands of Armenians from Azerbaijan. Azeris likewise fled Armenia. Armenian traders still form large minorities in other cities of the Caucasus.

Armenian in writing

The Armenian script was invented by Mesrop Mashtots' in 405 so that religious texts could be translated into the local language from Syriac and Greek. According to legend, he invented quite different alphabets for Georgian and for a third language of the Caucasus then called Albanian.

The first *original* text in Armenian, appropriately enough, was a biography of Mashtots by his pupil Koriwn. The usual Armenian text font is small and slanting. For clarity a larger, rounded font, more appropriate to newspaper headlines, is used in the box. The transliteration given, with its range of diacritical marks, is the one preferred by the majority of linguists.

Numerals in Armenian

մէկ	1	mēk
երկու	2	erkow
երեք	3	erek'
չորս	4	čors
հինգ	5	hing
վեց	6	vec'
եօթը	7	eōt'ə
ութը	8	owt'ə
ինը	9	inə
տասը	10	tasə

The Armenian alphabet

Ա Բ Գ Դ Ե Զ Է Ը Թ Ժ Ի Լ Խ Ծ Կ Հ Ձ Ղ Ճ Մ Յ Ն Շ Ո Չ Պ Ջ Ռ Ս Վ Տ Ր Ց Ի Փ Ք Օ Ֆ

ա բ գ դ ե զ է ը թ ժ ի լ խ ծ կ հ ձ ղ ճ մ յ ն շ ո չ պ ջ ռ ս վ տ ր ց ի փ ք օ ֆ

a b g d e z ē ə t' ž i l x c k h j ł č m y n š o č' p ǰ ř s v t r c' w p' k' ō f

AROMUNIAN

PERHAPS 200,000 SPEAKERS

Greece, Albania, Macedonia

Aromunian is one of the ROMANCE LANGUAGES, very close linguistically to ROMANIAN (see map there).

It is the most direct reminder of the fact that the Balkans belonged to the Roman Empire from the 1st century BC onwards. Latin was once spoken across much of south-eastern Europe. It is to be seen in the public announcements and private inscriptions still surviving in museums. It can be found in loanwords in Albanian, modern Greek and the south Slavonic languages.

The Latin speech of the Balkans was last recorded in the words of peasant soldiers in the Byzantine army in a battle of AD 587. And then it went underground for eleven hundred years.

The arrival of Slavonic speakers in large numbers from the 5th century onwards simply drove the Romance speech of the Balkans out of public view. Thus, while the medieval descendants of Latin became national languages in Spain, France and Italy, it shrank back to the more inaccessible mountain areas of north-western Greece, central Albania and southern Macedonia.

It is here – particularly in the Pindos mountains – that the *Aromunians* or *Vlachs* are now to be found. The word *Vlach* is the same historically as *Wallachian, Walloon* and *Welsh* – it had come to mean simply 'speakers of a strange language' – but, curiously, its origin appears to be the name of the Celtic tribe of eastern Gaul, *Volcae*, who were once on the linguistic frontier between Celtic and Germanic speech.

The Vlachs of northern Greece have been a highly prosperous community, prominent in local and long distance trade. The Gypsies of Turkey refer to Gypsies who are no longer nomadic as *Velakhos*.

There has been very little literature in Aromunian. A landmark is the Aromunian Haji Daniil's *Lexicon tetraglosson* 'four-language dictionary' (Voskopojë, 1764) whose aim was to teach Greek to the Albanian, Aromunian and Macedonian speakers of the region. In the 20th century Romanian scholars have been at the forefront of research on Aromunian, a language which gets no official recognition in its native territory.

Turn back! Turn back!

ἐπιχωρίῳ γλώττῃ εἰς τοὐπίσω τραπέσθαι ἄλλος ἄλλῳ προσέταττεν, **τόρνα, τόρνα** μετὰ μεγίστου ταράχου φθεγγόμενοι, οἷα νυκτομαχίας τινὸς ἐνδημούσης ἀδοκήτως αὐτοῖς.

In their peasant speech each man told the next to turn back, shouting *Torna, torna!* in great confusion, as if panicked by an unexpected night attack.

A unique record of the Romance speech of the Balkans, later to emerge as Aromunian, from the 7th-century Greek chronicler Theophylactus Simocatta.

Floară gălbinioară,	Yellow saw-wort,
dimând-a tutuloru,	ask them all,
dimând-a feateloru,	ask the girls,
se yină se-ñi me alumbă	to come to me
duminecă dimneaţa	on Sunday morning
şi luni de cătră seară,	and Monday in the evening,
cu roauă se-ñi-mi adună,	to gather me with the dew
ş-pre avră se-ñi-mi poartă	and bear me with the breeze
pre iapă nefitată,	upon an ass that has not foaled,
pre feată nemărtată,	a girl that has not married,
pre gione neinsuratu	a boy that has not taken a wife,
ş-pre cale necalcată.	and a road that is untrodden.

Aromunian folk song collected by C. Récatas. Every word is of Latin origin

After Th. Capidan, *Les Macédo-roumains* (Bucharest, 1937)

ASSAMESE

12,000,000 SPEAKERS

India

Assamese is the easternmost of the INDO-ARYAN LANGUAGES of India. It is spoken in the Indian state of Assam, in the middle Brahmaputra valley, where that wide river flows south-westwards eventually to reach the Bay of Bengal. Until modern times this was the eastern outpost of the whole Indo-European language family.

> *Assamese*, called by its own speakers *Asamiya*, is named after the Indian state (Assamese *Asam*, pronounced *Ohom*) which in turn gets its name from the Tai people who dominated the region from the 13th to the 19th centuries (see AHOM).

Assamese developed its special character because, unlike Bengali and Hindi, it was not simply a language of the Indian plains. Mountains shadow the lower Brahmaputra valley on both sides. Their inhabitants speak numerous quite unrelated languages, Tai, Austroasiatic and Sino-Tibetan. Assamese became the lingua franca of all these peoples, and in the process lost many of the features that almost all other Indian languages share – notably the retroflex consonants made by curling the tongue backwards towards the palate. Assamese, by contrast, shares with English the unusual feature of alveolar consonants (English *t, d*): these are formed when the tongue touches the alveolar ridge above the upper teeth.

Assamese vocabulary, basically inherited from SANSKRIT, includes borrowings from Khasi (*bhur* 'raft'), from Munda languages (*kadu* 'gourd') and from Ahom (*jeka* 'moist'). Bodo and related Sino-Tibetan languages are the source of many borrowed words (*celek* 'lick'; *gaba-mar* 'embrace';

thalamuri-mar 'slap') and apparently of the diminutive suffix *-ca* (e.g. *kala* 'black'; *kalca* 'blackish'). Bengali and English have both influenced Assamese strongly. For a table of numerals see BENGALI.

Assamese is first recognisable as a separate language from Bengali in poetry of about 1400 onwards. Sankara Deva, greatest of the Vaishnavite devotional poets, flourished around 1500. Assamese prose writing begins with translations of the Sanskrit *Bhagavadgītā* and *Bhāgavatapurāna* a century later. All this literature came from the small kingdoms of western Assam. Meanwhile at the Ahom court, to the east, Assamese became the court language in the 17th century, and prose chronicles, earlier composed in Ahom, began to be written in Assamese – of a noticeably modern form. Literature faded in the last half-century of Ahom rule, a chaotic period with rebellions, Burmese and British interventions, and massacres.

The British, who finally took control of Assam in 1826, tried to impose Bengali as the language of courts and education, but gave up in 1873 and made Assam a separate province of their Indian empire. *A few remarks on the Assamese language and on vernacular education in Assam*, by 'A Native' (Anandaram Dhekiyal Phukan), published at Sibsagar in 1855, influenced the change of policy. So did the publications of the American Baptists at the Sibsagar Mission Press, which encouraged the use of modern, colloquial language in Assamese literature.

Oriya, Bengali, Assamese: the map

Oriya is the language of Orissa State. *Sambalpuri* is the dialect of the Sambalpur lowlands, while

Bhatri, a quite distinct dialect, is spoken in Bastar District of Madhya Pradesh.

Malpaharia, an aberrant western dialect of Bengali, is spoken in the Rajmahal hills, in the Santal parganas of Bihar, where Malto was spoken until recently.

Bengali is divided into several dialect groups. Calcutta, whose language helps to form the standard in Indian West Bengal, belongs to the Central group; Dacca, which increasingly sets the standard for Bangladesh, speaks an Eastern dialect.

Sylheti, often counted as a separate language (see BENGALI), has many as 5,000,000 speakers in Sylhet District, a hundred miles north-east of Dacca.

Rajbangshi and a group of related dialects extend Bengali northwards from Rangpur in Bangladesh towards the Darjeeling Terai and south-eastern Nepal.

The *South-eastern Bengali* dialect of Chittagong and Noakhali is so different from the standard that it has been considered a separate language.

Chakma, spoken in the Chittagong Hills, has its own script, resembling that of some southeast Asian languages. It claims 68,000 speakers in Tripura and Mizoram, India, and more in Bangladesh.

The influence of the Mission Press at Sibsagar (continuing that of the Ahom court!) ensured that the dialect of eastern Assam would become the modern standard for *Assamese*. This eastern dialect, fairly uniform because the region has been politically unified for several centuries, is spoken on both banks of the Brahmaputra from Sadiya down to the modern capital Gauhati.

The western dialects of Kamrup and Goalpara Districts (historically separate small kingdoms) are very different from eastern Assamese and from one another. Kamrupi stresses initial syllables of words, like Bengali.

Naga Pidgin or *Nagamese* is a variety of Assamese – perhaps a kind of creole, but linguists differ over definitions here – that has become the lingua franca of the polyglot Indian state of Nagaland. It has at least 500,000 speakers. Among some Naga peoples it has been used for 150 years or more in trading with one another and with the valley of Assam. Although now used informally in many schools, Naga Pidgin has so many variant forms that it is difficult to produce an acceptable set of textbooks in it.

Assamese script

অ আ ই ঈ উ ঊ এ ঐ ও ঔ ক খ গ ঘ ঙ চ ছ জ ঝ ঞ ট ঠ ড ঢ ণ ত থ দ ধ ন প ফ ব ভ ম য র ল ৱ শ ষ স হ

a ā i ī u ū e ai o au k kh g gh ṅ c ch j jh ñ ṭ ṭh ḍ ḍh ṇ t th d dh n p ph b bh m y r l v ś ṣ s h

---

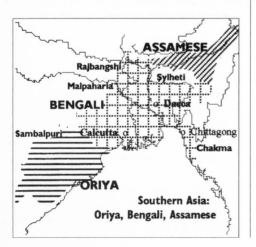

Southern Asia:
Oriya, Bengali, Assamese

Assamese in writing

The Assamese alphabet is almost the same as the Bengali, though the sound system is quite different. Assamese spelling is not phonetic, but it does help to show the origins and derivations of words. In the early 19th century the influential Baptist Mission Press introduced a modernised spelling closer to actual pronunciation, but then gradually reverted to the traditional Sanskritised spelling familiar to educated Assamese readers.

AUSTRALIAN LANGUAGES

When Europeans first began to explore and settle in Australia, about three hundred languages were spoken by the hunter-gatherer peoples (possibly 300,000 people in total) who inhabited the continent. Now there are fewer than 150 languages, and few indeed will survive beyond the next generation. The language that rules Australia is ENGLISH.

Australia is the 'Southern Land', already named *Terra Australis* in Latin on 16th-century maps, long before any European had seen it.

All but two or three of the recorded Australian languages can be confidently attached to a single family. Within it, a single branch, Pama-Nyungan, accounts for the indigenous languages of nine-tenths of Australia. Far greater linguistic diversity is found in the Arnhem Land region, the northern third of Northern Territory and the north-eastern segment of Western Australia.

The languages of Tasmania were perhaps not related to those of Australia. The two land masses were separated, 12,000 years ago, by a rise in sea level that flooded the Bass Strait. There were as many as twelve languages spoken on the island when Europeans began to settle there. Many speakers were exterminated, and the languages ceased to be spoken around 1900 before any serious linguistic records had been made, though a few amateurish wordlists and one or two recordings of songs do exist.

Research on Australian languages has been slow to develop, though some wordlists were made in the late 18th and 19th centuries. The first book about an Australian language was the Rev. L. E. Threlkeld's introduction to Awaba, a now extinct language of the Lake Macquarie region, published in 1827.

Australian loanwords in English

Kangaroo: Guugu Yimidhirr, the language of the Endeavour Bay district, is the source of the first Australian loanword to reach English. In that language *gangurru* is the term for a large black kangaroo, the male *Macropus robustus*. The word was noted down by Sir Joseph Banks, a member of Captain Cook's exploring party in 1770.

Boomerang: The *bumariñ*, as it is called in the Dharuk language of New South Wales, was first described in English in 1825: 'a short crested weapon which the natives of Port Jackson propel into a rotary motion, which gives a precalculated bias to its forcible fall'. By 1846 it was famous enough to find its way into a simile in an American poem:

Like the strange missile which the Australian throws,
Your verbal boomerang slaps you on the nose.

Based on *Australian words and their origins* ed. Joan Hughes (Melbourne: Oxford University Press, 1989) and other sources

In the last few decades much has been done to record dying languages, often by eliciting almost-forgotten vocabulary from the last one or two surviving speakers. A great deal of oral literature and music has been collected. Most Australian peoples tell legends in prose. Songs are reflective rather than narrative, but some genres of songs can be linked with the legend cycles.

In most or all Australian languages there is a separate speech register, with different vocabulary and sometimes a different sound pattern, used when speaking in the presence of a taboo relative such as a man's mother-in-law (see box). Special registers or secret languages may also exist for use among young men undergoing initiation.

The first external influence on Australian languages came from MAKASAR traders, who began to visit Arnhem Land in the 17th century. A few resulting loanwords have been identified in languages of the north-west, such as *rrupiya* 'money' which came via Makasar from Sanskrit *rūpya* 'wrought silver' (compare Indian English *rupee*).

The first English-speaking settlements, notably the prison camp at Botany Bay, followed soon afterwards. Interaction with settlers of Brit-ish and European origin, who now occupy most of Australia and rule it all, has been fatal for its indigenous peoples and cultures. The way of life of many tribes has been destroyed by disease, land seizure, forced migration, money and religion.

Australian languages are alike, historically, in having no numeral system: only 'one', 'two', 'several' and 'many' could be specified verbally in most languages. Days could also be counted in sign language by pointing at different areas of the palm of the hand. Many languages have now borrowed English numerals, which are necessary in dealing with money and other once-alien concepts.

'Mother-in-law language' in Dyirbal

The most extreme example of taboo language is that of Dyirbal-speaking tribes: here every single lexical word, except a few kin terms, has a different form in the *Jalnguy* 'avoidance' and *Guwal* 'everyday' styles. 'Blue-tongue lizard' is *banggara* in Guwal but *jijan* in Jalnguy, while 'ring-tail possum' is *midin* and *jiburray* respectively.

There are not, however, as many lexical forms in Jalnguy as there are in Guwal. Typically there is a one-to-many relationship: *jijan* is in fact the Jalnguy term for any lizard or guana, while *jiburray* covers all possums, squirrels and gliders. That is:

Guwal	Jalnguy
banggara 'blue-tongue lizard'	
biyu 'frilled lizard'	
buynyjul 'red-bellied lizard'	*jijan*
gaguju 'water skink'	
bajirri 'water goanna'	
midin 'ring-tail possum'	
jula 'striped blue possum'	
mungany 'Herbert River ringtail possum'	*jiburray*
yiwarrmany 'stinking honeysucker possum'	
burril 'flying squirrel'	

These correspondences reveal how speakers of Dyirbal, subconsciously, classify the natural world.

After R. M. W. Dixon, *The languages of Australia*
(Cambridge: Cambridge University Press, 1980) p. 61

Austroasiatic Languages

To trace the history of the Austroasiatic languages is a challenge that no linguist has yet faced up to fully. The membership of the family has, in part, been in doubt until very recently. Only two of the languages in the family, Vietnamese and Khmer, have national status, yet it extends across much of southern Asia. Its speakers are, some of them, hunter-gatherer peoples; some, mountain farmers highly unwelcoming to outsiders; some, bearers of old and long-recorded lowland civilisations. They seem to have little in common.

It has long been realised that KHMER and MON were related, and the well-established group of Austroasiatic languages typified by these two is universally known as *Mon-Khmer*. Both are recorded in early inscriptions as languages of medieval Buddhist kingdoms heavily influenced by the culture of classical India. Mon rule was supplanted by Burmese and Thai expansion, and the language is now in decline; Khmer survives. Close to Khmer are some minority and hill languages of south-east Asia, including Sre, Mnong, Stieng, Bahnar, Hrê, Sedang, Kuy, Bru, Sô and others.

The Mon-Khmer family was soon seen to include a northern group whose largest members are WA, Palaung, Khmu and – far off in north-eastern India – KHASI. Many languages of very small communities belong to this group, including Mlabri, spoken by 300 hunter-gatherers called 'Spirits of the yellow leaves'.

The *Aslian* languages of inaccessible districts in the Malay Peninsula include Sengoi (Semai), Temiar, Orang Benua and others with even smaller numbers.

More recently it has been shown that the *Munda* or Kharia group of languages, spoken entirely in east central India, is distantly related to Mon-Khmer, and the name Austroasiatic came into use to reflect this broader level of classification. The Munda group includes Korku, Bhumij, SANTALI, MUNDARI, Ho, Kharia, Sora and others. The division between the Mon-Khmer group and the Munda languages must have taken place many thousands of years ago.

Much more controversial has been the inclusion of VIETNAMESE and MUONG (with some tiny minority languages of Vietnam and Laos) in the Austroasiatic family. This is because Vietnamese – the only member of this *Viet-Muong* group on which much work has been done – has for two thousand years been under the influence of Chinese. Whatever its shape at the beginning of this period, Vietnamese is now a tonal language with a sound pattern rather resembling that of Chinese. Moreover, it was traditionally written in Chinese script and its grammar and style had adopted many Chinese features. Some thought it a Sino-Tibetan language or tried to trace links with the Tai group. The resemblances between Vietnamese and its Austroasiatic neighbours were hard to see; yet they have now been demonstrated to the satisfaction of nearly all specialists.

Nowhere do the speakers of major Austroasiatic languages appear to be recent migrants. This is a language family that must once have filled more of the map of south-east Asia and eastern India, now reduced to scattered islands by encroaching Indo-Aryan, Sino-Tibetan, Tai and Austronesian languages including Bengali, Assamese, Burmese, Thai, Lao and Cham.

Languages of the Andaman and Nicobar Islands

On the Nicobar Islands of the Bay of Bengal a Nicobarese group of Mon-Khmer languages is recognised – Car, Nancowry, Great Nicobarese and others. In these languages taboo leads to word avoidance on a considerable scale, and so to a rapid turnover of vocabulary. Thus, although they look very different from one another and from other Mon-Khmer languages, the relationships are historically closer than this would suggest.

On the Andaman islands two entirely separate language families exist – not clearly related to each other, or to the Austroasiatic languages, or to any other family, although Joseph Greenberg has postulated a relationship between these and the Papuan and Tasmanian languages. The first wordlist of an Andamanese language was made in 1795. The survival of the half dozen remaining Andamanese languages is now threatened, since there are fewer than 500 speakers in total.

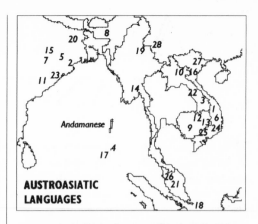

AUSTROASIATIC LANGUAGES

Austroasiatic languages on the ground			
Bahnar	1	85,000	Vietnam
Bhumij	2	200,000	India
Bru	3	120,000	Vietnam, Laos
Car	4	15,000	Nicobar Islands
Ho	5	750,000	India
Hrê and Sedang	6	150,000	Vietnam
Kharia	7	150,000	India
KHASI	8	500,000	India
KHMER	9	8,000,000	Cambodia
Khmu	10	350,000	Laos and other countries
Korku	11	300,000	India
Kuy	12	650,000	Cambodia
Mnong	13	200,000	Vietnam
MON	14	200,000	Burma, Thailand
MUNDARI	15	850,000	India
MUONG	16	800,000	Vietnam
Nancowry	17	5,000	Nicobar Islands
Orang Benua	18	10,000	Riau Islands
Palaung languages	19	500,000	Burma, China
SANTALI	20	4,000,000	India, Bangladesh
Sengoi or Semai	21	15,000	Malaysia
Sô	22	130,000	Laos, Thailand
Sora	23	270,000	India
Sre or Koho	24	100,000	Vietnam
Stieng	25	70,000	Vietnam, Cambodia
Temiar	26	10,000	Malaysia
VIETNAMESE	27	55,000,000	Vietnam
WA	28	1,000,000 or more	Burma, China

AUSTRONESIAN LANGUAGES

This is a family of over a thousand languages with a total of perhaps 270,000,000 speakers who live from Madagascar eastwards to Easter Island, and from Taiwan southwards to New Zealand.

Most of these thousand languages are spoken by very small groups in regions that are still almost untouched by world politics and communications. But one of them is Malay (Indonesian and Malaysian), which has long been crucial to the spread of trade and culture in the south-east Asian archipelago and is now a major international language.

Austronesian, a modern Graeco-Latin formation meaning 'of the southern islands', is a good name – accurate, yet not tied too tightly to any existing geographical or political label. It was devised by Wilhelm Schmidt in 1899. The first detailed reconstruction of *Uraustronesisch* 'proto-Austronesian' was worked out by the German scholar Otto Dempwolff between 1920 and 1938, but the family relationship had been noted as long ago as the 17th century. *Malayo-Polynesian* is sometimes used as a synonym for Austronesian, sometimes as a name for a grouping that excludes the languages of Taiwan.

When all these related languages are set side by side, there is the most striking diversity in the relatively small region of highland Taiwan. This diversity represents very long-established dialect divisions and separate development. It suggests that from Taiwan itself or somewhere nearby, in a series of seaborne migrations, the people who spoke early Austronesian languages migrated to spread their culture and language across the Indian and Pacific Oceans. Looking back to an even earlier stage of language prehistory, it is becoming accepted that Austronesian languages are distantly related to several language groups of southern China and south-east Asia in a larger family of AUSTRO-TAI LANGUAGES.

The proto-Austronesian language, then, is thought to have been spoken on Taiwan and perhaps on the adjacent coast of south-eastern China, and it may have begun to differentiate into four dialects about 6,000 years ago. Three of these long-forgotten dialects were the ancestors of the three language groups now spoken by the 'aboriginals' of Taiwan (see FORMOSAN LANGUAGES), which are now gradually giving way to elite Chinese. The fourth dialect is what would now be called proto-Malayo-Polynesian. It is the ancestor of all the remaining modern languages of the family – and its speakers were evidently mariners. For the distinctive feature of Malayo-Polynesian, as contrasted with all other major language groupings of the world, is that to reach their present locations, early forms of every one of these languages must have been carried across the sea.

The Austronesian family is a glorious laboratory for comparative linguistics. Groupings and subgroupings should be relatively easy to work out, because (1) few of the languages have been influenced, until very recently, by languages of other families, and (2) mutual influences ought to have been limited by the seas and mountains that separate many of them from one another. In practice, Austronesian subgroupings have been controversial.

What do the subgroupings mean in historical terms? In most cases – as with the Formosan languages – on one side of each successive dividing line will be the languages that 'stayed behind', and on the other side will be the single proto-language spoken by those who 'moved on', the ones who colonised a whole new island or island group.

Formosan languages

Philippine languages

CHAM

South Halmah

Central Malayo-Polynesia

W e s t e r n   M a l a y o - P o l y n e s i a n

MALAGASY

Taboos and secret languages

In many Austronesian languages, ethnologists have reported, taboo and forbidden topics force speakers to use circumlocutions or secret languages. The word *taboo* is a loanword in English, apparently borrowed from Tongan at the time of Cook's expedition.

As J. G. Frazer noted in *The Golden Bough* (London: Macmillan, 1911–15), Achehnese fishermen used a special language when fishing; Malay tin-miners and Sumatran gold-miners had a special language when at work, and collectors of aromatics, such as camphor and eagle-wood (see box at CHAM), whatever their religion, avoided offending forest spirits when gathering the valuable product.

In many parts of the Austronesian-speaking territory, from Madagascar to Tahiti and Maori New Zealand, names of parents-in-law, of children-in-law, of chieftains, and of the dead, are tabooed. They must be avoided in speech – and, often, words that sound like these names must be avoided as well.

Dusun and Kadazan dialects are spoken by the largest indigenous ethnic group of the east Malaysian province of Sabah. Priestesses, *bobohizan*, communicate with the dead using the so-called 'ancient Kadazan' language, which has a wholly different vocabulary.

AUSTRONESIAN LANGUAGE GROUPS

AMORRO

HAWAIIAN

Oceanic

New Guinea

SAMOAN

FIJIAN

TONGAN

Oceanic

MAORI

Austronesian languages: the major groupings

The map identifies the subdivisions of Austronesian that are now accepted by most linguists. It also shows by name some of the languages that have separate entries in this book.

The FORMOSAN LANGUAGES remain to show where the series of migrations began.

From here, by way of the Batan Islands, Austronesian speakers spread across the whole of the Philippines (modern languages include TAGALOG, PAMPANGAN, ILOCANO, PANGASINAN, BIKOL, CEBUANO and HILIGAYNON) and to Guam (CHAMORRO), then gradually expanded westwards to the western half of Indonesia (BUGIS, MAKASAR, SASAK, SUNDANESE, JAVANESE, MADURESE, IBAN, MALAY, MINANGKABAU, LAMPUNG, REJANG, BATAK, ACHEHNESE) with further migrations to the coast of Indochina (CHAM) and to Madagascar (MALAGASY). This first expansion formed what is now known as the Western Malayo-Polynesian (once called *Indonesian*) language group.

A new migration went from the Philippines southwards, and this is the origin both of the Central Malayo-Polynesian languages (which are spoken in the Moluccas and Lesser Sunda Islands) and the much larger Eastern Malayo-Polynesian group.

One Eastern subgroup expanded across South Halmahera and the western extremity of New Guinea (Irian). The other apparently moved along the northern coast of New Guinea – and that was where the next great migration began, in a gradual expansion across the islands of Melanesia, Micronesia and Polynesia that gave rise to the Oceanic group of languages. These include FIJIAN, KIRIBATI, MARSHALLESE, SAMOAN, TAHITIAN, TONGAN and many other languages with very small numbers of speakers. The most distant migrations were those that gave rise to HAWAIIAN, MAORI and the language of Easter Island, *Rapanui*. The remarkable Polynesian migrations took Austronesian languages across a vast area of ocean, 5,000 miles from north to south and 6,500 miles from west to east.

Austronesian languages: the individual languages

This is a list of all the languages of the vast Austronesian group that have more than 100,000 speakers.

Language name	Number of speakers	Location
Abung	500,000	southern Sumatra
ACHEHNESE	2,400,000	northern Sumatra
Aklanon	350,000	northern Panay
Amis (see FORMOSAN LANGUAGES)	130,000	Taiwan
Atoni or Timor	650,000	western Timor
Bajau and Mapun	115,000	Sulawesi, Palawan, Sabah
BALINESE	3,000,000	Bali, Lombok, eastern Java
Banggai	100,000	central Sulawesi
BATAK LANGUAGES	3,500,000	Sumatra
Biak	40,000 and as lingua franca	off Bird's Head
BIKOL	3,000,000	Luzon
Bima	500,000	eastern Sumbawa
Bingkokak	150,000	south-eastern Sulawesi
Blaan	200,000	Mindanao
Bolaang Mongondow	900,000	north-eastern Sulawesi
BUGIS	3,600,000	southern Sulawesi
Capiznon	450,000	north-eastern Panay
CEBUANO	12,000,000	Visayas, Mindanao
CHAM	235,000	Cambodia, Vietnam
Davaweño	125,000	Mindanao
Dobu	8,000 and as lingua franca	Milne Bay
Dusun and Kadazan	280,000	Sabah
Ende and Lio	220,000	central Flores
FIJIAN	340,000	Fiji
Gayo	180,000	northern Sumatra
Gorontalo	900,000	northern Sulawesi
HILIGAYNON	4,600,000	Visayas
Motu and HIRI MOTU	15,000 and as lingua franca	Papua New Guinea
IBAN and Sea Dayak languages	1,200,000	Borneo coasts
Ibanag	300,000	Luzon
Ifugao dialects	110,000	Luzon
ILOCANO	5,300,000	Luzon
Itawit	100,000	Cagayan Province
Jarai	200,000	Vietnam
JAVANESE	75,000,000	Java
Kankanaey	180,000	Luzon
Kei	85,000 and as lingua franca	Kei and Kur Islands
Kinaray-a	300,000	south-western Panay
Komering	700,000	southern Sumatra
Konjo	200,000	southern Sulawesi
Lamaholot	310,000	Solor, Lomblen, Pantar and Alor islands
Lauje	125,000	central Sulawesi
Lawangan	120,000	southern Kalimantan
Ledo	130,000	Sulawesi
MADURESE	9,000,000	Madura
Magindanaon	915,000	Mindanao

MAKASAR	1,600,000	southern Sulawesi
MALAGASY	10,000,000	Madagascar
MALAY and related dialects	30,000,000 and	
	as lingua franca	(see map at MALAY)
Mandar and Mamuju	345,000	western Sulawesi
Manggarai	400,000	western Flores
Manobo dialects	320,000	Mindanao
MAORI	100,000	New Zealand
Maranao	600,000	Mindanao
Masbateño	330,000 and as lingua franca	Masbate Province
Masenrempulu dialects	210,000	southern Sulawesi
MINANGKABAU	6,500,000	Sumatra
Muna	200,000	Muna and Buton islands
Ngaju	250,000	Borneo
Nias, Sikule and Simalur	600,000	off Sumatra
Pamona	105,000	southern Sulawesi
PAMPANGAN	1,850,000	Luzon
PANGASINAN	1,635,000	Luzon
Pesisir	400,000	southern Sumatra
Pubian	400,000	southern Sumatra
Rade	120,000	Vietnam
REJANG AND LAMPUNG	2,000,000	Sumatra
Romblomanon	200,000	Romblon and Sibuyan islands
Roti	130,000	Roti, Timor
Sama and Bajau	250,000	Philippines, Sabah; language of the 'Sea Gypsies'
SAMOAN	325,000	Samoa
Sangir	205,000	Sangir
SASAK	2,100,000	Lombok
Sawu or Hawuon	100,000	Sawu, Raijua, Sumba, Flores, Timor
Sikka	175,000	Flores
Subanun dialects	155,000	Mindanao
Sumba	200,000	Sumba
Sumbawa	300,000	western Sumbawa
SUNDANESE	27,000,000	western Java
TAGALOG	10,500,000 and as lingua franca	Philippines
TAHITIAN	100,000	Tahiti
Tausug or Sulu	480,000 and as lingua franca	Philippines, Borneo
Tetun	300,000	Timor
Tolai or Kuanua	60,000 and as lingua franca	Gazelle Peninsula
Tolaki	125,000	south-eastern Sulawesi
TONGAN	130,000	Tonga, Tuvalu
Tontemboan	150,000	Sulawesi
Toraja or Sadan	500,000	southern Sulawesi
WARAY-WARAY	2,400,000	Samar, Leyte, Sorsogon

AUSTRO-TAI LANGUAGES

A series of distant relationships may link the AUSTRONESIAN LANGUAGES, the KADAI LANGUAGES (including TAI LANGUAGES), the family consisting of MIAO and YAO, and possibly JAPANESE. The family relationship was proposed by Paul Benedict in a series of papers beginning in 1942, reprinted in his *Austro-Thai language and culture, with a glossary of roots* (New Haven: HRAF Press, 1975).

Benedict's idea cut across the once generally accepted link between Tai and SINO-TIBETAN LANGUAGES, for which, however, there had never been much evidence beyond a number of close word resemblances between Tai languages and Chinese. It also denied the family link ('Austric') which had long been suggested between Austronesian and AUSTROASIATIC LANGUAGES. This suggestion, made by Wilhelm Schmidt in 1906, is one which some Austroasiatic specialists still consider likely.

In both cases the resemblances, so Benedict argued, were due to borrowing. In later work he has argued more specifically for borrowing from an early Tai language into Chinese rather than from Chinese to Tai – an idea which in itself was controversial. Among the languages of his Austro-Tai family, meanwhile, Benedict was certainly able to list a surprising number of words that seem to go back to common roots: the monosyllabic words of the mainland languages corresponding, in most cases, to the stressed syllable of polysyllabic proto-Austronesian words.

Although few would consider it proved, the Austro-Tai hypothesis remains for the present the most promising of all the attempts to find distant family relationships among the languages of south-east Asia.

Languages of south-east Asia

By 3000 BC, rice cultivation was practised across the whole region from the Yangtze delta to northern Thailand. AUSTRONESIAN LANGUAGES, KADAI LANGUAGES, TAI LANGUAGES, MIAO and YAO may all derive from prehistoric languages spoken in this swathe of territory. Speakers of early SINO-TIBETAN LANGUAGES and AUSTROASIATIC LANGUAGES, with different cultures, may have bordered on these groups to the north and to the south-west.

Today the speakers of Austronesian languages have spread from island to island across the Indian and Pacific Oceans. The other language families mingle on the mainland in such a complex pattern, with such pervasive mutual influences, that their relationships and their prehistory are extremely difficult to trace.

AVAR

500,000 SPEAKERS

Russia, Azerbaijan

Avar is the best known of the North East Caucasian languages, spoken by mountain peoples in south-western Dagestan, the Russian republic beside the Caspian. There is an Avar-speaking minority in newly independent Azerbaijan.

> Speakers call themselves *Ma'arulal*; in Russian they are *Avartsy*. Historically, standard Avar is the dialect of Khunzakh and was known as *Bol mats* 'military language'.

The name 'Avar' has a long history: a tribe called *Avares* was linked with the Huns, who invaded the Roman Empire in the 5th century. These Avares were still a threat to Byzantium a hundred years later, but disappear from the historical record after being defeated by Charlemagne in 796. Their connection with the people now called Avar is uncertain.

In the last few centuries, Avar speakers have dominated the communications and trade of multilingual southern Dagestan, and the Avar Khanate was already establishing itself as a force independent of the Golden Horde by around 1500. It came under Russian control between 1803 and 1821.

Nowadays Avar is an official and literary medium shared by speakers of a group of languages – the 'Avar-Andi-Dido languages' – which are distantly related to one another but have clearly been developing separately for many hundreds of years. Even the four main dialects of Avar itself – Khunzakh, Antsukh, Charoda and Gidatl – are so distinct from one another that they are not mutually intelligible. In areas of linguistic fragmentation a lingua franca is needed, and this role was played by the dialect of Khunzakh in western Dagestan, a centre of trade and military activity since the 16th century. Essentially, the lingua franca based on the dialect of Khunzakh is what is now known as Avar. It serves also as a second or third language for highland speakers of DARGWA.

The local languages consist of the Andi group (Andi, Botlikh, Godoberi, Akhvakh, Bagulal, Tlisi, the eight Chamalal dialects, Karata and Tindi), the Dido or Tsez group (Tsez, Khvarshi, Bezheta, Hinukh and Khunzib) along with the more distantly related Archi: for a map see CAUCASIAN LANGUAGES. None has more than ten thousand speakers: some have only a hundred or so. After the Russian Revolution these small linguistic communities were at first recognised as separate 'nationalities' of the Soviet Union. They have been gradually brought together under the name of Avar, and the local languages are now in decline.

Numerals in Avar, Andi and Dido

	Avar	Andi	Tsez
1	ts'o	se-	sis
2	k'igo	ch'ègu	qano
3	l'abgo	l'òbgu	l'ono
4	unqo	-òqogu	uyno
5	shugo	ìnshtugu	l'eno
6	ant'go	ònt'gu	el'no
7	ankgo	hok'ugu	ot'no
8	mik'go	bìyt'ugu	bit'no
9	īch'go	hòch'ogu	och'ino
10	ants'go	hòts'ogu	ōtsino

Avar speakers are in general Muslims: they claim that Islam was introduced to the region as early as the 8th century. Until the beginning of this century the language of culture here was Arabic. Avar, occasionally written since the 17th century, traditionally used Arabic script. In 1928 the Latin alphabet was introduced. As with so many Soviet minority languages, Cyrillic script became standard in 1938.

AVESTAN

EXTINCT LANGUAGE OF IRAN

The sacred language of the Zoroastrian religion is known only from a single body of texts, the *Avesta*, with an adventurous history.

According to a late source Zarathustra (Greek *Zoroaster*) promulgated his religion three hundred years before the invasion of Alexander – thus around 630 BC. It soon achieved royal status, for the Persian Emperor Darius I (550–486 BC) and his successors were Zoroastrians.

Legends claimed that a vast body of sacred texts was written down at this early period: two copies existed, one of which was burnt accidentally while Alexander the Great destroyed the other. Some centuries after this first disaster a Parthian king, Vologeses, ordered all that could be found of the old sacred books to be collected; later still, around the 5th century, the Sassanian monarchs had a new edition made. The Islamic conquest of Persia led to fresh destruction, after which, once again, surviving fragments had to be pieced together.

Independently of these historical snippets we know that the surviving manuscripts of the *Avesta* texts are late and obviously incomplete. And we know the origin of the unique alphabet in which the *Avesta* is traditionally written: it is an enlargement of the kind of Aramaic alphabet used in Sassanid times. Finally, we know that the language of the older texts is much older than that – much nearer to proto-Iranian, ancestor of all the IRANIAN LANGUAGES. As we have them, the texts are accompanied by a translation and commentary, the *Zend*, in Middle Persian of the Sassanian period. By that time the real meaning was half-forgotten. Even if we cannot always understand the *Avesta* ourselves, we can tell that those Sassanian translations are, all too often, wrong!

Attempts to pin down the Avestan language geographically have not yet succeeded. It was not the language of the Persians of the Empire, for that was Old PERSIAN. It seems to have features of several of the Iranian dialects. No doubt the 'original' language will have been altered, repeatedly, in the course of oral transmission until, perhaps quite late in their history, the texts were fixed in writing.

There are modern Zoroastrian communities still surviving in the Iranian cities of Yazd and Kerman. A thriving Zoroastrian colony, the *Parsees*, has spread from its early centre of Bombay to

---

In praise of Mithra

Ahe raya xvarənaŋhača	For his glory and fortune
təm yazāi surunvata yasna	I will praise aloud
Miθrəm vouru-gaoyaoitīm zaoθrābyō.	Mithra of the wide pastures with libations.
Miθrəm vouru-gaoyaoitīm yazamaide	Mithra of the wide pastures we worship,
rāmašayanəm hušayanəm	giver of safe and comfortable dwellings
airyābyō daiŋhubyō.	to the Iranian lands.

Adapted from *The Avestan hymn to Mithra* ed. Ilya Gershevitch (Cambridge: University Press, 1967) pp. 74–5

Gershevitch uses the transliteration preferred by Iranian scholars. It is followed here and in the text. He suggests that the often-recurring epithet *vouru-gaoyaoitiš* 'having/providing wide cattle-pastures' is the origin of the by-name *Cautes* given to Mithras when he was adopted as a god of the Roman army.

other cities of the west coast of India, to East Africa and to many parts of the world. To all these the *Avesta*, in its mysterious original language, is still a holy book. Modern Parsees say their household prayers in Avestan, in words that they understand through traditional Gujarati translations and commentaries.

The first ten numerals in Avestan are: *aivas, duvā, trāyas̩, čatvāras̩, panča, xšvaš, hapta, aštā, nava, dasa.*

AYMARA

2,000,000 SPEAKERS

Bolivia, Peru

One of the AMERIND LANGUAGES, Aymara is spoken on the high Andes plateaus near Lake Titicaca (see map at QUECHUA).

Aymara shows many similarities with neighbouring Quechua. An argument continues as to whether the languages have the same origin, or have grown together in the course of shared cultural development. Hermann Steinthal, at the 8th International Congress of Americanists in Berlin in 1888, asserted the former. J. Alden Mason, in the *Handbook of South American Indians*, argued that in their basis the languages had 'little in common' but that they shared a large number of words, 'perhaps as much as a quarter of the whole, obviously related and probably borrowed'. Some modern researchers favour Steinthal, positing a 'Quechumaran' grouping to include both Quechua and Aymara; the majority, probably, agree with Mason.

At any rate, there certainly has been cultural influence between the two. A hundred years before the Spanish conquest, Aymara territory had become part of the Inca empire. The west Peruvian dialects of Quechua show strong Aymara influence, as if Aymara had once been spoken there.

The Aymara language has a traditional form of picture writing, used until quite recently to produce versions of Christian religious texts. This seems to represent an early stage in the typical development of writing – an aid to the memory, used for fixed texts such as catechisms and the Lord's Prayer, in which the texts are at least half-remembered. In this picture writing the characters are not standardised or used in the same way in different places. There are often fewer signs than words: just enough to recollect to the user's mind what he needs to say. The majority of signs are pictures of people and things. Some others are symbolic, and the meaning of signs can be stretched by means of puns and homophones. Aymara in this traditional script was at first written on animal skins painted with plant or mineral pigments: later, paper was used.

In modern Bolivia, where the largest community of speakers is to be found, Aymara is now written in the Latin alphabet. The orthography, introduced in 1983, follows Spanish practice. Books and magazines are regularly published, notably by the Evangelical and Catholic churches.

Many Bolivians are trilingual in Aymara, Quechua and Spanish. Thus, besides its Quechua elements, Aymara has now many Spanish loanwords, though they are much altered to fit the sound pattern: *winus tiyas* for Spanish *buenos dias*, 'good day'; *wisiklita* for *bicicleta*, 'bicycle'. The first ten numerals in Aymara are: *maya, paya, kimsa, pusi, phisqa, suxta, paqallqu, kimsaqallqu, llatunka, tunka*.

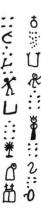

The Catholic sacraments in Aymara picture writing

AZERI

PERHAPS 14,000,000 SPEAKERS

Iran, Azerbaijan

One of the TURKIC LANGUAGES, Azeri is the national language of independent 'northern' Azerbaijan (once a republic of the Soviet Union) and is spoken in neighbouring districts of Georgia and Russian Dagestan. But the greatest number of speakers is in north-western Iran, in the province that will be called here 'southern' Azerbaijan (for map see TURKISH).

The place name *Azerbaijan* (local spelling *Azərbaycan*) derives from the Greek *Atropatene* – for this was once the kingdom of Atropates, a local Iranian ruler who established a dynasty on the south-western Caspian shores at Alexander the Great's death in 323 BC. *Azeri* has become the name of the Turkic language now spoken by the majority in the region. It is often called *Azerbaijani*, a term that misleadingly identifies the language with the political borders of Azerbaijan.

Speakers of a south-western Turkic dialect, the medieval ancestor of Turkmen, Azeri and Turkish, settled here between the 7th and 11th centuries AD. Some colonised the valleys and plains that border the Caspian Sea. Others turned to seasonal nomadism, their flocks grazing the Iranian and Caucasian highlands in summer and moving to the lowlands in winter.

Thus they range far beyond the borders of both halves of Azerbaijan. Apart from minorities in Georgia and elsewhere in Iran, there are 100,000 or more people of Azeri origin in Turkey, most of them belonging to the groups known as Karapapak and Terekeme, who migrated from northern Azerbaijan and Dagestan after 1828 and now live in Kars province. Their Karapapak language, originally a variety of Azeri, is gradually assimilating to the local dialect of Turkish.

Long disputed between Turks, Persians and Russians, Azerbaijan was divided between Russia and Persia (Iran) along the line of the River Araxes by the treaty of Turkmanchai, in 1828. In spite of an uprising against the Iran government in southern Azerbaijan in 1945, the border has held.

Briefly independent in 1918–20, northern Azerbaijan became independent again in 1991. Already Armenia's attempted annexation of the Armenian-speaking enclave of Nagorno-Karabakh, in the western mountains of Azerbaijan, has led to fierce fighting and eventually the expulsion of the hundreds of thousands of Azeris who formerly lived in Armenia. Meanwhile Azerbaijan has expelled the Lezghians from much of their former territory along its northern border, resettling this area with the refugee Azeris and with the Meskhetian Turks who have been driven out of Uzbekistan.

Some count the tales of *Dede Korkut* (see TURKISH) as the first classic of Azeri literature. In any case there has been an Azeri literary language, written in Arabic script, since the 14th century, and lively literary activity beginning in the 19th. Azeri oral epic poetry and romantic song is still a vigorous tradition – one that can be traced within Turkic cultures to the 11th-century performances of the *ozan* 'singer, storyteller'. Performances are now given by an *aşiq*, who improvises while playing on a stringed *kobuz*.

In Iran, Azeri education and publishing, outlawed under the Pahlavi monarchs (1925–79), revived in the 1980s: Arabic script is used. In the

1990s the Latin alphabet has become the standard in independent Azerbaijan. Azeri culture centres on Baku in the independent north and on Tabriz in the south, both cities of international importance.

Azari – confusingly – is the name of the Iranian language still spoken in parts of southern Azerbaijan (see map at GILAKI).

> Information on local languages is hard to find in Iran. Recent estimates of Azeri speakers there (including the closely related Qāshqāy, spoken in the southern mountains) range from 500,000 (P. Oberling in the 1960s) through 1 million (N. Poppe, 1965) and 3 million (B. Comrie, 1981) to 8 million (*International Encyclopedia of Linguistics*, 1982/86, and other recent sources). In Iran, Azeri has no official status, but it is the major language of the north-west.
>
> The Qāshqāy possibly number 100,000. They are traditionally seasonal nomads, keepers of horses, camels and cattle, whose lands are to the north-west and the south-east of Fars. They too had '*ashiqs*, who sang love poetry, battle songs and the epic tales of Köroghlu.

North of Azerbaijan lies Dagestan, a mountainous republic of Russia. In the scrambled terrain of Dagestan many peoples live and many languages are spoken. There had never been a single lingua franca for the region. High valley peoples learnt the languages of middle valley peoples; they in turn learnt lowland languages for trade and communication. 'Thus the Andi and Dido tribes used AVAR, while the Avars in turn used KUMYK or Nogai in their relations with the lowlands. In the same way, the Tabasarans in southern Daghestan used Lezgin [LEZGHIAN], and the Lezgins in turn used Azeri.'

In the 18th century classical ARABIC became the most-used lingua franca, and practically the only literary language, for Dagestan and neighbouring Chechnya. At the beginning of the 20th century the Young Turk movement, powerful here as well as in Turkey, urged the use of Azeri to replace Arabic. By the time of the Russian Revolution Azeri was in a strong position as lingua franca, especially in southern Dagestan.

Curiously, Soviet policy at first favoured Arabic as the second language of the region: it was seen as the choice of the 'masses' against the bourgeoisie. But this policy fell from favour, as it gave backing to traditional Islam and Sufism. Thus in 1923 Azeri was chosen as the preferred lingua franca, and the only school language, of Soviet Dagestan. Only five years later, policy changed again. There was now support for education and literacy in local languages. Dagestan (still staunchly Muslim) now has ten literary languages, and its usual lingua franca – naturally, since it is the language of government – is Russian.

Quotation from Alexandre Bennigsen, Chantal Lemercier-Quelquejay, 'Politics and linguistics in Daghestan' in *Sociolinguistic perspectives on Soviet national languages* ed. Isabelle T. Kreindler (Berlin: Mouton De Gruyter, 1985) pp. 125–42

Numerals in Turkmen, Azeri and Turkish			
	Turkmen	**Azeri**	**Turkish**
1	bir	bir	bir
2	iki	iki	iki
3	üç	üç	üç
4	dörd	dört	dört
5	beş	bäş	beş
6	altı	alty	altı
7	yeddi	yedi	yedi
8	səkkiz	sekiz	sekiz
9	doqquz	dokuz	dokuz
10	on	on	on

The Azeri alphabet

A B C Ç D E Ə F G H X İ I J K L M N O Ö P Q R S Ş T U Ü V Y Z

a b c ç d e ə f g h x i ı j k l m n o ö p q r s ş t u ü v y z

---

Writing in Azeri

Arabic script is still used by Azeris in Iran. In 1923 Soviet northern Azerbaijan adopted the Latin alphabet, which was called *Yanalif (yeni* 'new', *elifba* 'alphabet'). As elsewhere in the Soviet Union, the Cyrillic alphabet was imposed in 1939. In the 1990s the Latin alphabet has been reintroduced in independent Azerbaijan, in a form closely resembling Turkish, as shown in the box.

BAI

900,000 SPEAKERS

China

Bai is one of the SINO-TIBETAN LANGUAGES, or so most linguists believe. The older history of this language remains very mysterious. It is spoken in and around the city of Dali in Yunnan.

Speakers of *Bai* or *Pai* are called *Minchia* in older English writings, from local Chinese *min-jia* 'the common people'. The newly official term (from Chinese *bai* 'white') matches their own name for themselves, which is *pe-tsi* 'white people'.

Bai speakers, unlike most of the other minority peoples of Yunnan, are typically lowland dwellers and rice farmers, and they have adopted Chinese culture and Chinese beliefs quite comprehensively. Along with this, they have adopted Chinese words: most of the vocabulary of Bai is actually Chinese, some of it recent borrowing, some of it much earlier. Many Bai are bilingual in Chinese. Their cultural and economic links have been with Chinese, Tibetans and Burmese rather than with most of the hill peoples who surround them.

Can an older form of Bai be reconstructed? 'It would be difficult, because even those words which may be original Minchia vocabulary are difficult to interpret, as sound change seems to have proceeded radically to simplify the syllable structure of Minchia, thus eliminating contrasts that would have reflected proto-Tibeto-Burman and whichever subgroup of TB Minchia may belong to' (David Bradley).

It seems likely that the medieval kingdom of Nanchao, one of whose capitals was Dali, would have had Bai as one of its main languages. A Chinese text of the 9th century, *Man shu*, records several words in two Nanchao languages – but they do not coincide very much with Bai or with any of the other modern languages of Yunnan. Nanchao was conquered by Kublai Khan in 1253 and the Bai-speaking country has been part of China ever since.

Modern Chinese linguists regard Bai as a Burmese-Lolo language like YI. Scholars of Tai history sometimes take it to be a Tai language if they believe Nanchao to have been a Tai kingdom. The view was once popular that it was an Austroasiatic language of the Mon-Khmer group. In truth, no one knows the prehistory of Bai and no one at present can be certain with which language family to class it.

Bai has twenty consonants (a low number) and twelve vowels (a high number) including *v:* this is one of the few languages in the world in which *v* functions as a vowel. It has seven tones in open syllables. The first ten numerals are: *yi, go, sa, shi, ngur, fer, chi, bia, jiu, dser.*

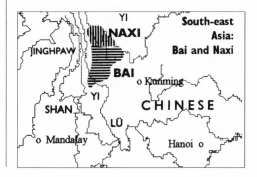

BALINESE

3,000,000 SPEAKERS

Indonesia

There was once a chain of Hindu and Maha-yana Buddhist kingdoms stretching east-wards from India across south-east Asia and the Malay archipelago. Their traces remain – in stone temples, in statues of lions and gods, in languages that are full of Sanskrit loanwords, in names and forms of address that suddenly recall an Indian original.

Many centuries ago, most of these kingdoms went along other paths. Theravada Buddhism, Islam and Christianity have all won converts. Bali is one of the last outposts of Hinduism in Indonesia. Thus Balinese, one of the AUSTRO-NESIAN LANGUAGES, is at the same time one of a chain of cultural links, and a unique survival.

Balinese, the language of Bali in Indonesia, is linguistically closest to its two neighbours to the east, Sasak and Sumbawa (see map at SASAK). But Bali learnt its civilisation from the great island of Java, directly to the west. The earliest stone inscriptions on Bali, dating from 914, are in scripts indistinguishable from those used in Java. These ancient texts are in two languages – Sanskrit and (already!) Balinese. The language has a history of more than a thousand years.

Along with writing (see box) a whole litera-ture, and a whole literary vocabulary, is shared between the two islands. Later Balinese inscrip-tions tend to be in Javanese, not Balinese. This interplay has its lucky side: if it were not for Bali's conservatism, the older Javanese literature would largely be lost and forgotten today. It was here that Javanese manuscripts were carefully preserved and recopied. It was through Balinese that western scholars, a century ago, discovered the old texts and learnt to read them.

Bali also learnt, and retained, a strictly hier-archical view of society, a view which is pre-served more clearly in Balinese than in almost any other language. Lowland Balinese has very distinct 'formal' (*basa madia*) and 'informal' (*basa ketah*) registers, which speakers switch between as necessary, depending on their relation to the person addressed. Within the formal register, numerous detailed distinctions are made: *basa singgih* is the most elevated variety and consists largely of words borrowed from Javanese. The vocabularies of the three varieties are often quite different: 'eat' is *naar* in Basa ketah, *neda* in Basa madia, *ngadjengang* in Basa singgih.

Javanese influence fell away in the 16th cen-tury. More recently Balinese has been influ-enced by Malay, which has been the language of trade and travel in the archipelago for many hundreds of years. Through Malay, loanwords have come from Dutch, Portuguese and Chi-nese.

Balinese numerals are somewhat varied in form. With '2' and '3', different words are used in formal and informal registers. All the numerals have slightly different forms depending on whether they are used before or after a noun. The basic forms of the first ten numerals are: *sa, dua* or *kalih, talu* or *tiga, pat, lima, nam, pitu, kutus* or *ulu, sia, dasa*. *Dasa* '10' is a loanword from Sanskrit.

Kawi in Balinese

Written Balinese begins in the 10th century, with inscriptions recording royal decrees, some on stone, the majority on copper plates. The script looks as though it developed in writing on palm leaf, not on stone – but in tropical conditions palm leaf manuscripts do not last for a thousand years, so we may never know.

The Latin alphabet is now used for Balinese.

| ha | na | ca | ra | ka | da | ta | sa | wa | la | ma | qa | ba | nga | pa | ja | ya | nya |

After C. Clyde Barber, *A Balinese-English dictionary* (Aberdeen: University Library, 1979)

BALTIC LANGUAGES

The Baltic languages (LATVIAN, LITHUANIAN and the extinct Old Prussian) are a compact group of INDO-EUROPEAN LANGUAGES, separate from but historically linked with their neighbours the Slavonic languages.

It is likely that as proto-Indo-European divided into dialects the linguistic ancestors of the Balts gradually moved northwards from an early location in what is now the western Ukraine. For a long period they must have remained in close touch with early Slavonic speakers. Eventually reaching the south-eastern Baltic shores, they settled in their present location without ever mingling with any large community of non-Indo-European speakers. Thus the Baltic languages – especially Lithuanian – seem closer than any other living tongues to the reconstructed proto-Indo-European of several thousand years ago.

Baltic languages on the ground

Latvian and Lithuanian descend from a hypothetical 'proto-East Baltic' language which will have begun to divide into dialects about AD 600 with a series of sound changes that have affected Latvian but not Lithuanian. They are the national languages of two republics both of which asserted their independence from the Soviet Union at the end of the 1980s.

Latvian has three main dialects. Livonian (*Tamnieks*) is spoken in the north-west; Central Latvian around Riga; Upper Latvian (*Augszemnieks*) in the east. Livonian is a confusing term as it is also used for an almost extinct Uralic language, related to Estonian, once the everyday language of north-western Latvia.

To the south-east, *Latgalian* is sometimes counted a separate language, midway between Latvian and Lithuanian, with a distinctive culture, Roman Catholic in religion.

Literary *Lithuanian* is based on the highland dialect of the *Aukstaiciai* of the south-east. The other major dialects are those of the *Zemaiciai* to the west and the *Suvalkieciai* south-west of the Nemunas river.

Two dialects of *Old Prussian* are known from a 14th-century glossary in Pomesan dialect and 16th-century catechism in Samland dialect. Soon after that the language must have become extinct, succumbing to the spread of German in East Prussia.

Numerals in proto-Indo-European and the Baltic languages		
	Lithuanian	**Latvian**
1	vienas	viens
2	du	divi
3	trys	trīs
4	keturi	četri
5	penki	pieci
6	šeši	seši
7	septyni	septiņi
8	aštuoni	astoņi
9	devyni	deviņi
10	dešimt	desmit

Baltic languages

BALUCHI

PERHAPS 4,000,000 SPEAKERS

Pakistan, Iran, Afghanistan

One of the IRANIAN LANGUAGES, Baluchi is a major language of south-west Pakistan, where it has over two million speakers, and can claim nearly a million speakers in south-east Iran.

There are about 200,000 Baluchi speakers in Afghanistan, where it is recognised as a 'national language'. (Quite distinct from them is the community of some thousands of Persian-speaking nomads in Afghanistan – called *Baluch* by themselves, *Jat* by others – who traditionally live by prostitution.) About 40,000 Baluchi speakers live around the Marw oasis in Turkmenistan: they migrated there from Afghanistan in the 19th century. Finally, there may be as many as half a million Baluchi-speaking migrant workers in Oman, Kuwait and the United Arab Emirates.

The name Baluchi or *Balōchī* is not found before the 10th century. It is believed that the language was brought to its present location in a series of migrations from northern Iran, near the Caspian shores: certainly it is more closely related to the north-west Iranian languages than to its neighbours.

For several centuries the speakers of Baluchi and BRAHUI have lived side by side. There are Brahui loanwords in Baluchi, and Brahui in turn is very heavily influenced by its neighbour. Baluchi naturally also contains loanwords from Persian – and from SINDHI, its eastern neighbour.

Written records of Baluchi date only from the 19th century. Quetta, in Pakistani Baluchistan, is now the centre of Baluchi culture and publishing. As with Sindhi and URDU, Baluchi is normally printed by lithography from handwritten copy in the *nasta'līq* form of Arabic script.

But quite apart from published prose and poetry there is a rich oral literature in Baluchi. Some of this has been collected in print – a major collection was made at Marw by the Soviet scholar I. I. Zarubin – but much remains to be done. Oral tradition preserves not only longer, anonymous tales and epics but also shorter lyrics by named poets of earlier centuries.

The first ten numerals in Baluchi are: *yak, dō, say, chīār, panch, shash, hapt, hasht, nuh, dah.*

Dialects of Baluchi

Rākhshānī is the major dialect group in terms of numbers. *Sarhaddī*, a sub-dialect of Rākhshānī, is used by Radio Kabul. Other sub-dialects are *Kalātī, Chagai-Khārānī, Panjgūrī*.

The *Kechī* dialect of Pakistani Makran is heard in Pakistani radio broadcasts; *Sarawānī*, of south-eastern Iran, is used in radio broadcasts there. *Loṭūnī* is a third distinct dialect of Iran. Historically important is the *Coastal* or *Rindī* dialect, which extends along the Indian Ocean shore in Iran and Pakistan: this is the language of a good deal of classical Baluchi poetry.

Eastern Hill Baluchi or *Northern Baluchi* is very different from the rest. It was the first Baluchi dialect that became familiar to the British in India, and is thus particularly well documented in older linguistic work.

The camel drivers of the Turkic-speaking Qashqai, who live in the Fars province of Persia, are said to speak a language all of their own – *Koroshi*, most closely related to Baluchi.

Based on J. Elfenbein, *The Baluchi language: a dialectology with texts* (London: Royal Asiatic Society, 1966) and other sources

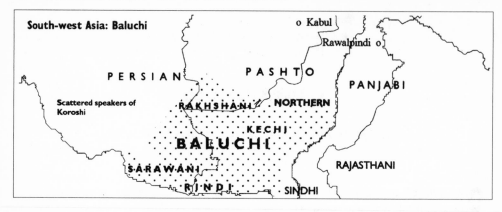

South-west Asia: Baluchi

o Kabul
Rawalpindi o

PERSIAN

PASHTO

PANJABI

Scattered speakers of
Koroshi

RAKHSHANI NORTHERN

KECHI

BALUCHI

SARAWANI

RAJASTHANI

RINDI

SINDHI

A riddle

Do gwahārāṇ dītha ambāzī,	I saw two sisters embracing,
ajab khush ant gwar-ambāzī,	Very happy at the embrace,
nēn-ī sūratā khamī,	Not the least difference in their looks,
yakē khor, dīgar chhamī.	But one is blind and the other can see.

The answer? A woman looking in a mirror.

M. Longworth Dames, *Popular poetry of the Baloches* (London: Royal Asiatic Society, 1907)

BANDA

1,000,000 SPEAKERS

Central African Republic, Congo (Kinshasa)

O ne of the Ubangi group of NIGER-CONGO LAN-
GUAGES, Banda is spoken across most of the
central and eastern districts of the Central African Republic, by a mainly agricultural population.

Gbaya and Banda are the two major hinterland
languages of the Central African Republic, now
overshadowed linguistically by their relative, the
national language, SANGO (see map there). Banda
has probably been spoken in roughly its present
location for as long as three thousand years, as
the result of an expansion of early Ubangian
languages from the west in the second millennium BC.

Its main dialects have thus gradually differentiated to the point where they are no longer
mutually intelligible. But there is much travel
and intermarriage among people of different
dialects, so many in practice understand two or
three. Most people are now bilingual in Sango; in
towns, some men (but few women) speak
French.

In Banda nouns a prefix marks the plural: *zu*
'man', *azu* 'men'. Banda is a three-tone language,
and the tones are essential in word formation:
kāngà 'to imprison', *kángà* 'prison', *kàngà* 'slave'.
In Banda country, long distance messages are
traditionally transmitted by three-tone drums,
using formulaic phrases that match the tones
of the spoken language.

BANTU LANGUAGES

A very large group of related languages of central and southern Africa. Their interrelationship, as a language group comparable to Semitic or Germanic, was obvious to early explorers and was demonstrated linguistically by Wilhelm Bleek in 1857 and more fully by Carl Meinhof, whose comparative grammar appeared in 1899. Meinhof was the first to attempt a reconstruction of *Ur-Bantu*, proto-Bantu. Scholars had already argued that Bantu languages were related to the more diffuse family now called the NIGER-CONGO LANGUAGES. Diedrich Westermann proved this in 1927.

Within the huge and very old Niger-Congo family, Bantu belongs to the Benue-Congo group, whose other members are spoken in south-eastern Nigeria and Cameroun. It was clearly in this district, about four thousand years ago, that 'proto-Bantu' – the direct ancestor of all the Bantu languages of today – was spoken.

It was from this point that speakers of Bantu languages began to spread across the whole southern half of Africa. South central Africa is one of the very oldest areas of human habitation: Bantu speakers were newcomers at the end of a long history now difficult to trace, spreading new kinds of agriculture in the region. In archaeological terms they were at that early time a 'neolithic' group of peoples who made pottery but did not work metal. Later, after their migrations reached the Great Lakes region, the Eastern Bantu were almost certainly instrumental in the spread of metal-working technologies across Africa.

The Pygmy peoples of central and southern Africa, ethnically quite distinct, do not in general speak different languages from their neighbours. Thus *Aka*, a language of the south-western Central African Republic, is unusual: a Bantu language spoken by Pygmies alone. It has eleven noun classes, not unlike neighbouring Bantu languages, based on categories such as countable/not countable, long/round, diminutive/augmentative.

Most Bantu languages are tonal: in the majority, tones are at least partly predictable from the grammatical shape of verbs and nouns, but in others tones serve to differentiate words that are otherwise identical. A few, such as Swahili, have stress accents and no tones.

They are notable for simple syllable patterns, which often include prenasalised consonants (the *Mp-, Mb-, Nt-, Nd-, Nj-* familiar from personal and place names from the southern half of Africa). Some sound changes recur in many Bantu languages, such as 'Dahl's Law', in which *k-* is voiced if the next syllable begins with an unvoiced consonant: hence the local name *Gikuyu* for the language known to most outsiders as *Kikuyu*.

The numerals '1' to '5' and '10' in most modern Bantu languages are traceable directly to proto-Bantu. '6' to '9' are usually formed as compounds, '5 + 1' and so on; sometimes they are borrowed from other languages (see SWAHILI for an example). Probably proto-Bantu itself counted on a base of five, like the majority of the modern languages.

Bântu is the word for 'people' in numerous Bantu languages including LUBA (see box there): the *ba-* prefix is normal for the plural of a noun denoting human beings. 'Bantu' was first used as a name for the language family by Wilhelm Bleek in 1857. He applied it essentially to what we now know as the Niger-Congo family: later scholars narrowed the term.

At present the word *Bantu* tends to be avoided in South Africa because in the all-too-recent days of apartheid it carried political overtones. In that country, Bantu languages are therefore often called *Sintu languages*. This new word simply incorporates a different noun class prefix, the one that is appropriately used for a language. It appears in many Bantu languages as *si-, se-, ki-*: *siLozi, seTswana, kiSwahili*.

Bantu grammar for Bantu languages

Clement M. Doke, a linguist at the University of the Witwatersrand from 1923 to 1953, was perhaps the first scholar to see clearly that grammar in the Greek and Latin tradition, as adopted by most European linguists, was inadequate to describe Bantu languages. His thesis, *The phonetics of the Zulu language*, was presented in 1924 and his *Textbook of Zulu grammar* first appeared in 1927. This gave a new classification of the 'parts of speech' in a Bantu language, and a new terminology that has been gradually applied, by Doke and many others, to the description of Bantu languages. Doke himself worked on Khoisan languages as well as on Zulu, Shona, Southern Sotho, Ila and other Bantu languages. The Zulu grammar reached its sixth edition in 1961.

Bantu migrations

Proto-Bantu was perhaps spoken in or near the Grassfields of western Cameroun. The general region of origin can scarcely be disputed now that the membership of Bantu in the Bantoid group of the Benue-Congo branch of the Niger-Congo family has been demonstrated, for this is where the other Bantoid languages, siblings of proto-Bantu and as varied as might be expected after four thousand years of independent development, are still spoken.

The modern Grassfields languages, all spoken by quite small communities, are hard to classify but it has been suggested that they are the residue of the very earliest Bantu expansion.

The speakers of three or four early Bantu dialects had begun by 2000 BC to colonise the rainforest of Cameroun, Gabon, Congo (Brazzaville) and the Inner Basin of Congo (Kinshasa). One very early migration was by sea, to the Gabon estuary and the island of Bioko (where *Bubi* is still spoken: see map at EWONDO). The main movement, however, was probably a steady expansion south-eastwards from Cameroun and along major rivers. Living by fishing, by agriculture and by river trade, and gradually adopting metal technology after about 300 BC, Bantu speakers established dominance over the remaining hunter-gatherer peoples of the rainforest, including the so-called 'pygmies', who now speak Bantu languages. The Bantu migrations into the rainforests were complete by about AD 300.

Meanwhile, perhaps as early as 500 BC, perhaps later, Eastern Bantu languages were spreading southwards from the region of the Great Lakes in modern Uganda, Tanzania and Kenya. They were eventually to reach the eastern half of what is now South Africa (the western half remaining the territory of speakers of KHOISAN LANGUAGES). They certainly interacted with, and perhaps mingled with, some of the Bantu languages of the rainforest, though the details here are much disputed. This migration reached the Atlantic along the coast of modern Angola. The Eastern Bantu expansion is usually linked with the spread of ironworking and of pastoralism across southern Africa, roughly two thousand years ago. A later archaeological break (the 'Later Iron Age' of southern Africa, with new pottery styles) at roughly AD 800 to 1000 may represent a second series of migrations.

What is not clear is the route by which early Eastern Bantu speakers migrated from the western plateaus to north-eastern Congo (Kinshasa) and the Great Lakes region in the first place. No solid archaeological evidence has been found for this migration, yet somehow it took place. Some think that it went almost due east, into the rainforest, and then up the Zaire and Uele rivers. Others believe that it was a gradual expansion of migrant cattle herders whose route kept to the north of the rainforest.

Linguists have made many sub-classifications of Bantu languages and their immediate relatives. One may see *Equatorial Bantu* (the rainforest groups), *Western Bantu* (sometimes the rainforest Bantu groups, sometimes others too), *Lacustrine* (including Luyia, Gusii, Nyankole, Ganda), the *East Highlands Group* (most of what is called Eastern Bantu above), *Narrow Bantu* or *Traditional Bantu* (excluding the Grassfields languages), the *Ungwa Group* (most Bantu languages and TIV), the *Bin Languages* and *Bane* and *Wide Bantu* (groupings of Bantu with Grassfields and some other Niger-Congo languages, separately known as *Bantoid* and *Semi-Bantu*). The continuing debate is highly important for the light that it may throw on African prehistory.

The Bantu spectrum

Detailed classification work on Bantu languages was done by Malcolm Guthrie. He assigned the five hundred languages and dialects of this group to lettered subdivisions A to S. Although superseded by later work, his classification is still sometimes used for reference so it is given for the languages listed here. A 'J' subdivision was introduced by Meeussen in 1953, incorporating some of the languages in Guthrie's subdivisions D and E; some other renumberings have been tried, but there is no standardisation about them, so it is Guthrie's own numbers (from his *Comparative Bantu* [Farnborough: Gregg, 1967–71]) that appear here.

The present list includes all Bantu languages with over a hundred thousand speakers – and gives cross-references to those which have a separate entry in this volume. More information on some of the smaller languages can be found through the index.

Guthrie was not in sympathy with modern comparative and historical linguistics. He believed that the Bantu language family, whose study he

BANTU LANGUAGES: THE SUBGROUPS

revolutionised with his work of reconstruction, was independent of other families and that modern Bantu languages represented various levels of decay from an original, fully logical proto-Bantu, spoken somewhere near the centre of the modern Bantu-speaking area. As an explanation of language change this approach was already outdated. Vestiges of it remain, however, not only in Guthrie's (indispensable) proto-Bantu reconstructions but in quite recent attempts by researchers to define what is 'a Bantu language'.

Asu	G22	315,000	Tanzania
Bangubangu	D27	120,000	Congo (Kinshasa)
Basaa (or Mbene) and			
Bakoko	A43	280,000	Cameroun
BEMBA	M42	1,850,000	Zambia and Congo (Kinshasa)
Bembe of Congo	D54	252,000	Congo (Kinshasa)
Bena	G63	490,000	Tanzania
Bera (or Bira), Komo and			
Nyali	D30	300,000	Congo (Kinshasa)
Bukusu	E31c	565,000	Kenya
Chagga or Chaga	E60	800,000	Tanzania
CHOKWE	K11	1,500,000*	Angola and Congo (Kinshasa)
Chopi or Lenge	S61	333,000	Mozambique
Chwabo or Cuabo	P34	665,000	Mozambique
Comorian	G44	450,000*	Comores

DUALA	A24	87,700	Cameroun
Embu	E52	242,000	Kenya
EWONDO, Bulu and Fang	A70	1,374,000	Cameroun, Equatorial Guinea and Gabon
Fuliru	D63	266,000	Congo (Kinshasa)
GANDA, Soga and Gwere	E10	3,542,000	Uganda
Gogo	G11	1,000,000	Tanzania
GUSII	E42	1,390,000	Kenya
Hehe	G62	630,000	Tanzania
Herero	R31	76,000	Namibia
Hunde	D51	200,000	Congo (Kinshasa)
Jita and Kwaya	E25	319,000	Tanzania
Kagulu	G12	217,000	Tanzania
Kalanga	S16	220,000	Botswana and Zimbabwe
KAMBA	E55	2,460,000	Kenya
Kami	G36	315,000	Tanzania
Kanyok	L32	200,000	Congo (Kinshasa)
Kaonde	L41	217,000	Congo (Kinshasa)
Kela	C75	180,000	Congo (Kinshasa)
Kele	C55	160,000	Congo (Kinshasa)
Kerebe	E24	100,000	Tanzania
KIKUYU	E51	4,360,000	Kenya
Komo	D23	150,000	Congo (Kinshasa)
KONGO	H16	4,720,000	Congo (Kinshasa), Angola and Congo (Brazzaville)
Konjo or Konzo	D41	250,000	Uganda
Kunda	N42	100,000	Zimbabwe
Kuria or Koria	E43	345,000	Kenya and Tanzania
Kwanyama	R21	150,000	Namibia
Lala and Bisa	M50	354,000	Zambia and Congo (Kinshasa)
Lamba and Seba	M50	170,000	Zambia and Congo (Kinshasa)
Langi	F33	275,000	Tanzania
Lega	D25	400,000	Congo (Kinshasa)
Lenje	M61	136,000	Zambia
LINGALA and Bangala	C36d	12,000,000 as a first or second language	Congo (Kinshasa), Congo (Brazzaville), Central African Republic
Logooli, Idakho, Isukha and Tirikhi	E41	503,000	Kenya and Uganda
LOMWE and Ngulu	P32	2,000,000	Mozambique and Malawi
LOZI	K21	450,000	Zambia
LUBA	L30	7,810,000	Congo (Kinshasa)
Luchazi	K13	125,000	Angola, Zambia
LUNDA	L52	550,000*	Congo (Kinshasa), Zambia, Angola
LUVALE	K14	600,000	Zambia, Angola and Congo (Kinshasa)
LUYIA, Nyore and Saamia	E30	3,734,000	Kenya
MAKONDE	P23	1,060,000	Tanzania and Mozambique
MAKUA	P30	3,540,000	Mozambique, Malawi and Tanzania

Mambwe-Lungu or Rungu	M15	307,000	Zambia and Tanzania
Masaba or Gisu	E31	500,000	Uganda
Matengo	N13	150,000	Tanzania
Mbala	H41	200,000	Congo (Kinshasa)
Mbola	D11	100,000	Congo (Kinshasa)
Mbunda	K15	102,000	Zambia and Angola
Benguela MBUNDU	R11	3,000,000	Angola
Luanda MBUNDU	H21	1,820,000	Angola
Mbwela	K17	100,000	Angola
MERU	E53	1,230,000	Kenya
Mijikenda	E72	988,300	Kenya, Tanzania
Mongo and Ngando	C60	216,000	Congo (Kinshasa)
Mpuono	B84	165,000	Congo (Kinshasa)
Mwanga	M22	223,000	Zambia
Mwera	P22	345,000	Tanzania
Nandi or Ndandi or Shu	D42	903,000	Congo (Kinshasa)
NDEBELE	S44	1,550,000*	Zimbabwe and South Africa
Ndengereko	P11	110,000	Tanzania
Ndonga	R22	240,000	Namibia and Angola
Ngando	C63	121,000	Congo (Kinshasa)
Ngindo	P14	220,000	Tanzania
Ngombe	C41	150,000	Congo (Kinshasa)
Ngoni	N12	205,000	Tanzania and Mozambique
Ngulu	G34	132,000	Tanzania
Nilyamba	F31	440,000	Tanzania
NKORE, Nyoro, Tooro, Kiga, Haya and Zinza	E10	4,668,000	Uganda, Tanzania and Congo (Kinshasa)
Nsenga	N41	250,000	Zambia
Ntomba	C35	100,000	Congo (Kinshasa)
Nyakyusa and Ngonde	M31	820,000	Tanzania and Malawi
Nyamwezi	F22	904,000	Tanzania
NYANJA or Chichewa	N30	4,000,000	Malawi, Zambia, Mozambique and Zimbabwe
Nyaturu or Remi	F32	490,000	Tanzania
Nyemba	K18	100,000	Angola
Nyiha	M23	306,000	Tanzania and Zambia
Nyungwe	N43	262,500	Mozambique
Pangwa	G64	185,000	Tanzania
Phende, Samba, Holu and Kwese	L10	492,000	Congo (Kinshasa)
Pogolo	G51	185,000	Tanzania
Rufiji	P12	200,000	Tanzania
Ruguru	G	506,000	Tanzania
RUNDI, Rwanda and Ha	D60	12,248,000	Burundi, Rwanda, Tanzania, Uganda and Congo (Kinshasa)
Safwa	M25	158,000	Tanzania
Sanga	L35	431,000	Congo (Kinshasa)
SENA	N44	1,200,000	Mozambique

Shambala	G23	485,000	Tanzania
Shi or Nyabungu	D53	654,000	Congo (Kinshasa)
SHONA	S10	7,950,000	Zimbabwe and Mozambique
Songe	L23	938,000	Congo (Kinshasa)
Northern and Southern			
SOTHO	S30	7,400,000*	South Africa and Lesotho
SUKUMA	F21	4,000,000	Tanzania
Sumbwa	F23	191,000	Tanzania
SWAHILI	G42	41,400,000 as a first	Tanzania, Congo
		or second language	(Kinshasa), Kenya and Uganda
SWAZI	S43	1,600,000*	South Africa, Swaziland
			and Mozambique
Taabwa	M	250,000	Congo (Kinshasa)
Taita	E74	153,000	Kenya
Teke dialects	B70	267,800	Congo (Brazzaville)
Tetela	C71	750,000	Congo (Kinshasa)
Tharaka	E54	100,000	Kenya
Tonga of Malawi	N15	200,000	Malawi
TONGA of Zambia	M64	880,000	Zambia and Zimbabwe
Tonga or Shengwe			
of Mozambique	S62	225,000	Mozambique
TSONGA, Ronga and Tswa	S50	4,095,200	Mozambique and South Africa
TSWANA	S31	4,500,000*	South Africa and Botswana
TUMBUKA	N21	1,500,000	Malawi and Zambia
VENDA	S21	850,000*	South Africa and Zimbabwe
XHOSA	S41	6,900,000*	South Africa
Yaka	H31	150,000	Congo (Kinshasa) and Angola
YAO (AFRICA)	P21	1,160,000	Malawi, Tanzania and Mozambique
Zalamo	G33	450,000	Tanzania
Zigula	G31	336,000	Tanzania
ZULU	S42	8,800,000*	South Africa and Lesotho

Dialect shades into language imperceptibly across this wide region. Some languages often spoken of as distinct are grouped into single entries in the present list.

The above population figures are in general adapted from the fuller list of Bantu languages in the *International encyclopedia of linguistics* (New York: Oxford University Press, 1992) vol. 3, pp. 31–53. Those marked * have been revised on the basis of other recent sources.

Bantu noun classes

Very striking in practically every Bantu language is an elaborate system of noun classes, differing for singular and plural. Typically these classes are marked by noun prefixes, with matching prefixes for adjectives and for verbs to mark agreement with noun subjects. In this book there are sample tables of these noun classes, with some examples, at EWONDO, LUBA, MAKONDE and SOTHO. Twenty-one classes are reconstructed in one version of proto-Bantu. Whichever Bantu language they are working on, scholars still usually label these noun classes in accordance with Wilhelm Bleek's numbering system, worked out in 1851. The twenty-one classes are set out in the box, with three alternative reconstructions of their proto-Bantu prefixes.

Bantu noun classes

Conventional number and probable area of meaning	Meinhof's 'Ur-Bantu'	Guthrie's 'Common Bantu'	Later work
1: person	umu	mu	mo
2: people (plural of 1)	aβa	ba	ba
3: animate, agent	umu	mu	mo
4: plural of 3	imi	m̩i	me
5: singular of 6	ili	di	de
6: paired things, multiples	ama	ma	ma
7: custom, method, tool	iki	j̩	ke
8: plural of 7	iβi	b̩i	be
9: animal	ini		ne
10: plural of 9	ilini		dine
11: one of many things	ulu	du	do
12: plural of 13 and 19	utu	ka	to
13: small thing	aka	tu	ka
14: abstraction	uβu	bu	bo
15: verb infinitive	uku	ku	ko
16: 'on'	apa	pa	po
17: 'outside'	uku	ki	ko
18: 'in'	umu	mu	mo
19: diminutive	ipi	p̩i	pi
20: pejorative	uɣu	gu	go
21: augmentative	iɣi	gi	gi

Carl Meinhof, *Grundzüge einer vergleichende Grammatik der Bantusprachen* (Berlin: Reimer, 1906) pp. 1–27; P. Alexandre in *Les langues dans le monde ancien et moderne* ed. Jean Perrot, Parts 1–2 (Paris: CNRS, 1981) pp. 355–6; and other sources

BASHKIR

1,000,000 SPEAKERS

Russia

One of the TURKIC LANGUAGES, Bashkir is spoken by about a quarter of the population of Bashkortostan, one of the self-governing republics within Russia, in the southern Urals (see map at TATAR). It is now classed with Tatar in the Western or Kypchak group of Turkic languages, but this classification belies its complex history.

A people called *Bashqurt* were ruled by the Volga Bulgars (see CHUVASH) in the 10th century. Their present territory, after Bulgar, Mongolian and Tatar domination, came under Russian rule in the late 16th century. Its capital, Ufa, was founded as a Russian fort in 1574. Bashkirs are traditionally Muslim, and Ufa is now a centre of religion and religious education for Muslims in many parts of Russia.

Bashkir shows strong evidence of its history in the form of loanwords from Mongolian, from one of the Ob-Ugric languages (see HUNGARIAN) and from Russian. In spite of long term Tatar influence, both medieval and modern, Bashkir remains quite distinct from Tatar.

Russian, Tatar, Bashkir and Chuvash are used in education and the media in Bashkortostan. The Bashkir literary language and its local adaptation of the Cyrillic script are quite new developments, dating only from 1923 and 1940 respectively. In the late 19th century Tatar was used, alongside Russian, as a literary language in the region, and it still has that role. But there is now a growing tendency to adopt Russian as the everyday language: only two-thirds of those who called themselves Bashkir, in the last USSR census, claimed Bashkir as their first language.

Numerals in Bashkir and Tatar		
Bashkir		**Tatar**
ber	1	ber
ike	2	ike
ös	3	öch
dürt	4	dürt
bish	5	bish
altı	6	altı
ete	7	jide
higedh	8	sigez
tughıdh	9	tugız
un	10	un

BASQUE

PERHAPS 660,000 SPEAKERS

Spain, France

Spoken in France and Spain, on either side of the Pyrenees, Basque is the only living language of Europe that has no known linguistic relatives.

Basque was once thought of as belonging historically to the Iberian peninsula; many viewed it as a descendant of ancient Iberian, the language spoken in parts of Spain at the time of the Roman conquest in the 2nd century BC. But Iberian inscriptions and coins show it to have been a quite different language. The tribal name *Vascones* is actually first met with in Latin texts concerning not the south but the north – Gaulish or 'French' – side of the Pyrenees. *Vascones* is clearly the equivalent of modern *Basque*, but it is also the ancient form of modern *Gascogne*, 'Gascony', the region of France that extends well to the north and east of the modern Basque country, the same region that the Romans called *Aquitania*. From the few sources for the ancient Aquitanian language it seems certain that it is, in fact, the ancestor of Basque.

In Basque itself, the Basque language is called *Euskara* and the Basque country *Euskal herria*. This may possibly be linked with the tribal name *Ausci* of Latin times, which also survives as the name of the French town *Auch*. Other theories exist, however.

There is no doubt that Basque was once spoken over a wider area of France and Spain than it is now. But it was never the language of a major state. Even the kingdom of Navarre, which once straddled the Pyrenees in the Basque country, gave more prestige to Latin and to local forms of Romance than to Basque.

The first book printed in Basque – though with a Latin title – was *Linguae Vasconum primitiae*, 'Elements of the language of the Basques', by Bernard Etxepare (1545). Serious research on the language may be dated from that time. Publishing in Basque flourished in the 17th century. Basque and its culture have suffered from periodic recrudescences of nationalism in both France and Spain, which have resulted from time to time in the outlawing of Basque in official contexts, in schools, and even in all public places.

Basque now has about 660,000 fluent speakers: the estimate results from adding the number of speakers in Spain to the guessed number in France, where linguistic censuses are not taken. As many as 500,000 others know something of the language.

Souriquois: Basque pidgin of the Canadian coast

Basque whalers and cod fishermen regularly spent their summers around the mouth of the St Lawrence river from the 16th century onwards. The French explorer, Jacques Cartier,

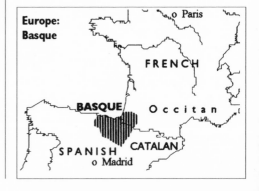

Europe: Basque

found in 1542 that the Amerindians of the St Lawrence shores could speak a kind of Basque. A similar report is made for Newfoundland by the historian Esteban de Garibay in 1571. More details of this pidgin language were recorded by later travellers. Having learnt it in contact with the early Basque mariners, the Indians naturally used it in speaking to the French and English explorers who came along later.

The name *Souriquois*, first reported in 1612, looks Indian. Far from it: it is a French spelling of Basque *zurikoa* 'language of the whites'.

Through these early voyages, which extended from Iceland across to New England, Basque pidgins may have had a significant influence on American English, as argued by J. L. Dillard: see his *A history of American English* (London: Longman, 1992) pp. 1–8.

The first ten numerals in Basque are: *bat, bi* (or *biga*), *hiru, lau, bost, sei, zazpi, zortzi, bederatzi, hamar*. A base of '20' is used to form higher numbers: *hogei* '20', *hogeitamar* '30', *berrogei* '40', *berrogei eta hamar* '50', *hirurogei* '60', *larogei* '80', *ehun* '100'.

There is no *f* in Basque. It is interesting that in a wide area around where Basque is now spoken, from the Garonne to Burgos, Latin *f-* has turned into *h-*. Does this mean that Basque was once spoken over all this area?

Souriquois on the St Lawrence river

A kind of jargon, *un certain baragouin*, assisted conversation between French and Algonquian language speakers in 17th-century Quebec. 'The Frenchmen who spoke it thought that it was good Indian, and the Indians thought that it was French,' said the missionary Paul le Jeune in a letter in 1632. L'Escarbot's *Histoire de la Nouvelle France* ('History of New France', 1612) explains the origin of this mixed language: 'The local people, to help us along, speak to us in a language with which we are more familiar, one in which a good deal of Basque is mixed. Not that they really want to speak our language – as they sometimes say, it was not *they* who came to look for *us* – but having been in such prolonged contact they are bound to remember some words.'

BATAK LANGUAGES

3,500,000 SPEAKERS

Indonesia

The Batak group of AUSTRONESIAN LANGUAGES is spoken in the highlands of north central Sumatra. The best known, with well over a million speakers, is Toba, usually called Toba Batak.

As the language of a longstanding independent written culture it has been much influenced by Sanskrit: see the section on 'The Batak script' for the word *si*, Sanskrit *śrī*, 'honoured', and the phrase *si raja*, 'honoured king, His Majesty', direct Sanskrit loans that are found in many languages of Indonesia. Other influences are Minangkabau, language of Sumatra's west coast,

and Malay, the lingua franca of the whole archipelago. Arabic, Portuguese and Dutch words are also to be found in Batak, many of them borrowed indirectly by way of Malay.

The Batak Lutheran Church, independent and locally organised since the 1930s, is the legacy of the work of the Rhenish Mission Society, begun in 1862. A translation of the Bible into Batak was completed in 1894, and schools spread rapidly.

The first ten numerals in Toba Batak are: *sada, dua, tolu, ɔpat, lima, ɔnɔm, pitu, ualu, sia, sappulu.*

The language of lamentation

At a death-bed and at a burial it is proper in Toba Batak to use a special form of language in chanted laments which narrate the life and achievements of the person mourned. Here are some examples of the traditional phraseology:

They are orphaned	Songon anak ni manuk na sioksiok i	They are like young chickens crying for help
I cannot speak	Songon sangge hinuntam, songon gansip na niodothon i	I am like a purse kept shut, like tongs squeezed tight
A scholar and speaker	Parjagajaga di bibir, parpustaha di tolonan i	One who is always watchful when speaking, and has the books in his throat
A headman or king	Sigongkonon bodari, sialopon manogot	The one who must be invited at night and met early in the morning

Examples from J. P. Sarumpaet, 'Linguistic varieties in Toba Batak' in *Papers from the Third International Conference on Austronesian Linguistics* ed. Amran Halim and others (Canberra: Australian National University, Research School of Pacific Studies, 1982) vol. 3, pp. 27–78

Toba Batak and its relatives

The Batak group consists of seven very similar languages or dialects of northern Sumatra: *Alas* or Kluet, *Karo Batak*, *Dairi* or Pakpak, *Simalungun* or Timur, *Toba Batak, Angkola, Mandailing.*

The Batak script

The Batak script is one of the offshoots of the ancient Brahmi alphabet once used for Sanskrit. Manuscripts (*pustaha*, from Sanskrit *pustaka* 'book') are written on bark. Texts may be in several of the dialects – Toba, Dairi, Angkola, Mandailing – and sometimes in Malay. Literacy in this traditional script is confined largely to *datu* 'priests', who use it for magical texts and diagrams, including calendars, which are important astrologically.

These texts are composed in a special language full of metaphor. A cooking pot is *si boru na birong panuatan, sitabo utauta*, 'her dark lady-

Insular South-east Asia: Batak languages

ship, source of things, whose emptying is tasty'. A lizard is *si raja ongkat di ruangruang, parbaju-baju bosi*, 'his majesty the king who lives in holes, who wears an iron coat'.

a ha ma na ra ta sa pa la ga ja da nga ba wa ya nya i u

BAULE

2,000,000 SPEAKERS OF BAULE AND ANYI

Ivory Coast and Ghana

Baule is one of the Kwa group of NIGER-CONGO LANGUAGES. Spoken by about one and a half million people of Ivory Coast, it is one of the two most important regional languages of the country (the other being Dyula, a variety of MANDEKAN). It was the mother tongue of the founding president of independent Ivory Coast, Félix Houphouët-Boigny (*ufue bwanyi*, literally 'white ram').

Until recently Baule was not a written language. It is now written in a 22-letter variety of the Latin alphabet, omitting *c h j q r x* but adding *ɛ ɔ*. As in French, an *n* following a vowel marks nasalisation.

Baule has twelve vowels, including five nasal vowels. All syllables end with a vowel. It has two basic tones, but modified in context, making for a fairly complex sound pattern. Two-tone drums are traditionally used to send messages between villages, mimicking the tone patterns of spoken phrases. Baule is more preponderantly monosyllabic even than its close relative Anyi: 'village' is *kulo* in Anyi, *klo* in Baule.

The first ten numerals in Baule are: *kun, nnyon, nsan, nnan, nnun, nsiɛn, nso, nmɔtyuɛ, ngwlan, blu.* Baule has borrowed heavily from French: *ekoli* 'school'; *loto* 'car' from French *l'auto* 'the car'; *amindi* 'noon' from French *à midi* 'at noon'.

Based on M. Malherbe, *Les langues de l'humanité* (Paris: Laffont, 1995) pp. 589–94 and other sources

Baule and Anyi on the map

Baule or Baoulé is a language of inland Ivory Coast, spoken in the regions surrounding Bouaké and Yamoussoukro and extending into western Ghana.

Anyi or Anyin is the eastern dialect of Baule, spoken on the left bank of the Comoé river. Anyi (under the name *Aowin*) and Sehwi (*Sefwi*) are the two Ghanaian dialects of Baule. There are perhaps 500,000 speakers of these dialects, including 200,000 in Ghana. Anyi includes the sub-dialects Nzema (or Nzima) and Ahanta.

Birthdays and names

In Baule, as in AKAN (see text there) and EWE, children are customarily named in accordance with the day on which they were born:

	Boys	Girls
Sunday	Kuame, Kuain	Amuin
Monday	Kuasi	Akisi
Tuesday	Kuadyo	Adyua
Wednesday	Konan	Amlan
Thursday	Kuaku	Au
Friday	Yao	Aya
Saturday	Kofi	Afue

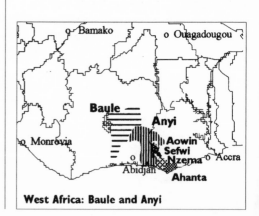

West Africa: Baule and Anyi

BEJA

PERHAPS 500,000 SPEAKERS

Sudan, Eritrea

Beja is spoken by a nomadic people of whom rather little is known. They live between the Nile valley and the Red Sea, in the arid hills of north-eastern Sudan (see map at AFAR); one tribe, the *Beni Amir*, are to be found in northern Eritrea. Few details of their history are recorded, but it seems likely that Beja speakers have been in this region for at least two thousand years, and that they are the *Blemmyes* of ancient Greek geographical texts.

Beja is the Arabic name for this people and their language. Their own name is *ti-Bedaawye*. The English term *Bedouin* derives from it, by way of Arabic and French. The Bedouin of the Arabian peninsula are actually Arabic speakers, but many of those of the western shore of the Red Sea speak Beja.

In Eritrea speakers call their language *Hadareb*. The tribal names *Bishari* and *Hadendiwa* have also been used to denote Beja.

At the end of the 19th century two linguists worked on Beja: Herman Almqvist published a description of the Sudanese dialect, Leo Reinisch of the dialect of the Beni Amir. Few outsiders have studied the Beja or their language since then, and too little is known of the boundaries between dialects to place them reliably on a map. In Eritrea, however, two dialects are said to be spoken – one by the aristocracy, the other by the serf class.

Beja speakers in Eritrea, the Beni Amir, are apparently fairly recent migrants, who have intermarried with Tigre speakers and are now largely bilingual in Tigre. The *Beni Kanz* were a Beja-speaking group who went through a similar development several centuries ago. By agreement with the Nubian kingdom of Makouria, they settled on the Nile, between the First and Second Cataracts, at a point where nowadays not Beja but a NUBIAN language, *Kenzi*, is spoken. As they settled, they evidently adopted – probably by intermarriage – the language of Makouria whose northern sentinels they had become: this language was *Dongolawi* Nubian, of which Kenzi is a dialect.

Beja has five vowels, a distinction of vowel length, and (according to a recent analysis by Richard Hudson) a pattern of word stress which is predictable but highly complex in its realisation in actual speech. The first ten numerals are: *ngaal, mhaloo-b, mhay, fadig, áy, asagwir, asaramaa-b, asamháy, as's'adig, tamin.*

BELORUSSIAN

7,500,000 SPEAKERS

Belarus

Belorussian is one of the three Eastern SLA-VONIC LANGUAGES, and has generally been overshadowed by its neighbours (for map see RUSSIAN).

Belorussian or *Byelorussian* means *White Russian*, and that name (or *White Ruthenian*) has sometimes been used for the language. It has nothing to do with the White Russian faction that attempted counter-revolution against Communism in 1918–22.

Belarus is divided from Ukraine by the vast Pripet Marshes. It seems likely that early Slavonic speakers slowly spread northwards from Ukraine to settle Belarus and Russia in the first millennium AD. The written Old Russian of Kiev (see UKRAINIAN) may be regarded as ancestor equally of Russian, Ukrainian and Belorussian. Modern Belorussian is part of a dialect continuum that links Ukrainian to the south and Russian to the east.

Little is known of the history of Belarus before it became part of the dominions of the pagan Lithuanians under Prince Gedymin in 1315. *Western Russian* or *Ruthenian*, an early form of Belorussian mixed with Old Slavonic, was the official language of Lithuania, which in due course became a Christian state and one half of the Polish-Lithuanian kingdom. This variety of Belorussian thus spread wider than any later form of the language, being spoken and written – in some contexts – all the way from the Baltic coast to Ukraine, where, gradually modified by Ukrainian, it was used administratively even in the 17th-century Cossack state in eastern Ukraine. It was often called *prostaya mova*, 'common tongue', to distinguish it from Church Slavonic.

However, Polish gradually supplanted Belorussian as the ruling language of Belarus and Belorussian peasants were increasingly subject to Polish landowners. At the end of the 18th century Russia annexed Lithuania, including Belorussia, and Russian became the new language of prestige.

A Belorussian translation of the Bible, by F. Skaryna, had been printed in Prague in 1517–19. There are important texts from the 16th century, including chronicles of Lithuania. The language and literature flourished in the 19th century, and even more with the establishment of an autonomous Belorussian Republic within the Soviet Union.

Belarus declared its independence in 1991 but remains on good terms with Russia, although Russia was blamed for the Chernobyl nuclear disaster which has left part of south-eastern Belarus uninhabitable. Most Belorussians speak Russian fluently, and some still regard their mother tongue as little more than a rustic dialect of Russian (as Russians themselves tended to do). The Belorussian press is more than half Russian in language, though the Russian minority forms less than a quarter of the population of the country.

The language differs from Russian not only by its characteristic sound pattern – there are examples in the table of numerals – but also because of the large number of Polish loanwords.

The Belorussian version of the Cyrillic alphabet is easily recognisable. It uses I i (in place of Russian И и) for *i* and Ў ў for *w*. Until the early 20th century, under Polish influence, some Catholic Belorussians wrote their language in the Latin alphabet.

Не зыч ліха другому, каб не давялося самому

Nye zich lyikha drugomu, kab nye davyalosya samomu

Don't wish ill on another, lest it fall on you

Numerals in East Slavonic languages

	Belorussian	Ukrainian	Russian	Russian in Cyrillic
1	adzyin	odin	odin	один
2	dva	dva	dva	два
3	tri	tri	tri	три
4	chatiri	chotiri	chetıre	четыре
5	pyats'	pyat'	pyat'	пять
6	shests'	shist'	shest'	шесть
7	syem	sim	sem'	семь
8	vosyem	visim	vosem'	восемь
9	dzyevyats'	devyat'	devyat'	девять
10	dzyesyats'	desyat'	desyat'	десять

In this table all three languages are given in Latin transliteration: Russian also appears in the original Cyrillic script.

BEMBA

1,850,000 SPEAKERS

Congo (Kinshasa), Zambia

One of the BANTU LANGUAGES, Bemba is the mother tongue of the largest single linguistic group of Zambia, where it is one of the eight official languages of the country and is spoken by many as a second or third language.

In its own region in north-eastern Zambia, Bemba is surrounded by related dialects. Its older history is uncertain: traditions speak of a migration from the west and of an origin among LUBA-speaking peoples. At any rate, the speakers of Bemba were, in the 19th century, the most powerful among their immediate neighbours. When the British South Africa Company took control here, in 1900, the Bemba king ruled the whole area between lakes Nyasa, Tanganyika, Mweru and Bangweulu, and even further to the east and the south-west.

The first ten numerals in Bemba are: *-mo, -bili, -tatu, -ne, -sano, mutanda, cine-lubali, cine-konse-konse, funai, ikumi.* English loanwords in Bemba include *shitoolo* 'store', *petulo* 'petrol'; from Portuguese *carreta* comes Bemba *iceleeta* 'cart'.

> The language is known to its own speakers as *chiBemba*; they refer to themselves as *ba-Bemba*. In older sources the form *Wemba* is found.

Languages of the Copperbelt

The earliest lingua franca of the Zambian Copperbelt was the pidginised ZULU known as Fanakalo. This was introduced at the end of the 19th century by the first European and Asian immigrants, who had learnt to use it in South Africa.

To the labourers in the mines, however, Fanakalo was both a foreign language and a colonial language: it was neither easy to learn nor socially acceptable. It continued to be used until the 1940s, by which time the ethnic profile of the mines had changed. Once, most workers had come from far away; now the majority of mine employees were speakers of Bemba and related languages. What was required was a language in which the minority of migrant workers could converse with this new majority.

Thus a simplified form of Bemba developed, known in English as *Town Bemba* (a term introduced by Irvine Richardson) or *Broken Bemba*; to its own speakers it is *ciKopabeeluti* 'Copperbelt language'.

Town Bemba is a good term, for this is a language of urbanism, a young people's language, the passport to the bustling life of Ndola, Mufulira, Chingola and neighbouring towns in the crowded Copperbelt. Here, speakers use it in work and leisure. Rural migrants learn it when they come to work in the city – and may cease to use it if they retire to their home villages. But with increased labour mobility it is now also spoken by significant minorities in Lusaka, Livingstone and Harare.

Town Bemba developed as a local lingua franca, easy to learn for speakers of a Bantu language (they take a few months to master it) but tending to exclude Europeans – and no less popular for that. It has superseded Fanakalo and was never seriously challenged by NYANJA (the police language). English, the fourth lingua franca of the Copperbelt, is used only by a minority.

Bemba and its relatives: the map

BEMBA has 1,850,000 speakers in Zambia and Congo (Kinshasa). *Taabwa*, with 250,000 speakers in Congo (Kinshasa), may be regarded as a northern dialect of Bemba.

Lala and Bisa, with 350,000 speakers, and Lamba with 175,000, are more distantly related to Bemba and are also spoken in Zambia and Congo (Kinshasa).

A third related group is formed by TONGA of Zambia, with 900,000 speakers in Zambia and Zimbabwe (divided into two main dialects, Plateau or Northern Tonga and Valley or Southern Tonga) and two smaller Zambian languages, *Lenje* (140,000 speakers) and *Ila* or *ciIla* (60,000). These are grouped as the 'three peoples', *Bantu Botatwe*.

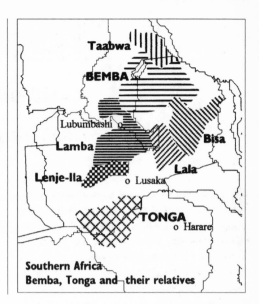

Southern Africa.
Bemba, Tonga and their relatives

BENGALI

180,000,000 SPEAKERS

Bangladesh, India

Bengali, the best known of the Eastern INDO-ARYAN LANGUAGES, is the national language of Bangladesh (formerly East Pakistan) and is also spoken by the great majority in the Indian province of West Bengal: for map see ASSAMESE. Differences are beginning to emerge between the colloquial standard Bengali used in the press and media in the two capitals, Calcutta and Dacca.

The country at the mouth of the Ganges was already called *Vaṅgāla*, 'Bengal', in an 11th-century inscription.

The region was apparently occupied by Indo-Aryan speakers for the first time in the course of the later first millennium AD.

The Middle Bengali period is dated to the 14th to 18th centuries. Hinduism was by now the religion of Bengal – soon to share its predominance with Islam – and literature of the period is religiously inspired. The *Brajabuli* literary dialect, a mixture of Maithili and Bengali, was used conventionally by Vaishnava poets in a wide area of India, as if it were thought somehow specially appropriate to the Braj homeland of Krishna.

Among the classics of modern Bengali are the historical novels of Bankimchandra Chatterji, which are set in a period of Bengali cultural renaissance in the 15th century, just before the spread of Islam: his first novel was in English (*Rajmohan's wife*, 1864), but he then turned to Bengali. Modern Bengali has had two literary standards, *sadhu bhāṣā*, which looked back to 14th- and 15th-century litera-

ture and to Sanskrit culture, and *colit bhāṣā*, based on the modern colloquial of Calcutta. Rabindranath Tagore, the greatest modern Bengali author, preferred *colit bhāṣā*. A range of spoken and written styles, more and less formal, has developed from it, and *sadhu bhāṣā* is now little used.

Bengali, like the other Eastern Indo-Aryan languages, has no grammatical gender. The verb has three separate inflexions in the 2nd and 3rd persons ('you, he, she') to indicate the relative status of speaker and subject.

There are marked regional dialects, including some which may be considered separate languages (see map at ASSAMESE).

Sylheti has about 5,000,000 speakers in Sylhet District of Bangladesh, a hundred miles north-east of Dacca. There is a large community, perhaps as many as 100,000, of Sylheti speakers in Britain – they are usually called *Bengalis* or even *Pakistanis*. The biggest concentrations are in the boroughs of Tower Hamlets and Camden in London.

Bishnupriya Manipuri (or Mayang) is historically a form of Bengali once current in Manipur. Its speakers were driven from there in the early 19th century, and it is now spoken in Tripura State, in Cachar District of Assam, and in Sylhet District of Bangladesh. There are thought to be 150,000 speakers. The two dialects – once divided geographically, but no longer – are *Mādai gāng* and *Rājār gāng*, 'Queen's village' and 'King's village'.

Caryāpada

Around 1000 AD, when Bengali, Oriya and Assamese were not yet distinguishable as separate languages, the remarkable, mystical Buddhist *Caryāpada* songs were composed. They were discovered in a manuscript at Kathmandu and first published in 1916. They are claimed as the foundation of the literary tradition of all three languages.

Gaṅgā Jaūnā majhem̐ re bahai nāī
tahim̐ buṛilā mataṅgī yoiā līle pāra karei.

Bāhatu Ḍombi, bāha lo Ḍombi; bāṭata bhaila
uchārā;
Sadguru pāapasāem̐ jāiba puṇi Jinaurā. . . .

Kabaḍī na lei boḍī na lei succhaṛe pāra karei;

jo rathe caṛilā bāhabā ṇa jāi kulem̐ kula buṛai.

Between Ganges and Jumna another river flows:
the outcaste woman easily ferries a sinking scholar
across it.
Row on, woman, row on, woman! It darkened
as we went;
by the grace of the Guru's feet I shall go again
to the City of the Jinas . . .
She takes no cowries, she takes no coppers: she
ferries whomever she pleases;
But if one mounts and cannot drive, he is set
back on the bank.

Caryāpada 14

Numerals in Bengali and related languages

	Bengali	Oriya	Assamese	Bishnupriya Manipuri
১	ek	eka	ɛk	ā
২	dui	dui	dui	dū
৩	tin	tini	tini	tin
৪	cār	cārī	sāri	sāri
৫	pānc	pañca	pās	pāz
৬	chay	chaa	say	soy
৭	sāt	sāta	khāt	hād
৮	āṭ	āṭha	āth	āt
৯	nay	naa	na	nau
১০	daś	daśa	dah	dos

The Bengali alphabet

অ আ ই ঈ উ ঊ এ ঐ ও ঔ কখগঘঙ চছজঝঞ টঠডঢণ তথদধন পফবভম যরল শষসহ

a ā i ī u ū e ai o au k kh g gh ṅ c ch j jh ñ ṭ ṭh ḍ ḍh ṇ t th d dh n p ph b bh m y r l ś ṣ s h

The Bengali alphabet is one of the local developments of India's early Brahmi. Like the others, it has numerous conjunct characters for doubled and adjacent consonants. When this alphabet is used for Sanskrit texts, the symbol ব serves for both *b* and *v*.

BERBER LANGUAGES

In the 18th and early 19th centuries linguists became interested in the distant relationships of well-known language families. The Semitic group, including Arabic and Hebrew, was found to have pervasive similarities with two language groups of north Africa: Egyptian and Berber. This was the beginning of the recognition of the 'Hamitic' or 'Hamito-Semitic' family, now most often known as the AFROASIATIC LANGUAGES.

Theories crop up from time to time linking Berber with the ancient Iberian language of Spain, with Basque, and with other linguistic survivals in Europe. They are generally short on evidence and probability.

Beraber is the name used for themselves by the speakers of TAMAZIGHT, one of the Berber languages of Morocco. The word has a long history: it was first used in northern Africa by Greeks or Romans, who referred to the local inhabitants vaguely as *barbari*, 'barbarians, foreign language speakers'.

Before the spread of Islam, and of the Arabic language that came with it, Berber languages were almost universally spoken across northern Africa and the Sahara from the Atlantic to the borders of Egypt: at least, this is what all surviving evidence suggests, for no other indigenous language group seems to be represented in early inscriptions or place names. Only limited inroads were made by Greek, the language of the founders of Cyrene and neighbouring cities in the 7th century BC; Punic, the Semitic language spoken by the Phoenician settlers at Carthage, near modern Tunis; and Latin, language of the Roman Empire. If a Romance language began to develop in Roman north Africa, it did not last long.

The mysterious *Guanche*, indigenous language of the Canary Islands, is generally thought to have been a Berber language, though perhaps long separated from the main group. It became extinct in the 16th century.

As the Islamic conquest swept across north Africa and onwards to Spain, Berber speakers were soon dominant in the armies, in government and culture. Through this channel Berber can be shown to have influenced modern Spanish and Portuguese, as well as the local Arabic of modern north Africa. Some of the greatest medieval Arabic scholars, such as Ibn Khaldūn and the traveller Ibn Baṭṭūṭa, were of Berber origin. Ibn Khaldūn, the great philosophical historian of the 14th century, wrote a history of the Berbers.

But, almost as quickly, Arabic, language of the prevailing culture and religion, became the lingua franca, and then the mother tongue, of an increasingly large proportion of the population. Since that time, Arabic has been the language of government, of education and of all written culture in north Africa: knowledge of the Berber script soon died in most places. The survival of the Berber languages of the north, still spoken by millions in north Africa though faced with official lack of recognition and sometimes active discrimination, is a tribute to the tenacity of traditional culture. It also has something to do with the seclusion of women, which ironically is a legacy of invading Islam: for, even today, while many Berber-speaking men are bilingual in Arabic, women are not. With the increasing reach of modern media, this situation is likely to change, and the position of these historic languages is under more serious threat.

It can be legitimately argued that one should still speak today of 'the Berber language', not of 'Berber languages'. The dialects spoken from Mauritania to Egypt remain identifiably alike. But it does not at present seem likely that a single literary standard will emerge; on the contrary, regional standards are tending to crystallise, with or without official support. That is why the major varieties of Berber have separate entries in this book.

In the Sahara, TAMASHEQ is the vehicle of a still vigorous nomadic culture – and the ancient script is still remembered. TAMASHEQ is a national language in Niger, Mali and Burkina Faso.

In all there are perhaps 12,000,000 speakers of Berber languages. Across all of north Africa, place names are largely of Berber origin. Many have the easily recognised double mark of feminine nouns, *t- -t* (Tamasheq *barar* 'son', *tabarart* 'daughter'). This characteristic shape is seen in the language names *Tamazight* and *Tashelhet* and in place names such as *Tamanrasset, Touggourt, Tanezrouft*.

Berber languages naturally have many loan-words from Arabic. Latin loanwords, from an earlier period of cultural influence, are also easy to find (see box at TASHELHET).

The Berber languages

Owing to the lack of official recognition of Berber languages in Morocco and Algeria, population figures are largely guesswork. The number of speakers in Libya and in the Siwa oasis of Egypt is also unknown (see map at TAMAZIGHT).

TAMASHEQ is the language of the *Tuareg* of the Sahara. It has perhaps 1,000,000 speakers in Niger, Mali, Burkina Faso, Algeria and Libya.

Chaoui or Shawia is the language of about 250,000 speakers in the Aurès mountains in south-eastern Algeria.

KABYLE has at least two million speakers (one recent estimate is 7,000,000) in north-eastern Algeria.

Mzab has about 80,000 speakers, centring on Ghardaia in the Mzab region of Algeria.

RIFIA or Northern Shilha has 1 to 2 million speakers near the northern coast of Morocco and in north-western Algeria.

TAMAZIGHT or Central Shilha is spoken by about 3,000,000 speakers, the *Beraber*, in north central Morocco.

TASHELHET or Southern Shilha has perhaps 3,000,000 speakers in southern Morocco, Algeria. The few speakers in Mauritania are a reminder that Berber speech was once widespread in that country, now supplanted by Hassaniya Arabic.

Siwa and *Zenaga*, at opposite extremities of the Sahara region, are the most isolated of today's Berber languages, each with a few thousand speakers.

Libyan and Berber scripts

Over a thousand stone inscriptions have been found in North Africa, dating from the 2nd century BC and into Roman times, in a script and language which is neither Punic nor Latin. Although they are mostly very short, consisting largely of names, it is clear that the language concerned (usually called 'Old Libyan') is a form of Berber.

The script is still used by TAMASHEQ speakers. The native name for it is *tifinagh*. Removing the *t*-prefix, this seems to derive from Latin *Punicae* 'Punic, Carthaginian'. The script shows Punic influence – and the Romans appear to have observed the fact.

· Φ Ϙ Π ⋮ ⁚ ⧻ Ⲭ Ⲭ ⁚⁚ Ǝ ⟨ ·· ‖ ⊐ ❘ ☉ ⁚ ⟩⟨ ⋯ ⤫ ◯ ℥ ✛

′ b ğ d h w z ž ẓ ẖ ṭ y k l m n s ǵ f q g r š t

BHOJPURI

PERHAPS 40,000,000 SPEAKERS

India, Trinidad, Guyana, Fiji, Mauritius, Suriname and other countries

One of the INDO-ARYAN LANGUAGES, Bhojpuri is spoken in the middle Ganges valley (for map see HINDI), both north and south of the historic city of Benares. Variant forms of Bhojpuri are the majority languages of Trinidad, Guyana and Fiji.

The ruined city of Bhojpur, near Shāhābād, was once the capital of a powerful Rajput principality. It fell foul of the Emperor Akbar, and later of the British Raj, and disappeared from the scene after 1857. Even at its climax, Bhojpur never ruled all the country where *Bhojpurī* is spoken. The language has also been called *Purbī* or *Purbiyā*, the language 'in front' or 'to the east' of Delhi.

Bhojpuri is not one of the established literary languages of India. The poet Kabir (1399–1518) claimed to write *Banārsī-bolī*, the 'language of Benares', his native city, but in fact his writing shows features that belong to Braj (see HINDI). Then and later, education here has been traditionally in Sanskrit and Hindi. Speakers of Bhojpuri nowadays will generally say that they speak 'Hindi'. There are relatively few Sanskrit loan-words; rather more are drawn from Bengali and Hindi, which are spoken in the cities from which government has emanated, Calcutta (the old capital of British India) and Delhi.

However, Bhojpuri has a strong tradition of oral literature. The plays called *Bidesiyā* are a reminder of the long history of emigration from the region, for they tell the distress of a wife whose husband has travelled far away to find work.

For a table of numerals see MAITHILI.

Sadānī or *Nāgpuriā* is sometimes considered a dialect of Bhojpuri, sometimes a separate language. It is the lingua franca of the eastern Chota Nagpur plateau, and is strongly influenced by the Austroasiatic language SANTALI that is still spoken there. There may be as many as 1,200,000 speakers. The name *Sadānī* means 'headquarters language', a reminder of how the language has gradually spread from local administrative centres in this jungle region.

Bhojpuri across the world

The Indians who were recruited to work in tropical plantations in the 19th century came, in their majority, from the middle Ganges region. There were speakers of Hindi dialects, of Bengali, of Maithili and Magahi, and of other Indian languages too. But in each major community a single language soon stabilised, to serve as a lingua franca among all Indian émigrés. Linguists who work on the languages of this diaspora today find that they have more of the special features of Bhojpuri than of any of its relatives.

The everyday name of these languages, however, is 'Hindi' or 'Hindustani'. If speakers are able to study their community language at school, standard Hindi is what they study. If they publish, standard Hindi is usually what they write. When their ancestors left India, Bhojpuri had hardly been identified as a separate language – and Hindi is still the Indian language of prestige, in literature, in education and in religion.

Mauritian Bhojpuri has about 300,000 speakers in Mauritius. Emigration took place between 1834 and 1900. Standard Hindi is used in school and in the media.

South African Bhojpuri is a threatened language, with fewer than 100,000 speakers: few children learn it. It contains loanwords from English (*afkaran* 'half a crown'), Fanakalo (*bagasha* 'visit') and Afrikaans.

Sarnami is the language of the Indian community of Surinam and the Netherlands, with about 180,000 speakers. There is some printed literature in Sarnami.

Guyanese Bhojpuri, locally best known as Hindi and Urdu, is the majority language of Guyana, with about 400,000 speakers.

Trinidad Bhojpuri or Hindi has been a major language of Trinidad, now in decline.

Fijian Hindustani (350,000 speakers, narrowly a majority of the population) seems to differ somewhat from the other Bhojpuri dialects of the diaspora, having more noticeable elements of 19th-century Bazaar Hindustani. Standard Hindi is sometimes used in Fiji in formal contexts: here English is tending to take its place. There is also a *Pidgin Hindustani*, commonly used in Fiji when Hindustani speakers converse with others who do not know the language.

The people down river

भागलपुर के भगोलिया ।	Bhāgalpur ke bhagoliyā	Bhagalpur are runaways,
कहलगाँव के ठग ॥	Kahalgāṅv ke ṭhag	Kahalgaon are thugs,
पटना के देवलिया ।	Paṭanā ke devaliyā	Patna are sharpsters,
तीनू नमजद ॥	tīnū namajad.	All three are known for it –
सुनि पावे भोजपुरिया ।	Suni pāvē Bhojpuriyā	If a Bhojpuri hears of them
त तीनू के तूरे रग ॥	ta tīnū ke tūrē rag.	He'll break the heads of all three.

Maithili is spoken at Bhagalpur; at Patna Magahi is spoken. Kahalgaon is where the Bengali language area begins. The English word *thug* is a loanword from Indian languages.

After U. N. Tiwari, *The origin and development of Bhojpuri* (Calcutta: Asiatic Society, 1970)

BIKOL

3,000,000 SPEAKERS

Philippines

One of the AUSTRONESIAN LANGUAGES, Bikol is the major language of the Philippine provinces of southern Luzon – unofficially referred to as *Bicolandia*. It is closely related to Tagalog, the *de facto* national language, spoken to the north, and to the Bisayan dialects of the Visayas islands to the south (see maps at TAGALOG and CEBUANO).

The language name can be spelt *Bikol, Bicol* (the Spanish form) or *Vicol*.

A fragment of Bikol oral epic, *Handiong*, was transcribed by the Franciscan priest Bernardino Melendreras (1815–67) and published in Spanish in 1895. Sadly, the Bikol text does not survive. It told of the Flood and the rising of three volcanoes, Hantic, Colasi and Isarog.

Numerals in Tagalog and Bikol

Tagalog		Bikol
isa	1	saro'
dalawa	2	duwa
tatlo	3	tulo
apat	4	apat
lima	5	lima
anim	6	anom
pito	7	pito
walo	8	walo
siyam	9	siyam
sampû	10	sampulo'

BISLAMA

PERHAPS 60,000 SPEAKERS OF BISLAMA AS A LINGUA FRANCA

Vanuatu

Like TOK PISIN of Papua New Guinea, Bislama is a modern form of *Beach-la-mar*, the English pidgin of the 19th-century western Pacific (see ENGLISH CREOLES AND PIDGINS). The influence of the old China Coast Pidgin can still be traced in the vocabulary and structure of the modern descendants of Beach-la-mar.

Bislama, the local pronunciation of *Beach-la-mar*, is now the preferred name; in French the modern form is *Bichelamar*. The word is said to derive from *bêche de mer*, the French term for the sea cucumber, which was gathered in the South Seas and marketed as a delicacy in China.

Bislama is the lingua franca of Vanuatu, formerly the New Hebrides. These islands were ruled as a 'condominium' by Britain and France between 1906 and 1980.

Originating in the mid 19th century as a language of labourers on European-owned plantations and of sailors on European-owned ships, Bislama became rapidly more important during the Second World War with increased population movement and the arrival of American military bases. In the 1960s New Hebrideans took part in local government, and Bislama was the available lingua franca. It is now an essential medium of communication among a population of 150,000 who speak 105 different local languages – though its English base makes it more accessible to the English-educated than to the French-educated Vanuatuans.

French and English remain official languages of independent Vanuatu, but Bislama now ranks as the national language. It is much used in government, press and broadcasting, as well as in trade.

The first ten numerals in Bislama, still close to English, are: *wan, tu, tri, fo, faev, sikis, seven, et, naen, ten*.

BODO-GARO LANGUAGES

PERHAPS 2,000,000 SPEAKERS

India

This group of SINO-TIBETAN LANGUAGES is spoken by hill peoples to the north and south of the Brahmaputra valley in Assam. The three major languages are Bodo, Garo and Tripuri. Two thousand years ago – before ASSAMESE arrived from the west and AHOM from the east – proto-Bodo was probably the language of the Assamese lowlands, the middle Brahmaputra valley.

Bodo or *Bāṛā* is the name for themselves of the Mec, Dimasa and Kachārī tribes. They are said long ago to have established an independent Buddhist kingdom: this was conquered by the AHOM of Assam. The Assamese language shows considerable Bodo influence; in turn, Assamese has influenced Bodo, particularly in its word structure.

Bodo peoples occupy what is in subcontinental terms a strategic location to the north of the Brahmaputra at the point where it narrows to a corridor linking Assam with the rest of India. They have taken full advantage of this location in agitating for political recognition. They won local autonomy in the early 1990s but a struggle for full independence continues, and many deaths resulted from the bombing of an Assam–Delhi train in December 1996.

Garo is spoken to the south of the Brahmaputra in the Garo Hills, at the western end of the Shillong plateau. Its speakers call themselves *Mande* 'man' or *A'chik* 'hillside': their neighbours to the east speak the quite unrelated Austroasiatic language KHASI.

'The Garo have long had market and headhunting relations with the surrounding plains people' (R. Burling in *Ethnic groups of mainland southeast Asia* ed. Frank M. LeBar and others (New Haven: HRAF Press, 1964) p. 56). Weekly markets are still a central feature of Garo culture. Garo speakers had no political units larger than the village, but they were generally independent until the British conquest in 1867: after that the Garo Hills formed a district within Assam, though with little outside interference, until the imposition of Assamese as official language led to demands for autonomy and the creation of the new state of Meghalaya in 1972. Garo and KHASI are its two main languages. As many as a third of Garo speakers are Christians, the majority of these being Methodists.

Speakers of Tripuri (or *Tipuri* or *Kok Borok*) are identified with the old state of Tripura, independent and sometimes powerful before the Mughal conquest in the 17th century. Tripura became a separate state of India in 1972. The majority of its inhabitants speak Bengali, a language of culture which was gradually spreading in Tripura under Mughal and British rule.

Bodo, Garo and Tripuri on the map

Bodo has 1,000,000 speakers in the Bodo hills of north-western Assam.

Garo has 500,000 speakers in the Garo Hills. *Atong* or *Koch*, to the south-east, with 50,000 speakers, is not mutually intelligible with Garo.

Tripuri (including the *Riang* dialect) is one of the three major languages of Tripura State, India, where it has 350,000 speakers. There are also 50,000 speakers in eastern Bangladesh.

Numerals in the Bodo-Garo languages

	Bodo	**Garo**	**Tripuri**
1	sè	sa	kai-sa
2	nè	gin-i	kun-nui
3	tham	git-tam	kā-thām
4	brè	bri	kai-brui
5	bā	bong-a	bā
6	ṛā	dok	dok
7	sni	sin-i	shini
8	zat	cet	cār
9	skhō	sku	cikuk
10	zi	ci-king	ci

Numerals are combined with classifiers: Robbins Burling, *A Garo grammar* (Poona: Schools of Linguistics, Deccan College, 1961) lists seventy-five of these. A few examples:

Classifier	**Range of meaning**	**Example**	**Example translated**
te-	hollow objects	me-dik te-sa	one rice-pot
dik-	potful	mi dik-sa	one pot of rice
kap-	cupful (English loanword)	ca kap-gin-i	two cups of tea
pak-	half of something	ku-mir-a pak-gin-i	two halves of an orange
cang-	times	cang-git-tam re-ang-a-ha	he went three times

South Asia:
Bodo, Garo and Tripuri

BRAHUI

1500,000 SPEAKERS

Pakistan

Brahui, a major language of western Pakistan, is an astonishing survival – utterly different from the Iranian languages that surround it. Most Brahui speakers are bilingual in Baluchi. There is no doubt that Brahui belongs to the family of DRAVIDIAN LANGUAGES of south India, though it is separated from the nearest of them by many hundreds of miles (see map at KURUKH). The relationship was first pointed out by the German linguist Christian Lassen in 1844.

One common guess is that early Dravidian speakers migrated southwards into the Indian peninsula thousands of years ago, and that Brahui (and perhaps Elamite) remain as a clue to show the route they followed. But it cannot be as simple as this: Brahui shares some innovations with northern Dravidian languages such as KURUKH so they must have separated from the other Dravidian languages before they themselves began to differentiate. In reality the early history of Brahui is quite unknown.

It is at least certain that the speakers of Brahui and BALUCHI have long lived side by side. Tradition tells of Hindu rule in medieval Kalat, the centre of Brahui and Baluchi culture, followed by a Brahui dynasty, followed by Mughal rule as elsewhere in India, followed by renewed Brahui domination. This last period contains a date –

1660, the accession of Mīr Ahmad as Khan of Kalat, ruling both Brahui and Baluchi tribes.

The pastoralist Brahuis traditionally migrate in large numbers in winter, the people called Sarāwān to Kacchī, the people called Jhalawān to Sind, where they have hereditary winter quarters. It has been suggested that their nomadic routes used to be westwards towards Afghanistan in earlier centuries, and that this explains why there are some 20,000 Brahui speakers now settled in Afghanistan, with a few further north in Tajikistan. At all events, Brahui is heavily influenced by Baluchi and by Sindhi, languages in which many Brahui speakers are necessarily bilingual. Although its Dravidian descent is still obvious, Brahui now has rather few inherited Dravidian words in its lexicon: Iranian, and specifically Baluchi, words predominate. Its sound pattern is most like that of Indo-Aryan languages such as Sindhi, without the short *e* and *o* and the multiple *r* sounds typical of Dravidian.

The first ten numerals in Brahui are: *asiṭ, iraṭ, musiṭ, chār, panch, shash, haft, hasht, noh, dah*. Only '1' to '3' are Dravidian – the higher numbers are borrowed from Baluchi or Persian.

O hilārki daun e ki ginjishk tūtaki – 'he's as fond of dates as a sparrow is of mulberries'.

BRETON

500,000 SPEAKERS

France

Celtic languages were once spoken all across the country that we now call France. They gave way before Latin, the language of education and government in the western Roman Empire. But as the empire faded and Saxon and other raiders attacked its northern provinces, Celtic speakers from Britain migrated in great numbers to northern France to fight and to settle.

These migrants were naturally called *Britanni*, 'Britons'. The great majority came to live in the north-western peninsula that was known to the Romans as Armorica – and was now renamed *Brittany*, or 'Little Britain', after the new inhabitants. This is how the island from which they set out gained its fuller name of *Great Britain*.

Perhaps this migration brought Celtic speech back to a country where it had already died out. More likely, it reinforced a surviving Celtic speech community and provided a new standard language, closer than before to Cornish and Welsh (see map at CELTIC LANGUAGES).

There was close contact between Wales, Cornwall and Brittany in early medieval times. Their religious communities were interwoven: students and missionaries were ever crossing the English Channel. Gildas, the 6th-century author of *The Ruin of Britain* (see box at WELSH), is commemorated as a saint in Brittany.

Even while Brittany was an autonomous duchy, in medieval times, French gradually became important there as a language of culture, of the nobility, and of the church hierarchy. As Norman dukes and French kings eroded the eastern frontiers of Brittany, the area of Breton speech gradually receded. In recent centuries French has been imposed as essential throughout Brittany by the highly centralised and nationalistic educational and legal systems of France. All speakers of Breton are now bilingual: it is said that there are 1,200,000 of them, but fewer than half of these use it daily as their first language.

The early literature of Brittany is in Latin – a series of religious texts and local saints' lives which contribute to the history of western France, south-west England and Wales. The 'Breton *lais*' written in French in the 12th and 13th centuries, by Marie de France and others, may be versions of oral poetry in Breton: as tales of Arthurian heroes they parallel the prose of the Welsh 'Mabinogion' and they inspired the better-known romances of the *Table Ronde* that were soon to be written in French, English, German and other European languages.

The first surviving Breton texts are some scraps of song inserted by a lonely Breton monk of the 14th century in a Latin manuscript that he was copying, Vincent de Beauvais' *Speculum historiale*, 'Mirror of history'. One of these reads:

Mar ham guorant va karantit
da vont in nos o he kostit . . .

> If my lover promises me
> I may lie beside her tonight . . .

A 15th-century text, a conversation between King Arthur and the prophet Guinclaff, long believed lost, was rediscovered in 1924 in an attic near Morlaix by the Breton scholar Francis Gourvil. The first printed text, a passion play, appeared in 1530. Breton literature revived in the 19th century (partly inspired by a collection of none too authentic folk poetry, *Barsaz Breiz*, published by Hersart de la Villemarqué in 1839) and flourishes today, though with no official encouragement.

Since its earliest speakers came from lowland Britain and from western Gaul, in both of which Latin had been widely spoken and Roman cul-

ture had long been in fashion, Breton has more Latin loanwords than any other Celtic language: *laer* 'thief', *koan* 'supper', *eured* 'wedding'. It is naturally full of French loanwords, some of which, to judge by their form, go back to a very early period: *fresk* 'cool', modern French *frais*, which was a late Latin borrowing from Germanic *frisk*; *brau* 'beautiful' from Old French *brave*.

Numerals in the Brythonic languages			
	Welsh	**Cornish**	**Breton**
1	un	onen, un	unan
2	dau, dwy	deu, dyw	daou, diou
3	tri, tair	try, tyr	tri, tair
4	pedwar, pedair	peswar, peder	pevar, péder
5	pump	pymp	pemp
6	chwech	whegh	c'hwec'h
7	saith	seyth	seizh
8	wyth	eth	eizh
9	naw	naw	nav
10	deg	dek	dek
20	dau ddeg, ugain	ugent	ugent

Welsh has two ways of counting from 11 to 20: the old-fashioned way, still heard in some dialects, makes 16 '1 on 15' and 18 'two 9s'. Here are the older forms: *un ar ddeg, deuddeg, tri ar ddeg, pedwar ar ddeg, pymtheg, un ar bymtheg, dau ar bymtheg, deunaw, pedwar ar bymtheg, ugain*. This can be compared with the 'North Country score' (see box at ENGLISH).

In Breton, counting from 21 to 99 goes not by tens but by scores, just as it does in French from 61 to 99. So 79 in Breton is *naontek-ha-tri-ugent* '19 on three 20s'; in French it is *soixante-dix-neuf* '60 + 19'.

BUGIS

3,600,000 SPEAKERS

Indonesia

One of the AUSTRONESIAN LANGUAGES, Bugis or Buginese is spoken in the southern peninsula of the spider-like island of Sulawesi (Celebes).

About three million Bugis speakers live in their historical homeland: many are rice farmers in the well-watered lowlands. They are also well known as seamen, and many speakers have settled in towns and cities elsewhere in the archipelago – other parts of Celebes, Borneo, Singapore, Java and Irian (New Guinea). The former principalities of Bugis have, at times, exerted power far beyond their linguistic boundaries: in the 18th century they dominated the seaways from the straits of Malacca eastwards.

Bugis, language of a Muslim culture, has loanwords from Arabic, Malay and the Dutch of the former colonial power. Like neighbouring MAKASAR (see script table there) Buginese has traditionally been written in *lontara* script, derived from the ancient Brahmi alphabet of India.

Many languages avoid the second person singular (older English 'thou') in polite address to strangers. The usual method is to substitute the second person plural (English *you*, French *vous*) or a third person form (German *Sie*, Italian *Lei*). Bugis uses the first person plural 'we': thus *idi'maning* means both 'we' and 'you [polite]', while *iko* and *iko'maning* are the singular and plural forms for 'you [familiar]'.

Bugis and Makasar on the map

These are the two major languages in a dialect chain covering much of south Sulawesi.

The principal dialects of *Bugis*, language of the former kingdoms of the centre of the peninsula, are Bone, Enna' or Sinjai, Camba, Soppeng, Barru, Sidrap, Wajo, Luwu and – in an enclave among Mamuju speakers – Pasangkayu. The north-western dialect *Sawitto*, spoken at Pinrang, is distinct from the rest. In *Pangkep* Bugis and Makasar are closely mingled, but their speakers live in separate villages.

Makasar is the language of the once influential Sultanate of Gowa, whose capital was at Sungguminasa near modern Ujungpandang (still a major trading port, called 'Makassar' or 'Macassar' on most maps). Gowa is the dialect of the old capital and its district. Other dialects are Maros-Pangkep, Turatea and Bantaeng.

Konjo is spoken in the south-east corner of the peninsula. Coastal Konjo, with about 125,000 speakers, and Mountain Konjo, with 75,000, are the main dialects.

Selayar has 90,000 speakers and is the language of Selayar island, off the southern tip of Sulawesi.

Mandar, a language of 250,000 speakers in coastal districts around Majene in western Sulawesi, is not part of the Buginese-Makasarese dialect group but has, likewise, been written in Lontara script. Napo was once the capital of the

Mandar kingdom, and its dialect, Balanipa, is still regarded as the standard. *Mamuju*, with 95,000 speakers, is the neighbour of Mandar to the north.

Based on Charles E. Grimes, Barbara Dix Grimes, *Languages of south Sulawesi* (Canberra: Australian National University, 1987)

	Numerals in Bugis and neighbouring languages				
	Makasar	**Konjo**	**Selayar**	**Bugis**	**Mandar**
1	se're	se're	se're	seddi	mesa
2	rua	rua	rua	duwa	da'dua
3	tallu	tallu	tallu	tıllu	tallu
4	appa'	'a'pa'	'appa'	'ıppa'	'ape'
5	lima	lima	lima	lima	lima
6	annang	annang	anang	ınnıng	'anang
7	tuju	tuju	tuju	pitu	pitu
8	sangantuju	karua	karua	aruwa	'aruwa
9	salapang	salapang	ka'assa	asera	amessa
10	sampulo	sampulo	sampulo	sıppulo	sappulo

BULGARIAN

8,500,000 SPEAKERS

Bulgaria, Ukraine, Moldova

Bulgarian, one of the South SLAVONIC LAN-
GUAGES, belongs to a dialect continuum that
includes Macedonian, Serbian, Croatian and Slovene. It is the official language of Bulgaria.

The people known as *Bulgars*, led by their
king Asparuch, conquered the eastern Balkans in AD 680. Their Turkic language was
soon forgotten (see CHUVASH), but their name
survives in *Bulgaria*. Whether Slavonic speakers arrived alongside them, or at a different
time, is not clear. Shortly afterwards, at any
rate, the usual language here was a Slavonic
dialect, and it was naturally called *Bulgarian*
after the name of the country.

The Slavonic speech of Bulgaria and Macedonia
(the two are hardly to be distinguished at this
period) was first recorded in the 9th century in
the form of OLD SLAVONIC or *Old Bulgarian*, in
Christian texts that were circulated throughout
the Slavic-speaking lands. *Middle Bulgarian* is the
local language that emerges – in grammatical
slips and spelling mistakes by scribes – in the
later Old Slavonic texts of the 11th to 14th
centuries. These are all in Cyrillic script, which
has continued to be used for Bulgarian ever
since. There is also plenty of evidence of Middle
Bulgarian in later Old Slavonic texts from
Wallachia and Moldavia (modern Romania),
though Bulgarian was never the everyday language there.

Between the 15th and 19th centuries Bulgaria
was under Turkish rule. Over this period the
three great influences on the language were
Turkish, Greek (as the language of Christian
education) and Old Slavonic (still used in the
Church). In particular, Bulgarian has been heav-

ily influenced by Turkish. For five hundred
years the local government, the elite and the
army were Turkish-speaking. Through all this
period Islam was spreading in Bulgaria, and
Turkish was the everyday language of that religion. Many Turkish speakers settled in the
country: some, in spite of recent discrimination,
are still there. This, too, brought loanwords into
Bulgarian.

Meanwhile there was regular interchange
between Bulgaria and the nearest Christian lands
to the north. In the 18th and 19th centuries
Bulgarians emigrated in this direction in some
numbers. There are now 275,000 speakers of
Bulgarian in southern Ukraine, centring on
Odessa, and 100,000 in Moldova.

Pomaks trace their origin to Bulgarian/Mace-
donian speakers who converted to Islam in
the 18th century. Some Pomak Muslims retain their distinct culture and dialect in Macedonia, Bulgaria and Greece. Others fled
from discrimination in Europe and settled
in Turkey, where the *Pomakça* dialect of
Bulgarian is still spoken, though it is not
likely to survive into future generations.

Modern Bulgarian texts, in a language already
significantly different from that of the medieval
manuscripts, begin to emerge in the 16th century. There was great interest in the language
from the beginning of the 19th century, with
grammatical studies by the Serbian Vuk Karadžić (1822) and the Bulgarian Neofit Rilski
(1835).

Modern Bulgarian has several striking differences from other Slavonic languages. One is
that nouns are no longer declined. As in Roma-

nian, however, there is a definite article suffixed to the noun: *grad* 'city', *gradăt* 'the city'; *gradove* 'cities', *gradovete* 'the cities'. For a table of numerals see SLOVENE.

The Cyrillic alphabet for Bulgarian

А Б В Г Д Е Ж З И Й К Л М Н О П Р С Т У Ф Х Ц Ч Ш Щ Ъ Ь Ю Я

а б в г е ж з и й к л м н о п р с т у ф х ц ч ш щ ъ ь ю

a b v g d e zh z i y k l m n o p r s t u f kh ts ch sh sht ă ' yu ya

The latest spelling reform, abolishing the letters Ѫ ѫ and Ѣ ѣ (see OLD SLAVONIC), took place in 1945.

BURMESE

21,000,000 SPEAKERS

Burma

One of a recognised Burmese-Lolo group of SINO-TIBETAN LANGUAGES, Burmese reached its present predominance in coastal and central Burma relatively recently.

> *Burma, Burman* (now less used) and *Burmese* are English approximations to the colloquial Burmese name for the speakers, their country and their language, *Bamā*. The stress falls on the final long *ā*, hence the old-fashioned English rendering *Burmah*.
>
> In Burmese formal speech and writing *Myanmā* is preferred to *Bamā*. *Myanmar*, the form at present encouraged in English and French, is a misspelling of the Burmese official name.

Burmese has been spoken in the middle Irrawaddy valley from at least the 9th century: its arrival there must have been the result of migrations from the north-east, where related languages are still spoken.

Anawrata, who ruled at Pagan from 1044 to 1077, established a lasting Burmese power one of whose effects was to spread the language westwards to Arakan (an independent kingdom until the 18th century) and southwards to the Irrawaddy delta region. Here it gradually replaced the mysterious Pyu language and eventually challenged MON. The relatively few remaining Mon speakers are now probably bilingual in Burmese.

But Burmese is pervasively influenced by Mon. Its script, its Buddhist religious terminology, its political vocabulary and its phonetics all demonstrate the long cultural supremacy of the Mon kingdoms of the Indian Ocean coast. Some Pali loanwords in Burmese have clearly been transmitted through Mon. At times Shan-speaking rulers held much of inland Burma, but the linguistic effect of this was relatively slight.

The Burmese cultural focus generally remained on the middle Irrawaddy – Pagan being eventually succeeded as capital by Ava, Amarapura and then Mandalay. Far beyond the area where it was a mother tongue, Burmese was a language of government and diplomacy in tributary states to west, east and south. The British, having annexed Arakan in 1826 and coastal 'Lower Burma' in 1852, retained Rangoon as their capital after conquering Upper Burma in 1885. Burma regained independence in 1947. This event has been followed by lengthy warfare with former tributary peoples, notably speakers of KAREN and SHAN. Burmese is now the official language of Burma, though primary education is sometimes in minority languages. It serves as national lingua franca – but only to the limits of government and army control.

The oldest written record of Burmese is the four-language Myazedi inscription at Pagan, dated to 1112. Royal inscriptions and the sacred texts of Buddhism were soon joined by a growing original literature, partly Buddhist in inspiration (there is a rich, often illustrated literature of *jataka* tales of the Buddha's former births), partly secular poetry and prose. At times Thai influence on Burmese literature has been powerful. Historical texts include the famous 'Glass Palace Chronicle', *Hmannan yazawindawgyi*, compiled from earlier sources in 1829–32. Printing in Burma began at the American Baptist Mission Press in 1816–17; it was also an American missionary, Adoniram Judson, who was responsible for the first major Burmese–English dictionary, published in 1852. The first non-Christian Burmese press began to issue a newspaper in Rangoon in 1868.

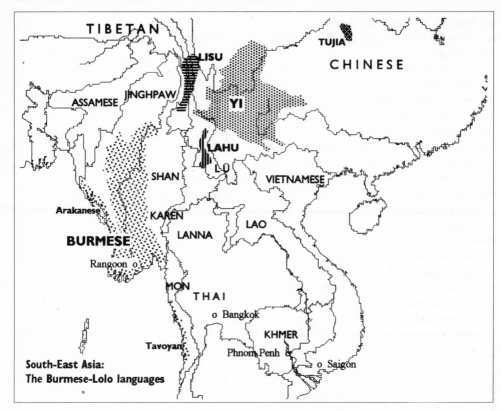

South-East Asia:
The Burmese-Lolo languages

There is a considerable difference between colloquial or 'spoken' Burmese – to be found in the dialogue passages of novels and on television – and the formal literary language, 'written' Burmese, used in most printed books, journalism and radio news bulletins. The two styles are no longer kept apart so completely as they used to be.

Burmese is a tonal language, but in a completely different way from Chinese or Thai. It has a high and low tone; also a 'creaky' tone resembling the 'breathy' register of Mon and Khmer, and a 'checked' tone representing a short vowel followed by a glottal stop.

'Pali, the language of Theravada Buddhism, was known to the Burmese since before our first records of the language and Pali loan words are found from the earliest times. The obvious need for loans was in the field of religion (for example, words for *nirvana*, *karma*, monk, hell) . . . Influence from English was inevitable during British rule. Loan words are found in the predictable fields (car, telephone, radio, plug, com-

mittee, cadre, coupon) . . . Loans from Mon are long-standing and are not nowadays generally perceived as loans by native speakers. They cover a wide range of fields, including flora and fauna, administration, textiles, foods, boats, crafts, architecture and music' (J. Okell in *South-East Asia languages and literatures: a select guide* ed. Patricia Herbert and Anthony Milner (Whiting Bay, Arran: Kiscadale, 1988) p. 5).

Burmese and the Burmese-Lolo languages: the map

Hani, Lahu, Lisu, Yi and others make up the 'Loloish' subgroup. Burmese and some minor hill languages make up the 'Burmish' subgroup.

HANI or *Akha* is spoken in south-western Yunnan, centring on Mojiang. There has been significant migration into mountain districts of Vietnam, Laos, Burma and Thailand.

The principal area of LAHU speech lies to the west of Akha territory, between the Salween and the Mekong, in Yunnan and north-eastern Burma. There are Lahu villages in several south-east Asian countries.

LISU originates to the north of Lahu, extending along the upper Salween and Mekong valleys from Burma and western Yunnan into Sichuan. There has been extensive migration into south-east Asia and even into India.

Burmese, after southward migration and expansion in medieval times, has become the major language of the Irrawaddy plain. Apart from the main dialect, spoken with little variation in Rangoon, Mandalay, and the country between, some significant regional dialects are known. *Arakanese* retains the *r* sound which in standard Burmese has coalesced with *y*. This is why the British, who had learnt their Burmese in Arakan, called their capital *Rangoon*: its name in standard Burmese, now official in English too, is *Yangon*. A 19th-century migration has spread Arakanese across the Indian border to the Chittagong Hills: the dialect of the 125,000 speakers here is known as *Marma* or *Magh*. *Tavoyan* is a long-established southern dialect, historically separated from the rest by an area of Mon speech. *Intha, Taungyo* and *Danu* are minor dialects, influenced by Shan, spoken in the south-western Shan State.

There are several 'hill languages' more closely related to Burmese than to the Loloish group. One, *Maru*, has about 100,000 speakers in the eastern districts of Kachin State and in neighbouring parts of Yunnan.

Tujia, a little-known language now in steep decline, still has about 200,000 speakers in Hunan and Hubei provinces of China. It is thought to belong to the Burmese-Lolo group: if so, it lies far to the north-east of all its relatives. As many as 3,000,000 people of the area identify themselves as Tujia, but most now have Chinese as their mother tongue.

Poet in exile

မဲဇာ တောင်ခြေ
From Me'-za mountain's jungle foothills,

စီ: တွေ့တွေ့ရတည်၊ မြစ်ရေ ဝန်:လည် မြင့်တော်စဉက်
Washed by the circling river constantly,

ရွှေပြည်ကိုသငၠ တရှာတောမီ။
My heart, against my will,
yearns for the Golden City . . .

Exiled to the jungle, far from the royal court, because of misbehaviour by one of his servants, Let-wè Thondará (1723–1800) wrote a series of poetic laments to his wife. The king was so moved by the verses that the poet was immediately recalled.

Hla Pe, 'Mind-bending Burmese poems and songs' in *Journal of the Burma Research Society* vol. 59 (1976) pp. 1–47

Burmese script

The thirty-three characters

ကခဂဃင စဆဇဈည ဋဌဍဎဏ တထဒဓန ပဖဗဘမ ယရလဝ သဟဠအ
k kh g gh ng c ch z zh ny ṭ ṭh ḍ ḍh ṇ t th d dh n p ph b bh m y y l w th h ḷ a

The twelve vowels shown with K

က ကာ ကိ ကီ ကု ကူ ကေ ကဲ ကော ကို ကာ: က်
ka kā ki kī ku kū kè ké kò kó ka: kā

Font: *Suu Kyi Burma* by Soe Pyne

Burmese numerals

	Transliteration	Actual pronunciation
၁	tac	ti'
၂	hnac	hni'
၃	sum:	thō'
၄	le:	lè
၅	nga:	ngà
၆	hkrok	chau'
၇	hku' hnac	hkú hni'
၈	hrac	shi'
၉	kui:	kò
၁၀	hcay	she

Writing in Burmese

Burmese script is a development of the Mon alphabet, Indian in origin, and is perfectly adapted for writing with a stylus on palm leaves: rounded shapes are necessary because straight strokes with a stylus would split the leaf.

The thirty-three characters are shown in the box in dictionary order (but some dictionaries begin with the vowel character, အ, and some end with it). There are many more than twelve possible vowel-tone combinations with each character – but those shown are the twelve that schoolchildren chant as they learn to read and write, beginning with *k* and running through each character in turn. The same vowel combinations, with each character in turn, are used in numbering manuscript pages from 1 to 396.

Owing to its complex and multilingual history, the match between characters in this script and the sounds of modern Burmese is very different from the match between the ancestral script and the sounds of Sanskrit and Pali. This is why such very different transliterations into Latin letters will be found. Some scholars use the original values of the characters: others are led by the modern pronunciation of Burmese.

BUYI

2,000,000 SPEAKERS

China

Buyi is one of the most northerly and, to scholars outside China, one of the least known of the TAI LANGUAGES. It is spoken by a minority population in south-western Guizhou province.

Buyi (older transliteration *Pu-yi*) is the official Chinese name. The language has been given many names by linguists and ethnologists: *Jui, Dioi, Yoi, Yay* are attempts at reproducing the speakers' own name for it, while alternative Chinese names have come across as *Zhongjia* or *Chung-chia* or *Yi-jen* or *I-jen*.

In their own heartland the speakers of Buyi are scarcely distinguishable culturally from Chinese – and most of them are bilingual in Chinese. They tend to be lowland farmers, living in stone-built villages off the main roads; but many settle in towns, where they gradually become Chinese. In this region the hill farmers are generally speakers of MIAO: they are quite distinct culturally as well as linguistically.

Buyi is a typically Tai language, with six tones. It is similar to its southern neighbour, ZHUANG (see map there), which is spoken by a much larger minority group. There is no old-established written form of Buyi: those who learnt to write used Chinese, and a form of Chinese is used in local forms of spirit worship. Buyi love songs, traditionally important in court-ship, often take the form of a question-and-answer dialogue.

Some hill peoples now living in Yunnan, northern Vietnam and Laos speak Tai dialects closely related to Buyi: they include *Nhang* (or Nyang or Giay or Yay) and the very archaic *Saek*, the recently discovered language of a small community in central Thailand. Linguists have occasionally worked on these displaced dialects of Buyi, but seldom on the language as spoken within China.

The first ten numerals in Buyi are: *nēu, lōng, lām, lī, hā, lɔk, shɛt, pēt, kū, ship*.

CATALAN

6,500,000 SPEAKERS

Spain

Like the other major ROMANCE LANGUAGES, Catalan grew out of the Latin of the Roman Empire, and it shows strong similarities both with Spanish to the west and with Occitan to the north. After centuries of decline Catalan has now emerged as the language of the autonomous region of Catalunya, established in 1979.

When the Kingdom of Aragon and the County of Catalonia were united in 1137 Catalan became the language of a major state, one with interests and connections far across the Mediterranean. The language remained important administratively until the 15th century, when the centre of power moved successively to Aragon and then to Castile, where Spanish was spoken. Since then the prestige of Catalan has depended on the success of movements for local autonomy, which first gained momentum in the late 19th century.

The language of lyric poetry in early medieval Catalonia was Provençal (Occitan). Catalan literature developed later, and is important for its prose, including the chronicles of Bernat Desclot and Ramon Muntaner and the political writings of Francesc Eiximenis.

Catalan and Occitan

Standard Catalan is based on the language of Barcelona, an *Eastern* dialect: others in this group are Roussillonais and Mallorquí. The dialect of Alghero in Sardinia also belongs here: Alghero has been a Catalan-speaking enclave since the 14th century. The major *Western* dialect is Valencian (see map at OCCITAN).

OCCITAN (Provençal) has no single widely accepted standard, in spite of the efforts of many activists. The numerous dialects range from *Provençal* and *Languedocien* in the south to *Limousin* in the neighbourhood of Limoges.

Quite distinct is Gascon, notable for its unusual sound changes, such as the replacement of Latin *f* by *h*, a feature shared with BASQUE.

A group of dialects transitional between French and Occitan, *Franco-Provençal*, is spoken in south-eastern France near the Swiss and Italian borders. Its territory covers the Italian autonomous district of Aosta, where there are about 70,000 speakers.

Numerals in the Iberian languages

Galician	Portuguese		Spanish	Catalan
un, unha	um, uma	1	uno, una	un, una
dous, duas	dois	2	dos	dos, dues
tres	tres	3	tres	tres
catro	quatro	4	quatro	quatre
cinco	cinco	5	cinco	cinc
seis	seis	6	seis	sis
sete	sete	7	siete	set
oito	oito	8	ocho	vuit
nove	nove	9	nueve	nou
dez	dez	10	diez	deu

CAUCASIAN LANGUAGES

The Caucasus mountains rise between the Black Sea and the Caspian. In geopolitical terms they help to divide the traditional spheres of influence of Russia to the north and Turkey to the south.

Like some other mountain ranges (the Hindu Kush, the Himalayas, New Guinea) the Caucasus has fostered the survival of a remarkable number of languages, most of them spoken by very small communities. Why? Because narrow mountain valleys hinder long distance communications, which help languages to spread; and because they provide excellent defences behind which relatively small communities can survive and prosper.

Since the maps in this book are at a standard scale, the map of the Caucasian languages is the most overcrowded of them all. In the Caucasus four completely independent language families are to be found – though evidence is accumulating that North Central and North East Caucasian are related, while some scholars, on evidence that is so far rather weak, add North Central and North West Caucasian to this grouping. Interspersed among these are also to be found members of other families well known elsewhere: Indo-European languages including Armenian, Russian and Tat (a variety of Persian), and Turkic languages including Azeri and Ossete.

If it is true, as many believe, that the ancient languages Hurrian and Urartian belong to the North East Caucasian family, the recorded history of Caucasian languages can be traced back over three thousand years. Otherwise, records begin with the invention of Armenian and Georgian scripts in the 4th century AD.

The mountain of tongues

'Caucasian languages' is a geographical grouping. It is customarily applied to the four independent

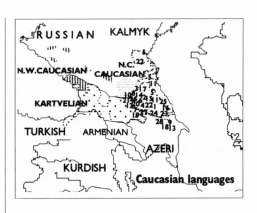

language families of the Caucasus, and not to the languages spoken there that belong to other well-known families. For completeness, some of the latter are marked on the map.

The *Kartvelian* or South Caucasian language family includes GEORGIAN (see map there), Svan (35,000 speakers in Georgia), MINGRELIAN and Laz.

For *Nakh* or North Central Caucasian see map at CHECHEN.

North West Caucasian includes Abkhaz, Abaza and the CIRCASSIAN languages (Adyge and Kabardian). For map see ABKHAZ.

The *North East Caucasian* or Eastern Caucasian or Dagestanian family includes the following languages, marked by numbers on the map and listed here with the number of speakers of each:

Agul	1	14,000
Akhvakh	2	7,000
Andi	3	12,000
Archi	4	1,000
Avar	5	500,000
Bagulal and Tlisi	6	7,000
Bezheta or Kapucha	7	2,000
Botlikh	8	2,000
Budukh	9	500
Chamalal dialects	10	6,000

Dargwa	11	300,000
Dido or Tsez	12	10,000
Dzhek or Gek or Kryz	13	1,000
Godoberi	14	2,000
Hinukh or Ginukh	15	200
Kaitak or Qaidaq	16	20,000
Karata	17	8,000
Khinalugh	18	2,000
Khunzib or Hunzal	19	1,000
Khvarshi	20	800
Kubachi or Ughbug	21	5,000
Lak	22	120,000
Lezghian	23	400,000
Rutul	24	20,000
Tabasaran and Khanag	25	90,000
Tindi	26	8,000
Tsakhur	27	12,000
Udi	28	5,000

For more on Dargwa, Kaitak, Kubachi and Lak, see DARGWA.

For more on the Avar-Andi-Dido group, see AVAR. It includes Andi, Botlikh, Godoberi, Akhvakh, Bagulal, Tlisi, the eight Chamalal dialects, Karata, Tindi, Dido, Khvarshi, Bezheta, Hinukh and Khunzib.

The remaining languages in the North East Caucasian family belong to the Lezghian or Samurian group. They have a particularly complicated political status.

LEZGHIAN itself is an official language in Russian Dagestan but not in Azerbaijan.

Russian has been imposed as literary language for speakers of *Agul* and *Rutul*. Agul is spoken by a fiercely independent and isolated group of clans, the Aguldere, Kurkhdere, Khushandere and Khpuikdere, on the upper Kurakh and Gyulgeri rivers. Rutul is spoken on the upper Samur, and Soviet policy had earlier been to assimilate its speakers to the Azerbaijani.

Tabasaran has separate official status in Dagestan. Its northern dialect, *Khanag*, is not mutually comprehensible with standard Tabasaran.

For any remaining speakers of the Shahdag languages *Budukh*, *Khinalugh* and *Dzhek* (which includes *Kryz*), Azeri is the official language. So it is for the *Tsakhur* speakers of Azerbaijan. For the 10,000 Dagestani speakers of Tsakhur, linguistic policy changed repeatedly. Tsakhur was briefly recognised as a literary language in the 1930s: Avar then took its place. Russian was finally imposed as their literary language in the late 1950s.

For *Archi*, Avar is the official language. Archi has a few hundred speakers only: it is the language of the single village of Ruch Archi in western Dagestan.

Udi, alone among North East Caucasian languages, is spoken by a people most of whom are Christians. Attached for thirteen hundred years to the Armenian church, this gradually shrinking community is settled around Vartashen and Nidzh in Azerbaijan.

CEBUANO

12,000,000 SPEAKERS

Philippines

One of the AUSTRONESIAN LANGUAGES of the Central Philippine group, Cebuano is the best known of the Bisayan languages.

These are the languages of *Visayas*, the group of mountainous islands, divided by narrow arms of the sea, lying between Luzon to the north and Mindanao to the south. The people call themselves *Bisayaq* and often call their language, collectively, *Binisayaq*, 'Visayan'. To eastern Muslims *bisayaq* came to mean 'slave', for the sultanates of the Malay archipelago raided these islands regularly. To its inhabitants now, the word signifies 'local, indigenous, native', with the implied warmth and pride of a phrase like 'home-grown' or 'home-made'. In Cebuano a local breed of chicken is *manuk bisayaq*; in Aklanon a local variety of rice is called simply *bisayaq*.

Cebuano, language of the island of *Cebu*, has also been called *Sebuano* (a simple spelling variant) and *Sugbuhanon*.

Bisayan language speakers have been fishermen and traders among the islands of the Philippine and Malay archipelagos since before the arrival of the Spaniards in the 16th century. Cebuano, Hiligaynon, Tausug and the rest, as vehicles of trade and culture, have influenced the languages of coastal and inland peoples of Mindanao, Palawan, Borneo, Mindoro, Luzon and many of the smaller islands on their trade routes. The effect of Bisayan oral literature has been traced in the *urukay* and *ambahan* songs of the Hanunoo speakers of Mindoro.

In its turn, Cebuano written literature developed under Spanish inspiration. A Christian manual of behaviour, *Lagda sa pagca maligdon sa tauong Bisaya*, published in 1734, is a landmark of Cebuano prose. Everyday language, too, is redolent of Spanish influence even to the greeting *kumusta*, Spanish *como esta*, 'How are you?' It has been calculated, by John U. Wolff, that a quarter of Cebuano vocabulary is of Spanish origin.

The Bisayan languages are certainly long-established in the Visayas region, but they have spread well beyond their original borders. The Cebuano of northern Mindanao, for example, shows the underlying influence of the various local languages from which the population has gradually shifted in order to adopt the more prestigious Cebuano. The same process can be seen at work still: smaller local Bisayan dialects, such as the *Porohanon* of the Camotes between Cebu and Leyte, gradually give way to the dominant Cebuano.

The effect of these long term influences is so pervasive, and the number of loanwords so great, that it is far from easy to ignore the later accretions and work out the original 'genetic' affiliations of the languages of the southern Philippines.

Based on David Zorc, *The Bisayan dialects of the Philippines: subgrouping and reconstruction* (Canberra: Australian National University, 1977) and other sources

Bisayan languages on the map

Seaborne trade is central to the culture of Visayas, and sea travel here is easier than land travel. This can be seen from the patchwork of languages and dialects, which tend to be

The Philippines: Bisayan languages

not divided but united by the arms of the sea that interpenetrate the archipelago.

Aklanon has about 350,000 speakers on the north-western shore of Panay.

Cebuano has spread more widely than the rest – in fact it has more native speakers than Tagalog, though this balance is likely to change. The mountain spine of Cebu itself faces south-eastern Siparay on one side, western Leyte and Bohol on the other (but some consider *Boholano* a separate language). Across the Mindanao Sea, much of the northern shore of Mindanao is also Cebuano-speaking.

Cuyonon, with 90,000 speakers, is the language of the Cuyo islands, also spoken on the coast of Palawan.

HILIGAYNON is spoken on eastern Panay and north-western Siparay. It is close to *Capiznon* of the north-eastern shore of Panay, and to *Masbateño*, the main mother tongue and lingua franca of Masbate island, which faces Panay and Siparay across the Visayan Sea.

Kinaray-a has about 300,000 speakers. It is the language of south-western Panay.

Romblomanon, with 200,000 speakers, is the language of the small island of Romblon and much of Tablas and Sibuyan islands on either side of it.

Tausug or Sulu, one of the two languages of Jolo and the Sulu islands, has a distinct history. The Muslim sultanate of Sulu was not conquered by Spain until 1878. There are nearly 500,000 speakers of Tausug as mother tongue, and perhaps as many again speak it as a second language. It is an important lingua franca of western and southern Palawan and the north-eastern coasts of Borneo.

WARAY-WARAY forms a dialect group including *Samar-Leyte*, *Northern Samar* and *Gubat*. These dialects are spoken on Samar, eastern Leyte and the south-eastern tip of Luzon.

Numerals in Cebuano and Tausug (Sulu)		
Cebuang		**Tansug**
'usa	1	'isa
duha	2	duwa
tulu	3	tuu
'upat	4	'upat
lima	5	lima
'unum	6	'unum
pitu	7	pitu
walu	8	walu
siyam	9	siyam
napulu'	10	hangpuu'

CELTIC LANGUAGES

The Celtic group of INDO-EUROPEAN LANGUAGES was once spoken across Ireland, Britain, Gaul (France), parts of Spain and Italy, much of southern Germany and the Danube valley. The Celts, farmers and brave warriors, were widely feared. Massive invasions had taken their language to Spain and northern Italy. There was even a Celtic-speaking enclave in classical Asia Minor: St Paul's Letter to the Galatians was addressed to the young Christian churches of this distant province. Place names across the Roman Empire testify to Celtic migrations: *Mediolanum*, Milan; *Singidunum*, the Latin name for Belgrade; *Laccobriga*, Lagos in southern Portugal.

Yet the four modern Celtic languages (BRETON, GAELIC, IRISH and WELSH) are now spoken only in scattered coastal and mountainous districts of north-western Europe – 'the Celtic fringe' in the jargon of centralist politics. All four survive only precariously. Languages of ancient and rich culture, they have been subject to centuries of social and political pressure from French and English. In the last hundred years two more Celtic languages, Cornish and Manx, have become extinct.

Manx

The Celtic tongue of the Isle of Man (*Ellen Vannin*) belongs to the group of *q*-Celtic languages like Irish: thus Manx *quig* (compare Welsh *pump*) 'five'.

Man was successively under Irish, Viking and Scottish domination, and was afterwards ruled by the Stanley family. The lordship of Man was sold to the English Crown in 1765. Under increasing English influence, Manx disappeared as a language of everyday life during the 19th and early 20th centuries: the last native speaker, Ned Maddrell, died in 1974. But it is still an official language: new laws must be promulgated in Manx and English.

Bishop John Phillips published the first Manx book, a prayer book, in 1611. He used English spelling rules as he devised a written form for Manx. The language showed strong English influence and also contained many Viking words: the Manx parliament, *Yn Kiare-as-feed* 'the Twenty-Four' (known in English as the House of Keys), meets annually at *Tynwald*, the same word as Icelandic *Thingvellir*, 'assembly ground'. The vocabulary of the English dialect of Man still includes Norse words: *clet* 'rock', *burrow* 'hill'.

Cornish: the once and future language?

The native speech of Cornwall is closely related to Welsh. It is closest of all, however, to Breton, the Celtic language of Brittany. Frequent contacts persisted, at least till the 16th century, between the priesthoods and the seagoing communities of these two peninsulas that face one another across the English Channel. Many place names are duplicated in Cornwall and Brittany, and many obscure local saints are commemorated in both.

The Celts of south-west England were geographically divided from those of Wales by the Saxon victory at Dyrham, near Bath, in 577. The West Saxons eventually advanced through Somerset and Devon. Cornwall itself was conquered in 936, but the Cornish language, without any official status, survived in daily use for nearly a thousand years after that date. From the 16th century come the *Ordinalia* and other religious plays in Cornish. But its survival was by now threatened: by 1600 it was said that nearly all Cornish speakers were bilingual in English. The last Cornish speaker who knew no English was said to be Dolly Pentreath: she died in 1777.

The very last native speaker of Cornish, John Davey of Zennor, died in 1891. Yet, in a modern revival movement, many Cornish children and adults now learn something of the language. Can it regain its position as a language of everyday life?

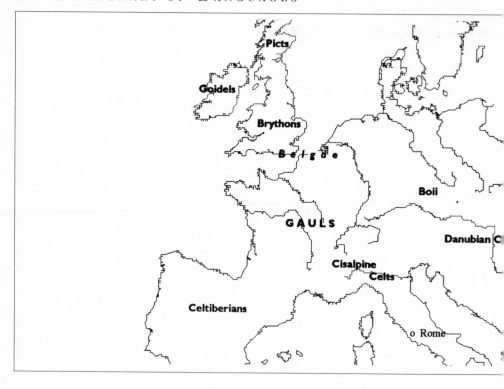

Twenty-three centuries of recorded Celtic

Dates AD	Goidelic	Continental	Brythonic	Dates AD
100–600	Primitive Irish	Gaulish	British	to 550
600–725	Archaic Irish	–	Primitive Welsh/Cornish/Breton	550–800
725–950	Old Irish	–	Old Welsh/Cornish/Breton	800–1150
950–1250	Middle Irish	–	Middle Welsh/Cornish/Breton	1150–1550
1250–	Modern Irish/Gaelic	–	Modern Welsh/Cornish/Breton	1550–

Brythonic and Continental Celtic are sometimes grouped together as *p*-Celtic, because Indo-European *q* became *p* in this group of dialects. Goidelic, more 'conservative', may be called *q*-Celtic.

For numerals in the Brythonic languages see table at BRETON; for numerals in the Goidelic languages see GAELIC.

Two worlds of Celtic languages

1st century BC

When the Roman Empire spread across Europe, two thousand years ago, three groupings of Celtic dialects can be distinguished – the evidence comes from place names, from the few words recorded in early inscriptions, and from reconstructions based on later texts. Scholars sometimes call *Goidelic*, or Gaelic, the language that was then spoken in Ireland (which remained entirely outside the Empire); *Brythonic* is the usual name for the Celtic of Britain; *Continental Celtic* is the general term for the dialects stretching from Spain to Galatia, of which the main group was *Gaulish*, spoken in what we now call France. *Pictish*, the language of the Scottish highlands in ancient times, may

bable areas of Celtic speech in the 1st century BC

Europe: Celtic languages

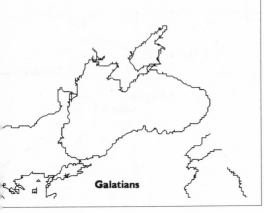

Galatians

have been a fourth subdivision of Celtic, but this is uncertain.

19th century AD

Continental Celtic disappeared completely: it was last spoken somewhere in northern France not long after the fall of the Roman Empire.

> *Cabmdhavas e metten, glaw yu etn* – 'a rainbow in the morning, rain is in it'. This rhymed Cornish proverb of about 1700, noted by William Gwavas of Paul, is close in rhythm to the English 'Red sky in the morning, shepherd's warning'.

Goidelic speakers invaded western Scotland in early medieval times, and their language replaced Pictish. Both Irish and Scottish Gaelic,

as well as the extinct Manx, are thus Goidelic languages.

In its heyday *Irish* had two main dialects, roughly corresponding to the legendary division of Ireland between *Leath Chuinn* and *Leath Mhogha*, Conn's half and Mogh's half. Others (such as Richard Stanyhurst, see box at IRISH) saw dialect boundaries corresponding to the four provinces, Ulster, Munster, Leinster and Connacht. Ulster Irish was continually influenced by the Scottish Gaelic of southward migrants. Unfortunately, very little of the Irish dialects was recorded before most of them died out.

In the 5th and 6th centuries Brythonic speakers migrated in large numbers from southern England to north-western France. This region, called *Brittany* after them, maintained close links with Cornwall for a long time. Welsh, Cornish and Breton are the three modern Brythonic languages. Welsh grew apart from Cornish and Breton, which are said to have been mutually intelligible. Cornish is no longer a mother tongue.

Celtic loanwords

Though they retreated before Latin, English and French, Celtic languages left their mark on the everyday vocabulary of all three.

camminus	road	French *chemin*, Italian *cammino*, Spanish *camino*
cerevisia	beer	Spanish *cerveza*
leuca	league [distance]	French *lieue*, Spanish *legua*, Portuguese and Occitan *legoa*, Italian *lega*

CHADIC LANGUAGES

The Chadic language group has around six hundred members, only one of which – Hausa – is at all well known. Half a dozen others are spoken by a hundred thousand people or more: most of the rest have quite small numbers of speakers. They are languages of Nigeria, Chad and Cameroun. The one Chadic language that is important on a world scale is HAUSA (see map there).

How do Chadic languages come to be spoken where they are? They form crucial evidence for the early history of one of the most important language families in the world: for (as was first observed by F.W. Newman in 1844) Chadic languages are related to the well-known Semitic group of languages. In fact Chadic is one of the six branches of the Hamito-Semitic or AFROASIA-TIC language family, whose other speakers are to be found in the Near East (e.g. Arabic, Hebrew), north Africa (e.g. Ancient Egyptian, Berber) and north-eastern Africa (e.g. Amharic, Somali). If it were not for Chadic, scholars might be able to argue that the Afroasiatic family originated in the Near East, spreading westwards and southwards. Some ignore Chadic and do argue this.

On this theory, the evidently ancient existence of Chadic languages at roughly their present location is almost impossible to explain: where would they first have differentiated from the other five branches, and why would their early speakers have migrated south-westwards across the Sahara? Chadic almost forces the adoption of a wholly different theory – the origin of Afroasiatic languages *in Africa* to the south and east of the Sahara. From there, the migrations that would produce Chadic, Berber, Egyptian and the Semitic languages are rather easier to explain.

In spite of differences resulting from some thousands of years of separate development, Chadic languages generally share some distinctive characteristics. They often have two classes of verbs, distinguished by the final vowel of the basic form, which may be –*ə* or –*a*: as in numerous other languages of the world, transitive verbs agree with the object, intransitive verbs with the subject. Verbs typically have distinct plural forms: singular *muri*, plural *mute* 'die'. Plural verb stems are often formed by replacing an internal vowel with -*a*- or by doubling an internal consonant. Intransitive verbs may be marked by a suffixed 'intransitive copy pronoun': *na ta-no* 'I went', *a ta-to* 'she went', *mə ta-mu* 'we went'. For the 'verbal extensions' reminiscent of English phrasal verbs, see HAUSA.

Examples from Paul Newman
in *Multilinguisme dans les domaines
bantou du nord-ouest et tchadique* ed.
Luc Bouquiaux (Paris: SELAF, 1979) p. 60

CHAM

230,000 SPEAKERS

Cambodia, Vietnam

Cham is unusual among AUSTRONESIAN LAN-GUAGES – for it is clearly long established on the Asian mainland. There, nearly two thousand years ago, it was the main language of the Hindu kingdom of Champa, founded, according to Chinese sources, in AD 192.

When this kingdom fell, as a result of a Vietnamese victory in 1471, many of its people migrated inland: this is the origin of the Cambodian speakers of Cham, now the largest group. Cham speakers are traditionally fishermen and traders along the waterways of Cambodia and Vietnam.

Islam had been adopted here in the 14th century and the speakers of Cham are still Muslims, though they have little contact with others of the religion. Malay is their language of religious education. A few still learn Arabic, but even fewer are able to make the pilgrimage to Mecca. Among the Vietnamese Cham, Muslim beliefs are mixed with Hinduism, and numerous gods have been recognised including *Po Haova* 'Eve' and *Po Adam* 'Adam'.

Proto-Chamic, linguistic ancestor of several scattered languages (see map), was influenced long ago by an early form of Khmer and perhaps other Austroasiatic languages. Sanskrit was the learned language of Champa, as of all the Hindu kingdoms of south-east Asia, and there are now many Sanskrit loanwords in Cham. More recently Malay, Arabic, Vietnamese, modern Khmer, French and English have all contributed loanwords.

Cham is one of the languages in which men's and women's speech differs most noticeably. Men, traditionally literate, use expressions from the older Cham literary language; women, traditionally not taught to read, speak in a 'modern' style.

Among the languages of the Malay Archipelago the closest linguistic relative of Cham is ACHEHNESE (see table of numerals there).

The Aceh-Chamic languages on the map

The languages related to Cham are widely scattered, and their early history is not fully known. Although Cham was the language of an early Hindu kingdom, the first four groups listed below are all now predominantly Muslim.

Western Cham is the modern form of the language as spoken in parts of Cambodia, along the Mekong and near Kompong Thom, by about 150,000 speakers.

Land of eagle-wood

Ves, corre a costa que Champá se chama,
    Cuja mata é do pao cheiroso ornada,

wrote Luis de Camões in his 16th-century epic of the Portuguese discoveries, 'see, here runs the shore called Champa, whose jungle is adorned with aromatic wood'. This is *Aquilaria agallocha*, aloes-wood or eagle-wood – an English term based on Portuguese *pao de aquila*, 'eagle-wood', which is borrowed from an Indian or south-east Asian language (compare Sanskrit *aguru*). When they go to the forest to gather eagle-wood, the Cham and Roglai are said to use a secret language, just as BATAK speakers do when collecting camphor.

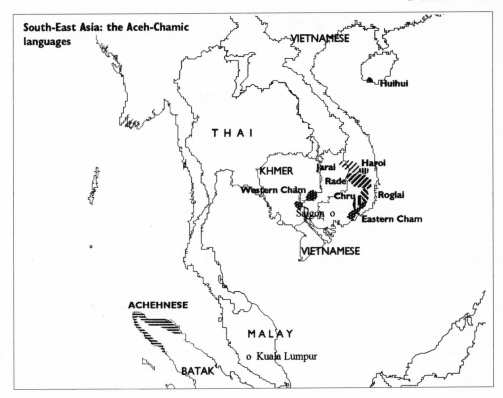

South-East Asia: the Aceh-Chamic languages

Eastern Cham is the language of the Phanrang district of southern Vietnam, with about 80,000 speakers.

Huihui or Utset is spoken by a migrant group whose linguistic ancestors settled, long ago, in Hainan (China). There are now only about 3,000 speakers.

ACHEHNESE is the language of a former independent kingdom of northern Sumatra (Indonesia).

Besides these, there are further related languages spoken by mountain peoples – non-Muslims – of central Vietnam. They include *Chru* (15,000), *Haroi* (15,000), *Jarai* (200,000), *Rade* (120,000) and *Roglai* (45,000). Speakers of some of these languages were once subject to the old Cham kingdom: others, including Rade, were its enemies.

Cham script

The beautiful Cham script is one of the less-known offshoots of the Brahmi script once used for Sanskrit in India. It is known from inscriptions of the first millennium AD, in both Cham and Sanskrit, and some eastern Cham speakers still use it. Among speakers of western Cham, whose Islam has been closer to orthodoxy, Arabic script has been used. Under French rule the Latin alphabet was introduced for both Cham communities.

k kh g gh ṅ c ch j jh ñ t th d dh n p ph b bh m y r l v ś s h a

CHAMORRO

72,500 SPEAKERS

Guam, Marianas

Unlike the languages of Micronesia, the three AUSTRONESIAN LANGUAGES of the Marianas and western Caroline islands are quite close linguistically to those of the Philippines – which lie fifteen hundred miles due west.

The islands came under Spanish influence in the 17th century. They passed successively to Germany, to Japan and then to United States suzerainty – Guam itself under direct US rule as a strategic air base, the other islands as a Trust Territory. The indigenous language of Guam, still a United States External Territory, is Chamorro, and it is still spoken by the majority of the inhabitants – but English is the island's only official language.

Chamorro shows strong influence both of Spanish and English. In vocabulary it is not very close to the Philippine languages, and its phonetics are unusual owing to a complex pattern of vowel harmony. All the modern Chamorro numerals are borrowed from Spanish: *un, dos, tres, kuatro, sinko, sais, siette, ocho, nuebi, dies.* Older sources, however, give native Chamorro forms: *hacha, hugua, tulo, futfat, lima, gunum, fiti, gualu, sigua, manot.* There are now so many Spanish loanwords in the vocabulary as a whole that some consider Chamorro a Spanish creole. However, Chamorro grammar remains very close to its Philippine relatives.

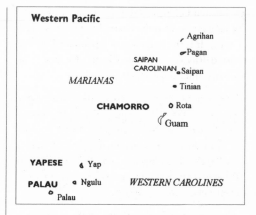

Chamorro, Palau and Yapese: the map

Chamorro or Tjamoro has about 60,000 speakers in Guam and over 10,000 in the Northern Marianas.

Palau or Palauan (15,000 speakers) is the language of Belau or Palau, a group of islands in the western Carolines, and also has some speakers in Guam.

Yapese has 5,000 speakers on Yap, one of the western Carolines.

Migrants from the Caroline Islands settled on Saipan, in the northern Marianas, in the 19th century. A Micronesian language, *Saipan Carolinian*, is now spoken there alongside Chamorro. The Northern Marianas are now a United States 'Commonwealth Territory', with three official languages: Saipan Carolinian, Chamorro and English.

CHECHEN

900,000 SPEAKERS

Russia

C hechen belongs to the small family of Nakh languages (North Central CAUCASIAN LANGUAGES). It is the language of a people who have resisted Russian expansion in the Caucasus for over two hundred years.

Chechen speakers call themselves *Nwokhchi* (singular *Nwokhchuo*) and their language *Nwokhchīn mwott*. The name *Chechen*, used in Russian and internationally, comes from a village in the Chechen lowlands; similarly, Russian *Ingush* comes from the lowland Ingush village name *Angusht*.

Chechnya is a firmly Muslim country: Arabic is still important in education. Russia has fought a bitter struggle for the conquest of Chechnya, a conquest which was still far from assured after the hundred years' Caucasian War of 1760–1860 and was challenged by fierce rebellions in 1860–1, 1864, 1877–8, 1917–18 and 1940–4. In that year of mass deportations, many Chechen speakers were killed and the whole of the surviving population was dispatched to central Asia: there were then about 400,000, of whom a quarter died in the first five years of exile. The personal dislike of Stalin, a Georgian, for Georgia's Muslim neighbours contributed to the merciless treatment of Chechens and some other Caucasian peoples in 1944.

Chechen speakers returned to their traditional lands after 1957. The old Chechen-Ingush republic was re-established, still within Russia, and gradually enlarged. The powerful Sufi brotherhoods of Chechnya fomented a new independence struggle at the collapse of the Soviet Union. In the course of the still continuing warfare of the 1990s, Chechnya and Ingushetia were separated administratively in 1992.

Arabic used to be the only literary language of Chechen speakers. The first orthography for Chechen itself was devised in 1923, in the Latin alphabet. This was replaced with Cyrillic script, after a shift in Soviet language policy, in 1938. Even with the addition of the letter I (not used in Russian) the present script is short of vowel symbols for Chechen: changes, including the use of double letters for long vowels, are talked of.

In general the dialects of Chechen are mutually intelligible. Slightly more distinct, though still closely related, is the neighbouring language Ingush. Many speakers of Ingush know enough Chechen to be able to understand it when spoken: some Chechen speakers are equally competent in Ingush. Ingush, too, first became a literary language in the 1920s.

Ingush was the language of 90,000 deportees to Siberia in 1944, who suffered a similar death toll to that of the Chechen speakers. They gradually returned to the Caucasus from 1957 onwards, and now number over 200,000: but much of their territory had been occupied by Ossete speakers meanwhile. The Ingush capital was once right-bank Vladikavkaz, while left-bank Vladikavkaz was the capital of North Ossetia.

The Nakh languages on the map

Chechen is the principal language of Chechnya. Literary Chechen is based on the central lowland dialect. There were once speakers in Georgia, in the upper valleys of the Assa, Argun and Alazani

Numerals in Chechen, Ingush and Bats			
	Chechen	Ingush	Bats
1	tsa'	tsha'	tsha
2	shii	shi'	shi
3	qwoa	qo'	qo
4	vii	-i'	-'iũ
5	p'khii	p'khi'	p'khi
6	yalkh	yɛlkh	yetkh
7	vworh	vuorh	vorl'
8	barh	barh	barl'
9	is	īs	is
10	it'	it	īt

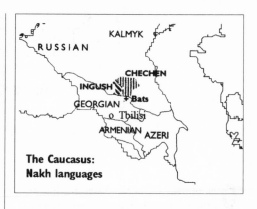

The Caucasus:
Nakh languages

rivers: few remain. Some Chechen speakers still live in Kazakhstan, to which they were exiled en masse in 1944.

Ingush has about 200,000 speakers in Ingushetia, which has now become a separate self-governing republic of Russia.

Bats (or Batsbi or Tsova-Tush) is the language of 2,500 cattle-farming people in the Akhmet region of Georgia. In winter and spring they are in the village of Zemo Alvani on the Kakhetian Alazani river; in summer they are in the mountain meadows on the upper Kakhetian Alazani and Tush Alazani.

CHEROKEE

10,000 SPEAKERS

United States

One of the AMERIND LANGUAGES, Cherokee is related to the Iroquoian group, as was first observed by Benjamin Smith Barton in *New views of the origin of the tribes and nations of America* (1797), though the Cherokee were not one of the original Five Nations of the Iroquois.

In the 17th century the Cherokee lived in the southern Appalachians, from which the spreading colonists expelled them in 1838. A few hid in the mountains, emerging in 1849 to settle in what is now the Qualla Reservation, North Carolina, but the great majority trekked to north-eastern Oklahoma. In 1821 a Cherokee, Sequoyah, devised a script for the language: this came at just the right time to be used by the first missionary to the Cherokee, Samuel Worcester, who began his work in 1825 and published translations, religious texts and almanacs in the script. It was widely used for a century or more. In the 19th century several short-lived newspapers – *Cherokee phoenix, Cherokee advocate, Cherokee messenger* – were published in the language.

Fewer Cherokee know the script now, though even in the 20th century there has been a *Cherokee newsletter* and a series of publications in the language sponsored by the Carnegie Cherokee Project.

Oklahoma Cherokee has become a tonal language: linguists recognise three level tones, a rising tone and two falling tones. Cherokee is important for its indigenous literature of myths and sacred ceremonial, recorded by ethnologists in the late 19th century. The first ten numerals in Cherokee are: *sawu, ta'li, tsō, nv̄g, hīsg, sudal, galquōg, tsunēl, sonēl, sgo.*

The Iroquoian languages

Cherokee is classed as the only Southern Iroquoian language. It is now spoken in North Carolina and Oklahoma.

The surviving *Northern Iroquoian* languages are Cayuga, Mohawk, Oneida, Onondaga, Seneca and Tuscarora. They are spoken by small communities in reservations and reserves in New York state, Ontario and Quebec.

Laurentian is the usual name for the extinct Iroquoian language spoken on the shores of the St Lawrence when Jacques Cartier explored the river in 1534 and 1535. The language had disappeared completely when later explorers visited the region. It was, however, closely related to *Huron*, also now extinct, once spoken in central Ontario between lakes Ontario and Huron. Samuel Champlain made notes on Huron in 1615 and a grammar was published in 1632.

North America: Iroquoian languages

The Cherokee syllabary

	a		e		i		o		u		v
D	a	R	e	T	i	Ꮵ	o	Ꮕ	u	i	v
S	ga	Ꭸ	ge	Ꮣ	gi			J	gu	Ᏼ	gv
Ꮒ	ka		ke		ki	Ꭺ	ko		ku		kv
W	ta	Ꮦ	te	Ꮝ	ti		to	S	tu	Ꮙ	tv
Ꮮ	da	S	de	Ꮪ	di	V	do		du		dv
Ꮂ	ha	Ꮀ	he	Ꮁ	hi	Ꮠ	ho	Ꮷ	hu	Ꮰ	hv
W	la	Ꮯ	le	Ꮲ	li	G	lo	M	lu	Ꮅ	lv
Ꮈ	ma	Ꮉ	me	H	mi	Ꮽ	mo	Ᏺ	mu		
Θ	na	Ꮑ	ne	h	ni	Z	no	Ꮐ	nu	Ꮕ	nv
Ꮃ	hna										
G	nah										
Ꮖ	qua	Ꮻ	que	Ꮗ	qui	Ꮴ	quo	Ꮘ	quu	Ꮛ	quv
Ꮍ	sa	Ꮞ	se	Ꮢ	si	Ꮖ	so	Ꮸ	su	R	sv
Ꮠ	s										
Ꮷ	dla	L	dle	C	dli	Ꮬ	dlo	Ꮷ	dlu	P	dlv
Ꮭ	tla		tle		tli		tlo		tlu		tlv
G	tsa	Ꮴ	tse	Ir	tsi	K	tso	J	tsu	Ꮶ	tsv
G	wa	Ꮾ	we	Ꮻ	wi	Ꮼ	wo	Ꮽ	wu	Ꮖ	wv
Ꮿ	ya	Ᏸ	ye	Ꭵ	yi	Ꭶ	yo	G	yu	B	yv

Font: *Cherokee.ttf* by Joseph LoCicero IV

Sequoyah's syllabary for Cherokee, invented in 1821, is quite independent of all other scripts, though some of its characters resemble Roman ones. In the transliteration *v* stands for a nasal vowel like the French *un*.

CHHATTISGARHI

PERHAPS 7,000,000 SPEAKERS

India

Although it can be called a dialect of Hindi in the widest sense (see map there), most linguists agree that Chhattisgarhi, like Bvhojpuri to its north, is best regarded as a separate language. It is one of the INDO-ARYAN LANGUAGES, and is spoken in south-eastern Madhya Pradesh in the districts of Raipur, Bilaspur, Raigarh, eastern Balaghat and northern Bastar.

Chhattisgarh is literally the 'country of the 36 forts'.

The first ten numerals in Chhattisgarhi are: *ek, dui, tīn, cār, pāṃc, che, sāt, āṭh, nō, das.*

CHINESE

PERHAPS 1,125,000,000 SPEAKERS OF CHINESE LANGUAGES

China, Taiwan, Hong Kong, Malaysia, Singapore and many other countries

Chinese is one of the SINO-TIBETAN LANGUAGES – or rather, it is a group of different languages, all descended from proto-Sino-Tibetan.

In origin, the Chinese languages are the speech of the farming communities of northern and south-eastern China and of the peoples of the coast as far as the borders of Vietnam. But one of them is also the language of a great and very long-lived empire. Fifteen hundred years ago, the northern Chinese – speakers of the language that is directly ancestral to 'Mandarin' – were already spreading their rule southwards and inland. In the 20th century the southern Chinese languages, like the unrelated minority languages of the south and south-west, are all of them threatened by the inexorable encroachment of the speech of the capital.

Chinese through history

Although the Chinese languages definitely belong to the same family as Tibetan, Burmese and their relatives, they differ radically. Proto-Sino-Tibetan must be dated many thousands of years ago. Possibly it was spoken in what is now southern China. Proto-Chinese, most likely, developed along the coast and the coastal valleys south of the *Yángzĕ* delta – the area of Chinese speech where dialect diversity is still at its peak.

The oracle bones of about 1400 BC, discovered at archaeological sites near the lower Yangze, are the oldest written documents of Chinese, which thus has a recorded history as long as that of Greek. True Chinese literature begins later: with collections of poetry, and with the works of Confucius and Mencius, around 500 BC. By that time Chinese was the language not only of the lower Yangze but of the wide lands to the north, in which the historic Chinese capitals, Beijing not the least of them, grew to eminence.

The classical literature of China is extremely rich, including short and long poetry, history, memoirs and many other prose genres. Chinese can claim the oldest printed literature in the world, dating back to a Buddhist sutra printed from wood blocks in AD 868.

Prose fiction has been cultivated in Chinese for much longer than in any other language. *The Water Margin* and *The Story of the Stone (Dream of the Red Chamber)* are, in their different styles, landmarks of world literature.

It is not surprising that there are several major languages extending across the vast and heavily populated region that is modern China. It is more surprising that one language alone – *Pŭtōnghuà*, the 'common language' or Mandarin – has so many hundreds of millions of speakers across northern China. Elsewhere in the world, single languages have not managed to extend themselves so far, except for rather brief periods. Examples are the Latin of the Roman Empire, the English of the British Dominions and the United States, the Russian of the Soviet Union: but not one of these languages has yet achieved such an enormous number of first-language speakers. Here Putonghua is unique, and its uniqueness must come from three factors: North China has been under a single government, most of the time, for well over a thousand years; administration and culture have shown impressive stability and uniformity over all this time; and, probably, northern peasants have found it more necessary than those in the south to travel and to resettle in order to escape famine and to find work.

In the modern context Putonghua has every reason to spread further and faster. It is propagated by the administration of a centralised state, by its media, by its education and by ever increasing nationwide travel and migration. In the past, very few people in southern China knew the language of the capital: nowadays, very many do, especially the young.

The 'internal' history of Chinese – the history of its words and its sounds – is very difficult to trace, since the script does not directly reflect the sounds of the language. A 'rhyming dictionary' compiled in AD 601 contributed to the researches of Bernhard Karlgren, who reconstructed the sounds of Ancient Chinese in *Grammata Serica* (1940) and *Grammata Serica recensa*. Karlgren's work has revolutionised many aspects of Chinese studies. Thanks to him we know far more about the patterns and forms of ancient poetry, the origins and histories of the other Chinese languages, and, much further back, the phonology and grammar of proto-Sino-Tibetan, the ancestral language out of which, many thousands of years ago, Chinese, Karen and the Tibeto-Burman languages all developed.

The best known of all monosyllabic languages, Chinese has about 1,600 possible syllables in its sound pattern. How can all the concepts of the modern world be specified in only 1,600 words? They cannot: although each syllable can be regarded as an independent word, Chinese strings them together, as would any other language, to specify ideas.

Varieties of Chinese

Together, the Chinese languages have more mother-tongue speakers than any other language on earth. Even on its own, Putonghua probably achieves this first place.

The Chinese languages are not mutually intelligible, but they share the Chinese writing system – and thus Chinese literature belongs to all of them equally, though in informal writing plenty of local variations may occur. That is why all the languages are treated here under the single heading 'Chinese'.

Putonghua or Mandarin first spread as the language of the capital, Beijing, and thus of administrators and scholars throughout the vast empire. China has for many centuries had a highly centralised system of higher education and centrally organised recruitment to the higher echelons of the civil service. The speech of Beijing has for all this time been the natural language for communication among Chinese from different regions, and the obvious first language to learn for non-Chinese living or working in China.

Putonghua is distinguished among the Chinese languages in having only four tones (high; high rising; falling-rising; falling), no voiced stops and no syllable-final consonants.

Wú is named after the old state of Wu, whose capital, two thousand years ago, was Soochow. Shanghai is nowadays the centre of Wu speech. The language has three ranges of stops – voiced, voiceless unaspirated, voiceless aspirated – as did middle Chinese. Like Putonghua it is one of the few languages of the world in which *z*, or a sound very like it, functions as a vowel.

Gàn is named after the river Gan, flowing through the province of Jiangxi.

Xiāng is the language of Hunan province: but while 'Old Xiang' of the mountains and valleys of the south and east is a quite distinct language, 'New Xiang' of the north-west and the cities is becoming a mixed language, not too different from neighbouring Putonghua dialects.

Yuè or Cantonese, named after the old southern state of Yue, is the major language of southern China, centred on the great trading city of Canton. Yue preserves all the middle Chinese syllable-final consonants, *p t k m n ng*. It sounds markedly different from Putonghua.

Kejia or Hakka is the language of northerners who moved south in medieval times. *Hakka* is in fact a Yue term meaning 'guests', and *Kèjiā* is the Putonghua reading of the same word. Kejia is close to Gan but with phonological and lexical differences.

Mǐn, Hokkien or Teochew is a group of nine mutually unintelligible dialects of Fújiàn and Taiwan. Min is the typical language of the Chinese fishing community of Singapore.

Abroad it is sometimes known as Swatownese, Swatow being the major emigration port for the speakers of this language. Swatow itself is in Guangdong province, but its cultural links are with Fujian to its north. The whole region is geographically isolated from the rest of China – except by coastal trade – and this has maintained its linguistic diversity.

North China and south China differ in more than their relative linguistic diversity. *Nán chuán, běi mǎ*, according to the Chinese proverb: 'in the south the boat, in the north the horse'. Travel, south of the Yangze, was traditionally by water.

Chinese in the Latin alphabet

Pinyin originated (as *Latinxua*) in the Soviet Union in 1931, at a time when most minority Soviet languages were being given Latin orthographies. A slightly revised form was named as China's official romanisation system in 1958. It is now very widely used both inside China, whenever transliteration is needed, and by people who write about China in other languages. It has taken longer to catch on in Hong Kong, Taiwan and Singapore. Some well-known Chinese place names are still familiar in an otherwise outdated mid-19th-century transliteration: *Peking* (Pinyin *Beijing*), *Fukien*.

The Wade-Giles system, developed by two British scholars in the late 19th century, is the earliest that is still in general use. It is often used in historical and literary texts about China in English, especially older ones. Those who study China and Chinese need to be able to convert between Wade-Giles and Pinyin. The most obvious difference between the two is that while Pinyin writes the commonest stop consonants *b d g – p t k*, Wade-Giles writes them *p t k – p' t' k'*.

The Yale system was devised in the 1940s when there was a sudden upsurge in Oriental language study in the United States. Other systems exist, such as *Gwoyeu Romatzyh*, but they are seldom met with except by specialists.

All the systems offer ways of writing the tones of Chinese, but most users omit the tone marks.

Periods of Chinese

Proto-Chinese: before 500 BC
Archaic Chinese: 500 BC to AD 1
Ancient or Middle Chinese: AD 1 to 1000
Modern Chinese: AD 1000 onwards

The Chinese languages on the map

Pǔtōnghuà or Mandarin (800,000,000 speakers) is in origin the language of the neighbourhood of Beijing. It is spoken in the north of China generally; by the 7,000,000 Chinese Muslims, an official nationality of Chinese Mongolia; and by rapidly increasing numbers throughout China. Overlying the regional languages, there are regional dialects of Putonghua. In its own homeland the major dialect divisions are *northern* (within which there is a distinct *north-western* dialect), *southern* or eastern – spoken around Nanking and the lower Yangze, and *south-western*, the language of Sichuan. Putonghua has also been called *Kuanhua, Pekingese, Kuo-yü* and by other names.

A medieval offshoot of what is now called Putonghua, the Chinese that is the language of traditional learning in Vietnam is pronounced on a system established in the 10th century: that was when Vietnam became independent and thus ceased to draw on the administrators and educators of the empire. More recently, Vietnam's Chinese community has used Yue (Cantonese) as its lingua franca.

Gàn (25,000,000 speakers) is the language of Jiāngxī.

Kèjiā (40,000,000 speakers), once well known as Hakka, is spoken throughout south-eastern China in agricultural communities in Yue and Min-speaking areas. It is the language of the New Territories of Hong Kong.

Mǐn (50,000,000 speakers) is the language of Fújiàn, also spoken across the water in Taiwan. It is the language of many Chinese speakers abroad, including some very important communities in south-east Asia, notably Singapore and

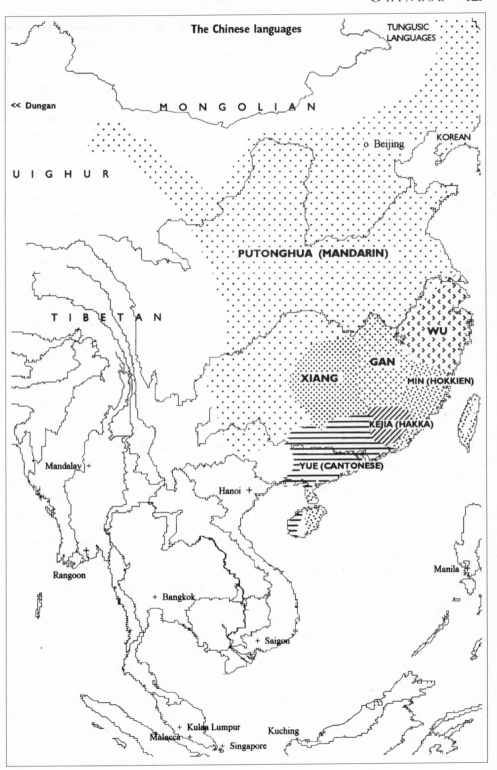

The Chinese languages

TUNGUSIC LANGUAGES

<< Dungan

M O N G O L I A N

o Beijing

KOREAN

U I G H U R

T I B E T A N

PUTONGHUA (MANDARIN)

WU

GAN

XIANG

MIN (HOKKIEN)

KEJIA (HAKKA)

Mandalay +

YUE (CANTONESE)

Hanoi +

Manila +

Rangoon

+ Bangkok

+ Saigon

+ Kuala Lumpur   Kuching

Malacca +

+ Singapore

Bangkok. It has had many names: Hokkien, Fukien, Teochew, Teochiu, Chiuchow, Cháozhōu, Taeciw, Swatownese. The coastal dialects of Swatow, Amoy and Foochow are the best known abroad: inland dialects are said to be quite distinct. *Mĭn Nán* ('Southern Min') extends along the coast of Guǎngdōng and is also spoken on Hǎinán island.

Wú (90,000,000 speakers) is the language of Shanghai, the heavily populated coastal districts nearby, and Zhejiang. With the recent vast growth of Shanghai, the dialect of the old Wu capital of Soochow is now 'old-fashioned' rather than standard.

Xiāng or Hunanese (55,000,000 speakers) is the language of Hunan.

Yuè or Cantonese (65,000,000 speakers) is spoken in a large area of southern China. A form of Yue, influenced by English and Malay, is the lingua franca of Hong Kong, and is the majority language of the Chinese communities in the United States and in Britain.

Dungan or Tung-an has about 50,000 speakers in Kyrgyzstan and Kazakhstan and was a national language of the Soviet Union. Unlike all other varieties of Chinese, Dungan is written in Cyrillic script.

The Chinese script

The oldest known passages of written Chinese are 'oracle bones' and inscriptions of 3,500 years ago. The brief texts scratched on bones were clearly used for fortune-telling.

In those 3,500 years Chinese script has developed massively: yet some characters are still recognisable. As shown in the box, they name concrete and familiar objects.

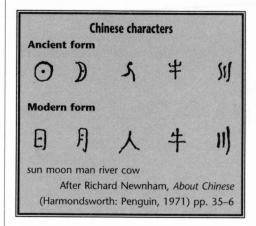

Chinese characters

Ancient form

Modern form

sun moon man river cow

After Richard Newnham, *About Chinese* (Harmondsworth: Penguin, 1971) pp. 35–6

A thousand years later, when Chinese literature had begun to be written down, all words – however abstract or concrete their meaning – could be recorded. The stock of characters had grown in several ways, but the most productive was by the doubling of characters: often the right-hand element was borrowed to give a sound or a 'sounds-like', the left-hand element to suggest a meaning.

Single or doubled, each character makes up a square block of text and each represents a single syllable of the spoken language.

In communist China a simplification of the individual characters and a reduction in the total number of characters have both been promulgated. Here Chinese is now normally printed from left to right across the page, like the Latin alphabet. The older pattern, still widespread in Taiwan, Hong Kong, Singapore and elsewhere, is to lay out the page with lines read vertically and following from right to left.

Most Chinese dictionaries arrange characters

Numerals in Chinese

yī	一	1
èr	二	2
sān	三	3
sì	四	4
wǔ	五	5
liù	六	6
qī	七	7
bā	八	8
jiǔ	九	9
shí	十	10

not by sound but according to the number of strokes (from 1 to 17) used to write the character, or used to write the 'radical' element of a doubled character.

CHOKWE

1,000,000 SPEAKERS

Angola, Congo (Kinshasa), Zambia

Chokwe, one of the BANTU LANGUAGES, is spoken in the upper Kasai valley and along the left bank tributaries of this river.

Chokwe speech has spread to its present territory in the last two hundred years. Tradition speaks of a Chokwe origin in the old Northern LUNDA state of Mwata Yamvo, perhaps in the 16th century, and of a migration from there to the area of Kangamba in south-eastern Angola: but this may be the history of a ruling group rather than of the whole people. At any rate, speakers of the related Mbwela, Luchazi and Mbunda (see map) are now to be found around Kangamba, and Luimbi is the dialect of a smaller group to the north-west. Chokwe itself has spread along the river valleys northwards, westwards and southwards, for its speakers were travellers and traders, particularly active in the slave trade. To the west they traded with the MBUNDU of Luanda. In the north they eventually conquered their traditional point of origin, the Lunda empire, in 1885–8: there is now a belt of Chokwe speech dividing Northern Lunda from Southern Lunda.

Soon afterwards, with the colonial partitions, Chokwe territory was divided between Angola and the Congo Free State, now Congo (Kinshasa). Some eastward migrants later settled in Northern Rhodesia (now Zambia). LUVALE, language of the upper Zambezi, is important as a second language for many speakers of Chokwe, Mbunda and Luchazi who inhabit the surrounding hills.

The first six numerals in Chokwe are: *-mu, -ali, -tatu, -wana, -taanu, sambano*. It is unusual among Bantu languages in the number of nouns that require no class prefixes. In some verb forms, tone is used to distinguish between negative and positive – not an easy feature for the foreign learner.

'There are almost as many variations on the word *Chokwe* as there are writers on this area,' wrote Merran. McCulloch in 1951 'Practically every combination of the prefixes *ba-, ka-, u-, tu-, va-*, or *wa-* with the roots *choko, cokwa, chiboque* (used by Livingstone), *chivoque, chiboqwe, chioko, chiokwe, djok, jok, kioko, kioque, quioco, tsioko, tshioko, tshiokwe, tshoko, tsiboko, tschibokwe, tschiwokwe* or *tschivoque* has been used. Reasons for this variation include the adoption by writers of the names used by neighbouring tribes in referring to the Chokwe, and the correspondence of some of the forms with dialectal differences within Chokwe itself ... The most correct rendering of the name is *Kachokue* in the singular, *Achokue*, or in the north *Tuchokue*, in the plural. Chokwe in Angola are occasionally included in the term *Ganguella*, and Chokwe immigrants in [Zambia] are included by the LOZI in the term *Wiko*, and by Europeans as well as by other tribes in the term *Balovale*' (M. McCulloch, *The Southern Lunda and related peoples* (London: International African Institute, 1951) p. 28)

The speakers of Luimbi, Luchazi, Mbunda and Mbwela were despised by the MBUNDU-speaking slave traders of the Benguela highlands to their west. They were given the general label *ovi-Ngangela*, also applied to the smaller Nyemba community. 'As a grass hut is not a house, so an *ociNgangela* is not a person,' the proverb said. This derogatory term recurs as *Ganguella* in Portuguese ethnographical sources.

Luvale, Chokwe, Luchazi and Mbunda: the map

Chokwe territory is in Lunda province of Angola and Kasai Occidental and Bandundu provinces of Congo (Kinshasa).

Mbwela, Mbunda, Luchazi and *Luimbi*, with an additional 350,000 speakers in Angola and Zambia, may be regarded as co-dialects with Chokwe. Luchazi has two dialects, those of the *vaka-ntunda* 'river people' and *vaka-ndonga* 'bush people', differing in phonetics and in vocabulary. The smaller Mbunda and Luchazi population in Zambia was reinforced by refugees in 1917, after a Mbunda-Luchazi uprising in Angola was brutally suppressed.

LUVALE is the language of the headwaters of the Zambezi. Politically, Luvale speakers are divided between the North Western province of Zambia and México province of Angola.

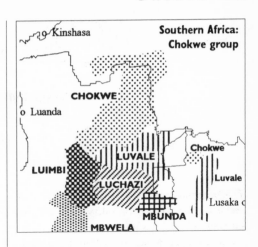

CHUVASH

1,500,000 SPEAKERS

Russia

Chuvash is one of the TURKIC LANGUAGES – but so different from the rest that a few linguists prefer to count it as a separate branch of the ALTAIC family. It is spoken in Chuvashia, a self-governing republic of Russia.

> Modern Bulgarian is a Slavonic language. But the Bulgars, after whom Bulgaria is named, spoke a language related to Turkic. While one group established themselves in the southern Balkans – and eventually lost their language – a second group remained on the banks of the Volga. The Volga Bulgar state disappeared from history. But it is now believed by many scholars that one dialect of the Volga Bulgars' language of medieval times survives. It is what we call Chuvash (*Chăvash*).

Much earlier than the Turkic migrations and conquests that spread other Turkic languages across Asia, the 'Bulgars' first appear in historical records, living on the steppes north of the Black Sea. They were allies or subjects of the mysterious Khazar Empire of the 7th to 10th centuries AD. While the Khazars ruled the lower Don and Volga valleys and the steppes between, the Bulgars' homeland was to the north, in the middle Volga valley, roughly where the Chuvash now live. The ruins of their old capital city, Bolgar, are still to be seen just south of the confluence of the Volga and the Kama.

The Volga Bulgars used Arabic script. Their language is known from tomb inscriptions and from the many Volga Bulgar loanwords in modern HUNGARIAN. Early Hungarian speakers clearly lived and fought beside the Bulgars in the Russian steppe in the centuries before they reached their own new home in the middle Danube valley – modern Hungary.

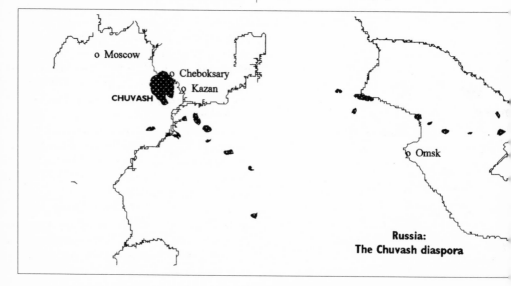

**Russia:
The Chuvash diaspora**

Making do

Akh mochi, kvartir yar,	Uncle, give me shelter,
Kvartir yar-ta khərne par.	Give me shelter and let me have the girl.
Khərə pultır tüshekle,	The girl will be my pillow,
tüshekki pultır syittila,	The pillow will be my blanket,
syitti pultır syüsyele,	The blanket will be my bedspread,
syüsyi pultır okala,	The bedspread will be my braid,
oki pultır syarsam.	The braid will be my knapsack.

Folk song sung by a Chuvash prisoner of war. From Robert Lach, *Gesänge russischer Kriegsgefangener*. Vol. 1 pt 4: Chuvash songs (Vienna, 1940) p. 126

In later medieval times the Mongol Khanate of Kazan' ruled the middle Volga. The Russian Emperor Ivan the Terrible took control in the mid 16th century. From then on, Russian administration and Russian immigration gradually linked the region more and more closely with the heartland of Russia. The process was not trouble-free. The 'Cossack' rebel, Stepan Razin, emerged from Chuvash country to challenge Russian rule in a series of bloody adventures in the 17th century.

Like the speakers of Mordvin, Chuvash speakers were converted to Orthodox Christianity by Russian missionaries. The Chuvash had not until now written their own language, but a form of the older Cyrillic alphabet was introduced by the missionaries about 1730. Active development of the literary language came only in the later 19th century, particularly after Y. Y. Yakovlev refined the alphabet in the 1870s. The script was revised again, based on modern Cyrillic, in 1938. For this alphabet see TURKIC LANGUAGES.

The language is used in schools and in the local press. It differs considerably from other Turkic languages, having long been influenced by neighbouring Uralic languages and by Russian. The first ten numerals are: *pər, ikə, vizhə, tavat, pilək, ult, zhits, sakar, takhar, vun.*

The Chuvash diaspora

Chuvash speakers form over two-thirds of the population of Chuvashia, in the middle Volga valley, with its capital at Cheboksary (Chuvash *Shupashkar*). But half the speakers of Chuvash live outside the republic, in a series of enclaves stretching eastwards across Russia and to Krasnoyarsk and beyond.

In Chuvashia itself two dialects are commonly recognised, *Anatri* or 'downstream' (in territory of the old Simbirsk province) and *Viryal* or 'upstream' (in the old Kazan province). Literary Chuvash is based on Anatri.

Medieval relatives of Chuvash were once spoken further down the Volga valley – in the extensive state of the Volga Bulgars – and far to the west, where Bulgar conquests reached the southern Balkans.

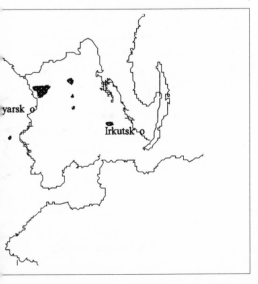

CIRCASSIAN

PERHAPS 1,500,000 SPEAKERS

Turkey, Russia and other countries

A group of dialects of the North West CAUCA-SIAN LANGUAGES are often referred to together as Circassian or Cherkess. In Russia they have officially been regarded as two separate languages, Adyge and Kabardo-Cherkess.

There are nearly a million 'Circassians' in Turkey, where many of their ancestors fled to escape Christian rule when Russia conquered this part of the Caucasus in 1864. Others came to Turkey as slaves or 'migrant workers': in some roles Circassians were much in demand, young men as soldiers, young women as domestic servants and concubines. King Hussein of Jordan's personal guard is manned by Circassians.

Most who call themselves Circassians in Turkey nowadays are probably still speakers of a dialect of Adyge, Cherkess or Kabardian – but the language gets no encouragement in Turkey and is now in steep decline. Smaller numbers had settled in the regions that are now Syria, Jordan, Israel, Serbia and Bosnia. Circassian was taught in schools in Syria till the 1950s, and is still taught in a few schools in Israel.

The speakers now to be found in Russia number about 500,000: Adyge (West Circassian) in the Adyge Republic, Kabardian (East Circassian) for those who shared the Kabardo-Balkar ASSR but who have now voted to establish an autonomous republic of Kabarda. Other speakers of Kabardian live in the Cherkess Republic: they are known as Cherkess. For a map see ABKHAZ.

In the 19th century Circassian was occasionally written in Cyrillic, more often in Arabic script. Adyge and Kabardian were both written in Latin script in the 1920s and in Cyrillic from the mid 1930s.

Literary Adyge in Russia is based on the Temirgoi dialect. Literary Kabardian is based on the Baksan dialect.

Ubykh was once a quite separate language of this family, spoken on the east coast of the Black Sea by as many as 50,000 people. Practically all of them fled in 1864: the language is now extinct in the Caucasus. In former Ubykh-speaking districts a distinct dialect of Circassian is now to be heard. In Turkey, Ubykh speakers turned to Turkish and Circassian (in the latter they were already bilingual), but, according to sources down to 1989, Ubykh was spoken in Turkey by one old man, the then 82-year-old Tevfik Esenç, of Tepelik Hacı Osman Köyü, Bandırma. The language has the astonishing total of 83 consonants.

Numerals in Abkhaz and Circassian

Abkhaz		Circassian
akà	1	zə
üba	2	t'ü
khp'a	3	śə
p'śba	4	ptə
khuba	5	tkh'u
fba	6	khə
bzhba	7	blə
ābà	8	jji
zba	9	bʏu
z'abà	10	pś'ə

Based on Adolf Dirr, *Einführung in das Studium der kaukasischen Sprachen* (Leipzig: Asia Major, 1928) p. 358

COPTIC

CLASSICAL LANGUAGE OF EGYPT

After the conquests of Alexander (died 323 BC), Egypt was ruled by Greek-speaking monarchs, and ancient EGYPTIAN eventually ceased to be a language of government and prestige. Greek spread rapidly. It was to remain the lingua franca of Egypt and the eastern Mediterranean even under Roman rule.

Meanwhile, Egyptian remained the majority spoken language of Egypt. It was a new form of Egyptian, however: a language with an increasing number of Greek loanwords, and one that was no longer written in the hieroglyphic or demotic scripts, but in an alphabet based on Greek. This new form of Egyptian is called Coptic.

As the everyday speech of the Christians of Egypt, Coptic soon became a language of Bible translations and religious texts. The oldest Coptic texts are writings by early Christian saints and hermits, including St Antony of Egypt and St Pachomius. With the Arab conquest of Egypt, in the 7th century, Greek was soon forgotten and Coptic became all the more important as the special and unifying feature of the distinctive, eventually independent, 'Coptic Church'. Hymns of the 7th and 8th centuries demonstrate the power of Coptic religious poetry.

In Greek the language and its speakers were *Aigyptioi*, 'Egyptian'. In Arabic this became *Qibṭ*. *Coptic* is a later Latinisation of the Arabic form.

Although religious texts in Bohairic Coptic are still used by the Christians of Egypt, they no longer understand the language. Arabic is now their spoken tongue. For modern scholars, meanwhile, Coptic has gained a new significance with the discovery of the Nag Hammadi library of sacred texts of the Gnostic religion. To linguists, Coptic is important as the only form of Egyptian in which the vowels were written: thus it helps in the reconstruction of the sound pattern of hieroglyphic texts.

Coptic dialects

Several dialects are recorded in early Coptic texts. As the language lost the official role that Egyptian had held, no single dialect was able to maintain its position as the standard.

The best-known dialect of Upper Egypt was *Sahidic* (Arabic *al-Ṣaʿīd* 'Upper Egypt'), essentially the dialect of Thebes, the southern capital. After the 5th century AD this was the only southern dialect still used in writing. Others known from earlier manuscripts are *Fayyūmic*, *Asyūṭic* and *Akhmīmic*.

The major Lower Egypt dialect was *Bohairic* (Arabic *al-Buḥairah*), reflecting the speech of Alexandria and Memphis. After the 11th century this became the standard dialect for all Coptic Christian texts.

Numerals in Coptic		
Masculine		**Feminine**
oуа	$\bar{\text{a}}$	oуеі
снау	$\bar{\text{в}}$	снтє
ϣомнт	$\bar{\text{г}}$	ϣомтє
qтооу	$\bar{\text{λ}}$	qтоє
†оу	$\bar{\text{є}}$	†є
сооу	$\bar{\text{ѕ}}$	соє
сашq	$\bar{\text{z}}$	сашqе
ϣмоун	$\bar{\text{н}}$	ϣмоунє
ѱіс	$\bar{\text{ө}}$	ѱітє
мнт	$\bar{\text{і}}$	мнтє

The Coptic alphabet

ⲁ ⲃ ⲅ ⲇ ⲉ ⲍ ⲏ ⲑ ⲓ ⲕ ⲗ ⲙ ⲛ ⲝ ⲟ ⲡ ⲣ ⲥ ⲧ ⲩ ⲫ ⲭ ⲯ ⲱ ⲱ ϥ ϣ ϩ ϫ ϭ ϯ

a v gh dh e z ē th i k l m n x o p r s t w ph kh ps ō sh f ch h j g ti

---

Writing in Coptic

The alphabet is Greek – though it is usually printed in a different style, as shown in the box – with seven extra characters representing sounds unknown in Greek. The extra symbols are borrowed from the Demotic form of Egyptian script.

CREE

70,000 SPEAKERS

Canada

One of the Algonquian languages, Cree was spoken by an Amerindian people who occupied a vast territory in western Canada in the 17th and 18th centuries. In terms of population it remains Canada's largest indigenous minority language.

At their greatest reach Cree speakers ranged from Hudson's Bay westwards to Alberta, and prospered in the fur trade with the British and French. There is some Cree vocabulary (along with several other languages) to be found in James Isham's *Small account of the Indian language in Hudson's Bay*, written as long ago as 1743.

In the 19th century, somewhat reduced in numbers by smallpox epidemics and by war with Dakota and Blackfoot peoples, Cree speakers became of interest to missionaries. It was for Cree that the most important of the special scripts for North American Indian languages was first devised: it survives, though not all Cree speakers use it, and with modifications it also serves for Ojibwa and Inuit.

Some publications have appeared in Cree, both in the Cree syllabary and in the Latin alphabet (in various spellings). There was even a Cree newspaper, the *Native people*.

As a reminder of the importance of French trade contacts with American Indians, *Mitchif* or *French Cree* is the most long-lasting of all the mixed languages of Amerindian North America. It still has a few hundred speakers in North Dakota and Canada, who are 'Métis', descendants of French fur traders of the 17th and 18th centuries who married Amerindian women. Nowadays, speakers know neither French nor Cree.

There are four main dialect divisions of Cree but the two important ethnic divisions historically were the *Swampy Cree* of the forests of Manitoba and Ontario and the *Plains Cree* of Saskatchewan and Alberta. The latter were traditionally bison hunters, while the Swampy Cree hunted more generally: hare was a main constituent in their diet.

The Plains Cree were the more warlike of the two. Perhaps their dialect had already in the early 19th century become recognised by other Cree speakers as the most prestigious, the 'standard language'. For whatever reason, it was chosen by missionaries to be used for the Cree translation of the Bible, and this has had the effect of maintaining its prestige, so that when Swampy or Woods Cree speakers are asked for a Cree word they may well give the Plains Cree form rather than that of their own dialect.

The first ten numerals in Cree are: *peyak, nisho, nisto, newaw, niyalan, nikotwas, niswas, niyananew, shank, mita*.

The Cree syllabary

The Cree syllabary was invented in 1840 by James Evans, a Wesleyan missionary who had already worked with Ojibwa. It is partly inspired by English shorthand, partly by Evans' knowledge of Devanagari and other Indic scripts.

In an adapted form it is used for OJIBWA and for INUIT. The Ojibwa form is also used for 'Eastern Cree', the dialect of James Bay, and for Atikamek: for these Cree dialects see map at ALGONQUIAN LANGUAGES.

There is a special sign X for 'Christ'. Added characters for *r*- and *l*- syllables are found in the version of the script used by Roman Catholics.

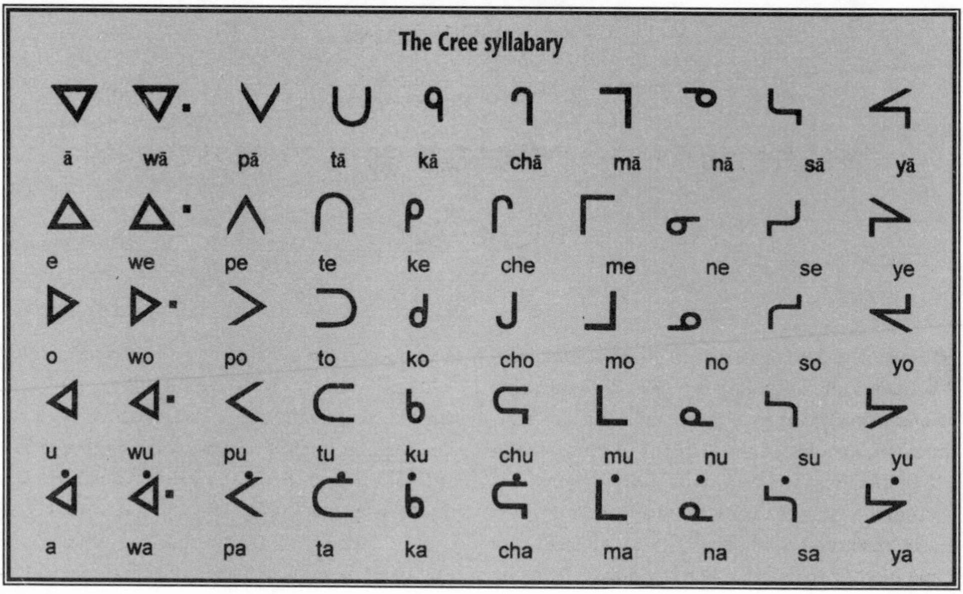

The Cree syllabary

▽	▽·	∨	∪	९	ᖏ	ᒪ	ᓇ	ᒪ	⌄
ā	wā	pā	tā	kā	chā	mā	nā	sā	yā
△	△·	∧	∩	ρ	ᒉ	Γ	σ	ᒉ	ᒉ
e	we	pe	te	ke	che	me	ne	se	ye
▷	▷·	>	⊃	ḍ	J	ᒍ	ᒧ	ᒎ	ᒋ
o	wo	po	to	ko	cho	mo	no	so	yo
◁	◁·	<	⊂	ḅ	�978	L	ᒣ	ᒧ	ᒷ
u	wu	pu	tu	ku	chu	mu	nu	su	yu
◁̇	◁̇·	<̇	ḍ̇	ḅ̇	ᒼ̇	L̇	ᒣ̇	ᒧ̇	ᒷ̇
a	wa	pa	ta	ka	cha	ma	na	sa	ya

CRIOULO

PERHAPS 750,000 SPEAKERS OF CRIOULO AS A LINGUA FRANCA

Guiné, Cape Verde Islands, Senegal

A creole based on PORTUGUESE, Crioulo has been called by linguists *Kryôl* and *Upper Guinea Creole Portuguese* to distinguish it from the island creoles of the Bight of Benin.

Crioulo grew up as a pidgin used between Portuguese and Africans in the former Portuguese territories of Guiné Guinea-Bissau and Cape Verde. Nowadays in Guiné the creole is known to the great majority of inhabitants as a lingua franca, but it has also become the first language of many in towns.

The vocabulary of Crioulo is largely Portuguese but the grammar is closer to that of African languages of the hinterland: the influence of Mandekan is noticeable. Verb tenses are formed with prefixes and suffixes: *i bay* 'he went', *i ka bay* 'he didn't go', *i bay ba* 'he had gone', *i na bay* 'he is going'. The first ten numerals in Crioulo, still very similar to those of Portuguese, are: *un, dus, tris, kwatru, sinku, seis, seti, oytu, nobi, des*.

The majority of speakers, about 400,000, are in Guiné. In the Cape Verde Islands two dialects are recognised, *Sotavento* 'Leeward' and *Barlavento* 'Windward'. There are perhaps 50,000 speakers in the Basse-Casamance region of Senegal. There are still a few speakers of Crioulo in New Bedford, Massachusetts, to which a community of 'Bravas' emigrated in the 19th century.

CUSHITIC LANGUAGES

One of the major groups of AFROASIATIC LAN-GUAGES, Cushitic languages are spoken in Ethiopia, Somalia, Sudan, Kenya and Tanzania. According to one theory, this is the very region from which, many thousands of years ago, the earliest Afroasiatic languages began to spread. No Cushitic language was recorded in writing before recent times – yet Cushitic words have been recognised in ancient Egyptian references to southern peoples, a sign of the early presence of these languages in roughly their present location.

The language group is named after the ancient kingdom of *Kush* which once ruled the middle Nile valley (see NUBIAN LANGUAGES) – but the undeciphered 'Meroitic' language of this kingdom's inscriptions has no proved link with the Cushitic group.

Statistical work on their vocabularies suggests that the Cushitic languages began to differentiate – 'proto-Cushitic' began to divide into dialects – about seven thousand years ago. Beja, the northern Cushitic language, has probably never migrated very far: the rest perhaps spread generally southwards, and a notable migration must have led to the present isolation of Iraqw and the other Southern Cushitic languages in distant Tanzania.

Cushitic languages were almost certainly spoken, until less than two thousand years ago, in the parts of central Ethiopia where Semitic languages – such as Amharic – now predominate. The considerable differences between these 'Ethio-Semitic' languages and their close relative Arabic are to be explained by the influence of a Cushitic substrate, as linguists would say. In human terms, this means that an early form of Ethio-Semitic very rapidly became a language of communication for speakers whose mother tongue had been Cushitic.

Quara or *Felasha*, a dialect of western Agew, is the traditional language of the Falashi or 'Black Jews', a people of the central Ethiopian mountains remarkable for their adherence to a pre-Muhammadan religion closely resembling Judaism. The language is said to be now chiefly used in religious ritual: most Falashi speak Amharic or Tigrinya in daily life – or, since a recent mass migration to Israel, modern Hebrew.

Based on M. Lionel Bender, 'Introduction', Andrzej Zaborski, 'Cushitic overview' and Christopher Ehret, 'Cushitic prehistory' in *The non-Semitic languages of Ethiopia* ed. M. L. Bender (East Lansing: African Studies Center, Michigan State University, 1976) with other sources

Major Cushitic languages

The Cushitic languages of today may be divided into four subgroups. *Northern Cushitic* has just one member, BEJA, in north-eastern Sudan. *Central Cushitic* or *Agew* is a small group in northern Ethiopia: the language of the Falashi belongs to this group. *Southern Cushitic* consists of Iraqw and other little-known languages of Tanzania. Largest of the subgroups is *Eastern Cushitic*, divided in turn into *Highland* and *Lowland*. Major Lowland East Cushitic languages are AFAR, Konso, OROMO or Galla, Saho and SOMALI. Highland East Cushitic (including some of the languages once called *Sidama*) includes Gedeo, Hadiyya, Kembata and Sidamo.

In the absence of reliable linguistic censuses, estimates of numbers of speakers vary wildly, as indicated in the table.

AFAR	100,000–700,000	Eritrea, Djibouti, Ethiopia
BEJA	up to 1,000,000	Sudan, Eritrea
Bilin with Agw and Quara	200,000	Ethiopia, Eritrea
Darasa	250,000	Ethiopia
Gedeo	500,000	Ethiopia
Hadiyya	100,000–2,000,000	Ethiopia
Iraqw	111,000–338,000	Tanzania
Kambata (Timbaro and Alaba)	250,000–1,050,000	Ethiopia
Konso	60,000–150,000	Ethiopia
OROMO	7,500,000	Ethiopia, Kenya
Saho	120,000	Eritrea
Sidamo	650,000–1,400,000	Ethiopia
SOMALI	5,500,000	Somalia, Ethiopia

CZECH

12,000,000 SPEAKERS

Czech Republic

Czech is the official language of the Czech Republic, a mountain-ringed country of central Europe. It and its relative Slovak belong to the Western SLAVONIC LANGUAGES.

The traditional name of the region where Czech is spoken is *Bohemia*, after the tribe *Boii* who possessed the territory in the 1st century AD, according to Roman sources. The dialects of *Moravia* to the south-east are also counted as Czech: this province occupies the valley of the *Morava*, a tributary of the Danube.

Some think that Czech speakers' own name for themselves, *češi* (singular *čech*), derives from the word *četa* 'group', but this is uncertain. They call their language *česky*. The unusual English spelling, with its initial *Cz-*, comes via Polish: in other languages the word looks very different, French *Tchèque*, German *Tschechisch*. The term *Bohemian* was standard until the early 20th century.

Most scholars believe that the Boii were not Slavonic-speaking: but *when* Slavonic speakers first came to Bohemia is quite unknown. Some say they came westwards in the 5th century with Attila's Huns, and remained when Attila's invading force melted away.

A state of Bohemia can be traced from about 900 AD, when it freed itself from the short-lived and newly Christianised realm of Great Moravia. The roles were soon reversed: since that time Moravia has usually been ruled from Bohemia. The Kingdom was in general under German influence until the 17th century, when it became part of the Austrian Empire. Independence from Austria, and union (which lasted until very recently) with Slovakia, came at last in 1918.

Thus, for nearly a thousand years, German was the language of power in Czech-speaking lands. Yet Czech survived and flourished. Czech literature first appears in the 13th century. Prague University was founded under King Charles IV (1346–78), a patron of Czech culture. But the greatest figure of early Czech literature is the religious reformer Jan Hus (1369–1415: see box). The first Czech printed book, retelling the story of the Trojan War, appeared at Plzeň (German *Pilsen*, where the beer comes from) in 1468.

The decline of Czech literature under Austrian rule was stemmed by a national revival that began at the end of the 18th century. Folklore was a powerful influence on writers (and on composers such as Antonín Dvořák). Twentieth-century authors include the playwright, and now President, Václav Havel.

In the last hundred years, as many as 1,500,000 Czech speakers can be traced in the United States, not all of them still speakers of Czech.

Jan Hus (1369–1415)

Jan Hus, the religious reformer who gave his name to the Hussite movement, contributed important works to Czech literature – and also reformed Czech spelling. He identified the significant sounds (phonemes) of the language and prescribed one symbol per sound, adding diacritics to the Latin alphabet. His new letters are still used, some slightly modified: his ſ and ż are now š and ž. Owing to his work, a page of Czech looks very different from a page of Polish, in which digraphs (double letters) such as *sz* and *rz* are used for similar sounds.

Numerals in West Slavonic languages

	Czech	Slovak	Polish	Upper Sorbian	Lower Sorbian
1	jeden	jeden	jeden	jedyn	jaden
2	dva	dva	dwa	dwaj	dwa
3	tři	tri	trzy	tři	tśo
4	čtyři	štyri	cztery	štyri	styŕo
5	pět	pät'	pięć	pjeć	pěš
6	šest	šest'	sześć	šěsć	šesć
7	sedm	sedem	siedem	sedm	sedym
8	osm	osem	osiem	wosm	wósym
9	devět	devät'	dziewięć	dźewjeć	źewěš
10	deset	desat'	dziesięć	dźesać	źaseś

In Czech and Sorbian, as in German, numbers such as '23' are formed on the pattern 'three-and-twenty' (German *dreiundzwanzig*, Czech *třiadvacet*, Upper Sorbian *tři a dwaceci*). In Slovak – as in English – such forms are thought old-fashioned or literary.

DANISH

5,500,000 SPEAKERS

Denmark, Greenland

Danish is a descendant of OLD NORSE. As Old Norse began to differentiate into dialects, the lowlands of southern Sweden and the crowded islands of Denmark allowed readier travel and communication than the backbone mountain chain of Scandinavia. So the 'East Norse' dialect of later Old Norse is the ancestor both of SWEDISH (see map there) and of Danish, a pair of languages that make up a single dialect continuum.

Danish has been the language of a powerful kingdom. In the 8th and 9th centuries Danish speakers ranged widely over England. At the Treaty of Wedmore, in 878, all England northeast of a line from Chester to the Thames was ceded to them. Although Norse speech did not survive for long in this 'Danelaw' which they settled and ruled, modern English has many loanwords, Norse, East Norse or Danish in character, as a result of the episode. *By-law* is a Norse loanword in English, meaning literally 'town law'.

The full union of England with Denmark, under Cnut (Canute) in the 11th century, was transitory. Meanwhile, the Viking conquests in Normandy must have retained their Norse speech for only a short time, though Norman French is still distinctive. From 1397 Denmark ruled Norway and Sweden: Sweden regained independence in 1523, but Norway remained under Danish political and cultural domination for four hundred years, and Norwegian still shows the signs of heavy Danish influence.

Danish, in turn, was influenced by the Low German of the Hansa cities, whose trade network criss-crossed the Baltic and the Danish islands.

Danish is distinguished from the other Scandinavian languages – from its close relative Swedish in particular – by its softened consonants. The stops *p t k*, between vowels, became *b d g* in Danish, and the *d* and *g* are pronounced as fricatives. For Swedish *kaka* (English *cake*) Danish has *kage*, pronounced with a light *gh*. Standard Danish also has a uvular *r*, like that of French, and many words end in a glottal stop. Together these phonetic characteristics give Danish a soft yet guttural sound pattern very different from all its neighbours.

The three principal dialects of Danish are Jutish (of the Jutland peninsula), Island Danish and the South Swedish or Dano-Swedish dialect group, which includes the island of Bornholm. This region of Sweden, the provinces of Skåne, Halland and Blekinge, was part of the Danish kingdom until 1658.

For historical reasons Danish has had an extensive reach as a literary language. Its range has gradually been shrinking since the 17th century. Until a separate Norwegian literary language was developed, from about 1830 onwards, Danish was the official language of Norway and Norwegians were prominent as Danish authors – Holberg was one. The best-known authors in the language are Søren Kierkegaard, the philosopher, and Hans Christian Andersen, whose folk tales were originally intended for adult reading though English versions are usually aimed at children.

Danish is still one of the official languages of the Faroes (see FAROESE) and of Greenland (see INUIT). It was the official language of Iceland until 1944.

Danish numerals

For the numerals from '1' to '10' see table at SWEDISH. Danish is unusual in the way that the tens from '50' to '90' are expressed. The recently devised 'new form' is used for writing cheques.

	Traditional forms	Literal meaning	New official form
10	ti	ten	ti
20	tyve	twenty	toti
30	tredive	thirty	treti
40	fyrretyve, fyrre	forty	firti
50	halvtredsindstyve, halvtreds	half the third twenty	femti
60	tresindstyve, tres	three twenties	seksti
70	halvfjerdsindstyve, halvfjerds	half the fourth twenty	syvti
80	firsindstyve, firs	four twenties	otti
90	halvfemsindstyve, halvfems	half the fifth twenty	niti
100	hundrede	hundred	hundrede

DARGWA

300,000 SPEAKERS

Russia

Dargwa or Dargin belongs to the North East CAUCASIAN LANGUAGES (see map there). It is the official and literary language for a group of peoples speaking related dialects, the most distinct of which are Kaitak or Qaidaq (with perhaps 15,000 speakers) and Kubachi. Standard Dargwa, however, is based on the dialect of Akusha.

The 2,500 inhabitants of the village of Kubachi were once famous in Russia, the Caucasus and the Middle East as goldsmiths and silversmiths. Their own name for themselves is *Ughbug*. Among Persians and Arabs they got the name *Zirekhgeran*, 'makers of chain mail'.

The Muslim speakers of Dargwa, Kaitak and Kubachi once used Arabic as their literary language. Dargwa became a written medium in the late 19th century, at first using Arabic script. As with so many minority languages of the Soviet Union, the Latin alphabet was introduced in 1928, to be abandoned in favour of Cyrillic script in 1938.

Lak is the language of about 120,000 people originating in the Kazi Kumukh valley in southern Dagestan. Related to Dargwa, Lak has separate official status as a literary language. Its speakers have moved repeatedly with the vagaries of Soviet ethnic policy. When the Chechens were deported en masse in 1944, many Lak moved from their high valleys to the newly empty town of Aukhov, renamed Novolak 'New Lak'. In 1992 a second Lak migration, to the Caspian coast near Makhachkala, allowed the Chechens to return.

'The Lak are among the most multilingual of all Dagestanis. They frequently know Kumyk and Russian as well as their native Lak language. Many are also fluent in Azeri, Avar and/or Dargwa' (R. Wixman, *The peoples of the USSR* (London: Macmillan, 1984) p. 122).

Numerals in Dargwa and Lak		
Dargwa		**Lak**
tsa	1	tsa-
k'wel	2	k'i-
hɛwal	3	shan-
aw'al	4	muq-
shwal	5	khyo-
urighal	6	rakhy-
werhal	7	arul-
gahal	8	myay-
urch'imal	9	urch'-
wits'al	10	ats'-

DINKA

1,350,000 SPEAKERS

Sudan

One of the Nilotic group of NILO-SAHARAN LAN-GUAGES, Dinka is spoken in the upper Nile valley in southern Sudan.

> Dinka speakers call themselves *Jieng*. The Arabic version of this is *Denkawi*, whence English *Dinka*.

A warlike and previously independent people, the Dinka were raided for slaves and exploited commercially by Egypt, supported by British adventurers, in the 19th century. The pattern thus established of exploitation from the north, punctuated by revolt, has continued.

Arabic and English have been used as lingua francas among the Dinka. Their closest linguistic relatives are their traditional enemies, the speakers of Nuer, whose territory is said to have expanded rapidly westwards, at the expense of Dinka speakers, in the 19th century.

Dinka and Nuer have a distinction of vowel register, contrasting 'hard' or 'clear' with 'breathy', comparable to that of south-east Asian languages such as KHMER.

The first ten numerals in Dinka are *tok, róu, dyak, 'nguan, wdyech, wdetem, wderóu, bêt, wde-nguan, wtyer*.

How Dinka and Nuer became rivals

'A legend relating the common ancestry states that in the past Dengdit, the great spirit of the Dinka, married a woman called *Alyet* in Dinka dialect and *Lit* in that of Nuer. Alyet gave birth to Akol who married Garung from whom were descended Deng and Nuer, brothers and ancestors of the Dinka and Nuer tribes respectively. When Garung died he left behind a cow and a calf, the former being bequeathed to Deng and the latter to Nuer. Deng stole the calf of Nuer and Nuer resorted to raiding Deng – just as today the Nuer raid Dinka cattle.'

Audrey Butt, *The Nilotes of the Anglo-Egyptian Sudan and Uganda* (London: International African Institute, 1952) p. 26

Dinka and Nuer on the map

There are four main dialects of Dinka: *Northern Dinka* or Padang; *Western Dinka* or Rek; *Central* or *South-western Dinka* or Agar; Eastern or *South-eastern Dinka* or Bor.

Nuer has 850,000 speakers on the Upper Nile and the Sobat river: their territory extends into Ethiopia. Their own name for themselves is *Naath; Naath cieng*, 'Homeland Nuer', for those west of the Nile; *Naath doar*, 'Bush Nuer', for those to the east. *Atuot* or *Thok cieng* is an isolated dialect spoken in the Lau valley.

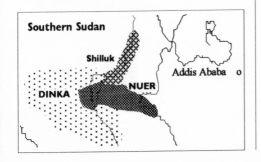

DIOLA

500,000 SPEAKERS

Senegal, Guiné, the Gambia

Diola or *Jola* has about 500,000 speakers on either side of the lower Casamance river, which reaches the Atlantic in southern Senegal. To the north the language extends, across a mainly rice-growing lowland zone, to the Gambian frontier; to the south it is also spoken at the mouth of the Cacheu river, in northern Guiné. It belongs to the Atlantic group of NIGER-CONGO LANGUAGES, and is one of the regional official languages of Senegal. Speakers call themselves *Kuyolāk*.

Diola was important in the early history of European exploration and exploitation of the West African coast. Two of its dialects can be traced in very early records. *Floup*, spoken at the mouth of the Cacheu, long an artery of Portuguese trade, is first recorded in a wordlist made for the French Royal Senegal Company in 1690. *Kasa* or Carabanne is the dialect of the Senegalese river towns on the Casamance, from Ziguinchor down to the Atlantic ports.

The major dialect in Senegal nowadays is the majority *Fony* or Fogny, spoken all the way from the Ziguinchor district to the Gambia border: it is the official standard, used on radio and television. For a table of numerals see WOLOF.

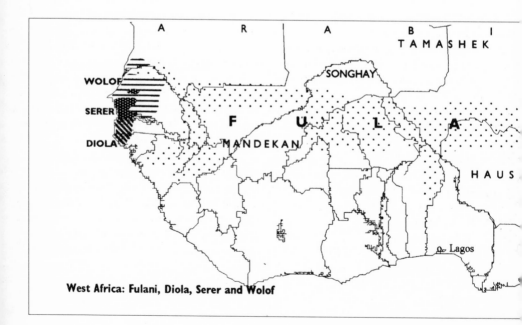

West Africa: Fulani, Diola, Serer and Wolof

A sentence from J. David Sapir's *Grammar of Diola-Fogny* (Cambridge: Cambridge University Press, 1965) shows how loanwords can change so much in sound as to be scarcely recognisable. *Babay bukanak kariem pɔntitɛr ning Kuyɔlāk mankuriem ɛmānɔ*, 'There are people who eat *potatoes* the way the Diola eat rice.' 'Pɔntitɛr' is borrowed from French *pommes de terre*.

Fulani, Diola, Serer and Wolof

In spite of their scattering, the FULANI dialects remain in general mutually intelligible.

The dialect of the Futa Sénégalais is sometimes called *Poular*.

The dialect of the Futa Djallon is sometimes called *Fula*.

East of these a major Fulani centre extends from Macina to the Niger bend.

The major Nigerian dialects are those of Kano and the north, of Sokoto, and of Adamawa. There are two *Adamawa* dialect divisions, 'East Fulani' or *Foulbéré* or *Fulfulde Funaangere*, centred on Diamaré in Cameroun, and 'West Fulani' or *Fulfulde Hiirnaangere*.

Two other members of the Atlantic group are especially closely related to Fulani.

Serer, with 650,000 speakers, is one of the six official languages of Senegal. Its main dialects are the coastal *Serer Non* and *Serer Sin* of the Saloum river valley. A word-list in this language (as *Séraire*) was made for the French Royal Senegal Company as early as 1690.

WOLOF, with over two million speakers, is in practice Senegal's national language. Both of these are also spoken in the Gambia.

More distantly related are Diola, Balanta and Mandyak.

Diola or Jola has about 500,000 speakers. It also belongs to the Atlantic group, but is less closely allied to the other three. The major dialect of Senegal is *Fony* or Fogny, extending from the Ziguinchor district to the Gambia border. *Kasa* is the dialect of the river towns on the Casamance, including Ziguinchor itself. *Floup* is the main dialect of Guiné.

Balanta or Brassa has about 300,000 speakers, most of them in northern Guiné.

Mandyak (Portuguese *Manjaco*, French *Mandjaque*) has 150,000 speakers north-west of Bissau, the capital of Guiné.

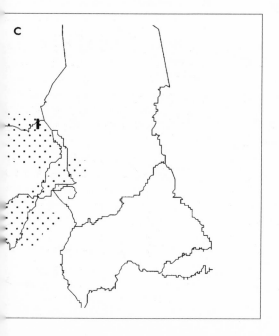

DIVEHI

100,000 SPEAKERS

Maldives

One of the INDO-ARYAN LANGUAGES, Divehi or Maldivian is the everyday language of the Maldives, now an independent state in the western Indian Ocean.

It has been suggested that the language was brought here by colonists from Sri Lanka, perhaps sixteen hundred years ago. At any rate, Divehi shows a closer relationship with SINHALA (see map there) than with the rest of the Indo-Aryan group: dialects of the southern islands show additional Sinhalese influence from later contacts. The Maldives were at first Buddhist, like Sri Lanka: Islam reached the islands in the 10th century and is still the majority religion.

The first twelve numerals are: *eke, de, tine, hatare, fahe, haye, hate, ashe, nuvaye, dihaye, ekolahe, dolahe*. These basic numerals resemble those of Sinhala, but larger numbers used to be built on a duodecimal base: '13' was *dolos-eke*, '14' was *dolos-de*, '24' was *fassehe*. A base of ten is now used.

The Tana script

Divehi shows its independence from Indian cultural influence partly in its script, called 'Tana' or 'Thaana'. This is quite different from Indic scripts in structure. Like Arabic script it is written from right to left, and its unknown inventor borrowed the shapes of the Arabic numerals and of some other Arabic characters. The script has been in use since about 1700: earlier Maldivian inscriptions, which date back to the 12th century, are in Indic-type scripts.

／ 𝒴 𝓂 𝓇 ☉ 𝒴 ∨ ∧ 9 ＞ 𝓅 𝒮 𝒴 𝒮 ⍩ 𝒴 ㇄

h ś n r b ḷ k a v m f d t l g ñ s ḍ

DOGRI

1,300,000 SPEAKERS

India

One of the INDO-ARYAN LANGUAGES, and sometimes regarded as the most aberrant of the dialects of PANJABI, Dogri is the language of the small former state of Jammu – which is now part of the resolutely Indian segment of the divided state of Kashmir.

Older Dogri texts can be found written in a distinctive script, related to the Gurmukhi script that is used for Panjabi. Nowadays Dogri is written in the Devanagari script familiar from Hindi. Dogri is rich in folk literature – from riddles to long tales and ballads – but there was little written literature before Indian independence in 1947. The

Jammu radio station, opened in 1948, broadcasts in Dogri and encouraged local literature, as did the Cultural Academy founded in 1958.

The first ten numerals in Dogri are: *ik, do, trai, cār, pañj, che, sat, aṭh, nau, das.*

Hāṃ-re, kar-ke mahabbat mānue de rāh vic rahnde;
tāre gindī nūṃ raiṇ bihāwe.
Once having loved, she always longs for her man;
she passes the night counting the stars.

Couplet from a Dogri folk song

DONG

1,500,000 SPEAKERS

China

Dong is the most important language of the Kam-Sui group of KADAI LANGUAGES. The comparative linguist Fang Kuei Li discovered this language group, or at least brought it to the attention of European scholars for the first time, and demonstrated its distant relationship to the Tai languages.

Dong is the official Chinese name of the language. Its speakers call themselves *Nin-kam* and their language *Kam. Tung, Tung-chia* and *Tung-jen* are found in older sources. Chinese records sometimes confuse the Dong with the MIAO.

All the Kam-Sui languages are spoken by minority peoples of southern China. Dong is to be found further north-east than any other language of the Kadai family, where the borders of Hunan, Guizhou and Guangxi meet. Dong speakers are well known as musicians and singers – and as weavers of a specially fine cloth. The majority are wet rice farmers: MIAO speakers are their hill-farming neighbours.

'The Kam language is noteworthy for its extraordinarily large number of tone distinctions. Counting six pitch distinctions in "checked" syllables [ending in a consonant or glottal stop], most dialects of Kam are said to have fifteen different tones. This is surely close to a record.

(S. Robert Ramsey, *The languages of China* (Princeton: Princeton University Press, 1987) p. 244).

The first ten numerals in Sui are: *dau, gha, ham, hi, ngo, lyok, shet, pat, chu, sup.*

Songs at the drum tower

'Villages are located near water if possible. A unique structure is the so-called drum tower [*ta lei*]. These towers, of wood with tiled roofs, may reach 100 feet in height. The ground floor space serves as a combination village meeting hall and men's house. A wooden drum, suspended from the roof, is beaten in times of emergency and as a preliminary to village meetings. During the period between planting and harvesting, when farmwork is light, villagers gather at the drum tower, often inviting young people from neighbouring villages. On these occasions the two sexes may sing antiphonally throughout the night.'

Frank M. LeBar and others, *Ethnic groups of mainland southeast Asia* (New Haven: Human Relations Area Files Press, 1964) p. 231, based on work by Chen Kuo-chün and Inez de Beauclair

---

The Kam-Sui languages

The two important languages of this small group are Dong and Sui. *Dong* or Kam has about 1,500,000 speakers. *Sui* or Shui or Pa-shui has perhaps 200,000 speakers in Guizhou and Guangxi provinces – and a magical writing system all of its own. Speakers of Sui are said to have been settled in Guangdong province until they were forced to move in 1732.

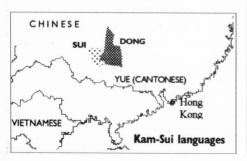

Kam-Sui languages

DRAVIDIAN LANGUAGES

The Dravidian languages of southern India have a total of well over 170,000,000 speakers. They include four state languages (Malayalam, Telugu, Kannada and Tamil) the last of which is also an important language of Sri Lanka.

Drāviḍa is a Sanskrit name for the old Tamil kingdom whose capital was at Kancipuram near Madras. Already in the 8th century a Sanskrit writer had grouped the languages of the south as *Andhradrāviḍabhāṣā*, 'languages of the Telugu-Tamil group'. On this basis, *Dravidian* was suggested as a convenient label for the whole family by Robert Caldwell, Bishop of Madras, who published his *Comparative grammar of the Dravidian or South-Indian family of languages* in 1856.

They are unrelated to the Indo-Aryan languages to their north, which belong to the Indo-European family as do Greek, Latin and English. But there are tantalising similarities between the two groups (see box). Some period of shared development, or some episode leading to close mutual influence, must have produced this effect – at a date in prehistory which is now difficult to pin down.

There are minority Dravidian languages to be found far north of the line that marks the Dravidian/Indo-Aryan boundary, notably Brahui of western Pakistan. There is evidence that Dravidian once stretched further still: many linguists, ever since Caldwell's *Comparative grammar*, have believed that the family includes the mysterious, ancient Elamite language known from inscriptions and clay tablets from western Iran.

How early, then, did speakers of Indo-Aryan dialects meet speakers of prehistoric Dravidian? Or did other, now forgotten, languages transmit the same typical regional features to both groups? Is Burushaski a surviving specimen of

such a language? For even Vedic Sanskrit, spoken in the far north-west of India as long ago as 1000 BC, had already adopted the retroflex consonants so typical of Indian languages.

India has been a single cultural area for most of two millennia, and all the Dravidian-speaking region is heavily influenced by Sanskrit, the universal learned language of the subcontinent. Three of the major languages, Malayalam, Kannada and Telugu, have such a large proportion of Sanskrit loanwords that early Western linguists believed the whole family to be an aberrant group of Indo-Aryan languages, directly descended from Sanskrit, like those of the north.

The retroflex consonants

'Most of the languages of India have a set of retroflex, cerebral or domal consonants [formed by turning the tip of the tongue towards the roof of the mouth] in contrast with dentals. The retroflexes include stops *ṭ ḍ ṭh ḍh*, nasals *ṇ*, also in some languages sibilants *ṣ*, laterals *ḷ*, tremulants and even others. Indo-Aryan, Dravidian, Munda and even the far northern Burushaski form a practically solid bloc characterised by this phonological feature. In Dravidian it is a matter of the utmost certainty that retroflexes in contrast with dentals are proto-Dravidian in origin . . . In Southern Dravidian, moreover, several languages have three phonemic series in the front of the mouth – dental, alveolar, retroflex – a possibility hardly envisaged by the makers of the International Phonetic Association's alphabet.'

Murray B. Emeneau, *Language and linguistic area* (Stanford: Stanford University Press, 1980) pp. 110–11

English has alveolar and not dental consonants (in other words, the English *t d* are formed by touching the alveolar ridge with the tongue, while in French and many other languages the comparable *t d* sounds are formed by touching the upper teeth with the tongue). To Indians, these English alveolar consonants sound more like the retroflex consonants *t̠ d̠* than the dental consonants *t d*. So, in speaking English, most Indians are likely to pronounce *t d* as retroflex consonants – the characteristic feature of what the English call an 'Indian accent'.

Dravidian languages and others

Northern Dravidian languages include BRAHUI and KURUKH. The most important Central Dravidian language is GONDI: see the map there for information on others. Some include Telugu in Central Dravidian, but this is to overstate its differences from the other major languages of the Southern group.

The Southern Dravidian languages include KANNADA, MALAYALAM, TAMIL, TELUGU and TULU. Tamil is the only one with large numbers of speakers outside the Indian subcontinent – in Sri Lanka, Vietnam, Malaysia, Singapore, Zanzibar and even further afield.

Dravidian languages are not as well mapped as those of northern India. The great *Linguistic Survey of India* did not explore the states now called Tamilnadu, Andhra Pradesh and Karnataka: it missed some Dravidian languages even north of this.

The *Kurumbar*, nomadic shepherds of the mountains of southern India, have no separate language but speak dialects of those in their neighbourhood (see box at Kannada).

Several 'language isolates', apparently not belonging to any known language family, survive in India as reminders that the linguistic history of the subcontinent is more complicated than we can now reconstruct.

Burushaski, with 40,000 speakers in Kashmir valleys, is the most famous. The first ten numerals in Burushaski are: *hin, altan, iskin, walto, sundo, mashindo, thalo, altàmbo, huncho, tormo*.

The language of Elam

The great three-language inscription of King Darius at Behistun, in Iran, was the key that eventually allowed scholars to decipher all three languages. The most mysterious – at first with no recognised links to any other tongue – was Elamite, later found in a series of inscriptions and tablets dating from about 2200 to about 400 BC. They are the records of a once independent people, of what are now the provinces of Khuzestan and Fars in Iran, who were eventually incorporated in the great Persian Empire. Their language must have died out not long afterwards.

Bishop Caldwell, the 19th-century Dravidian scholar, was struck by the similarities between Elamite grammar and that of the DRAVIDIAN LANGUAGES. Scholars still pursue this insight – but without as yet reaching an agreed conclusion.

The cuneiform script is based on AKKADIAN, simplified, yet clearly not well adapted to Elamite sounds. Linguists have to work from scribes' spelling mistakes or variations to puzzle out the existence of such features as nasal vowels and final consonant clusters.

DUALA

80,000 SPEAKERS

Cameroun

Duala, one of the BANTU LANGUAGES, is spoken in the once-famous trading city of Duala on the coast of Cameroun (for map see EWONDO).

European traders began to visit this coast in the late 15th century; the slave trade was established by 1500. These may have been the impulses that brought Duala speakers from an earlier inland territory to colonise the coast and found Duala around 1650. The city soon became a major exporter of slaves, ivory and aggrey, a blue coral-like rock much prized on the Gold Coast. Duala speakers made long trading journeys, inland and along the coast of Calabar, and their language became familiar to many other tribes as a lingua franca of trade.

Once fabulously wealthy, Duala crumbled, from about 1840, as the external market for slaves died. When the Germans invaded Cameroun in the late 19th century they themselves began to develop the inland trade of the region, displacing Duala speakers. At the same time, however, Duala was taken up by the Basle mission, which built on its existing position as a second language of trade to make it the vehicle of education in the districts of Victoria, Kumba and Mamfe – well beyond the area where Duala was a first language. Thus Duala became the first African language of Cameroun to be used for literature, and it provided the standard for official spellings of place names. The Bible was translated into Duala in 1862–72; the first grammar, by Alfred Saker, had appeared in 1855.

However, even in its heartland, Duala was in competition with another lingua franca – the Cameroun variety of pidgin English now usually known as KAMTOK. The German rulers, though they did not approve of Kamtok, found it easier to learn than Duala, and in practice they used it regularly. It became the language of plantations and of the market place in coastal Cameroun, while Duala became once more the local language of the city of Duala and its neighbourhood.

Duala has been influenced by neighbouring EFIK. Loanwords include Efik *makara*, Duala *mukala*, 'white man'. The first ten numerals are: *èwɔ, bebǎ, belalò, benèi, betanù, mùtoba, sàmba, lɔ̀mbì, dìbùa, dôm.*

DUTCH

20,000,000 SPEAKERS

Netherlands, Belgium

O ne of the GERMANIC LANGUAGES, Dutch is in
origin the western extremity of the dialect
spectrum of Low GERMAN. It is the national
language of the Netherlands. It is also one of
the two national languages of Belgium, and there
is a small Dutch-speaking minority in northern
France near Dunkerque.

Nederland, or in full *Koninkrijk der Nederlande*,
'Kingdom of the Low Countries', is the official name of the country; *Holland* is sometimes used in English as shorthand for this. In
French it is called *Pays-Bas*, a direct translation of the native name. *Belgium*, French
Belgique, Flemish *België*, is a revival of a tribal
and provincial name from the time of the
Roman Empire – but the *Belgae* of that period
spoke a Celtic language.

The native name of the language is *Duits*,
which is in origin the same as *Deutsch* (see
GERMAN). As a national language, however,
Dutch is called *Nederlands*. *Vlaams* (*Flemish*)
used to be the standard name in Belgium.

Most of the Netherlands, and almost all of
Flemish-speaking Belgium, belong to the Lower
Franconian dialect division of Low German.
Standard Dutch originates as a variety of this –
the language of the cities of Holland and Flan-
ders, notably Amsterdam, Utrecht and Antwerp.
As they passed through the hands of various
European dynasties in medieval times, these
centres of world trade became more prosperous
and more powerful. Their independence, largely
established by William of Nassau, Prince of
Orange, in the 16th century, was recognised at
the Treaty of Westfalia in 1648.

Belgium seceded in 1830 and became an
officially bilingual state – one in which the
language boundary is not to be ignored and
linguistic rivalry sometimes borders on civil
war. Brussels, its capital, forms an enclave where
French is now the majority language in a region
which is historically Flemish-speaking.

Belgium once ruled Zaire, Rwanda and Burundi, but French rather than Flemish served as
the administrative language there. Dutch, however, was once the official language of a colonial
empire and trade network that has included
Indonesia, Sri Lanka, parts of South Africa, a
varying number of possessions on the Indian and
African coast, Suriname and some Caribbean
islands. Names such as *Nassau* (capital of the
Bahamas), *New Amsterdam* (the early name of
New York) and *New Zealand* are reminders of
the historical extent of Dutch exploration and
trade.

Several local and mixed forms of Dutch grew
up in the Dutch East Indies (Indonesia): all are
now on the way to extinction, if they are not
already extinct. *Petjo* was spoken by 'Indos',
descendants of Dutch men and Asian women,
in Batavia (Jakarta). *Javindo*, the mixed Dutch-
Malay language of Semarang, was also known
as *Krom-Hollands* 'Bad Dutch'. But AFRIKAANS,
an offshoot of Dutch, now one of the major
languages of an independent South Africa,
stands as the greatest linguistic monument to
Dutch expansion, trade and settlement overseas.

Linguists speak traditionally of *Old Franconian*
but of *Middle* and *Modern Dutch*. The oldest, 9th-
century, manuscript sources of Old Franconian
are translations inserted in the Latin text of the
Laws of the Salic Franks: there are also translations

of the Psalms. There is some 12th- and 13th-century poetry in Middle Dutch. The full Bible translation of 1619–37, called *Staten-Bijbel*, is a landmark of Modern Dutch literature.

Nederlands and Vlaams

The boundary between the Netherlands and Belgium is of recent origin and has nothing to do with major dialect divisions. However, differences do exist between the two national standards of the Netherlands and of Belgium. Amsterdam and the Hague are in the *Hollands* dialect zone, while Antwerp and Brussels are in *Brabant*. Manuals are published for Flemish speakers, urging them to avoid 'Brabantisms' or regionalisms. For 'sandpaper' they are told to use the Standard Dutch *schuurpapier*, not the Brabantism *zandpapier*.

Low German, Dutch and Frisian on the map

FRISIAN has significant dialect divisions. *West Frisian* is spoken in the Netherlands (some linguists distinguish *West Frisian* of the coast and the island of Terschelling from *Central Frisian*, spoken inland). *East Frisian* is spoken in a small moorland enclave in Saterland (the language of the East Frisian islands is Low German). *North Frisian* is spoken on the islands of Sylt, Amrum, Föhr and Helgoland (*Island Frisian*) and on the neighbouring Schleswig coast.

Low GERMAN consists of a series of dialects extending from east to west along the Baltic coast and its hinterland. *Niederpreußisch* and *Ostpommersch* are on the way to extinction as the German-speaking populations of the Königsberg (Kaliningrad) enclave and Poland were expelled at the end of the Second World War. Most now live in Germany. At the other end of the range, *Nordsächsisch* or *Niedersächsisch*, 'Lower Saxon', extends into the Netherlands, but the three most westerly dialects, *Limburgisch*, *Brabantisch* and *Holländisch*, grouped together as *Niederfränkisch* 'Lower Franconian', are spoken almost wholly in the Netherlands and Belgium and form the basis of modern Dutch.

Dutch as a world language

Throughout the former Dutch empire Dutch was an administrative language and was spoken by expatriates and mixed populations. In particular the local forms of Dutch in Indonesia were once varied and important, but they are now almost forgotten.

The most lasting linguistic legacy of Dutch expansion is certainly AFRIKAANS, the modified or creolised Dutch of South Africa.

New Amsterdam Dutch was spoken in parts of New York and New Jersey until about 1900. The dialects of Dutch settlers and of their black slaves were said to be noticeably different. Although the English took New Amsterdam (New York) in 1664, Dutch remained the official school language till 1773.

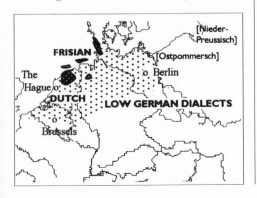

Numerals in Dutch, Afrikaans and Frisian		
Dutch	**Afrikaans**	**Frisian**
1	een	een	ien
2	twee	twee	twa
3	drie	drie	trije
4	vier	vier	fjouwer
5	vijf	vyf	fiif
6	zes	ses	seis
7	zeven	sewe	saun
8	acht	agt	acht
9	negen	nege	njuggen
10	tien	tien	tsien

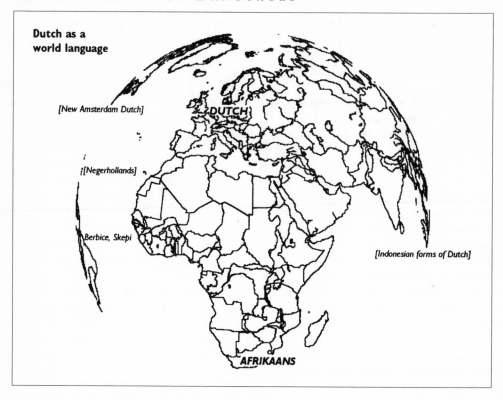

Dutch as a
world language

[New Amsterdam Dutch]

DUTCH

[Negerhollands]

Berbice, Skepi

[Indonesian forms of Dutch]

AFRIKAANS

Negerhollands was the Creole Dutch of the Virgin Islands and Puerto Rico, now United States territories. Some publications appeared in Negerhollands in the 19th century, including a New Testament translation in 1818. It is probably now extinct.

In Guyana two Dutch creoles, *Berbice* and *Skepi*, have been discovered recently, both spoken by small communities in inland river valleys. They, also, are nearing extinction. But Dutch has had a considerable influence on PAPIAMENTO, the creole language of Curacao, and on Sranan, the lingua franca of Suriname (see ENGLISH CREOLES AND PIDGINS).

DZONGKHA

PERHAPS 500,000 SPEAKERS AS A SECOND LANGUAGE

Bhutan

As Mongolia, Tibet and other strongholds have succumbed to invasion and annexation, Bhutan is the one surviving independent state that continues the political and religious traditions of northern Buddhism. It became a unified state in the 17th century and a hereditary monarchy early in the 20th century.

Two of the three major regional languages of Bhutan (see map) belong to the 'Bodish' or Tibetan group: in other words, they are descended from the earliest reconstructable form of Tibetan (and are thus SINO-TIBETAN LANGUAGES). Pronunciation has changed so far, however, that they are mutually unintelligible with one another and with modern central Tibetan. After long and relatively undisturbed development in a country where inter-valley communication is not easy, numerous local dialects have grown up.

Classical Tibetan was, and still is, the language of religious education and culture across the whole of Bhutan. With unification, however, the need for an everyday lingua franca must have increased. The origin of Dzongkha can thus be traced to the 17th century, when it began to develop as a second language of army, administration and trade on the basis of Ngalong, the language of Thimphu.

Dzongkha (sometimes called *Bhutanese*) is, in written Tibetan, *rDzong-kha* 'language of the fortress'. It is now taught in all Bhutanese schools, as is English; a written form of it has been developed, a new use of the existing Tibetan script, which is most often seen in its local cursive form *rgyug-yig*.

For a table of numerals see TIBETAN.

Information from Michael Aris,
Bhutan: the early history of a Himalayan kingdom (Warminster: Aris & Phillips, 1979)

Languages of Bhutan

Ngalong is the language of the six valleys of western Bhutan, including Thimphu, the capital. Dzongkha originates as a lingua franca form of Ngalong.

Bumthang or Kebumtamp is spoken in central Bhutan; its territory also extends beyond that of Tsangla into the Indian state of Arunachal Pradesh, where it is sometimes known as 'northern Mon-pa'. Close to Bumthang is the language of the *Dag-pa* or Dap or Adap, a pastoralist community on the eastern edge of Bhutan. Earlier studies of this language called it 'Takpa' and 'Dwags', but it is quite different from the dialect of the *Dwags* province of southern Tibet.

Tsangla or Sharchagpakha or Sharchop, still a Sino-Tibetan language but more radically different from Tibetan than the other two, is the largest of the three regional languages, with perhaps 600,000 speakers in eastern Bhutan. There is a local assumption that Tsangla is the 'oldest' or 'original' language of the country.

NEPALI is spoken across a belt of south-western Bhutan.

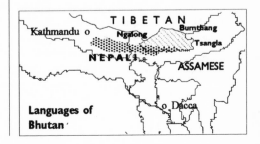

Languages of Bhutan

EDO

1,350,000 SPEAKERS

Nigeria

One of the Benue-Congo group of NIGER-CONGO LANGUAGES, Edo was spoken in the once powerful and long-lasting Kingdom of Benin. It is now the major language of Bendel State, Nigeria.

Edo is the old local name of Benin City, capital of the kingdom. The language has also been called *Bini* and *Benin* by Europeans.

Oral tradition traces the historical kingdom back fifteen generations before the first European contact, the Portuguese visit to Benin in 1485. There are Edo legends of an older, mythical dynasty of sky kings, *ogiso* (see box) whose adventures linked them with personified animals and plants and pitted them against the animal trickster, the tortoise, *egwi*.

Benin grew rich in trade with the Portuguese, Dutch and British, exporting slaves, leopard skins and Guinea pepper. Its borders fluctuated and are now difficult to reconstruct – but Lagos is said to have been a Benin foundation and Onitsha was once under Benin suzerainty. IGBO titles of nobility are of Edo origin. Through the slave trade Edo exerted an influence on European creole languages, notably the Portuguese Creole of São Tomé.

The British conquered Benin in 1897, but reestablished a titular kingdom. Though not one of the national languages of Nigeria, Edo is today a major regional language and is used in education and the media.

The Edo and the Yoruba

'According to Edo mythology, the Benin kingdom was founded by the youngest of the children of *Osanobua*, the high god. With his senior brothers, who included the first kings of Ife and other Yoruba kingdoms and the first king of the 'Europeans', he was sent to live in the world (*agbõ*). Each was allowed to take something with him. Some chose wealth, material or magical skills or implements but, on the instructions of a bird, the youngest chose a snail shell. When they arrived in the world they found it covered with water. The youngest son was told by the bird to upturn the snail shell and when he did so sand fell from it and spread out to form the land. So the first *Oba* of Benin became the owner of the land and his senior brothers had to come to him and barter their possessions in return for a place to settle. Hence, though he was the youngest son, he became the wealthiest and most powerful ruler'.

R. E. Bradbury, *The Benin kingdom* (London: International African Institute, 1957) p. 19

Edoid languages

Edo, with 1,000,000 speakers, is spoken across the central territory of the old kingdom.

Esan or Ishan, with 200,000 speakers, is locally an official language, used in primary schools and on television. It is said to originate with emigrants from Benin who established their own domains along the lower Niger.

Yekhee, Etsako or 'Kukuruku', with 150,000

speakers, is said to mark the position of a sub-
ordinate kingdom. Esan and Yekhee may be
regarded as dialects of Edo.

South West Edoid languages are *Urhobo* and *Isoko*.
Together they have 650,000 speakers. They are
not close enough to be intelligible to Edo speakers; the same applies to the *North West Edoid* and
Delta Edoid (including *Engenni*) languages, which
are spoken by much smaller communities.

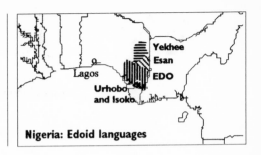

Nigeria: Edoid languages

EFIK AND IBIBIO

2,750,000 SPEAKERS

Nigeria

One of the NIGER-CONGO LANGUAGES, this is a language of the Cross river shores and a lingua franca of Cross River State in Nigeria – a role that Nigerian Pidgin English may now begin to take over. Efik is used in education up to university level.

> *Efik* is properly the name for the language spoken as a mother tongue in Calabar, Creek and along Cross river as far as Itu. *Ibibio* and *Annang* are a series of dialects partly mutually intelligible with Efik.

Ibibio traditions claim that they have been settled in their present location for many centuries, and this is likely to be true. Ibibio speakers were once numerous in the Atlantic slave trade. Ibibio speakers were reluctant colonials, continuing to resist the British until 1929 and after.

Missionaries began to work and teach in Efik at Calabar in 1846. As a vehicle of trade, Efik was already known along the routes that Calabar traders used. It now became a language of religion and culture, used in church, in education and in print. So although Efik has a relatively small number of speakers, it is nowadays ac-

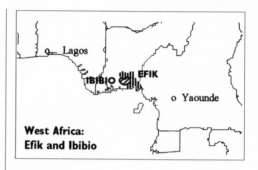

West Africa: Efik and Ibibio

cepted as the standard language among Ibibio speakers generally, and continues to be used in the press and media.

Efik has four tones. An initial nasal, *m* or *n*, functions as a vowel and can take a tone. The first ten numerals in Ibibio are: *kèt, ìba, ìtá, ìnā, ìtyō, ityôket, ìtyâba, ìtyâitá, ùsúkkèt, dwòp.*

Ibibio dialects on the map

Efik is accepted as the standard throughout Ibibio country. *Andoni* of the Atlantic coast and the western *Annang* are the most aberrant of the dialects.

EGYPTIAN

EXTINCT LANGUAGE OF EGYPT

Egyptian is one of the AFROASIATIC LANGUAGES, and the second oldest of all written languages. In its later form, COPTIC, Egyptian survived as a spoken language until a few hundred years ago: some Coptic texts are still used in the Christian churches of Egypt.

In its unmistakable hieroglyphic script, Egyptian was already being recorded in stone inscriptions before 3000 BC. It was the language of government and of the all-pervading state religion throughout the long life of the Egyptian kingdom, which eventually succumbed to Persian and then to Macedonian conquest in the 4th century BC. The fate of the dead was an abiding preoccupation of Egyptian culture – a preoccupation that resulted not only in the pyramids, but also in the lengthy historical, ritual and magical texts that make up the majority of surviving Egyptian literature.

The classical form of the language is Middle Egyptian, reflecting spoken Egyptian of about 2200 BC but formalised and frozen in official use for two thousand years.

The last important text in Middle Egyptian is the Rosetta Stone. Erected in 196 BC, this is inscribed in Middle Egyptian (hieroglyphic script), in Demotic and in Greek – the three written languages of prestige in Greek-ruled Egypt. It was crucial to the decipherment of the Egyptian scripts. In 1822 Jean-François Champollion identified the names in the Hieroglyphic and Demotic versions, showing that some signs were alphabetic while others were classifiers or represented whole words. The work of decipherment, following Champollion, was largely completed in the course of the 19th century.

The first ten numerals in Egyptian are – as written – *w*, *snw*, *ḥmt*, *fdw*, *diw*, *sisw*, *sfḫ*, *ḫmn*, *psd*, *mj*. For the vowels as recorded in a later form of the language, see table at COPTIC.

Periods of written Egyptian
Old Egyptian: 3100 to 2200 BC
Middle Egyptian: 2200 to 200 BC or later
Late Egyptian: 1600 to 700 BC
Demotic: 700 BC to AD 400
COPTIC: AD 200 to 1400 or later

The Hieroglyphic script: the main alphabetic signs

ʼ i y ʼ w b p f m n r h ḥ ḫ ẖ s š ḳ k g t ṯ d ḏ

ENGLISH

350,000,000 SPEAKERS

United States of America, United Kingdom, Canada, Australia, South Africa, India, Ireland, Malaysia, Singapore, Sri Lanka and many other countries

One of the GERMANIC LANGUAGES, English is rather different from the other members of the group (Dutch, German, Danish and the rest) – different in its early history and unique in its status in the 20th-century world.

Although Chinese has more mother-tongue speakers, no language rivals English in the extent to which it is used across the world. There are probably 800,000,000 people who speak English either as a first or second language. All available evidence tells us that this number will go on growing.

The history of English

English and Frisian must both have grown out of the unrecorded lingua franca of the North Sea seaways in the 4th and 5th centuries AD, when Germanic mercenaries fought for and against the Roman Empire, eventually overwhelming it. In Italy, southern France and Spain their migrations had come overland. To the north, in northern France and Britain, the lands of the empire were approached by sea.

Out of this ethnic and linguistic melting-pot, Frisian was to emerge in the mainland ports: but Frisian is now nothing more than a regional language in districts of the Netherlands and north-western Germany. English owes its origin to the migrants ('Angles, Saxons and Jutes') who crossed the sea and settled in the Roman provinces of Britain, particularly after the Roman army had withdrawn, from 449 onwards if the traditional dating is correct.

By about 600, Anglo-Saxon kingdoms covered most of what is now England, though not Cornwall or the Lake District. The Latin of the lowlands had died away (there are no direct traces of it in English loanwords), as would the Celtic language that had once been spoken there. Wessex (*West Seaxe*, the 'West Saxons') became the most powerful of the new kingdoms, the only one able to withstand the Viking invasions that followed in the 9th century. It was in Wessex that a written language first flourished, at the court of Alfred (849–99). Alfred himself was a capable poet and a translator from Latin.

The dialects of the kingdoms of Mercia, Northumbria and Kent, rather different from 'West Saxon', are known from a few literary texts and documents.

Anglo-Saxon poetry

Lytle hwile leaf beoð grene,	A little while leaves are green,
ðonne hie eft fealewiað, feallað on eorðan	Then they go yellow, fall to earth
and forweorniað, weorðað to duste . . .	and die, turn to dust.

Solomon and Saturn

Old English verse is not rhymed: each line is alliterated on two or three stressed syllables. Similar patterns are found in the oldest German and Old Norse poetry.

England (medieval Latin *Anglia*; French *Angleterre*, 'land of the Angles') comes from the most obscure of the three tribal names associated with the Germanic migration. It is the land that the Angles and Saxons conquered for themselves, out of the larger territory that the Romans had called *Britannia*, 'Britain'. *English* is its language; but its culture before the Norman conquest is traditionally called *Anglo-Saxon*, and the same name used to be used for the language at that period. Linguists now prefer to emphasise the continuity between it and later periods and to call it *Old English*.

The greatest Old English literature consists of epics (*Beowulf*) and shorter poems in alliterative verse. Their makers were Christians, but Christianity was new to Anglo-Saxon England and had not yet overlaid the ethos of its traditional heroic poetry.

The Norman Conquest in 1066 drew a line under Anglo-Saxon literature and so, as far as we are concerned, under the Old English language as well. For the next two centuries the language of the court was French, and very little English was written – or at least very little survives. When 'Middle English' is again recorded, it had become a different language, heavily influenced by Norman French (for the first century of the conquest) and by Parisian French (from the mid 12th century onwards). The language is full of French loanwords – as it still is. In Old English there were several ways of forming the plural of nouns: in later English there is practically only one, -*s*, the same as in medieval French.

The Middle English period may be said to begin in 1066 and end with the introduction of printing in English in 1475. Alliterative verse was still written, such as the anonymous 14th-century masterpiece *Sir Gawain and the Green Knight*, but fashion turned to rhymed verse and to poetry and prose based on, or simply translated from, French. The most original writers – Geoffrey Chaucer (died 1400) in verse, the 15th-century 'knight prisoner' Sir Thomas Malory in prose – transformed these foreign influences into characteristic English forms. In the 12th and 13th centuries some of the greatest writers used not English but French (its English form is known as Anglo-Norman). Others wrote in Latin, the language of historical prose and of 'serious' and scholarly writing in many subjects.

The history of modern English has three important themes. The first is the extension of the language into new subject areas. Three crucial dates are the first printed English translation of the Bible, in 1525, the 'Authorised Version' of the English Bible in 1611, and the revised *Book of Common Prayer* in 1662. The latter two texts were in everyday use in Anglican churches until the 1970s: they influenced the speaking and writing of English for over 300 years. As in religion, so in science and scholarship, English came to take the place of Latin in the 16th century and after. Vast numbers of loanwords have been added to the language to make this possible.

The second theme is the spread of English to many parts of the world. It is the native language of English-speaking colonies, which have become independent and powerful states. Spread by British trade and influence, it is the second language of many other states that continue to need English because it is an international language and because, within their arbitrary excolonial frontiers, they have no better choice as national language. Worldwide, English is by far the most popular second language. It is the universal language of diplomacy and science (roles once played by French and Latin). It is the language that people usually try first when talking to 'foreigners'.

The third theme is the growth in England of a new and more widely accepted standard language, the language of London and its elite, nowadays identified as 'Standard British English', 'the King's (or Queen's) English', 'BBC English' and 'Received Pronunciation'. This has gone hand in hand with the spread of education and literacy, the extension of printing and publishing, and recently the influence of radio and television. All these influences have tended to freeze pronunciation, spelling, and spoken and written style.

But 'Standard British English' is now only one focus out of many.

Modern English, as it has gradually developed over the last five or six centuries, has some striking differences from earlier forms of the language. Final unstressed -*e*, a very common feature, was dropped; most former long vowels underwent a sound shift, the 'English Vowel Shift', and became diphthongs. Some examples: *dame*, *mole*, *pure* and *five*, and hundreds of words like them,

used to be pronounced as two syllables. They used to have a simple long first vowel (*a* as in *father*, *o* as in French *pôt*, *u* like the *oo* in *boot*, *i* like the *ee* in *been*). Now they are one-syllable words whose vowel sound has turned into a diphthong. But, when the change in pronunciation took place, English spelling did not change to reflect it: we do not write *deym*, *meul*, *pyur*, *fayv*.

Modern English noun forms

girl	singular base form
girl's	singular possessive
girls	plural base form
girls'	plural possessive

The last three of these have the same pronunciation. The distinction between them is a spelling rule that is taught by schoolteachers, with varying success: misplaced apostrophes have long been a common feature of public notices and of everyday writing. Copy editors and sub-editors maintain the rule in published books and newspapers.

Over-use of the possessive is a feature of unskilled writing in English by non-native speakers (*dog's food* for *dog food*; *the paint's colour* for *the colour of the paint*).

In marketing in France, English words are fashionable. The apostrophe is a reliable marker of English, and is favoured in hybrid forms such as *jean's* 'jeans', *pin's* 'lapel badge'.

Modern English verb forms

'Weak' verbs	'Strong' verbs	
play	take	1. base form
plays	takes	2. 3rd person singular, present
playing	taking	3. present participle
played	took	4. past
played	taken	5. past participle

Forms 2 and 3 can practically always be predicted from form 1. Forms 4 and 5 are identical, and predictable, in the so-called 'weak' verbs (the majority); they sometimes differ, and always have to be learnt individually, in the so-called 'strong' verbs. Young children sometimes get these wrong (*taked*). The past tenses of strong verbs tend to vary from dialect to dialect (*brung* for *brought*; *blowed* for *blew* and *blown*). There are even a few differences among the standard varieties of English (US *dove*, *gotten*; British *dived*, *got*).

English has developed far from a proto-Indo-European structure, in which both nouns and verbs had many possible forms defining their function in the sentence. In English most nouns only have two forms in speech, four in writing; verbs have four or five forms (see box).

Influences on English

The oldest external influences on English come from the language that was spoken in England

when English first began to develop – its Celtic speech, a variety of early Welsh. Many river names came from Celtic, like *Avon* from Welsh *afon* 'water'. Some other place names are Celtic too: the town names typically derive from the Latin version of an even older Celtic name, which had been adopted by the Romans at the time of their conquest, like *Londinium*, modern *London*. In the form in which they were learnt by the Anglo-Saxons, some of these included the Latin word *castra* 'fort', which comes through as modern *chester, -caster*: thus *Exeter* comes from the Latin (originally Celtic) town name *Isca* plus the Latin label *castra*, all passed on to the Anglo-Saxon invaders by no doubt Celtic-speaking inhabitants.

Few other English words are of early Celtic origin. Numerous examples have been proposed (*lad, lass, trudge, whap, mattock, drill, bran, bodkin*) but some have been disproved and most others are doubtful. A group of words including *bogey, boggle* and *bugbear* certainly has Welsh relatives. Other likely cases are *brisk, hog*. Additional Celtic words can be found in the western and northern dialects of English: sometimes, like *combe* (Welsh *cwm*) and *glen* (Gaelic *gleinn*), these eventually become known by speakers of standard English.

After the Anglo-Saxon settlements came the Viking raids and invasions of eastern England. It is because of these that English has a strong element of Norse words: Old Norse was a Germanic language, like Old English, but its forms were already quite distinct. Sometimes the Norse loanwords form 'doublets', when the same Germanic word already existed in Anglo-Saxon with a slightly different sense, as with Anglo-Saxon *shirt* and Norse *skirt*. Northern and eastern dialects have more Norse loanwords than standard English: Yorkshire *lake* 'play'; *gate* 'street' in place names.

Next came the single most powerful influence on English, that of French. The long term linguistic effect of the Norman Conquest was the incorporation of hundreds, even thousands of French loanwords in Middle and Modern English. Many of these are semantic doublets of existing Germanic words, with essentially the same meaning but with a cultured or elevated nuance: *clean* from Germanic, *pure* from French; *song* from Germanic, *chant* from French; *bed* from Germanic, *couch* from French.

In recent centuries English has drawn new words from most of the languages of Europe but, perhaps even more important, from the languages of other parts of the world: *chocolate* from Nahuatl; *jaguar* from Tupi; *curry* from Tamil or Kannada; *springbok* from Afrikaans.

Scientific terms: where from?

In the Western Roman Empire, Latin was the everyday language but Greek was the language of science and technology. If you spoke or wrote on scientific subjects in Latin, you would use Greek technical terms: *arithmetica, astronomia*.

In medieval western Europe, Greek was no longer widely known. Latin survived as the spoken and written language of scholarship. As new progress came in philosophy and science, in later medieval times, the Greek loanwords of older Latin were revived and new ones were wanted. Greek became the primary source for loanwords in medieval and modern Latin.

After the Renaissance, with the spread of literacy and printing in the modern languages of Europe, Latin gradually lost its role as the language of science. Science was now taught and written about in English, French, Italian, Spanish and other languages. New words were needed in these languages to cope with new subject areas; naturally the loanwords came from Latin – and naturally many of them were based on Greek – because these were the words that had already been used, by the same writers or by their forerunners, in scientific Latin.

New words are still invented all the time in science and technology. Most of them are still put together on the basis of Latin and Greek roots: *astrophysics, biomedicine*. This is the way it has always been done, and scientists are just as conservative as other people.

In German and Russian the tendency has been not to make up new words on Latin roots but to use the language's own resources. This can be seen in the language of psychoanalysis, a theory and technique developed by the Viennese Sigmund Freud (1856–1939). In his own writings Freud used ordinary German words in special senses for many of his new technical terms: *das Ich, das Es*. Freud's English translator, Ernest Jones, found it best not to use parallel English expressions (*the I, *the It*) and not to borrow the German words directly (*the Ich, *the Es*) but to use new *Latin* loanwords that matched Freud's terms. This is why English-speaking psychoanalysts talk of *the Ego* and *the Id*.

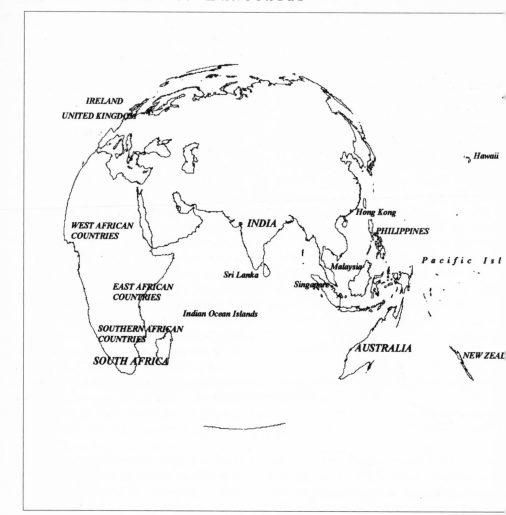

IRELAND
UNITED KINGDOM
Hawaii
WEST AFRICAN COUNTRIES
INDIA
Hong Kong
PHILIPPINES
Sri Lanka
Malaysia
Pacific Isl
EAST AFRICAN COUNTRIES
Singapore
Indian Ocean Islands
SOUTHERN AFRICAN COUNTRIES
SOUTH AFRICA
AUSTRALIA
NEW ZEAL

'Englishes' across the world

Neither American nor British English is noticeably more 'modern'. Each preserves features of older English which the other has lost. The regional dialects of North America and Britain are full of older words and forms that have disappeared from the standard varieties of English.

The Americas

Speakers of many languages crossed the Atlantic, voluntarily or involuntarily, to trade and settle in what are now the United States and Canada: English, French, Basque, Spanish, Dutch, German, Wolof, Akan, Yoruba, pidgin English and pidginised versions of several others. English arrived with John Cabot's expedition in 1497. From all the languages used there, English had emerged by the 18th century as North America's lingua franca.

Its history has been the merging of the languages of individuals and communities into a larger unity. But the unity of North American English has its own subdivisions: regional variants on an educated standard, regional dialects, city colloquials, an easily identifiable 'Canadian English', a range of forms grouped as 'Black English'. There has been plenty of room for these modern American dialects to retain fea-

been entirely shaped by migration. Nowadays, with powerful centralised media influences, the trend is strengthening, though speakers of highly distinct varieties – jargons of black city youth, 'hillbilly' dialects – may find the use of an almost private language advantageous and attractive.

English is a major language of communication in the central and eastern Caribbean, in a range of forms, from the regional standard (which has its slight variations from Standard American or British English) to local dialects of the island creoles.

Guyana is the furthest point south for the English language in the Americas (except for English-speaking minorities in Argentina and other South American countries). The furthest west is marked by two detached states of the US, Alaska and Hawaii: in the latter, standard English coexists with an English creole.

The British Isles

Standard British English differs from the American standard in its pronunciation (which Americans often describe as 'clipped'), in its written style, and in its vocabulary: *van* for *truck; tights* for *pantiehose; jam* for *jelly.*

The local dialects of England have been developing without interruption for 1,500 years – while continually influenced by the standard language and by one another. It is impossible to draw boundaries around them: every small locality has its own peculiarities of accent and vocabulary. On the larger scale, however, it is easy to recognise West Country, West Midland, East Midland, East Anglia, Cheshire, Lancashire, Yorkshire and North East dialects: cities such as London (*Cockney*), Bristol, Birmingham, Liverpool (*Scouse*) and Newcastle (*Geordie*) have their own colloquials. The country dialects are in a slow decline: increased population mobility, schools and broadcasting all work against them. The city dialects, along with the varieties of 'British Black English', are still vigorous. The Black English of British cities has close historical links with Jamaican and other Caribbean creoles – but its musical and poetic traditions have developed new and original features.

English: the world language

tures of the original languages and dialects of the migrants. Black English, in particular, is partly shaped by the creoles that were the everyday speech in slave communities of the American South and the Caribbean.

On the margins of North American English, numerous other languages survive in local use: French, Spanish, German, Yiddish, English creoles such as Gullah, the French creole of Louisiana, Amerind languages. All these can still provide new loanwords in regional American English dialects.

The trend is towards standardisation rather than fragmentation. Perhaps it has always been so in these two countries whose demography has

The English of Wales has been developing for some hundreds of years. Two main dialects can be recognised: the southern is closer to English dialects of the West Midlands and the West Country; the northern is closer to north-west England and shows continuing strong influence from Welsh. Both have a characteristic sentence intonation comparable to that of Welsh.

English in Ireland dates from the English settlements of the 16th century and after. True Irish English is somewhat different from the conventional 'brogue' of fiction and theatre. The standard language of broadcasting and government incorporates Irish loanwords such as *garda* 'police', *Dáil* 'Parliament'. The Northern Irish variety is different again. The two religious communities of Northern Ireland have lived side by side for four hundred years, yet they are distinguished by certain features of accent.

The North Country score

Yan, tan, tethera, methera, pimp, teezar, leezar, cattera, horna, dik, yandik, tandik, tetherdik, metherdik, bumpit, yan-a-bumpit, tan-a-bumpit, tethera-bumpit, methera-bumpit, jigot. There are many versions of this counting jargon, used until quite recently in the north of England for special purposes – to count sheep; to count stitches; and in skipping games. My mother came from Lancashire, and this is the version that she knew.

Clearly it has something to do with the Welsh numerals. But it is hard to know whether it was remembered in the hills through a millennium and more, ever since Cadwallader fell and the Welsh were driven out of northern England; or whether it was learnt in some later contact between Wales and the North Country. The really striking feature is the way of saying 'sixteen' to 'nineteen'. The compound words mean 'one-and-fifteen', 'two-and-fifteen' and so on. This is exactly what is done in modern Welsh – but not, it seems, in very early Welsh.

The special history of Scots

The Anglo-Saxon settlements, from which the English language originated, actually extended north of the present border between England and Scotland. Gradually, both before and after the Norman conquest of England, English speakers went on spreading into the Lowlands of Scotland. They became a majority, though no one knows when this milestone was reached. Their form of speech eventually became the official tongue of the Scottish court and government.

In later medieval and early Renaissance times this language, Scots, was used not only in documents of all kinds but also in a great literature, from the poetry of Barbour (14th century) and Dunbar (c. 1320–95) to the prose of *The Kingis Quair* (whose author is usually thought to be James I of Scotland, 1394–1437).

When James VI of Scotland succeeded his cousin Elizabeth and became James I of England, the two courts became one. The political and cultural centre moved from Edinburgh to London. The Authorised Version of the Bible (1611), which was in the English of the South, was to have an enormous influence on literature all over Britain.

As an official and literary language, Scots quickly lost ground, though still used not only by Robert Burns (1759–96) but by other major writers such as the 19th-century novelist John Galt and the 20th-century poet Hugh Macdiarmid.

In Scotland now there is a continuum of speech forms. At one extreme is broad Scots, the descendant of the language of the medieval kingdom, strikingly different from southern English – and varying considerably across the geographical spread of Scotland. At the other is standard English spoken with a 'Scottish accent' and a few distinctive words such as *outwith*.

Scots, which in past times was the language of an independent government and a rich culture, is discouraged in schools and has no official status.

Africa and Asia

A highly distinctive standard is that of South Africa – the only one in Africa in which English serves as a mother tongue. The vowel sounds of South African English are immediately recognisable to English speakers from other parts of the world. The standard English of South Africa shows the influence of Afrikaans, Zulu, Xhosa and other local languages.

In the other African countries of the Commonwealth, in India, Sri Lanka, Malaysia and Singapore, English is not generally a mother tongue but a national auxiliary language used to varying degrees in education, government and business.

Malaysian and Singaporean varieties range from a standard very close to British English (as used in publishing) to forms of speech that would be barely intelligible to an English-speaking visitor. Spoken Malaysian English often omits the verb *be/is: He very stupid*. Only one verb form is used: *He call out*, a natural development since many final consonants are dropped. Spoken sentences are often completed by an expressive particle, *la* (a loan from Min Chinese) or *man*.

Within Sri Lankan English, regional differences can be recognised between the north-east and the south: there are also differences between Sinhala and Tamil speakers.

Indian English

In the 17th century, Englishmen who went to India needed to learn Portuguese, or, better, the Indo-Portuguese pidgin which was then the lingua franca of trade. Persian, as the language of local diplomacy and the elite, was equally important.

English gradually replaced Portuguese, and English itself became a ruling language in India, in the course of the 18th century. From the beginning it required a special vocabulary for hundreds of details of Indian administration and the Indian way of life which were wholly different from those of England. These loanwords came from Portuguese, Persian, Arabic, Bengali, Tamil, 'Hindustani' (Hindi and Urdu) and from many other languages of southern Asia. Ever since that time, Indian English has been distinguished less by its accent than by its vocabulary: *lathi* 'baton'; *out of station* 'away on business'; *tiffin* 'lunch'.

The Indian English accent is also distinctive: along with nearly all Indian languages it has the retroflex *t, d, n* sounds pronounced with the tip of the tongue turned upwards. These form a handy substitute for the alveolar *t, d, n* sounds of other varieties of English, in which the tongue points to the alveolar ridge behind the upper teeth.

In standard Indian English high numbers are counted in a special way. *Millions* are not used. Instead, *one lakh* is 'one hundred thousand' and *one crore* is 'ten million'. Numerals are punctuated to match. 1,27,55,380 is read in Indian English as *One crore, twenty-seven lakhs, fifty-five thousand, three hundred and eighty*: in British English it is *Twelve million, seven hundred and fifty-five thousand, three hundred and eighty*. American English omits the two *ands*.

'With the establishment of the first universities in 1857 English for all practical purposes became an Indian language' (S. Mathai). By the time British rule in India had flourished and declined, to end with independence in 1947, the English language was so solidly entrenched in education and in communications among speakers of the various indigenous languages that it was impossible to do without it. Its constitutional position has varied – but English remains, in practice, an essential lingua franca of India.

Australasia

New Zealand English is perhaps not easily distinguished from that of Australia by non-Antipodeans, though in fact the two regional forms have their differences. New Zealand English has naturally borrowed from Maori: *pakeha* 'white man', literally 'flea-bringer'. It has its own favoured phrases, such as *fire in the fern* 'wildfire'. Forenames drawn from Maori, such as *Ngaio*, have been fashionable at times.

Australian English has a history of almost two hundred years, and already has its own regional dialects. It has many loanwords from aboriginal Australian languages (and *Kylie* is a name borrowed from an aboriginal source), but it is best known for its distinctive colloquialisms at various levels of fashion and status: *sanga* 'sandwich', *the big spit* 'vomit', *sheila* 'woman'.

ENGLISH CREOLES AND PIDGINS

MANY MILLIONS OF SPEAKERS

This is a survey of the offspring of ENGLISH: the languages that have grown up in various parts of the world, in the last few centuries, wherever English, spoken in trade and conquest, has met other languages and mixed with them.

Why pidgins and creoles?

Pidgin languages are likely to develop wherever groups of speakers of two different languages need to communicate – and there is not the time or incentive for in-depth language learning. Typically this happens in the course of travel, trade, migration and conquest.

Pidgins tend to have limited vocabularies: enough for the circumstances in which they are used, buying and selling, giving and receiving orders, but no more.

Creoles are the offspring of pidgin languages. When pidgins for some reason become so essential to a community that they begin to be the first, and the only, language of at least some speakers, they are called creoles. Unlike most pidgins, creoles become capable of carrying the full range of information that members of any human community need to exchange: they are potentially as varied and as complex as any other language.

Pidgin languages are common: creoles less so. Not all pidgins ever become so essential within a community as to be the first language that children learn. But when migration throws speakers of different languages together permanently, then the conditions exist that make it likely that a creole will develop.

The Atlantic slave trade that began in the 16th century, and the 19th-century Pacific labour trade, both created these conditions. In many third world countries today, countries in which numerous regional and local languages are spoken, the powerful pull of city life and of industrial wages brings speakers of different languages together in a similar way. There, too, in great cities and busy towns, on marketplaces and at bus stations, pidgins are needed: in mixed-language communities they may develop into creoles.

There have been many guesses at the origin of the term *Pidgin*. The word is first found in N. Berncastle's *Voyage to China* (1850), and it is often said to derive from a Chinese pronunciation of the English word 'business' – or of the Portuguese word *ocupação*, which means the same. Others say that it comes from a Chinese phrase *pú-ts'ín* 'paying up'; or from the Portuguese expression *pequeno Portugues*, 'little Portuguese', which was used as a name for the Portuguese pidgin spoken in the coastal cities of Angola; or from the same Portuguese word *pequeno* in its Sranan form *pɔɔ́ɾī*. There are other, less likely, suggestions, including a derivation from Hebrew *pidjom* 'ransom'.

The word *Creole*, French *créole*, Spanish *criollo*, originates in Portuguese. The form found there, *crioulo*, meant 'home-bred' (Portuguese *criar* 'breed' from Latin *creare*, 'create'). Creole was viewed, in the period of Portuguese conquests, as the language spoken by slaves who had been brought up in the household rather than captured as adults.

Pidgin English is often called *Broken English*. Creoles are sometimes known, especially in the Caribbean, by the French name *Patois* 'peasant dialect'.

The tongues of European trade

The English-speaking traders who explored the Atlantic and Indian Ocean routes from about 1600 onwards found pidgin PORTUGUESE and SPANISH spoken. As the English prospered, their Amerindian, African and Asian trading partners and employees soon realised that they could make themselves better understood by using English words. Thus the oldest recorded English pidgins of the Atlantic and Indian Oceans are not really new inventions: they consist, in essence, of the Portuguese West African pidgin, 're-lexified' with English words, but still retaining Portuguese features – and still showing, in simplified form, a structure reminiscent of the NIGER-CONGO LANGUAGES of West Africa, notably WOLOF, one of the first with which the Portuguese had come into contact.

These first English pidgins, carried around the world by seamen, migrant workers and slaves, are the linguistic ancestors of several major languages of today – and of a host of less-known creoles and pidgins of small, isolated, half-forgotten communities in every continent.

Languages of the Atlantic

In and around the Caribbean, the destination of so many African slaves in the 17th and 18th centuries, there grew up a family of English creole languages, each of which has had its own history, though all are closely related. None of them is an official language, but the creoles of Jamaica (see separate entry), several Antillean islands, the Bahamas, Belize, Guyana and Suriname are indispensable languages of national communication and cohesion. In most countries where English is official, speakers nowadays learn to adopt a range of spoken styles from 'standard English', or a local standard, all the way to 'pure creole'.

First there are JAMAICAN CREOLE and the languages of the English-speaking Leeward Islands, Antigua, St Kitts, Nevis, Montserrat, Anguilla, Barbuda, and of the Virgin Islands. Barbadian or Bajan Creole played a pivotal role in the development of these creoles in the 17th century, though it is now scarcely spoken on Barbados itself. Related English creoles are also spoken in the Dutch Windward Islands, and in Tobago, St Vincent and Grenada. Trinidad Creole, though linked with Barbadian, was also influenced by BHOJPURI (better known locally as Hindi) and by KRIO, because of later migration from India and Sierra Leone. Echoes of all these Caribbean creoles can be heard in the Black English of modern Britain.

To the south-east, Guyanese Creole, like that of Trinidad, has been influenced by 19th- and 20th-century labour migration as well as by the earlier slave trade. Again, strong recent links exist with the Krio of Sierra Leone and with Bhojpuri.

To the west, in the former British Honduras, Belize Creole is the mother tongue for most of the urban population of Belize City, while country people, whose first languages are Spanish or Mayan languages or Black Carib, learn the creole as their second language. An offshoot, Miskito Coast Creole, has long been spoken in harbour towns and villages along the north coast of Nicaragua. There is a Panama variety of Caribbean Creole, with as many as 100,000 speakers, in Panama City, Colón and Bocas del Toro.

To the north, Bahamas Creole is sharply distinct from Caribbean varieties – for good historical reasons. The Bahamas were long ago united administratively with the British colony of Carolina; later, after the American Revolution, Loyalists from the southern states, and their slaves, settled in the Bahamas in large numbers. This explains why Bahamas Creole has a close relative in *Gullah* or Geechee, still spoken in the Sea Islands and along the southeastern United States coastline from Florida to North Carolina. Otherwise, the 18th- and 19th-century creole of slave communities in the southern United States does not survive directly – but it is not forgotten. Modern Black English of the United States retains some features of this language, as does Liberian Creole.

Church Creole in Suriname

The Moravian Missionaries started about 1780 to use creole in church. They translated the Bible, compiled a hymnbook, published a monthly paper and countless pamphlets, tracts and edifying stories.

Foreign missionaries have not always been gifted language learners. Their pronunciation of creole was not always correct. They were not corrected by their congregations, but imitated. So, by institutionalised mispronunciation, they created a creole variety which was then imitated by others as more fashionable and given superior status, because it was used on solemn occasions by people belonging to the former upper caste.

Church Creole	English	Common Creole (Sranan)
pikin	small child	pikiẽ
belə	belly	bere
tem	time	tẽ
helpi	help	yepi
rœstə	rest	lostu

After Jan Voorhoeve in *Pidginization and creolization of languages* ed. Dell Hymes (Cambridge: Cambridge University Press, 1971) pp. 310–13

The lingua franca of Suriname

Sranan (sometimes called Taki-Taki or Negro-English) is the lingua franca of Suriname, the mother tongue of most city and coast dwellers, known as a second language to many who live upriver.

Sranan is important in the study of Creole history because DUTCH, not English, is the standard language of Suriname. Sranan is not continually subject to the normalising influence of a closely related standard, as Jamaican Creole is. Thus to the creole specialist Sranan seems 'conservative', even 'archaic', in comparison with its Caribbean relatives.

The English ruled Suriname for only twenty-six years, from 1651 to 1667. Most of the English planters left soon afterwards, and took many of their slaves with them. Why has an English creole remained the normal, everyday language of the country ever since? For the next two hundred years, Dutch slave-owning society maintained a caste system charged with symbolism. Slaves were not allowed to learn Dutch (or to wear shoes, or to become Christians). The English creole, known to existing slaves, learnt by new arrivals from Africa, was thus necessary to everyone.

At emancipation in 1863 the same symbolism determined policy. Since all were free, all must now use Dutch. Creole (Sranan) was outlawed in education: even the Moravian missionaries, who alone had used it in their mission schools, had to turn to Dutch. The result was a bilingual society in which almost everyone learnt to switch at will from Dutch to Sranan and back. In the 1960s there was a move to raise the status of Sranan, and non-religious literature appeared in it for the first time.

The Bush Negro languages

Sranan is not the only creole of Suriname. Already in the 17th century runaway slaves had set up tribal societies in the river valleys of the interior. The first, probably, were the *Saramaccan* and *Matuari*. Having broken away from the pidgin-creole continuum so early, these two languages are now quite distinct from their relatives. They have tones, like many West African languages; their vocabulary seems almost evenly split between Portuguese and English words, but there is also a strong KONGO element. These are important clues to the nature of the 17th-century Atlantic pidgins.

Historical facts are scarce, but linguistic evidence suggests that the Ndjuka, Paramaccan and Boni (or Aluku) tribes were founded by runaways of a slightly later period, perhaps the early 18th century, when English was closer to replacing Portuguese on Atlantic trade routes. Of these three languages *Ndjuka* (also called Aukaans) is the best known. It has a syllabic writing system related to those of some West African languages – compelling evidence that some of the escaped slaves who formed this tribe had been literate in an African language before their enslavement.

Song and story in Saramaccan

In Saramaccan storytelling, often performed at funerals, songs are interspersed with the prose narrative. Many are at least partly in an obscure poetic language quite different from that of everyday life. Here, in the course of storytelling, a woman character is introduced to the audience:

Agangaai, i sá kíi m. Mhmm.
Agangaai, i sá kíi m. Mhmm.
Di hánse fa a du m te. Mhmm.
A du m te mooi ta yáa sónu. Mhmm.
Agangaai, i sá kíi m. Mhmm.

Agangaai, you could kill me –
Agangaai, you could kill me –
Your beauty does something to me,
It's enough to make the sun come up,
Agangaai, you could kill me!

Richard Price, Sally Price, *Two evenings in Saramaka* (Chicago: University of Chicago Press, 1991) p. 87

African English creoles and pidgins

Liberian English has well over a million speakers. It has also been called Merico, Americo, Brokes, Waterside English and Settler English. Spoken especially in Monrovia and other coastal towns, it was implanted on the creation of this 'homeland' for freed American slaves; it naturally derives from the creole of United States slaves of the 19th century, though it shows signs of strong influence from the local languages of Liberia.

Liberian English is thus distinct from the KRIO of Sierra Leone and from the other English creoles and pidgins of West Africa. These form a sequence along the Guinea coast: they include the old-fashioned 'Krio' used by the Kru fishermen (originating in eastern Liberia) in their work and trade along the West African coast. They also include the West African Pidgin English or Nigerian Pidgin English that is a major lingua franca of Nigeria.

As elsewhere, creole languages are more likely to achieve stability and permanence if no longer in competition with the standard language from which they derive. An example is Fernando Po Creole or 'Porto Talk', which derives from Freetown Krio and West Indian Creole English, brought by immigrants who came to Fernando Po in 1830. It is now conservative, even archaic, and easily distinguished from its neighbours, since Spanish, not English, is the standard language of Fernando Po. A better known example is KAMTOK, now a language of communication in much of Cameroun.

Indian Ocean and Pacific Ocean pidgins

Until recently, the various kinds of pidgin English of the Indian and Pacific Oceans had not developed into stable creoles. There have been many of them: the so-called *Babu English* of northern British India, supposed typical of Indian clerks writing English; the Madras Pidgin or *Butler-English* of the south, English-based but much influenced by Dravidian languages; the famous *China Coast Pidgin*, now perhaps spoken only in Taiwan and on Nauru, surviving till recently in Hong Kong and among old people in Shanghai, once so essential that Chinese tradesmen and servants in some cities could not avoid learning it if they were to deal effectively with non-Chinese, and that manuals were compiled to teach it to 19th-century English-women.

Far more recent, but already lost in history, are the Bamboo English of the Korean War, the Vietnam Pidgin of the Vietnamese War, and the so-called Japanese Pidgin of the 19th century and of the Second World War.

Of more lasting importance than any of these is *Beach-la-mar*, the English pidgin of the 19th-century western Pacific, with its modern descendants: Melanesian Pidgin English, TOK PISIN, BISLAMA and Solomons Pidgin or *Pijin*. Another offshoot was the older Australian Pidgin and the *Kriol* to which some Australian speakers are moving. Hawaiian English, with its 500,000 speakers, is usually considered a creole: it shows the influence of Chinese, Japanese, Hawaiian, Portuguese and various Philippine languages. The language of Pitcairn Island, with its offshoot on Norfolk Island, is an English-based creole with Tahitian elements – the inhabitants are descendants of the mutineers of HMS *Bounty*.

Many of the English creoles and pidgins are on record in travellers' memoirs, old and new. But these records depend on authors' varying linguistic skills. Some, clearly, heard incorrectly, or tried to reconstruct conversations heard long ago and did so inaccurately. Few if any had a clear understanding of the structure of the language they were attempting to write. Naturally, novelists' 'Pidgin English' is to be taken with a pinch of salt. The same goes for novel and film versions of American Indian Pidgin English, a language first recorded in 1641 and now extinct.

ESKIMO-ALEUT LANGUAGES

From Greenland across the Arctic edge of America to eastern Siberia, speakers of Eskimo-Aleut languages have established cultures perfectly adapted to a harsh environment. The languages have no close relatives elsewhere. The family includes the eastern Eskimo language INUIT, the language of western Alaska and St Lawrence Island known as Yupik (18,000 speakers), and a much more distant connection, Aleut.

Eskimo, by way of French *Esquimaux*, is a loanword from an Athabaskan language of North America. The word meant 'stranger'.

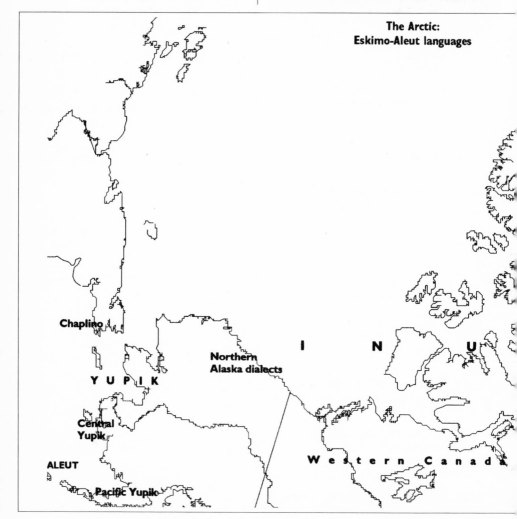

**The Arctic:
Eskimo-Aleut languages**

Chaplino

Northern
Alaska dialects

Y U P I K

Central
Yupik

ALEUT

Pacific Yupik

I   N   U

Western Canada

Aleut is now spoken by only 500 or fewer people in the Aleutian and Pribilof Islands, Alaska (especially at Atka), and perhaps by a few in the Commander Islands, Siberia. In the 19th century, when Alaska was still Russian territory and Aleut speakers were much more numerous, some were literate. Aleut was written in the Cyrillic alphabet with extra characters. This tradition is dead, and the language itself dying, both in Siberia and in Alaska.

Yupik is a group of Eskimo dialects of western Alaska and the eastern tip of Siberia. In Siberia and in St Lawrence Island, Alaska, the majority dialect is Chaplino or Ungazik (1,500 speakers). Schoolbooks, grammars and dictionaries used to be published in Siberia in Chaplino: at first in a phonetic script; after 1936, for political reasons, in Cyrillic. A few texts in Roman script have been issued in St Lawrence Island. On the Alaskan mainland the majority dialect is Central Yupik, which has a tradition of religious and educational publications. Pacific Yupik (sometimes confusingly called Aleut) is spoken by 2,000 or fewer speakers especially at English Bay, Alaska.

In the 18th and 19th centuries Eskimos developed pidgin versions of their languages to help speakers of English, Russian, Danish and NA-DENÉ LANGUAGES to understand them. More recently research on Eskimo-Aleut languages has taken place in Russia, the United States and Canada, and all three governments have presided over a rapid decline in the daily use of these inconveniently international languages of tiny minorities. In Greenland, INUIT has a fuller place in official and everyday life. Even there, the difficult accommodation between Eskimo and 'Western' ways of life results in a gradual reduction in the number of Inuit speakers.

ESTONIAN

1,100,000 SPEAKERS

Estonia

With Finnish, Estonian is one of the twin Balto-Finnic languages divided by the Gulf of Finland. They belong to the wider family of URALIC LANGUAGES.

> The Estonians, *Eesti*, may possibly be the *Aestii* of the Latin writer Tacitus (1st century AD) and are certainly the *Eistneskr* of the Norwegian poet Þjóðólfr's *Ynglingatal* (11th century). The meaning of the word is unknown. Traditionally, Estonians called themselves *maa rahvas*, 'people of the country'.

Estonia was apparently warlike and independent at the end of the first millennium AD. After Danish raids in the 12th century, the country was conquered by German knights in the 13th. Estonia was subject to German landowners – and generally under Swedish or Russian government – till the late 19th century. Thus, while Finnish was influenced by Swedish, Estonian was for many centuries under strong German influence. Estonian bulges with German loanwords – including many from the Low German of the Baltic trading ports (see box at FINNISH).

There are a few medieval records of the language, such as the Estonian personal names in the *Chronicle* of Henry of Livonia. The first known printed book was the bilingual German-Estonian catechism, by S. Wanradt and J. Koell, which appeared (in far-off Wittenberg) in 1535. No complete copy survives. An Estonian grammar was printed in German, for the use of priests, in 1637.

As a serf population, few Estonians received education before the 19th century. The emergence of Estonian as a literary language can be dated by the publication of a language magazine, *Beiträge zur genauern Kenntniss der ehstnischen Sprache*, 'Studies towards better knowledge of the Estonian language' edited 1813–32 by the clergyman Heinrich Rosenplänter – and by the *Ehstnische Litterarische Gesellschaft*, 'Estonian Literary Society' which was founded in Kuressaare in 1817. A sign of the continuing domination of German, even under Russian rule, is that both these institutions had German names. It was only around 1840 that Estonians themselves began to predominate as authors of works in and about their language.

Estonian literature now flourished, notably with F.R. Kreutzwald's *Kalevipoeg* (1857–61), a literary epic emulating the Finnish *Kalevala*. It is based on Estonian prose legends and on the metres of oral lyric poetry: these resources were needed because Kreutzwald found that unfortunately there were no Estonian oral epics to draw on!

Estonia was independent from 1918 to 1940, and has been independent again since the break-up of the Soviet Union. In this century literary Estonian has been almost rebuilt, many loanwords eliminated, and others replaced by dialect words or Finnish loans. The language is now emerging once more from a period of heavy Russian influence.

Standard Estonian is based on the midland dialect of North Estonian, spoken in Tallinn and its hinterland (see map at FINNISH). It has four (some linguists say three) possible lengths for both vowel and consonant sounds. Length variations often change the meaning completely and are difficult for foreign learners to distinguish. The four lengths are not fully marked in normal spelling, but are specially written in these examples: *sadaa* 'hundred', *saaadaa* 'send!', *tahab saaaada* 'want to get'; *kanu* 'of hens', *selle kannu* 'this jug's', *seda kannnu* 'of this jug'. Nouns have 14 cases, and verbs change form to show person, tense, mood and the active/passive opposition.

Examples based on Aimo Turunen, 'The Balto-Finnic languages' in *The Uralic languages: description, history and foreign influences* ed. Denis Sinor (Leiden: Brill, 1988) pp. 58–83

Numerals in Estonian, Finnish and SAMI

	Estonian	Finnish	Sami
1	üks	yksi	åkta
2	kaks	kaksi	guokte
3	kolm	kolme	gålbma
4	neli	neljä	njællje
5	viis	viisi	vitta
6	kuus	kuusi	gutta
7	seitse	seitsemän	čieža
8	kaheksa	kahdeksan	gávci
9	üheksa	yhdeksän	åvci
10	kümme	kymmenen	lågi

The name of Estonia's capital, *Tallinn*, is a reminder of the country's history of foreign domination. Originally it was *Taani linn*, 'Danes' town'.

South Estonian

'In the 17th to 19th centuries South and North Estonian emerged as distinct languages, and there is some printed literature in South Estonian. The New Testament appeared in South Estonian in 1686, in North Estonian only in 1715. Even nowadays, if south Estonian youngsters return from study with a standard (northern) accent, they may be greeted with the rebuke *Kas ma' su tuuperäst kuuli saadi, et sa' mul sääl joba rääkmä nakkat?* "Do you think I sent you to school for you to start *talking*?" '

From Alo Raun, Andres Saareste, *Introduction to Estonian linguistics* (Wiesbaden: Harrassowitz, 1965) p. 82

ETHIOPIC

Classical language of Eritrea and Ethiopia

O ne of the SEMITIC LANGUAGES, Ethiopic is a relative of Arabic and Hebrew, but most closely related to the South Arabian languages and to the modern South Semitic languages of Ethiopia, notably AMHARIC. Ethiopic is the traditional language of the Ethiopian Christian church.

Ethiopic is often called *Ge'ez*, the local term for a letter of the Ethiopic script – and thus for the classical written language of the country.

South Semitic languages have gradually spread southwards across Ethiopia from the Red Sea coastal region. Ethiopic is recorded in stone inscriptions from the 3rd century onwards, linked with the kingdom of Axum in what is now Eritrea. Ever since the conversion of King Ezana in the 4th century, Axum and Ethiopia have been a stronghold of Christianity, though long isolated from the rest of Christendom by the Islamic conquests to the north.

Ethiopic literature began with translations of the Bible and of Christian texts of all kinds: early translations were made from Greek, but many later ones came from Arabic versions, and in many cases the intermediate texts do not survive. So Ethiopic preserves a record of early Arabic Christianity, which has long since been overlaid by Islam. Original writings in Ethiopic include important histories, such as the legendary *Kebra Negast*, 'Glory of the Kings', which tells of the Queen of Sheba's visit to Solomon, and of their child, Menelik, mythical founder of Axum.

As a spoken language Ethiopic gave way to later local standards which developed into modern TIGRINYA, Tigre and Amharic. As an official language, and especially as the language of church worship, Ethiopic has lasted far longer. The classic period of Ethiopic literature was the 13th to 17th centuries. *Weddase Mariam* 'Praise of Mary', a 14th-century poetic collection, accompanies the Psalms in the Ethiopic canon. The law code *Fetha Negast* 'Justice of the Kings' dates to the 17th century.

Ethiopic was still the language of literature, religion and official documents in the 19th century, but Amharic has now invaded all these fields.

The Ethiopic alphabet

The distinctive Ethiopic script was developed from an alphabet used for an early South Arabian language. In this script, which is written from left to right, the original consonant signs are modified in a fixed pattern to indicate one of seven following vowels. Thus, unlike the other writing systems used for Semitic languages, that of Ethiopic represents the sounds of the language fairly fully. The 'first order', shown in the box, is of consonants followed by the vowel ä.

Ethiopic script: the 'first order'

ሀ ለ ሐ መ ሠ ረ ሰ ቀ በ ተ ኀ ነ አ ከ ወ ዐ ዘ ፐ የ ደ ጠ ጸ ፀ ፈ ፐ ጰ

h l ḥ m š r s k' b t ḫ n ʾ k w ä z y d g t' p' c z f p

Ethiopic script: 'h' with the seven vowels

ሀ ሁ ሂ ሃ ሄ ህ ሆ

hä hu hi ha he hə ho

EWE AND FON

4,000,000 SPEAKERS

Togo, Benin, Ghana

Ewe and Fon are the best-known names for one of the Kwa group of NIGER-CONGO LAN-GUAGES. Linguists call it Gbe. Dialects of this language are spoken in south-eastern Ghana – east of Lake Volta – and across southern Togo and Benin to south-western Nigeria.

Tado and Notse in Togo, sites with impressive ancient earthworks, are said to be the ancestral homes of Gbe-speaking peoples, from which they spread southwards and to east and west. They had reached the Atlantic coast, and begun to come into contact with European traders, over five hundred years ago. A Gbe wordlist (the language is called *Mina*) was put together for Portuguese traders in 1480.

Gbe speakers later had no overarching political systems. Their one hundred and twenty small chieftainships were in British, German and French possession at the end of the 19th century.

The form of Gbe spoken on the Togo coast, at Anécho and Lomé, was perhaps already somewhat distinct from those of the hinterland because its population had been built up by 18th-century migrants from southern Ghana. Gbe, in the form of the Gĕ-Anglo dialects of the so-called Slave Coast, became a lingua franca of the inland trading routes as they were developed by the German administration of Togo in the late 19th century. Along the railway line inland from Lomé, Ewe was the usual means of communication, spreading to become the trade language of the major towns Atakpamé and Sokodé. Its expansion westwards towards the Volta valley was promoted in German times by both missionaries and administrators, who actively discouraged trading contacts with the Twi (AKAN) speakers of the British-dominated Gold Coast.

The modern standards

The Anglo dialect of coastal Togo is now the standard form not only for Togo itself but also for the Ewe-speaking districts of Ghana, where – spoken with a local accent – it is used in broadcasting, in churches and in schools. In Togo, too, there is an Ewe press in the Anglo dialect. At home, local dialects continue to be used.

The most widespread dialect of Benin, the one that has become an official and literary language there, is Fŏ. Within this Gŭ is the most used sub-dialect, heard at the capital, Porto Novo, and along the coast into western Nigeria.

Typical of Gbe phonetics are the labiovelar sounds *kp*, *gb*, *ngm* – the unfamiliarity of these sounds explains the wide variation in European attempts to spell Gbe words. The language has four tones and is largely monosyllabic: only compounds and foreign loanwords have more than one syllable. Unusually for African languages, tone in Gbe is 'lexical' only – it distinguishes between words of different meanings, not between different forms of the same word. The suffix *–wo* marks the plural of nouns and is also the third person plural pronoun 'they'. In Gbe, *ètsò* means both 'yesterday' and 'tomorrow' – but the context makes the meaning clear.

Gbe is the local term for 'language'. It was adopted by linguists in 1980 as an overall term because neither 'Ewe' nor 'Fon' was acceptable to all speakers of the language. *Ewe (Ephe* in German writings, *Eve* in French) is the traditional name for the standard form which is closest to *Anglo* and *Gĕ*: its proper local name is *Evegbe*, while the Gĕ dialect is properly called *Gẽgbe* and the Fon dialect *Fõgbe*.

'The Ewe are called *Bubutubi* by the Anglo, *Benigbe* by the Avatime, *Bayikpe* by the Santrokofi, *Manyigbe* by the Akpafu, *Bowli* or *Ayigbe* by the Gã and Dangme. In the west they are called *Hua* by the Akan. The central and eastern Ewe, especially those near the coast, are called *Popo* by the Yoruba and *Ima* by the Kposo. Other names found in older literature are *Eibe, Krepi* and *Krepe*' (Madeline Manoukian, *The Ewe-speaking people of Togoland and the Gold Coast* (London: International African Institute, 1952) p. 10).

The earliest extended text, and the first printed book, in any language of West Africa is a bilingual Spanish–Gbe catechism printed in Madrid in 1658: *Doctrina christiana . . . en nuestra idioma Español y en la lengua Arda*, 'Christian teaching in our Spanish language and in the Arda tongue'. *Arda* is the name of a now-forgotten Gbe-speaking kingdom that then ruled the coast hereabouts.

This milestone in African language history 'was lost for nearly three centuries, partly because the surviving copy was catalogued under "languages of America" . . .' (P.E.H. Hair in *Language and history in Africa* ed. D. Dalby (London: Cass, 1970) p. 53. There is indeed an obscure and now extinct Amerindian language of Peru with the same name *Arda*.

The Gbe dialects

Ewe (or *Vhe*) is the usual name for the western dialect group, spoken in Ghana and Togo. The most important of these, the one from which a written form was developed, is *Anglo* (or Anlo or Awuna), spoken along the coast between the mouth of the Volta and Lomé. *Gẽ* (or Gen or Guin or Gain or Mina) is the name for the Togo group of dialects. *Adja* is the dialect spoken from Natja eastwards. There are about 1,200,000 speakers in Togo and 1,500,000 in Ghana.

Further east, *Fon* (or Fõ or Dahoméen) is the

dialect group from which the standard language used in Benin originated. Local dialects include *Gũ* (or Goun or Egun), spoken in the immediate neighbourhood of Porto Novo, capital of Benin, and the north-eastern dialect *Mahi*. There are 1,000,000 speakers of Fon as a mother tongue; at least half a million more speak it as a second language.

As can be seen from the many alternative spellings, the sounds of this essentially monosyllabic, four-tone language, with its complex initial consonants and its nasal vowels, are difficult at first for western European language speakers to catch.

Numerals in Ewe and Fon		
Ewe		**Fon**
ɖékà	1	ɖòkpó
èvè	2	we
ètɔ̀n	3	àtɔ̀n
ènĕ	4	ɛ̀nɛ̀
àtón	5	àtɔ́n
àdé	6	àyìzɛ́n
àdré	7	tɛnwɛ
ènyí	8	tântɔn
ènyíɖé, àsièkè	9	tɛnnɛ
èwó	10	wŏ

In Fon, '3' and '5' differ only by the tone of the second syllable.

M. Malherbe, *Les langues de l'humanité* (Paris: Laffont, 1995) pp. 829, 855 and other sources

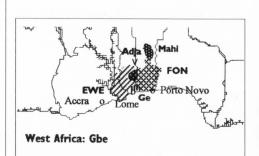

West Africa: Gbe

EWONDO, BULU AND FANG

1,350,000 SPEAKERS

Cameroun, Equatorial Guinea

Ewondo and its relatives are BANTU LANGUAGES spoken in the valleys of western Cameroun, Gabon and Equatorial Guinea. Speakers of early western Bantu languages settled here well over three thousand years ago. This particular group of dialects probably spread to its present inland locations in the 14th and 15th centuries. With colonial political frontiers, several closely related languages emerged as local standards. Speakers of any one can quite easily understand the others.

Together the languages are sometimes called the 'Sanaga-Ntem group' after the rivers that define their territory to north and south. But *Yaoundé* (German spelling *Jaunde*) was the name that the Germans learnt from coast-dwellers for the inland region where they planned to establish their new trading post. Yaoundé has remained the official name of what has now become the capital of independent Cameroun. It is really a 'foreign' version of the name that the people of the district give to themselves and their language, which is *Ewondo*.

Fang is locally known as *Fangwe* or *Mpangwe*. This last form gave rise to the older French name – utterly different at first sight – *Pahouin*.

Bulu, the language of Ntem, Dja and Lobo divisions of South Province, Cameroun, was increasingly important in the early 20th century, when Cameroun was a German colony. The American Presbyterian missionaries in southern Cameroun published a Bible translation and textbooks in the dialect, and used it in their schools: speakers of other local languages found that Bulu was the route to education. Some resisted this development – the Ngumba, for example, who left the Presbyterian church because the missionaries would not use their language. However, some of those whose languages were closest to Bulu, such as the section of the Fang that live in Cameroun, accepted Bulu from its use in school and church as their standard language. For these it is now a mother tongue.

Bulu as a second language has given way before the spread of French and Ewondo.

Ewondo or Yaoundé is the language of the neighbourhood of the capital of Cameroun, Yaoundé, which began its history as the trading post from which the Germans advanced into inland Cameroun. The Ewondo were at hand to be employed as labourers, porters and soldiers. They and their language spread with the growth of the colony: when French replaced German as the language of government in 1918, Ewondo was already familiar to many as a second language throughout southern Cameroun, though not on the coast, where DUALA and KAMTOK were the lingua francas.

A pidgin language with its roots in Bulu and Ewondo has rapidly developed to permit easy communication among migrant workers, rail-waymen and truck drivers in Cameroun. This is known as *Ewondo Populaire, Bulu beDiliva* ('Bulu of the drivers') or – by linguists with a liking for classification – *Pidgin A70*, because

A70 is one way of designating the Ewondo group of Bantu languages. This pidgin began before 1930, when the construction of the railway inland to Yaoundé attracted migrant labour, and it is now much used in market-places and on transport routes throughout the country. It can also be heard in Gabon and Congo (Brazzaville). Ewondo Populaire is still a pidgin or jargon of men's employment, little used by women, children or old people.

Fang, like Bulu and Ewondo, spread in the 19th century, when, with coastward migrations, it became the language of the Gabon and Ogooué estuaries at the time when the Spanish and French interests in the region were first being asserted. Fang had clearly followed the local trade routes that had developed between coast and hinterland, in a region where European colonisation did not immediately follow European trade. Fang was the language of Catholic missions, in contrast with the Presbyterian use of Bulu.

So Fang, earlier spoken in inland southern Cameroun and northern Gabon, is now also the major language of Mbini, the mainland territory of Equatorial Guinea. On independence in 1969 it was abortively named the sole official language of the whole country, temporarily supplanting Spanish, much to the dissatisfaction of inhabitants of the island of Annobon, where Spanish is the language of culture and Fang was little known.

Ewondo, Duala and some relatives: the map

Ewondo, of the Yaoundé region, has 575,000 speakers and is one of the national languages of Cameroun.

Bulu is the major language of South Province, Cameroun, with about 175,000 speakers. *Beti* and *Eton* belong to the same dialect continuum: they are languages of central Cameroun. Ewondo is the language of education and administration here.

Fang and *Ntumu*, with 525,000 speakers, spread towards the coast in the 19th century where Fang is the principal language of Mbini (formerly Rio Muni or Spanish Guinea, a Spanish possession from 1778 to 1969). For speakers in Gabon and Cameroun Ewondo serves as the standard language.

DUALA, a distant relative of the Ewondo-Bulu-Fang group, is the language of the old trading city of Duala, once important regionally but now restricted to Duala and its neighbourhood. It has 80,000 speakers.

The island of Bioko (Fernando Póo), the other half of Equatorial Guinea, has a language of its own, *Bubi* (once spelt *Booby*: 20,000 speakers), representing an extremely early Bantu migration. The British naval base of Clarence, occupied 1827–44, brought rapid migration of West African peoples: as a result an English creole is the main language of coastal regions. On independence from Spain in 1969 there was an unpopular attempt to impose Fang as sole official language.

Numerals in Ewondo, Bulu, Fang and Bubi

	Ewondo	Bulu	Fang	Bubi
1	fóg	fok	fokh; -boré	-de
2	be	-bae	-bè	-ba
3	lá	-lal	-lal	-cha
4	nyie	nyin	-né	-ñe
5	tan	tan	-tan	-chio
6	saman	saman	-samé	lade
7	zamgbál	zangbwal	nžañ gwal	la ba
8	moom	mwôm	oñwam	la cha
9	ebul	ebul	ébul	la am
10	awóm	awôm	awôm	lēño

Information from Jeanne d'Arc Lacoin and others in
M. Malherbe, *Les langues de l'humanité* (Paris: Laffont, 1995)

Noun classes in Bulu

As in other Bantu languages, nouns in Ewondo, Bulu and Fang belong to classes marked by prefixes:

	Singular			Plural	
Class		**Example**	**Class**		**Example**
I	m-ongo	child	VII	b-ongo	children
V	əm-vu	dog		bə-mvu	dogs
	ən-jo	scissors	IX	mə-njo	scissors
III	ə-ci	egg		mə-ci	eggs
II	n-tomba	sheep	VIII	min-tomba	sheep
IV	e-mvang	calabash	X	bi-mbang	calabashes
VI	o-non	bird	XI	a-non	birds

From Yashutoshi Yukawa, 'A tonological study of Bulu verbs' in
Studies in Cameroonian and Zairean languages (Tokyo: ILCAA, 1992) pp. 67–93

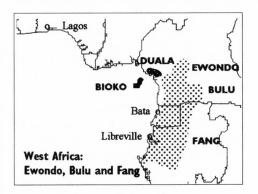

West Africa:
Ewondo, Bulu and Fang

FAROESE

50,000 SPEAKERS

Faroe Islands

Except for a few communities of Celtic monks, Vikings from south-western Norway were the first inhabitants of the Faroe Islands (see map at NORWEGIAN), which they colonised in the 9th and 10th centuries. Faroese is thus a direct descendant of OLD NORSE, and it does still contain a few Celtic words. Like Icelandic, it has undergone very little influence from any other language – except Danish, since the Faroes were long treated as a Danish colony and are still linked politically to Denmark.

The name of the Faroes, *Føroyar*, means 'sheep islands'.

Although there were only about 9,000 Faroese in the 1850s, when the movement for national and linguistic self-assertion began in the islands, it has been far more successful than many similar movements in Europe. It is now the language of the press, of a very small but thriving publishing industry, and of local government and education. Danish is taught as a second language.

For a table of numerals see SWEDISH.

FIJIAN LANGUAGES

350,000 SPEAKERS

Fiji

Fijian is the national language of the Fiji island group. Because of massive Indian migration to the islands in the 19th century under British rule, Fijian is spoken by less than half the population. It is a Polynesian language, belonging to the Oceanic branch of AUSTRONESIAN LANGUAGES.

There is such great dialect variation in Fiji, which was traditionally divided into small chiefdoms, that Fijian is usually considered to be at least two languages. The development of a single literary language is due to early 19th-century missionaries. They arrived by way of Tonga and first learnt their Fijian in the Lau islands, close to Tonga. However, as they prepared to work on the larger islands, they found it best to start from Bau, the most powerful chiefdom at the time. The missionary language, Old High Fijian, used in church and in the Fijian Bible translation, was thus *Bauan* with some residual *Lauan* features. Its style was also noticeably influenced by the missionaries' mother tongue, English.

The long term result is that Bauan became the prestige dialect all over Fiji, and it remains so to this day. It is used in literature and the media, in religion, and very largely in schools. By now most if not all Fijians are able to understand Bauan, even if they cannot speak it. It is also the basis of the Colloquial Fijian that is the everyday speech of town-dwellers.

Tongans ruled much of Fiji in the 19th century: British rule followed in 1874 and lasted until independence in 1970. Fijian has borrowed extensively from both Tongan and English. Western Fijian and other country dialects are now gaining loanwords from Standard Fijian.

The local 'Hindustani' language of mainly BHOJPURI origin, spoken by half the population, has also supplied some loanwords.

> Pidgin Fijian has grown up as the language of markets and village centres, used for daily contact among speakers of Fijian, 'Fijian Hindustani' and Chinese. It is highly simplified: where Bauan has 135 distinct forms of pronouns, Pidgin Fijian has only six.

The first nine numerals in Fijian are: *dua, rua, tolu, vā, lima, ono, vitu, walu, dhiwa*. '10' is *tini* in Eastern Fijian, *chini* in Western Fijian.

Based on Paul Geraghty, 'Eastern Fijian' in *Comparative Austronesian dictionary* ed. Darrell P. Tryon (Berlin: Mouton De Gruyter, 1995–) pt 1 pp. 919–23 and other sources

Languages of Fiji

Eastern Fijian is a group of dialects spoken in Vanua Levu, the eastern half of Viti Levu, and most of the smaller islands. *Bauan*, the dialect of a small island off Viti Levu, is the basis of standard written Fijian.

Western Fijian (50,000 speakers) is a group of dialects of western Viti Levu. Western and Eastern Fijian are not mutually intelligible.

The other major language of Fiji is *Fijian Hindustani* (see BHOJPURI), spoken by the descendants of labourers imported by the British rulers of Fiji in the 19th century. Many still work in the sugar-cane plantations. Most also speak Fijian or Pidgin Fijian. *Chinese, Rotuman* and *English* are also spoken in Fiji by small communities.

Rotuman, related to Fijian, has about 8,500 speakers on the nearby island of Rotuma.

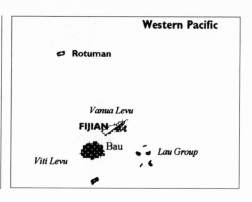

FINNISH

5,000,000 SPEAKERS

Finland, Sweden, Russia

Finnish belongs to the URALIC LANGUAGES and, with Swedish, is one of the two national languages of Finland. It has two close relatives, spoken by much smaller numbers in north-west Russia: Karelian and Veps. Otherwise, the nearest relative of Finnish is Estonian. These two languages, spoken in neighbouring countries on either side of the Gulf of Finland, are almost similar enough to be mutually comprehensible (for a table of numerals see ESTONIAN).

Finn was originally the name for the SAMI or Lapps. The country that was seen as their homeland came to be called *Finnland* by Scandinavians. Its settled inhabitants, in distinction from the nomadic Sami, were then logically named *Finnlendingar* 'Finlanders' in Old Norse – whence the usual modern name *Finnish* for their language. In Finnish itself the country and language are called *Suomi*. This derives from older Swedish *somi* 'mass', a reminder that Swedes once classed Finlanders disparagingly as 'the masses, the plebs'.

In the first millennium BC speakers of proto-Finnic were already settled around the southern Baltic shores – and certainly extended much further east into Russian lands, as surviving Finnish place names show.

Karelian, which may be described as a sequence of eastern Finnish dialects, is actually recorded earlier than Finnish itself (see box). The differences between present-day Finnish and Karelian come largely from their contrasting history. Finnish has been influenced by Sweden, by western Europe and by Protestantism; Karelian by Russian and by the Russian Orthodox Church.

Finnish written literature did not begin to develop till the Reformation, with Michael Agricola's Finnish translation of the New Testament in 1548. As Bishop of Åbo (Finnish *Turku*), Agricola based his written Finnish on the south-western dialect, relatively close to Estonian. A complete Finnish Bible appeared in 1642 at Stockholm.

Meanwhile, long a part of the Kingdom of Sweden, Finland began to lose its linguistic autonomy in the 17th century, under King Gustavus Adolphus. Centralisation led to the dominance of Swedish in public life and culture. Even after the Russian conquest of Finland in 1808, Swedish speakers remained in local control.

Then the nationalist movement began to gain strength. Its most famous exponent was certainly Elias Lönnrot (1802–84). He was Professor of Finnish at Helsingfors (Helsinki) University: much more important, he collected folk songs from Karelia and remoulded them into the most successful 'epic' of the whole Romantic period, the *Kalevala*, a poetic retelling of Finnish mythology. Later written Finnish has gradually incorporated more features of the eastern (Karelian) dialects: the *Kalevala* is essentially in northern Karelian.

Finland asserted its independence at the time of the Russian Revolution in 1917, but its eastern boundary, especially after Russian gains in 1944, left most speakers of Karelian dialects inside the Soviet Union. Finnish speakers in Sweden face discrimination.

Finnish and related languages

Finnish, Estonian and their relatives form the surviving western end of a dialect continuum that once probably stretched, unbroken, across European Russia as far as MARI and MORDVIN territory – an area now long since occupied by Russian speakers. Though crossed frequently by travellers, the Gulf of Finland eventually effected the separation between early Finnish (with Karelian and Veps) and early Estonian (with Livonian and Vote).

Estonian dialects are strongly marked, from the conservatism of the south (separated from the rest by moorland and forest) to the Finnish-like character of the north-east, where only two vowel and consonant lengths are distinguished.

There are two dying languages related to Estonian. In western Latvia lived the *Livonians*: fewer than 200 people now speak this language. In Ingria, to the east, the *Vote* language is now spoken by about ten old people.

Finnish is the majority language of Finland. A very distinct dialect, Tornedal Finnish, has about 75,000 speakers, mainly inhabitants of the Torne valley in Sweden. There are also tens of thousands of Finnish migrants and settlers in central Sweden.

Karelian has about 120,000 speakers. Religious and other texts have been printed in Karelian for two hundred years, but the Soviet attempt to establish a Karelian literary language independent of Finnish was a failure. Russian and Finnish are the usual written languages of Karelia, a self-governing republic within Russia which has a strong Russian majority.

Karelian has several major dialect divisions. To the south, *Olonets* and *Ludian* (or Lydian) are sometimes considered separate languages. So is *Ingrian*, the Karelian dialect spoken until 1944 in 'Ingermanland' to the south of St Petersburg. That was when the Ingrians (*Iz-horas*), numbering 12,000, were deported to labour camps in the Kola Peninsula and Kazakhstan. As a result, Ingrian now has only a few hundred speakers. Even further south lay a community of Karelian speakers whose ances-

tors migrated from the western part of Karelia in 1617, when their homeland was ceded by Russia to Sweden, and settled near Tver, not far from Moscow.

Curiously, this event was repeated in 1944, when a tranche of western Karelia was ceded by Finland to the Soviet Union. This time, all Karelian and Olonets speakers in the district moved en masse to Finland.

Veps is spoken by fewer than 8,000 people living around Lake Onega. In the 1930s there was some publishing of textbooks in Veps, using the Latin alphabet, but nowadays children in these districts are taught in Russian.

Loanwords in Finnish and Estonian

Proto-Finnic, ancestor of Finnish and Estonian, was in contact with Baltic and Germanic languages in the first millennium BC. Baltic loanwords from this period include Finnish *meri* 'sea', *herne* 'pea', *lohi* 'salmon', *tuhat* 'thousand'. Germanic loanwords include *raha* 'money' (originally 'squirrel skin'), *leipä* 'bread' (cf. English *loaf*), *tunkio* 'dung heap' (cf. English *dung*).

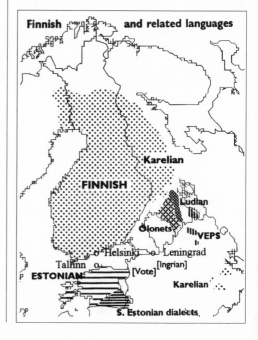

Finnish and related languages

Around 500 AD speakers of Slavonic languages, spreading north-eastwards, were in touch with early Finnish and Estonian for the first time. Some later Slavonic loanwords demonstrate the introduction of Christianity to Finland by missionaries from Russia. They include Finnish *pappi* 'priest', *raamattu* 'book' – and Estonian *roosk* 'whip', *turg* 'market'.

Swedish and German domination gave rise to a large number of recent loanwords in Estonian, such as *värdjas* 'bastard', *piibel* 'Bible', *pööbel* 'mob'.

Kalevala and its children

Kalevala is the name of the legendary country where the mythological tales unfold. Lönnrot's long poem is full of brief magic charms, spells and lyric songs – sometimes disrupting the flow of the story – but perhaps its most valuable component, for they are wholly authentic records of the oral poetry of Karelia and Finland.

Ohrasta oluen synty,	The origin of beer is barley,
humalasta julkijuomen,	Of the high drink the hop plant,
vaikk' ei tuo ve'että synny,	Though it is not made without water
eikä tuimatta tuletta.	And a good hot fire.
Humala, Remusen poika,	Hop, son of Remunen,
piennä maahan pistettihin,	Was put into the ground when small,
kyynä maahan kynettihin,	Was ploughed into the ground like a snake,
viholaisna viskottihin . . .	Was tossed away like a nettle . . .

'The origin of beer': *Kalevala* 20, lines 139–46.

The success of *Kalevala* found echoes in English literature. Several translators tried successively to recreate its simple but haunting rhythm and insistent parallelism. Then the same rhythm was used in a new romantic 'epic' that achieved vast sales – Longfellow's *Hiawatha*. Longfellow's verse form and style were inspired by a German translation of *Kalevala* by his friend Ferdinand Freiligrath, though the story of Hiawatha is based on folk literature of the Ojibwa as retold by H. R. Schoolcraft in *Algic researches* (1839).

FORMOSAN LANGUAGES

PERHAPS 200,000 SPEAKERS

Taiwan

Three separate groups of AUSTRONESIAN LANGUAGES are spoken in the inland regions of Taiwan. The long separate linguistic development of each group makes them coordinate with the huge Malayo-Polynesian group to which belong all the remaining thousand Austronesian languages, with their 270,000,000 speakers, extending from Malagasy to New Zealand and Easter Island. These fascinating 'aboriginal' languages have apparently been spoken in Taiwan for at least six thousand years, and it must be from here that the first major Austronesian migration embarked on its southward route to the Batan islands and the Philippines.

The island was called *Formosa*, 'beautiful', by the first Portuguese mariners who reached it, in 1498. Now outdated as a place name, this word still serves to identify the language group.

Chinese speakers began to settle in the lowlands of Taiwan in the early 17th century. But the fate of the Formosan languages was sealed when Taiwan became the haven of the ousted Nationalist government of China. This brought an alien, top-heavy national bureaucracy to Taipei, previously a rather isolated provincial capital. It also brought settlers from the mainland, rapid commercial development and a large international presence. Chinese, already the language of the elite, is spoken by an ever-increasing majority: it is the language that brings success and prosperity in the capital, Taipei, which lies all too near the remaining districts of 'aboriginal' speech. There were once twenty-five Formosan languages, but several have already become extinct.

The first studies of Formosan languages were made during a brief period of Dutch rule in the mid 17th century. The island belonged to Japan from 1895 to 1945 and some Japanese research took place then. More recently, research on these languages has been supported by Taipei's Academia Sinica. Politically, they have no status.

They are utterly different from Chinese and very far removed from the minority languages of mainland southern China. The typical word in the Formosan languages has more than one syllable, and there are no tones. Word stress falls on the last syllable in Atayal, on the last-but-one in Paiwan.

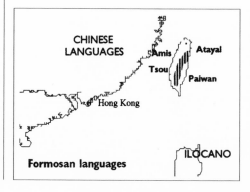

Formosan languages

The Formosan languages

Amis (136,000 speakers, in the plains along the railway from Hualien to Taitung) and *Paiwan* (53,000, in the southern and south-eastern mountains) are classified in the Paiwanic group.

Atayal or Tayal (41,000 speakers, in the northern mountains) is the best-known member of the Atayalic group.

The Tsouic language group is closer to extinction. *Tsou* itself has about 4,000 speakers on the western slopes of Mount Yu in south central Taiwan.

Numerals in Atayal and Paiwan		
Atayal		**Paiwan**
qun	1	ita
rusha'	2	ḍusa
tū'	3	cəḷu
shupat	4	səpac
tima'	5	ḷima
matū'	6	unəm
pitu'	7	picu
pat	8	aḷu
qishu'	9	siva
pugh	10	ta-puḷuq

Comparative Austronesian dictionary ed. Darrell P. Tryon, (Berlin: Mouton De Gruyter, 1995)

FRENCH

70,000,000 SPEAKERS

France, Belgium, Canada, Switzerland, Italy, United States and many other countries

French is the most northerly of the ROMANCE LANGUAGES that descend from Latin, the language of the Roman Empire. Historically it is the language of northern France: it became France's national language, and spread to many other parts of the world with French conquest and trade.

> In Roman times the part of Europe in which French is now spoken was called *Gallia*, 'Gaul'. When the empire succumbed to 'barbarian' conquerors most of Gaul became the kingdom of the *Franci*, 'Franks'; they soon forgot their Germanic language, but the name of their kingdom survived as *France*. Its national language is therefore *Français* or *French*.

The Celtic-speaking inhabitants of Gaul were among the first non-Italians to take a full part in the culture of the Roman Empire. Not surprisingly, there are Celtic loanwords in Latin and in all the Romance languages. But there are more of them in French: they include *chemise* 'shirt'. The language of the Franks, which was close to Old High German, also contributed loanwords to French, including *fauteuil* 'armchair', originally **faldistôl* 'folding stool', an item of army equipment; *rôtir* 'roast', a cooking method more familiar to the invaders than to the Roman Empire; *houx* 'holly'; *marais* 'marsh'.

For reasons which have not been fully worked out – but must be linked with the speech patterns of Celtic and Frankish speakers – early French underwent a process of more rapid change than did the other Romance languages of the period. The final result is that French now looks and sounds far more different from Latin than do other modern Romance languages such as Spanish, Italian and Romanian.

As in the rest of western Europe, Latin remained in use as a written language while everyday speech continued to develop. The earliest clear evidence of a new language in the making in northern France is in the Strasbourg Oaths of 842 (see box at ROMANCE LANGUAGES), because the words of the agreement were faithfully recorded, in French and German, in Nithard's Latin history.

There are a few documents and religious texts in French of the 10th and 11th centuries, but the first real flowering of French literature is in epics, the first and greatest being the *Chanson de Roland* 'Song of Roland' of around 1200. They were recorded in manuscript form for oral recitation. From this beginning, French poetry soon became more varied and more consciously literary.

Although the language of Paris and of the neighbouring royal monastery of Saint-Denis was already influential, medieval French texts have varied dialect links. This is natural since Paris was not the only major centre of French cultural life. After the Norman conquest in 1066, London was another: for nearly two centuries after that date not English but the Anglo-Norman variety of French was the usual language of literature in England (alongside Latin). The oldest and best manuscript of the *Chanson de Roland* is Anglo-Norman.

As the connections between England and France grew more distant, Anglo-Norman – instead of developing into a new modern Romance language – regressed to a jargon of lawyers and courtiers. Its descendant, 'Law French', can still be found in fossilised phrases in modern English legal terminology. But English, now revived as a language of culture and literature, had taken in a mass of loanwords from French, involving most aspects of everyday life, often providing near-synonyms to Germanic words: thus while English still uses Germanic terms such as *ox*, *sheep*, *pig* for the domesticated animals, it uses the French loanwords *beef*, *mutton*, *pork* (modern French *boeuf* 'ox', *mouton* 'sheep', *porc* 'pig') for their meat.

Meanwhile Paris was asserting its position at the centre of French culture. The central role of French, the French of Paris, followed from this. Two landmarks are the foundation of the University of Paris, chartered in 1231; the spread of printing, at the end of the 15th century; and the *Ordonnance de Villers-Cotteret*, 1539, which ruled that legal proceedings in France must be *en langaige maternel françois*, 'in the French mother tongue'. In practice, this asserted the uniquely privileged status of French not only against Latin but also against OCCITAN, BRETON, BASQUE and the local dialects or *patois* of French.

Yet French does borrow from its regional languages: *bijou* 'jewel' is a Breton loanword, while *bouillabaisse* 'fish soup' is one of many food words borrowed from Occitan dialects.

By the 16th century, French was the language of an astonishingly rich literature – and writings in French were read, admired, translated and imitated across all of western Europe. Among the greatest of older classics had been the poetic *Romance of the Rose* (adapted in English by Chaucer), the Arthurian romance sequence *Lancelot* (the main source for Malory's English *Morte Darthure*) and the vivid chronicles of the Hundred Years War written – in French that was influenced by his native Picard dialect – by Jean Froissart. The 16th century was a period of exciting and varied experiment, and also of much linguistic borrowing from Latin and from Italian.

A reaction followed, often identified with the influence of François de Malherbe (1555–1628). Written French became a rule-bound language, with an artificially restricted vocabulary. In spite of the Enlightenment (French was the language of the great *Encyclopédie* of Diderot and others), in spite of the French Revolution and all that has followed, in many ways written French is still rule-bound. Spelling and usage are overseen by the Académie Française, a self-elected college of eminent authors and intellectuals, under government patronage. Standard French differs rather widely from most people's everyday speech. Traditional French verse, which some still write, demands a special pronunciation (see box). For all this, French remains the language of a very rich and flourishing literary culture, in some ways the most vital in Europe.

Counting in French

Une, deux, trois,	One, two, three,
J'irai dans les bois –	I'll go to the woods –
Quatre, cinq, six,	Four, five, six,
Cueillir des cerises –	To pick cherries –
Sept, huit, neuf,	Seven, eight, nine,
Dans un panier neuf:	In a new basket:
Dix, onze, douze,	Ten, eleven, twelve,
Elles seront	
toutes rouges!	They will all be red!

This traditional children's song has a regular 3-syllable/5-syllable rhythm – only if one does not count the 'mute' *es*. Thus it breaks the basic rule of written French poetry. In reciting literary French poems, the final *es* must be sounded.

Europe: French

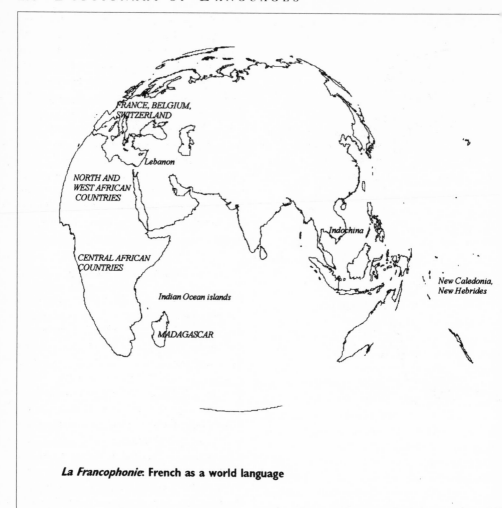

FRANCE, BELGIUM, SWITZERLAND

Lebanon

NORTH AND WEST AFRICAN COUNTRIES

CENTRAL AFRICAN COUNTRIES

Indian Ocean islands

MADAGASCAR

Indochina

New Caledonia, New Hebrides

La Francophonie: French as a world language

Unchallenged as the national language of France, French is also one of the major languages of the world. Until recently its status as the worldwide language of diplomacy was unrivalled: in practice this role has now been taken over by English. For most children of the former French Empire it is the national language, used in school from an early age; for many other children across the world it is the first foreign language that they learn, but, once more, this role is more and more taken by English.

The cultural role of French as a foreign language has a long history. William the Conqueror found that Edward the Confessor's court, in London in 1051, spoke French. Franco-Italian, the literary French of northern Italy, goes back at least to the 13th century. In this distinctive form of French were written not only a major variant of the *Chanson de Roland* but also the record of Marco Polo's travels (known as *Il Milione*).

Much later the Venetian adventurer Giacomo Casanova (1725–98) chose French as the language for his memoirs. This was far from unusual: in the 17th and 18th centuries French was the first language of culture in many European courts. Frederick the Great of Prussia, tutored by Voltaire, wrote a history of German literature in French. French was the favoured language of the 18th- and 19th-century Russian court; in the 19th and early 20th centuries French was cultivated

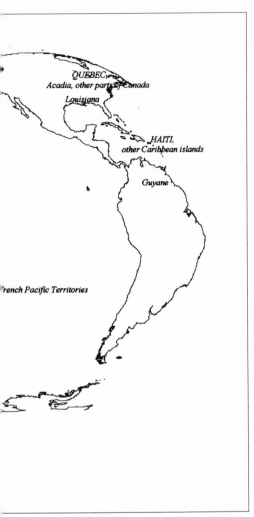

QUEBEC,
Acadia, other parts of Canada
Louisiana

HAITI,
other Caribbean islands

Guyane

French Pacific Territories

original borrowing took place. *Eventuellement* must be translated not 'eventually' but 'possibly'; *sensible* not 'sensible' but 'sensitive'; *librairie* not 'library' but 'bookshop'. Even recent English loanwords emerge as false friends: *slip* is not 'slip' but 'panties, knickers'; *parking* is 'parking lot, car park'.

French spelling differs almost as wildly from the real pronunciation of the language as does that of English. This is a legacy of the printers and scholars of the 16th century, who – instead of adapting spelling to changing speech habits, as earlier writers had done – tried to embody the origins and history of words in their spellings.

French and its dialects

France still has over a million native inhabitants whose mother tongue is not French: the significant minority languages are Basque, Breton and the Alsatian dialect of German. In this context no figure can be given for the Occitan-speaking minority, because Occitan is popularly felt to be a French patois and very few parents will now encourage their children to speak it.

Across the borders of France, French is also one of the official languages of Belgium, Luxembourg and Switzerland. French is particularly vigorous as a language of culture and literature in southern Belgium. It is the everyday language of the Belgian capital, Brussels, which is now also the de facto capital of the European Union. French is naturally one of the working languages of the Union.

The Channel Islands, once part of the Duchy of Normandy, became English possessions around 1200. Yet *Les Îles Normandes* (as they are known in France) were still largely French-speaking at the beginning of the 20th century.

After eight hundred years of political separation, the French of Jersey and Guernsey (now spoken only by older people in country districts) is rather different from the dialects of modern Normandy, and still more different from standard French.

Each island has its own constitution. Guernsey

enthusiastically by courts and intellectuals in the new states of eastern Europe. Practically all European languages have numerous French loanwords for items of culture and fashion.

The difficulty for English speakers in learning French comes at the beginning, with the pronunciation and the spelling. French vocabulary seems familiar to English learners because, although the languages are only distantly related, English has borrowed a great number of words from French and both languages have borrowed freely from Latin. But there are 'false friends', words that look the same but mean something different, usually because their meaning has changed in one or both languages after the

has its *Douzaines*, 'parish councils', and Sark has its *Greffier* or Registrar. The local Protestant tradition is signalled by the word for 'church', *église* in mainland French, *temple* in the Islands.

French outside Europe

With the explorations and conquests of the last few centuries French has spread far across the world. The ugly but necessary word *Francophonie* designates the world community of French-speaking countries.

French is one of the two official languages of Canada. The French-speaking community there, centred on Quebec, feels (and is) threatened by the attractions of the English-speaking culture of North America: the province of Quebec legislates incessantly to give the advantage to French. Parisian French is official, but there is a local colloquial standard and also local dialects, which show special affinity with the Normandy dialect, since the majority of migrants to Canada came from Normandy and northern France.

There is also an old-established French minority in *Acadie*, a district of New Brunswick. Many Acadians migrated to the French colony of Louisiana in the late 18th century, and they now form the main French-speaking minority in the United States. Their dialect is *Cajun*. Also in Louisiana a FRENCH CREOLE is spoken, a result of migration from the Creole-speaking islands of the Caribbean.

Elsewhere French is the standard language of French colonies and conquests, both those which remain under French rule (known as the *DOM-TOM*, *Départements et Territoires d'Outre-Mer*) and those which have become independent. Naturally, local colloquials become established, influenced by the various local languages of these countries: for example, the French of Guinea has a sound pattern clearly related to that of WOLOF.

> ## The 'Servants' French' of Vietnam
>
> *Tây Bôi*, 'boys' French', was a pidgin spoken in Vietnam under French rule from about 1860. French words were cut down to fit Vietnamese sound patterns: the coin *piastre* became *bi-at*, while *ordre* 'order' became *ot*. (One sees why the French used to call the Vietnamese *mangeurs de syllabes*, 'syllable-eaters'.) Vietnamese classifiers accompanied French nouns, *trai coco* 'coconut fruit'. Numbers were reorganized: eleven was *dit-ong*, derived from French *dix-un* 'ten-one'. The French departed in 1947 and *Tây Bôi* was already almost forgotten by 1960, when an American army pidgin was beginning to take its place.
>
> After John E. Reinecke in *Pidginization and creolization of languages* ed. Dell Hymes (Cambridge: Cambridge University Press, 1971) pp. 47–56

Pidgin forms of French developed in contacts between Europeans and Indians in Quebec and Louisiana in the 17th and 18th centuries: two survivals are *Mitchif* (see CREE) and *Métis French* of the Canadian West, both of which became the language of mixed French-Amerindian communities. In Africa, *Petit Mauresque* 'Little Moorish' was a pidginised French that seems to have emerged from the old Lingua Franca (see box at ROMANCE LANGUAGES) eventually to merge into the local colloquial French. *Petit-Nègre* 'Little Negro' was a similar temporary development in West Africa, especially Ivory Coast. Both were most used in and around the French Army. More important than these pidgins are the FRENCH CREOLES dealt with in the next article, for these serve as mother tongues for many millions of people and some of them have reached official status.

FRENCH CREOLES

SEVERAL MILLION SPEAKERS

A s FRENCH was used across the world in trade and empire, a group of creole languages developed from it, mainly used by mixed communities arising from intermarriage and slavery.

For the origin of the name *Creole* see ENGLISH CREOLES AND PIDGINS. In the Caribbean, everyday Creole may be called *kreòl rèk* 'crinkly Creole' or *gwo kreòl* 'fat Creole'. Elevated Creole, closer to French, may be called *kreòl swa* 'silky Creole' or *kreòl fen* 'thin Creole'.

While some creoles struggle for any form of recognition, others have become official languages, like SEYCHELLOIS. HAITIEN is so universally used in Haiti that its status is no longer threatened by French. The varying status of creoles has much to do with local history and attitudes.

In Martinique and Guadeloupe, where schooling and administration are in French, self-conscious attempts to make the Creole a literary language have failed. Yet Creole does appear in everyday writing more and more – in advertisements, in several very popular comic strips – and Creole is the language of local popular music. In Dominica (French 1632–1732, 1778–83, British at other periods, now independent), English is the formal language. There is a strong movement to give some recognition to the Creole, with an annual *Jounen Kwéyòl* (Creole Day).

The first ten numerals in the Creole of Guadeloupe are: *an, dé, twa, kat, sen, sis, sèt, uit, nèf, dis*.

French creoles: the Caribbean and Indian Ocean groups

French creoles are classified by linguists into *New World Creoles* and *Isle de France Creoles* – the latter group named after an insignificant island in the Indian Ocean.

Major New World Creoles include HAITIEN, French Guyanese (50,000 speakers) and the well-known *Louisiana Creole* (40,000 speakers), sometimes called Gumbo. The gift of Louisiana Creole to world children's literature is Brer Rabbit. These traditional tales were told in the 19th century and appeared in print, in Creole, in local newspapers from about 1875 onwards.

The subgroup of Lesser Antillean Creoles (*Antillais* or *Kwéyòl* or *Patwa*) has at least 1,000,000 speakers. It includes the creoles of Martinique and Guadeloupe, which are French départements, and those of St Lucia, Dominica, Désirade, Marie Galante, St Martin, Les Saintes and St Barthélemy. San Miguel Creole, now spoken in Panama, originates from St Lucia and belongs to this subgroup.

Isle de France Creoles include Réunion Creole or *Réunionnais* (once called Bourbonnais:

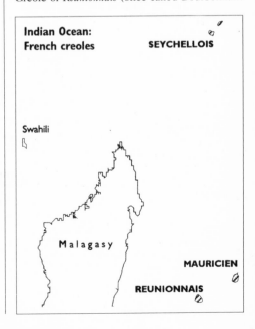

Indian Ocean: French creoles

SEYCHELLOIS

Swahili

Malagasy

MAURICIEN

REUNIONNAIS

550,000 speakers), *Mauricien* (600,000 speakers) and SEYCHELLOIS. Mauricien and Réunionnais are also used as trade languages on the Malagasy coast and in the Comoro Islands. Réunion is a French département; Mauritius and the Seychelles, formerly under British rule, are now independent states.

Brer Rabbit: smartened up?

Frère Lapin stories are still told in Louisiana Creole, but the language now shows heavy English influence:

> Lapẽ mõjé tu lafer. Lapẽ smart!
>
> Rabbit eats the whole lot. Rabbit's smart!

Creole in Mauritian politics

The linguist Peter Stein arrived in Mauritius on 3 February 1975, the day on which MBC broadcast its first-ever programme in Creole: a political debate on the American takeover of Diego Garcia. He switched on his tape recorder just in time. Anerood Jugnauth, party leader of the Mouvement Militant Mauricien, was speaking:

> . . . Sa mem ase pu fer nu fremir: Amerikẽ ule fer en baz militer lor Dyego Garsya; zot ule ãpil ban bom atomik laba.

That itself is enough to make us tremble:
> the Americans want to make a military base on Diego Garcia; they want to fetch in some atomic bombs down there.

> After Peter Stein in *Les créoles français entre l'oral et l'écrit* ed. Ralph Ludwig (Tübingen: Narr, 1989) pp. 217–18

Jugnauth's name – and his effective oratory – are a reminder of the quadrilingual nature of Mauritian society. It is an Indian name, deriving from the Hindu god Jagannātha, but the spelling is 19th-century English: compare the English word *juggernaut*, which has exactly the same origin.

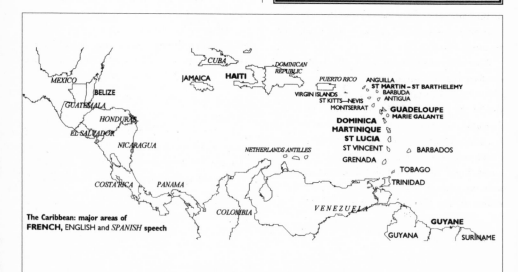

The Caribbean: major areas of FRENCH, ENGLISH and *SPANISH* speech

FRISIAN

750,000 SPEAKERS

Netherlands, Germany

One of the GERMANIC LANGUAGES, Frisian is a regional language of the province of Friesland in the Netherlands, spoken by about 5 per cent of the whole population of the country. It is also spoken by scattered and shrinking communities along the north German coast (see map and table of numerals at DUTCH).

> The Germanic tribe *Frisii* are recorded by a 1st-century Latin source as already settled north-east of the mouth of the Rhine. The language is now known to its speakers as *Frysk*.

It is no coincidence that Frisian is the closest relative of English: it was from this coast that the 'Angles, Saxons and Jutes' of traditional history set out in the 5th century. Frisian was evidently the language of the coast dwellers and seamen in those times, and easily became the lingua franca of the miscellaneous population that crossed from here to take army service – and eventually to settle – in Britain.

This is reconstruction, but it is supported by the fact that for three centuries after the migration Frisian certainly was a crucial language of the North Sea and Baltic seaborne trade. The Frisians' commercial centre was Dorestad, near Utrecht. Their power was destroyed by the Franks and the Vikings. Frisia remained a fairly autonomous but gradually shrinking political unit, extending from northern Holland to the mouth of the Weser, until the early 16th cen-tury, since when the western half of it has been more and more closely linked with the Netherlands.

'Old Frisian' was regularly used administratively until about 1500: it was then supplanted for most purposes by Dutch and German. But West Frisian, the dialect of Friesland, has been a literary language since the 17th-century writings of Gysbert Japicx, and has a small but flourishing publishing industry today.

Most speakers of West Frisian nowadays are bilingual in Dutch. True Frisian is a language of the small towns and villages of Friesland: in Leeuwarden and other large towns *Town Frisian*, a mixture of Frisian and Dutch, is the everyday speech.

The Frisian dialects of Germany are unlikely to survive long. All are heavily influenced by the surrounding Low German dialects and by Standard (High) German. North Frisian also shows the influence of Danish and English, a reminiscence of the English occupation of Helgoland, which contributed such friendly terms as *blakhol* 'prison cell' and *laisen* 'boat licence'.

> *Bread, butter and green cheese / Is good English and good Friese*, says the proverbial rhyme, a reminder that Frisian is closer to English than any other language of Europe. Nowadays, though spelling sometimes looks different, pronunciation is still close: Frisian *ikker*, English *acre*; Frisian *sliepe*, English *sleep*.

FULANI

PERHAPS 15,000,000 SPEAKERS IN THE COUNTRIES OF WEST AFRICA

Historically the Fulani have been a migrant, pastoral people. With their migrations the Fulani language, one of the Atlantic group of NIGER-CONGO LANGUAGES, has spread widely across the Western Sudan, the inland plains of West Africa. It is now a national language in Guinea, Niger and Mali and important regionally in several other countries (see map at DIOLA).

Ful, Fula, Fulani are English forms, based on the Hausa name for the speakers of this language, *Filani*. In Kanuri they are called *Felata*, in Mōōre the term is *Silmiigá*. *Peul* and *Toucouleur* are the usual French names.

Speakers in Senegal call their language *Pulaar*, in Guinea *Pulle*, and in areas further east *Fulfulde*. They call themselves *Pullo* (singular), *Fulɓe* (plural).

Some Fulani words are noted by Arabic authors who had travelled in the Western Sudan in the 12th to 14th centuries. European records of the language date from the 17th century.

Fulani was (and is) the language of a pastoral people who gradually spread eastwards over these centuries across inland West Africa, from a starting point in lower Senegal. By the 16th century they were at Macina and the middle Niger.

At the beginning of the 19th century the Fulani Osman dan Fodio founded an empire among the Islamic peoples of what is now northern Nigeria. His follower Adama, who came from the plateaus to the east, was sent by Osman back to his own lands to stir up the Fulani of the region, to spread Islam and to extend the boundaries of the empire. The Adamawa plateau of eastern Nigeria and northern Cameroun is now named after him.

Adama was so successful that, in the area of the emirate that he established, Fulani are still the dominant group. They encouraged the growth of Islam among the peoples of the plateau, and their language became more and more widely used as lingua franca among them. There is also a pidgin version of it, *Kambariire*. This name comes from the Hausa *kambari* 'a Muslim living among non-believers'.

Thus Fulani speakers are now to be found all over West Africa, from the Gambia to Cameroun. They are not in a majority anywhere, but countries in which there are significant minorities include Senegal, the Gambia, Guinea, Mauritania, Mali, Sierra Leone, Liberia, Ivory Coast, Ghana, Burkina Faso, Niger, Benin, Togo, Nigeria, Chad, Sudan and Cameroun.

A literary form of Fulani, used in the oral recitation of texts, has special grammatical features and can serve as a 'secret language'. There are also pidginised forms of Fulani spoken by those who use it as a trade language.

Linguists once doubted the relationships of Fulani, partly because of the distinctive appearance of typical Fulani speakers. Meinhof, in the 19th century, classed it as a Hamitic (AFRO-ASIATIC) language. Its link with the languages now classed as the Atlantic group within Niger-Congo was first stated by the French linguist Faidherbe in 1875 – yet it is possible to read, even in books published in the 1990s, that Fulani 'originated in Egypt'.

Printed literature in Fulani was slow to develop, though missionaries produced Bible translations and Christian books in the dialects of Adamawa, Macina and Futa Djallon.

A remarkable feature of Fulani is initial consonant alternation. Related words have varying initial consonants, in a complex but regular pattern, depending on their grammatical status: thus *jeso* 'face', *gese* 'faces', *ngesa* 'big face'. Noun classes, as in other Niger-Congo languages of

West Africa, are marked by suffixes, which are different for singular and plural. The two factors combine to make plural forms very different from singular forms for many nouns: *gorko* 'husband', *wor ɓe* 'husbands'; *linngu* 'fish', *liddi* 'fishes'.

Fulani has borrowed from Arabic and, more recently, from French and English: *nuuru* 'light' from Arabic *nur; galaas* 'ice' from French *glace; teebur* 'table' from English. For a table of numerals see WOLOF.

The Fulani alphabet

a e i o u b ɓ mb c d ɗ nd f g ng h j nj k l m n ŋ ny p q r s t w x y ỹ z

---

Writing in Fulani

Fulani is most often written in a variant of the Latin alphabet. But the usual alphabetical order is quite specific to Fulani: the vowels come first, and nasalised consonants follow immediately after corresponding non-nasalised consonants. ɓ and ɗ are 'explosives'; ŋ is a velar nasal, like English *ng* in *singing*, and it is sometimes written

ng. Long vowels are written doubled.

This script derives from the 'Africa alphabet' once championed by the International African Institute in London, now taken up by Unesco. The problem with it has always been that special equipment or software is needed to type or print it. None of the many fonts used in this book contains the curled y which is the last-but-one letter of this Fulani alphabet.

GÃ

1,000,000 SPEAKERS

Ghana

Gã and Dangme are two closely related NIGER-CONGO LANGUAGES spoken in the south-eastern corner of Ghana. *Gã*, variant of *Nkrã*, is the name of the city now better known in its Europeanised form *Accra*.

According to local tradition Gã speakers brought their language southwards to the coastal towns of what is now eastern Ghana in a series of migrations down the Volta valley in the 16th and 17th centuries. The towns were traditionally small independent units: the Gã state was a British colonial creation.

A grammar of *Acraisk* or Gã, by C. Protten, was published in Danish in 1764, reminder of former Danish interests on the West African coast. Gã came to greater prominence when German missionaries began to work on the Danish Gold Coast in 1826. From then onwards, under Danish, British and independent governments, Gã has been a language of education and religion. Its special importance nowadays comes from the fact that it is the local language of Accra, the capital, and of a compact district immediately surrounding the city. For the majority of inhabitants of this district it is either a first or a second language, necessary at Accra markets.

Dangme or Adangme is a group of dialects closely related to Gã and spoken to the east and north-east. Until a few years ago, Gã was the standard language used in education and written contexts in both areas – and so most people there are bilingual in Gã – but a standard written form of Dangme has now been established.

Gã has two tones, Dangme three. Gã has borrowed heavily from Akan and will no doubt continue to do so: thus its vocabulary, in such details as the names of foodstuffs, is quite distinct from that of the Dangme dialects, which show less external influence.

The first ten numerals are: *eko, enyõ, etē, e'fe, enũo, ekpa, kpawo, kponyõ, nehũ, nyongmã*.

Gã and Dangme on the map

The *Gã* towns are Accra, Osu, Labadi, Teshi, Nungwa and Temma. Accra itself is in origin a federation of seven quarters, three of which once formed Jamestown or 'English Accra', the other four 'Dutch Accra'. There is a distinct pidginised form of Gã used by non-native speakers as a lingua franca in the streets and markets of the city.

The six dialects of *Dangme*, as usually counted, correspond to traditional political units. The inland dialects are Shai, Krobo and Osudoku. The coastal ones, from west to east, are Kpone (where speakers now use Gã or are bilingual in it), Prampram (close to Gã), Ningo and Ada (the last strongly influenced by EWE).

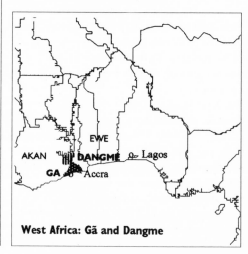

West Africa: Gã and Dangme

GAELIC

80,000 SPEAKERS

Scotland

Scottish Gaelic, one of the *q*-CELTIC LANGUAGES (see map there) and historically an offshoot of Irish, spread into western Scotland from the 4th century onwards. There was heavy migration across the narrow straits that separate Ulster from Galloway, and settlement spreading from south-western Scotland over land that had formerly belonged to the Picts and the Vikings. The even heavier influx of English speakers, which began a few centuries later, has in turn almost overwhelmed Gaelic, which is now commonly spoken only in some of the western islands and the most isolated parts of the western Highlands. It was never the language of the whole of Scotland.

Gaelic is known to its own speakers as *Gàidhlig; Hielans*, the 'language of the Highlands', is a term that has been used in Scots.

Celtic Christianity reached Iona with Columba's arrival from Derry in 563 and spread across Scotland and beyond. The Gaelic-speaking realm of the west gradually absorbed the old Pictish kingdom, the British kingdom of Strathclyde (which spoke a variant of Welsh), and part of Northumbria, by the 11th century, but Gaelic was never widely spoken over this large territory. Norman French was adopted, as in England, as the court language, while the Scots variety of English gradually spread north-westwards in everyday speech.

By the 17th century Gaelic had retreated to the Highlands and the Hebrides, where it had meanwhile absorbed the remaining Scandinavian-speaking territory: Norse rule in the Hebrides had ended in 1266. Independent Gaelic culture was gradually undermined by central government: *bards*, the itinerant poets and story-

tellers, were outlawed. The voluntary Gaelic schools of the early 19th century were replaced by English-speaking state schools after 1872.

In the first centuries of publishing, Irish was regarded as the literary standard for Gaelic: the Liturgy of 1567 and the Bible of 1690 are both essentially in Irish. Gaelic literacy is at its strongest now in northern Skye, Lewis, Harris and North Uist, where a Calvinist religious tradition encourages home worship and Bible study. The language is also spoken in Tiree, Mull, the remainder of Skye and parts of the western Highlands. These districts are the *Gàidhealtachd*, corresponding to the *Gaeltacht* of western Ireland. There is now some bilingual primary education in these areas. Practically all speakers of Gaelic are bilingual in English.

Comhairle nan Eilean, the Western Isles Island Area Council, created in 1975, has a bilingual policy, using both Gaelic and English in its activities and on public signs. There is broadcasting in Gaelic, but there has never been a generally accepted standard spoken dialect, and listeners tend to dislike hearing dialects that are not their own.

There are small communities of Gaelic speakers in Glasgow, Edinburgh, London and in the Canadian province of Nova Scotia. It was in Cape Breton Island, Nova Scotia, that the first all-Gaelic newspaper was published: *Mac Talla* 'The Echo' ran from 1892 to 1904.

Little is known of the language of the *Picti* 'painted people' who were the Romans' main opponents across the Imperial boundary that was marked by Hadrian's Wall. Some scholars believe that this early language of Scotland will have belonged to the Celtic family, though not especially close to the Gaelic of today.

Scottish Gaelic has many Scandinavian loan-words: *ób* 'creek', *mód* 'court', *úidh* 'ford'. Scottish names such as Lamont, MacCorquodale and MacLeod (*Mac Laomuinn, Mac Corcadail* and *Mac Leóid* in Gaelic) are ultimately Norse. As many as half of the place names of the western Highlands and the Hebrides are Gaelic versions of originally Norse names.

Numerals in Manx and Scottish Gaelic		
	Manx	**Scottish Gaelic**
1	unnane	aon
2	daa, ghaa	dà
3	tree	trì
4	kiare	ceithir
5	queig	céig
6	shey	sia
7	shiaght	seachd
8	hoght	ochd
9	nuy	naoi
10	jeih	deich

GALICIAN

3,000,000 SPEAKERS

Spain

One of the ROMANCE LANGUAGES, Galician is a twin language with Portuguese – but their later histories have been very different. It is spoken in the north-west corner of Spain, and until recently has had no official recognition as a minority language.

Galicia (in Roman times the territory of the *Gallaeci*) was the western extremity of that mountainous strip of northern Spain which never came under Muslim rule. Instead, in early medieval times, Galicia was the realm of the Suebi, one of the Germanic peoples who had invaded and parcelled the western Roman Empire. Galician *laverca* 'lark' may possibly be a loanword from Suebic.

In the 11th century Galicia was divided, along the River Minho, from a new province of *Portugal* to the south. Both were fiefs of the kingdom of Castile. But in 1143 Portugal became an independent kingdom.

The medieval language of the two provinces is often called Galician-Portuguese: no significant dialect difference existed between them. Since then, Portuguese, as the language of an independent country and a world empire, with a

Europe: Portuguese and Galician

flourishing literature, has gradually grown apart from Galician, which remains of local interest only. The two are still much closer to each other than Galician is to Spanish.

For a table of numerals see CATALAN.

Galician and Portuguese are divided by the political boundary which follows the River Minho.

GANDA

3,750,000 SPEAKERS OF GANDA, SOGA AND GWERE

Uganda

One of the BANTU LANGUAGES, Ganda was the ruling language of the Kingdom of Buganda. Ganda, counted together with its eastern relatives Soga and Gwere, is spoken by a quarter of the population of Uganda.

'Readers who are unfamiliar with Bantu languages should note that these languages use systematic alternations of prefixes. The *Baganda* are the people who speak *Luganda*; they live in *Buganda*; and a single member of the tribe is a *Muganda*' (Peter Ladefoged and others, *Language in Uganda* (London: Oxford University Press, 1972) p. 17). In most cases the official English name of Bantu languages now omits the prefix: thus *Ganda*, not *luGanda*.

Early European explorers, approaching East Africa from the Swahili-speaking coast and guided by Swahili travellers, often used Swahili forms of proper names. The Swahili name for the kingdom of the baGanda was *uGanda* – hence the modern official name for the country. When the explorer J. H. Speke reached the outflow of the Nile on the northern shore of Lake Victoria, in 1862, he was told to call the place *uSoga*.

Ganda and related languages are now to be heard close to the point from which Eastern Bantu languages began to disperse, well over two thousand years ago. At that period there appears to have been some interaction near here between speakers of early Bantu, Nilo-Saharan and Afroasiatic languages, resulting among other things in the spread of iron-working and of banana cultivation among Eastern and other Bantu-speaking peoples.

However, the older history of the kingdoms north of Lake Victoria and of their languages is not known. They do not show strong influence from the other language families of eastern Africa: the old theory that the kingdoms are 'Hamitic conquest' states is unfounded. There are *baHima* cattle-farmers among the speakers of Ganda, but – by contrast with NKORE – no evidence that they were ever dominant or even respected.

In the late 18th century, from Egypt to the north and from the East African coast, Arabic and Swahili-speaking traders began to exert influence in the powerful kingdom of Buganda (whose language was Ganda) and its eastern neighbours, about twenty much smaller kingdoms now forming the district of Busoga. There came to be a royal monopoly on trade with the Arabs. They were followed, from the mid 19th century, by English-speaking travellers, traders and conquerors. Captain F. D. Lugard, of the British East Africa Company, dominated Kampala in 1890–2 (and wrote *The rise of our East African Empire*, 1893).

Buganda was the first of the states of modern Uganda to attract Arabic and Swahili trade, and eventually the first to submit to British government suzerainty in 1894. As a result, Kampala was already a regional centre of influence, and schools, roads and colonial administration naturally developed here first. Ganda speakers made ideal 'advisers' and civil servants in Busoga and other neighbouring states when they in their turn were taken over and developed. Thus Ganda gradually became the major language, a kind of lingua franca, in the whole of Uganda.

There was no conscious policy in this. Indeed, the British tried in the 1920s to make SWAHILI the official language of Uganda. But Ganda had too strong a hold. It was and is widely used in religion and in education from primary level onwards: Soga, by contrast, is scarcely used in these contexts.

Ganda is also, alongside English, the principal language of the media. The first grammar of Ganda appeared in 1882, and it was soon followed by a growing range of publications in the language. At first this was missionary-inspired, but much traditional literature and history has appeared in print. For many decades Catholics and Anglicans kept to their own slightly different spelling rules.

Ganda is easily learnt by most Ugandans because their own languages are closely related to it: they include the speakers of Soga and the group of dialects related to NKORE. RUNDI and Rwanda also belong to the same branch of Bantu languages. In northern Uganda, where unrelated languages are spoken, Ganda is less used as a lingua franca.

> 'The Luganda word *èmmûndú* 'rifle' looks like a loan from Swahili *bunduki*, itself a loan from Turkish via Arabic. The ultimate origin of this word is the Greek *pontikòn* 'hazelnut', referring to the shape of a musket bullet.'
> Jan Knappert in D. Dalby and others, *Language and history in Africa* (London: Cass, 1970) p. 82

Ganda, Soga and Gwere on the map

'If the political divisions could be disregarded, Luganda and Lusoga might just be considered to be very different dialects of the same language'

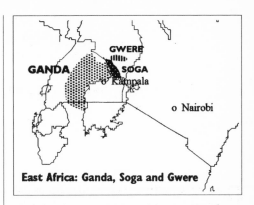

East Africa: Ganda, Soga and Gwere

(P. Ladefoged (1972)). For all that, *Soga* speakers consider Ganda an alien language, one that they need to know for political and religious reasons. Their kingdoms were historically independent of Buganda. The two, together with Gwere, can be called the North Nyanza group of Bantu languages, and form a dialect continuum.

Ganda is best defined as the language of the Kingdom of Buganda, with its capital at Kampala. About 2,300,000 speak it as a mother tongue.

Soga is the language of the following former kingdoms: Bugabula, Luuka, Bulamogi, Bugweri, Bukoli, Busiki, Kigulu, Butembe (around the town of Jinja), Bunya and Bunyuli, with at least ten other very small states. There are perhaps 1,200,000 speakers. Two main dialects are recognised, *luPakoyo* in the north and *luTenga* in the south.

Gwere, with about 250,000 speakers, is the dialect of Bugwere and is the easternmost of the group.

	Numerals in Ganda, Nkore and Rundi		
	Ganda	**Nkore**	**Rundi**
1	-mu	emwe	limwe
2	-biri	ibiri	kabiri
3	-satu	ishatu	gatatu
4	-nya	ina	kane
5	-taano	itaano	gatanu
6	mukaaga	mukaaga	gatandatu
7	musanvu	mushanju	karindwi
8	munaana	munaana	umunani
9	mwenda	mwenda	icyenda
10	ekkumi	ikumi	icumi

GARHWALI

1,200,000 SPEAKERS

India

One of the INDO-ARYAN LANGUAGES (see map there), Garhwali is the local language of the former state of Garhwal, now part of Uttar Pradesh. Garhwal has a place in three mythologies. To Hindus it is *Uttarakhāṇḍa*, 'the last stage' on the pilgrimage to the sources of the Ganges and the Jumna: both great rivers rise in this small Himalayan region. To the colonial British, Garhwal was the state in which the proud administrative centre of Dehra Dun and the fashionable hill station of Mussoorie lay close together, within easy reach of Delhi. And at Rishikesh, where the Ganges flows out of the mountains into the North Indian plain, the Beatles met their Indian teacher, the Maharishi Mahesh Yogi.

Garhwali, like its neighbour Kumauni, belongs to the Pahari subgroup of Indo-Aryan. Difficult communications in the Himalayan valleys have led to the crystallisation of several distinct languages with relatively small numbers of speakers. The Garhwali numerals, however, are identical with those of KUMAUNI.

Numerals in Nepali, Kumauni and Garhwali		
Nepali		**Kumauni and Garhwali**
ek	1	ek
dui	2	dvī
tin	3	tīn
chār	4	cār
pāñch	5	pāṃc
chha	6	chai
sāt	7	sāt
āṭh	8	āṭh
nau	9	nau
das	10	das

GBAYA

PERHAPS 1,200,000 SPEAKERS

Central African Republic, Cameroun

Gbaya belongs to the Ubangi group of NIGER-CONGO LANGUAGES, and, like BANDA, has been spoken in its present location for about three thousand years.

Gbaya was apparently once the ruling language of a state in what is now the western part of the Central African Republic and south-eastern Cameroun; at any rate it became the second language for people of several different mother tongues in this region.

In the 19th century the Gbaya were subject to slave-raids. This was why Gbaya was also known in Ngaoundéré in northern Cameroun, the principal market for Gbaya slaves.

Gbaya speakers live on both sides of the River Kadei, which roughly corresponds to the frontier between Cameroun and the Central African Republic. Gbaya and Banda are the two major hinterland languages of the Central African Republic, now overshadowed linguistically by the national language, SANGO (see map there).

In Gbaya nouns and noun phrases a prefix marks the plural: *wi* 'man', *yowi* 'men'; *polombo wi* 'young man', *yopolombo wi* 'young men'. The first ten numerals are: *kpém, rííto, tar, nar, mɔɔrɔ́, 'dong kpém, 'dong rííto, nú-nãá, kusi, 'bú*.

GEORGIAN

3,500,000 SPEAKERS

Georgia

One of the Kartvelian or South CAUCASIAN LANGUAGES, Georgian is the national language of independent Georgia, in the Caucasus, formerly one of the constituent republics of the Soviet Union. Apparently unrelated to all other languages except its three close neighbours, Georgian is the vehicle of an ancient Christian culture and of a literature that goes back to the 5th century AD.

Modern Georgia (*Sak'art'velo*) includes both ancient *Iberia* (modern Georgian *K'art'li*) and ancient *Colchis* (later *Lazica* and *Abasgia*, modern Georgian *Egrisi*) from which, according to Greek legend, the Argonauts brought home the Golden Fleece. These territories were politically united in 1008 under King Bagrat III.

For some centuries before that unification, K'art'li had been under Muslim rule; it now became the heart of an independent kingdom, but one that was soon to fragment. Georgia allied itself with Russia in the late 18th century, for Russia was also a Christian state, a potential protector in view of the threat of Turkish conquest. In due course Russia became ruler rather than ally. Georgia asserted independence in 1918 after the Russian Revolution, but was reconquered by the Soviet Union in 1921. Georgians were prominent in Soviet politics: Yosif Vissarionovich Stalin (Joseph Djugashvili) was a Georgian; Aleksandr Shevardnadze, once foreign minister of the Soviet Union, was to become president of newly independent Georgia. Independence was achieved once more in 1991, since when Georgia has been beset by civil warfare.

Christianity in Georgia is traditionally dated to the conversion of King Mirian in 337 and Georgian literature began with religious texts, most of them translated from Greek: the 5th-century *Martyrdom of Shushanik* is identified as the earliest original work. Thus there is a very long tradition of native literature in Georgian, including royal chronicles and epic poetry. The 12th-century poem by Shota Rustaveli, *The Man in the Panther's Skin*, is the best known work of Georgian literature.

Georgian serves as the official and literary language for speakers of Svan and Mingrelian. Many Abkhaz speakers are bilingual in Georgian. The Jewish community in Georgia has had a distinct language, Judaeo-Georgian, which may still have as many as 10,000 speakers – many of them now in Israel.

There is also a population of Georgian-speaking Muslims: these are the *Ach'areli* (Russian *Adzhartsy*), about 150,000 of whom live in the Ach'ar autonomous republic on the Black Sea coast near the Turkish border. Their religious culture has been Turkish-speaking, and many Ach'ar are bilingual in Turkish. There are at least 50,000 Ach'ar in Turkey: their ancestors fled Christian Georgia in fear of religious persecution in 1877–8.

Georgian shows the influence of Greek, Turkish, Armenian, Persian and Russian. It remains a typically Caucasian language: although the Caucasian language families have not yet been shown to be related to one another, they share such features as a very large inventory of consonants and a complicated 'agglutinative' word structure.

For a table of numerals see MINGRELIAN.

The Kartvelian languages

Georgian is the national language of Georgia. The *K'art'li* dialect of Tbilisi and its region is the basis of standard Georgian. The western dialects, including *Ach'ar*, show the influence of MINGRELIAN and Laz, two related languages, which are spoken at the western extremities of the Georgian-speaking area.

Svan has about 40,000 speakers in Svanetia, the sequence of inaccessible high mountain valleys whose streams feed the Inguri and Kodori rivers, in north-western Georgia. Related to the other Kartvelian languages, Svan has probably been growing apart from them for over three thousand years.

Mxedruli: the Georgian alphabet

Mxedruli gradually came into use for Georgian between the 9th and 13th centuries. It replaced an older script, quite different in shape, now known as *asomtavruli*, which is first found in a

stone inscription of AD 430 and was clearly invented at about the time of the conversion of Georgia to Christianity in the 4th century.

The alphabetical order is that of Greek – but the additional consonant sounds of Georgian have been fitted in, with newly invented letters, towards the end of the sequence. The alphabet still begins with *a* (Greek *alpha*) and ends with o (Greek *omega*), though the last letter is now obsolete.

Mxedruli

ა ბ გ დ ე ვ ზ ჱ ჲ თ ი კ ლ მ ნ ჳ ო პ ჟ რ ს ტ ჳ უ ფ ქ ღ ყ შ ჩ ც ძ წ ჭ ხ ჴ ჰ ჵ

a b g d e v z ē t i ḳ l m n y o p̣ ž r s ṭ ü u p k ğ q̇ š č c j ç č̣ x q ǰ h ō

GERMAN

120,000,000 SPEAKERS

Germany, Austria, Switzerland, Russia, Kazakhstan, Romania, United States

One of the GERMANIC LANGUAGES, German is in origin the language of the tribes that stayed put – east of the Rhine, north of the upper Danube – while Germanic mercenaries and warlords were parcelling out the Roman Empire among themselves between AD 300 and 500.

German has many different names. *Germania* was the Roman name for the country, and *Germani* for its people. They now call themselves and their language *Deutsch* – a word first used in medieval Latin documents of the 8th century in the rather different form *theodisca lingua,* 'language of the tribes'. *Deutsch* is also the origin of the English word DUTCH.

In French, Germany is named *Allemagne* and its language *Allemand,* after the *Alemanni,* one of the prominent tribal groups of the 4th century AD. The usual eastern European term (Czech *Němec,* Romanian *Neamţ*) comes from a Slavonic word meaning 'mute', i.e. 'not speaking our language'.

The first records of a German language come from the 8th century. They amount to the so-called *Song of Hildebrand* (a few lines of an epic poem), some magical charms, and a collection of German glosses – translations between the lines – in Latin manuscripts. There is even a short Latin–German dictionary, now called *Abrogans* from its first Latin word, written in the 760s. But the usual written language in Germany, for many centuries yet, was Latin, and students of 'Old High German' (700–1100) have to study a fairly small number of texts. The emperor Charlemagne, around 800, ordered the ancient German epics to be written down in a book – but, if this was ever done, the book has long ago disappeared.

The Strasbourg Oaths

In AD 842 an alliance between Charles the Bald and Louis the German was sealed by the taking of mutual oaths by the French and German monarchs and by their armies. So that everyone could understand what was going on, the oaths were taken in the everyday languages of the two countries, and not in Latin. The official chronicler Nithard recorded the proceedings word for word. Charles took the oath in German:

In Godes minna ind in thes christianes folches ind unser bedhero gehaltnissi, for thesemo dage frammordes, so fram so mir Got gewizci indi mahd furgibit, so haldih thesan minan bruodher, soso man mit rehtu sinan bruher scal, in thiu thaz er mig so sama duo, indi mit Ludheren in nohheiniu thing ne gegango, the, minan willon, imo ce scadhen werdhen.

For God's love and for the salvation of the Christian people and ourselves, from this day onward, so far as God gives me knowledge and power, I will aid this my brother Charles, as a man in justice ought to do for his brother, so long as he does the same to me, and I will enter no talks with Lothar which might, by my will, damage him.

For the French text as sworn by Louis, see box at ROMANCE LANGUAGES.

Nithard, *Histoire des fils de Louis le Pieux* ed. Ph. Lauer (Paris: Les Belles Lettres, 1926) p. 106

KAZAKHSTAN

mus' based on Afrikaans *seekoei*; *Armstuhl* 'arm-chair'.

Examples from Claus Jürgen Hutterer, *Die germanischen Sprachen* (Budapest, 1975) pp. 342–7; Philip E. Webber, *Kolonie-Deutsch: life and language in Amana* (Ames: Iowa State University Press, 1993); Elizabeth De Kadt in *Language and social history: studies in South African sociolinguistics* ed. Rajend Mesthrie (Cape Town: David Philip, 1995) pp. 107–15

The dialects of High and Low German

Low German is divided from High German by an 'isogloss', a line on a dialect map – or rather by a bundle of isoglosses, all following roughly the same path. The most important of them is the northern limit of the area in which the High German Sound Shift took effect.

The south

German also spread to other continents. Pidgin varieties of German existed briefly in short-lived German colonies such as North West New Guinea, Tanganyika, South West Africa, Togo and Cameroon, though they never displaced the already established lingua francas of these countries. German influence can be traced in TOK PISIN, the national language of Papua New Guinea: *mak* 'shilling' from German *Mark*; *gumi* 'rubber'.

Some Germans settled in these colonies: others emigrated to Australia, Chile, Argentina and Brazil, in all of which cohesive but small German-speaking communities still exist.

At the end of the 18th century more than half the European population of the Cape Town region was German in origin, and there are still about 40,000 German speakers in South Africa, with some German schools and churches, most of the latter originating in the 19th-century Lutheran missions in Natal. Most immigrants probably spoke varieties of Low German – but modern *Springbockdeutsch*, thanks to German schooling, has turned into a regional variant of standard High German. It has numerous loanwords and calques from Afrikaans and English: *Fenz* 'fence'; *Seekuh* 'hippopota-

Low German

Almost as old as the oldest literature in German are two poems in what is now called Old Saxon – the language of northern Germany in the 9th century AD. They are called *Heliand* ('The Healer') and *Genesis*, and were composed at the request of King Louis the Pious, son of Charlemagne. Even in those days Old Saxon was quite distinct from the 'High German' of the south.

In its later forms the speech of the lower Rhine and the north German plains is known as *Plattdeutsch, Low German* (because it is the language of the low-lying country). Until the 16th century it was used in official documents by northern courts, and in particular in the business of the Hansa cities, which dominated Baltic trade. Low German influence can be traced in Norwegian, Danish, Swedish, Latvian and other languages of northern Europe. It might easily have become the standard dialect, the German that everybody learnt, if German cultural history had taken a different course – if medieval German courts had not patronised the poetry of the south, and if Luther's Bible translation had not dominated writing and literature in the 16th century. But it was not to be: for centuries now the Low German dialects have been seen as homely, rustic forms of speech, seldom written down except in folk tales and consciously 'folkloric' literature.

With one exception. DUTCH is in origin one of the Low German dialects: for centuries, Dutch has counted as a language in its own right.

Why did Louis the Pious commission *Heliand* and *Genesis*? 'He instructed a certain Saxon, considered by his own people no mean seer, to turn the Old and New Testaments into German poetry, so that the lessons of the Divine Teachings should be revealed not only to those of his subjects who could read but also to those who could not . . . The stories were expressed in German of such clarity and elegance that all who listened to them took no little pleasure in their style' (*Heliand*, Latin prose preface).

Low German consists of several quite distinct dialects, some of which were used as written languages in late medieval times. None ever became a standard language for the whole area. The main modern dialects are DUTCH (or Low Franconian), *Niedersächsisch* or Low Saxon and *Ostniederdeutsch* or East Low German. Where the isogloss bundle splays out – in real human terms this is along the Rhine valley, where north–south communication encouraged dialect mixture – some linguists distinguish two West Middle German dialects. These are *Mittelfränkisch* or Middle Franconian (which includes the Moselle Valley and LUXEMBURGISH) and *Rheinfränkisch* of the Palatinate. These are important dialects because they formed the basis for others: Pennsylvania Dutch; Transylvanian Saxon; Volga German; and also YIDDISH, the language of German-speaking Jews, a language that gradually spread from the medieval Rhine across large areas of eastern Europe.

High German dialects include Thuringian and Upper Saxon (but these are sometimes grouped as 'East Middle German'), Upper Franconian, Alemannic (including Swiss German), Bavarian and Austrian. Both Alemannic and Austrian dialects extend southwards across the Italian border.

The further east

The geographical range of Yiddish was merely one result of the vast, long-lasting migration that

left central and eastern Europe, at the beginning of the 20th century, studded with large and small German-speaking communities of farmers, miners and others. There were heavy concentrations of German speakers in Silesia and Pomerania, now Polish-speaking; from Pomerania German speech extended by way of Danzig eastwards to East Prussia (now divided between Poland and Russia) and into the Baltic states.

Halbdeutsch 'Half-German' was the simplified German that was spoken by Estonians and Latvians who settled in the German-dominated towns of that region, until Russian influence increased in the 19th century.

The Sudetenland, the regions of Bohemia (now the Czech Republic) bordering on Germany, had a German-speaking majority. Unusually extensive also were the German settlements in Transylvania (*Siebenbürgen*: now in Romania) and on the lower Volga in southern Russia.

As the ruling language of the German and of the Austro-Hungarian Empire, the language of their armies, and the vehicle of higher education, science and scholarship, German was uniquely respected. Thus, however isolated, German settlements tended to retain their language for centuries.

The fate of German in the east

The Second World War was fomented by nationalist agitation concerning the German-speaking populations of Czechoslovakia and Poland. Ironically, in the course of the war eastern European speakers of the Yiddish form of German were almost completely wiped out as a matter of German policy. The outcome of the war was a catastrophe for most of the remaining German-speaking communities of eastern Europe. Many died; most others were uprooted. Many of these, as refugees in Germany, have learnt to lose their local dialects and culture.

Germans in the Baltic republics were moved en masse to Germany in 1939 after the German–Soviet Pact placed these republics in the Soviet sphere of influence.

German rural settlement in Russia itself had been concentrated in the lower Volga valley around Saratov. The Volga German Autonomous Republic, established soon after the Revolution, was broken up on the German invasion of the Soviet Union in 1940 and its whole German-speaking population exiled to Kazakhstan and Siberia. There were still about a million German speakers in Kazakhstan, and over 800,000 in Russia (mostly in Siberia), in 1989; the numbers are steadily declining as German speakers are allowed to emigrate to Germany.

In 1945 the German population was expelled from East Prussia, which was divided between Poland and the Soviet Union. German speakers were also expelled en masse from western Poland up to the new Oder-Neisse border, and from Sudetenland.

Numerals in German and Luxemburgish		
German		**Luxemburgish**
eins	1	eent
zwei	2	zwee, zwou
drei	3	dräi
vier	4	véier
fünf	5	fënnef
sechs	6	sechs
sieben	7	siwen
acht	8	aacht
neun	9	néng
zehn	10	zéng

German fonts

𝕬𝕭𝕮𝕯𝕰𝕱𝕲𝕳𝕴𝕵𝕶𝕷𝕸𝕹𝕺𝕻𝕼𝕽𝕾𝕿𝖀𝖁𝖂𝖃𝖄𝖅

a b c d e f g h i j k l m n o p q r s t u v w x y z

𝔄𝔅ℭ𝔇𝔈𝔉𝔊ℌℑ𝔍𝔎𝔏𝔐𝔑𝔒𝔓𝔔ℜ𝔖𝔗𝔘𝔙𝔚𝔛𝔜ℨ

a b c d e f g h i j k l m n o p q r s t u v w x y z

A B C D E F G H I J K L M N O P Q R S T U V W X Y Z

a b c d e f g h i j k l m n o p q r s t u v w x y z

Printing in German

The two 'Gothic' font families shown in the box are known as *Fraktur* (lines 1–2) and *Schwabacher* (lines 3–4). Until the 1930s they were typical of German language printing. When quoting single words or longer texts in other languages, printers would normally switch to a Roman font.

Research showed that reading in Fraktur was significantly slower than in Roman, and by a decision of the National Socialist government the Gothic fonts were abandoned. Younger Germans now find pre-war printed books difficult to read.

GERMANIC LANGUAGES

A mong the language groups that derive from proto-Indo-European, the Germanic languages have a very clear geographical base and several features that distinguish them from their relatives. English and German are among the major modern languages belonging to this group.

> *Germanic* has long been the international term for this language family: it derives from the usual Latin name, *Germani*, for a group of peoples coinciding more or less with the speakers of early Germanic dialects. It is not a native but a Latin word: it meant 'relatives'. *Teutonic* has occasionally been used as an alternative: it is the name of one tribal group at the same period – but it is quite possible that this group spoke a Celtic language! Another alternative is *Gothic*, outdated in English (where it is the name of one particular, extinct, Germanic language) but, as *gottonsk*, favoured by some Scandinavian scholars.

Proto-Germanic, ancestor of all the modern Germanic languages, must have been spoken on the shores of the western Baltic in the last few centuries BC. There are no records of it, but Germanic scholars have been able to reconstruct its forms, probably with fair accuracy, through working backwards from the known Germanic languages of later periods. Additional evidence comes from loanwords in Finnish and the Baltic languages.

The early records of Germanic languages are inscriptions on stone and wood in Runic script. The very oldest Runic inscriptions, such as that on the horn discovered at Gallehus, go back to AD 200 or soon after, and they are very close indeed to the reconstructed proto-Germanic. A slightly later example appears in the box at OLD NORSE.

The Germanic languages in 1000 BC

In the first millennium BC the early Germanic dialects had been surrounded by other INDO-EUROPEAN LANGUAGES, Celtic, Baltic and perhaps Illyrian and Slavonic. To the north, the North Germanic dialect (prehistoric OLD NORSE) may already have been close to areas of SAMI and FINNISH speech.

Some important words were borrowed into Germanic from neighbouring languages: they include modern German *Reich*, Dutch *rijk* 'kingdom', a Celtic word in origin.

Germanic languages in Europe today

Icelandic

NORTH GERMANIC

Faroese

Norwegian

Swedish

Danish

WEST GERMANIC
Frisian

English   Low German

Dutch

German SLAVONIC
LANGUAGES

ROMANCE LANGUAGES

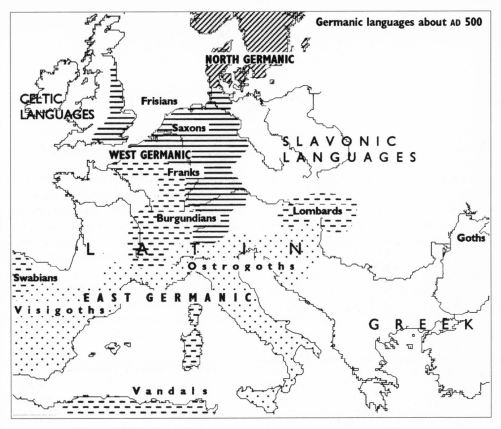

Germanic languages about AD 500

The Germanic languages in AD 500

By AD 500, East Germanic (GOTHIC) was being carried through the Roman Empire as a language of mercenary troops who were already beginning to conquer territory for themselves. Many West Germanic speakers, who included Angles, Saxons, Burgundians and Franks as well as the direct forerunners of modern Dutch and Germans, were also within the boundaries of the Roman Empire. Both these branches of Germanic show heavy influence from Latin. One early Latin loanword surviving in modern Germanic languages is Latin *vinum*, German *Wein*, English *wine* – but the name of a different fermented drink is inherited directly from Indo-European, German *Met*, English *mead*.

Speakers of North Germanic would soon begin their expansion across the north Atlantic to the Scottish and Irish coasts, the Isle of Man, the Faroes, Iceland and Greenland.

The Germanic languages today

The East Germanic branch has died out. To West Germanic belong GERMAN, YIDDISH, DUTCH, LUXEMBURGISH, FRISIAN, ENGLISH and the ENGLISH CREOLES AND PIDGINS. To North Germanic belong SWEDISH, DANISH, NORWEGIAN, FAROESE and ICELANDIC.

GILAKI

PERHAPS 4,250,000 SPEAKERS OF 'CASPIAN DIALECTS'

Iran, Azerbaijan

The 'Caspian dialects' are IRANIAN LANGUAGES quite distinct from Persian, spoken in northern Iran and Azerbaijan near the shores of the Caspian. None of them is recognised as an official language: many younger speakers are thus bilingual in Azeri or in Persian.

Some 16th-century poetry from Ardebil, in north-western Iran, is in a dialect very close to modern Talysh (see map). There is old poetry in Mazandarani too, by Amir Pazvari and others. In general, however, very little has been written in any of the Caspian dialects.

With the growth of education and press in Persian, these survivals of the very early spread and differentiation of Iranian languages are likely to disappear.

In Gilaki the first four numerals are *i, do, sǝ, čār*. In Mazandarani they are *atto, detto, se, čār*. The Caspian dialects retain more than Persian does of the noun declension system that was characteristic of older Iranian.

The Caspian and north-western dialects: the map

Talysh or *Taleshi* is the language of the Caspian coastal plain in southern Azerbaijan and north-west Iran. There may be 250,000 speakers.

Gilaki is spoken along the western half of the Caspian's southern coastline. Its natural centre is the city of Rasht. One estimate suggests 2,000,000 speakers.

Mazandarani borders the south-east Caspian, and includes *Gorgani*. There may be 1,500,000 speakers. The Elburz mountains mark the southern limit of Gilaki and Mazandarani.

Scattered among speakers of Turkic AZERI, in inland north-western Iran, are the Iranian dialects known confusingly as *Azari* or *Tati* (see box at PERSIAN for the other language known by this name). They include *Takestani*. There are perhaps 250,000 speakers.

Semnani is the language of the city of Semnan, east of Tehran.

There are further dialects of central Iran, insufficiently known, gradually retreating before the advance of Persian.

Iran: Caspian dialects

GONDI

3,000,000 SPEAKERS OF CENTRAL DRAVIDIAN LANGUAGES

India

The family of DRAVIDIAN LANGUAGES includes not only the state languages of southern India, but also a number of minority languages of hill and jungle peoples scattered over much of the subcontinent. *Gōṇḍī* is the most important of the Central Dravidian group, which must have separated from southern languages such as Kannada and Tamil well over two thousand years ago.

The hills and jungles where the Gōṇḍ tribes live were once called after them Gondwana (Sanskrit *Goṇḍavana* 'forest of the Gonds') – a name which, before it was forgotten, was borrowed for a geological stratum typical of the region, and then borrowed again by the proponents of the geological theory of continental drift. So Gondwanaland is now the agreed name of the supercontinent that existed hundreds of millions of years ago before South America split from Africa, Antarctica, Australia, Arabia and India. Most Gond tribes call themselves *Kōī, Kōītōr* and other similar names.

There is no written literature in Gōṇḍī. The language is spoken in several large enclaves of jungle country, separated from one another by settled lands where Marathi, Chhattisgarhi and Telugu are spoken. There is no doubt that some of these settlements are relatively recent: Gōṇḍī speakers, as they settle to agriculture, turn to speaking these languages of 'civilisation'. Gōṇḍī clearly forms the linguistic substrate underlying the distinctive features of the Bhatrī dialect of ORIYA and the Halbī dialect of MARATHI.

In these languages the three-way gender distinction of early Dravidian has given way to a two-way distinction between masculine (male humans) and non-masculine (all other nouns).

The first ten numerals in Gōṇḍī are: *undī, rend, mūnd, nālūng, siyāng, sārūng, ērūng, armur, anma, putth*. For the higher numerals – from '8' up – borrowed Marathi forms are usually used.

The Central Dravidian languages

The islands of *Gōṇḍī* speech, with about 1,900,000 speakers, are in the Indian states of Maharashtra, Madhya Pradesh and Andhra Pradesh. About 5,000,000 people in India class themselves as Koitor or Gonds, but many speak Hindi or Telugu and not Gōṇḍī. The Muria Gonds of the Bastar district are well known among anthropologists for the *ghotul*, the young peoples' dormitory, in which sexual promiscuity before marriage is encouraged.

Kui (500,000 speakers) and *Kuvi* (300,000 speakers), similar to each other and fairly close linguistically to Gōṇḍī, are spoken in a hill and jungle region of southern Orissa state.

Kōlāmī (90,000 speakers) and *Parjī* (or Duruwa, 90,000 speakers) form a separate subgroup, spoken in hill districts to the south of the Gōṇḍī-Kui area.

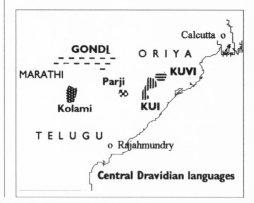

Central Dravidian languages

GONGA LANGUAGES

PERHAPS 200,000 SPEAKERS

Ethiopia

A group of now-scattered languages belonging to the OMOTIC group of Afroasiatic languages, Gonga is the speech of a series of old kingdoms of south-western Ethiopia.

The best-known kingdom, the best-known language and a popular name for the whole group is *Kefa* or *Kaffa* (the double *f* shows this to be an Amharic form). However, *Gonga* is a name known ever since the oldest reports of travellers to the region.

Christianity was introduced to Kefa and other Gonga kingdoms from Ethiopia about 1590. In the early 17th century, when Europeans first travelled through the region, the Gonga kingdoms were already under attack from Oromo-speaking invaders. In the late 19th century they were conquered by the Ethiopian Empire of Menelek. Meanwhile, in 1855 a Roman Catholic mission entered the religious scene. An early wordlist of Gonga had been published by the explorer Charles Tilstone Beke in 1846.

Kefa is remarkable among minor African languages in having had a detailed study made of its erotic vocabulary – could this have been a special enthusiasm of the Austrian explorer F. J. Bieber? He published his work in the pioneering journal of sexology, *Anthropophyteia*, in 1903.

Gonga languages have two or three tones, and also distinguish vowel length and syllable stress. Already in the 17th century Gonga languages included Amharic loanwords in fields such as politics and religion: the kingdoms were then self-governing but tributary to the King of Ethiopia.

The major Omotic languages

The Gonga languages include Kefa, Moca, Anfillo and Shinasha. *Kefa* is the language of the old kingdom of Kefa. *Moca* or Mocha is spoken to the west of Kefa. *Anfillo* or Southern Mao, a dying language, is spoken in Anfillo forest in an area now predominantly Oromo-speaking. *Shinasha* or North Gonga or simply Gonga is a group of languages spoken in the Blue Nile valley.

The Ometo languages include *Basketto*, of the east bank of the Omo; *Kullo*, the dialect of Jimma and its neighbourhood; and, WOLAYTTA or Welamo, the main dialect and now the basis of a literary language.

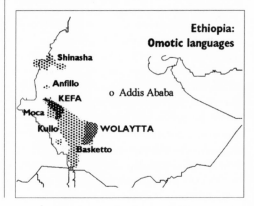

Ethiopia: Omotic languages

GOTHIC

EXTINCT LANGUAGE OF EUROPE

Gothic is the only member of the East Germanic branch of the Germanic languages in which any continuous texts are recorded.

The name of the Goths can still be traced in their earliest recorded territory, southern Sweden and the Baltic shores – it survives in the island of *Gotland* and the Swedish districts of *Götland*. The Goths of Roman history were divided into two 'tribes', *Ostrogothi* or *Greutungi* 'dune-dwellers' and *Visigothi* or *Tervingi* 'steppe-dwellers'.

Three peoples whose dialects were very close to one another – Goths, Burgundians and Vandals – were prominent in the invasions and mercenary warfare that marked the decline of the Western Roman Empire, between about AD 350 and 500 (see maps at GERMANIC LANGUAGES).

The major Gothic text is a translation of the Bible, the work of Bishop Ulfilas (*Wulfila*), the religious leader of the Visigoths when they first settled within Roman borders, in what is now Bulgaria, after 348. It is the earliest literary text in any Germanic language.

The Visigoths eventually established a kingdom in 5th-century Spain: their language had some influence on the late Latin of Spain, and thus eventually on Spanish. The Ostrogoths – who also used Ulfilas' Bible translation – ruled Italy about the same time, and again some Gothic vocabulary can be traced in modern Italian. The name of the French province of Burgundy, *Bourgogne*, is the last reminiscence of the Burgundians, who settled in that region. The Vandals briefly established an empire in North Africa; their earlier dominion in southern Spain was still remembered when the Arabs conquered the region and named it, after them, *al-Andalus* (modern Spanish *Andalucia*).

Some Goths, meanwhile, remained on the shores of the Black Sea, where their migrations had taken them before they entered the Roman orbit. Until the 15th century there was a Gothic principality in the Crimea. Even in the 16th and 17th centuries, European travellers were surprised to find *Crimean Gothic* still spoken by small communities. The language is now extinct.

The first ten numerals in Gothic are: ΑΙΝS TΥΑΙ ΦΚΙGΑ FΙΑΥΩΚ FΙΜF SΑΙhs SΙΒΝΝ ΑΗΤΑΝ ΝΙΝΝ ΤΑΙhΝΝ or, in transliteration, *ains, twai, thrija, fidwor, fimf, saihs, sibun, ahtau, niun, taihun.*

The Gothic alphabet

ΑΒΓΔΕUΖhΦΙΚΛΗΝGΠΠΥΚSΤ
ΥFΧΘΩ↑

a b g d e q z h th i k l m n j u p – r s t w f ch wh o –
1 2 3 4 5 6 7 8 9 10 20 30 40 50 60 70 80 90
100 200 300 400 500 600 700 800 900

Font: *gothicl. ttf* from
'Dr Berlin's Foreign Font Archive'

The Gothic script

'Gothic' is a word that has been used with many meanings, in history, in art, in architecture and in typography. Quite different from the black-letter scripts of medieval Europe, and the Fraktur typefaces of German printing, both of which have sometimes been called 'Gothic', what is shown in the box is the alphabet invented for the Gothic language by Ulfilas in the 4th century. It is based on Greek scripts of his day (with added letters from Latin and Runic alphabets). Just as in Greek, the 25 letters of the alphabet, with two special added characters U and ↑, served also as numerals from '1' to '900'.

GREEK

11,500,000 SPEAKERS

Greece and Cyprus

Greek is an INDO-EUROPEAN language, the sole descendant of one of the original dialects of proto-Indo-European. In its mountainous homeland in south-eastern Europe, from 700 to 300 BC and after, ancient Greek was the language of philosophers, historians, poets and playwrights whose works have been read ever since. Greek has had a continuous and eventful history from that time to the present day.

Greek is known to its own speakers as *Eliniki* (the word is borrowed from ancient Greek *Hellenikê*). This name is formed from the native name of the country, ancient *Héllas*, modern *Elládha*. The traditional term for Greek in medieval and early modern times was *Romaikí*, as the language of the 'Romans' of the later empire: fewer speakers use this term now. Most foreign names for the language and the country derive from the Latin word *Graecus*, 'Greek'.

3,300 Years of History

Greek was first recorded about 1300 BC on clay tablets in Linear B script (see box). Then there is a six-hundred-year gap in the record. Greek has an uninterrupted recorded history from about 700 BC – the date of the earliest surviving texts in the Greek alphabet – down to modern times.

By that time it was the majority language of the Greek peninsula and islands and a major language of Cyprus, and it has held these positions ever since. It was the language of scores of independent Greek cities founded along the Mediterranean and Black Sea coasts in the cen-

turies after 750 BC. It was the ruling language of the great 'Hellenistic' kingdoms of the Near East that lasted for several centuries after the death of Alexander the Great in 323 BC and stretched as far as the Indus valley. It was the lingua franca of the whole eastern half of the Roman Empire.

Periods of Greek

Mycenaean: about 1300 BC

Ancient: 700 BC to AD 500

(Archaic, 700 to 500 BC; Classical, 500 to 300; Hellenistic, 300 to 1; Roman, AD 1 to 500)

Byzantine: 500 to 1450

(early Byzantine, 500 to 1100; late Byzantine: 1100 to 1450)

Turkish and Venetian: 1450 to 1800

Modern: from 1800

Even after the long domination of the Romans, Greek eventually supplanted Latin, and became once more the single ruling language of the 'Byzantine' Empire, which fell to the Ottoman Turks in AD 1453. Greek was at first the language of diplomacy for the Seljuk and Ottoman Turkish kingdoms. Greeks retained the status of an autonomous minority, *millet*, under the Ottoman Empire. Many ancient communities of Greek speakers, all over the empire and especially in the coastal regions of Anatolia, survived and prospered. Greek retained wide importance as the language of the Greek Orthodox Church; Greek literature flourished in Venetian-ruled Crete, and Greek culture and education prospered in Bucharest (Romania).

St Andrews professor receives national honour

Professor Stephen Halliwell

Professor Stephen Halliwell of St Andrews University's School of Classics has been elected a Fellow of the British Academy.

The British Academy is the premier national body representing the humanities and the social sciences, the counterpart of the Royal Society for the natural sciences.

Professor Halliwell's research ranges widely across the study of ancient Greek literature, especially tragedy and comedy, and philosophy with a focus on Plato and Aristotle, as well as the influence of Greek cultural ideas and practices on later periods. He is also a Fellow of the Royal Society of Edinburgh.

Professor Halliwell commented: "It is an honour to be elected to the Academy but all the more gratifying because it helps to mark St Andrews' outstanding record of achievement in the study of the ancient world."

Professor Halliwell's election maintains a remarkable St Andrews tradition going back almost a century - he is the university's sixth professor of Greek in succession to become a Fellow of the British Academy.

1/8 '2014

What was once a very large minority in Asia Minor, numbered in millions, declined rapidly with the 'population exchanges' that followed the disastrous Greek invasion of Turkey in 1923. Although the balance was redressed slightly by Greek-speaking Muslims who were expelled from Greece at the same time, the total Greek-speaking community in Turkey now is estimated at well under 50,000.

The refugees from Greece to Turkey in 1923 included *Valakhádhes*, people of AROMUNIAN origin who had become town-dwellers, adopting Islam and the Greek language. Their dialect is unlikely to survive long. The same is true of several Greek communities of Asia Minor itself that adopted Islam in Ottoman times – they look on themselves as Turks and did not migrate in 1923.

The changing Greek language

There are great differences between Mycenaean and ancient Greek – differences that are only underlined by the utterly different writing systems. There is no surviving Mycenaean literature: the clay tablets are accounts and inventories. When ancient Greek emerges, around 700 BC, it is in the form of the great epics attributed to Homer, the *Iliad* and the *Odyssey*, which have influenced European literature ever afterwards.

Ancient Greek is recorded in several dialects (see map), but the Attic dialect of Athens of the 4th century BC gained cultural prestige and became a standard, adopted in the new Hellenistic monarchies of the Near East and, gradually, in Greece itself. Classical Attic continued to be the usual language of education and written culture until almost AD 1500. Its derivative, the koiné ('common') dialect, was the ordinary spoken language of Hellenistic and Roman times: the Hebrew Old Testament was translated into the developing koiné of 250 BC and the New Testament was written in the koiné of about AD 100.

Yet almost at the same date Lucian was writing satirical pieces and Plutarch was composing his biographies of Greeks and Romans, both in skilful pastiches of classical Attic. Meanwhile, narrative poetry – from the limpid, romantic *Hero and Leander* of Musaeus to the florid *Dionysiaca* by Nonnus, both written around AD 500 – would still be composed in a metre and a dialect close to those of the *Iliad* and *Odyssey*, which were by then twelve hundred years old.

'The Greeks had a word for it'

The proverb is a reminder of the richness of the Greek vocabulary: Liddell and Scott's *Greek–English Lexicon* has about 300,000 entries. Like modern German, ancient Greek was a language in which any speaker or writer might invent new compound words with the confidence that they would be understood.

In the Byzantine Empire, too, it came naturally to the educated to write in a kind of classical Attic, though writings for a less courtly milieu, such as saints' lives, were in a language closer to that of every day.

Through the Roman and Byzantine centuries the development of the spoken language can be traced in informal writings (for example, in papyri from Egypt). At last satire and fiction in a recognizably modern form of Greek emerge around 1150, throwing off the classical and ecclesiastical straitjackets. At the centre of the linguistic revolution, it has been argued, were French and German empresses and princesses, familiar with the new romantic literature of their home countries. Since that time, creative writers have increasingly used the language of every day.

Modern Greek looks very like ancient Greek, but it probably sounds very different. Greek as spoken in classical Athens in 400 BC had a front-rounded vowel like German *ü*, several diphthongs (*ai, au, eu, oi, ui*), aspirated stops (*ph, th, kh*, like those of Hindi), a distinction between long and short vowels, and, perhaps most important of all, a distinction between high and low pitch, which must have given a musical quality to the spoken language comparable to that of Welsh. All these features disappeared in the centuries after Alexander. High pitch was replaced by syllable stress, and many changes occurred in vowel sounds. Modern spoken Greek has 5 vowels and, by one count, 22 consonants.

The basic vocabulary of Greek was inherited from Indo-European. The names of cultural innovations were borrowed, often from languages to the south and east: ancient *oînos* 'wine', *asáminthos* 'bathtub', *tyrannos* 'dictator'. Names of native plants and animals come from some other source, presumably from earlier languages of Greece or Turkey now lost: *amygdále* 'almond', *koríannon* 'coriander', *sepía* 'cuttlefish'. In later times Greek has borrowed words from Latin, French, Turkish and English: *tavérna* 'restaurant', *kafé* 'coffee', *yaúrti* 'yoghurt', *flért* 'flirtation'.

A form of ancient Greek was revived in the 19th century in the stiff and artificial katharévousa, the 'purified' language of modern officialdom, occasionally reimposed in schools by right-wing governments. It is used in some technical writing but not in literature, which is written in dhimotikí, the demotic or 'popular' tongue.

Greek in the wider world

Greek was one of the two great languages of the Roman Empire, very widely used among both the upper and the lower classes: it was the first or second language of a large proportion of slaves. Any educated Roman, between about 100 BC and AD 300, was expected to know Greek. Many Romans studied in Greek 'university' cities, especially Athens. Greek had a powerful influence on Latin and Arabic, the medieval languages of international learning and science. This influence continues today as ancient Greek words and affixes, often in Latinised forms, are borrowed and compounded to create new international technical terminology in pharmacology and medicine, in the sciences and social sciences (Greek *tékhne*, skill; *phármakon*, drug).

The majority language of Greece and Cyprus, Greek is spoken by minorities in Georgia, Egypt, Albania, southern Italy and many other countries. There were once flourishing Greek communities in Odessa (Ukraine), in Alexandria and Cairo (Egypt) and in the old Byzantine capital, Istanbul. These are now in decline: in recent years, particularly large Greek and Cypriot colonies have grown up in Chicago, London and elsewhere across the world. The Greek speakers of London, numbering well over 100,000, are mostly of Cypriot origin and came between 1955 and 1974 with the political upheavals that culminated in the Greek and Turkish interventions and the division of Cyprus.

The first ten numerals in modern Greek are: *ena, dhio, tria, tessera, pende, exe, efta, ohto, enya, dheka*.

Greek dialects: ancient and modern

During the early centuries of recorded Greek numerous dialects were spoken. Their mapping is a complex task as migrations and colonizations multiplied. At first no single dialect was standard. In official inscriptions recording laws and religious ceremonies, each city would use its own local dialect. So it was in literature, too, at first. The love poetry of Sappho was written in the Aeolic of Lesbos, her native island. For choral lyrics Doric seemed natural – the legacy of Alcman, who had written songs of matchless beauty for the girl choirs of Doric-speaking Sparta. Tragedy and comedy belonged to the Athenian stage, and were in Attic: so were the writings of the philosophers Plato and Aristotle, who taught in Athens. Medical treatises and notes, traditionally unsigned, were written in the Ionic dialect of Cos, even if Ionic did not

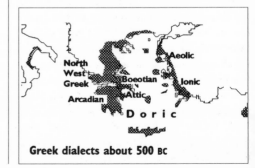

Greek dialects about 500 BC

Greek in the 20th century

come naturally to their authors: Cos was where Hippocrates, father of medicine, had lectured and practised around 500 BC. Thus the use of dialects easily slipped into a stylistic convention. Even the early epics, *Iliad* and *Odyssey*, are recorded in a mixed Ionic/Aeolic dialect which was no one's mother tongue.

The true ancient dialects disappeared as the koiné spread: they have only one modern survival, Tsakonian, descendant of the Laconian variety of Doric. But eventually dialect differences developed in the koiné itself, encouraged by political fragmentation as the Byzantine Empire declined and was extinguished. Modern standard Greek is based on the dialect of Athens. Cyprus has its own local standard. Modern dialects spoken outside Greece and Cyprus include Italiot and Pontic. Italiot is spoken in two small districts in southern Italy, south of Lecce in Apulia and near Bova in Calabria. Greeks had settled in southern Italy by the 7th century BC, but the Greek spoken there will have remained close to standard Greek until the Byzantine Empire lost its Italian foothold around AD 1100. Pontic and Cappadocian were spoken by Greeks who were expelled from northern and central Turkey in 1923, in the 'exchange of populations' that followed the disastrous Greek invasion of Asiatic Turkey. Pontic is still spoken by a few communities in southern Russia, especially near Rostov. Again, the first settlements of Greeks in these regions took place in the 7th century BC and after: under the later Roman Empire almost all of Asia Minor (modern Turkey) was Greek-speaking. Cappadocian Greek communities were Turkish-ruled from 1071 onwards, and their dialect became strongly influenced by Turkish. Pontic grew apart from standard Greek with the decline of Byzantium and the establishment of the independent Empire of Trebizond after the Crusaders captured Constantinople in 1204.

Traditionally, students of Greek have been taught to speak and write classical Attic. An early textbook was composed around AD 170 by Julius Pollux for the future Roman emperor Commodus. Unfortunately, Commodus was more interested in ceramics, dancing and martial arts: 'subjects unsuitable for an emperor,' said his biographer.

In recent times, all over western Europe, Greek has been one of the two 'classical' languages of a full education, though Ben Jonson, a classical scholar, thought none the worse of his contemporary Shakespeare because the latter knew 'small Latin and less Greek'. The writing of classical Attic prose and verse is still a common exercise for students of classics at school and university.

Tsakonian: survival of an ancient dialect

Tsakonian is spoken in an inaccessible mountainous district of the Peloponnese (southern Greece), north of Leonidhi. It is the direct descendant of the Doric dialect of ancient Greek. The link can be seen in the preservation of the old long *a* sound so typical of Doric: Attic *mêlon*, modern standard Greek *mílo*, Doric *mâlon*, Tsakonian *máli* 'apple'. Development in isolation has made Tsakonian very different from modern Greek.

The Tsakonian-speaking villages were listed in a local song:

Alepú tta Síkina	Foxes at Sitena
ke liúko tta Kasténitsa	and wolves at Kastenitsa
ke kukuváya ttom Prasté,	and owls at Prastos –
ke més ta Meliyítika	and up at Meligou
pidhúnde fardakláne.	it's the frogs that dance.

Greek in Writing: 1. the Linear B script

Michael Ventris (1922–56) was an English architect with a flair for languages and cryptography. His discovery that Greek was the language of the Linear B tablets was the culmination of twelve years of interest in the mysterious script, beginning with a paper 'Introducing the Minoan language' published in the *American journal of archaeology* in 1940, when he was 18. Although it contradicted current opinions (classicists used to think that 'the Greeks' could not have invaded Crete until after the time of the tablets) Ventris's insight was soon taken up by others,

notably John Chadwick of Cambridge (see his *The decipherment of Linear B*, 2nd edn, 1967) and Emmett L. Bennett of Yale. Linear B is a syllabary, combining consonant with following vowel in each character.

The Greek alphabet developed out of a Phoenician script that had symbols for consonants only. In the Greek alphabet, vowels were written as well – a spectacular advance. At first, local alphabets varied widely: almost every city seemed to have its own. But by about 400 BC most of them were already using something very like the present upper-case Greek alphabet of 24 characters.

The Greek alphabet

Α Β Γ Δ Ε Ζ Η Θ Ι Κ Λ Μ Ν Ξ Ο Π Ρ Σ Τ Υ Φ Χ Ψ Ω

α β γ δ ε ζ η θ ι κ λ μ ν ξ ο π ρ σ τ υ φ χ ψ ω

a b g d e z ē th i k l m n x o p r s t y ph kh ps ō

Greek in Writing: 2. From alpha to omega

Some argue that it was first used for writing down poetry (notably the epics, *Iliad* and *Odyssey*), while others think that laws and official

inscriptions came first. But the earliest surviving examples of the Greek alphabet are actually 8th-century BC graffiti on a rock face on the island of Thera, mostly recording homosexual encounters.

GUARANÍ

3,000,000 SPEAKERS

Paraguay

Tupí and Guaraní form a closely related group, possibly belonging to the family of AMERIND LANGUAGES. When the Spanish and Portuguese began to explore the south-eastern parts of South America, they found that the languages of Para-guay and coastal Brazil were no more different from one another than were Portuguese and Spanish. Guaraní, the language of Paraguay, was at the eastern end of a dialect chain that stretched unbroken from what is now southern

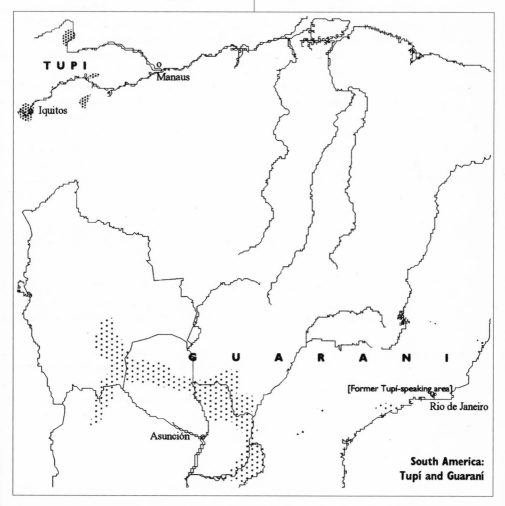

South America:
Tupí and Guaraní

Bolivia to the southern Brazilian coast: the Tupí dialects extended from here north-eastwards.

The later history of these two important languages has been very different. As early as 1583 the Spanish-speaking Jesuits of Paraguay began a programme of settlement and education for the speakers of Guaraní, their converts and subjects. The long term result is that although Guaraní has practically disappeared from the rest of its old territory, Spanish and Guaraní are now the two national languages of Paraguay. Religious texts have been published in Guaraní since the 18th century.

Four centuries of coexistence, during all of which time Spanish has had a higher status, have led to considerable changes in what was at the outset a major language of inland South America, a language relatively uninfluenced by others. Guaraní is now stuffed with Spanish loanwords: in some subject areas the whole vocabulary is Spanish. Even the numeral system is largely Spanish. The common numerals in Guaraní are: *peteĩ, mokõi, mbohapy, irundy, sinko, sei, siete, ocho, nueve, diez*. '5' to '10', and all the higher numerals, are Spanish loanwords, though the old Guaraní word for '5', *pekua*, can still be heard.

As the major language of its region Guaraní has contributed loanwords to several European languages. Those to be found in English include *cougar, jaguar, toucan*. The Guaraní word *petun*, once a synonym for 'tobacco' in English, survives in the name of the botanical genus *Petunia. Para*, a common element in South American place names, is the Guaraní word for 'river'.

The Tupian languages on the map

Guaraní is one of the national languages of Paraguay. There are small communities of speakers in Argentina and Brazil.

Tupi, once a lingua franca of Brazil, now has only a few thousand speakers on the banks of the Vaupés, Içana and Rio Negro in Amazonas state.

Tupian languages once extended from the Amazon southwards to the border of Uruguay.

GUJARATI

45,000,000 SPEAKERS

India, Great Britain

Gujarati is the Indo-Aryan language of the Indian state of Gujarat – and of numerous migrant communities in many parts of the world.

The name is undoubtedly that of the *Gujjars*, a widespread caste, traditionally cattle-farmers. Nomadic members of the community are nowadays most commonly found far to the north, in Kashmir and Himachal Pradesh, where they speak *Gujuri* (see INDO-ARYAN LANGUAGES).

Old Gujarati, ancestor of both Gujarati and Rajasthani, is recorded in texts of the 12th to 14th centuries. Gujarati literature really begins in the 15th century, however, with mystical poets such as Mirabai. Both Persian-Urdu and Sanskrit traditions of poetry continue to influence Gujarati authors. The statesman and writer Mohandas Karamchand Gandhi (1869–1948), born in the Gujarat town of Porbandar, helped to inspire a 20th-century renewal in the literature of his mother tongue.

Although the major regional dialects differ little, there are also social dialects of several kinds. There are strong differences in intonation between men's Gujarati and women's Gujarati. Among tribal dialects are the mountain languages Bhili and Khandesi (see map). An important caste dialect is that of the Parsis, clustering in the southern part of the state. They have a press and literature of their own, quite distinct from standard Gujarati in style and idiom. Muslim speakers of Gujarati – now mostly settled in Pakistan, Bangladesh and Britain –

tend to be at least trilingual, being familiar also with Urdu and having studied classical Arabic. Their Gujarati, like that of the Parsis, contains many Persian loanwords. Another dialect of historical importance is that of Kathiawari sailors, who travelled all over the world as steamship crewmen. Their speech included loanwords from Urdu and several European languages.

In Kutch, in north-western Gujarat state, the 500,000 speakers of the Sindhi dialect *Kacchī* use Gujarati as their literary language.

Outside the borders of Gujarat state, Gujarati speakers are widely scattered: in Maharashtra state; in Pakistan and Bangladesh; in South Africa; in Singapore. One of the oldest communities of the diaspora is in East Africa, where Indian traders (Gujarati, Kacchī and Konkani) were already established in the 1490s when Portuguese explorers reached the Indian Ocean. This linguistic enclave was reinforced when Gujaratis were recruited in large numbers by both British and German governments to work in East Africa around 1900. East African Gujarati became a distinct dialect. Many East African Gujaratis, faced with an increasingly uncertain future and mounting discrimination in newly independent East African countries – especially Uganda – migrated to Britain, where there are now a third of a million speakers of the language, many of them in the London areas of Wembley, Harrow and Newham and in Leicester, Coventry and Bradford.

The Gujarati alphabet

અ આ ઇ ઈ ઉ ઊ ઋ એ ઐ ઓ ઔ કખગઘઙ ચછજઝઞ ટઠડઢણ તથદધન પફબભમ યરલવ શષસહ

a ā i ī u ū ṛ e ai o au k kh g gh ṅ c ch j jh ñ ṭ ṭh ḍ ḍh ṇ t th d dh n p ph b bh m y r l v ś ṣ s h

Numerals in Gujarati

એક	૧	1	ek
બે	૨	2	be
ત્રણ	૩	3	traṇ
ચાર	૪	4	cār
પાંચ	૫	5	pāñc
છ	૬	6	cha
સાત	૭	7	sāt
આઠ	૮	8	āṭh
નવ	૯	9	nav
દસ	૧૦	10	das

The Gujarati Script

The Gujarati script, which is similar to Devanagari but without the headstrokes or 'washing line', was standardised in its present form in the 19th century. The usual transliteration is given in the box. Both script and transliteration are poor at representing the vowel sounds of Gujarati, which actually has 8 normal vowels əaɛeiɔou, no distinction of vowel length, but (especially in the standard and central dialects) a range of breathy vowels.

Gujarati and Rajasthani on the map

Standard literary Gujarati is based on the central dialect of Baroda and Ahmadabad. Other dialects of Gujarati are Pattani (north), Surati or Surti (south) and Kāṭhiyāwaḍī of Saurashtra. They differ relatively little from the standard.

Bhīlī is spoken by the mountain tribes of Bhil, to the east and north-east of Gujarat state. It has numerous dialects: Wāgdī alone claims 750,000 speakers. The whole dialect group may have as many as 2,500,000. Bhīlī is often counted a separate language.

To the south of Bhili, *Khandesī* is another group of hill dialects, with up to a million speakers. Khandesī is heavily influenced by Marathi.

RAJASTHANI, by contrast with Gujarati, has no strong modern literary tradition. Its main dialects are Marwari, Jaipuri, Mewati and Malvi. Nimadi, an isolated southern dialect in a mainly 'tribal' area, has developed special peculiarities.

Gujuri is the language of nearly half a million semi-nomadic herdsmen in Indian and Pakistani Kashmir and in Himachal Pradesh. Gujjars keep buffaloes and cows, while Bakarwals, who speak the same language, keep goats and sheep. Most speakers own their winter pastures, moving to high meadows, *ṭok*, during the summer season, April to August. The language is close to Rajasthani.

Parya is a recently discovered Indo-Aryan language spoken by about 1,000 people in the Hissar valley, Tajikistan. Its history is unknown – but linguistically it seems to belong with Rajasthani and Panjabi.

Rule of thumb

Aro gharo ne, nhālli va'w par āvine paro.
Whatever happens, the youngest
daughter-in-law gets the blame.
Shrikrishna N. Gajendragadkar,
Parsi-Gujarati (Bombay:
University of Bombay, 1974) p. 153

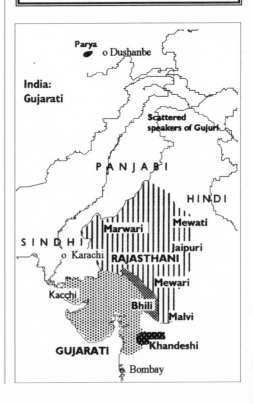

GUSII

2,000,000 SPEAKERS

Kenya

G usii or Kisii is one of the BANTU LANGUAGES, spoken in a heavily populated region of Kenya, the Kisii highlands – two thousand metres high – of Nyanza province. Its speakers trace their history to a migration five hundred years ago. They are predominantly arable farmers and cattle-breeders.

Gusii is remarkable for the low number of words that it shares with other members of the Bantu family, even with neighbours to which it is considered closely related, such as LUYIA (see map there). In fact Gusii has been described as having 'one of the most interfered-with vocabularies in East Africa' (Derek Nurse). It seems to have borrowed from Cushitic languages at some earlier period, and more recently from Nilo-Saharan languages – indeed its territory is entirely surrounded by those of LUO, Kipsigis (see KALENJIN) and MASAI.

HAITIEN

6,000,000 SPEAKERS

Haiti

One of the FRENCH CREOLES, and very close historically and linguistically to the forms of Creole spoken in Guadeloupe, Martinique and other Caribbean islands, Haitien has developed a separate identity thanks to the long independent history of Haiti. It is the one essential everyday language, used throughout the island, but until very recently it had no official recognition, French being regarded as the sole language of government and culture in Haiti. The Haitien spoken in the capital, Port-au-Prince, still shows relatively greater influence from French because of the concentration there of educated speakers and of government offices.

In Haiti, the educated language of the urban elite is French. To reach a wide audience, you write Creole. But a writer's Creole will be influenced, more or less intrusively, by French. For example, in US Embassy publicity, the phrase 'to the United States' may appear in a form closer to standard French, *Ozetazini* (French *aux Etats-Unis*), rather than in the everyday Haitien *peyi Zetazini* (from French *pays* 'country' + *les Etats-Unis* 'the United States').

In the same way, spoken Creole may include more or fewer French features – such as the front-rounded vowel in elevated Creole *zeu* (ordinary Creole *ze*), from French *les oeufs*, 'eggs'.

The Haitian audience

Literacy remains low. Yet Haitian Creole authors still reach a mass audience, as Franketienne, author of *Dezafi* (Port-au-Prince, 1975), explained in an interview:

'Bon, dapre ou menm, konben moun kapab li sa – bagay tankou *Dezafi*, sa ki fèt an kreyòl?'
'Sa k'fèt an kreyòl? M fè eksperyans deja. E gen anpil zanmi ki fè eksperyans nan sèten pwovens.
   Pèp-la pa konn li. Yo li l pou yo. Yo li *Dezafi* nan sètenn rejyon pou de san, sen senkant moun ki reyuni:
   yo konprann tou sa k'ladan yo.'

'Well, according to yourself, how many people are capable of reading it – something like *Dezafi*,
   that's written in Creole?'
'Written in Creole? I have already proved that. I have plenty of friends who have proved that, in
   various parts of the country. People there can't read. They read it for them. They read *Dezafi* in
   some places to two hundred, a hundred and fifty, people at once. They understand everything in it.'

From *Les créoles français entre l'oral et l'écrit* ed. Ralph Ludwig (Tübingen: Narr, 1989) pp. 53–4

If you know French, you will find that this text begins to seem familiar if you read it aloud, making sure that the stress falls on the last syllable of each word as it does in French. A vowel followed by *-n* is nasalised. Notice the following words: *zanmi* (from French *les amis*) 'friends'; *moun* (from French *du monde*) 'people'; *tankou* (from French *tant que*) 'like'; *de san* (from French *deux cents*) 'two hundred'.

HANI

PERHAPS 1,300,000 SPEAKERS

China and south-east Asia

Hani is spoken by mountain-dwellers who live in a compact region of western Yunnan, China, and in scattered villages in four other countries – Vietnam, Laos, Burma and Thailand. It is the main language in the 'southern Loloish' subgroup of SINO-TIBETAN LANGUAGES (see map at BURMESE). Hani speakers are an official nationality of China, with a population there of over 1,000,000. It is only recently that the size of this language community has been realised: earlier estimates were closer to 200,000.

Hani is the official Chinese name for the language and people best known internationally as *Akha*. In Burmese and Shan (and in older English writings) Hani speakers are called *Kaw*, in Lao (and French) *Kha Kaw* or *Kha Ko*, in Thai *Ikaw*, in Vietnamese *Hanhi*.

Hani speakers in southern Yunnan have traditionally been rice farmers, building narrow, irrigated terraces on steep mountainsides; they are also among the growers of Pu'er tea, so named because it is traditionally marketed through the city of Pu'er.

Their migration southwards from Yunnan appears to be quite a recent phenomenon. In the south-east Asian countries Hani speakers are often bilingual in the local majority language such as Shan or Thai. Hani men are often familiar with LAHU, using Lahu loanwords freely in their own language. Roman Catholic missionaries have had some success among Hani speakers and have published religious texts in the language.

For a table of numerals see LAHU.

Hani genealogies and personal names

'Akha culture differs in many ways from that of other Loloish groups such as Lahu. The Akha are preoccupied with religious ritual. The religious leader or *dzŏema* is usually a person of considerable importance, as his title, which includes the verb "rule", implies.

'The village is sited above, not near or below, its water source. At the main entry there is a gate, renewed each year with considerable ritual. Near the centre of the village there is a "swing", which is used only at the New Year, when the gate is renewed. [Villagers take turns swinging, in a ceremony lasting three days, while sacrifices are performed to expel evil spirits.]

'The Akha clans are named according to their common ancestor, and members of a clan are thought to constitute a more or less homogeneous group, speaking a distinct dialect. Every individual has his own genealogy, which includes a series of mythical ancestors preceding the clan founder, then the "common ancestor", and then a series of increasingly more recent ancestors, who are more and more likely to be real, named individuals, until the father is reached. As in the case of genealogies among other Loloish groups, the final syllable of one name is the initial syllable of the following name – unless an individual has been renamed. Thus the son's name normally begins with the last syllable of the father's name.'

David Bradley, *Proto-Loloish* (London: Curzon Press, 1979) pp. 33–4, abridged

Hausa

25,000,000 SPEAKERS OF HAUSA AS A MOTHER TONGUE

Nigeria, Niger, Cameroun

Hausa is the most widely known of the CHADIC
LANGUAGES, which belong to the Afroasiatic
family. Once the language of the Empire of
Sokoto, it is now spoken in the Northern Region
of Nigeria and across most of neighbouring
Niger.

> In Kanuri the Hausa language is *Afŭno* – hence
> its name in some medieval Arabic and 18th-
> century European sources, *Afnu*. The term
> *Hausa* is first recorded, as a tribal name, in a
> 13th-century Arabic text. Speakers call them-
> selves *Háusáawáa* (singular *Bàháushè*).

In medieval times Hausa was the language of
seven states of the 'central Sudan' – in terms of
modern political geography, northern Nigeria.
They and their neighbour Bornu, where KANURI
was spoken, were scarcely known to the outside
world except for the description by the young
Arabic-speaking traveller 'Leo Africanus', written in the early 16th century when he was a
captive in Italy. Some Europeans probably lived
as slaves in the Hausa states in recent centuries,
but none returned.

However, there have always been trade routes
across the Sahara, and in North Africa the de-
voutly Muslim Hausa are still renowned as traders. Their home territory has been a crossroads.
Trade goes from the Niger valley eastwards and
(even more important) from the West and Central African forests northwards, along the Sahara
caravan routes to the Mediterranean. Hausa
themselves, in considerable numbers, have
settled in West and North African cities at the
nodes of these trade routes.

Thus the extent and diversity of the Hausa
country is as striking as the diaspora of Hausa
communities elsewhere. The language is an
indispensable medium of communication for
all inhabitants of northern and central Nigeria
and Niger and for many in Benin, Togo, Ghana,
Chad and Cameroun.

Groups of the essentially nomadic FULANI pastoralists had long settled in the Hausa country. In
1804 a Fulani priest, Osman dan Fodio, founded
the Empire of Sokoto. Through the 19th century
this ruled what is now northern Nigeria. Although
Fulani became the dominant language of the state
of Adamawa, Hausa, language of the great majority elsewhere, maintained its position as the ruling
language of the new empire – and flourished as a
language of written poetry, in the Arabic script
known as *ajami*.

Under British rule Hausa retained official
status – jointly with English – in northern Nigeria, and with their departure it became one of
the official languages of Nigeria. In the early
years of independence there was even a movement to make Hausa the single national language, though against the opposition of most
Ibo and Yoruba speakers (not to mention the
many smaller linguistic groups) this was doomed
to fail. It is, however, used as a second or third
language by a large proportion of the population
of northern Nigeria. As many as 40,000,000
people probably use Hausa on a daily basis.

Hausa has a long tradition of literacy and of
written (mostly religious) literature in ajami script.
Under British rule a Roman alphabet for Hausa
was developed and assiduously encouraged: this
boko script (from English *book*) was made official in
1930. The Hausa Language Board, established in
1955 on the model of other British colonial com-
mittees, worked towards the standardisation of

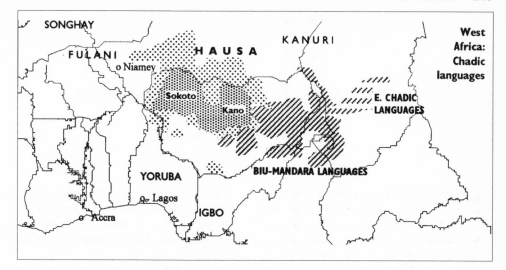

the written language on the basis of the Kano dialect. Literary Hausa is enriched with idioms and phrases drawn from other dialects. There is now a strong press in Hausa and the language is well represented in the media.

Barikanci, a pidgin form of Hausa, grew up around army barracks in northern Nigeria in the early twentieth century and came to be used as a lingua franca by the armed forces. Simplified Hausa is also used on the desert route to Mecca.

Hausa has three tones, high, low and falling. Like other Chadic languages it has a characteristic set of verbal extensions, the effect of which has been compared to the phrasal verbs of English such as *give away, finish up*. There are six verbal extensions in Hausa, including -*a* 'down, properly', -*e*, -*nye* 'completely, all over', -*o*, -*wo* 'towards', -*n* 'to, for'. The first ten numerals are: *ɓaya, biyu, uku, huɓu, biyar, shidà, bakwày, takwàs, tarà, gomà*. Some higher numerals are Arabic loanwords.

Pure Hausa – impure Hausa

As far back as tradition serves, the language was spoken in the 'Hausa seven', *Hausa bakwai*: these seven states are Biram, Daura, Rano, Kano, Zazzau (Zaria), Gobir and Katsena. Here dialect differences are few: the main dialects are those of *Sokoto* and *Kano*.

Nowadays Hausa is spoken, or at least serves as a lingua franca, far beyond this region. Tra-

ditionally Hausa speakers give a list of the *banza bakwai* or 'false seven' states that have adopted something of Hausa language and culture: Zamfara, NUPE, Kebbi, Gwari, Yauri, YORUBA and Kororofa (the *Jukun*-speaking region).

There are long-established Hausa communities in many Ghanaian towns, speaking their own dialect. The Hausa used as a trade language in Ghana is a pidginised form, largely lacking the masculine/feminine distinction (as does the usual spoken English of the area). It is one of the three most important lingua francas of Ghana, along with AKAN and English.

The subgroups of Chadic

The Biu-Mandara languages include *Bura* (250,000 speakers in Bornu State, Nigeria), *Kilba* (100,000 in Gongola State), *Mafa* or Matakam (125,000 in Far North State, Cameroun), *Margi* (200,000 in Bornu and Gongola States, Nigeria), and many smaller languages.

The numerous East Chadic languages are spoken in southern Chad, Cameroun and the Central African Republic. None has more than 50,000 speakers.

West Chadic languages, all spoken in Nigeria, include *Angas* (100,000 speakers), *Bade* (100,000), *Tangale* (100,000) and Hausa. Hausa has 20,000,000 speakers in Nigeria, 2,000,000 in Niger and probably 3,000,000 in other countries.

HAWAIIAN

2,000 SPEAKERS

Hawaii

One of the AUSTRONESIAN LANGUAGES, the most northerly by far of the Polynesian group, Hawaiian was still the language of an important independent kingdom in the early 19th century. Newspapers and a range of publications appeared in it. A Bible translation was published in 1839. It was a language of oral literature, too, notably the creation myth *Kumulipo*.

Now it has been swamped by English, and is spoken only by the two hundred people on Ni'ihau island and by not more than two thousand people in total. Even these are bilingual in English, or in the Hawaiian Creole variety of English.

Hawaiian is studied – along with other languages of Oceania – at the University of Hawai'i. The language is still used in some state ceremonies and in church services, and Hawaiian phrases still impress tourists.

Hawaiian, like other languages of the Polynesian group, has a simple sound pattern, with five vowels and only eight consonants, ' *h k l m n p w*. The first ten numerals in Hawaiian are: *kahi, lua, kolu, haa, lima, ono, hiku, walu, iwa, 'umi*.

HEBREW

3,000,000 SPEAKERS

Israel

One of the SEMITIC LANGUAGES, Hebrew has an astonishing history. It was the language of the early Jews, the language in which the books of the Old Testament were written. Two thousand five hundred years ago, ultimately as a result of the Jewish 'captivity in Babylon', Hebrew ceased to be an everyday spoken language – replaced, naturally enough among a displaced and scattered people, by Aramaic, the lingua franca of the Babylonian and Persian empires.

But Hebrew remained the sacred language of the Jewish religion: and in the early 20th century, as Jews from all over the world began to settle once more in Palestine, Hebrew was revived, from the old texts, as a spoken language. It became an official language in 1922 and is now the everyday speech of Israel and the mother tongue of a growing number of Israelis.

> The English name *Hebrew* comes, by way of Latin and Greek, from Aramaic *'Ebrāyā*. The original is ancient Hebrew *'ibrī* 'from the other side of the river'. Some linguists prefer to distinguish modern Hebrew under the name *Ivrit* (which is the modern pronunciation of its name in Hebrew).

Modern Hebrew necessarily differs from the ancient language. It differs in pronunciation, since it had to compromise with the speech habits of its first new users, mainly Yiddish-speaking, and of more recent immigrants to Israel; in any case the details of ancient pronunciation are not fully known, and it was necessary to build on traditional Hebrew pronunciations used in the religious schools. It differs from ancient Hebrew in vocabulary, too, because

modern life demanded numerous new words including many English loans.

The writings included in the Jewish Bible (the Christian 'Old Testament') were first composed between 1200 and 200 BC, and there are also a few Hebrew inscriptions from this period.

The Hebrew literature of the next period includes the Mishna, Tosephta, Midrash, and various texts called 'apocryphal' (which is essentially a negative term meaning that, though in some ways comparable to Biblical texts, they were not included in the Bible). Although Hebrew had ceased to be used as the mother tongue, it was still the language of scripture and law, and for many centuries also of poetry and philosophy. There was a notable flowering of Hebrew poetry and scholarship in Muslim-dominated Spain, in the 10th and 11th centuries.

By now Jews were writing in other languages too: not only Aramaic and Greek but also JUDEZMO (the Romance language of the *Sephardim* exiled in 1492 from Spain to Turkey) and YIDDISH (the Germanic language of the *Ashkenazim* who spread eastwards from Germany into central and eastern Europe). There are several more Jewish languages, including varieties of ARABIC, PERSIAN and OCCITAN. As migration to Israel has increased, so modern Hebrew is supplanting these other languages, none of which has official status in Israel. There is a growing modern literature in Hebrew.

Like Arabic, Hebrew is a language whose vocabulary is largely built on three-consonant roots. Because of its status as the language of the Old Testament, details of Hebrew and its structure permeate into modern Western languages. Many are aware of the typical Hebrew noun plural suffix *-im* (*cherub, cherubim*).

The first ten numerals in Hebrew are: *akhat, shtayim, shalosh, arba, khamesh, shesh, sheva, shmone, tesha, esser.*

The script

The earliest Hebrew alphabet was derived directly from a Phoenician script. The familiar square Hebrew alphabet of classical and modern times developed out of an Aramaic script, itself originally based on Phoenician.

Vowels can be fully marked in Hebrew writing by the use of additional signs, but this is normally done only in texts of the Bible, where correct pronunciation is essential for religious reasons. Even when using these vowel signs, no distinction is made between the central vowel ə and the absence of a vowel.

The Hebrew alphabet

א ב ג ד ה ו ז ח ט י כ ל מ נ ס ע פ צ ק ר ש ת

'b g d h w z ḥ ṭ y k l m n s ġ p ṣ q r š t

HILIGAYNON

4,600,000 SPEAKERS

Philippines

One of the Bisayan languages, like CEBUANO (see map there), and thus a member of the larger family of AUSTRONESIAN LANGUAGES, Hiligaynon is spoken on the islands of Panay and Siparay (Negros) in the southern Philippines.

There are about 4,600,000 speakers of Hiligaynon. The language is close to *Capiznon* (450,000) of the north-eastern shore of Panay, and to *Masbateño* (350,000) of Masbate, which faces Panay and Siparay across the Visayan Sea. Masbateño in turn is linked with *Northern* or *Masbate Sorsogon* (100,000) of the city of Sorsogon in south-eastern Luzon.

Hiligaynon has become the dominant language in the whole of Panay Island. Speakers of Kinaray-a, to the south-west, and Capiznon, to the north-east, tend to be competent also in Hiligaynon and the national language, Tagalog.

Hiligaynon soldiers were recruited by the Spanish in their conquest of the southern Philippines in the 17th century. This explains the Hiligaynon influence that is evident in the SPANISH creole now spoken in Zamboanga at the western end of Mindanao.

The first ten numerals in Hiligaynon are: *'isah, duhah, tatloh, 'apat, limah, 'anom, pitoh, waloh, siyam, napulo'*.

HINDI

180,000,000 SPEAKERS

India

One of the INDO-ARYAN LANGUAGES, Hindi is cultivated in two forms which may be called two languages, though there are no significant differences of grammar or pronunciation between them. The twin language of Hindi is URDU (see table of numerals there). Hindi contests with English the position of India's principal language.

Hindi is so called as the language 'of India', from the Mughal point of view (Persian *Hind* 'India') – because it was the vernacular of the Delhi region, from which the Mughal Sultans ruled.

The history of Hindi, with the closely related dialects Braj and Awadhi, can be traced to the 12th century: earlier writings from the Hindi-speaking region are in middle Indo-Aryan dialects (Prakrits and Apabhramsas). Until the 19th century Hindi was important only as a spoken language and in literature – nearly all of it in verse, for Hindi has 'a system of versification which for inexhaustible variety, as well as for its intrinsic beauty, is probably unsurpassed' (S.H. Kellogg, *A Grammar of the Hindi Language* (London: Routledge, 1938). In the government of northern India Persian ruled. Under the British Raj Persian eventually declined, but, the administration remaining largely Muslim, the role of Persian was taken not by Hindi but by Urdu, known to the British as Hindustani. It was only as the Hindu majority in India began to assert itself that Hindi came into its own.

As spoken languages, Hindi and its close relatives meanwhile continued to grow as the north Indian population grew. Under British rule millions of speakers found work abroad, and many of them established permanent colonies which still prosper. However, linguists regard the Indo-Aryan languages of these overseas settlements as closer to Bhojpuri than to any other Hindi-like language (see BHOJPURI).

Standard Hindi and Urdu are structurally alike. Both are literary languages based on the spoken dialect of Delhi, known as *Dihlavi* or *Khari Boli* 'standard speech'. But in terms of vocabulary there are strong differences. Urdu draws official, scholarly and religious vocabulary from Persian and, through Persian, from Arabic. Hindi draws on the resources of Sanskrit for learned and technical vocabulary of all kinds. Thus the difference between them is essentially a religious and cultural one, underlined by the fact that they use different scripts.

While the independence movement attempted to unite Hindus and Muslims politically, Mahatma Gandhi urged speakers of Hindi and Urdu to merge their languages in a shared 'Hindustani' – a name which continued to be emphasised in linguistic writings of the period. However, when Pakistan and India were separated on religious lines, Urdu was left as a relatively minor language within India, and Hindi became paramount.

Hindi (*Modern Standard Hindi*, to be precise – *High Hindi*, as it used to be called) is the standard and official language of a vast inland region of India: Delhi and the states of Uttar Pradesh, Bihar, Madhya Pradesh, Rajasthan, Haryana and Himachal Pradesh. Throughout these states it is the language of administration, the press, schools and literature. More than that, Hindi has official status, alongside English, throughout India – unlike all the other official languages of

India, which are recognised only in their own states or districts. This special position of Hindi is a compromise. Proponents of Hindi wanted it to take the place of English as India's lingua franca. It may still do so: but as yet speakers of the other state languages of India generally prefer English, not Hindi, to be their second language.

Hindi literature is taken, these days, to include the classics written in the older standard languages Braj and Awadhi. Old Hindi literature, antedating these, is relatively small in bulk (it includes two short pieces in the *Adi Granth* of the Sikhs, attributed to the Sufi saint Baba Farid, who died in 1266). Braj was the language for praises of Krishna; traditionally associated with the cities of Mathura and Vrindaban, it was used for poetry from the 16th to the early 20th century. Awadhi belongs to literature in praise of Rama, legendary king of Ayodhya, and was used for poetry between the 16th and 18th centuries. The great *Ramcaritmanas* of Tulsidas is in Old Baishwari or Old Awadhi of the late 16th century. The oral epic *Alhakhand* is traditionally sung in Banaphari, a mixed Bundeli-Bagheli dialect of Hamirpur where the action of the epic takes place.

The *Sadhu Bhasha*, the fluid mixed literary language of the Nirguna tradition of mystical poets, beginning with Kabir in the late 15th century, incorporated some elements of *Khari Boli*, the local language on which Hindi is directly based. But the creation of modern 'High Hindi' as a literary language in the early 1800s is credited to Lallu Lal, author of *Prem Sagar* and *Rajniti*, retellings of Sanskrit classics which immediately achieved classic status themselves. Hindi is now the language of a prolific literature in prose as well as verse.

Hindi *-vālā*, English *wallah*

Hindi has the unusual distinction of having contributed a (now rather old-fashioned) loan suffix to English: this is the form *-vālā* added to a noun, English *wallah*. Hindi examples: *dudhvālā* 'milkman', *Dihlīvālā* 'man from Delhi', *Kābulvālā ghoṛā* 'horse from Kabul'. One of the oldest Anglo-Indian examples is *competition-wallah* 'one who got his job by competitive examination'.

Hindi is an easy language for the average West European learner. It is clearly Indo-European in much of its structure, but, as with English, un-

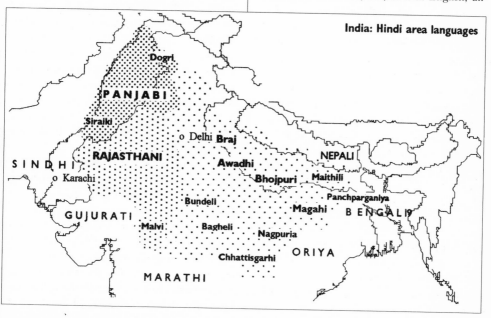

India: Hindi area languages

varying prepositions and particles tend to replace the complex noun and verb inflections of older forms of the language. It has two genders (Sanskrit and Pali still retained three from Indo-European).

The Hindi language area

The linguistic map of the north Indian plains cannot be drawn in sharp lines. In the neighbourhood of Delhi, the local speech varieties (*Khari Boli*) would be regarded by everybody as dialects of Hindi. Almost as close to Standard Hindi is Eastern PANJABI, yet that is treated – here and elsewhere – as a separate language. As one moves outwards from Delhi, one comes to other dialects which have had claims to the status of 'language': *Braj* (centred on Agra, capital city from 1566 to 1658) and *Awadhi* (of the old kingdom of Oudh). Then come some language varieties that are rather more distinct from Hindi: BHOJPURI, MAGAHI and MAITHILI, the three once grouped together as *Bihari*, but that was a name dreamed up by a linguist which has no cultural validity; CHHATTISGARHI; RAJASTHANI.

Bhojpuri is spoken in the middle Ganges val-ley, both north and south of the historic city of Benares. Sadani or *Nagpuria* may be regarded as a dialect of Bhojpuri: it is the vernacular and lingua franca of the eastern Chota Nagpur plateau.

Magahi is spoken in the southern half of Bihar, notably the cities of Patna and Gaya. *Panchparganiya* is the eastern dialect of Magahi.

Maithili is the language of northern Bihar and southern Nepal.

Chhattisgarhi is spoken in south-eastern Madhya Pradesh in the districts of Raipur, Bilaspur, Raigarh, eastern Balaghat and northern Bastar.

Rajasthani is itself a grouping of quite varied dialects, a reflection of the long political fragmentation of what is now the state of Rajasthan.

The script

The most striking difference between Hindi and Urdu is in their scripts. Urdu uses a form of Arabic script. Hindi is written in the Devanagari alphabet which is also used for Nepali and Marathi and is the usual choice for printing Sanskrit.

The Devanagari alphabet for Hindi

अ आ इ ई उ ऊ ऋ ऌ ए ऐ ओ औ क ख ग घ ङ च छ ज झ ञ ट ठ ड ढ ण त थ द ध न प फ ब भ म य र ल व श ष स ह

a ā i ī u ū ṛ ḷ e ai o au k kh g gh ṅ c ch j jh ñ ṭ ṭh ḍ ḍh ṇ t th d dh n p ph b bh m y r l v ś ṣ s h

---

Like all the major languages of south Asia, Hindi can be written in any south Asian script. The Indian prime minister H. D. Deve Gowda, a native Kannada speaker, gave the traditional Independence Day speech in 1996 in Hindi – but he is said to have read from a text converted for him into Kannada script.

HIRI MOTU

PERHAPS 250,000 SPEAKERS OF HIRI MOTU AS A LINGUA FRANCA

Papua New Guinea

Motu, which belongs to the Oceanic group of AUSTRONESIAN LANGUAGES, is one of the two local languages of the Port Moresby region in Papua New Guinea. In this linguistically fragmented region the speakers of Motu appear to have developed in contact with their immediate neighbours a pidginised or simplified form of their language which was used in local trade.

'This Foreigner Talk or Simplified Motu is presumed to have been taken up, used and spread by relatively large numbers of foreigners who settled or traded in the Port Moresby area in the late 1870s and throughout the 1880s, some . . . later employed by the Government as interpreters, guides, boatmen and unofficial policemen' (Dutton).

Police Motu was traditionally looked down on by external observers, who viewed it as a 'corrupt' Motu. But Seventh Day Adventist missionaries found it indispensable in missionary work. The first study of Police Motu, published as late as 1962, found that the so-called Central dialect, in general used by speakers of Austronesian languages related to Motu, differed from the non-Central dialect used by speakers of Papuan languages both in phonetics and grammar – for example, in having a range of possessive suffixes, *-gu* 'my',*-na* 'your', *-na* 'his, her, its'.

The first three numerals are: *ta, rua, toi*. Numerals above '3' are English loanwords.

When Papua became a British colony in 1888, this language soon became indispensable to the local administration and particularly to the police force that was established in 1890. *Police Motu* – as it was still called until recently – gradually spread all over Papua with government control and peacekeeping.

Until recently, Police Motu had no official recognition or encouragement. It is now accepted alongside English and TOK PISIN, the local English-based creole, as a national language of Papua New Guinea and an important medium of communication across language boundaries. However, it is in practice less used officially than the other two, and is seldom heard in Parliament. The new official name, *Hiri Motu*, comes from the probably mistaken belief that Motu speakers once used this language on their long distance trading voyages, *hiri*.

Based on Thomas E. Dutton, 'Police Motu of the Second World War' in *Pacific linguistics*, A 76 (1988) pp. 133–79 and other sources

HITTITE

Extinct language of Turkey

'Hittites' were known only from references in the Bible and other ancient Near Eastern sources until the beginning of the 20th century. Then clay tablets written in an unknown non-Egyptian language were found at Amarna in Egypt. Soon afterwards, great numbers of tablets in the same language were found in the excavation of what was evidently a royal capital, Boğazköy in north central Turkey. The history of this kingdom can now be traced in documentary and literary texts in its local language from about 1780 to 1200 BC.

An unrelated people of central Turkey are called *Hatti* in the texts: the capital city now known as Boğazköy had the related name *Hattušas*. But the name that speakers of what we call 'Hittite' gave to their language is not known.

The tablets could not at first be read. The Czech scholar Bedřich Hrozný showed in 1915 that they were a very ancient record of an Indo-European language, from a branch hitherto completely unknown.

Hittite texts include laws, myths (some of them Hattic and Hurrian in origin), historical texts and poetry. The Hittite law texts are organised in two series, the first known as *If a man . . .*, the second *If a vineyard . . .*, from the first words of each. Hittite religious poetry includes passages in the older Hattic language.

The Hittite kingdom in its heyday was in close touch with other Near Eastern peoples. The Assyrian trading colony of Kanesh was not far to the south. The Hurrians to the east (see CAUCASIAN LANGUAGES) were conquered around 1380 BC, and many Hurrian loanwords are found in Hittite texts. By about 1300 the Hittite kingdom dominated nearly all of Anatolia, and contested Syria with the Egyptians.

After the destruction of Hattušas by invaders, around 1200, Hittites gradually disappear from the historical and linguistic record.

The language of the tablets is usually divided into three periods, Old Hittite (to about 1550 BC, coinciding with what historians call the Old Kingdom), Middle and Late Hittite. Hittite was in many ways very close to reconstructed proto-Indo-European. Famously, it alone retained the postulated laryngeal consonants of the ancestral language (see box at INDO-EUR-OPEAN LANGUAGES). However, Hittite does not have the dual number or the masculine/feminine gender distinction which are otherwise typical of Indo-European languages, especially at earlier periods.

The numerals in Hittite are not fully known, because they were usually written in 'figures' rather than words in Hittite texts.

The Anatolian languages

There is evidence of two other languages in the Hittite texts. *Palaic* was spoken in northern Anatolia in Hittite times. *Luwian*, to the south, is known from cuneiform texts and also from a few hieroglyphic inscriptions (sometimes called 'Hieroglyphic Hittite'). Palaic and Luwian were both related to Hittite, and are grouped with it as 'Anatolian languages' within the INDO-EUROPEAN family (see map there). At least two languages contemporary with classical Greek – *Lydian* and *Lycian* – also belonged to the Anatolian branch; Lycian was in essence a later form of Luwian.

Hittite cuneiform

Hittite cuneiform script originated as an adaptation to a completely different language of the script that was first devised for Sumerian and later used for Akkadian. The script carries its history with it: partly phonetic, it also includes word forms taken directly from Akkadian cuneiform script, and more than a thousand word forms ('Sumerograms') inherited from Sumerian by way of Akkadian. The way that Hittite scribes and readers would have pronounced these words is often unknown.

The cuneiform script was never well suited to Hittite, whose sound pattern was evidently very different from that of Akkadian. The native 'hieroglyphic' script actually survived longer, continuing to be used by speakers of Hittite in northern Syria long after the Hittite kingdom and Hittite cuneiform had passed into history.

HUNGARIAN

15,000,000 SPEAKERS

Hungary, Romania, Slovakia

One of the URALIC LANGUAGES, Hungarian is separated by thousands of miles from its close linguistic relatives, Khanty and Mansi, the 'Ob-Ugric' languages of the Ob valley in western Siberia.

Hungarians may be identifiable in history in the 5th century AD, as *Onogouroi*, a tribe driven from their Siberian home by a series of migrations of other peoples. If the identification is correct, then for some centuries thereafter Hungarian horsemen roamed the Russian steppe and the plains of central Europe, fighting variously for Romans, Khazars, Franks and others. At any rate, Hungarian speakers conquered the Pannonian plains, the country now called Hungary, in 895–6.

Here the Hungarian language developed under the influence of Old Slavonic, of medieval Latin and of German. In the 16th and 17th centuries Hungary was divided between the Holy Roman (German) and the Ottoman Empires. As Ottoman power waned, an Austrian Empire grew, an em-

pire which eventually had two governing languages, German and Hungarian, and many less privileged minorities. A policy of 'Magyarisation' imposed Hungarian as the first language of the south-eastern half of the empire: but this policy remained unpopular with most of the minorities, and in practice German remained the first lingua franca of Austria-Hungary. Many Hungarians have themselves been bilingual in German.

> Hungarians call themselves *Magyar* (and their country *Magyarország*). This may be in origin a tribal name – identical with *Mansi* and with *Måsy*, which is the name of one of the two formerly exogamous clans of the Khanty.
> All three peoples, Mansi, Khanty and Hungarians, were called *Ugri, Yugra* in early medieval times. From this useful word come the linguists' terms for several language groupings – Finno-Ugric, Ugric, Ob-Ugric – and also the usual foreign name for *Hungarian*.

Hungarian and the Ob-Ugric languages

After 1918 Austria-Hungary was broken up. The boundaries then drawn, which left many Germans and Hungarians in the novel position of minorities in new nation-states, have been a source of dissatisfaction for Hungarians ever since. Several major Hungarian settlements exist well beyond the borders of modern Hungary. The largest such group lives in northern and eastern Transylvania (*Erdély*, 'the forest country' in Hungarian). Hungarian speakers there number well over 1,500,000, the majority in a compact enclave in the south-east: these are known as *Székely* in Hungarian, *Secui* in Romanian. There are others in north-eastern Serbia, Ukraine and southern Slovakia. Those who lived in the *Csángó* enclave in Moldavia migrated en masse to western Hungary early in the 20th century, but perhaps 50,000 remain.

There are now many Hungarian émigrés in Britain, other European countries, Australia and the Americas. Mass emigrations took place after 1918, during the 1930s (particularly of Jews), after 1945, and after the 1956 uprising.

The early literature of Hungary was in Latin, from the Anonymous Chronicle of the 12th century to the classicising poetry of Czesmicze János (1434–1472; his Latin name is Janus Pannonius, 'John the Hungarian') under King Matthew Corvinus, a patron of scholarship. But some texts in Hungarian survive from as far back as the 13th century. The first Hungarian printed book appeared – at Krakow in modern Poland – in 1527.

> In Hungarian, surnames precede Christian names; -*né* means 'Mrs'. *Platt Jánosné*, 'Mrs John Platt', was how one 19th-century authoress, who happened to be married to an Englishman, signed her novels.
> Traditionally a Hungarian's full name included the village of origin. *Misztótfalusi Kis Miklós* is the full native name of the 17th-century typographer known abroad as 'Nicholas Kis', who was born in the small mining town of Misztótfalu (Tăuţii) in present-day Romania.

Literature in Hungarian flourished in the late 18th and 19th centuries. Hungary's 'national poet', Petöfi Sándor (1823–49), a fanatical democrat, rose to the rank of major in the revolutionary army of the 1848 uprising and was killed at the battle of Segesvár (Sighişoara) in Romania.

Hungarian has 7 short vowels *a e i o ö u ü* and 7 long vowels *á é í ó ő ú ű*. Nouns and verbs are highly inflected, nouns having at least 238 possible forms.

Loanwords in Hungarian

Older Turkic loanwords in Hungarian are evidence that Hungarian nomadic horsemen worked with and learnt from the Volga Bulgars, who spoke a Turkic language (see CHUVASH). They include *alma* 'apple', *árpa* 'barley', *ökör* 'ox', *bor* 'wine', *tyúk* 'hen'.

Slavonic loanwords are a reminder that Pannonia had been Slavonic-speaking when the Hungarians occupied it, and that Slavonic-speaking missionaries converted them to Christianity: *káposzta* 'cabbage', *pohar* 'glass', *szent* 'holy', *templom* 'church'.

German loanwords (for example, German *Graf*, Hungarian *gróf* 'Count') demonstrate Hungary's long political coexistence with Germany and Austria. *Kávé* 'coffee' is a later loanword from Turkish: it arrived under Ottoman rule.

Hungarian and the Ob-Ugric languages

Speakers of Mansi, only about 4,000 in total, live among the eastern foothills of the Urals in the valleys of the Sos'va, the Konda and other tributaries of the Ob. They were traditionally called *Vogul* by outsiders after another river, the Vogulka, flowing through their territory.

Khanty or Ostyak speakers occupy a much larger but even more thinly populated region to their east, in the middle and lower Ob basin. They number over 15,000. *Khanty* means 'people': it is probably related to Hungarian *had* 'fighting men'. *Ostyak*, from Tatar *istäk*, was an outsiders' name for all the indigenous peoples of Siberia and their languages, sometimes applied also to Selkup (see SAMOYEDIC LAN-

GUAGES) and to one of the PALAEOSIBERIAN LANGUAGES.

Linguistic renewal – 18th-century style

There are fewer German words in Hungarian than there used to be, thanks to a movement begun in the late 18th century to reduce the German element in the language. 'Old words were revived, and full use was made of the resources of derivation. New compounds were fabricated, sometimes by mutilation, e.g. *csőr* "bill, beak, nib" from *cső* "tube" and *orr* "nose". Folk etymologies were invented, e.g. *szivar* "cigar" from the verb *szív-* "suck". The most remarkable example of successful rashness in these endeavours is *minta* "sample, model, pattern", which is a most current and indispensable word in modern Hungarian. It was taken from a Lapp [SAMI] dictionary – it is, as a matter of fact, a Norwegian loanword in Lapp, now obsolete in both languages – under the false pretence that it has a Hungarian etymon: *mint* "as, like" + *a* "that one".'

Bjorn Collinder, *An introduction to the Uralic languages* (Stockholm: Almqvist & Wiksell, 1960) pp. 32–3

Two thousand years ago, early Hungarian speakers, too, must have lived in the neighbourhood of the Urals. They occupied modern Hungary after a series of epic wanderings.

Numerals in Hungarian, Khanty and Mansi

	Hungarian	Khanty	Mansi
1	egy	ĭt	akwa
2	kettő	katən	kitıgh
3	három	khutəm	khūrŭm
4	négy	nyătə	nyila
5	öt	wet	at
6	hat	khut	khōt
7	hét	tapət	sāt
8	nyolc	nyŭwtə	nyollow
9	kilenc	yĭryan	öntəllow
10	tíz	yang	low

IBAN

Perhaps 1,200,000 speakers

Indonesia, Malaysia

Iban, formerly known as *Sea Dayak*, is the mother tongue of about a third of the population of Sarawak, and of a large, scattered population in western and southern Kalimantan. It is one of the AUSTRONESIAN LANGUAGES, close to Malay and the Malayic languages of Sumatra. For a map and table of numerals see MALAY.

Dayak was once used to denote several peoples of the rivers of Borneo, whose languages are not closely related. *Land Dayak*, as the name suggests, is an inland language of the valleys where Sea Dayak or Iban is spoken: it has about 50,000 speakers. *Ngaju Dayak*, a Barito language related to MALAGASY, is a language of 250,000 speakers in the valleys of south-western Kalimantan.

Speakers of Iban have traditionally settled in river valleys and are traders along river and coastal routes. Their language is a lingua franca throughout these valleys. They have a rich oral literature of ritual and epic, not all of which has been recorded. Their religion is strongly influenced by the Hinduism that came to the Malay Archipelago two thousand years ago, and the language shows Sanskrit influence.

Dialects of Iban

'It is homogeneous: dialect words are few and differences between areas of settlement are differences of accent, and of detail in custom and ritual. The extremes are, on the one hand, the so-called "Saribas" Iban of the northern Second Division, who have combined with the previous inhabitants, have long been closely associated with Malays, and were the first to profit from extensive rubber plantations and the opportunities of literacy afforded by mission schools; and, on the other, the pioneer communities of the Ulu Ai and Bajleh on the eastern flank of migration whose manner is bluff and whose language is short and rapid. The latter tend to regard the former as precious and a little comic; the former see the latter as uncouth and rustic. In between are the great majority known by the names of the other rivers of the Second Division.'

Anthony Richards, *An Iban–English dictionary* (Oxford: Clarendon Press, 1981) p. ix

Ngaju Dayak and the language of praise

Ngaju communities hold ceremonies at which oral poetry is performed in a traditional language 'for discussing the gods', *Sangiang*. Verses are spoken by an expert poet, and repeated in turn by four or six apprentices, who also accompany the words with a rhythmical drum beat. This poetry, usually celebrating or mourning a contemporary, is marked by two-line parallelism and by pervasive internal rhyme:

lii . . .

Nyaho hai mamparuguh tungkupah,
Kilat panjang mamparinjet ruang!

The great thunder exerts its power,
The long lightning ignites the heaven!

lii . . .

Tesek bewey kalingun Sambang hariak nanjulu,	Memory of Sambang begins to ripple like the
kilaw riak kalawaw kabantukan danaw,	ripples of a fish on the surface of a lake,
Pandang tege karendem garu haringki, tingkah	Knowledge of him starts to well up like the
pahi laut Bukit Liti!	waves of a river fish off Bukit Liti!

From Kma M. Usop, 'Karunya: the Ngaju Dayak songs of praise' in *Papers from the Third International Conference on Austronesian Linguistics* ed. Amran Halim and others (Canberra: Australian National University, Research School of Pacific Studies, 1982) vol. 3 pp. 319–24

ICELANDIC

250,000 SPEAKERS

Iceland

A descendant of OLD NORSE (see map at NORWE-GIAN), Icelandic developed from the speech of the Vikings who settled Iceland from 870 onwards and officially adopted Christianity in the year 1000.

The island was self-governing until 1262. Thereafter it was ruled by Norway, and along with Norway was transferred to Danish rule in the 14th century. Iceland became fully independent only in 1944. The revival of Icelandic as a literary and official language is thus a very recent event. The language is still in general closer than any of its relatives to Old Norse.

Icelandic names

Most Icelanders do not have surnames but patronymics. Forenames are followed by 'son of . . .' or 'daughter of . . .' and the father's name. The system is no different from that to be found in the sagas, and it was once used throughout Scandinavia.

Hansen is now one of the commonest surnames in Denmark and Norway. Its origin was as a 'special case' in the system of patronymics. It meant 'his son', that is, 'God's son': it was an indication that the child's true father was unknown or unacknowledged.

In the absence of surnames, the Icelandic telephone book lists subscribers under their forenames.

The great literary works of Iceland – its prose sagas – date from the 12th and 13th centuries. They were written for recitation, in a simple and vivid language that had as yet hardly differentiated from Old Norse. Many, including *Brennu-*

Njals saga 'The story of the burning of Njal' and *Laxdaela saga*, are anonymous. Ari the Learned (1068–1148) and Snorri Sturluson (1179–1241) were the greatest named authors of medieval Iceland. Snorri, with his *Heimskringla*, was responsible for the gathering of the histories of the Norwegian kings; in the so-called *Prose Edda* he set out a schema of Norse mythology, with many illustrative quotations from Old Norse poetry.

The study and printing of medieval Icelandic literature began in the 18th century. The priceless manuscripts collected by Arne Magnusson (the Arnamagnaean collection) were for a long time held at the Royal Library in Copenhagen, but have now returned to Iceland.

For a table of numerals see SWEDISH.

Entertainment with a purpose

Ketill Flatnefr hét einn ágætr hersir i Noregi. Hann var sonr Bjarnar Bunu, Gríms sonar hersis ór Sogni. Ketill var kvángaðr; hann átti Ingvildi dóttur Ketills veðrs, hersis af Raumaríki . . .

Ketil 'Flatnose' was a famous chieftain in Norway. He was the son of Bjorn 'Roughfoot', the son of Grim, a chieftain of Sogn. Ketil was married; he had as his wife Ingvild, daughter of Ketil 'Wether', chieftain of Raumarik . . .

Eyrbyggja saga, 1

Icelandic sagas kept alive the knowledge of how, and by whom, the country had been settled, and how each farming family was related to its neighbours. Typically a saga covers several generations of the local history of a district of Iceland – and deals with disputes over land ownership and status that result in litigation, feud and murder.

IGBO

12,000,000 SPEAKERS

Nigeria

Igbo is one of the four national languages of Nigeria, alongside Hausa, Yoruba and English. It belongs to the family of NIGER-CONGO LANGUAGES, and it is likely to have been spoken in its present location for many hundreds of years.

The meaning of *Igbo* or *Ibo* is uncertain: perhaps 'people', or possibly 'slaves', a name that might have been applied to Igbo speakers in the neighbouring Igala language. Certainly many of them suffered enslavement; Igbo speakers were already, perforce, crossing the Atlantic in the 17th century.

The absence of a centralised state among earlier Igbo speakers has contributed to dialect differentiation (see map). Neighbouring languages, including Isoko, Edo, Igala, Idoma, Ibibio and Ijo, have influenced the dialects to which they lie closest. English, more recently, has been a powerful influence on all Igbo dialects and on the standard language.

Retaining power

okwuru akaa onye kuru ya, 'Okra never grows taller than the one who plants it'. A useful proverb, but is it literally true? Yes – because the farmer can always bend the plant to a convenient height.

The dialect used for the earliest religious publishing was not the mother tongue of any Nigerian. Originating in Freetown, Sierra Leone, it was a mixed dialect or lingua franca spoken among ex-slaves of Igbo origin who worked with European missionaries to bring Christianity to the Igbo speakers of Nigeria, beginning in 1841. The first printed book in Igbo, a primer and prayer book compiled by the YORUBA linguist Samuel Crowther, appeared in 1857 in this *Isuama* dialect, which was difficult for native Igbo speakers to understand.

Igbo in writing

For a long time two different Igbo spellings were in competition. The Old orthography, developed by Samuel Crowther and J. F. Schön, represented only six vowels, *a e i o o u*. The New orthography of Ida Ward and R. F. G. Adams, developed in the 1930s, gave all eight, but used three characters that were difficult to type and print, *a e i o u ɛ ɔ ɸ*. The Catholics accepted it but the Protestants did not. Finally, in 1961, the Official orthography devised by S. E. Onwu and others satisfied all difficulties. It represents all eight vowels, and its dotted vowels mark Igbo vowel harmony effectively: the 'odd' vowels *i e o u* have no dots, while three of the four 'even' vowels *i a o u* are dotted.

Southern dialects have a separate set of nasal consonants, but these are usually not written. Nor are the high and low tones that are an important feature of the language.

'Union' Igbo was devised soon after 1900, as a mixture of five dialects, and was used for a Bible translation. 'Central' Igbo was a conscious development of the 1930s: it was another artificial standard, but a more successful one, based essentially on the Umuahia and Owere dialects.

This has been used even by some speakers of Onitsha Igbo, though Onitsha has a rather different consonant pattern: *l* for Central *r, n* for *l, f* for *h*. Standard Igbo, encouraged by the Society for Promoting Igbo Language and Culture, has been the most successful written standard of all. It shows relatively greater influence of the Onitsha dialect.

Since the introduction of the Official Orthography in 1961 (see box) the Igbo press and publishing have grown rapidly. Onitsha, centre of the earliest missionary activities, is a major market city and still a focus of Igbo written culture.

Igbo has three verbs 'to be': *-bu* to identify, *-no* to locate animate subjects, *-di* to locate inanimates. The first ten numerals are: *otu, abua, ato, ano, ise, isi, asa, asato, iteghete, iri.*

Igbo and its dialects

The major dialect division is between *Onitsha* to the north and *Owere* to the south. The dialect of Onitsha city is distinct, and has strong links with those of the west bank of the Niger. The old city of Bonny, on the coast, has its own Igbo dialect: it was once a major centre for the export of slaves.

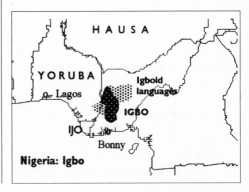

Nigeria: Igbo

IJO AND KALABARI

600,000 SPEAKERS

Nigeria

Ijo, one of the most important regional languages of southern Nigeria, belongs to the
NIGER-CONGO LANGUAGES.

The name has been spelt in many ways: *Ijo,
Ijaw, Izon, Udso, Djo* will all be found. Some
members of the Ijo dialect continuum have
been regarded as separate languages, including *Brass* or *Nembe* (see map) and the *Kalabari*
of the old trading ports of Calabar and its
neighbourhood.

Ijo speakers live in the Niger Delta, where
travel is often easiest by water. Inland there is
rich farmland, replenished by the Niger's regular
floods; in the tidal regions near the coast the local
economy depends on fishing and on trade.

The language is usually regarded as a separate
branch of Niger-Congo, not closely linked to any
of its neighbours. Its early history is unknown.
The first recorded Ijo word occurs in Duarte
Pacheco Pereira's geographical survey, *Esmeral-
do de situ orbis*, in 1500: by this time, at any rate,
Ijo speakers already lived where they do now.
From the 16th to the early 19th centuries their
trade flourished, as they held the middle ground
between European mariners and the inland
kingdoms. Calabar is only the most famous of
the Ijo city states. It was also a slave port, from
which many, Ijo and others, were sold across the
Atlantic, where they were called *Caravali, Kal-
bary* or *Calabars*. With the British annexation of
Nigeria, Ijo prosperity declined.

Writing and publishing in Ijo was begun by
missionaries, who have used many dialects. Ibani
or 'Bonny' was the first dialect to be used for
Bible translations, beginning in 1870. In 1956
the complete Bible appeared in Nembe, which

was then expected to become the universal
written language for all Ijo. This did not happen,
but it remains a major standard alongside Kolokuma and Kalabari.

Kalabari itself has nearly a million speakers
and is one of the languages used in broadcasting
in Nigeria. There is some publishing in Kalabari,
which is a lingua franca for speakers of smaller
neighbouring languages such as Ido.

Ijo speakers are traditionally traders, and
frequent travel has helped to keep dialect
divergences within bounds. There is also intermarriage, and thus bilingualism, between Ijo and
IGBO. English, and Nigerian Pidgin English, are
widely known.

The first ten numerals in Ijo are: *kẹnẹ, mamọ,
taro, nẹyi, shọnrọ, shendiye, shonoma, ningina, essiẹ, oyi.*

Dialects of Ijo

Ijo is spoken in many dialects, most often known
by the name of their *Ibe* 'clan'. In general the
dialects are mutually intelligible, but, for example, while Nembe speakers understand Kalabari

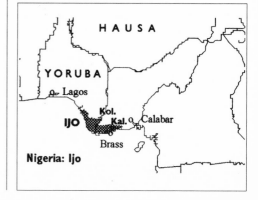

Nigeria: Ijo

without difficulty, Kalabari speakers have more difficulty with Nembe.

Nembe or Brass-Nembe is the Southern Ijo standard language. *Akassa* is close to Nembe.

Kolokuma or Patani is the Northern Ijo standard. Two related dialects are *Gbanran* and *Ekpetiama*.

Kalabari forms a single dialect group, called 'Eastern Ijo', with *Okrika*, *Ibani* and *Nkoro*. Ibani, important in the 19th century, is now spoken only in part of Bonny town and a few villages; it has been supplanted by Igbo. In Calabar town EFIK is also spoken.

South Eastern, South Central, North Eastern and North Western dialect groups are also distinguished.

ILOCANO

5,000,000 SPEAKERS

Philippines

One of the AUSTRONESIAN LANGUAGES, Ilocano is the major language of the northern provinces of the Philippine island of Luzon (see map at TAGALOG). Its closest linguistic relative is Pangasinan.

> *Ilocano* – a Spanish form of the word – is the language of *Ilocos*. There are several variant spellings of the language name, including *Ilokano, Iloko*. An alternative name in local literature is *Samtoy*.

Ilocano is the everyday language in the provinces of La Union, Ilocos Sur, Ilocos Norte and Abra, but not in Batanes, where Ivatan is the local language. It is also widely spoken in Pangasinan, except the central region, where PANGASINAN retains its dominance. Ilocano had been studied by Spanish missionaries and was naturally one of the first languages in which the United States Army, newly charged with the rule of the Philippines, took an interest. Henry Swift, in his *Study of the Iloko language* (Washington, 1909), wrote of the people of the Philippines, 'he is best equipped and prepared to do his work, especially a government official, who

can meet them on their own ground', and the army offered incentives to its officers to study Ilocano and other Philippine languages. Later, the syntax by Leonard Bloomfield, published in the journal *Language* in 1942, was a landmark in the study of Ilocano.

Ilocano is unique among the major Philippine languages – those of large, partly urbanised and mainly Christian peoples – as being the language of a traditional oral epic which survived long enough to be recorded by modern folklorists and anthropologists. Five versions of the story of *Lam-ang* were collected between 1889 and 1947.

Why did *Lam-ang* survive? Its setting is the frontier between Ilocano speakers and the 'blackest mountain', home of the Igorot tribe, who were never subdued during the four centuries of Spanish rule – and who had killed Don Juan, Lam-ang's father, before the hero was born. The threat of the Igorots was a real one until quite modern times, and the epic was as relevant as ever.

The first ten numerals in Ilocano are: *maysa, dua, tallo, uppat, lima, innem, pito, walo, siam, sangapulo*.

Ilocanos and Igorots

Ta idintocan a magtengnan	And when he reached
ti bantay a cangisitan	The blackest mountain
idiai Mamdili ken Dagman	In the towns of Mamdili and Dagman
dimmagus iti tallaongdan.	He went straight to the gathering.
Ket inna met nakitan	There he saw
daydi bangabanga ni amanan	His father's skull
ta napanda met sinarucang	Which had been placed on a stick
nga impasango iti dayaan.	And made to face the feast.

Text edited by Leopoldo Y. Yabes, 1935. From *Epics of the Philippines* ed. Jovita Ventura Castro and others (Quezon City: ASEAN Committee on Culture and Information, 1983) p. 72

INDO-ARYAN LANGUAGES

The history of the Indo-Aryan group of languages goes back four thousand years. About that time, somewhere in central Asia, the speakers of 'Indo-Iranian' – one of the early INDO-EUROPEAN LANGUAGES or dialects – divided. The divergent group was to make its way towards northern India. Its dialect was an ancestral form of the modern Indo-Aryan languages, which are now spoken by over 600,000,000 people, in the northern part of the Indian subcontinent and in many other parts of the world.

The dialects of those left behind, who continued to occupy the central Asian steppe, and eventually spread into Iran, were the earliest distinct form of the IRANIAN LANGUAGES. The name *Ārya* was used by both groups. *Indo-Aryan* was invented by modern scholars to mean 'the Aryan languages of India' as opposed to those of Iran.

India itself is a Greek and Latin term for 'the country of the River *Indus*'. The official name of India is *Bhārata*, the land of the Bharata tribe whose legendary story is told in the Sanskrit epic *Mahābhārata*.

The Indo-Aryan languages occupy a region where DRAVIDIAN LANGUAGES and AUSTROASIATIC LANGUAGES (and perhaps others now quite unknown) were spoken before them. They show influences from both these families. Development of written culture influenced other south and south-east Asian cultures as far away as Cham and Javanese.

Old, Middle and New Indo-Aryan

SANSKRIT is the earliest Indo-Aryan language of which texts survive. It may possibly date from 1000 BC or even earlier (though the written records are not so old). As a language of culture it has continued to influence the modern languages, its descendants, to this day.

Sanskrit was standardised by about 500 BC, and was no longer current in everyday speech. By that time spoken dialects, 'Prakrits', were developing very distinct forms. Prakrit dialects were written in the inscriptions of the Emperor Asoka (see below). Some of them also became literary languages in their own right, notably PALI and ARDHAMAGADHI. There are also texts in Niya Prakrit, the language of a community in Chinese Turkestan in the 3rd century AD, and in Maharashtri. This was the language of the Andhra or Satavahana Empire, centred on Paithan, in the 1st century BC to 2nd century AD.

Two of the Prakrits, called *Sauraseni* and *Magadhi*, are known for a special reason. In Sanskrit plays these dialects were put into the mouths of low class characters, who were not supposed to have learnt the 'Perfect' language of the well educated. They may be as close to the real speech of their day as are the country dialects of modern radio drama.

The root of all languages

Magadhi, one of the Prakrits, was the mother tongue of the Buddha according to a Pali commentary. It must therefore logically be the *mulabhasa*, the language which a child would naturally speak if it heard no other language spoken (*Vibhaṅgatthakathā* 387–8).

Some features of Maharashtri reappear in modern Marathi. Maharashtri was used in lyric poetry and in Jain literature. Sauraseni Apabhramsa, based on a dialect of the Hindi area of about 600 AD, was later used for literature all the way from Bengal to Gujarat, with some local variations. The period of the Prakrits and their successors, from 500 BC to AD 1000, is known to linguists as Middle Indo-Aryan.

New Indo-Aryan is the period of development of the modern languages of the group. They begin to occur in literary texts from AD 1000 or soon after.

Modern Indo-Aryan languages cover a vast region of inland northern India across which dialects shade gradually into one another so that language boundaries are difficult to draw. For more information on the languages in this central zone see MAITHILI and MAGAHI (together called *Bihari*), BHOJPURI and CHHATTISGARHI (together called *Kosali*), HINDI, URDU, PANJABI, DOGRI. On the edge of this central zone to east, south and southwest are ASSAMESE, BENGALI, ORIYA, MARATHI, KONKANI, GUJARATI, RAJASTHANI and SINDHI. Geographically separated, SINHALA and DIVEHI also belong to the group. So does *Saurashtri*, spoken by a colony of silk-weavers at Madurai.

Several Indo-Aryan languages are difficult to map as they are spoken by nomadic peoples. ROMANI, language of the Gypsies of Europe and America, is the most important. For *Gujuri*, spoken by 500,000 seasonal nomads of Indian and Pakistani Kashmir, see map at GUJARATI.

Lamani, also called Banjari, is spoken by well over a million nomadic people who call themselves Gormati – now mostly construction workers, noted for the colourful dress of their women – in Andhra Pradesh, Karnataka and Maharashtra, and elsewhere in India.

> Linguistic influences are so complex in India that Indian linguists long ago set up a classification of word origins in the spoken languages of India. *Tadbhava* words are inherited from Sanskrit and have gone through normal processes of historical change; *deśya* 'country' words are at home in later Indo-Aryan yet they do not derive from Sanskrit; *tatsama* words are medieval or modern scholarly borrowings direct from Sanskrit. These distinctions are basic to modern research into linguistic history in many parts of the world – wherever a widely known language of culture, such as Old Slavonic, Latin or Sanskrit, has continued to influence the speakers of modern languages related to it.

In Himalayan valleys

In the wide north Indian plains easy communications have helped to reduce language differentiation. But in deep Himalayan valleys in Nepal, India, Pakistan and Afghanistan there are many little-known Indo-Aryan languages, spoken individually by small numbers.

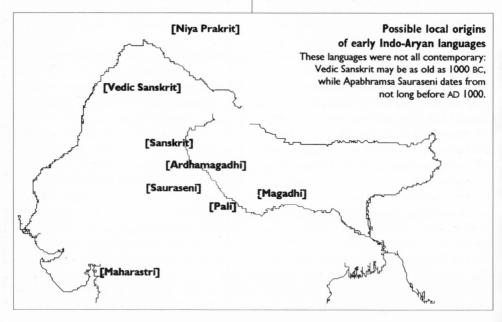

[Niya Prakrit]

**Possible local origins
of early Indo-Aryan languages**
These languages were not all contemporary:
Vedic Sanskrit may be as old as 1000 BC,
while Apabhramsa Sauraseni dates from
not long before AD 1000.

[Vedic Sanskrit]

[Sanskrit]

[Ardhamagadhi]

[Sauraseni]

[Magadhi]

[Pali]

[Maharastri]

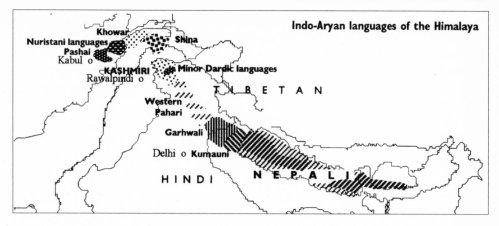

Indo-Aryan languages of the Himalaya

Pahari means 'of the hills', and is the convenient name for a group of Indo-Aryan languages from the Himalayan foothills north of the Ganges plain.

Languages of the Himalaya

The easternmost is NEPALI, and next to it lie the 'Central Pahari' languages, KUMAUNI and GARHWALI. The 'Western Pahari' languages have fewer speakers. Several were once the languages of small independent principalities. They include Jaunsari, Sirmauri, Baghati, Kiunthali, Sodochi, Mandeali (the largest, with over 200,000 speakers), Kului, Chameali and Bhadrawahi.

The Dardic languages, of which KASHMIRI has a separate entry, are spoken by small communities in Kashmir and north-eastern Afghanistan. The dialect of Srinagar is the main ingredient of Standard Kashmiri; to north and south, *Maraz* and *Kamaraz* dialects are distinguished. Other Dardic languages are Shina, with about 300,000 speakers, Kalami, KHOWAR and Torwali. Khetrani of Baluchistan may also be a Dardic language. For a table of numerals in Dardic languages see KASHMIRI.

Pashai, a group of mutually unintelligible dialects spoken in the smaller valleys north of Kabul, had a total of about 100,000 speakers before the current civil war.

The *Nuristani* languages, so different that they are usually considered a separate branch parallel with Indo-Aryan and Iranian, are spoken in remote valleys of north-east Afghanistan by a total of about 60,000 speakers. They include Kati or Bashgali, Waigali, Prasun and Ashkun.

Greeks in the Hindu Kush?

Nuristani (or *Kafir*, 'pagan') languages may belong to Indo-Aryan – or they may have separated even earlier from the mainstream, forming a separate small branch midway between Indo-Aryan and Iranian languages. Their discovery in the 19th century caused excitement.

'The more or less exact rumours about their fair complexion and hair and "Nordic" type, their wine-drinking and other European customs, their age-long resistance to the advance of Islam, have stirred the imagination of others beside the specialists; missionaries have cherished the hope that they were Christians of sorts; others have seen in them the descendants of Alexander's Greeks – an imaginative German traveller and scientist has [spoken of] "this Homeric island in the interior of Asia", and Kipling has based a romantic story, "The Man Who Would Be King", on the rumours abroad in India about these little known, but fascinating tribes . . . The geographical seclusion in which the Kafirs live in their inaccessible alpine valleys, and the religious and racial opposition between them and their Islamic neighbours, have deeply affected [their] social structure.'

Georg Morgenstierne, *Irano-Dardica*
(Wiesbaden: Reichert, 1973) p. 298

Indian onomatopoeia

Among the words that are most clearly shared between Dravidian and Indo-Aryan languages are onomatopoeic terms. These are clearly not freshly invented in each language: their sound changes are regular, and in general they appear to be borrowed by early Indo-Aryan from an early Dravidian language. Some examples:

'Chew, grind the teeth'

Dravidian	Indo-Aryan
Kannada *katakata kadi* 'grind the teeth', Tulu *katukatu* 'crunching noise'	Pali *katakatāyati* 'snaps, crushes', Hindi *karkarānā* 'chatter [of teeth]', *katkatī* 'grinding of teeth'

'Jingle, tinkle'

Tamil *kanakana-* 'to sound, rattle, jingle', Kannada *ganagana* 'ringing of bells'	Sanskrit *kanakanāyita-* 'tinkling', Nepali *khankhanāunu* 'jingle', Marathi *ghanghan* 'jingle'

'Rustle, murmur'

Tamil *kalakalam* 'chirping of birds, murmur of a crowd', Kannada *kalakala* 'confused noise of a crowd'	Sanskrit *kalakala-* 'confused noise', Gujarati *kalkalvum* 'to murmur', *khalkhalvum* 'to rumble'

Examples from Murray B. Emeneau, *Language and linguistic area* (Stanford: Stanford University Press, 1980) pp. 269–71

Numerals in Nuristani languages and Pashai

	Bashgali	Waigali	Prasun	Pashai
1	ē, ev	ī, ek	ipin	ī
2	diu, du	du	lūe	dō
3	treh	trē	chī	hlə, hlē
4	što	štā	cipū	cār
5	puc	pūc	uc	panj
6	šo	šū	ušū	sə, khē
7	sut	sōt	sete	sat
8	ošṭ	ošṭ	aste	ašt, akht
9	noh	nū	nūh	nō
10	dič	dōš	leze	dē

From G. A. Grierson, *The Pisaca languages of north-western India* (London: Royal Asiatic Society, 1906) p. 37

Indo-Aryan in writing: 1. The Edicts of the Emperor Asoka

Asoka (c. 274–32 BC), grandson of Chandragupta Maurya, was one of the greatest of all rulers of India, and became a fervent believer in Buddhism. In many parts of India he erected stone inscriptions in the colloquial dialects of his time, the Prakrits, with instructions on *dharma*, or, to use a roughly equivalent Christian term, 'righteousness'. The Edicts of Asoka are the first surviving contemporary records of any of the Indo-Aryan languages of India.

In north-west India Asoka's stonecutters used an alphabet called Kharoṣṭhi, derived from an Aramaic script. Soon afterwards this is found on coins issued by Greek and Iranian monarchs in Central Asia. Kharoṣṭhi fell out of use long ago.

Elsewhere Asoka's inscriptions are in the Brahmi script. This survived. Gradually modified and adapted to different languages and writing materials, Brahmi is the ancestor of many alphabets used in south and south-east Asia.

Indo-Aryan in writing:
2. The children of Brahmi

The scripts that descend from Brahmi are more logical than any other. Devised over two thousand years ago on the basis of an accurate analysis of the sounds of Sanskrit and Prakrit, these alphabets have been adapted to very different languages, Indo-Aryan, Tai, Sino-Tibetan, Austroasiatic and Austronesian. All follow a similar alphabetical order, which is itself systematic and thus easy to remember. The box shows the basic *Devanāgarī* alphabet of Hindi (almost identical with those of Marathi and Nepali) alongside corresponding characters in Bengali, Gujarati and *Gurmukhi* (for Panjabi). Ten vowels come first (there are additional vowel signs for *r* and *l* in most of the languages, but these are not shown here); then 25 stop and nasal consonants, in groups of five according to point of articulation, from the velars at the back of the mouth to the labials formed by the lips; then four fricatives; then four sibilants.

अ आ इ ई उ ऊ ए ऐ ओ औ कखगघङ चछजझञ टठडढण तथदधन पफबभम यरलव शषसह

অ আ ই ঈ উ ঊ এ ঐ ও ঔ কখগঘঙ চছজঝঞ টঠডঢণ তথদধন পফবভম যরলব শষসহ

અ આ ઇ ઈ ઉ ઊ એ ઐ ઓ ઔ કખગઘઙ ચછજઝઞ ટઠડઢણ તથદધન પફબભમ યરલવ શષસહ

ਅ ਆ ਇ ਈ ਉ ਊ ਏ ਐ ਓ ਔ ਕਖਗਘਙ ਚਛਜਝਞ ਟਠਡਢਣ ਤਥਦਧਨ ਪਫਬਭਮ ਯਰਲਵ ਸ਼ਸਹ

All scripts of the Brahmi family are based on the concept of one complete character per syllable: usually a central consonant shape to which vowel and second-consonant signs may be added, above, below or beside. The reader soon learns to dismantle these compound characters.

In Sanskrit, in each syllable in which no other vowel sign was added, the so-called 'inherent vowel', short *a* or *ə*, was to be read. This is one way in which the modern scripts are not so easy as they might be: nowadays one needs to know some fairly complicated rules, differing for each language, before one can tell whether an inherent vowel is to be read, or no vowel at all.

The Sanskrit word कात्स्न्र्य, *kārtsnya* 'fully', written in Devanagari script, is made up of two compound characters: the first is क *k* + आ *ā*, the second is र *r* + त *t* + स *s* + न *n* + य *y*. To the second character no vowel sign is added, so the vowel *a* is to be read. The *r* is written as a semicircle above the line.

The standard romanisation for Indic scripts, agreed by a congress of Orientalists in the late 19th century, can be applied to Sanskrit, to Pali and to many of the modern languages written in these scripts.

The standard romanisation

अ आ इ ई उ ऊ ए ऐ ओ औ कखगघङ चछजझञ टठडढण तथदधन पफबभम यरलव शषसह

a ā i ī u ū r̥ l̥ e ai o au k kh g gh ṅ c ch j jh ñ ṭ ṭh ḍ ḍh ṇ t th d dh n p ph b bh m y r l v ś ṣ s h

INDO-EUROPEAN LANGUAGES

Indo-European languages are spoken on every continent and by members of every racial group. English, Spanish, French and Russian have some official status in dozens of countries worldwide. Hindi, Bengali, Portuguese and German are just as essential in many multinational contexts. Latin, Greek, Sanskrit, Pali and Avestan are classical languages of religion, philosophy and culture. Greek, Armenian, Yiddish and Romani are the languages of worldwide diasporas. There are many other Indo-European languages, from Icelandic to Italian and Persian, whose literatures enrich humanity.

How is it known that all these languages are related to one another?

In the 17th and 18th centuries a European scholar, having begun to master Latin and Greek and one or two modern European languages, might well go on to learn Hebrew – the language of the Old Testament – and perhaps Arabic. These were readily seen to be wholly different in their structure from the ancient and modern languages of Europe. Then European interest in India began to grow, and there was the opportunity to study Sanskrit, the classical language of India, under the guidance of Indian teachers. It was realised that Sanskrit – quite unlike Hebrew and Arabic – showed pervasive similarities with Latin and Greek and other languages of Europe. How did this come about? The speakers of these languages lived thousands of miles apart, and history told of no early contact between them. It was a puzzle that Indo-European scholars, ever since, have continued to explore.

Though not the first to notice the link between European and Indian languages, Sir William Jones put it most clearly into words, in his presidential address to the Asiatic Society of Bengal in 1786:

'The *Sanscrit* language, whatever be its antiquity, is of a wonderful structure; more perfect than the *Greek*, more copious than the *Latin*, and more exquisitely refined than either, yet bearing to both of them a stronger affinity, both in the roots of verbs and in the forms of grammar, than could possibly have been produced by accident; so strong indeed, that no philologer could examine them all three, without believing them to have sprung from some common source, which, perhaps, no longer exists: there is a similar reason, though not quite so forcible, for supposing that both the *Gothick* and the *Celtick*, though blended with a very different idiom, had the same origin with the *Sanscrit*; and the old *Persian* might be added to the same family'. (Sir William Jones, 'Third anniversary discourse, 1786' in *Asiatick researches* vol. 1 (1788) pp. 415–31).

The 'common source' that Jones deduced is now called proto-Indo-European. This may be the first time in English that the word *family* was applied to a group of languages.

Persian and Gothic had already been compared, as long ago as 1723, by the Swedish linguist Olaus Odhelius Andersson.

To the branches of the Indo-European family that Jones listed, later research has added Baltic, Armenian and Albanian; also some extinct languages rediscovered in the 19th and 20th centuries, such as Hittite and Tocharian.

In the 18th century the languages of Europe had sometimes been grouped together as *Japhetic*, named after one of Noah's three sons in the Biblical story of the Flood and its aftermath. To replace this name and to make clear the newly recognised link between European and Indian languages, the term *Indo-European* was coined by Thomas Young in 1818 in a review of Adelung and Vater's multilingual compilation *Mithridates*. German scholars have traditionally preferred *Indogermanische*. In the excitement engendered by the decipherment of Hittite, the term *Indo-Hittite* was briefly used as a statement that Hittite had separated from the Indo-European dialects slightly earlier than the remaining branches of the family. *Aryan* ('noble', the term that Vedic Sanskrit speakers used for themselves) was once popular as an alternative to Indo-European – but no longer, because of the racial connotations it picked up in European extremist politics.

It was clear that the known Indo-European languages must have gradually grown apart through changes in sounds: hence the difference in the initial consonants of English *brother*, Latin *frater*, Greek *phrater*, Sanskrit *bhrātṛ*, words that were clearly related both in sound and meaning. The essential breakthrough in Indo-European research was the gradual realisation that these sound changes were *regular*. In the development of each particular language or dialect they took place invariably, whenever a certain sound occurred in defined surroundings; if there appeared to be exceptions, the exceptions should in principle have explanations. In this way Indo-European studies helped to galvanise historical work on other languages too, for the same principles can be applied in all language families.

Once the regularity of sound change was accepted, it was possible to set up hypotheses about the sounds and the words of the parent language, 'proto-Indo-European': to make a formula (for example, **bhrāter* for 'brother') to which word forms in the known languages could be traced back.

The rebuilding of proto-Indo-European

One line of this research led to the gradual reconstruction of proto-Indo-European as an apparently natural language, with a complete sound system and a vocabulary to match. This is not a simple task. Some of the pitfalls become obvious as one studies the result.

The formulae or reconstructed forms are, in general, the most economical possible: such that the simplest possible series of changes will link them with known language forms. This makes them efficient as formulae, but it does not prove that they really existed in a parent language. The sound system of proto-Indo-European, variously reconstructed by generations of scholars, and sometimes given as many as four 'laryngeal consonants' (see below), differs noticeably from the sound systems of natural languages. The real proto-Indo-European can never have been a unitary form of speech but always a bundle of varying speech forms, 'sociolects' and dialects, as all real languages are.

The reconstructed vocabulary of proto-Indo-European is a collection of words that continued to be used, for some thousands of years, in *at least two* of the later branches of Indo-European. In the case of words that continued to be used in only one branch, there can usually be no proof of their ultimate origin, so they have to be discounted. Vocabulary is never static, especially as speakers migrate and as their economy and their society changes. Words are forgotten, new words are invented, and words are given new meanings. It is not surprising, after all this, that there are far fewer words in the proto-Indo-European dictionary than there are in any natural language.

Finally, proto-Indo-European itself was the product of a history, probably involving earlier migrations, certainly involving changes in society and economy. In all natural languages, history is reflected in inconsistencies, words whose meanings are undergoing change, words that some speakers misunderstand.

Still, linguists and archaeologists do try to pin down, from the vocabulary of proto-Indo-European, where its speakers lived, what kind of society they lived in, how they farmed, how

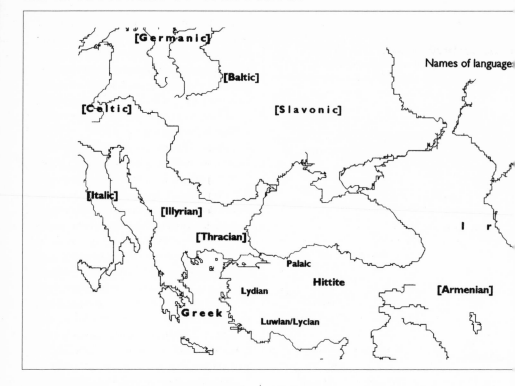

[Germanic]

[Baltic]

[Celtic]

[Slavonic]

Names of language

[Italic]

[Illyrian]

[Thracian]

Palaic

Lydian

Hittite

[Armenian]

Greek

Luwian/Lycian

they lived and even (Emile Benveniste, *Indo-European language and society*, 1973) how they thought. They try to identify a 'homeland' or (to use the German term) *Heimat* for the Indo-Europeans.

Heimat: the 'homeland'

Very different results have been reached. In the early 19th century some thought that Sanskrit itself, first spoken in north-west India, was the parent tongue. Sir Monier Monier-Williams, author of the great Sanskrit dictionary, saw the vast ruins of Balkh in Afghanistan as the city from which all Indo-Europeans traced their origin. Others looked to the north German plain.

In the 20th century none of these views has found favour. For several decades now the majority of scholars has placed the 'homeland' on the south Russian steppes. The theory is particularly identified with the work of Marija Gimbutas, who presses the identification of the proto-Indo-Europeans with the builders of *kurgans* – burial mounds – in the eastern Ukraine.

A persistent minority looks south of the Black Sea. But these do not agree among themselves. The archaeologist Colin Renfrew (*Archaeology and language: the puzzle of Indo-European origins*, 1987) identifies the proto-Indo-Europeans with the earliest neolithic farmers of central Asia Minor, between 7000 and 6000 BC. Tomas Gamkrelidze and Vyacheslav Ivanov argue for an origin in what is now Armenia, perhaps equally early, followed by migration to the Ukraine, which then became a secondary 'homeland' and point of dispersal for the speakers of early Indo-European dialects. Robert Drews (*The coming of the Greeks*, 1988) also looks to Armenia – but as late as 1700 BC, when, he suggests, a chariot-riding elite spread their Indo-European speech across southern Europe and southern Asia.

The dialects of proto-Indo-European

Meanwhile, there has been work on the lines of descent from proto-Indo-European: how early, unrecorded dialects gradually differentiated into the widely different languages later known, and

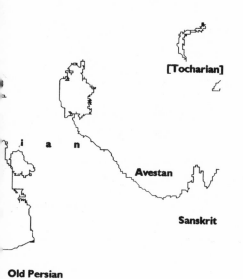

do-European languages about 1250 / 750 BC
recorded at this period are in square brackets

[Tocharian]

Avestan

Sanskrit

Old Persian

how these dialects were interlinked. They did not suddenly split. Just as with modern languages, there must for a long time have been a dialect continuum within Indo-European, marked by a succession of changes that affected different groups of dialects. On a modern dialect map the divisions are called *isoglosses*.

One, immediately noticeable, is called in linguists' shorthand the *centum/satem* split (see below). The innovation of the *satem* dialects – a very common one in language history – was the regular change from velar stops to dental fricatives when followed by a front vowel: thus, from proto-Indo-European *ḱmtom*, Avestan *satəm* contrasts with Latin *centum* (pronounced *kentum*).

Keywords of proto-Indo-European research

Laryngeals: The Swiss linguist Ferdinand de Saussure (1857–1913) developed a theory that proto-Indo-European had a series of throaty consonants, 'laryngeals', which had disappeared in all the descendant languages but had left indirect evidence in the length and type of vowels that had preceded them. Saussure could not specify how his laryngeals would have been pronounced, and the theory remained controversial – until the decipherment of Hittite, which turned out to have voiced and voiceless consonants (transliterated *ḫ*, *ḫḫ*) in exactly the position where Saussure had predicted his laryngeals.

*Loḱsos, salmon or trout? This word is found in many Indo-European languages, including German *Lachs*, Icelandic *lax*, Polish *osoś*, Russian *losos'*. In these it means 'salmon'. If proto-Indo-European had a word for 'salmon', surely the language must have been spoken somewhere where salmon were to be found, that is, in northern Europe or Siberia. The argument has sometimes been thought powerful. But in other modern languages the same word means 'a kind of trout', Latvian *lasis*, Ossete *læsæg*, or simply 'fish', Tocharian A *laks*. This example shows how difficult it can be to place the proto-Indo-Europeans on the map: too often it depends on arbitrary decisions as to whether the meaning of words has shifted or remained fixed.

*Eḱwos, horse: The proponents of 'linguistic palaeontology' (research on proto-Indo-European society through the rebuilt vocabulary of the ancestral language) are roused to enthusiasm by the evident existence of a word for 'horse' in pIE, reconstructed from Sanskrit *aśvah*, Greek *hippos*, Latin *equus*, Old Irish *ech*, Anglo-Saxon *eoh*, Tocharian A *yuk*. They visualise the horse as a major element of pIE culture – a culture perhaps spread by warriors who conquered from horse-drawn chariots (like the Greek heroes imagined in Homer's *Iliad*) and who sacrificed horses (like those for whom a Vedic Sanskrit poet wrote the 'Hymn to the Horse', *Ṛgveda* 1.163). Some more cautious scholars consider that the horse was known, but not especially important, to the speakers of proto-Indo-European – and may have been known at first as a wild rather than a domesticated animal.

*kṃtom, the centum/satem split: The word for 'hundred' is an example of a sound change shared by almost half the descendant languages of proto-Indo-European (see above). *K* followed by a front vowel became *s* or *sh* in Indo-Aryan (Sanskrit *śata*), Iranian (Persian *sad*), Slavonic (Russian *sto*), Baltic (Lithuanian *simtas*), Albanian (*qind*, pronounced *chind*) and Armenian. It remained *k* in Celtic (Welsh *cant*), Italic, Tocharian (*känt*), Greek (*hekaton*) and Germanic (with a subsequent move to *h*, English *hundred*).

This is a very common sound change in linguistic history: in fact a similar change has actually taken place, later, in many languages of the *centum* group. For example, Latin *centum* has become French *cent* (pronounced *sã*) and Spanish *cento* (pronounced *thento*).

Germanic, Baltic and Slavonic share some interesting features, such as the way in which the numerals '20' to '90' are built up. In the other Indo-European languages old compound words exist, such as Latin *triginta*, Greek *triákonta* for '30'. The corresponding terms in these north European languages are newly coined, and they have the obvious meaning 'three tens': Gothic *threis tigjus*, Lithuanian *trýs dẽšimtys*, Old Slavonic *triye desęte, tri desęti*.

What was proto-Indo-European like?

Like Sanskrit, Old Slavonic, Latin and Greek, proto-Indo-European had numerous forms for nouns (incorporating the notions of number and 'case') and for verbs (marking 'person', number, time and 'mood'). At some time in distant prehistory, an agglutinating language – in which these notions were separately identifiable as affixes – had become a synthetic language, in which they were fused with one another and with the noun or verb root. What is more, the fusion took different forms depending on the shape of the root. Students of Latin and Greek are all too familiar with the resulting noun declensions and verb conjugations whose forms cannot be wholly predicted and must be separately learnt. Proto-Indo-European, it seems, was already like this.

The later history of all the languages of the family has been of a gradual reduction in this complexity, and thus of a long term change of character. While the early Indo-European languages were largely *synthetic*, English and Hindi (to take two examples) are largely *isolating* languages.

The first ten numerals in proto-Indo-European may be reconstructed as **oinas, *dwō, *treyes, *qwetwōr, *penkwe, *sweḱs, *septṃ, *oḱtō, *enewen, *deḱṃ*.

How did Indo-European languages spread so widely?

Colin Renfrew has argued that the spread of neolithic farming from central Anatolia to northern Greece and the Balkans is the archaeologically visible sign of the earliest Indo-European expansion. Most Indo-European specialists have not yet accepted Renfrew's argument, but it cannot be said to have been disproved. Renfrew's more tentative hypothesis that Indo-European languages spread also to Iran and northern India at this early period, along with neolithic farming, goes against the grain of the evidence.

The theory accepted by many linguists, though not by all, is that around 4000 BC an early group of Indo-European dialects was spoken across a wide swathe of central and eastern Europe, perhaps extending into southern Siberia and central Asia. The theory is often linked to the domestication of the horse – and certainly horsemanship has helped the spread of languages and empires, in this same steppe region, ever since.

Not long after 2000 BC the first surviving written records of Indo-European languages document HITTITE – the language of a powerful kingdom in Asia Minor – and the influence of an early form of Indo-Aryan on the Hurrian-speaking Mitanni in the Middle East. It is likely, meanwhile, that other Indo-European dialects were gradually spreading further into western Europe. Outlying and less accessible regions – Spain, Italy, southern Greece, northern Scandinavia – retained their non-Indo-European speech for rather longer. The speakers of early

Indo-Iranian dialects must by now have been approaching Iran and north-western India from the north. The hypothesis of their long-distance migration seems necessary to explain the links between Indo-Iranian languages on the one hand and Slavonic and URALIC LANGUAGES on the other.

At the time when the Romans were establishing their empire, early texts from Europe and Asia show with fair certainty the location of most of the then surviving branches of Indo-European: CELTIC LANGUAGES, GERMANIC LANGUAGES, BALTIC LANGUAGES, SLAVONIC LANGUAGES, LATIN and the other Italic languages, Illyrian (possibly the ancestor of ALBANIAN), Thracian, GREEK, ARMENIAN, the IRANIAN LANGUAGES, the INDO-ARYAN LANGUAGES and – far away to the north-east – the TOCHARIAN languages. The latter are not especially similar to Iranian and Indo-Aryan: their geographical location must result from a quite different migration.

Latin, spread widely by trade and empire, gradually evolved into the ROMANCE LANGUAGES. More recently English, French, Spanish and Russian have spread across the world: will they, in turn, split into daughter languages?

INUIT

ABOUT 65,000 SPEAKERS

Greenland, Canada and Alaska

Inuit is the only language of the Eskimo-Aleut family that is in widespread everyday use. It is often called Eskimo or Greenlandic, and is the language of one of the few peoples who have developed a way of life admirably suited to Arctic conditions. Their habitat, untrammelled by national frontiers, stretched from Greenland (where they are the majority population) across the northern edge of Canada and Alaska to the Diomede Islands (for map see ESKIMO-ALEUT LANGUAGES). The Eskimos of Big Diomede were moved to mainland Siberia and dispersed in 1948.

The East Greenland dialect, spoken around Angmagssalik and Scoresbysund, far across the icecap from the settled districts on the west coast, differs quite strongly from West Greenland – because of a persistent custom of word avoidance. Taboo has meant that new expressions are invented, old words are forgotten, and the whole vocabulary is renewed at a rapid rate. Knut Bergsland has used East Greenland to show how risky is the statistical approach to language history called glotto-chronology, a method that relies on counting similar words to estimate how many hundred years ago a pair of languages began to grow apart.

The West Greenland dialect is one official language of Greenland, the other being Danish. It is a language of education, publishing, broadcasting and administration, though it does not threaten the East Greenland (3,000 speakers) and Polar (700 speakers) dialects, which remain in daily use in their regions. In Greenland, Inuit is officially *Kalaallit Oqasii*, 'Language of the Greenlanders'.

Publishing in Canadian Inuit began in Labrador in the 18th century. At first it was entirely religious. There are now newspapers, government publications, schoolbooks and some creative literature.

A few Inuit words have been borrowed into English, including *kayak* and *anorak*. On maps of the Arctic, Inuit place names mingle with names imposed by explorers from the south. The northern Greenland settlement Thule (so named by classically minded Europeans after the legendary 'farthest north' of ancient Greek geography) is called *Qâmâq* in Inuit.

Numerals in Alaska and Greenland Inuit		
Alaska Inuit		**Greenland Inuit**
atautseq	1	ataasiq
matleruk	2	marluk
pingayun	3	pingasut
stauman	4	sisamat
tatlîman	5	tallimat
aravinligin	6	arvinillit
matlerunligin	7	arvini-marluk
pingayunligin	8	arvini-pingasut
qulingúneritâran	9	qulingiluat
qulin	10	qulit
In Greenland, numerals above '12' are now usually borrowed from Danish.		

The Inuktitut syllabary

In Greenland, Inuit is written in the Roman alphabet: so it is in Alaska and by some Canadians. In these countries there are several different spelling systems depending on the nationality of the missionaries who first began to write the language and on later changes of practice – linguists in Alaska and Canada have treated Inuit as a laboratory for spelling reforms. In Siberia, meanwhile, Inuit is (or was) written in Cyrillic. In Canada, since the mid 19th century, a syllabary (based on the one used for CREE) has competed with the Roman alphabet. The syllabary is most used by writers of the Inuktitut dialect as spoken in Quebec. The current version, called ᑎᑎᕋᐅᓯᖅ ᓄᑖᖅ *Titirausiq Nutaaq* or 'New Writing System', was adopted by the Inuit Cultural Institute in 1976.

ᑎᑎᕋᐅᓯᖅ ᓄᑖᖅ The Inuktitut syllabary

ᐃᐱᑎᑭᒋᒥᓂᓯᓕᔨᕕᕆᕿᖏᖠ
i pi ti ki gi mi ni si li ji vi ri qi ngi łi

ᐅᐳᑐᑯᒍᒧᓄᓱᓗᔪᕗᕈᖁᖑᖢ
u pu tu ku gu mu nu su lu ju vu ru qu ngu łu

ᐊᐸᑕᑲᒐᒪᓇᓴᓚᔭᕙᕋᖃᖓᖤ
a pa ta ka ga ma na sa la ja va ra qa nga ła

ᕼ ᑉ ᑦ ᒃ ᒡ ᒻ ᓐ ᔅ ᓪ ᔾ ᕝ ᕐ ᖅ ᖕ ᖦ
h p t k g m n s l j v r q ng ł

A dot above a symbol stands for a long vowel: ᐲ *pii*, ᖔ *ngaa*. The last row, in the table above, gives the small symbols that are used for consonants not followed by a vowel.

IRANIAN LANGUAGES

As the INDO-EUROPEAN LANGUAGES gradually differentiated, several thousand years ago, the earliest precursors of Balto-Slavonic and Indo-Iranian languages must have been spoken side by side. Already distinct from one another, the two groups show evidence of long term mutual influence.

If Indo-European speakers in general were an agricultural people, the ancestors of Indo-Iranian language speakers, occupying the plains north of the Black Sea, may have adopted the nomadism of the steppes.

All this is hypothetical. What is known is that when they first emerge into recorded history, over 2,500 years ago, *Old Iranian* languages were spoken and written in Persia, thousands of miles to the south-east of the Baltic and Slavonic peoples, their former neighbours. Some of them, not long afterwards, were certainly spoken by nomadic peoples. At the same date the INDO-ARYAN LANGUAGES come to light even further off, in northern India. And the agricultural terminology that is shared by most of the other Indo-European languages seems to be forgotten, or to have changed meaning, in Iranian and Indo-Aryan.

> *Īrān* was so named, long ago, as the country 'of the Arya', *erānām*. This name *Ārya* was used of themselves by speakers of several Iranian and Indo-Aryan languages (and was more recently taken up in Europe by racial theorists). The use of 'Iran' in place of 'Persia' as the name of the modern state is slightly misleading: Iranian languages have been, and still are, spoken over a much wider area than this.

The first Iranian people recorded in history are the Medes, who must have been in north-western Iran by the beginning of the first mil-

lennium BC. Almost all that remains as evidence of their language is a corpus of place names and personal names found in Akkadian and Greek texts. Around the same time the *Parsa*, Persians, are heard of, first in Kurdistan, then in south-western Iran: there are important inscriptions in Old PERSIAN, dating from the 5th and 4th centuries BC, when the Persian Empire, efficient and decentralised, extended its rule from Greece to the borders of India. Some AVESTAN texts – the sacred books of Zoroastrianism – are at least as old as this, though the manuscripts in which they now survive were copied many centuries later. Meanwhile the Scythians and Saka – still nomadic steppe-dwellers – ranged an even wider swathe of territory from the Black Sea coast to the borders of China.

The fall of the Persian Empire to Alexander the Great (died 323 BC) is a convenient beginning for the *Middle Iranian* period, which is considered to last until the Islamic conquest in AD 640. Texts are known in several Middle Iranian languages, including Middle PERSIAN, Parthian, Chorasmian, Bactrian and SOGDIAN. Further east, KHOTANESE is considered a late variety of Saka, the only one in which literary texts are known.

The modern Iranian languages

New Iranian languages are still spoken in Iran and central Asia. Nearly all of them have absorbed Arabic influences through the medium of Islamic culture. Those of Iran are now heavily influenced by Persian. The basic dialect division is between East and West Iranian.

Old Persian is already identifiable as a Western language. Its best known modern relative is PERSIAN, an official language in Iran, Afghanistan and Tajikistan. The provincial languages of Iran are numerous – it is wrong to class them simply as dialects of Persian. This book deals with them under the headings LURI and GILAKI. Important beyond the borders of Iran are KURDISH and BALUCHI.

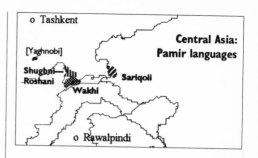

The Eastern group includes Avestan, Sogdian and Khotanese. Its major modern representatives are PASHTO, official language of Afghanistan, and the long-isolated OSSETE, which descends from the language of the Alans, a Scythian people. Sogdian's modern descendant is Yaghnobi, now found in Tajikistan. There are many other East Iranian languages spoken by small communities in the valleys of the Pamir mountains.

The Pamir languages and Yaghnobi

Spoken in the mountains of north-east Afghanistan, Tajikistan and a tiny corner of China, the Pamir languages have a total of fewer than 100,000 speakers.

Shughni has at least 40,000 speakers in the valley of the Panj, which divides the Mountain Badakhshan district of Tajikistan from Badakshan province of Afghanistan. It is a second language in many of the Pamir valleys. *Roshani*, mutually comprehensible with Shughni, has about 12,000 speakers downstream.

Sariqoli is the Pamir language of China, with 10,000 speakers in Tashkurghan and the villages around. Their ancestors migrated from Shugh-

nan in Tajikistan. The language is sometimes misleadingly called *Tajiki*. It is historically close to Shughni, but is influenced by Uighur, the administrative language of Xinjiang.

Wakhi is spoken by about 25,000 people settled in the upper valley of the Panj, in south-east Tajikistan and the 'Wakhan corridor' of Afghanistan. The language is also spoken in high valleys of Hunza district in Kashmir.

The Pamir languages belong to East Iranian, but they have archaic features indicating that they split from the main body of Iranian dialects in very early times.

Yaghnobi, the modern descendant of SOGDIAN, was until 1971 spoken by about 2,500 people in the upper Yaghnob valley. The speakers then moved en masse to Zafarobod, still in Tajikistan, where they retain their language.

There are several other Pamir and East Iranian languages with no more than a few hundred speakers each.

Numerals in the Pamir languages

	Shughni	Roshani	Sariqoli	Wakhi
1	yīw	yīw	iw	yiw
2	dhu	dhaw	dhεw	buy
3	aray	aray	aroy	truy
4	cavōr	cavūr	cavur	cəbır
5	pīnzh	pīnzh	pinzh	panzh
6	khōgh	khūw	khel	shad
7	wūvd	wūvd	ıvd	ıb
8	wakht	wakht	wokht	at
9	nōw	nāw	new	naw
10	dhīs	dhos	dhes	dhas

From John Payne, 'Pamir languages' in *Compendium linguarum iranicarum* ed. Rüdiger Schmitt (Wiesbaden: Reichert, 1989) pp. 417–44

IRISH

PERHAPS 80,000 SPEAKERS

Ireland

Irish is the only survivor among the CELTIC LANGUAGES (see map there) whose speakers remained outside the Roman Empire. It has the oldest literature in Europe after Greek and Latin.

> The language is often known as *Irish Gaelic* or simply *Gaelic*: the Irish spelling is *Gaeilge*. In this book GAELIC is used as the name of its Scottish offshoot.

Christianity was introduced to Ireland from Roman Britain: St Patrick, who lived in the early 5th century, was himself a Briton, and wrote in Latin. Irish authors were prominent in the Latin literature of Europe in the next three centuries. Meanwhile a literature in Irish was developing. Early hymns, including one attributed to Patrick, seem to go back to the 5th century. Heroic tales in prose, quite non-Christian in inspiration, were being written down by the 7th century, no doubt on the basis of earlier oral traditions. But most surviving manuscripts were written after the destructive Viking invasions of the 9th and 10th centuries.

Early Irish literature is prolific and varied. The best known of the prose tales (often called sagas) is *Táin Bó Cuailnge*, 'the *Táin*' for short, the 'Cattle Raid of Cooley'. The oldest form of this survives in the Book of the Dun Cow or *Lebor na hUidre*, compiled at the Monastery of Clonmacnoise in the 12th century. Alongside many other tales and rich lyric poetry there are chronicles, historical narratives, law codes and texts on grammar and poetics. *Dinnseanchus* is a book of place names – their etymologies and their legends – and there are other traditional dictionaries.

English colonisation began in the 16th century. Many chiefs, at whose courts the language and its literature had been cultivated, emigrated after the defeat at Kinsale in 1601. In the 17th to early 20th centuries Irish gradually gave way to English, which was now the only language of government. In the 19th century, with very few remaining monolingual speakers, schools worked to eradicate Irish. Famine and labour migration contributed to its decline, for English was needed by migrant workers.

At the division of Ireland in 1922 Irish gained the position of official language. As a symbol of independence it has had strong official encouragement. Government and civil service are, at least theoretically, bilingual. The language and its distinctive uncial script are widely seen in public. The Irish form of public titles and names has been borrowed into Irish English (and into the international English of television reporting): *Garda* 'police', *Taoiseach* 'Prime Minister', *Dail* 'Parliament'. Around 1,000,000 people claim to speak Irish.

But the officially defined *Gaeltacht*, the area where Irish is the majority everyday speech, is small and fragmented, with about 80,000 inhabitants. Even here modern population mobility threatens the survival of the language. The only Irish weekly (Sunday) newspaper, *Anois*, has a circulation of 5,000.

In 1922 Irish was still spoken by 20,000 people in remote areas in the six counties of Northern Ireland that remained British. Very few speakers remain there in the 1990s. There are communities of Irish speakers in London, Liverpool and Birmingham.

Sheldru or *Shelta* (also known as *Cant, The Old Thing* and *Gammon*) is a secret language that has long been used by Irish travellers and their descendants in England (where there has certainly been an Irish 'tinker' community since the late 16th century) and also in the United States. Its structure is English: its vocabulary is largely Irish, and many words are altered to ensure that outsiders cannot understand it.

Irish and English have coexisted for centuries and have influenced each other. Irish loanwords in English include *slogan* from *sluagh ghairm* 'army shout, war cry'; *whiskey* from *uisge bheatha* 'water of life, aqua vitae'; *bard*, a traditional oral poet.

According to Richard Stanyhurst in the *Description of Ireland* (1577), 'As the whole realme of Ireland is sundred into foure principal parts, so eche parcell differeth very much in the Irish tongue, euery country hauing his dialect or peculiar maner, in speaking the language.' There was a common saying, he added, that Ulster has only the right grammar, Munster has only the true pronunciation, Leinster has neither, and Connacht has both.

Sweeney mad

Ó'dchuala trá Suibhne sésdan na sochaidhe & muirn an mór/lúaigh nostógbaidh uime asin mbile re fraisnéllaibh na firmaiminti ós mullaighibh gacha maighni & ós fhégi gacha ferainn.

    Baoi fri ré chéiniarsin seachnóin Érenn ag tadhall & ag turrag a sgalpaibh cruadhcharrag & a ndosaibh crann urard eidhneach & i ccuasaibh caolchumhguibh cloch ó inber do inber & ó binn do binnd & ó glinn do glionn go ráinic Glenn mbitháluinn mBolcáin.

When Sweeney heard the shouts of the soldiers and the big noise of the army, he rose out of the tree towards the dark clouds and ranged far over mountains and territories.

    A long time he went faring all through Ireland, poking his way into hard rocky clefts, shouldering through ivy bushes, unsettling falls of pebbles in narrow defiles, wading estuaries, breasting summits, trekking through glens, until he found the pleasures of Glen Bolcain.

The legend of Sweeney, who was defeated at the battle of Moira in AD 637 and was driven mad, is told in mixed prose and verse in a 17th-century manuscript – but it is of much older origin. The prose passage quoted here is marked by rhythm and parallelism. Translation after Seamus Heaney, *Sweeney Astray* (Derry: Field Day Theatre Co., 1983).

Ogam script

b l v s n h d t c q m g ng z r a o u e i ch
Font: *Beth Luis Fearn*, blf.ttf
by Curtis Clark (jcclark@csupomona.edu)

Ogam script

Apparently based on late Latin handwriting, Ogam script may have been developed for writing on wooden message-sticks: straight lines are easier to carve than curves. About a hundred stone inscriptions from Ireland are known in Ogam script, probably dating from the 5th and 6th centuries. In Britain some bilingual Ogam/Latin inscriptions have been found. The script may be called *beth luis fearn* and *beth luis nion* after the names of the first few letters.

In the version shown in the box the letters ⊥, ＃ and ＃ are given their values in later manuscript texts: their values as originally used on stone inscriptions are not known. The script was usually written vertically, bottom to top, in inscriptions, horizontally in manuscripts. Ogam was still studied in scribal schools in Ireland down to the 17th century.

The Irish alphabet

Modern Irish script is a local variant of the Latin alphabet, originating in medieval manuscripts. Irish can also be printed in Latin typefaces, and often is, but the script is seen on road signs and public notices throughout Ireland.

Upper and lower case scarcely differ except for ʀ and s . An acute accent on a vowel marks length. Consonants may be written with a dot above to mark aspiration. When Irish is written in Latin script the dot is replaced by *h*, and there are other differences between the usual spellings in Irish and Latin scripts.

Modern Irish script

ᴀ b c ᴅ e ꜰ ᵹ h ɪ ʟ m n o p ʀ s ᴛ u

ᴀ b c ᴅ e ꜰ ᵹ h ɪ ʟ m n o p ꞃ ꞃ ᴛ u

Italian

60,000,000 SPEAKERS

Italy, Switzerland, Eritrea

One of the ROMANCE LANGUAGES, Italian is a direct descendant of Latin – and is spoken in the same region where Latin first spread, in the peninsula of Italy, the Po river valley to the north, and the island of Sicily to the south.

> The peninsula was known as *Italy* even before Rome's power had spread across it, over two thousand years ago. *Italian* has become the usual term for the dialects spoken here, and for the standard language of united Italy – though this standard language is still sometimes called *Tuscan* and was once better known as *lingua Fiorentina*, the language of Florence, the cultural and political centre from which the standard variety of Italian has gradually spread.
>
> In Polish the term *Wloch* is used for 'Italian' – a word of the same origin as *Welsh* and *Vlach*, historically meaning 'speakers of a strange language'.

In the first few centuries after the collapse of the Roman Empire, those who wrote anything in Italy continued to write Latin. In fact there are few signs that a new language was developing: yet it was, for in the tenth century a few short texts, inserted in Latin documents (see box), show how far the language of everyday speech had changed from that of the Roman Empire.

Thus Italian emerges as fragments of real speech in records of lawsuits – and then as poetry. Led by King Frederick II, himself a poet, the 'Sicilian school' of the 11th century composed lyric verse that was influenced by the emerging poetry in OCCITAN. In the following centuries there was at first no standard Italian language. Instead, a succession of writers in different regions formed for themselves written dialects that were more or less strongly influenced by one another, by Latin (which continued to be the language of the great majority of texts) and by other languages.

Although it appears to outsiders to be a united country, Italy is historically a group of small and large states which were not politically united and some of which were under foreign rule or influence for long periods. There was every reason for local dialects to continue to differentiate. Besides, in northern Italy, often French-ruled, both French and Occitan were cultivated as literary languages.

The impulse towards an Italian linguistic standard was cultural rather than political. Crucial was the work of Dante Alighieri (1265–1321), who not only wrote the *Divine Comedy* – still the classic of Italian literature – but also, in his Latin study *De Vulgari Eloquentia* 'On Vernacular Literature', explored, in a wholly original way, the spoken languages of medieval Europe, especially the dialects of Italy, and their suitability for literature. Perhaps predictably, his choice fell on his own – the speech of Florence, capital of a small state and cultural focus of Tuscany in central Italy. Dante, Petrarch and Boccaccio, author of the *Decameron*, all wrote in the Tuscan of Florence. It was no coincidence that Tuscan gained respect in the 14th century, and that political and cultural circles elsewhere in Italy began to speak and write in varieties of Tuscan.

Latin was still pre-eminent (all three of these authors also wrote in Latin). It was only in 1495 that Leon Battista Alberti compiled the first grammar of Italian, a manuscript to which he gave the Latin title *Regule lingue florentine* 'Rules of the Florentine language'.

In the 15th and 16th centuries Italian and Latin were both used for technical and scientific writing. Scholars spoke both languages: macaronic poetry made fun of the unskilled ones whose Latin was full of Italian words, while the Fidenzian style (named after the 16th-century pedant Pietro Giunteo Fidenzio of Montagnana) was an Italian full of Latin words and Latin forms. But the spread of printing slowly gave the advantage to Italian, which many more people could read and understand.

At the same time, Italian itself was becoming more standardised. The bitter argument of the 16th century – whether to write in Tuscan or in the 'language of the courts' – was a non-argument, for the courts were using a form of Tuscan. It was no longer the language of Florence, or even *lingua fiorentina in bocca sanese* 'Florentine words in a Siena mouth' (one 16th-century definition of the best Italian): Tuscan had become a lingua franca for cultured Italy, as it remains today. Out of many experiments with writing and printing Italian came the idea of using the Greek epsilon, ε, for the open *e* sound, a usage introduced by Giangiorgio Trissino in his play *Sophonisba* in 1524 and nowadays widespread among linguists.

Music, painting and architecture, fields in which Italy was at the forefront of European culture, had emerged as subjects for which Italian was the best language to choose. Italian terms are still used internationally in music – *cantata, allegro, andante* – and have to be learnt by students as they learn musical notation.

With the political upheavals of the Napoleonic period (when northern Italy once more came under French rule) and the unification of Italy around 1860 language questions were renewed. Once more, no alternative existed to Tuscan as a national language. Tuscan is in general the language of modern broadcasting and the press: of films, too, though the film industry, centred on Rome, has raised the profile of the city dialect of Rome. Local and regional forms of speech, within the spectrum of Italian, remain more distinct and more

Europe: Italian

important in Italy than in some other European countries.

Italian is now the official and everyday language of Italy itself and of the two small enclaves of the Vatican City and San Marino. It is one of the official languages of Switzerland, where there are half a million speakers. Italian is still spoken as a second language by many people in Malta (where it was once official).

Italian is still an important language of Eritrea, an Italian colony from 1890 to 1941. The press and education used standard Italian until, as an Islamic country, independent Eritrea recently began to favour Arabic. The Italian of everyday conversation in Eritrea is rather different from the Italian standard. Phonetically it resembles TIGRINYA: *borta* for *porta* 'door'; *tərobbo* for *troppo* 'very'.

Italian has spread widely across the world as the language of Italian émigré communities. The largest and longest-established are those of Chile, Argentina, Brazil (where *Fazendeiro* used to be the creole of a mixed Italian-Negro community in Sao Paulo), Australia, Canada and the USA. The Italian population of Britain numbers 200,000, and has been building up for several centuries, though larger numbers arrived from the mid 19th century onwards. Clerkenwell is the centre of the bilingual Italian community of London.

A distinct Jewish variety of Italian once had

many speakers in the Jewish quarters of north Italian cities such as Modena. There are now no more than a few hundred speakers at the most. A Jewish variety of the Venetian dialect used to be spoken by the Jews of Corfu: this community was wiped out during the Second World War.

Italian is the source of many loanwords in English and other European languages. They include military terms such as *colonello* 'colonel', *sentinella* 'sentinel'; words linked to the arts like *sonetto* 'sonnet', *pantalone* 'pantaloon' (originally a character in comedy); and many others, such as *cortigiana* 'courtesan' and *influenza*, literally 'influence'.

For a table of numerals see SARDINIAN.

Italian, Sardinian and Corsican on the map

Italian is the majority language of Italy, also spoken in part of Switzerland. Standard Italian is based on the Tuscan dialect of Florence. Regional varieties of Italian shade into the city dialects (including that of Rome) and into strongly marked local dialects. The northern dialects share some important features with French and Occitan. Sicilian, sometimes regarded as a distinct language, has a literary tradition older than that of Italian itself.

Sardinian is the regional language of Sardinia, though it has little official recognition. The major dialects are Campidanese and Logudorese. Gallurese has many links with Corsican, while Sassarese is influenced by the mainland dialects of Pisa and Genoa. In Alghero the local language is Catalan; in Calasetta and Carloforte the Ligurian dialect of Italian is spoken.

Corsican is the regional speech of Corsica, where the official language is French. In Bonifacio in Corsica a Ligurian dialect of Italian is spoken, implanted long ago by colonisation from Genoa.

The Voice of the Lombard People

The 'Northern League', which presses for autonomy or independence for the Italian North, has an ambiguous attitude to the northern dialects. These are satisfyingly distinct from standard Italian – but lack the cultural cachet of the language of Dante. Some separatist writing does appear in dialect form, such as the small-circulation paper *Lombardia Autonomista: la vus del popul lumbard*. One 1986 issue opened with the following clarion call:

Lumbard, muvemas tücc, e drelamen, perchè Roma l'autonomia ghe la regala minga de sücür. O semm bun de cunquistala nun, o'l noster popul el scumpariss de la storia.

Lombards, let us move forward, and quickly, because Rome will not serve us autonomy on a plate. Either we are up to conquering it for ourselves, or our people will be erased from history.

Indovinello Veronese: the 'Veronese riddle'

The oldest Italian text is generally said to be the riddle that a scribe of the 9th century inserted in the margin of a religious manuscript:

Se pareba boves,	The oxen were driven out;
alba pratalia araba	they ploughed a white field
e albo versorio teneba	and held to a white furrow
e negro semen seminaba.	and sowed a black seed.

The answer, appropriately, is the scribe's own hand as he writes his text.

JAMAICAN CREOLE

2,200,000 SPEAKERS

Jamaica

One of the ENGLISH CREOLES AND PIDGINS of the Caribbean, Jamaican Creole originated in the heavy immigration of African slaves to Jamaica after the English took the island in 1655. The slaves came from many different African cultures: at certain times, to judge by word origins in the modern Creole, AKAN and TEMNE speakers must have been strongly represented. But the English pidgin of the Atlantic trade was their only means of communication, and this soon developed into a new language that mixed English elements with Portuguese, African and others – a language as necessary to the white inhabitants of Jamaica as to the slaves.

Through all the centuries that followed, English has been the language of officialdom and educated culture on the island. The creole has historically been despised by teachers and by educated Jamaicans, who, in speaking to outsiders, often found it best to deny any knowledge of it. In fact there are many language varieties (see box) between 'pure creole' and standard English, and skill in switching between them is learned early in life: children speaking to a teacher will use neither creole nor standard, but something between.

A sociolinguistic continuum

'The varieties of Jamaican English differ to the point of unintelligibility. There are many middle-class St Andrew housewives who claim that they can speak the broad creole because they can converse with their maids, yet they can understand very little of the conversation if they hear the maid talking with the gardener.

'In Jamaica there is no sharp cleavage between creole and standard. Rather there is a continuous spectrum of speech varieties ranging from the 'bush talk' or 'broken language' of Quashie to the educated standard of Philip Sherlock and Norman Manley. Many Jamaicans persist in the myth that there are only two varieties: the patois [Creole] and the standard. But one speaker's attempt at the broad patois may be closer to the standard end of the spectrum than is another speaker's attempt at the standard. Each Jamaican speaker commands a span of this continuum, the breadth of the span depending on the breadth of his social contacts; a labor leader, for example, commands a greater span of varieties than does a suburban middle-class housewife.'

David DeCamp in *Pidginization and creolization of languages* ed. Dell Hymes (Cambridge: Cambridge University Press, 1971) p. 350, abridged

JAPANESE

120,000,000 SPEAKERS

Japan

Japanese is something unique: one of the major languages of the world, spoken by well over a hundred million people, yet with no known linguistic relatives.

Naturally, attempts have been made to find links between Japanese and other languages. Research has concentrated on an apparent, very distant, relationship that might exist with the ALTAIC language family. But the results so far are anything but certain, as can be seen from a recent survey article which speculates whether Japanese may be 'a mixed language, deriving its lexical and grammatical properties from both Austronesian and Altaic, possibly with additions from Austro-Asiatic and Dravidian' (M. Shibatani). To have undergone such varied influences a language would have to be sited at a crossroads of Asia, rather than on an offshore archipelago. In fact, in historic times, the Japanese islands have been involved rather little in migration and ethnic mixture – a fact that certainly helps to explain why Japanese has no obvious links to other known languages.

Japanese is known to its own speakers as *Nihongo*.

Although the two languages are utterly different from each other, Chinese has exerted enormous cultural influence on Japanese throughout its known history – from the very beginning, the 8th century AD, when the first two Japanese texts were written down in Chinese script. These were *Kojiki*, 'Records of Antiquity', a miscellany of myths and legendary history; and *Manyōshū*, 'Collection of Ten Thousand Leaves', an anthology of poetry. Some of the texts in these collections are clearly rather

older than the 8th century. Japanese has been a written and literary language for about as long as English.

In later centuries Chinese loanwords multiplied, yet the styles and genres of Japanese literature tended to remain distinct from those of Chinese – indeed, Japanese intellectuals also wrote in Chinese. Medieval Japanese poetry and prose have one striking feature which makes them a landmark in world culture: many of the greatest masterpieces were written by women. This includes the single greatest classic of Japanese literature, the 11th-century *Tale of Genji* by Lady Murasaki.

Japanese and Chinese continued their symbiosis until the mid 19th century: Chinese loanwords are said to amount to more than half of the Japanese vocabulary. Then Japan opened itself to Western influence, almost for the first time. It now has numerous loanwords from European languages, notably English: tēburu 'table', wāpuro 'word processor', *rampu* 'lamp'. Kōhī 'coffee' is an older loanword, from Dutch.

With political and commercial expansion, Japanese became a major language in the western Pacific and eastern Asia at this period. It was an official language in Korea, Malaysia, Indonesia, Singapore and other countries while they were under Japanese rule.

In spite of the collapse of Japanese imperialism at the end of the Second World War, Japanese remains an important language of worldwide trade: two Japanese daily newspapers, *Asahi shinbun* and *Nihon keizai shinbu*, are now published simultaneously in Europe.

Japanese is a language in which politeness,

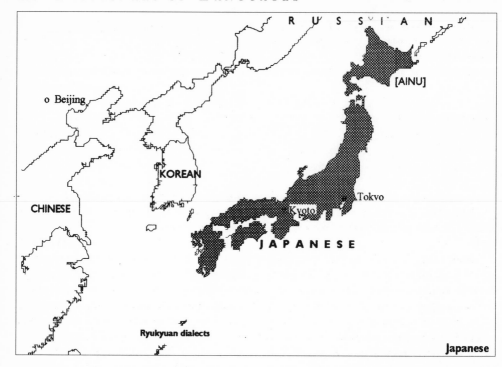

Japanese

deference and euphemism are built in very firmly. So are distinctions between men's and women's speech; there are words categorised as 'rough' which women do not use, and women's speech tends to have fewer Chinese loanwords than men's.

One feature of the Japanese sound pattern is well known: it has only one phoneme corresponding to the *l* and *r* of many other languages. Japanese speakers of foreign languages find the distinction between these two sounds difficult to make.

Japanese dialects

Over most of Japan dialect differences, though significant, do not impede understanding because a standard form of Japanese (*kyōtūgo* 'common language'; *hyōzyungo* 'standard language') based on the Tōkyō dialect is used in broadcasting and education and is generally understood. The major dialect division is between Western dialects, including that of the old capital Kyōto, and Eastern, including Tōkyō.

Ainu

A second language native to Japan, once spoken in northern Honshū and the islands of Hokkaido and Sakhalin but now practically extinct, Ainu is quite unrelated to Japanese. Like Japanese it has no proven links with any other language of the world. The Ainu were distinctive in their language, their culture – and in being hairier than any other human population. Once an independent fishing and hunting people, they were conquered by Japan in 1669–72 and have very slowly assimilated to Japanese culture.

There was no written literature in Ainu but rich collections of oral epic poetry have been made. Ainu epics were usually in the first person, the imagined speaker being sometimes a god or goddess, sometimes a human being or an animal. They were most often performed by women: one, Imekanu (1875–1961), after her retirement from work as a Christian missionary, wrote down more than 20,000 pages of epics from her own repertoire.

Javanese has western, central and eastern dialect groups. The dialect of the former government centres of Surakarta and Yogyakarta sets the standard. *Osing*, spoken around Banyuwangi, is particularly distinctive. Tengger has 500,000 speakers on the slopes of Mt Bromo in eastern Java.

SUNDANESE dialect groupings follow traditional administrative subdivisions: Banten, Priangan, Bogor and Krawang, and Cirebon.

MADURESE is usually divided into western, central and eastern dialect groups, though communications on the island are easy and sharp dialect differences have not emerged. The Madurese of the Kangean islands is so different from that of Madura that some would class it as a separate language. That spoken on the north-east coast of Java is apparently the result of relatively recent migration: separate mainland dialects have not been recorded.

The speech levels of Javanese

Javanese speech takes account, in every sentence that is spoken, of the relative status of speaker and hearer. The practice is sometimes said to have been learnt from the Hindu caste system – but it has perhaps nowhere been built into spoken language so thoroughly as in Java. It affects tone of voice (which varies between *alus* 'refined' and *kasar* 'crude') and, most especially, vocabulary. Choice of words ranges between *ngoko* 'low' and *krama* 'high'. *Ngoko* is a complete language, in which everything can be said that one ever needs to – but it cannot be used in formal situations. In talking of social superiors, even more formality is needed – *krama inggil*, 'high *krama*', referring to the honoured person's actions; *krama andhap*, 'humble *krama*', referring to one's own.

For a table of numerals in Ngoko and Krama see SUNDANESE.

Ngoko, high krama and humble krama

Ngoko	Aku **negekeki** kancaku buku	I **gave** my friend a book
Krama andhap	Aku **njaosi** bapakku buku	I **gave** my father a book
Krama inggil	Bapak **maringi** aku buku	My father **gave** me a book

English speakers can and do make such distinctions – 'I **was privileged to offer** . . .', 'The Director **was kind enough to give** . . .' but in Javanese they are far more systematic. There are dialect distinctions in the *krama* language, which has a larger vocabulary in eastern Java than in the west of the island.

Example from Elinor Clark Horne, 'Javanese' in *International encyclopedia of linguistics* (New York: Oxford University Press, 1992) vol. 2 pp. 254–9

The Javanese alphabet

Alphabetical order, in this script of Indian origin, does not follow the otherwise universal Indian rule. Instead, the following doggerel verse acts as a mnemonic:

hana c̀araka,	ꦧꦤꦲꦗꦤꦩ	There were two envoys,
data sawala;	ꦝꦠꦱꦮꦭ	They began to fight;
padha jayanya,	ꦥꦝꦗꦪꦚ	Their prowess was equal,
maga bathanga!	ꦩꦒꦧꦛꦔ	Both fell down dead!

After J. C. Kuipers and R. McDermott in *The world's writing systems* ed. P. T. Daniels, W. Bright (New York: Oxford University Press, 1996) p. 478

JINGHPAW

700,000 SPEAKERS

Burma, China, India

One of the SINO-TIBETAN LANGUAGES, Jinghpaw is a major language of Kachin state, Burma. It has been described as the 'linguistic crossroads' of the Sino-Tibetan family, showing similarities with Tibetan to the north, with Burmese to the south and with Yi and its relatives to the east.

Edmund Leach, in *Political systems of highland Burma* (London: Bell, 1954), has shown that the cultural and linguistic position of its speakers is equally fluid. There is a continuing, complex pattern of change in which Kachins may adopt a new language, Jinghpaw, Shan or Burmese, which tends to go with a new social orientation.

Jinghpaw is the local form of the name. *Singpho*, *Chingpho* and *Jingpo* are spellings adopted in various foreign sources; the Burmese form is *Theinbaw*. Jinghpaw has sometimes been called 'the *Kachin* language' (*Kakhyen* is an older form of this name): the majority of inhabitants of Kachin state speak either Jinghpaw or Burmese or both.

Kachin country is mountainous, with deep valleys. The two major towns are Myitkyina and Bhamo, both of them traditional nodes of long distance land trade. But little is known of the history of Jinghpaw and its speakers before the 19th century. The border between China and British Burma, cutting through Jinghpaw-speaking country, was fixed in the 1890s.

Jinghpaw has borrowed vocabulary from Shan and, rather less liberally, from Chinese and Burmese. It has also borrowed from English, particularly for religious and cultural concepts, as a result of the work of American Baptist missionaries who were active in Bhamo by 1900. They devised the Latin orthography in which Jinghpaw is normally printed.

The first ten numerals are: *ləngai*, *ləhkawng*, *məsum*, *məli*, *mənga kru*, *sənit*, *məcat*, *jəhku*, *shi*.

Three uses of traditional Jinghpaw literature

'Traditional Kachin culture tolerates premarital sexual relations. The front apartment of a house is the *nla dap* where adolescents gather in the evening for singing, recitation of poetry, and, finally, lovemaking.

'The priest's chief task is to offer sacrifices to the spirits with appropriate invocations. Most of his training consists in learning prayers and formulas, some of which are quite long, in a special, obsolescent style of speech. The priest is recompensed with a part of the sacrifice. An additional specialized status is that of *jaiwa*. Although older sources regard this as a religious status, their descriptions support the term 'saga-teller' used by Leach. Certain rites are accompanied by lengthy recitations of traditional cosmogony and history, of which the saga-teller is the repository.'

Frank M. LeBar and others, *Ethnic groups of mainland southeast Asia* (New Haven: Human Relations Area Files Press, 1964) pp. 15, 17

Jinghpaw on the map

In Kachin state, Burma, where over 500,000
Jinghpaw speakers live, the language serves as
lingua franca for speakers of the minority hill
languages of the Burmese-Lolo group, Atsi (Tsai-
wa), Lashi and Maru. In China there are about
100,000 speakers: Jinghpaw (*Jingpo*) is an official
nationality in China. For Jinghpaw speakers in the
northern Shan state no figures are available. The
number of speakers in Assam is relatively small.

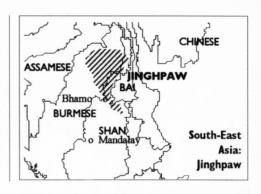

JUDEZMO

150,000 SPEAKERS

Israel and other countries

Judezmo is the SPANISH-like language spoken by descendants of the Jews who were exiled from Spain and Portugal at the end of the 15th century. Most of them settled in the western parts of what was then the Ottoman Turkish Empire – but in this century the majority have migrated again, this time mainly to Israel.

Its most obvious difference from Spanish is that Judezmo is written in the Hebrew alphabet.

The Iberian peninsula had been divided politically and religiously, and there is some evidence that Jews of the peninsula, in the centuries that preceded their exile, spoke both Spanish-related and Arabic-related dialects. Although Spanish (including MOZARABIC), Hebrew and Aramaic are the principal constituents of Judezmo, Arabic elements can also be traced in it, such as *alxá* 'Sunday' from Arabic *al-akhad*.

In 1492 most of the Jews of Spain fled the persecution of the Inquisition and found refuge in the Ottoman Empire; in 1497 the Jews of Portugal, equally threatened, followed them. They settled in Istanbul, the empire's new capital, as well as in Saloniki (where for a while they formed a majority of the population) and in many other towns of the Balkans and Anatolia.

Engaged in business and trade, gradually prospering, these Sephardic Jews became the dominant group of the very diverse Jewish communities of the empire. Their language has continued to differentiate gradually from Spanish and Portuguese, and eventually became the lingua franca of nearly all Ottoman Jews.

By 1948 there were probably over 150,000 speakers of Judaeo-Spanish or Judezmo, including large communities in the United States and Latin America and about 70,000 in Turkey. Half of these moved to Israel in that year, and the Turkish community has continued to shrink: there are now only 15,000 or fewer in Istanbul, where they are known as *Spañoles*.

Sepharad is the classical Jewish name for the Iberian peninsula: thus the members of this ancient exile community are the *Sephardim*. Their language was named *Judezmo* 'the Jewish language' from the Iberian point of view, *Ladino* 'the Romance language' from the Jewish point of view. But in practice these two names are used for two different forms of the written language.

Judezmo emerged as a widely used written language, as well as a spoken language, in the later 19th century, in the western cities of the Ottoman Empire. There was a lively press in Sarajevo and Constantinople and places between. There was considerable variation in written forms – from a Westernised Judezmo, *Lingua Franqueada*, typical of a French-educated intelligentsia, to styles that were much closer to everyday popular speech.

Ladino was a somewhat artificial development – a language used specifically for the translation of Hebrew and Aramaic liturgical texts. In Ladino texts, the Hebrew and Aramaic elements of Judezmo are consciously avoided.

There is a Judezmo newspaper in Istanbul, *Şalom*: it nowadays publishes articles in Turkish as well as Judezmo. In general Judezmo is now in steep decline both as a written and as a spoken language: in Israel, modern Hebrew tends to take its place.

KABYLE

2,500,000 SPEAKERS

Algeria, France

Kabyle is one of the BERBER LANGUAGES (see map there). It has at least two million speakers (one recent estimate is 7,000,000) in northeastern Algeria. There are half a million Kabyle-speaking migrants in French and Belgian cities. Its speakers call themselves *Qbaili*, from the Arabic *qbaila* 'tribe'.

Although some information on Kabyle and other Berber languages is recorded by medieval Arabic authors, serious study of Kabyle followed European interest in North Africa in the 18th and 19th centuries. Adolphe Hanoteau's grammar of Kabyle, aimed at French administrators, was published in 1858.

Male speakers of Kabyle are generally bilingual in Arabic, the language of education; many also speak French. Women are more likely to be monolingual. The active Kabyle resistance movement urges the adoption not of Kabyle but of the Algerian dialect of Arabic as the national language in place of the official classical Arabic. But the Algerian constitutional amendment of 1996, declaring Arabic the sole language of business, education and administration, poses a new threat to the survival of Kabyle culture.

Kabyle has numerous Arabic loanwords (sometimes difficult to recognise after phonetic reshaping) as a result of the centuries-long co-existence of the two languages: *ṭeffaḥ* 'apple' from Arabic *tuffāḥ*. Latin loanwords, dating from the Roman Empire, include *tifirest* 'pear tree', from Latin *pirus* with the Berber feminine affixes *t- -t*.

The first ten numerals in Kabyle are: *yiwen, sin, tlata, rewâa, xemsa, setta, seṭḥa, tmanya, tesâa, âaṣra*.

The Kabyle alphabet

a â b c č d ḍ e f g g gw ǧ h ḥ i j k k kw l m n q ɣ r ṛ s ṣ ṣ t ṭ ṭ u w x y z ẓ ž

Kabyle script

Among Kabyle speakers, knowledge of the ancient Libyco-Berber alphabet, still used by the Tuareg, has long disappeared. Although nowhere an official language, Kabyle is beginning to find its way into print, in a newly standardised Latin alphabet of 37 letters.

After M. Malherbe, *Les langages de l'humanité* (Paris: Laffont, 1995) p. 1008

KADAI LANGUAGES

Kadai is the name usually applied to a language family that consists of the TAI LANGUAGES, the Kam-Sui languages (see DONG) and some other distantly related, little-known languages of Hainan and southern China. For more information on these, and a map, see LI. Paul Benedict demonstrated the relationship in 1942 in a paper entitled 'Thai, Kadai and Indonesian; a new alignment in southeastern Asia' in the *American anthropologist*. He argued that the Kadai family was linked to a wider grouping of AUSTRO-TAI LANGUAGES, and a growing number of linguists agree.

The family called *Kadai* or *Tai-Kadai* by western linguists is also recognised in China, where it is known as the *Zhuang-Dong* family, ZHUANG being the name of the largest Tai-speaking minority in China, while Dong is the name of the most important language in the Kam-Sui group.

KALENJIN

2,500,000 SPEAKERS

Kenya

O ne of the NILO-SAHARAN LANGUAGES, Kalenjin is spoken by a group of traditionally pastoralist peoples in north-western Kenya.

Kalenjin, meaning 'I tell you', is a term coined by the speakers themselves in the 1940s to emphasise their linguistic and cultural unity. They were earlier grouped as the *Nandi dialects*: the separate dialects include Nandi, Kipsigis, Päkot and others (see map at TURKANA).

The migration that brought a language of the Nilo-Saharan family to this region may have taken place in the 14th century. In the 19th century the Nandi were the best known of the Kalenjin-speaking peoples. They were then a fiercely independent people, defeating the Masai in the 1870s after long warfare, and successfully preventing Swahili caravans from taking Nandi slaves and even from travelling through their country. They resisted British administration for fifteen years, from 1890 to 1905.

The savagery of the final British conquest and deportations left a legacy of lasting hostility.

A. C. Hollis's book *The Nandi: their language and folk-lore* (Oxford: Clarendon Press, 1909: revised by G. W. B. Huntingford, 1969) is still cited by anthropologists, but Hollis wisely found his informants outside the borders of Nandi country. Indeed, 'his principal informant, Arap Chepsiet, sometimes introduced himself to visiting officials as "the man who wrote Bwana Hollis's book" '.

Kalenjin has ten vowels and three tones. The language is unusual in having a three-way distinction of vowel length. It has no distinction between voiced and unvoiced consonants. Nouns have separate indefinite ('primary') and definite ('secondary') forms, and sex or gender prefixes, *ki-*, *ce-*: *kípnándíín* 'Nandi man', *cèpnándíà* 'Nandi woman'; *kibléngwa* 'hare', *cepkoikòs* 'tortoise'.

The first ten numerals are: *akenge, aeng, somok, angwan, mut, kullo, tisap, sisiit, sokol, taman*.

Atinye cheptánnyō nepiiyonyi mutai, korukut lakat – 'I have a daughter who gets plenty to eat every morning and goes to bed hungry every night.' The answer? A broom.

KAMBA

2,500,000 SPEAKERS

Kenya

Although clearly related to its neighbours MERU and KIKUYU (see map there), Kamba may, to judge from its well-established dialect divisions, be among the oldest established of the BANTU LANGUAGES of northern Kenya.

The local name of the language is *kiKamba*, of its speakers *aKamba*, and of their country *uKamba*. They were called *waringao*, 'naked people', in Swahili.

Kamba speakers were once an important trading people of inland Kenya: their colony in Rabai, near coastal Mombasa, was perhaps established for trade reasons and certainly kept up trade links with the homeland. Swahili traders, too, came to the edge of Kamba country but did not enter it. Kamba shared a local market system with the Masai and Kikuyu areas to the west. In the 1920s travellers still found Kamba a particularly useful language, known as a lingua franca by many Kikuyu and Masai speakers and by the smaller peoples around the foothills of Kilimanjaro. For Kamba speakers themselves Swahili was the most useful second language, followed later by English.

The British East Africa Company set up a trading post at Machakos in 1892. The country became a British 'protectorate' in 1895 and some land was taken by English and Afrikaans speakers from 1903 onwards.

Kamba has a seven-vowel system, sometimes written *i ī e a o ū u*, though the accents marking open *i* and *u* are often omitted in print. The first ten numerals are: *īmwe, ilī, itatū, inya, itaano, thanthatū, mūonza, nyanya, kenda, īkūmi*.

KAMTOK

PERHAPS 2,000,000 SPEAKERS OF KAMTOK AS A LINGUA FRANCA

Cameroun

One of the ENGLISH CREOLES AND PIDGINS, this language has had many names in its short life: *Cameroons Pidgin, Wes Cos* ('West Coast'), *Broken English. Kamtok* ('Cameroun talk') has now caught on.

At the eastern end of the continuum of English creoles that begins with KRIO of Sierra Leone, there is little difference between Kamtok and the West African Pidgin English of Nigeria: the two are in general mutually intelligible. Both serve principally as an everyday medium of trade and interchange among speakers of different local languages – but with the linguistic fragmentation of coastal Cameroun there is a growing number of first-language speakers of Kamtok in the larger towns.

Kamtok and Krio proverbs

Kamtok		Krio
alata neva hapi wen pusi bɔn pikin	Mouse is never pleased when Cat has kittens	arata nɔba gladi we pus bɔn pikin
trɔki wan fait bɔt i sabi se i han sɔt	Tortoise wants to fight but (he knows) his arms are short	trɔki wã bɔt i an shɔt
wan han no fit tai bɔndu	You can't tie a bundle with one hand	wan an nɔ ebul tai bɔndul

From Loreto Todd, 'Cameroonian' in *Readings in creole studies* ed. Ian F. Hancock (Gent: Story-Scientia, 1979) pp. 281–94

KANNADA

27,000,000 SPEAKERS

India

Kannada (Canarese, to give its older English name) belongs to the DRAVIDIAN LANGUAGES of southern India. It is the state language of Karnataka.

As a language of the Rashtrakuta and Yadava dynasties in Maharashtra, used in inscriptions along with Sanskrit, the influence of Kannada once reached further north than it does now. Indeed, MARATHI shows strong evidence of co-existence with its Dravidian neighbour. In turn Kannada has been influenced by Sanskrit, the learned language of India, and later by Portuguese, radiating from nearby Goa, the metropolis of Portugal's eastern possessions.

Known from inscriptions of the 6th century and after, Kannada has a surviving literature from the 9th century onwards. Some early texts are lost – their existence known or surmised through such sources as Kēśirāja's 13th-century grammar ('Jewel mirror of grammar') and the 9th-century textbook on poetry, *Kavirājamarga*. The *campu* epic, of mixed prose and verse, was a major genre in the 10th to 12th centuries. Lyric poetry came later. Kannada was a major language of literature under the Empire of Vijayanagar, from 1336 to 1575. The beginnings of a modern literary language can be traced to the middle of the 19th century.

Great numbers of Indo-Aryan loanwords, especially from Sanskrit, have brought into educated Kannada speech a contrast between aspirated and unaspirated stops (e.g., *ph bh* contrasting with *p b*) which is foreign to Dravidian languages. The typical Dravidian rolled *r* and fricative *l* are no longer distinguished in modern Kannada. For a table of numerals see TELUGU.

Kannada, Telugu and Tuḷu

Standard spoken *Kannaḍa* is based on the colloquial language of Bangalore and Mysore City. The Dharwar dialect of the north of Karnataka, beyond the former borders of Mysore, forms a regional standard of its own. The coastal dialects are also quite distinct.

Languages of the Nīlgiri Hills

Besides the languages of the Todas and the Kōtas, two other languages are vernacular on the Neilgherry Hills – viz., the dialect spoken by the Burghers or Baḍagars (the northern people), an ancient but organised dialect of the Canarese; and the rude Tamil spoken by the Irulars ('people of the darkness') and Kuruburs (Can. *Kurubaru*, Tam. *Kurumbar*, shepherds), who are occasionally stumbled upon by adventurous sportsmen in the denser, deeper jungles, and the smoke of whose fires may occasionally be seen rising from the lower gorges of the hills.

Robert Caldwell, *Comparative grammar of the Dravidian or South-Indian family of languages*, 3rd edn (London: Kegan Paul, 1913) p. 34

Baḍagaga bāḍāse,   The Baḍaga wants mutton,
Kōtaga pōtāse,   The Kōta wants beef,
Todavaga hālāse,   The Toda wants milk,
Kurumaga jēnāse.   The Kurumba wants honey.
Paul Hockings, *Counsel from the ancients: a study of Badaga proverbs, prayers, omens and curses* (Berlin: Mouton De Gruyter, 1988)

Kannada has two close relatives which are sometimes counted as dialects. *Baḍaga* is a language of the Nīlgiri Hills, now with 100,000 speakers, descendants of 16th-century emigrants from Mysore.

Kōḍagu or Coorg, with 90,000 speakers, is the language of the old hill state of Coorg, independent until British annexation in 1834.

Telugu dialects are usually classed in four groups: Northern, Southern, Eastern and Central. The last-named, the speech of East and West Godavari, Krishna and Guntur, has contributed most to the modern standard.

Tuḷu is spoken in a coastal region of southern Karnataka, around Mangalore.

Toda and *Kōta*, mentioned in the Baḍaga proverb (see box), are Dravidian languages of small tribal groups, with less than a thousand speakers each.

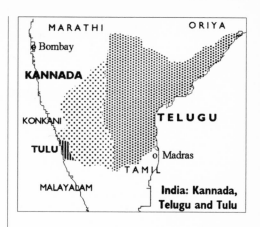

India: Kannada, Telugu and Tulu

Writing in Kannada

The Kannada alphabet is in all essential features identical with that of Telugu, though it has its own typical printed style. Consonants are combined with following vowels to form a single symbol. Most compound consonants involve the writing of one element below the line.

Kannada script: the consonant characters

ಕಖಗಘಙ ಚಛಜಝಞ ಟಠಡಢಣ ತಥದಧನ ಪಫಬಭಮ ಯರಱಲವ ಶಷಸಹಳ

k kh g gh ṅ c ch j jh ñ ṭ ṭh ḍ ḍh ṇ t th d dh n p ph b bh m y r ṟ l v ś ṣ s h ḷ

KANURI

4,000,000 SPEAKERS

Nigeria, Niger, Chad and Cameroun

Kanuri is a language of the Saharan group of NILO-SAHARAN LANGUAGES.

Kanurí is the local name of the language, *Kanúri* that of the speakers: their homeland is *Kanem*, east of Lake Chad. *Bornu*, name of a second traditional state, is the name of the Kanuri language in some 19th-century English records.

Legends tell of Kanuri origins in a migration from Arabia, the migrants intermarrying with the indigenous people of the shores of Lake Chad. In fact the history of the Kanem-Bornu Empire may go back to the 8th century, but it became an Islamic state in the 11th and remained a major force in central Africa for eight hundred years. Originally centred on Kanem, east of Lake Chad, internal power shifted to Bornu (north-eastern Nigeria, west of the lake) in the 14th century. The empire's power reached its zenith under Prince Idris Aloma (ruled 1571–1603), whose conquests and long distance diplomacy encouraged trade and cultural development.

The names of the old tribes incorporated in the empire are still remembered, but their languages disappeared over the centuries as Kanuri, the prestigious language of court and government, took their place. Across southern Chad the territories of vassal states of the later empire can be traced – Logone, where the native language is SARA; Wandala in the northern salient of Cameroun, where they speak Mandara, a Niger-Congo language; Bagirmi in central Chad, where the main language, Bagirmi, is Nilo-Saharan; Kanem itself; Damagherim; and even Wadai, where the local language is MABA. In these, the provincial languages remain in use, though for some centuries Kanuri was the language of diplomacy, education and long distance trade. Arabic, the language of the Qur'ān and of religious education, is widely known in the lands of the former empire.

Kanuri has six vowels and a complex tone pattern based on two main tones, high and low. Suffixes, such as the plural *-a*, alter the tone of preceding syllables: *fèrò* 'girl', *fèrò-á* 'girls'. The first ten numerals in Kanuri are: *tílō, ndī, yásqo, dēgu, ūgu, rásqo, tullur, usqu, legár, mēgū*.

The first printed record of Kanuri, a list of numerals, appeared in 1790. A fuller printed vocabulary, collected from a Bornu traveller by

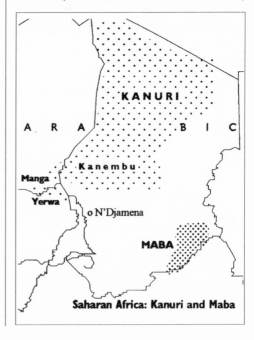

Saharan Africa: Kanuri and Maba

J. L. Burckhardt in Cairo, was published in 1819; but the best early work on Kanuri was by Sigismund Koelle, author of the *Polyglotta Africana*. In 1854, the same year in which this great work appeared, he also published a *Grammar of the Bornu or Kanuri language* and a collection of folklore, entitled *African native literature, or proverbs, tales, fables and historical fragments in the Kanuri or Bornu language, to which are added a translation of the above and a Kanuri–English vocabulary.*

Kanuri and MABA

The three dialect groups of Kanuri are: *Yerwa Kanuri* (or Bornu) of north-eastern Nigeria, the centre of the empire; *Manga Kanuri* of southwestern Niger, the old northern province; and, *Kanembu*, the language of the ancient heartland of Kanem, now in Chad.

MABA, once the language of the state of Wadai, is also a member of the Nilo-Saharan family, but is only distantly related to Kanuri.

KAREN LANGUAGES

PERHAPS 4,000,000 SPEAKERS

Burma, Thailand

The largest ethnic minority in east central Burma are the speakers of Karen languages, which form a sub-group of the Tibeto-Burman Languages, or, some would say, a branch of the family of SINO-TIBETAN LANGUAGES on an equal level with Chinese on one side and the Tibeto-Burman languages on the other. This is a measure of the long independent history of the Karen languages, which must stretch back several thousand years, but not of the current number of speakers. There are no more than a few million.

Kareang, Karieng, are names used in Mon and Thai for Karen speakers and their languages: the English name derives from these. In Burmese they are called *Kayin* and in Shan *Yang*. The old-fashioned name *White Karen*, in Burmese *Kayin byu*, in Thai *Yang khao*, was often used for the lowland Karen, speakers of Pwo and Sgaw.

Karyan 'Karens', and *Cakraw* perhaps 'Sgaw', are found in Burmese records of the 13th century, and there is no reason to suppose that they were new arrivals even then. Little is known of their history till the early 19th century, when missionaries in British-occupied Tenasserim began to work with speakers of Sgaw and Pwo, devising scripts (based on Burmese) for these two languages. Translations and other publications were soon appearing. A vast *Thesaurus of the Karen knowledge*, by Sau Kau-too and the Rev. J. Wade, was published at Tavoy in 1847–50.

Karen speakers now occupy two quite distinct kinds of terrain: the flat coastal plains of the Irrawaddy, Sittang and Salween deltas, and the abrupt hills and valleys of the Tenasserim range that marks the border between Burma and Thailand.

Lowland Sgaw, and most Pwo speakers, are merged – administratively and to some extent culturally – with Burmese. They tend to be Buddhists, and to be bilingual in Burmese: indeed, the Karen languages may well be in steep decline in these areas, but no recent information is available. Karen State, established in 1952, includes many of the speakers of Sgaw who are hill dwellers. Kayah State marks the territory of Kaya (Karenni) speakers. With continuing warfare and oppression in Burma the numbers of Karen language speakers in Thailand has increased massively in recent years.

Karen languages – like Chinese – are overwhelmingly monosyllabic. Pwo and Sgaw both have four tones in open syllables. The object normally follows the verb, and modifiers (adjectives and adverbs, in our terms) follow the word that is modified, much as in Thai. There are a great many Burmese loanwords in Karen, mostly quite recent loans of cultural terms. Some loans from Mon and Thai are also found.

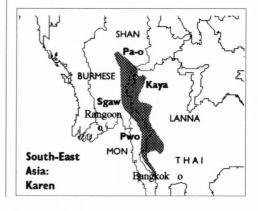

South-East Asia: Karen

A lullaby

'When playing with the chickens, children sometimes catch one of them and pretend to rock it to sleep, droning the while:

Hsaw po, mi, mi –	Sleep, sleep, little chick,
n'mo n'pa leh hsu Yo.	mother and father have gone to Shanland.
Heh ke so ne na	They will come back
p'theh tha wa ko lo.	and bring you plenty of betel nuts.
Aw gha lo gha lo –	You can eat them one by one –
me aw, hsaw hpo.	sleep, little chick.'

Harry Ignatius Marshall, *The Karen people of Burma* (Ohio State University, 1922) p. 174

The Karen languages on the map

Sgaw has possibly 2,000,000 speakers. They call themselves *Kanyaw*; in Burmese they are often known as *Bamā Kayin*, 'Burmese Karen' because their territory is close to the central areas of Burmese speech.

Pwo has possibly 1,250,000 speakers, often called in Burmese *Talaing Kayin*, 'Mon Karen': they are lowlanders in regions that are or were Mon-speaking.

Pa-o has perhaps 500,000 speakers in southern Shan State. In Burmese its speakers are called *Kayin net* 'Black Karen' or *Taungthu*, 'hill people', and in Shan *Tongsu*.

Kayā speakers, of whom there may be about 300,000, used to be called *Kayin ni* in Burmese with the equivalents *Red Karen* and *Karen-ni* in English. *Kayah* is now the usual English form.

Numerals in Karen languages

	Sgaw	Pwo	Pa-o
1	ta'	là'	tà'
2	khí	nì	nì
3	thö`	thàn	thòm
4	lwì	lí	lít
5	yὲ	yɛ´	ngát
6	khü´	khù	thù
7	nwí	nwè	nö´t
8	khɔ'	kho'	thɔt
9	khwí	khwí	kút
10	shí	shì	chì

Numerals follow the noun and are followed by classifiers: thus Pwo *li' la bi* 'one book', literally 'book one flat-item'; *ghi ni phlo* 'two houses', literally 'house two round-items'.

Paul K. Benedict, *Sino-Tibetan: a conspectus* (Cambridge: Cambridge University Press, 1972) pp. 129, 131 and Robert B. Jones, *Karen linguistic studies* (Berkeley: University of California Press, 1961)

KASHMIRI

3,000,000 SPEAKERS

India, Pakistan

Kashmiri is the best-known member of the Dardic group of INDO-ARYAN LANGUAGES – the only one that has unequivocally reached the status of a literary language.

The Kashmir Valley has probably spoken Kashmiri for a long time: it is reasonable to suppose that the Dardic languages have been here as long as the main group of Indo-Aryan languages has been spreading from north-western India, that is, for three thousand years or more. There is a venerable literary tradition, going back to the 13th century, when the poet Sitikantha chose 'the language of the people, understood by all' for his manual of Tantric worship, *Mahanaya-prakasa*. From the next century come the verses of the great woman poet of Kashmir, Lalla Ded. Later, Persian literature had a pervasive influence: there is even a Kashmiri translation of Firdausi's vast epic *Shah-nama*.

Through all this time the government of Kashmir has been conducted in other languages. For many centuries it was Sanskrit, and the early history of Kashmir is recorded in the Sanskrit chronicle compiled by Kalhana in 1148, *Rājataraṅgiṇī* 'Ocean of Kings'. After Akbar conquered Kashmir in 1589, Persian became the language of government (as it was for the whole of northern India), and remained so until the early 20th century. It was then replaced by Urdu, which still functions as the government language both in Pakistani Kashmir, where it is also the national language, and in Indian Kashmir. Many speakers of Kashmiri use Urdu as their literary language.

There is, however, literature and a press in Kashmiri, which is normally printed in a form of Perso-Arabic script similar to that used for Urdu. The official post-1950 version of this script (which some writers have not fully adopted) includes diacritical marks for all the vowels of Kashmiri. The *Sharada* alphabet, a descendant of ancient Brahmi, is not so often seen.

Numerals in the Dardic languages and Khowar			
Kashmiri	**Shina**	**Kalami**	**Khowar**
1 akh	ek	ā, ak	ī
2 zəh	dū	dū	jū
3 trih	trē	ṭhā	troi
4 chōr	cār	cōr	cōr
5 pānch	push	panj	pōnj
6 sheh	shah	shō	choi
7 sath	sat	sat	sot
8 aiṭh	ach	aṭh	osht
9 nav	nau	num	nəoh
10 dah	dāī	dash	josh

The Dardic languages include several of those spoken in the valleys of Kashmir (see map at INDO-ARYAN LANGUAGES). Their distinctive feature, among the Indo-Aryan group, is precisely the extent of their differences from the rest of the group and from one another – a sign of their long history of separate development in a region where communications are far more difficult than in the Indian plains. Shina, with about 300,000 speakers, is relatively close to Kashmiri but much less influenced by the languages of 'civilisation' such as Persian and Sanskrit. It is spoken to the north, west and east of the Kashmir Valley. Kalami is also known as Garwi or Kohistani. For KHOWAR see separate entry.

KAZAKH

8,000,000 SPEAKERS

Kazakhstan, Russia, China

One of the TURKIC LANGUAGES, Kazakh is spoken by a very widespread, traditionally nomadic people of the Central Asian steppe. There are over five million speakers in Kazakhstan and about a million each in neighbouring areas of Russia and the Chinese province of Xinjiang.

The vast steppes of Kazakhstan were the scene of successive migrations of Turkic and other peoples for many centuries. Historical atlases show one government after another holding sway here, but none – at least until Soviet rule in this century – really ruled the nomadic population, whose name *Qazak* ('vagabond', see below) suggests their miscellaneous origins and rebellious character. If a single origin is to be assigned to the Kazakh and their language, they should perhaps be considered as a more widely ranging offshoot of the already nomadic KYRGYZ.

Until the 18th century, Chagatai (see UZBEK) was the written language used in the region. Russian political domination of the Kazakhs developed in the early 19th century. At the same time Islamic TATAR missionaries, speakers of a related Turkic language, began to set up religious schools among the Kazakhs.

Kazakh is a language with a long tradition of oral epic. But the first published Kazakh-language poetry was that of the *Zar Zaman* 'Time of Trouble' poets in the 1840s: notable among them was Muhammad Utemis uli (1804–46). Educated in the Islamic schools, they naturally wrote Kazakh in Arabic script – and incited revolt

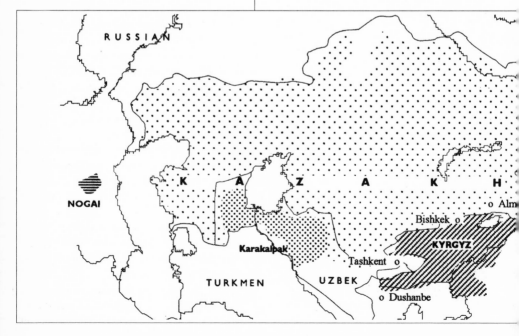

KHASI

500,000 SPEAKERS

India and Bangladesh

K hasi is one of the main Mon-Khmer group of AUSTROASIATIC LANGUAGES, spoken well to the north-west of all other members of the group. It is the state language of the Indian state of Meghalaya, whose capital is Shillong (see map at MUNDARI).

Medieval Indian legends of a land of female magicians, Kudali, may very well have something to do with the matrilineal and, some would say, matriarchal society in which Khasi speakers still live, and with the sorcery which some Khasi women still practise.

When they are first heard of in historical records, in the 16th century, Khasi speakers already made up twenty-five chiefdoms, which persisted through British times into the period of Indian independence. The Kingdom of Jaintia, more outgoing than the rest, paid tribute to the Ahom kingdom to the north and made conquests and raids into the Sylhet region (in modern Bangladesh) to the south. Jaintia came under British rule in the 1850s, but the other Khasi chiefdoms remained nominally independent, and as such were transferred to the suzerainty of the Governor of Assam in 1947 as the United Khasi-Jaintia Hills District, later to be joined with the Garo Hills in the state of Meghalaya.

Yet Shillong, in the temperate Khasi hills, had made an ideal provincial capital for all of British Assam. There was also early interest in Khasi speakers on the part of Welsh Presbyterian missionaries, who devised a Latin orthography for Khasi in 1842, on the basis of the dialect of Cherrapunji, which preceded Shillong as a radiating point for British influence. The missionaries also introduced primary and secondary education and founded a theological seminary. Thus, though politically independent, Khasi speakers in fact underwent significant English-speaking cultural and linguistic influence. Meanwhile, Bengali-speaking Sylhet had long been the centre of trade penetration into the Khasi hills. Thus Khasi has numerous loanwords from Bengali, Urdu and English. It has also been influenced by neighbouring Sino-Tibetan languages.

The system of eight-day markets is so central to Khasi rural life that in each country district the days of the week are named after the eight accessible market villages. Markets are centres for recreation (notably archery contests), courtship and the transmission of news.

Welsh missionaries and Khasi spelling rules

The Latin alphabet as used for Khasi has some most unusual features – which turn out to correspond with features of WELSH spelling, because the system for writing Khasi was devised by Welsh missionaries. In the Khasi words *dap* 'full' and *dab* 'bullock', there is no difference in the final consonant sound: it is a voiceless *-p* in both. The difference is in the vowel sounds: a long *a* in *dab*, a short *a* in *dap*. The missionaries thought they heard different final consonants because, in Welsh, a voiced consonant like *-p* is preceded by a shorter vowel sound, while a voiceless consonant like *-b* is preceded by a longer one. Unique among South Asian scripts, this odd way of writing the difference between short and long vowels is perfectly efficient: it is easier than writing a diacritic and shorter than doubling the vowel letter. Many Khasi words begin with a two- or three-consonant cluster. Where these did not match Welsh or English consonant groups, the missionaries pronounced and wrote the words with two syllables, inserting the neutral vowel *shwa* (the vowel of English *the*) where they thought they heard it. This vowel is written *y* in Welsh, as in *mynydd*, 'month': hence Khasi *bndi* 'mortgage' is usually spelt *byndi*, and *bna* 'hear' is often spelt *byna*.

After Eugénie J. A. Henderson in *Austroasiatic languages: essays in honour of H. L. Shorto* (London: School of Oriental and African Studies, 1991) pp. 61–6

KHMER

8,000,000 SPEAKERS

Cambodia

Khmer belongs to the Mon-Khmer group of languages within the Austroasiatic family. Khmer and Vietnamese are the only two AUSTROASIATIC LANGUAGES that are national languages in a modern state.

> The language name is *Khmae* in the standard language but is still *Khmer* in 'Northern Khmer', the dialect spoken in eastern Thailand.
> *Cambodia* is the Latinised form, used internationally, of Sanskrit *Kamboja*. Other modern variants of the name are French *Cambodge* and Khmer *Kampuchea*. The medieval Hindu and Buddhist kingdoms of south-east Asia often labelled themselves with classical names out of Sanskrit literature: this was one. Two thousand five hundred years ago Kamboja was the name of a minor kingdom somewhere in north-west India.

Khmer has a history traceable to the 7th century. It is the language of the great culture that built the sacred capital of Angkor, centre of a powerful kingdom between the 9th and 15th centuries. Its bilingual culture was a strong, continuing influence on Thailand. The monuments were abandoned to the jungle, but the language continued to be a vehicle of Buddhist and Hindu scripture and poetry. For ninety years from 1864 the weakening Cambodian kingdom was a French protectorate: it regained independence in 1954, but collapsed in anarchy in the early 1970s after American air attacks.

The oldest dated Khmer inscription goes back to AD 611. Hundreds of inscriptions from the following centuries allow the development of the language to be divided into periods: 'pre-Angkorian Old Khmer' to 802, 'Angkorian Old Khmer' from then till 1431, 'Middle Khmer' until the 18th century, then 'Modern Khmer'. As the monumental civilisation of Angkor fell into senescence, Middle and Modern Khmer were recorded less in inscriptions than in palm leaf manuscripts – and eventually in printed books. The traditional literature of Khmer shows early Indian inspiration transformed by its southeast Asian context. The story of Rama, the *Ramakirti* or *Reamker*, is an enduring classic. Royal chronicles are an important historical source.

Khmer words have one or two syllables: if two, the first is unstressed and may be skipped in colloquial speech. But Pali and Sanskrit loanwords can have several syllables. These loanwords are found in large numbers, with other special vocabulary, in the 'monks' language' and the now obsolescent 'royal language', special speech registers used in polite address.

Linguists find many similarities between the structures of Khmer and of Thai, two unrelated languages which coexisted for many centuries, exchanging literary and cultural influences. In modern times Khmer has borrowed scientific and cultural terms from French and has continued to build neologisms on the basis of Sanskrit and Pali.

The first ten numerals in Khmer are: *muəy, pii, bəy, buən, pram, prammuəy, prampii, prambəy, prambuən, dəp.*

Register: clear and 'breathy' vowel quality

The concept of 'register', distinct from 'tone' and now considered central to the phonetic study of many south-east Asian languages, was first introduced and defined in an innovative study of Khmer.

'The Cambodian 'registers' differ from tones in that pitch is not the primary relevant feature. The pitch ranges of the two registers may sometimes overlap, though what I shall call the *Second Register* tends to be accompanied by lower pitch than the *First Register*.

'The characteristics of the first register are a 'normal' or 'head' voice quality, usually accompanied by a relatively high pitch.

'The characteristics of the second register are a deep, rather breathy or 'sepulchral' voice, pronounced with lowering of the larynx, and frequently accompanied by a certain dilation of the nostrils. Pitch is usually lower than that of the first register in similar contexts . . .

'In sentences the word registers are modified according to intonation and by emotional factors. Register may be used, as in many other languages, to express emotion, and when this happens the emotional register may overlie the lexical register, much as in many tone-languages intonation may overlie lexical tone.'

Eugénie J. A. Henderson, 'The main features of Cambodian pronunciation' in *Bulletin of the School of Oriental and African Studies* vol. 14 (1952) pp. 149–74

According to one recent phonemic analysis, the concept of register is valid for earlier forms of Khmer but not for the 20th-century language, in which, instead, there is a huge number of vowels – as many as thirty.

Mon and Khmer

Modern MON can be divided into three dialect groups: Pegu, Martaban and Moulmein, and Ye. Mon villages in central Thailand – resulting from settlements in the last three or four hundred years – speak dialects close to those of Martaban and Moulmein.

Khmer is the majority language of Cambodia.

In eastern Thailand there are 500,000 speakers of 'Northern Khmer'

Khmer vowels

អា អិ អី អឹ អឺ អុ អូ អួ ចើ ចើៀ ចឿ ចេ ចែ ចៃ ចោ ចៅ អំ អំ អាំ អះ អុះ ចះៈ ចោះៈ

Twenty-three written Khmer vowels in traditional order are shown here with the character *a*. Fewer vowels are found in Old Khmer texts.

Khmer script

Khmer script, like others of south and south-east Asia, descends from the Brahmi of ancient India – in this case by way of the *Pallava* script which was used both in south India and in Indochina in the 5th and 6th centuries AD. It has continued to develop through the centuries.

From the beginning Khmer script was used both for the classical tongues – Sanskrit and Pali – and for the contemporary local language, Old Khmer. It provided the immediate inspiration for the invention of the THAI alphabet, which was specifically designed for the very different sound patterns of Thai. In the Thai kingdom (until a few decades ago) Khmer script continued to be used, in the traditional way, for writing and printing Pali.

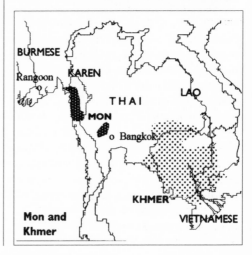

Mon and Khmer

KHOISAN LANGUAGES

Three language families remain in southern Africa as a reminder that its linguistic history is more complex than the story of the Bantu expansion of the first millennium AD.

For convenience these three are grouped together as Khoisan or Khoesan languages, after the Khoe names for themselves, *Khoe* (plural *khoekhoe*), and for their longstanding enemies, *San*. The word *khoe-i* 'person', origin of the language name, also survives as a loanword in Xhosa, *ikwayi* 'commoner, deposed chief'. *San*, like *Bushman* (Dutch *Bosjeman*), is a derogatory term for a despised people.

Modern *Namibia*, covering part of what has been known for longer as *Namaland*, bears the name of the *Nama* people and their language, which is spoken by larger numbers than any other survivor of the Khoisan families.

Until their modern decline, Khoisan speakers were highly important transmitters of culture in southern Africa. The word for cattle in the Nguni languages (Zulu, Xhosa and others) is borrowed from a Khwe language: was the agricultural practice of cattle-keeping borrowed, along with the word, by Bantu speakers from Khwe speakers? Was the keeping of sheep – older here by some centuries than that of cattle – introduced to the southern edge of Africa by Khwe speakers, two thousand years ago, and from whom had they got the idea? Alongside these subsistence necessities, luxuries may also be traced to Khoe and its relatives. For 'smoking of tobacco or cannabis' southern Bantu languages use a verb *-daka* (Zulu), *-dzaha* (Tsonga) apparently borrowed from a Khwe language, which itself must have borrowed from Arabic *dakkhana* 'to puff'.

Khoe and Nama, the two best-known members of the Khwe family, have a long history in what is now South Africa. It has been calculated that the Khoe dialect chain (of which practically nothing now remains) had been developing *in situ* for at least fifteen hundred years. Khoe and Nama arrived where they now are as the result of an expansion or migration through south-eastern Africa. Kwadi speech probably reached southern Angola by way of a westward movement to the Atlantic coast. These movements may have begun about 2,500 years ago somewhere near the Limpopo valley – and a further Khwe language, 'Limpopo Khoi', extinct and unrecorded, can be resurrected from loanwords in proto-Southeastern Bantu, linguistic ancestor of Sotho, Tsonga, Zulu and other modern languages.

Kwadi is recently extinct. The use of Nama seems to be in rapid decline. Khoe, a language of what is now Cape Province, was gradually replaced by *Khoe Dutch*, and eventually by AFRIKAANS: place names and plant and animal names survive as reminiscences of Cape Khoe.

Oblique strokes are usually used to write the click sounds that are typical of Khoisan languages. The first ten numerals in Nama are: /*gúi*, /*gàm*, /*nòna*, *hàga*, *góro*, /*náni*, *hũ*, /*khéisa*, //*khòise*, *dìsi*. If they have worked in the South African mines, !Kung speakers count with Fanagalo (see ZULU) numerals, ultimately from English: *wán*, *thú*, *trí*, *fóri*, *fáifi*, *síkisì*, *sébhènì*, *èitì*, *náinì*, *téni*. The traditional numeral systems of Khoe and !Kung are more complicated than this: '3' literally 'it's a few', '4' literally 'it's many' or 'it's two and two', '5' literally 'it finishes the hand', '10' literally 'both hands dead and finished'.

The Khoisan language families on the map

The Khwe or Khoe or Hottentot or Central Khoisan languages are spoken by small groups in Angola and South Africa, and by as many as

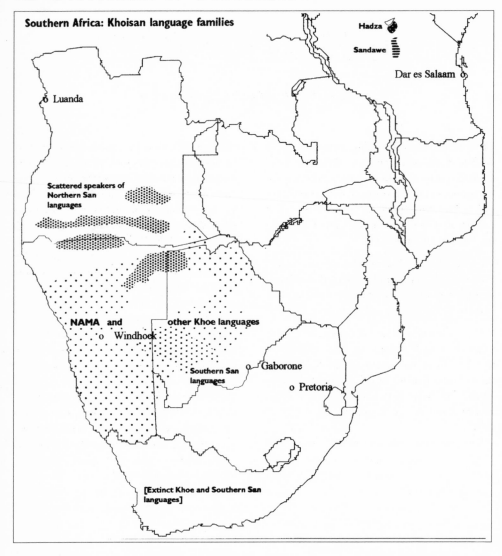

Southern Africa: Khoisan language families

Hadza

Sandawe

Dar es Salaam o

o Luanda

Scattered speakers of
Northern San
languages

NAMA and   other Khoe languages
o Windhoek

Southern San   o Gaborone
languages

o Pretoria

[Extinct Khoe and Southern San
languages]

150,000 speakers of *Nama* in Great Namaland, southern Namibia. *Khoe*, a language of what is now Cape Province, once had an equal number of speakers, and a chain of dialects stretching from the Cape itself to the Kei river and beyond. A great number of Khoe speakers died in small-pox epidemics in the 18th century. *Kwadi* and other Khoe languages have ceased to be spoken in the course of the 20th century.

The Southern Bushman or Southern San languages are now almost extinct; there are a few hundred speakers in Namibia and Botswana. The *!Xam* or 'Cape Bushman' language was wiped out between 1750 and 1900 by Khoekhoe and Europeans, who gradually enslaved and exterminated its remaining speakers.

The *!Kung* or Ju or Northern Bushman or Northern San languages have a few thousand speakers in northern Namibia and southern Angola.

Sandawe, with as many as 70,000 speakers in far-off Tanzania, may be a long-separated relative of the Khwe languages. Its neighbour *Hadza* may be a linguistic isolate. It has only 200 speakers, hunter-gatherers in inhospitable country near Lake Eyasi.

KHOTANESE

Extinct language of Central Asia

Belonging to the multilingual history of the Silk Road in Central Asia, Khotanese is the name given to a group of Eastern Iranian dialects, now extinct, rediscovered in documents and literary texts from the neighbourhood of Khotan in Chinese Xinjiang, dated between the 7th and 10th centuries.

Khotana was the Prakrit (Indo-Aryan) name for this city-state. The people themselves called it *Hvatana*: its Chinese name now is *Hotan*.

Since it was located well to the east of all other recorded IRANIAN LANGUAGES, scholars guessed that Khotanese was related to the language of the nomadic Iranians of the steppes, the *Saka*, *Skythoi* and *Scythi* of Persian, Greek and Latin history – and the guess appears to have been right.

Some Khotanese vocabulary seems to go back to a period when its speakers were Zoroastrians, like *urmaysde* 'sun' from the name of the Zoroastrian supreme deity *Ahuramazda*. But the Khotanese were early converts to Buddhism, and a large proportion of the vocabulary comes from Prakrit dialects, like *ṣṣamana* 'monk', or from Buddhist Sanskrit. In late Khotanese, political terms are borrowed from Tibetan: *śkyaisa* 'official gift'. The Tumshuqese dialect of Khotanese has borrowings from TOCHARIAN B – business words such as *kapci* 'finger seal'.

The first ten numerals in Khotanese are: *śśau / śśa, duva / dvi, drai, cahora, paṃśa, ksǝtǝ, hauda, hasta, nau, dasau*. The script – alongside other influences – came from northern India. It is a variant of the early Brahmi script.

Based on R. E. Emmerick, 'Khotanese and Tumshuqese' in *Compendium linguarum iranicarum* ed. Rüdiger Schmitt (Wiesbaden: Reichert, 1989) pp. 204–29 and other sources

KHOWAR

PERHAPS 100,000 SPEAKERS

Pakistan

Khowar, the everyday language of the remote valley of Chitral, is one of the INDO-ARYAN LANGUAGES (see map there). Its closest linguistic relationships are not clear, because – though influenced by several of its neighbours, Iranian, Nuristani, Dardic and Burushaski, and by languages of culture such as Sanskrit, Persian and Urdu – it also shows many striking differences from neighbouring languages. A table of numerals is given at KASHMIRI.

Alongside the Urdu that is Pakistan's national tongue, a place has been made for Khowar as a standard local medium of communication. There is now some writing and publishing in the language, and a strong tradition of oral poetry.

A fawn and its mother

Nan-ei, nan-ei, af hera mosh goyan –
Nano zhan-ei, ano pazhal no-a?
Nan-ei, nan-ei, thuek lapheika prai –
Nano zhan-ei, yoro zahri no-a?
Nan-ei, nan-ei, ta pazo lei goyan –
Nano zhan-ei, tambuso xel no-a?
Nan-ei, nan-ei, coghuwan pon kuri?
Nano zhan-ei, Phureto an no-a . . .

Mother, mother, there's a man coming –
'Mother's love, is it not the mountain shepherd?'
Mother, mother, a rifle's flashing –
'Mother's love, is it not the sun's rays?'
Mother, mother, blood runs down your breast –
'Mother's love, is it not the sweat of summer?'
Mother, mother, where is the orphan's road?
'Mother's love, is it not the Purit Pass . . .'

The passes from the Chitral to the Panjkora valley are the only land link between Chitral and the rest of Pakistan.

'Some Khowar songs' collected by Wazir Ali Shah, translated by Georg Morgenstierne, in *Acta orientalia* vol. 24 (1959) pp. 29–58

KIKUYU

4,300,000 SPEAKERS

Kenya

K ikuyu, which belongs to the BANTU LAN-GUAGES, is one of the major languages of Kenya, spoken in a swathe of territory between Nairobi and Mount Kenya and by many inhabitants of the capital.

The local names for the people, *aGikuyu*, the country, *uGikuyu*, and the language, *kiGikuyu*, demonstrate a local sound change, 'Dahl's Law', that is found in several Bantu languages. Some linguists use the form *Gikuyu* or *Gekoyo*, but most prefer *Kikuyu*, which is usual among speakers of other Kenyan languages.

Historically Kikuyu speakers were a fiercely independent, indeed militaristic, people, growers of sorghum and millet, keepers of goats and sheep, and collectors of honey. The Swahili slave trade route from the Uganda region and Lake Victoria crossed the southern tip of Kikuyu country, but the Kikuyu themselves were too formidable to be seriously threatened by slavers. In the late 19th century they resisted the British invasion violently, but in vain: the best land was seized for large scale farming, and many Kikuyu, classed as 'squatters', took work as farm labourers or in the colonial capital, Nairobi. The attempt by the invaders to rule them through appointed 'chiefs' had little success.

Kikuyu speakers were prominent in the Mau Mau and other resistance movements. Jomo Kenyatta, president of independent Kenya, was Kikuyu in origin and was the author of the best available study of Kikuyu society (*Facing Mount Kenya*, 1938).

Between Kikuyu and English speakers Up-Country SWAHILI was the usual lingua franca, and Swahili remains essential in modern Kenya, though English is also widely known. Kikuyu has numerous English loanwords, sometimes hard to recognise at first sight, such as *njanji* 'judge'. Kikuyu itself is necessary as a second language to speakers of the smaller languages of the neighbourhood, such as Chuka, Embu and

Kikuyu, Kamba and Masai

'The Kikuyu and Masai were constantly at war, raiding for cattle. The Masai were invincible on their own terrain, the plains, but were easy victims for the Kikuyu if they ventured into the forests, where they were killed by the arrows and staked war-pits which awaited them. At times, however, peace was made and relationships established by intermarriage. Trade also occurred between the tribes, women being able to pass freely from one to the other [even when they were at war]. Stigand states that Kikuyu often "lent" their cattle to be tended by the Masai, and Eliot writes that in the great famine of 1882 Masai settled in Kikuyu and took Kikuyu wives, sometimes entering the service of Kikuyu as "a sort of mercenaries" . . .

'The Kikuyu have various myths of origin which reflect their relations with other peoples. One tells that the three sons of Mumbere, the creator of the world, Masai, Gikuyu and Kamba, were given a choice by their father of a spear, bow, and digging-stick: Masai chose the spear, Kamba the bow, and Gikuyu the digging-stick.'

John Middleton, *The central tribes of the North-Eastern Bantu* (London: International African Institute, 1953) pp. 13, 15

Tharaka. There has been long term mutual interaction between Kikuyu and MASAI (see box).

The first ten numerals in Kikuyu are: *īmwe, igīrī, ithatuñ, inya, ithano, ithathatuñ, mungwanja, inyanya, kenda, ikunmi.*

The Thagicu languages

Thagicu is the name of the region from which speakers of Kikuyu and related languages may have dispersed. It was suggested as a name for the language group by P. R. Bennett in 1967.

The *West Thagicu* branch includes Kikuyu and three smaller Kenyan languages, *Embu*, with 250,000 speakers, *Cuka* or Chuka, with 70,000, and *Mwimbi*, with 70,000.

The Thagicu group also includes three other languages, MERU (1,250,000 speakers), *Tharaka* (100,000) and KAMBA (2,500,000). Meru serves as

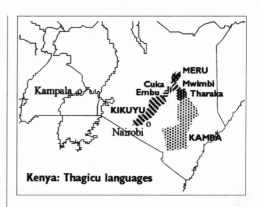

Kenya: Thagicu languages

a second language for some speakers of Chuka and Tharaka. Kamba has two main dialects, *Machakos* and *Kitui*, each subdivided: people of *Ulu*, the 'high country', call those of Kitui *aDaisu*, 'lowlanders'. There are Kamba speakers in Rabai near Mombasa.

KIRIBATI

70,000 SPEAKERS

Kiribati

One of the Micronesian group of AUSTRONE-SIAN LANGUAGES, Kiribati takes its name from the chain of atolls that form the republic of Kiribati. As British possessions these were known as the Gilbert Islands.

Gilbertese and *Kiribati* are two versions of the same word – for Kiribati is the local language form of 'Gilbert'. Captain Thomas Gilbert put the main island of the group on the map in 1788: its older name is Tarawa. The people now call themselves *I-Kiribati*, with the same ethnic prefix that is seen in *I-Aotiteria* 'Australian'. In modern sources *I-Kiribati* is often wrongly given as the name of the language.

The Gilbert Islands were British-ruled from 1892 until 1979, interrupted by Japanese occupation during the Second World War. English was and is the main foreign influence on the Kiribati language.

Kiribati (see map at MARSHALLESE) is spoken in the Kiribati chain itself, in Banaba (Ocean Island) and now also in the Line Islands, one of which is Kiritimati (Christmas Island). All these form part of the Republic of Kiribati. The language also extends to Niu, which belongs to Tuvalu. Resettlement and work migration have taken Kiribati speech to Gizo and Wagina in the Solomon Islands, to Rabi in Fiji, and to Nauru.

Kiribati is unusual among Micronesian languages: it has only five vowels, where most have seven to twelve; it retains final vowels; its usual word order is verb-object-subject. These details have been seen as showing Polynesian influence – but Sheldon Harrison argues that they are conservative features, retained from the proto-Oceanic which is the ancestor of both Micronesian and Polynesian languages.

Yet linguistics shows that Kiribati was once under strong Polynesian – perhaps TONGAN – influence. There are numerous Polynesian loanwords, suggesting trade and cultural penetration, such as *moa* 'chicken', *baurua* 'sailing canoe', *rongorongo* 'news'.

Examples from S.P. Harrison, 'Linguistic evidence for Polynesian influence in the Gilbert Islands' in *Language contact and change in the Austronesian world* ed. Tom Dutton, Darrell T. Tryon (Berlin: Mouton De Gruyter, 1994) pp. 321–49

KITUBA

PERHAPS 4,000,000 SPEAKERS

Congo (Kinshasa), Congo (Brazzaville)

A creole based on KONGO (see map there), Kituba originated in the 16th century as a language of trade on the routes that led to the kingdom of Kongo. Kongo traded with the Portuguese of Angola, whose demand for ivory, slaves and other products of the centre of Africa was insatiable.

Kituba is often known in Congo (Kinshasa) as *Kikongo ya letá* or *Kileta*, 'language of government' (from French *l'état* 'the state'), or *Kisodi*, 'language of soldiers', or in French as *Kikongo véhiculaire* 'trade Kongo' or *Kikongo simplifié*. In Congo (Brazzaville) its usual name is *Munukutuba*.

Although the kingdom of Kongo and its overland trade have disappeared, Kituba remains – in three distinct regions radiating from Malebo Pool. South-east of Kinshasa, along the southern tributaries of the lower Congo, in a region where many languages cluster together in a small area, Kituba is the means of communication, the most-used second language, known in town and country alike. Missionaries use it for preaching and teaching. In Brazzaville, Kituba is an urban language, used by the majority of inhabitants and important in broadcasting. Downriver in Dolisie and Pointe-Noire in Congo (Brazzaville), and in Boma, Matadi and Thysville in Congo (Kinshasa), Kituba is the mother tongue of many speakers.

In the surrounding country, however, Kituba has not spread. Kongo, Kituba's parent tongue, remains vigorous in and around these lower Zaire towns and is favoured in education, though local officialdom uses Kituba. In Kinshasa itself and its suburbs, those who have moved from the surrounding countryside tend to use Kongo while those who come from upriver use LINGALA: Kituba is less known.

Kituba has been influenced by French and Lingala, the other lingua francas of the lower Congo. It is also influenced by Zaire Swahili and by Portuguese. But it grew up as a trade language for speakers of Kongo and other Bantu languages, and remains closer to its roots than many other creoles. It even retains a limited set of noun class prefixes.

Verb tenses in Kongo and Kituba

I am eating	ndiá	móno kéle diâ
I will eat	nìdiá	móno áta diâ
I ate	ndîidì	móno dià-áka
I have eaten	nádià	móno méne diâ

In Kongo persons and tenses are built into single-word verb forms by internal changes of sound and tone. This kind of word-building is also typical of the older Indo-European and the Semitic languages, called by linguists 'synthetic'.

In Kituba, as in many other lingua francas and creoles, separate, unchanging words are combined to indicate person and tense alongside a verb. This structure, also familiar from English and Chinese, is called 'isolating'.

Example from S. S. Mufwene in *Substrata versus universals in creole genesis* ed. P. Muysken, N. Smith (Amsterdam: Benjamins, 1986) pp. 129–62

KOMI

360,000 SPEAKERS

Russia

O ne of the URALIC LANGUAGES, Komi is spoken in the Komi Republic in north-eastern European Russia along river valleys that drain into the Barents Sea.

Spreading northwards in prehistoric times from the territory of the related UDMURT, the speakers of Komi once traded in fur all the way from the old city of Perm' to the White Sea and the Arctic Ocean. They were known as *Beormas*, 'Permians', to the Norwegian Ohthere, who described his travels to the English King Alfred around AD 900 (see box at SAMI). Loanwords in Komi are evidence of early contacts with Karelian and Veps dialects of FINNISH. They were also in close contact, across the northern Ural Mountains, with the Khanty and Mansi of the lower Ob valley (see HUNGARIAN), notably at the old market city of Salekhard where the 'Permians' traded with Russia too.

In the Soviet period there were several very large prison camps in Komi territory. The social problems of the modern Komi Republic come partly from the large number of former camp inmates, Russian-speaking and with a criminal history, who have settled locally after release.

Komi was first written as long ago as the 14th century, when the missionary St Stephen of Perm' devised the Abur alphabet, used for three hundred years. Little remains of early Komi writings, but there is a rich oral literature. The most typical form of Komi traditional poetry is the *berdedchankiv* or lament, clearly related to the *yarabts* sung by the Nenets of the northern tundra.

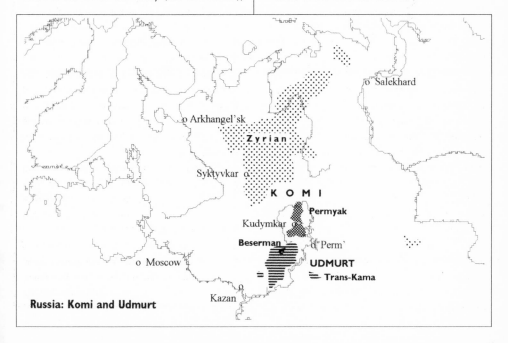

Russia: Komi and Udmurt

Komi nouns have seventeen cases and a singular/plural distinction. With possessive suffixes (*pi* 'son'; *piey* 'my son'; *piid* 'your son'; *piis* 'her son') the theoretical number of noun forms rises to 136, most of which can actually be heard in everyday speech. The first ten numerals are: *ömi, kık, kuim, nyol', vim, kvaim, sizim, kök'yamıs, ökmıs, das.*

Komi and Udmurt on the map

Since the Russian Revolution in 1917 there have been two Komi literary languages. *Zyrian* (perhaps meaning 'sea people') is based on the middle Vychegda dialect of Syktyvkar, the capital of the extensive, very sparsely populated Komi Republic. *Permyak* ('Permian') is based on the southern dialect of Kudymkar. The Southwest and Trans-Kama dialects of *Udmurt*, now far separated from the rest, have many Bashkir and Tatar loanwords. So has the distinctive Besermen dialect, spoken in the north of the Udmurt Republic by people of Tatar origin who long ago took to speaking the local language.

At a wedding

Syoyim da yuvim	We have eaten and drunk
(pasyibe da pomesyibe)	(Thanks to our host)
keres shər shobdıse,	The best wheat of the hill,
shobdə shər tusyse,	The best ear of the wheat,
tusy shər yadrese,	The best grain of the ear,
yadre shər pirogse.	The best cakes of the grain.
Syoyim da yuvim	We have eaten and drunk
tsyəskid ıreshse,	Sweet light beer,
kurid vinase,	Strong brandy,
tsyəskid yaya shıdse.	Sweet meat soup.
Pasyibe da pomesyibe	Thanks to our host
Syoyim da yuvim!	We have eaten and drunk!

Once sung by girls at a Komi wedding, this song was collected by Robert Lach, a folklorist who worked with Russian prisoners of war around 1918.

Robert Lach, *Gesänge russischer Kriegsgefangener, Vol. 1 pt 1: Udmurt and Komi songs* (Vienna, 1926) pp. 59, 115–16

KONGO

3,200,000 SPEAKERS

Congo (Kinshasa), Angola and Congo (Brazzaville)

One of the BANTU LANGUAGES, Kongo attained significance as the state language of the kingdom of Kongo, already the greatest power on the south-western coast of Africa at the time of the early European explorations.

Political units became gradually larger, in the region that is now northern Angola, Congo (Brazzaville) and western Congo (Kinshasa), until, in the 14th and 15th centuries, the substantial and powerful kingdoms of Kongo, Loango and Tio were established. Loango occupied much of the coast between the mouths of the Ogooué and the Zaire, controlling the road from Malebo Pool (Stanley Pool) through a copper-mining region to the coast at Loango city, long a port of call for Dutch traders. Kongo straddled the lower Zaire and held the Atlantic coast and hinterland to the south, where Portuguese ships dominated trade. Inland, from the present sites of Kinshasa and Brazzaville northwards, was the kingdom of Tio, which lasted till the 19th century.

Language spread with government and trade: there was a four-day week with weekly markets. But Kongo became economically dependent on the increasing European demand for slaves, and collapsed in 1665, when the king fell in battle against the Portuguese at Ambwila. The small successor kingdoms eventually succumbed to the European adventurers of the 'Congo Free State' in the late 19th century. After a period of Belgian rule, this has now become an independent state, Congo (Kinshasa).

The first information about the Kongo language to reach Europe was F. Pigafetta's 'Report of the Kingdom of Congo', published in Italian in 1591, largely based on the reports of the Portuguese mariner Oduardo Lopez, who had visited Luanda in 1578. In 1624 a bilingual catechism in Portuguese and Kongo, *Doutrina christãa*, was published in Lisbon – probably the oldest printed book in any African language. A Latin–Spanish–Kongo dictionary was compiled in manuscript about 1650.

The oldest African grammar

'The year 1659 saw publication in Rome of the first known grammar of a sub-Saharan African language, a 98-page study of Kongo by Giacinto Brusciotto. This Italian Capuchin is known also by the Latin and Portuguese renderings of his name as Hyacinthus Brusciottus a Vetralla and Jacinto Brusciato de Vetralha. The title of his book is *Regulae quaedam pro difficillimi Congensium idiomatis faciliori captu ad grammaticae normam redactae* [Some rules compiled in the form of a grammar for the easier understanding of the very difficult language of the Congolese]. Brusciotto recognised and described the system of noun classes, which he termed "principiations", and of concordial agreements. It is significant that his division into "principiations" was determined by the concordial agreements and not by the form of the noun prefix, thus revealing deeper linguistic insight than some of his successors up to the present day!'

Desmond T. Cole, 'The history of African linguistics to 1945' in *Current trends in linguistics* vol. 7 ed. Thomas A. Sebeok (The Hague: Mouton, 1971) pp. 1–29

Kongo dialects are spoken on both banks of the lower Congo, west of Kinshasa, and a creole of Kongo origin, Kituba, is used in part of the region as a lingua franca. After massive recent migrations Kongo is spoken by about three-quarters of the vast population of Kinshasa itself. Lingala, however, remains the single most important lingua franca of the city.

For a table of numerals see LINGALA. Examples of Kongo verb forms are given at KITUBA.

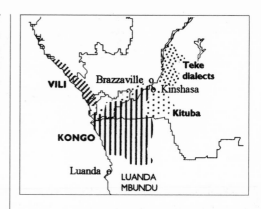

Kongo: languages and kingdoms

Kongo was once the language of the Kingdom of Kongo. *Kituba*, a creole based on Kongo, initially spread with Kongo trade through regions not originally Kongo-speaking.

Vili is now the usual name of the language of coastal Congo (Brazzaville) (the former Kingdom of Loango) and its speakers. It once meant 'caravan trader', evidence of the centrality of long distance trade to this pre-colonial state. *Luanda Mbundu* was the language of the southern region of the old Kingdom of Kongo (see map at MBUNDU).

Teke is a group of dialects, with about 300,000 speakers, whose present location helps to show the old extent of the kingdom of Tio.

KONKANI

1,500,000 SPEAKERS

India

K onkani is the southernmost of the contiguous INDO-ARYAN LANGUAGES. Its chief centre
is the old Portuguese possession, Goa (an Indian
state since 1987) – and this is the clue to the
separate identity of Konkani. Linguistically close
to the Marathi of the state of Maharashtra, it is a
language of the western coastal strip of India: not
of the whole of it, but of the northern third –
coastal Maharashtra – spreading southwards to
many large and small harbour towns. It grew up
alongside the Portuguese development of Indian
coastal traffic, and is now in decline as the reason
for its separateness has disappeared.

Konkan is the coastal strip between the Western Ghats of Maharashtra and the Indian
Ocean, running southwards as far as Goa.
Konkanī (Portuguese *Concani*, a name already
used in the oldest, 16th-century publications
in the language) is thus the speech of this
coastline: later, more specifically, the speech
of Goa and its daughter settlements, when
that came to be seen as a distinct language.

From south to north (see map at MARATHI)
eight Konkani dialects can be identified along
the coast of Kerala, where the surrounding language is MALAYALAM. Of these the major one is at
the long term Portuguese colony of Cochin. On
the coast of Mysore, whose majority language is
KANNADA, Mangalore has a large Konkani community. The territory of Goa itself is the largest
enclave of all. From Kerala northwards to Goa,
then, Konkani is surrounded by Dravidian
speech. Onwards again, the Konkani of coastal
Maharashtra gradually – north of Ratnagiri –
shades into the Konkan dialects of Marathi.

Goa was captured by the Portuguese in 1510,
becoming the metropolis of their Eastern possessions, the seat of a Viceroy and of an archbishop. Konkani literature begins in the 16th
century, as early as the language itself. It is
Christian in inspiration, with religious texts,
Bible translations and grammars. Konkani served
the Portuguese as a missionary language, while
administration was carried on in Portuguese.
Traditionally Konkani speakers – here and in
East Africa, where many are settled – have had a
knowledge of Latin, the religious language of
Catholic Christianity. Latin is still used in some
religious rituals, though worshippers in general
no longer understand it.

Recently there has been an attempted revival
in writing in modern Konkani dialects, alongside
an effort to create a unified literary language. For
all that, most Konkani speakers consider Marathi, Kannada and Malayalam to be their literary
languages.

In keeping with its multicultural context,
Konkani has been written in four scripts: Latin,
Devanagari, Malayalam and Kannada (now the
commonest). The Latin orthography, based on
Portuguese, was devised in the 16th century and
is still sometimes used. Retroflex consonant
sounds are marked by a double letter (in Portuguese a doubled *r* has this same meaning): this
leaves double length consonant sounds to be
marked with a hyphen, rather as they are in
Catalan. There is no indication of vowel length.

The first ten numerals in Konkani are: *yek, don,
tīn, cār, pānz, sa, sāt, āṭ, nou, dhā.*

KOREAN

63,000,000 SPEAKERS

South Korea, North Korea, China, Japan, Uzbekistan, Kazakhstan, Russia

Korean is thought by some linguists to be a member of the ALTAIC family of languages. If so, it must have separated from the remainder of the family many thousands of years ago. It is now the national language of North and South Korea. There are considerable Korean minorities in Manchuria and (as a result of recent migration) in Japan and central Asia.

Before the 15th century, when Korean was first written phonetically, little in the history of the language is certain. Scholars generally suppose that an early form of Korean was already spoken in Korea and parts of Manchuria two thousand years ago. The small states in the region, often subject to China, were beginning to merge. In the 7th century the southern kingdom of Silla succeeded in unifying the peninsula, and Korean apparently descends from the old 'Han' dialect spoken in Silla.

Since then, Korean has undergone strong po-

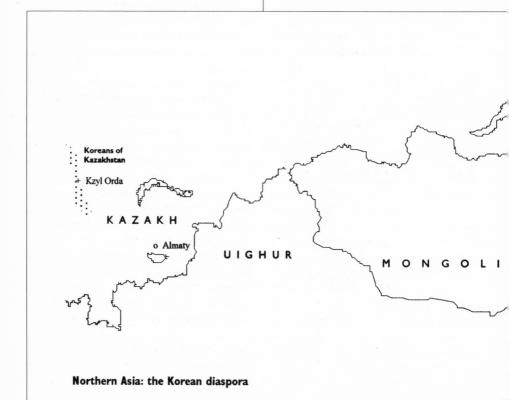

Koreans of Kazakhstan

⊹ Kzyl Orda

KAZAKH

o Almaty

UIGHUR

MONGOLI

Northern Asia: the Korean diaspora

litical, religious and literary influence from China. This is reflected in huge numbers of Chinese loanwords in the language. They have been customarily written in Chinese characters, which thus appear interspersed with Korean script in every older text.

> *Koryŏ* (whence *Korea*) and *Chosŏn* (which, as *Chosen*, is the Japanese name for Korea) are in origin the names of two successive dynasties that ruled Korea. The Koryŏ capital, Songdo, is near modern Seoul.

A collection of ancient songs is dated to the Silla period, which ended in 935 when the Koryŏ began to rule the country. The literature of Koryŏ included new genres, notably the dramatic poetry that celebrated the Buddha and the local gods of Korea. *Sijo*, a poetic form consisting of three-line stanzas, is traced to the 12th century and is still current. Narrative prose first became popular in the 17th century.

Korea fell under Japanese rule from 1910 to 1945. With the ensuing division of the country between regimes of opposing political philosophies, the written languages of North and South have diverged. In the North the Korean alphabet is mandatory. Chinese characters have not been used officially since 1949, and Chinese loanwords are officially discouraged – yet many remain, and expressions modelled on Chinese ('calques') permeate writing and political discourse. In the South, Chinese characters continue to be used, though less than before. Schoolchildren still need to learn nearly two thousand of them. Meanwhile American English influence on the language increases.

The first ten numerals in Korean are: *hana, tul, set, net, tasŏt, yŏsŏt, ilgop, yŏdŏl, ahop, yŏl.*

Korea and the Korean diaspora

Korean emigration is one of the less-known diasporas of recent history. Already extending across the Korean borders into Manchuria, Korean farmers began to settle the Pacific coast of far eastern Russia after 1863. From 1924 other pioneers were encouraged to colonise parts of Uzbekistan and Kazakhstan. With a sudden change of Soviet policy under Stalin, the Pacific coast settlers were deported en masse to central Asia in 1937. During the Second World War, Koreans were recruited to settle and farm the island of Sakhalin, then under Japanese rule.

Today substantial Korean minorities are to be found. There are 2,000,000 in Chinese Manchuria, and Korean counts as one of the 'major nationalities' of China. Recent migration to Japan has resulted in a minority of 700,000 there. The 100,000 *Korei* of northern Sakhalin are now under Russian rule. There are 200,000 Koreans in Uzbekistan, most of them at the Amu Darya delta, and 150,000 in Kazakhstan, concentrated near Tashkent, Kuygan, Taldy-Kurgan and Kzyl Orda. At Kzyl Orda there is a Korean newspaper, radio station and theatre. Many of these Korean farmers developed desert lands with water drawn from the Amu Darya and Syr Darya, and are now threatened by their own success, which is leading to the drying up of the Aral Sea.

The Korean alphabet

ㄱ ㄲ ㄴ ㄷ ㄸ ㄹ ㅁ ㅂ ㅃ ㅅ ㅆ ㅇ ㅈ ㅉ ㅊ ㅋ ㅌ ㅍ ㅎ
k kk n t tt l m p pp s ss ng ch tch ch' k' t' p' h

ㅏ ㅐ ㅑ ㅒ ㅓ ㅔ ㅕ ㅖ ㅗ ㅘ ㅙ ㅚ ㅛ ㅜ ㅝ ㅞ ㅟ ㅠ ㅡ ㅢ ㅣ
a æ ya yæ ŏ e yŏ ye o wa wæ oe yo u wŏ we wi yu ŭ ŭi i

Hangŭl – Chosŏngŭl

All writing in Korea was in the Chinese script – whether the author was writing Korean, or whether the Chinese language itself, culturally and politically dominant, was being recorded – until 1443/4. That was when King Sejong, of the Chosŏn dynasty, invented the remarkable alphabet now known to southerners as *Hangŭl* 'Korean writing', to northerners as *Chosŏngŭl*.

The Korean alphabet did not emerge from Sejong's unaided imagination, as is sometimes implied. Compare the letter forms with TIBETAN (and an old Mongolian script) and similarities begin to appear. Two further strands of inspiration can be identified. First, a careful analysis was made of the sounds of the language, in the Indian (Sanskrit) tradition transmitted via nor-

thern Buddhism. Secondly, the use of an independent character block (for example, 발 *pal* 'foot'), usually a visible combination of more than one letter, is typical of Chinese even more than of Indic scripts: and the character blocks stand well alongside true Chinese characters, as they need to do in written Korean. But the result – a phonemic script in which each sound is represented by a single, always identifiable letter form – was indeed remarkable, and has been rightly hailed as one of the most scientifically designed and efficient scripts in the world.

The alphabetical order of the vowels given in the box is the one that is standard in North Korea. The transcription is a basic form of the most widely accepted standard, called 'McCune-Reischauer'.

KRIO

350,000 SPEAKERS OF KRIO AS A MOTHER TONGUE

Sierra Leone, the Gambia

One of the ENGLISH CREOLES AND PIDGINS, Krio ('Creole') is the first language of many inhabitants of Freetown and the lingua franca of as many as three million people in Sierra Leone. A variant form, called *Krio*, *Aku* or *Patois*, is spoken in the Gambia. There, however, a pidginised form of WOLOF is in the ascendant.

Was Krio first introduced to Sierra Leone by the freed slaves from the Caribbean who were resettled here in the 18th century? Or did their speech merge with an already existing creole stemming directly from the English West African pidgin? Krio has strong links with the Caribbean creoles. Its grammar in many ways resembles West African languages: some researchers emphasise its similarity to YORUBA (of Nigeria), others to varieties of AKAN; but neither of these languages belongs to Sierra Leone itself.

The early 19th-century Krio speakers of Sierra Leone were evidently a mixed group. Akan was the language spoken when early English trade had concentrated on the Gold Coast (modern Ghana): it thus influenced the pidgin, and all the creoles that stem from it, directly. It contributed to the oldest layer of Krio. The new linguistic influences that came to Sierra Leone with the migration of freed slaves in the early 19th century were themselves complicated: while migrants of older Caribbean background already had an English creole as their mother tongue, many of those of recent African origin had certainly come from Nigeria, to which some, such as the linguist Samuel Crowther (see box at YORUBA), would return.

English dialects and the Atlantic creoles

'In the sixteenth century,' Ian Hancock observed, 'the crews of English ships would have included men speaking a gamut of widely differing English dialects. In Sierra Leone Krio there are preserved dialect forms from as far south as Cornwall and as far north as Scotland. Krio words such as *fitrí* (Yorkshire *fittery* "with legs akimbo") and *gánga* (Yorkshire *ganger* "little girl's dress") are still used in Yorkshire today and are quite unintelligible to a modern Devonian or Cornishman. Given also the admixture of non-English speakers in the crews, and the long history of specialized nautical lingo, the form of English heard first by West Africans must have been itself a somewhat flexible compromise'

Hancock in *Pidginization and creolization of languages* ed. Dell Hymes (Cambridge: Cambridge University Press, 1971) p. 290).

The serial verbs of Krio

Typical of Krio is the use of English verbs to mark direction, and the development of additional auxiliary verbs:

A bring di kasada **kam** na os	I brought the cassava **to** the house
A **bin tek** di buk **go** na skul	I **took** the book **to** school
Wi **go tray** fo push di trak	We **will try** to push the truck
I **don was** di klos	He **has washed** the clothes

After I. T. Givón in *Readings in creole studies* ed. Ian F. Hancock (Gent: Story-Scientia, 1979) pp. 16–18

KRU LANGUAGES

PERHAPS 2,000,000 SPEAKERS

Ivory Coast, Liberia, Sierra Leone

The KRU LANGUAGES are spoken in the forests of southern Liberia and Ivory Coast. They belong to the NIGER-CONGO family.

Although none has as many as a million speakers individually, Kru languages remain important on a regional scale; many speakers now know some English or French. Historically, Kru languages are crucial for their position at the crossroads of African-European interaction.

Oral tradition suggests that speakers of these languages migrated southwards in medieval times from an earlier habitat well inland. What is certain is that Kru languages (often called *Kra, Krumen*) were among the first to be encountered by European voyagers on what was then known as the Pepper Coast, centre of the production and export of Guinea pepper or melegueta pepper, once a staple of the African seaborne trade. The oldest Kra wordlist is in a French manuscript of the 1540s, where it is called *langaige de Guynee* 'language of Guinea'.

Bété, of the Ivory Coast, has the largest number of speakers of any Kru language today – yet it is not an official language and seldom appears in print. Bété has borrowed heavily from French, the ruling language of Ivory Coast, in which many speakers are now bilingual. It has also borrowed from English, long a major language of the coastal trade: *bogu* 'book'; *copu* 'glass' from English *cup*. The first ten numerals in Bété are: *bolo, so, ta, mona, ghi, gbopolo, gbiso, gbota, gbomona, kuba.*

Kru people themselves worked on European ships as early as the 16th century, and there are still Klao, Grebo and Bassa-speaking communities in several West African port cities as a lasting sign of their participation in long distance sea travel.

Major Kru languages

Bassa has 300,000 speakers in Liberia.

Bété dialects are spoken by 700,000 people in central and western Ivory Coast. *Dida*, with about 150,000 speakers, is sometimes regarded as a dialect of Bété.

Grebo of eastern Liberia, and *Krumen* or Kroumen of western Ivory Coast, form a dialect group with a total of perhaps 250,000 speakers.

Guéré (with *Wobe*) of Ivory Coast, and Krahn of Liberia, form a similar dialect group, with as many as 450,000 speakers.

Klao or Kru has its territorial base in eastern Liberia, where there are 150,000 speakers.

The Kru or *Kra* language communities in West African port cities such as Freetown, Lagos and Accra have diverse dialect origins but their lingua franca is generally closest to Klao and Bassa.

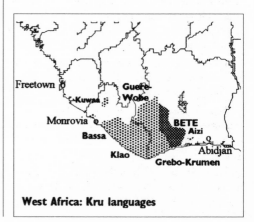

West Africa: Kru languages

KUKI-CHIN AND NAGA LANGUAGES

PERHAPS 2,000,000 SPEAKERS IN TOTAL

India, Burma

In the Chin Hills of western Burma, and the Indian states of Mizoram and south-eastern Assam, a group of SINO-TIBETAN LANGUAGES is spoken. Their fragmentation – most have only between 10,000 and 50,000 speakers – has three causes: the broken landscape, the absence until very recently of large-scale political units, and the fact that the speakers have evidently been settled over most of their present habitat for many centuries. Thus early dialects gradually differentiated until they reached the point of mutual unintelligibility.

There has, however, been a gradual movement westwards. The name of the Chindwin river, the greatest Irrawaddy tributary, means literally 'Hole of the Chins'; yet the deep Chindwin valley now lies well to the east of almost all Chin populations.

Indian and Burmese rulers tended, until the British advances in the 19th century, to leave the Chin Hills alone. On the Indian side of the hills the inhabitants were grouped under the name *Kuki*; on the Burmese side the usual name was *Chin* (spelt *khyang* in Burmese, and meaning 'friend'). In older English sources the forms *Kookie* and *Khyeng* can be found.

The speakers gave to their own communities and languages names that often included the element *-zo*: among them were the *Mizo*, known to others as *Lushei*, who have given their name to an Indian state. *Zo* is said to mean 'wild' or 'independent', by contrast with *vai* 'civilised' or 'ruled'.

Lushei was almost the only exception in this region to the rule of linguistic fragmentation. Here, approaching the 'Mizo Hills' from Assam, explorers and British administrators – who established control in 1890 – found a language that had become a local lingua franca of inter-community travel and trade. Lushei, with about 350,000 speakers, is now the official language of the Indian state of Mizoram, established, after a long struggle, in 1987. It has a Christian majority.

North of Mizoram are a series of tribes known as Old Kuki and New Kuki – because they form two separate ethnic and linguistic groupings and New Kuki is the later arrival. Old Kuki languages are all spoken by very small communities. The major New Kuki languages are Thado and Paite, both closely related to Tiddim, largest of the languages of the northern Chin Hills in Burma. Somewhat further south in Burma is Falam or Hallam, and this is close linguistically to the Old Kuki languages of India.

On both sides of the Chin Hills, the gradual advance of 'pacification', followed by 'administration', was scarcely complete when the Japanese occupation of Burma foreshadowed the end of British rule. The Burmese side became the Chin Special Division of independent Burma; on the Indian side the state of Mizoram was established, other Kuki peoples being divided among Assam, Manipur and Nagaland.

Although political relations were minimal, local trade routes have long criss-crossed the Chin Hills. Kuki-Chin languages show the influence both of Burmese and of Assamese (and to some extent of Bengali).

The Naga languages

North of the Chin languages extend two further groups of related languages, spoken in Nagaland, Manipur and eastern Assam. They are grouped by linguists as 'Naga' and 'Konyak'. Here, too, little political organisation above the village level existed until recently. Naga peoples did pay tribute to the AHOM kingdom of Assam, and in some cases to the king of Manipur. British rule, at least nominal, came in 1881. The Indian state of Nagaland was created in 1963 after a bitter struggle for Naga independence. The multiplicity of local languages has led to the increasing use of *Naga Pidgin* or *Nagamese*, a creolised form of ASSAMESE, which developed at least 150 years ago as a result of local trade patterns. It is now the lingua franca of Nagaland.

> ### The introduction of writing: two perspectives
>
> 'Why did Naga languages have no traditional script or writing? Speakers explained that a god once gave them writing, on skins, but a dog ate the skins and since then they had not been able to write.'
>
> J.P. Mills, *The Rengma Nagas*
> (London: Macmillan, 1937) p. 286
>
> 'With the suppression of headhunting and the establishment of law and order by the British Raj – followed almost immediately by the arrival of the late Rev. F. W. Savidge and myself as Christian missionaries [1892] – a new day dawned upon the Lushai Hills . . . It fell to our lot to reduce the language to writing in such a way that our system could be readily adopted by the people themselves. For this purpose we chose the simple Roman script, with a phonetic form of spelling . . . still used throughout the tribe.'
> James Herbert Lorrain (Pu Buanga), *Dictionary of the Lushai language* (Calcutta: Royal Asiatic Society of Bengal, 1940) p. vii

Among these languages there is no indigenous tradition of writing. But Naga languages have a wealth of folk tales and oral poetry; while Lushei is rich in similes. Events that happen 'in turn' are *a tui kang nghâkin* – 'like girls at a drying-up spring'.

The Kuki-Naga language group

Southern Kuki-Chin includes Khumi, Matu, Mün and other smaller languages.

Central Kuki-Chin includes Lushei or Lushai or Mizo (350,000 speakers), Haka and Hmar.

Old Kuki includes Falam (100,000 speakers) and many smaller languages.

Northern Kuki-Chin includes Thado (150,000 speakers), Tiddim (100,000), Paite and Zome.

The *Naga* languages include Angami, Lotha, Mao and Sema, the largest, with over 60,000 speakers.

The *Konyak* languages include Konyak itself, with nearly 100,000 speakers, Ao and Tangkhul. Throughout their territory the Ao people are actually divided into two subgroups, speaking very different dialects, Chongli and Mongsen.

Also part of the Kuki-Naga group are the *Mikir-Meithei* languages, Mikir (200,000 speakers) and MANIPURI, which has a separate entry.

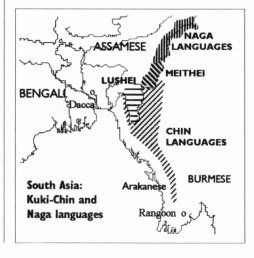

South Asia:
Kuki-Chin and
Naga languages

Numerals in Kuki-Naga languages					
Lushei	**Falam**	**Thado**	**Angami**	**Tangkhul**	**Mikir**
-khat	-khāt	-khat	po	kha	sī
-nhih	-ni	-ni	nā	ni	nī
-thum	-thūm	-thūm	sē	thum	thām
-lī	-li	li	dā	li	lī
-ngā	-ngā	-ngā	ngu	ngā	ngō
-ruk	-ruk	-gūp	ru	ruk	rāk
-sarih	-rī	-sagi	nā	shini	rāksī
-riat	-riet	-gēt	thā	shat	nəkep
-kuā	-kūok	-kū	kü	ko	səkep
shom	sām	-som	kö	tharā	kep

KUMAUNI

1,200,000 SPEAKERS

India

Kumauni belongs to the Pahari group of INDO-ARYAN LANGUAGES (see map there), like Nepali and Garhwali, its neighbours on either side.

Kumaūn was once the small area around Champāwat: the local dialect here is still called *Kumaiyyā*. The land dominated by the 'fortress of Kumaūn', first mentioned by the 12th-century poet Chand Baradai, gradually expanded until under British rule the principality stretched from the Tarai foothills to the heights of the Himalaya.

In the mountain passes and the higher valleys the *Bhoṭiā* people speak Tibetan dialects. In the lowlands, recent migrations have led to the use of Hindi as a lingua franca. Between the two, Kumauni remains the everyday language of more than a million people. Beside Hindi as the language of education and government, and the local dialects of which as many as fifteen have been counted, there is an identifiable Standard Kumauni spoken by educated classes over most of the former state, deriving from the dialect of the old capital at Champawat.

There are inscriptions, erected by local rulers, dating from the 17th century. Since 1800 a small body of written poetry in Kumauni has dev-eloped, but the language is especially important for its oral literature, which includes legends, romances and shorter ritual songs.

जो औरों उपर खाड़ खनछ | ऊ आफी वीमी पड़ैछ ||
Jo aurom upar khāṛ khanch, ū āphī vī-mī paṛamch.
One who digs a pit for others will fall into it himself.

Numerals in Nepali, Kumauni and Garhwali

Nepali		Kumauni and Garhwali
ek	1	ek
dui	2	dvī
tin	3	tīn
chār	4	cār
pāñch	5	pāṃc
chha	6	chai
sāt	7	sāt
āṭh	8	āṭh
nau	9	nau
das	10	das

KUMYK

200,000 SPEAKERS

Russia

One of the TURKIC LANGUAGES of the Kipchak group, Kumyk is spoken by the fourth largest ethnic unit of the multilingual Russian republic of Dagestan. There are no historical records of their origins, but the speakers of *Qumuq* or Kumyk appear to have been established here, between the northern Caucasus mountains and the Caspian Sea, at least since the 11th and 12th centuries when the region was conquered for Islam. They can clearly trace their history to the empires of the steppes, like the Tatars, and thus have quite a different origin from that of the AZERI speakers to their south.

In recent centuries, however, Kumyk has been strongly influenced by the culturally dominant Azeri and by the neighbouring Caucasian language DARGWA. Long threatened by Russian expansion, the region was conquered by Russia in 1867. The coastal plains of central Dagestan, once sparsely populated by Kumyk, were re-settled with Avar and Dargwa speakers in the 1950s to 1970s – a knock-on effect of the return of mass exiles, such as Chechen, Karachai and Balkar speakers, to their homelands.

The Kumyk capital and cultural centre is Buinaksk (Temir Khan Shura). Oral and traditional poetry was collected in the 19th century. The founder of Kumyk literature, it is usually said, is Yırçı Qazaq, born in 1839, who was exiled to cold Russia as punishment for an illicit love affair and from there wrote a lyrical poetic letter to his beloved Rayḥānat, begging her father's forgiveness.

There is now some publishing in Kumyk: the first magazines and newspapers appeared in 1917–18. Arabic script was used until 1928, the Latin alphabet for the next ten years; the Cyrillic alphabet was introduced in 1938. Russian is increasingly the language of culture, education and politics in modern Dagestan.

Two other small Turkic language communities of the northern Caucasus can be grouped with Kumyk. Both, like Kumyk itself, have been written in three successive alphabets since the Russian Revolution.

Karachai and Balkar: 'punished peoples'

Karachai and Balkar are usually regarded as a single language, though the speakers see themselves as distinct peoples. They have been settled, side by side, in the northern Caucasus at least since the 14th century, and began to adopt Islam, under Nogai and Crimean Tatar influence, in the 18th. Russia conquered the region in 1827–8. One phonetic feature easily distinguishes the two dialects: the Karachai say *ch* when the Balkar say *ts* (Karachai *küchük*, Balkar *kütsük* 'small').

Speakers of Karachai were among the Muslims of the northern Caucasus who incurred Stalin's distrust. Soon after the German occupation of 1942, the whole population, numbering 75,000, was deported from the Caucasus to the Soviet East in 1944. A quarter of them died on the journey or in the first five years of exile. The survivors and their children returned in 1957, and Karachai speakers now number 160,000. The former republic of Karachaevo-Cherkessia has now been divided, and the Karachai have self-governing status within Russia.

The 43,000 speakers of Balkar were also dispatched eastwards en masse in 1944, and many died. The remnant were allowed to return in 1956 and their descendants now number 85,000. Once sharing the Kabardino-Balkar autonomous region, Balkar speakers now have a self-governing republic within Russia.

KURDISH

PERHAPS 14,000,000 SPEAKERS

Iraq, Turkey, Iran, Syria, Armenia

Kurdish is the second largest of the IRANIAN LANGUAGES in terms of population – but its political position is wholly different from that of Persian, the largest of the group. While Persian is the national language of Iran and Tajikistan, Kurdish language and culture struggle for recognition in all the states in which its speakers live.

Kurds are possibly first named in surviving records of about 400 BC, as the *Kardoukhoi* encountered by Greek mercenary soldiers, led by Xenophon, on their march from Mesopotamia to the Black Sea – or possibly four hundred years later, as the *Kyrtioi*, a Median population, listed by the Roman geographer Strabo. At any rate, Kurds occur frequently in historical sources from the time of the Islamic conquest onwards. Redoubtable mountaineers with a nomadic lifestyle, they were independent most of the time. At the end of the First World War, at the Lausanne Conference, Kurdish territory was parcelled out to Turkey, Iran and Iraq, with a promise of autonomy only for the Iraqi section.

Kurds have been authors in Arabic, Persian and Turkish for about a thousand years, while Kurdish written poetry – in Arabic script – goes back to the 15th century. The classic text is the epic *Memozîn* by Ehmedî Khanî (1650–1706). Kurdish oral literature is remarkably powerful and varied.

In Iraq Kurdish has in general been recognised as a language of education and the press. The struggle for political autonomy has, however, led to bitter warfare recently. In Turkey Kurdish is outlawed in official use and in the press: even tape recordings are not allowed.

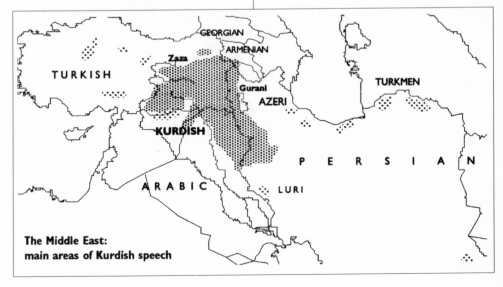

The Middle East:
main areas of Kurdish speech

Kurdish, Gurani and Zaza

The major geographical division within Kurdish is between Northern and Central dialects.

The principal Northern dialect is *Kurmanji*. This is the Kurdish of eastern Turkey, north-eastern Syria and Iranian Azerbaijan. It is also spoken, as a result of recent migrations, in Khorasan, Baluchistan and Afghanistan. It is the usual speech of Kurdish communities in Middle Eastern cities, from Beirut to Istanbul. North-eastern Kurdish includes the *Badinani* of the Mosul region of north-west Iraq. To the same group belongs the dialect spoken in Armenia and independent Azerbaijan. After forced migrations from Soviet Transcaucasia during the Second World War, this dialect is also spoken in Kyrgyzstan and Kazakhstan.

The principal Central dialects are the *Sorani* of Iraqi Kurdistan and the closely related *Kurdi* and *Sine'i* of Iranian Kurdistan.

To the south there are more scattered Kurdish-speaking groups in Luristan, including the Lak tribes.

Gurani and *Zaza* are two quite separate Iranian languages, spoken by as many as two million people (there are no reliable figures) in Iran and Turkey. They consider themselves, and are often considered by outsiders, to be Kurds. A considerable number of the 'Turkish workers' living in several countries of western Europe are Kurds – and a high proportion of these are actually Zaza speakers. The *Bajalani*, who speak a Gurani dialect, live in northern Iraq and form an esoteric Islamic sect with a special devotion to the Imam 'Ali, 'black 'Ali' as they call him. Gurani has an established tradition of oral poetry, once performed at princely courts.

Numerals in Kurdish and LURI		
Kurdish		**Luri**
yek	1	yak
du	2	du
sê	3	se
çar	4	châr
pênc	5	panch
şeş	6	shish
heft	7	haft
heşt	8	hash
neh	9	nuh
deh	10	dah

Kurdish in writing

Kurdish as a literary language can be found in three different scripts. The Latin alphabet now used for Kurmanji is similar to that of Turkish. An additional character ẍ is sometimes used.

The Kurdish alphabet: Latin, Arabic and Cyrillic scripts

A B C Ç D E Ê F G H I Î J K L M N O P Q R S Ş T U Û V W X Y Z

a b c ç d e ê f g h i î j k l m n o p q r s ş t u û v w x y z

ا ب ج چ د ه ة ز م ل ك ي ژ ك پ و ن ه ك گ ه ى ي ك ل ا ق ر س ش ت و وو و خ ي ز

А Б Щ Ч Д Э Е Ф Г Гь Ь И Ж К Л М Н О П Q Р С Ш Т Ö У В W Х Й З

а б щ ч д э е ф г гь ь и ж к л м н о п q р с ш т ö у в w х й з

Until the 20th century Kurmanji was written in the Arabic alphabet. Arabic script is still used for publications in Badinani, Sorani and Sine'i. Arabic script is read from right to left, but in the box the letters are given from left to right, corresponding to the latin script above.

A form of the Cyrillic alphabet was assigned to Kurdish speakers in the Soviet Union in 1945. The box shows it in Latin alphabetical order.

KURUKH

1,200,000 SPEAKERS

India

Kurukh is spoken well to the north-east of the main body of DRAVIDIAN LANGUAGES, on the borders of the Indian states of Orissa and Madhya Pradesh, extending as far as the southern edge of Bihar.

Kurukh is the speakers' own name for their language. Outsiders spell it in various ways – *Kurux* and even *Khurñk* will be found – or may use the alternative terms *Orāon, Urāon.*

Like other northern and central Dravidian languages it is spoken by hill and jungle dwellers and has no written tradition. Kurukh speakers who settle in the plains turn to other languages of their neighbourhood, such as Oriya, Bengali or Magahi. The number of speakers has, however, remained constant or even increased over the past decades.

The first ten numerals in Kurukh are: *onṭā, ēmr, mūnd, nākh, pancē, soyyē, sattē, aṭṭhē, naimyē, dassē.* Only '1' to '4' are Dravidian: the rest are borrowed from Magahi or a related dialect.

The northern Dravidian languages on the map

Kurukh is spoken from the Sambalpur district of eastern Orissa northwards to the Chota Nagpur region. Its speakers have a tradition that they originated in the hills north of Patna. A small number of speakers of a related dialect has in fact been identified in the Nepalese Terai: it is called *Dhangar* or *Nepali Kurukh.* The same tradition speaks of a party who went further east, to the mountains of Rajmahal. These will have been the linguistic ancestors of the 50,000 speakers of *Malto.* It is sometimes called *Rajmahalia* or *Malpaharia* – a name also given to the local creolised Bengali which appears to be replacing Malto on the lips of many.

BRAHUI, completely isolated from the rest of the Dravidian family, is spoken in western Pakistan, and is heavily influenced by the Iranian languages that surround it.

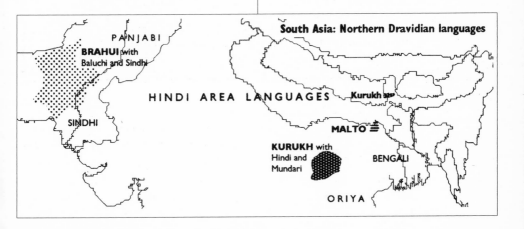

KYRGYZ

1,500,000 SPEAKERS

Kyrgyzstan, China

Speakers of one of the TURKIC LANGUAGES, which is now the national language of Kyrgyzstan, the *Kyrgyz* (or Kirghiz or Qırχız) burst into history as the opponents, and eventual destroyers, of the old Uighur empire in western Mongolia, which fell in 842 AD.

They did not found an empire of their own in its place. At that time the Kyrgyz were apparently forest dwellers of the upper Yenisei valley: to their north, an Arabic source reported, were 'frozen desert lands'. It was probably some time later that they began to migrate south-westwards to their present location in the Tien Shan mountains (see map at KAZAKH). Here, after subjection to successive transitory central Asian empires, and after becoming tributary to China in the mid 18th century, they were conquered by Russia in the 19th. Kyrgyzstan was one of the republics of the Soviet Union. It became independent at the end of 1991.

The first Kyrgyz speaker to visit Europe was probably a slave-girl, θεράπαινα δωριάλωτος ἐκ τῶν λεγομένων Χερχίρ, 'a prisoner of war from the people called *Kherkhir*', given to the Greek envoy Zemarchus in 569 AD on his visit to the Türk emperor Ishtemi (Menander the Guardsman, *History*, fragment 10.3; see also box at TURKIC LANGUAGES).

Kyrgyz is the vehicle of magnificent epic poetry.

Written Kyrgyz literature, at first in Arabic script, began to appear only around 1910. With changes in Soviet policy, a Latin alphabet, introduced in 1928, was abandoned in favour of Cyrillic in 1940.

Altın iyerning kashı eken:	A golden saddle has its pommel:
ata jurtnung bashı eken.	a people has its chieftain.
kümüsh iyerning kashı eken:	A silver saddle has its pommel:
tün tüshkön kalıng köp Nogay	the Nogay teeming as shadows
jurtnung bashı eken.	at nightfall have their chieftain.

The memorial feast for Kökötöy-khan: a Kirghiz epic poem ed. and tr. A. T. Hatto (London: Oxford University Press, 1977) lines 1–4

Kyrgyz epic

The *Memorial Feast* for Kökötöy-khan (see box) is 'the earliest and one of the best of a group of ten oral heroic poems recorded among the northern Kirgiz tribes between 1856 and 1869' (A. T. Hatto). Variant versions were collected from oral poets about seventy-five years later. It was first published by V. V. Radlov in 1885. Radlov supplied a rough German translation and a study of the nature of improvisation in oral poetry, making interesting comparisons with the ancient Greek epics attributed to Homer. Later, an edition with a Russian translation was published by the original collector, the Kyrgyz nobleman Chokan Valikhanov, in 1904. These editions were abridged. The full original text had been noted down in Arabic script for Valikhanov. Long believed lost, it was rediscovered in a Leningrad manuscript in 1964.

Numerals in Kazakh and Kyrgyz

Kazakh (Latin transcription)	Kyrgyz (Cyrillic script)	Kyrgyz (Latin transcription)
bir	бир	bir
eki	эки	eki
üsh	уч	üch
tört	төрт	tört
bes	беш	besh
altı	алты	altı
zheti	жети	zheti
segiz	сегиз	segiz
toghız	тогуз	toguz
on	он	on

from Kurtulus Öztopçu and others, *Dictionary of the Turkic languages* (London: Routledge, 1996)

LAHU

500,000 SPEAKERS

China and south-east Asia

One of the Burmese-Lolo group of SINO-TIBETAN LANGUAGES, Lahu is spoken by a high mountain population in south-western Yunnan, between the Salween and Mekong rivers (see map at BURMESE).

In older sources the *Lahu* are often called *Muhsö*, originally a Tai term, 'hunter'.

Like their neighbours who speak Wa, the Lahu have been among the chief producers of opium for the world market. They are divided into subgroups with different costumes and somewhat different customs, Black Lahu (*Lahu na*), Yellow Lahu (*Lahu shi*) and others. Each has its distinct dialect.

There is some evidence of a once-autonomous state of the Black Lahu, ruled by thirty-six *fu* or priests, north of Xishuangbanna and east of the Wa country in western Yunnan. If this ever existed, it succumbed to Chinese rule at the end of the 19th century. It would at least help to explain why a 'Black Lahu' dialect, *Meuneu*, remains a kind of standard language and has served as a lingua franca of local trade and communication in the Mekong valley and the mountains to the north of the Golden Triangle.

It is certainly true that religious leaders, *paw-ku*, exert great power among Lahu communities, sometimes claiming apotheosis and inspiring holy war. Baptist missionaries have worked for many years among the Lahu, devising an orthography for the language in Latin script and publishing religious texts.

New Year is the time for courtship among the Lahu and AKHA. Young men are always on the move, visiting neighbouring villages. Boys and girls camp out, close together but in separate groups, around bonfires, and sing alternate verses of traditional love songs.

Numerals in Loloish languages

	Akha	Black Lahu	Lisu	Yi
1	ti ˆ, ti ˇ	te ˇma ˍ	hti ˋ	t'a ˋ
2	nyi ˆ, nyi ˇ	nyi ˇma ˍ	nyi ˋ	nyi ˋ
3	sm ˆ, sm ˇ	sheh:leh ˇ	sa	sɔ
4	oe ˇ	awn_leh ˇ	li	lye
5	nga ˇ	nga ˇma ˍ	ngwa ´	ngɪ
6	k'o ˆ	hkaw ˍma ˍ	hchaw ˋ	fu ¯
7	shi ˆ	suh ˍma ˍ	shi ˋ	she
8	yeh ˆ	hi ˍma ˇ	h'i ˋ	hi ¯
9	g'oe ˇ	k'aw ˇma ˍ	ku ´	gu
10	tse ˇ	te ˇchi:	htsi	tshi

From David Bradley, *Proto-Loloish* (London: Curzon Press, 1979) pp. 338–41, 382, and other sources

LAMPUNG

1,500,000 SPEAKERS

Indonesia

One of the AUSTRONESIAN LANGUAGES, Lampung is the regional language of Lampung province at the southern end of Sumatra. The province is heavily overpopulated as a result of government-directed resettlement from Java: speakers of Lampung are outnumbered, at least five to one, by migrants who speak Javanese or Indonesian.

Contacts with Malay, the trade language of the archipelago, go back hundreds of years. There is much bilingualism in Indonesian, now the official form of Malay.

Lampung has its own script, an offshoot of the Brahmi script of ancient India: this has been taught in schools and some people use it for personal letters.

The first ten numerals in Lampung are: *sai, ghua, talu, pa, lima, onom, pitu, walu, siwa, sapuluh*.

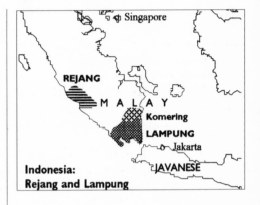

Indonesia: Rejang and Lampung

Rejang and Lampung

There are about 1,000,000 speakers of Rejang and perhaps 1,500,000 of Lampung, related languages of south-western Sumatra. *Komering*, with a further 700,000 speakers, is a variety of Lampung spoken in the Komering Ilir and Komering Ulu districts of South Sumatra province.

LANNA THAI, KHÜN AND LÜ

PERHAPS 6,500,000 SPEAKERS

Thailand, China, Burma, Laos

The *Lanna* or *Tai Yuan* language of northern Thailand, with its main centre now at Chiangmai, is very close to the *Lü* of the autonomous region of Xishuangbanna in south-western Yunnan. Between the two territories lies the state of Kengtung, at the eastern extremity of Burma: this was counted in British times as one of the 'Shan States' but its ruling language was *Khün*. Kengtung claimed a tributary state, Muong Sing, which is now at the north-western corner of Laos (for map see LAO).

Under its many names, the majority language in these areas is recognisably one; it is written in the same traditional script; and it is the vehicle of the same Buddhist culture. It belongs to the TAI LANGUAGES. Tai Yuan is the term preferred by some linguists.

Xishuangbanna is the Chinese form of the native Lü name, *Hsip hsong pan na*, 'Twelve thousand rice fields', for the historic state whose capital is at Jinghong (Shan *Kenghung*, Thai *Chiengrung*, older Chinese name *Ch'eli*).

Lü is commonly known in Chinese as *Baiyi* (older transliteration *Pai-i*), as *Xishuangbanna Dai* or simply as *Dai*. In Thailand the term *Lanna Thai* is now most used. British and Burmese have often confused Khün with *Shan*.

Local chronicles take the history of the three main states back to the 12th century, when Patseng ruled the Hsip Hsong Pan Na, and the 13th, when Mangrai founded the kingdom of Lanna at Chiangmai and its offshoot at Keng-

tung. The relations between the old Yunnanese kingdom of Nanchao and the Hsip Hsong Pan Na state are unknown, but it, along with neighbouring smaller states, has been tributary to China since the Mongol conquest of Nanchao in 1253. In more recent centuries, these Tai states paid occasional tribute to China, to Burma and to Thailand, retaining local autonomy, until colonial frontiers were drawn in the 1890s. Local relations among them have been maintained as much as possible, and their language and culture still give evidence of the multiple influences of their past.

Like its relatives, Tai Yuan is a tonal language: the Lü variety has six tones. It contains many loanwords from Pali, the language of the Buddhist scriptures. The *Jātaka* tales of the Buddha's former lives, originally written in Pali, have had a strong influence on local traditional literature.

'Northern Thai' script

The traditional script for Lanna Thai, Khün and Lü is similar to that used for Lao: both derive from the Khmer alphabet. Pali texts, the scriptures of southern Buddhism, can also be written in this script. There was once metal type capable of printing this script at a press in Kengtung: its fate is unknown. In Xishuangbanna a simplified version has recently been introduced, and textbooks and traditional literature have been published. At Chiangmai, offset printing from handwritten calligraphy has been the rule;

but computer typesetting now permits high quality printing of this complex script.

LAO

PERHAPS 15,000,000 SPEAKERS

Thailand, Laos

Lao, one of the TAI LANGUAGES (see table of numerals there), is spoken along both banks of the middle Mekong. The majority of speakers, along the right bank and the southern tributaries, are in Thailand and their official and literary language is Thai. The Lao language in Thailand is sometimes called *Isan* or *North-eastern Thai*. The other speakers of this language, those along the more mountainous left bank of the Mekong and its northern tributaries, are the *Lao* or *Laotians*, and they form the largest linguistic group in Laos, whose national language this is.

In the 14th century the powerful state of *Lan Xang* was established; its ruler, at Luang Phrabang, exacted tribute from the other smaller Tai states that already encircled it. Lan Xang declined in the 18th century, and the states of the middle Mekong were fought over by Thailand and Annam. A century later, the French colonial administration in Indochina, asserting the claims of Annam (which they had already annexed), seized the states on the left bank of the river, leaving the right bank to Thailand. The kingdom of Laos, thus created as a French protectorate, became independent in 1949 and the scene of a long civil war.

Lao is the language of a strongly Buddhist culture. Traditionally most young men spend some time as monks, and learn to read, if not to translate, the Pali scriptures, which are written in Lao script. The rich older literature of Lao, preserved in palm leaf manuscripts, includes religious and secular poetry as well as chronicles.

All dialects of Lao are tonal: some dialects have five tones, some six. Lao has borrowed cultural and religious vocabulary from Sanskrit, Pali, Khmer and French. Under French rule many Vietnamese were employed in Laos. Thai, the closely related language of a much more powerful state, is now a strong cultural influence on Lao.

Thai, Lanna Thai, Lao and the Tai languages of Vietnam

THAI or Central Thai is the national language of Thailand. The dialect of Bangkok forms the standard. The dialect of *Khorat* shows some Khmer influence. The *Pak Thai* or Southern Thai dialect, with Malay loanwords, is spoken in Chumphon and Nakhon Si Thammarat.

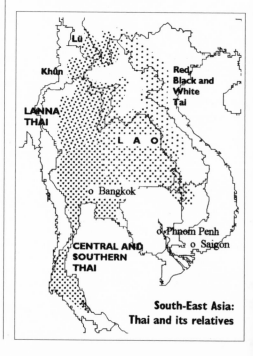

South-East Asia: Thai and its relatives

Tai Yuan or LANNA THAI or Northern Thai is the language of north-western Thailand, including the old principalities of Chiangmai, Lamphun, Lampang, Nan and Phrae; slightly varying dialects are spoken in Kengtung, Muong Sing, Jinghong and other, smaller neighbouring states.

Lao is the lowland language of Laos, the country once ruled from Luang Phrabang but now from Vientiane. It is also spoken in the north-eastern Thai provinces.

Red Tai, *Black Tai* and *White Tai* are all spoken by minorities in Laos and North Vietnam.

The Lao alphabet

ກຂຄງ ຈສຊຍ ດຕຖທ ບປຜຝພຟມ ຢຣລວຫ ຫງຫຍຫຍ ຫຫງອຣ

g kk ng c ss ny d t tt n b p pfp f m y ll w h ng ny n m l w a h

---

In the box are shown, above, the thirty-three characters and their Latin equivalents.

Below are the thirty-eight vowel-tone combinations, shown here with the character ອ *a*.

Lao script is a variant of Thai. As with other scripts of Indian origin, characters are combined into compounds to make up a syllable, including one or more initial consonants, a vowel and a tone mark.

ອະ ອໍອ ອາ ອິ ອີ ອຶ ອື ອຸ ອູ ເອະ ເອໍອ ເອ ແອະ ແອໍອ ແອ ໂອະ ອໍອ ໂອ ເອາະ ອອໍອ ອ

ອອອ ເອີ ເອີ ເອໍຽະ ອໍຽອ ເອໍຽ ອຽອ ເອຶອ ເອືອ ອົວະ ອົວອ ອົວ ອວອ ໄອ ໄອ ເອົາ ອໍາ

Font: *alice-4.ttf* by Ngakham Southichack

LATIN

Classical language of Europe

One of the INDO-EUROPEAN LANGUAGES, Latin was the language of the ancient city of Rome. Rome became the capital of an empire that embraced all the Mediterranean countries and most of western Europe. In this way, Latin became a language of world importance, with a literature that is still read today. Latin was, and to some extent still is, the international language of the Catholic Church, the Christian sect out of which all others grew. It has been used as an official international language in many academic and scientific fields. Latin has had an influence on all the modern languages of Europe and the Mediterranean, and is the direct ancestor of French, Spanish and the other ROMANCE LANGUAGES.

The Latin or Roman alphabet was a local variant of Greek script. It has had even wider influence than the Latin language, being used in all continents for writing hundreds of languages. It is still spreading.

Two thousand five hundred years ago, Italic languages, a branch of the INDO-EUROPEAN family, were spoken in central Italy. They include Oscan, Umbian, Sabine and Latin: inscriptions, in alphabets based on Greek, record the distinctive features of these and other dialects. Latin was the Italic dialect of the district called Latium (modern *Lazio*). Rome, with its seven hills on the south bank of the Tiber, was simply one of the towns of Latium.

The growth of Rome and of Latin may be traced to the city's emergence from the cultural and political influence of Etruria, to the north. Etruscan, a language unrelated to Latin, not yet fully deciphered, and now long extinct, can be seen to have had a heavy influence on Latin in its early stages. The Roman emperor Claudius (ruled AD 43–56) was one of the last professed experts on Etruscan. Latin loanwords from Etruscan include *caerimonia* 'ceremony', *persona* 'mask', *histrio* 'actor', *baro* 'strong man, lout, baron'; all these, incidentally, were later borrowed into English.

The last of the Italic languages to challenge the position of Latin was Oscan, the official language of the anti-Roman allies in the Social War of 91–88 BC. Latin loanwords from Oscan include *popina* 'cookshop': Oscan had *p* where native Latin had *q*, and this word is cognate with Latin *coquus* 'cook'.

By the 1st century AD Rome ruled not only Italy but all the countries that surround the Mediterranean. Latin was the ruling language of the empire. It gradually extended its range as everyday spoken language, helped by its status in law and administration, by population mobility, by army recruitment and resettlement. The Latin of the empire borrowed a good deal of vocabulary from local languages: from Celtic, for example, came *carrum* 'wagon', *camminus* 'road', *cerevisia* 'beer'.

Greek, which was already the lingua franca of the eastern Mediterranean, retained its position and even increased in importance, for Greek literature, philosophy and science were admired. Well-educated Romans learnt Greek as well as Latin. Greek was also a lingua franca among slaves, and between slaves and owners. Greek loanwords in Latin include *persica* 'peach', *balneum* 'bath' (see box).

Greek had been the first major international language of Christianity, but Latin was soon to claim this role as the Bible and many other texts were translated into Latin and as the bishop of Rome came to be recognised as leader of the church. Christian Latin borrowings from Hebrew and Greek include *sabbatum* 'sabbath', *episcopus* 'bishop'. The Latin Bible in its *versio vulgata*, 'common translation, Vulgate' of about AD 405

LATVIAN

1,500,000 SPEAKERS

Latvia

Latvian and Lithuanian are the two surviving BALTIC LANGUAGES (see map and table of numerals there). Latvian is the official language of the Republic of Latvia, which became independent from the Soviet Union in 1991.

The name of *Latvia* derives from the speakers' own name for themselves, *Latvis*. The language was once better known in English as *Lettish*; in French it is still called *Letton*.

Latvian speakers, expanding northwards from neighbouring Lithuania, were in this region by the 10th century, and probably rather longer if, as linguists believe, Latvian began to separate from Lithuanian around AD 600.

Latvia was under the rule of the Teutonic knights, largely German-speaking, and then of German landowners and bishops, from 1158 to 1562: during much of this time it was divided between two states, Courland and Livonia. Riga, now capital of Latvia, was in its origin a Hanseatic port and its everyday language was Low German. Poland ruled Courland from 1562; Livonia was ruled by Sweden from 1629. But both territories eventually fell to Russia, which eventually governed the whole of Latvia until 1918 and seized it again in 1940. Germans occupied Latvia in 1941–4. This complex history led to a division in Latvia between Orthodox, Catholic and Lutheran Christianity: the majority of the population is Lutheran.

Hundreds of thousands of Latvians died in the Second World War and its aftermath. After 1944 the ethnic situation was complicated by mass deportations of Latvians to Siberia and Kazakhstan, and mass immigration of Russians. The Russian minority amounted to 40 per cent of the population on independence.

A Lutheran catechism was published in Latvian in 1586. In the 19th century Latvian speakers became increasingly aware of their national and linguistic distinctness and their folklore.

Latvian reflects its history in its numerous loanwords, from Swedish, German, Polish and particularly Russian.

LEZGHIAN

400,000 SPEAKERS

Russia, Azerbaijan

One of the Lezghian or Samurian group of North East CAUCASIAN LANGUAGES (see map there), Lezghian has been one of the official languages of Dagestan since soon after the Russian Revolution. Its status in Azerbaijan is far more precarious.

Islam was introduced in the 15th century to this part of the Caucasus. The territory was annexed by Russia between 1812 and 1865.

Arabic was the language of literature and education for this Muslim mountain people; Azeri was becoming the lingua franca of everyday life. In turn, Lezghian served as a lingua franca for the smaller number of speakers of Agul, Rutul and Tabasaran. On the occasions when Lezghian was written, Arabic script was used.

With the development of Soviet nationality policy, Lezghian was recognised as a literary language both in Dagestan and Azerbaijan, and a Latin orthography was introduced in 1928 – followed, as usual, by a Cyrillic alphabet in 1938. The number of Lezghian speakers grew steadily through Soviet times, although in 1939 Lezghian lost its position as an official language in Azerbaijan, and in the 1950s Russian was made the educational and official language for speakers of Agul, a position that Lezghian had formerly held.

Since Azerbaijan became independent in 1991 many Lezghian speakers from northern Azerbaijan have fled northwards to Dagestan. Their lands have been resettled with Azeri refugees from Armenia and with Meskhetian Turks, exiled from Georgia to Uzbekistan in Stalin's time, now fleeing ethnic hostility there. Lezghian speakers remain dissatisfied with the division of their territory between Russia and Azerbaijan.

The three main dialects of Lezghian are Kürin, Akhty and Kuba, the latter spoken in Azerbaijan. The literary language is based on Kürin.

There are a few thousand Lezghian speakers in villages near Balıkesir and İzmir in Turkey. The Muslim migrants settled there in 1865, after the Russian conquest of their homeland, and are said to cling tenaciously to their language and culture with its traditions of hospitality.

The first ten numerals in Lezghian are: *sad, qwed, pud, qud, wad, rughùd, erìd, muzhùd, k'ud, ts'ud.*

LI

800,000 SPEAKERS

China

L i is a language of Hainan Island, and is one of the KADAI LANGUAGES (known in China as Zhuang-Dong languages). It is thus distantly related to the Tai group.

Li is the Chinese form of the speakers' own name for themselves, which varies according to dialect: Hlai, Dli, B'li, Le, Lai, Loi, Day, K'lai are all found.

Traditionally, trade in Li villages was in the hands of Chinese shopkeepers and pedlars. Li, particularly the southern dialect spoken by the Ha Li, has been noticeably influenced by Chinese: a large number of speakers are now bilingual. This is not to say that Li speakers were easily brought under Chinese rule. The 'Wild Li of Hainan' were famous for their long resistance to conquest – and, fairly or unfairly, for cannibalism too. Fifty rebellions can be found in the history books, extending over the 2,100 years since the first Chinese colonies were established on Hainan.

The last rebellion was the most decisive. In 1943 Wang Guoxing, the leader of Li resistance to the Nationalist Chinese government, made contact with the Communist guerrilla forces on the island. Li speakers were thus among the very few Chinese minorities to ally themselves with the Communists, and the Li Column was soon celebrated in Chinese legend for its contribution to the struggle. The former 'Wild Li' are now much more highly regarded. The Hainan Li and Miao Autonomous Region was created in 1952.

Li is a tonal language, and in essence monosyllabic, like its Tai relatives. The proportion of vocabulary shared between Li and the Tai languages – the vocabulary from which their histor-

ical relationship is demonstrated – is actually quite small, indicating a very long separation.

Li had no traditional writing system: if Li speakers became literate, they wrote Chinese. The language shows some influence from the YAO dialect (inaccurately called 'Miao') that has been spoken on Hainan since the 16th century.

Li and related languages

There is little detailed information as yet on dialect divisions of Li. *Southern Li* is in broad terms the dialect of the Ha, who live in the southern part of Hainan near the coast. *Northern Li*, or Loi to some authors, has numerous tribal and dialect divisions, largely to be found inland. Five Li dialect groups are generally recognised.

Other Kadai languages, related to Li but at some distance in time, are spoken by small and remote communities of the southern Chinese

China: Kadai languages

mainland. They include *Kelao* or Gelo, *Lakkia* or Laqua, and *Lati*. None has as many as ten thousand speakers; Lati has only a few hundred, in the Vietnamese hills just south of the Chinese border.

Ong-be or Bê, a language of obscure origins, possibly Kadai but with numerous loanwords from Chinese, is spoken by a fairly large population, perhaps as many as half a million, on the northern coasts of Hainan. Speakers of Ong-be are very much Chinese in their culture, and are not recognised as an official minority.

LINGALA AND BANGALA

PERHAPS 12,000,000 SPEAKERS, MAINLY AS SECOND LANGUAGE

Congo (Kinshasa), Congo (Brazzaville), Central African Republic

One of the BANTU LANGUAGES, Lingala developed in the 19th century from dialects spoken by the Ngala people, inhabitants of the banks of the middle Zaire near Mbandaka and Nouvelle Anvers. It appears closest to the now-minor languages Boloki and Bobangi.

The Ngala, originally fierce opponents of Stanley's advance, eventually became allies of the European colonists. Their trade language, Mangala, had already spread upriver and downriver before European soldiers and traders arrived in large numbers. When they did, they took up Mangala as a medium of communication over an even wider region. As new towns and trading posts developed along the Zaire and its tributaries, a creolised Mangala, called Lingala, became the preferred language among migrants of varying mother tongues who had to find a living there. Much army recruitment also took place among Ngala speakers near Nouvelle Anvers, and Lingala became the language of the army. Soon new recruits were required to know 600 words of Lingala.

Lingala – language of local government, the army and the new towns – appeared so important in official eyes that in 1918 the Belgian government tried to make it the official language of the whole of Belgian Congo.

As development continued to encourage migration and intermarriage, Lingala rapidly became a mother tongue in towns and cities. It is now the predominant language of the middle Congo, upriver almost to Kisangani and downriver all the way to Kinshasa, and is spoken by many inhabitants of the big city. Even the speakers of Kongo dialects – the majority in Kinshasa – need Lingala as a second language. Originally a language of trade and employment, Lingala is now a major mother tongue of modern Congo (Kinshasa). It is also spoken by some in Brazzaville (though KITUBA is the majority lingua franca there) and along the line of the railway to Pointe Noire on the Atlantic coast.

Its use as a language of trade, of education and religion, and of the home has led to the rapid development of varieties of Lingala: in Kinshasa, for example, 'street Lingala' or 'river Lingala' is quite different from the *Langue scolaire* or 'school Lingala'.

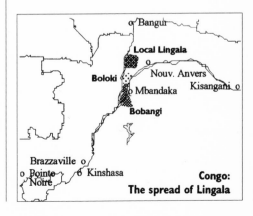

Congo:
The spread of Lingala

Originating as an inter-Bantu lingua franca, Lingala remained difficult for others – hence the emergence from it of Bangala. This, with 3,500,000 speakers in Congo (Kinshasa) and the Central African Republic, is a pidgin form of Lingala which arose in contact between Africans and Europeans. It is now a language in its own right, characterised by much-simplified grammar and word formation. Use in the army has spread Bangala in the Uele area and in the north-east of Congo (Kinshasa) among a mainly non-Bantu-speaking population.

Lingala and Bobangi

In the 19th century *Lingala* was still merely the language of one of several trading communities on the middle Congo. Its growth since then has been astonishing.

Bobangi or Bangi, a related Bantu language, was spoken by the traders of the river Ubangi, who also ranged the Zaire as far as Malebo Pool (Stanley Pool) where Kinshasa and Brazzaville now stand. It now has about 70,000 speakers in Congo (Kinshasa) and Congo (Brazzaville).

Numerals in Kongo, Lingala and Bobangi			
	Kongo	**Lingala**	**Bobangi**
1	-mosi	m-ókó	-oko
2	-ole	mi-balé	-bale
3	-tatu	mi-sáto	-sato
4	-ya	mi-nei	-nei
5	-tanu	mi-táno	-tano
6	-sambanu	motóbá	motoba
7	nsambwadi	nsambo	ncambo
8	nana	mwambi	mwambi
9	vua	libwá	libwa
10	kumi	zómi	zomu

LISU

650,000 SPEAKERS

China, Burma and south-east Asia

One of the SINO-TIBETAN LANGUAGES, Lisu is spoken in the upper valleys of the Salween and Mekong rivers, and by numerous migrant communities in the mountains of south-east Asia.

> Speakers call themselves *Lisu*; Chinese, Lanna, Lahu and other neighbours tend to use a form such as *Lishaw*. An older Chinese term is *Yeh-jen* 'wild men'. This may be the origin of Kachin and Burmese *Yawyin*, *Yawyang*, a name often found in older English writings on the Lisu.

The first published wordlist of Lisu appeared in 1871, in a report by a British explorer of the Burma–Yunnan route.

The 'wild Lisu' or Black Lisu of the north are traditionally fiercely independent, living in easily defended villages and – at least until recently – exacting tribute from traders who passed below them. They practised slash-and-burn agriculture, hunted, and collected wild honey. Above Lisu villages that adhere to the traditional religion there will be a spirit grove of sacred trees. Lisu priests were said to have a secret religious language, and, according to Erik Seidenfaden, a hieroglyphic script in which sacred texts were recorded: if this exists, no details of it have been published.

There have been massive conversions of Lisu speakers to Christianity: the mission of the Church of Christ has been particularly successful among them. The dialect of west central Yunnan, very similar to that of the northern Shan State, acts as a standard language, with an orthography in a missionary-devised extension of Latin script in which both Christian and secular texts have been published. For a table of numerals see LAHU.

Northern dialects show a characteristic sound change: initial *py- by- my-* become *c- j- ny-*.

'Chinese Lisu', spoken by the people who used to be called 'tame Lisu' in central Yunnan and in some communities in northern Thailand, is a creolised variant of the language, resulting from extensive intermarriage with Yunnanese Chinese speakers.

The Lisu alphabet

BPᗡDT⅂GKꓥJCꓛZFꓤMNLSRΛXWYꓭVH
ΛVEꓱIOUꓵ꓄BꓦO . , ꞏ ꞏ ꞏ , : ;

b p ph d t th g k kh j c ch dz ts tsh m n l s r ng sh
v y h nh kh a æ e ö i o u ü ghı gha ghe ´ ˇ ˆ ˉ ˋ ˎ

In standard Lisu only the upper-case Latin letters are used; additional sounds are symbolised by upside-down letters. The six tones of Lisu are marked by punctuation symbols. The vowel *a*, when it follows a consonant, is unmarked (just as in Indic scripts). This unusual writing system was devised by the highly successful missionary J. O. Fraser, whose *Handbook of the Lisu (Yawyin) language* appeared in Rangoon in 1922.

A second writing system for Lisu is a syllabary of several hundred characters, apparently devised by a Lisu peasant, Wang Renbo, around 1925. It looks a little like Chinese script, but is not really based on it or any other, because Wang Renbo was illiterate. Although unsystematic and therefore hard to learn, Wang Renbo's script continued to be used in the neighbourhood of his home town, Weixi.

LITHUANIAN

3,500,000 SPEAKERS

Lithuania

Lithuanian is one of the BALTIC LANGUAGES (see map and table of numerals there). It has the distinction of being the language that has changed least over the several thousand years since proto-INDO-EUROPEAN began to split up into the dialects and languages now spoken in a wide swathe across Europe and southern Asia. Lithuanian is the official language of Lithuania, which was the first constituent republic of the Soviet Union to make good its escape from the collapsing superpower.

The *Litva* were already here, at the south-eastern corner of the Baltic, in the 10th century. Their earlier history is really unknown, though archaeologists consider it likely that their ancestors had occupied the region for a long time: certainly a Baltic language influenced an early form of FINNISH and Estonian over two thousand years ago, suggesting that the two language groups were adjacent at that time.

In the 14th century the Grand Duchy of Lithuania had become the largest state in Europe, stretching all the way from the Baltic to the borders of the Khanate of Crimea. The country was still pagan, but on the marriage of Queen Jadwiga of Poland to Grand Duke Jagiello of Lithuania (in 1385) it became officially Catholic, almost the last European nation to adopt Christianity. It now formed part of a double Polish-Lithuanian state in which Polish became the ruling language (until very recently Polish was the majority language of the Lithuanian capital, Vilnius). When this state was broken up, in the 18th century, Lithuania was annexed by Russia and Russian was the new language of prestige. Lithuanian sank into the status of a peasant tongue. After rebellions in 1830, printing and

teaching in Lithuanian were outlawed and many schools and Roman Catholic monasteries were closed. The German occupation of 1915–18 was equally oppressive.

Independent from 1918, Lithuania was once more seized by the Soviet Union in 1940, and suffered a second German occupation in 1941–4. The ethnic situation was complicated by mass deportations of Lithuanians to Siberia and Kazakhstan, and mass immigration of Russians. There was meanwhile considerable emigration of Lithuanian speakers to western Europe and America – in 1830 to 1910 these were mostly unskilled workers; in the 1940s they were refugees from Soviet occupation. Many rapidly assimilated to their new linguistic environment; others were ready to return as Lithuania declared its independence once more on 11 March 1990 and Russia ceased to dispute the position in September 1991.

The first Lithuanian printed text, a catechism, appeared in 1547. The first dictionary was printed in the 17th century. A more extensive publishing trade developed in the 19th century – and at this period there was already a vigorous press serving Lithuanian communities in the United States. As the nationalist movement flourished under Russian repression, Jonas Mačiulis (1862–1932), 'prophet of the Lithuanian renaissance', emerged as perhaps the greatest 19th-century poet.

Lithuanian vocabulary has striking points of similarity with the most ancient known Indo-European languages: *ašis*, Latin *axis* 'axle'; *avis*, Latin *ovis* 'sheep'; *katras*, Sanskrit *kataras* 'which'. Lithuanian is a tonal language, as ancient Greek and Sanskrit were and as proto-

Indo-European probably was. Nouns have seven cases. There are three numbers, singular, dual and plural. Verb forms, however, are much simpler and more regular than the usually reconstructed proto-Indo-European forms.

In modern literary Lithuanian there has been a concerted attempt to supersede the loanwords from German, Polish, Ukrainian and Belorussian that are found in early texts.

LOMWE

2,000,000 SPEAKERS

Mozambique, Malawi

Lomwe, one of the BANTU LANGUAGES, is spoken in inland Mozambique and in parts of neighbouring Malawi (for map see MAKUA).

The speakers of Lomwe are sometimes called *Manguro* and *Alolo* in older narratives. Alolo is a YAO name for them.

Their older history is unknown. They are traditionally farmers, and the rich, fertile Lomwe valleys of Mozambique are heavily populated. There has been long interaction between Lomwe and Nyanja speakers, and apparently much migration in both directions. The Mihavani, a trading group from the west of the Lomwe-speaking country in Mozambique, are said to be a 'mixture' of Lomwe and Nyanja. After a famine in 1900, however, many Lomwe speakers settled in Nyasaland (now Malawi). More went there later as migrant labourers.

There are now about a million Lomwe speakers in each country. In Malawi they are called *Nguru* or *Anguru*.

LOZI

450,000 SPEAKERS

Zambia, Zimbabwe, Angola

Threatened by the Zulus under their great ruler Chaka, in 1823 thirty thousand Sotho people of the Kololo group, led by the twenty-year-old Sebitwane, marched away from their homeland on the north banks of the Vaal in modern South Africa. Their long march westwards and northwards, involving a great deal of fighting, ended when they conquered the Luyi-speaking Lozi, whose lands were in the upper Zambezi valley in modern Zambia. The Kololo became the ruling caste, and their own dialect of Sotho – one of the BANTU LANGUAGES – was their language of empire (for map see SOTHO). It was already the court language, and a lingua franca of the Upper Zambezi, when David Livingstone visited Sebitwane's capital in 1853.

The Lozi rose against the Kololo in 1864, and ruled from then onwards. The language of the Kololo had already spread widely. The result of the political reversal was not, as might have been expected, a resurgence of the local Luyi language. The Lozi victor, Lewanika (ruled 1878–1916), expanded the boundaries of his kingdom. Lewanika's policies encouraged the spread of the language of the former conquerors even further. Until 1941 Luvale and Southern Lunda speakers of northern Barotseland were ruled by the Lozi under British suzerainty.

Originally known as *siKololo*, this linguistic offshoot of Sotho is now called *Lozi* after its speakers, or *Rozi* or (in their own language) *siLozi*. The first missionaries who worked with this language spelt its name *Rotse*, and that of the tribe *baRotse*. That is how the Lozi territory in Northern Rhodesia, nowadays Zambia, came to be called *Barotseland*.

Lozi speakers are traditionally gardeners of the margins of the Central Barotse Plain through which the Zambezi flows. They cultivate at least eight different kinds of gardens, distinguished by soil, fertilisation and irrigation. Fishing and cattle-herding are also commonly practised.

Lozi is widely used as a lingua franca of south-western Zambia, understood by many men who are speakers of other regional languages. The number of women who speak it is smaller, since women travel less. Lozi is the main language of Livingstone and one of the eight official languages of Zambia, used beside English in local administration and education. The first ten numerals in Lozi are: *ngwi, -peli, -talu, -ne, ketalizoho, ketalizoho ka alimungwi, ketalizoho ka zepeli, ketalizoho ka zetalu, ketalizoho ka totune, lishumi. Ketalizoho* means literally 'finish the hand'.

There are still some speakers of the old language of the valley, Luyi, a dialect of Luyana, which is related to LUVALE to the north. Luyi survives in religious ceremonies and in traditional songs.

Why did Lozi survive?

'The Sotho speakers, a minority, brought with them only a few women, and most of those were rendered barren by the endemic malaria of the Zambezi flood plains. One would expect the language of these conquerors to disappear without trace, especially after the return of the old Luyi dynasty. But Lozi is alive and well, still a typical Sotho dialect, mutually intelligible with Southern Sotho to this day.

'A factor which may have made the difference here is the early and continuous presence of missionaries. They used a Sotho Bible in their work: to this day Lozi is the only liturgical language in Barotseland, the only literary language in the region, and in fact for decades the only African language in Zambia committed to print.'

I. T. Givón in *Readings in creole studies* ed. Ian F. Hancock (Gent: Story-Scientia, 1979) pp. 11–12, modified

Noun classes in Lozi

As in other Bantu languages, nouns in Lozi belong to classes marked by prefixes:

Class	Singular Example		Class	Plural Example	
I	mu-tu	person	IX	ba-tu	people
II	mu-lomo	mouth	X	mi-lomo	mouths
III	li-lundu	mountain	XI	ma-lundu	mountains
VI	lu-limi	tongue		ma-limi	tongues
IV	si-shimani	big boy	XIV	bi-shimani	big boys
	si-katulo	shoe	XII	li-katulo	shoes
V	kuhu	chicken		li-kuhu	chickens
IV	ka-twa	trap	XIII	tu-twa	traps
VIII	bu-ta	bow			

From Yashutoshi Yukawa, 'A tonological study of Lozi verbs' in *Studies in Zambian languages* (Tokyo: ILCAA, 1987) pp. 73–128

LUBA

7,800,000 SPEAKERS

Congo (Kinshasa)

The speakers of Luba, one of the BANTU LAN-GUAGES, inhabited the plateaus of southern Congo (Kinshasa) from the upper Sankuru to the upper Lualaba valleys.

In 1869 Swahili-speaking adventurers from Zanzibar founded the stronghold of Nyangwe on the Lualaba as a centre for trade and slaving raids. The 'Congo Free State' and Belgian colonial governments inherited the Zanzibar trading networks here. Roads, railways, river harbours and mines were developed: the baLuba people, formerly a source of slaves, still provided labourers and, eventually, office and transport workers. Wherever the new arteries went, Luba speakers settled and worked. Luba speakers multiplied in local administration, teaching and the clergy. Thus Luba is not only a local language but has become a lingua franca whose territory covers the two Kasai provinces: in other words, much of southern Congo (Kinshasa), from the Lubilash valley to the Lualaba valley. There are Luba-speaking communities in the big cities of Kinshasa, Kisangani and Lubumbashi, too. In Kinshasa, however, LINGALA is the usual lingua franca. Luba is now one of the national languages of Congo (Kinshasa).

The lingua franca is clearly based on western Luba, the dialect adopted in education and the church. Christian missionaries encouraged this by using western Luba in teaching and preaching. Luba includes loanwords from Portuguese (see box), from English (*sisibete* 'bedsheet'; *mbulankeci* 'blanket'), from Zaire Swahili and nowadays increasingly from French, the ruling language of Congo (Kinshasa).

The first ten numerals in Luba are: *u-mwe, i-bidi, i-satu, i-naayi, i-taanu, i-sambombo, muanda mutekete, muanda mukulu, citeema, diikumi.*

The geographical spread of Luba

The major dialects of Luba are the central (*kiLuba*, Luba-Shaba or Luba-Katanga) and the western (*ciLuba*, Luba-Kasai or Luba-Lulua).

Luba belongs to a larger dialect continuum. This also includes *Bangubangu* (120,000 speakers), *Hemba* or Luba-Hemba or Eastern Luba, *Kanyok* (200,000 speakers), *Sanga* or Luba-Sanga (450,000 speakers), *Songe* or Luba-Songi or North-east Luba (nearly 1,000,000 speakers) and *Kaonde* (220,000 speakers) in Zambia, where it is one of the eight official languages of the country.

Kuba or Luna or Northern Luba also belongs to the group. The Kuba kingdom was an independent power in the 18th and 19th centuries. Hence this was once an influential language, and features of Kuba can be found in the variety of Luba that is now used as lingua franca.

Noun classes in Luba

Like other Bantu languages, Luba nouns belong to classes marked by prefixes:

Class	Singular Example		Class	Plural Example	
I	mu-untu	person	IX	ba-antu	people
II	mu-keta	arrow	X	mi-keta	arrows

III	di-laandi	snail	XI	ma-laandi	snails
VIII	bu-ta	bow		ma-ta	bows
IV	ci-laamba	clothing	XII	bi-laamba	clothes
V	n-koonko	finger ring	XIII	n-koonko	finger rings
VI	lu-kasu	hoe		n-kasu	hoes
VII	ka-minyiminyi	scorpion	XIV	tu-minyiminyi	scorpions

From Yashutoshi Yukawa, 'A tonological study of Luba verbs' in *Studies in Cameroonian and Zairean languages* (Tokyo: ILCAA, 1992) pp. 303–62

Loanwords and noun classes in Luba

'The Luba word for "box" or "chest" is *mushete*. Its meaning aroused my suspicion [as a potential loanword] from the start, but I was unable to pin down its origin. When I found it in KIMBUNDU as well, I was certain that it must be a loanword and that its origin must be Portuguese. The Portuguese word for this article is *caixete* and this would become something like **kashete* in a Bantu language. But the Bantu speakers seem to have rejected this form of the word since the first syllable *ka-* has the shape of the prefix of class 12 [of Guthrie (see box at BANTU LANGUAGES); VII in the table above], which denotes only small things; for big things and for things made of wood, the *mu-* prefix [II above] is used and has therefore been substituted.'

Jan Knappert, 'Contribution from the study of loanwords to the cultural history of Africa' in D. Dalby and others, *Language and history in Africa* (London: Cass, 1970) pp. 78–88

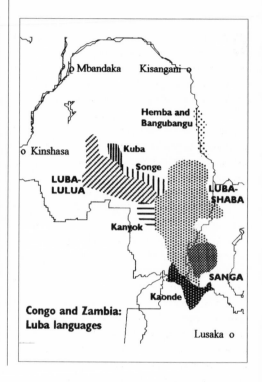

Congo and Zambia: Luba languages

LUNDA

550,000 SPEAKERS

Congo (Kinshasa), Zambia, Angola

O ne of the BANTU LANGUAGES, Lunda is spoken in the wooded plateau north and west of the headwaters of the Zambezi river. Once the language of the Lunda empire of Mwata Yamvo (ruled from what is now Kapanga district of the Shaba region of Congo (Kinshasa)), Lunda has since the European conquest and partition been spoken by almost equal numbers in Congo and Zambia and a smaller population in the Móxico province of Angola. It is one of the eight official languages of Zambia.

Genealogies preserved in oral tradition take Lunda history back to the 16th century, when a King Mwaku ruled a Lunda population in Congo (Kinshasa). The Southern Lunda people (and also the CHOKWE) are said to derive from migrations southwards in the 17th century. The Northern Lunda of Mwata Yamvo meanwhile came to be ruled by a LUBA dynasty: the southerners, who customarily inherit in the female line, claim to preserve the traditions of the early Lunda more fully than the northerners, who adopted male inheritance from their Luba overlords. In the late 19th century Chokwe speakers, expanding northwards once more, conquered Mwata Yamvo. Even then the Southern Lunda were not quite cut off from the old empire of the north, to which they still occasionally paid tribute. The Chokwe expansion covered much of 'Lunda' province of Angola, a region once subject to Mwata Yamvo: there are few Lunda speakers in this province now.

Northern Lunda is naturally influenced by Luba and Chokwe; Southern Lunda shows strong Portuguese influence, even in Zambia, because of continuing migration across frontiers. The first six numerals in Southern Lunda are: *-mu, -yedi, -satu, -wana, -taanu, itaanu naciimu.*

Two genres of Lunda oral literature

'The Southern Lunda fall into about twelve named matriclans, which are dispersed and not localised units. As most of the clan names are also common among Luena [see LUVALE], Chokwe and Luchazi, they were presumably known among the Lunda prior to their emigration. Possessors of the same clan name were formerly forbidden to marry . . .

'Common possession of the clan name implies the obligation to give assistance and hospitality. When a stranger from another village with the same clan name arrives, he quotes his clan name and the clan "formula". The formula consists usually of names of some of the clan progenitors and references to their exploits, and often contains archaic terms.

'*Senseka* is a mutual assistance agreement which holds, not between clans, but between the Ndembu and Akosa groups of Lunda. A member of one, visiting the other, calls them *asense nindi*, while they call him *asense netu*. They have an obligation to offer him hospitality, including a hut, food, and a mat to sleep on, while the *asense netu* has theoretically a right to do almost anything, from committing adultery to mere reviling, without incurring penalties. In practice he will often make outrageous jokes, e.g. with the women, forbidden among the members of the groups concerned.'

Merran McCulloch, *The Southern Lunda and related peoples* (London: International African Institute, 1951) citing work by C. M. N. White, F. H. Melland and J.C. Sakatengo

Northern, Eastern and Southern Lunda

The three groups speak rather different dialects. Northern and Southern Lunda are said to be no longer mutually intelligible.

The 250,000 speakers in Congo (Kinshasa) are divided between Northern, Eastern (*Luwunda*) and Southern Lunda. In Zambia and Angola all but a few speak Southern Lunda.

Northern Lunda is sometimes called *Luunda* or *Ruund*: among Bible translators it was traditionally *Lunda of Kambove*, where the first translators worked. The name *Ndembu* or *kiNdembu*, belonging to a single population group in north-western Zambia, has often been used as an alternative for *Southern Lunda* as a whole. This dialect was

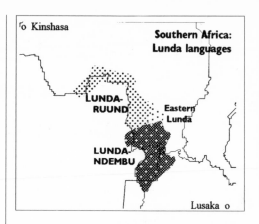

called by translators *Lunda of Kalunda*, after a missionary centre in eastern Angola.

LUO LANGUAGES

PERHAPS 5,800,000 SPEAKERS

Uganda, Kenya, Sudan, Ethiopia, Tanzania

A subdivision of the Western Nilotic group of NILO-SAHARAN LANGUAGES, Luo in its various related forms is spoken by a scattered series of peoples extending from western Ethiopia to the northern extremity of Tanzania. Traditionally, most speakers of Luo languages are cattle herders.

These languages differ from one another largely as a result of their linguistic and social environment – most of them are surrounded by other, quite unrelated languages. Anywa, for example, has borrowed vocabulary from Amharic, English and Oromo. Luo has interacted closely with Luyia, Karamojong (see TURKANA), Swahili and English. Shilluk shows Arabic influence: it is said that Shilluk speech once extended further north towards Khartoum, and has retreated before the advance of Arabic.

There is a press in Lango-Acholi and a small-circulation press in Alur. Anywa is an official language in Ethiopia, and the New Testament has appeared in Anywa in a variant of Ethiopic script.

Luo distinguishes between dental and alveolar consonants (dental *t d* pronounced as in French; alveolar *t d* pronounced as in English). The language has a sing-song sound, with two pitch levels. Among other things, the tone pattern serves to distinguish between the complete and incomplete tenses of verbs. Anywa also has high and low tone, with a similar distinction in verb tenses: *àn ònák kàcì* 'I shall be hungry'; *àn ónàk kàcì* 'I am hungry'. Anywa vowels may be either clear or 'breathy'; in Luo a similar distinction of vowel register is between clear and 'hollow' (on vowel register see box at KHMER).

The first ten numerals in Anywa are: *aciel,*
ariio, adak, angween, abiic, abiciel, abiriio, abara, abingween, apaar. As can be seen, the numeral base is '5': '6' is '5 + 1', and so on.

Shilluk is rich in metaphor. *Adúk góngó lùyì,* 'the grey one going under a pool', is a riddling term for a loaf which is ready to be baked under ashes.

> 'Anywa is spoken with the tongue forward in the mouth. One of the Nilotic customs of this tribe is to remove the lower incisor and canine teeth, and the characteristic position of the tongue at rest is lying against the lower lip in the space vacated by these teeth. This tongue position is difficult for some foreigners to master, and we seem to them to be talking "in our throats".'
>
> Marie Lusted, 'Anywa' in *The non-Semitic languages of Ethiopia* ed. M. L. Bender (East Lansing: African Studies Center, Michigan State University, 1976) pp. 495–512

Names and peoples

Jo Luo, 'Luo people', is the local name of the speakers of Luo, on the Kenyan and Tanzanian coast of Lake Victoria. They are known as *aba-Nyoro*, people of Nyoro, by their neighbours who speak the Bantu language LUYIA. English speakers sometimes called them *Nilotic Kavirondo* in contrast with the Luyia or *Bantu Kavirondo*. *Jo Luo* is also the local name of the speakers of Lwo, near Wau in Sudan: from this phrase derives *Jur*, their name in Arabic and in some English writings.

Jo Anywa is the name that speakers of another

of these languages, in Ethiopia and Sudan, use for themselves. 'They have been much oppressed by the neighboring tribes throughout the years; which has no doubt increased their own solidarity, and their name *anywa*, from *nywak* 'to share', reflects their practice of sharing food and all their belongings with the other members of the group' (M. Lusted, 1976). In Amharic and Oromo they are called *Yambo*, in Nuer and Dinka *Ber*. *Anuak* is an alternative English form.

Shilluk comes from an Arabic adaptation of *Colo*, the name that the Shilluk give to themselves.

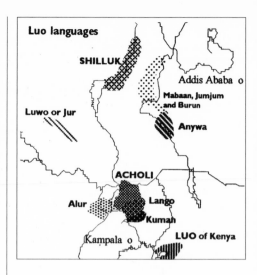

Luo, Shilluk and their relatives

Mabaan, *Jumjum* and *Burun*, with possibly 75,000 speakers, are to be found in the plains of Dar Fung, in Sudan, between the two branches of the Nile.

Shilluk of Sudan has roughly 175,000 speakers, largely surrounded by territories where DINKA is spoken.

Luwo or Jur of Sudan has 50,000 speakers.

Anywa or Anuak of Ethiopia and Sudan has perhaps 66,000 speakers (an estimate by M. L. Bender). There are four dialects, *Adongo*, *Ciro*, *Lul* and *Opëno*, all close enough to be mutually intelligible without difficulty. Some speakers consider Adongo to be 'good Anywa', the best dialect.

Acholi, with 700,000 speakers, *Lango*, with 800,000, *Kuman*, with 150,000, and *Alur* form the central group of Luo languages. The first three are all spoken in northern Uganda; Acholi extends into Sudan. Alur is spoken in Congo (Kinshasa) and Uganda by roughly 800,000 people. These four are sometimes regarded as a single language, *Lwo*.

Luo (sometimes distinguished as 'Luo of Kenya') has about 3,000,000 speakers in Kenya and 200,000 in Tanzania.

LURI

PERHAPS 4,000,000 SPEAKERS

Southern Iran

Luri is one of the IRANIAN LANGUAGES, spoken by a mainly nomadic people in south-western Iran.

The mountain peoples of Luristan have a long history of fierce independence. Alexander the Great was among the many military leaders who have found themselves in danger in these mountains. 19th- and early 20th-century travellers tell of adventures and dangers in Luristan. Surprisingly little up-to-date information is to be found. The government of modern Iran is gradually imposing subjection and conformity on Luristan, and Luri is now heavily influenced by Persian, the national language. It is also full of Arabic loanwords. Mongolian loans include *tushmāl* 'chief of a clan'; *kūrän* 'encampment'.

'Down to the beginning of the 20th century, our knowledge of the Lur dialects was confined to 88 words collected by Rich, to four Bakhtiyari verses in Layard [*Description of Khuzistan*] and to some thirty words collected by Houtum-Schindler. As late as 1901 we find the thesis stated that Luri is closely related to Kurdish and may even be described as one of its dialects. The merit of having first established the important fact that Kurdish and Luri are quite separate is due to O. Mann. Although there are Kurd tribes in Luristan, the true Lurs speak dialects which belong to the south-western Iranian group, like Persian and the dialects of Fars' (V. Minorsky, 'Lur' in *Encyclopaedia of Islam*, 2nd edn, vol. 5 (Leiden: Brill, 1986) pp. 821–6).

Luri is an unwritten language, but there is a rich oral literature. Some has been published, notably from the Bakhtiari dialect. There are fairy stories, love songs, wedding songs (*wāsī-nak*), lullabies (*lālā'ī*) and epic poetry celebrating semi-legendary heroes.

For a table of numerals see KURDISH.

The Lurs in 1932

'The handsomest people in Baghdad are the Lurs of Pusht-i-Kuh. They stride about among the sallow-faced city Shi'as in sturdy nakedness, a sash round the waist keeping their rags together, a thick felt padded affair on their backs to carry loads, and their native felt cap surrounded by a wisp of turban. They . . . sleep in the shade on the pavement, careless of the traffic around them, and speaking their own language among themselves: and you will think them the veriest beggars, until one day you happen to see them shaved and washed and in their holiday clothes, and hear that they belong to this tribe or that tribe in the mountainous region that touches Iraq's eastern border, and find that they are as proud, and have as much influence in their own lonely districts, as any member of a county family in his. They own three hostels, or "manzils", in Baghdad . . .

'Once a year the Lurs of Pusht-i-Kuh who work in the Baghdad custom house give a theatrical performance and show to a small audience the life and traditions of their province. There are bandits in white, with faces [covered] all except the eyes . . . there are songs on the high sobbing note like yodelling of the Alps.'

Freya Stark, *The valleys of the Assassins* (London, John Murray, 1934)

Languages of southern Iran

Luri or *Lori* is spoken in the regions of Fars, Khuzestan and Ispahan. The *Great Lur* dialects are those of Fars, the *Little Lur* those of Khurramabad.

Bakhtiari, the best-known Great Lur dialect, is spoken by as many as 650,000 seasonal nomads who occupy Bakhtiari and Ispahan in the summer and Khuzestan in the winter.

In the province of Fars several other dialects are spoken in enclaves surrounded by Persian. They have been called – confusingly – *Tajiki* dialects.

The old languages of the southern Persian cities are lost, supplanted by Persian, except for the dialects of the Jews of Ispahan, Yazd and Kerman and those of the Zoroastrians of Yazd and Kerman.

To the south-east, *Larestani* or *Lari* and the dialects of Bashakerd (*Bashkardi*) are also wholly

Languages of Southern Iran

distinct from Persian. There is no clear information on the number of speakers of these dialects.

Kumzari is an Iranian dialect spoken at the tip of the Musandam Peninsula in northern Oman.

Bakhtiari couplet

Khīnum chi āu gulōu zi gar tukiste,	My blood like rosewater flowed from the mountains;
heme jūnum tash girih, dabem pukiste.	Fire seized my soul; my powder-flask is broken.

After I. M. Oranskij, *Les langues iraniennes* (Paris: Klincksieck, 1977) pp. 144–6

LUVALE

600,000 SPEAKERS

Angola, Zambia, Congo (Kinshasa)

One of the BANTU LANGUAGES, Luvale is spoken around the headwaters of the River Zambezi (see map at CHOKWE). As a result of colonial partition, Luvale speakers are split between the North-western province of Zambia and Móxico province of Angola, with a smaller number further north in Shaba province, Congo (Kinshasa).

Luvale and *Lovale* are the names used in Zambia for this language; its own speakers call themselves *vaLuvale* and their language *chiLuvale*. Balovale Province is named after them. In Angola the language is called *Luena* or *siLuena* and the people *vaLuena*.

The Luvale language and people, like the closely related Southern Lunda and Chokwe, whose territories lie to the east and north-east, have a traditional origin in the LUNDA empire of Mwata Yamvo. As this empire spread its rule southwards, in the 16th and 17th centuries, it is said that Lunda invaders mixed with longer-established inhabitants, speakers of Mbwela.

But Mbwela, Luvale and Chokwe are more closely related to one another than they are to Lunda, so the invaders may in truth have had little linguistic influence.

Many Luvale speakers keep cattle and grow cassava. They are known outside their own territory as traders in these products – and as brothel-keepers. Others live by fishing and hunting. Those initiated into these skills are given a second name, a 'hunter's name', to be used when they are on an expedition.

Luvale is used as a second language by some speakers of Southern Lunda and CHOKWE. Luvale is also a close relative of the Luyi language once spoken by the LOZI, and still used by a small number of speakers immediately to the south on the Upper Zambezi. It is one of the eight official languages of Zambia.

The first ten numerals in Luvale are: *-mwe, -vali, -tatu, -wana, -tanu, -tanu na -mwe, -tanu na -vali, -tanu na -tatu, -tanu na -wana, likumi*. The correct noun class prefix, singular or plural, is inserted at each hyphen.

LUXEMBURGISH

300,000 SPEAKERS

Luxembourg

The Grand Duchy of Luxembourg is one of the smallest independent states in Europe. It has a long history, going back at least to the 10th century, when Luxembourg was a feudal province of the 'Holy Roman Empire' of Germany. In later centuries the state belonged to Burgundy, to Germany, to the Spanish Netherlands, and to newly independent Belgium. In 1839 Luxembourg was divided from north to south: the western half, mostly French-speaking, became the Belgian province of Luxembourg, while the eastern became fully independent.

Luxembourg is now a trilingual state. French is the language of government; German is the language of business and of the press. But nearly all the people of Luxembourg speak another language at home: this is *Letzeburgisch*, 'Luxemburgish', a local dialect of German which has – quite recently – been recognised as the third official language. Children study all three at school, and Luxemburgish is heard alongside German and French on radio and television.

Scholars have traced the Luxemburgish dialect, or something very close to it, a thousand years back in occasional written documents. But there is only a limited literature in modern Luxemburgish, mostly 'folk' poetry. After the Second World War there was a local movement to drop Standard German entirely and to make Luxemburgish the main official language. A new spelling system was invented: *Letzeburgisch* was to become *Lezebuurjesh*. Nobody took any notice.

For a table of numerals see GERMAN.

LUYIA

3,750,000 SPEAKERS

Kenya, Uganda

Luyia or Luhya forms a generally accepted grouping of BANTU LANGUAGES of western Kenya. They are the dialects of the region once called 'Bantu Kavirondo' and now buLuyia; their speakers may be called abaLuyia, and form the third largest language community in Kenya.

The early history of these languages is unknown. Oral tradition tells of settlement in this region only in the 15th century by peoples who had migrated over great distances, yet buLuyia is actually close to a very early centre of Bantu dispersion. There has been interaction with speakers of the neighbouring Nilo-Saharan languages LUO and KALENJIN, most noticeable in the Nyore, Logooli, Isukha, Idakho and Tiriki dialects: among these communities some clans are historically Kalenjin. It was shortly after 1900 that Luyia-speaking territory came under British rule.

Luyia dialects are rich in folk-tales and legends, and narrative skill was traditionally much admired. Songs are incorporated at fixed points in the oral narratives.

In the early 20th century Christian missionaries began to write religious texts and Bible translations in several of these dialects. The Friends' African Mission was established at Kaimosi in 1902, and its home dialects were Logooli and Tiriki. The Church Missionary Society began work in 1912 and developed a unified dialect based on Wanga, Marama, Kisa and Tsotso, with elements of Samia and Khayo: this new literary form of Luyia was named luHanga. The Church of God worked in Nyore. The Roman Catholic missionaries used Wanga, Isukha, Bukusu and other dialects. The 'Lumasaba' or Gisu dialect was used by missionaries in Uganda, who began

work with this 'cannibal tribe' (as local rumour described it) in 1899. The first grammar appeared in 1904.

The newly written dialects were so close to one another that in the 1930s some missionaries, particularly of the Church Missionary Society, pressed for the adoption of a unified literary Luyia which could be used by all (or at least all in Kenya). But the dialects corresponded closely with local administrative divisions and had firm support among speakers: although mutually intelligible, they had distinctive local features which were already enshrined in writing. Much work was put in on Standard Luyia from 1942 for about twenty years, notably by a missionary linguist, Deaconess L. L. Appleby. However, two major dialect districts, Bukusu and Logooli-Tiriki, never accepted the proposed standard; elsewhere enthusiasm gradually waned, and schools never adopted Standard Luyia.

GANDA is the lingua franca for Gisu speakers in Uganda: their everyday speech includes Ganda loanwords as well as many from Swahili and

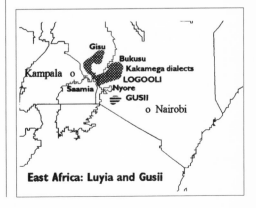

East Africa: Luyia and Gusii

English. Swahili is the language of religious education in the many Islamic schools of buGisu.

Based on P. A. N. Itebete, 'Language standardization in western Kenya' in *Language in Kenya* ed. W. H. Whiteley (Nairobi: Oxford University Press, 1974) xpp. 87–114 and other sources

The Luyia dialects and Gusii

Logooli or Maragoli is the southern dialect, and one that is often regarded as a separate language. Close to it, and mutually almost indistinguishable, are the three eastern or Kakamega dialects, *Isukha* (or Besukha), *Idakho* (or Bedakho) and *Tiriki*. Together these four have 500,000 speakers.

Nyore and *Saamia*, with their separate written traditions, are occasionally counted apart from the other central Luyia dialects.

The remaining central dialects are Nyala, Khayo, Wanga, Tachoni, Kabras, Tsotso, Marama and Kisa. The central dialects have 3,750,000 speakers.

The northern dialects of Luyia are *Bukusu* or Vugusu of Kenya (once called baKitosh) and *Gisu* or Kisu or Masaba of Uganda. Together these dialects have about 1,000,000 speakers. Although *luMasaaba* is often used as a name for the Gisu language, the term *baMasaaba* really means 'people of Mount Elgon' – which is called *Masaaba* locally – and thus includes the speakers of Sebei, a Nilo-Saharan language related to KALENJIN.

GUSII, another Bantu language of Kenya, is sometimes considered very closely related to Luyia and particularly to Logooli.

Numerals in Logooli and Isukha		
Logooli		**Isukha**
-ala	1	-ala
-bili	2	-bili
-bhaga	3	-bhaka
-ne	4	-ne
-tano	5	-rano
sita	6	sita
saba	7	saba
munane	8	munane
tisa	9	tisa
kumi	10	khumi

As in many other Bantu languages, a noun class prefix is added to the numerals '1' to '5'. Numerals above '10' are borrowed from Swahili.

R. A. Kanyoro, *Unity in diversity: a linguistic survey of the Abaluyia of western Kenya* (Vienna, 1983) p. 118

Three Luyia written languages

The written language in most of the dialect areas was that of the dialect in which the first materials had been written by the mission which was operating in that area – and not necessarily that of the area itself. In a dialect area which was under the influence of two or more missions, then two or more written forms of the language co-existed. In Bwisukha the Catholics, Friends' African Mission and Church of God operated:

The Son of God took on a human body

Friends' African Mission Logooli form Mwana wa Nyasaye yavugula muvili gu mundu

Catholic Isukha form Mwana wa Nasayi yabukula mubili ku mundu

Church of God Nyore form Omwana wa Nyasaye yabukula omubili kw'omundu

Example from P. A. N. Itebete (1974)

MABA

PERHAPS 300,000 SPEAKERS

Chad

Maba is one of a small group of NILO-SAHARAN LANGUAGES only distantly related to the rest. All are spoken in the highlands of eastern Chad and south-western Sudan (see map at KANURI). It is called by its speakers *Bura Mabang*.

Historically Maba is the most important of its group because it was the language of the Islamic state of Wadai, founded by a certain Abd al-Karim in the 17th century. From their old capital of Wara and their later capital Abéché, the Wadai rulers encouraged trade and Islamic culture. Maba, language of the ruling class, and Arabic, language of religion, were the two lingua francas of this remote empire. Later, when the Empire of Bornu reduced Wadai to vassal status, KANURI became a third language of power there.

Maba is still widely known in south-eastern Chad and in the neighbouring borderlands of Sudan.

The first ten numerals in Maba are: *tek, bar, kungāl, asāl, tor, settāl, mindrī, īya, adoī, atuk*.

MACEDONIAN

2,250,000 SPEAKERS

Macedonia, Bulgaria, Greece

Macedonian was the last of the SLAVONIC LAN-GUAGES to gain official recognition – in 1944, when Yugoslavia was reconstituted as a federal republic. Macedonian dialects form part of the South Slavonic continuum that extends from Bulgarian to Slovene. Standard Macedonian is now the language of the independent Republic of Macedonia. It is written in the Cyrillic alphabet.

Macedonia (*Makedoniya*) takes its name from the ancient kingdom ruled in the 4th century BC by Philip II and his son Alexander the Great. The early core of this kingdom fell within the borders of modern Greece, but later conquests took in much of the valley of the River Axios or Vardar, thus partly coinciding with the modern Republic of Macedonia. Slavonic speakers settled here in early medieval times. Until the 20th century their language was usually called Bulgarian.

OLD SLAVONIC, the language of the religious texts through which Christianity spread among Slavonic speakers, was actually based on the Slavonic dialect spoken in the 9th century in Macedonia, in the country near Saloniki. Thus modern Macedonian may be regarded as today's nearest relative of the classical language of the Slavs. Ironically, it was the last of the modern Slavonic languages to develop a literary form.

In the valley of the Vardar, until the beginning of the 20th century, there were three languages of culture. Turkish ruled, for this was part of the Turkish Empire till 1912. Church Slavonic was used in religion. Greek was the language of Christian education. Also spoken were Albanian, Aromunian, Romani and – the language of the

majority – Macedonian. There was a great corpus of oral poetry in Macedonian, and in the 19th century some poetry was printed, but a movement to foster the local language in education and culture was slow to develop.

In 1912 the territory where Macedonian was spoken was split between Yugoslavia, Bulgaria and Greece. The national languages, Serbian, Bulgarian and Greek, were imposed in education and administration.

In spite of temporary shifts in policy Macedonian remains out of favour in Bulgaria and Greece. The minority in Greece numbers almost 200,000. In Bulgaria, speakers are officially regarded as Bulgarian and no census figures are available. However, the great majority of Macedonian speakers, in Macedonia itself, have since 1944 been able to regard their language as a fully fledged medium of national communication.

The Western dialects of Macedonian, spoken over most of the Republic of Macedonia itself (for map see SERBIAN), are the basis of the standard language. They have the unusual feature of not one but three definite articles – all suffixed to the noun, as in other Balkan languages – to indicate distance from the speaker: *vol* 'ox', *volot* 'the ox', *volov* 'the ox here', *volon* 'the ox there'. For a table of numerals see SLOVENE.

Ancient Macedonian

Little is known of the language of ancient Macedonia. The royal family spoke Greek – the elite language of the whole region – and patronised Greek culture. Their official genealogy traced their descent from Greek heroes. *Alexandros* and *Philippos* are actually Greek names. But plenty of

Macedonian rulers and military figures had non-Greek names, and Greek never spread widely among the ordinary people of Macedonia. Alexander's Macedonian troops got their commands in 'Macedonian', and some words of this language survive in Greek historical texts and glossaries.

Macedonia was annexed by the Roman Republic in the 2nd century BC. Ancient Macedonian was eventually supplanted by Latin, and it has no connection with modern Macedonian.

The political ideology of modern Greece sets store by its ancient heritage. The view accepted by most Greek historians is that Philip and his family 'were Greek' (after all, they spoke Greek) and that, in any case, ancient Macedonian was a form of Greek. In fact the recognised ancient Greek dialects, such as Doric, Ionic and Aeolic, were already so different from one another that, looking only at their forms and setting aside their cultural interconnections, modern linguists might well have defined them as separate languages. Macedonian was very different again from any of these. Many scholars outside Greece prefer to say that it was Indo-European (like other languages of the ancient Balkans) but not Greek.

MADURESE

9,000,000 SPEAKERS

Indonesia

Madurese is one of the AUSTRONESIAN LAN-GUAGES, spoken on the island of Madura, north-east of Java, and on nearby smaller islands.

It is usually said to be very close linguistically to Javanese. Linguists have disputed the precise relationships among the languages of the Greater Sunda Islands. What is in no doubt is the long history of mutual interaction between Javanese and Madurese. They share many aspects of culture – including the traditional script or *aksara*, ultimately of Indian origin, and the separate 'formal' and 'informal' registers of normal speech. Within the formal register, speakers mark, by the choice of a whole range of words, the relative social status of themselves and their hearers. The words of the formal register are almost all borrowed from Javanese. The same is true in Balinese, incidentally, and it indicates that the social levels so carefully distinguished were learnt, by speakers of both languages, from speakers of Javanese.

Apart from these loanwords Madurese has borrowed quite extensively from Malay, as well as from Arabic and Dutch.

Madurese is now written in the Latin alphabet, as used for Indonesian, more often than in the old script. The first ten numerals in Madurese are: *settong, dhuwa, tello, empa, lema, ennem, petto, ballo, sanga, sapolo*. For a script table and a map see JAVANESE.

MAGAHI

PERHAPS 20,000,000 SPEAKERS

India

The three INDO-ARYAN LANGUAGES of Bihar, Bhojpuri, Maithili and Magahi, are often thought of as dialects of HINDI (see map there). No statistics are available: the census reports this language as 'Hindi'. Yet in many ways it is closer to Bengali, its eastern neighbour. For a table of numerals see MAITHILI.

Magahi is spoken in the southern half of Bihar, and extends across the border of West Bengal and Orissa, where the Eastern Magahi dialect (*Pañcparganiyā* 'of the five districts') shows Bengali and Mundari influence. If a standard Magahi can be recognised, it is that of the cities of Patna and Gaya.

There is no real tradition of written literature in modern Magahi. Educated speakers will tend to incorporate Hindi words and turns of phrase in their speech, and to use standard Hindi on formal occasions.

For a table of numerals see MAITHILI.

Magadha has been the name of this region for over two thousand years, and gave its name to *Magadhī*, one of the Prakrit dialects of ancient India. This is regarded as the linguistic ancestor of six modern languages – Bengali, Assamese, Oriya and the three languages of Bihar. A typical sound change of Magadhī was the shift of *dh* to *h*, of which the modern language name itself provides an example.

MAGINDANAO

1,000,000 SPEAKERS

Philippines

The Danao languages – Magindanao, Iranun and Maranao – are spoken in south-western Mindanao, in the Philippines. All three are languages of Muslim peoples; together, their speakers make up the largest Muslim community in the Philippines.

The history of these peoples is traced in the 19th-century *tarsilas*, manuscripts containing genealogies that go back five hundred years to the arrival of Islamic proselytisers in Mindanao. Even then, it seems, there were three adjacent peoples here, linked by trade relations through the speakers of Iranun, who were perhaps always the intermediaries, and whose dialect shows the influence of both the others.

The first ten numerals in Magindanao are: *sa, dua, talu, pat, lima, nɪm, pitu, walu, siaw, sa-pulu*. In Maranao '1' is *isa* and '10' is *sa-wati*. In Iranun '3' is *tulu*.

The Philippines: Danao languages

The Danao languages

Magindanao, with 1,000,000 speakers, is the language of the Pulangi river basin, often inundated – hence their name, which appears to mean 'liable to flood'. It was originally the name of a town founded by the Iranun at the site of modern Cotabato City.

Iranun or Ilanun is spoken on the coast of Illana Bay and to some distance inland. There is an émigré community of Iranun speakers in Sabah, Malaysia.

Maranao has 600,000 speakers around Lake Lanao. The name means 'lake people'.

MAITHILI

PERHAPS 22,000,000 SPEAKERS

India, Nepal

Like its neighbours Bhojpuri and Magahi, Maithili is one of the INDO-ARYAN LANGUAGES, and is sometimes regarded as a dialect of HINDI (see map there). Many speakers call their language Hindi, and Hindi is the usual language of education and literature.

Maithili is spoken in the northern half of the Indian state of Bihar and across the border into Nepal, where it is the second most widely spoken language of the country. Maithili was first recognised as a separate language in G. A. Grierson's *An introduction to the Maithilī language of North Bihār* (1881–2).

The name is a recent invention derived from *Mithilā*, a semi-legendary city and kingdom of classical Sanskrit literature. The term *Bihari* has been used (for example, in the *Linguistic survey of India*) to cover all three languages, Maithili, Magahi and Bhojpuri. There is, however, no particular reason to treat them as one.

Indo-Aryan speakers are thought to have been already dominant in Mithilā by the 6th century BC – the time of the Buddha, who lived and preached here. In succession to SANSKRIT and Magadhī Prakrit, *Avahattha*, a mixed language containing Apabhramsa and Maithili elements, was once used for literature. The oldest literary text in an identifiable Maithili is the 14th-century *Var ṇa-ratnākara*, 'a sort of lexicon of vernacular and Sanskrit terms, a repository of literary similes and conventions dealing with the various things in the world and ideas which are usually treated in poetry' (S. K. Chatterji).

Maithili was once written in *mithilakṣar* script, resembling that of medieval Bengal; it is still in use in some religious contexts. The language is nowadays normally written in Devanagari script, like Hindi. Like Bengali to the east, Maithili has lost the gender distinction in nouns (though local grammars, under Hindi and Sanskrit influence, still claim to distinguish masculine and feminine genders). Its vocabulary shows the influence of the Austroasiatic language SANTALI, which is spoken in the southern hills.

Numerals in Bhojpuri, Maithili and Magahi

	Bhojpuri	Maithili	Magahi
1	ēk	ekə	ek
2	dūi	dui	dū
3	tīni	tini	tīn
4	cāri	cari	cār
5	pāñc	pañcə	pāñc
6	chav	chɔɔ	chau
7	sāt	satə	sāt
8	āth	aṭhə	āṭh
9	nav	nɔɔ	nau
10	das	dəsə	das

MAKASAR

1,600,000 SPEAKERS

Indonesia

Makasar, one of the AUSTRONESIAN LAN-GUAGES, is the language of the old Sultanate of Gowa, at the south-western tip of Sulawesi (Celebes). The city of Ujungpandang, near old Makassar, is still an important stopping place on the sea routes among the islands of Indonesia.

Makasar traders have been long distance travellers. Makasar words have been identified in AUSTRALIAN LANGUAGES, evidence of contacts established before Europeans began to explore Australia. Ujungpadang remains a multiethnic market centre, used by numerous speakers of Chinese, Malay and the many local languages of Sulawesi. Makasar remains the lingua franca of the city. Fishing is a source of wealth here: in the countryside rice is grown in the irrigated fields of the coastal strip.

Makasar is one of a group of related dialects, all spoken in south-western Sulawesi. Its neighbour BUGIS (see map and table of numerals there) stands somewhat apart linguistically; Mandar, to the north-west, belongs to a third subgroup. In

all three languages there is a traditional literature of epic tales and chronicles, recorded in Lontara script, retelling the adventurous history of the small kingdoms of Sulawesi.

Lontara script

Lontara script, originating like so many others from the Brahmi alphabet of ancient India, has been the traditional form of writing for Buginese, Makasarese and Mandar. In Bugis it was once used for laws, treaties, trading contracts and maps, but is now confined to purely ceremonial uses – it can be seen in use at marriage ceremonies, for example. In Makasar, however, the script is still used by young and old, for such things as personal letters and students' notes, though officially the Latin alphabet, as used for Indonesian, is favoured.

Lontar is the Malay name of the palmyra palm, whose leaves are traditionally used for manuscripts in India, south-east Asia and Indonesia.

The Lontara script

ka ga nga nka pa ba ma mpa ta da na nra ya ra la wa sa a ha

MAKONDE

1,100,000 SPEAKERS

Tanzania, Mozambique

Makonde is spoken in south-eastern Tanzania, along the Ruvuma river, and also on the northern edge of Mozambique (for map see MAKUA). Its speakers are traditionally farmers, growing maize and sorghum on the dry but fertile plateaus of the region. They also sold rubber, gum-copal and ivory at the market of Mikindani, an important slaving port. They suffered repeatedly from slave raids and invasions in the 19th century, until the Sultan of Zanzibar established peace in 1876.

The Makonde of Tanganyika joined in the unsuccessful Majimaji rebellion against the invading Germans in 1905. Makonde is now the second largest regional language of Tanzania. The Makonde of Mozambique were among the staunchest fighters for the liberation movement of the 1960s led by Frelimo.

Speakers call their language *chiMákonde*. The Portuguese spelling is *Maconde*.

Like some other BANTU LANGUAGES of the Tanzanian coast, Makonde has word stress instead of the tones that are such a prominent feature in most languages of the family. It shows Swahili influence – though its speakers, unlike some of their neighbours, have not adopted Islam.

In turn, *kiMwani*, a local form of Swahili spoken on the coast of northern Mozambique, is much influenced by Makonde.

The secret songs

'The girls' initiation is called *ciputu*. The girls of a village are initiated together; they are taken to the bush by a chief instructress, each girl assisted by a sponsor [a sister, aunt or friend]. Each mother, when she comes to take her daughter home, receives a burning brand from a fire which has previously been carried round the village in procession. With this she lights new fire in her hut. After the initiation each girl is semi-secluded for a month. At the end of the time there is a reunion in the *ciputu* house, the girls are bathed and taught secret songs; beer is brewed for the sponsors, and when the sponsors are finally paid they reveal the meaning of the secret songs.'

Mary Tew, *Peoples of the Lake Nyasa region* (London: Oxford University Press, 1950) pp. 28–9

Two Makonde riddles

Kunchuma nchagwa wangu ku Ñambela, ndila kupita alila – 'I bought a slave in Tanganyika: he walked along crying': the bells on a dancer's costume.

Chindjidi nkanywa mene kulova – 'What goes into the mouth does not get chewed': tobacco smoke.

M. Viegas Guerreiro, *Os Macondes de Moçambique*, vol. 4 (Lisbon: Junta de Investigações do Ultramar, 1966) p. 328

MAKUA

3,500,000 SPEAKERS

Mozambique, Malawi, Tanzania

Makua or *eMakua* is a major language of northern Mozambique, and serves as a lingua franca for speakers of minority languages in its neighbourhood. It is one of the BANTU LANGUAGES.

Traditionally a farming people, Makua speakers controlled trade routes between the southern end of Lake Nyasa and the Indian Ocean. They dealt with Swahili and Gujarati traders at the coast: their stock was groundnuts, sesame seeds, castor-oil seeds and maize, and they were prominent in the slave trade. Those living near the coast adopted Islam under Swahili influence.

Makua and its relatives

One subgroup of the Bantu languages of Mozambique consists of Makua with LOMWE (2,000,000 speakers, half in Mozambique, half in Malawi) and *Chwabo* or Cuabo (650,000).

A neighbouring group, not quite so closely related, consists of MAKONDE (1,100,000 speakers,

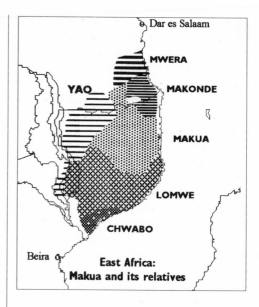

East Africa:
Makua and its relatives

Tanzania and Mozambique) with *Mwera* (350,000, Tanzania) and YAO (1,200,000 in Malawi, Tanzania and Mozambique).

MALAGASY

10,000,000 SPEAKERS

Madagascar

Malagasy is the national language of Madagascar. The geographically unexpected link between it and the AUSTRONESIAN LANGUAGES was noted as long ago as the 18th century.

Linguistic comparison has now shown beyond a doubt that Malagasy is a language of the otherwise obscure South-east Barito group: its linguistic relatives are thus to be found in a region of southern Kalimantan (Borneo) in Indonesia. It is not clear when or why migrants from this area colonised the great island of Madagascar, but this is what must have happened. Otto Christian Dahl, who demonstrated the link in 1951, suggested that Madagascar was colonised by traders from the Hindu kingdom of southern Borneo around the 4th century AD.

Certainly Malagasy now shows the influence of Malay, Javanese and Sanskrit, evidence of early involvement in the developed culture of the Indonesian islands. Easily traceable, too, are loanwords from Swahili and Arabic – the trading languages of the East African coast – Ngazija of Grande Comore, French of the former colonial rulers of Madagascar, and English of the pirates whose headquarters it was in the 18th century. Loanwords include *dité* 'tea' from French *du thé* 'some tea'; *mompera* 'priest' from French *mon père* 'my father', used in addressing Catholic priests.

Written literature in Malagasy goes back to the 15th century, when the Arabic *ajami* script was used for astrological and magical texts. In 1823 King Ramada I decreed that the Latin alphabet should be used, and Christian missionaries set to work on translations from the Bible.

Malagasy has a complex system of personal and demonstrative pronouns, varying with the distance between the speaker and the person or thing denoted. The first ten numerals in Malagasy are: *iray, roa, telo, efatra, dimy, enina, fito, valo, sivy, folo.*

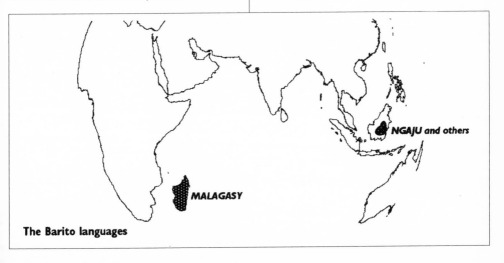

NGAJU and others

MALAGASY

The Barito languages

Place names of Madagascar

Malagasy forms long compound words easily. Nouns referring to a place are prefixed *an-*. These two facts explain the striking form of many names on the map of Madagascar. The capital city, *Tananarive* in French, is more correctly called *Antananarivo*, 'the village of a thousand'.

Malagasy and the Barito languages

Merina 'the high people', dialect of the central highlands, is the basis of standard Malagasy. There has been controversy over the grouping of other dialects, but *Sakalava*, of the west coast, is also important.

The Barito languages of Kalimantan include several small language communities – and *Ngaju* or Land Dayak, which has a quarter of a million speakers: see also box at IBAN.

Ibonia: epic hero of Madagascar

Hoy Iboniamasoboniamanoro:
'Izaho no taranaky ny omby mahery.
Raha tezitra aho
sokina an-tampon-doha,
mitraka aho vaky ny lanitra,
miondrika aho vaky ny tany,
hitsahiko ny hazo mibaraingo,
hitsahiko ny tany mitriatra,
hitsahiko ny tanitra manao vara-maina.'

He of the clear and captivating glance said:
'I am the descendant of powerful bulls.
When I am angry
The top of my head bristles,
When I raise my head the sky bursts open,
When I bend the earth bursts open,
When I trample on trees they twist,
When I trample on the earth it splits,
When I trample on the sky it thunders.'

The Merina people of inland Madagascar have rich historical and poetic traditions. The 'Royal histories of the Merina', *Tantaran'ny Andriana*, collected by François Callet in 1864, are said to be the most comprehensive oral history ever collected in any part of Africa.

Many tales and poems cluster around the figure of Ibonia. The epic of Ibonia, collected and published by the Norwegian missionary Lars Dahle in 1877, is the undisputed classic of Malagasy literature. The text quoted here is from a shorter folk poem, *hainteny*, which alludes to the epic hero.

Ibonia tr. Lee Haring (Lewisburg: Bucknell University Press, 1994); text from Jean Paulhan, *Les hain-teny merinas* (Paris: Geuthner, 1913) pp. 268–9; translation from Leonard Fox, *Hainteny: the traditional poetry of Madagascar* (Lewisburg: Bucknell University Press, 1990) p. 215

MALAY, INDONESIAN AND MALAYSIAN

PERHAPS 35,000,000 SPEAKERS

Indonesia, Malaysia, Singapore, Brunei, Thailand

For at least a thousand years Malay has been the principal lingua franca of 'insular southeast Asia', of the great Malay Archipelago which is now politically divided between Indonesia and Malaysia.

The lands on either side of the Straits of Malacca have been called the Malay country for all this time. The origin of the name is uncertain, though it may possibly come from a Dravidian word by way of Sanskrit *Malaya* 'mountain'. Malay is locally known as *bahasa Melayu* 'Malay language' (*bahasa* deriving from Sanskrit *bhāṣah* 'language'); its speakers are *orang Melayu* 'Malay people'.

For the designated national language of independent Indonesia the old name, redolent of the British-controlled Malay peninsula, was thought inappropriate. So this form of Malay is called *bahasa Indonesia* 'Indonesian language', a term introduced around 1930. In due course independent Malaysia followed suit with *bahasa Malaysia* 'Malaysian language'. *Malay* is still a term that we cannot do without – for Singapore and Brunei, and for the many regional and non-standard varieties of the language.

Malay is one of several related AUSTRONESIAN LANGUAGES that originate in the arc between western Sumatra and eastern Borneo: they are now believed to have come here, three thousand years ago or more, as the result of gradual, prehistoric migration from the Philippines, and ultimately from Taiwan.

Two other members of the group are MINANGKABAU and IBAN. These two, also, have spread as vehicles of trade and water travel – but Malay itself, from its early homeland on either side of the Straits of Malacca, has spread much further.

Old Malay is first recorded in the early inscriptions of the kingdom of Śrīvijaya. They are found near Palembang in southern Sumatra and on the nearby island of Bangka, and are dated to 683–6. Later inscriptions come also from the Malay peninsula, just across the straits. Singapore's history might have begun with a 12th-century inscription – but the British, frightened that it would excite anti-colonial feeling, destroyed it before it had been deciphered. By the 12th century 'Malaya' – perhaps the same kingdom, under a different name – was well known to Arabic and Chinese travellers, from whom even Marco Polo heard of it. Its language had certainly already become a lingua franca of trade in the archipelago. In a different form, 'Classical Malay', it was to be a language of literature, rich in historical texts.

In the Malay peninsula the great trading city of Malacca, founded in 1403, was briefly dominant throughout the region. It retained some importance even when ruled by European powers, successively Portuguese, Dutch and British. In Java the old capital of Jakarta fell to the Dutch in 1619 and for more than three centuries was renamed *Batavia* after a Latin name sometimes used for the Netherlands. It was in the early 19th century that the British made inroads into Dutch influence in the archi-

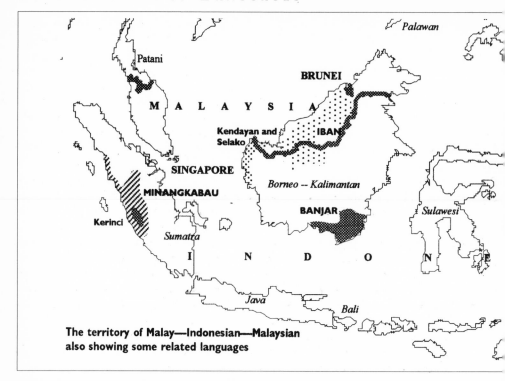

The territory of Malay—Indonesian—Malaysian also showing some related languages

pelago. The position of both colonial powers was undermined by Japanese occupation in the early 1940s. Indonesia became independent in 1945 and Malaysia in 1957. Thus the long term result of British–Dutch competition is the modern divide between Malaysia, formerly a group of British territories and protectorates, and Indonesia, formerly the Dutch East Indies.

Malay, in slightly different forms, became the national language of both states.

In Malaysia it is the majority language, though there is also a large Chinese-speaking population and some significant indigenous linguistic minorities. In Indonesia the number of regional and local languages is very large indeed. Javanese is actually the largest linguistic community, but Malay, or rather *bahasa Indonesia*, is the only language with the potential to draw the country together, a potential that has been energetically tapped by the resolutely nationalistic policies of Indonesian governments.

The Śrīvijaya inscriptions are in an Indian script. With the arrival of Islam, Arabic (*jawi*) script was being used for Malay by the 14th

century. Under British and Dutch influence Latin script has now become standard.

Malay at the crossroads

Malay is a spectrum of many dialects and registers. There are the formal, official languages of Indonesia, Malaysia and Brunei; the varieties used in the press, broadcasting, schools and religion in these three countries and in Singapore; the everyday colloquial of great cities including Kuala Lumpur and Jakarta (whose local speech is sometimes called *Batawi*); the lingua franca used in towns and markets by people with different mother tongues, *Bazaar Malay*; the local speech of scattered trading ports and colonies, most of them bilingual, from *Ambon Malay* to *Sri Lankan Creole Malay* (which alone has 50,000 speakers); major regional varieties including *Banjar* of eastern Kalimantan and *Patani Malay* of southern Thailand; local varieties spoken by peoples far from the mainstream of Malay culture, including the 'aboriginal' Malay of inland districts of the Malay peninsula. Tin-

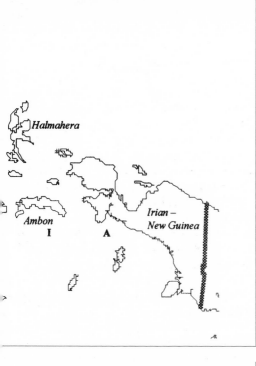

Halmahera

Ambon
I

Irian –
New Guinea

A

tic language, cf. Khmer *ktam*, Mon *gatam*. *Pasar* 'market' comes from Persian *bāzār*, which has been borrowed into many languages of the world. A 'fair' is picturesquely called *pasar malam*, 'night market', in Malay. The black market is *pasar gelap*, 'dark market'.

Local forms of Malay have other loanwords. In Larantuka Malay *nyora* 'woman' comes from Portuguese *senhora;* *om* 'uncle' comes from Dutch *oom*.

As the one essential language for trade and administration in the archipelago, Malay has contributed many loanwords to English. They include *compound*, which with the meaning of 'yard, enclosure' comes from Malay *kampong* 'enclosure, quarter of a city'; *gong; rattan; sago; orang utan*, literally 'people of the forest'.

The Malayic languages

Standard MINANGKABAU is based on the dialect of Padang. Four dialect groups are usually distinguished: Tanah Datar, Limapuluh Kota, Agam, Pasisir.

Kerinci has 300,000 speakers in inland Sumatra, on the slopes of mount Kerinci.

Banjar, the major eastern Kalimantan dialect of Malay, sometimes regarded as a separate language, has around 2,000,000 speakers centred on the city of Banjarmasin. It shows strong Javanese influence.

The speakers of IBAN and related 'Ibanic' or 'Malayic Dayak' languages (including *Kendayan* and *Selako*) are to be found along the rivers of western Sarawak and western Kalimantan.

Malay itself began its spread, perhaps two thousand years ago, from the lowlands of central eastern Sumatra, southern Malaya and southwestern Borneo. On the mainland it extends to the southern Thai province of Patani. By sea, Malay gradually reached as far as Sri Lanka, the Mergui archipelago (where it is spoken by the so-called Sea Gypsies) and the northern coast of New Guinea.

Local varieties of Malay have grown up at several points in the archipelago. Each has its history, often several centuries long, and its own blend of loanwords which may come from Por-

miners of Malaya traditionally used a 'secret language', a special form of Malay with arcane vocabulary, to avoid offending the spirits that guard the ore. *Baba Malay* is a term sometimes used for the pidginised Malay, strongly influenced by Min (see CHINESE), that is spoken by communities of southern Chinese origin in Malacca and other Malaysian cities.

Malay is a language of state education throughout Indonesia and Malaysia. It is also the traditional language of religious education for some Muslim peoples of the archipelago and for the CHAM Muslims of Cambodia.

Malay is still quite recognisably a member of the Malayic group of Austronesian languages: but in some ways it is now rather different from the rest. A lingua franca needs to be easy to grasp, and Malay has a more approachable structure than its relatives. It has undergone extremely varied external influences, with loanwords from many local languages of the archipelago (notably Javanese), from Sanskrit, Chinese, Arabic, Portuguese, Dutch and English. *Ketam* 'crab' comes from an Austroasia-

tuguese, Dutch, Chinese, local languages, and now from standard Indonesian as well. *Larantuka Malay, Ambon Malay, Kupang Malay*, are among better-known examples. Speakers are now usually bilingual in Indonesian, which they use for more formal and prestigious purposes.

Languages of Timor

In a multilingual archipelago, Timor is one of the most multilingual of islands.

The Austronesian languages of Timor belong to the Timor-Flores group. They include *Timor* (650,000 speakers), *Tetun* (300,000), *Galoli* (50,000) and *Mambai* (80,000). *Rotinese* or Roti (120,000) is spoken both on Roti itself and on the nearby western tip of Timor. *Lamaholot* (300,000 speakers) is a language of Solor, Lomblen, Pantar and Alor islands.

The Timor-Alor-Pantar family of languages is quite independent of Austronesian: it may have distant relatives in north-western Irian Jaya. It includes *Makasai* (70,000 speakers), *Bunak* (50,000) and *Kolana* (50,000), the majority language of Alor island.

	Minangkabau	Malay	Jakarta Malay	Banjar	Iban
	Numerals in Malay				
1	cie'	satu	atu	asa	satu
2	duo	dua	duɛ	dua	dua
3	tigo	tiga	tigɛ	tiga	tiga
4	ampe'	empat	əmpat	ampat	ampat
5	limo	lima	limɛ	lima	lima'
6	anam	enam	ənəm	anam	nam
7	tujuəh	tujuh	tuju'	pitu	tujoh
8	(sa)lapan	(de)lapan	dəlapan	walu	lapan
9	sambilan	sembilan	səmbilan	sanga	semilan
10	sa-puluəh	sepuluh	sə-pulu	sa-puluh	sa-puloh

From K. Alexander Adelaar, *Proto Malayic: the reconstruction of its phonology and parts of its lexicon and morphology* (Canberra: Australian National University, 1992) and other sources

MALAYALAM

22,000,000 SPEAKERS

India

Malayalam is one of the DRAVIDIAN LANGUAGES of India, the state language of the mountainous south-western coastal state of Kerala (for map see TAMIL).

Malei means 'hill country' in Tamil: Kerala was 'Male, where pepper comes from' to a Greek geographer of the 6th century. The name *Malabar*, evidently derived from this native word, was applied to the region in Persian and then in European geographical texts. It is now old-fashioned, but the related form *Malayalam* 'mountain region' has remained as a name for the language.

Until around AD 1000 Malayalam was not a separately identifiable language. Early inscriptions from Kerala are in Old Tamil, which was spoken both in Kerala and in the state now called Tamilnadu.

From that date onwards, Tamil and Malayalam have grown apart – most obviously in the matter of loans from Sanskrit. Later Tamil, unusual among the cultivated languages of India, has not been receptive to Sanskrit loans. Malayalam is so full of Sanskrit words, and even of Sanskrit forms and syntax, that the two are inextricably interwoven. The acknowledged masterpieces of Malayalam literature are the 16th-century versions of the Sanskrit *Mahābhārata* and *Rāmāyaṇa* by Tuñcattu Eḻuttacan. But even in spoken Malayalam Sanskrit words are to be heard in practically every sentence.

Numerals in Malayalam and Tamil		
Malayalam		**Tamil**
oru	1	oṇṇu
raṇṭu	2	ireṇṭu
mūnnu	3	mūṇu
nālu	4	nālu
añju	5	añcu
āṟu	6	āṟu
ēṟu	7	ēḻu
ettu	8	eṭṭu
ompatu	9	ompatu
pattu	10	pattu

Malayalam script

Malayalam script achieved its present form in the 17th century. Although showing a clear underlying resemblance to the Tamil-Grantha alphabet it looks very different in print, heavy and blockish where Tamil is light and angular. Some letters are used mainly in Sanskrit loanwords.

Malayalam is spoken by sizeable communities in Singapore and Malaysia. Here the Arabic script is in regular use: in Kerala, too, among Muslims, Malayalam is occasionally printed in Arabic script.

Malayalam consonants

കഖഗഘങ ചഛജഝഞ ടഠഡഢണ തഥദധന പഫബഭമ യരറലവഴളഷശസഹ

k kh g gh ṅ c ch j jh ñ ṭ ṭh ḍ ḍh ṇ t th d dh n p ph b bh m y r ṟ l v ḷ ḻ ś ṣ s h

MALTESE

350,000 SPEAKERS

Malta

One of the SEMITIC LANGUAGES, Maltese originates in the Arabic conquest of the island of Malta in AD 870. It is thus a direct offshoot of ARABIC, but is now very distinct from its parent because of Malta's later history.

> Some now prefer to replace the English form *Maltese* with the local *Malti*.

European political influence and Christianity arrived with the Norman conquest in 1090. For more than three centuries, from 1530 to 1798, Malta was the stronghold of the former crusading order, the Knights Hospitaller of St John. The island was taken by Britain in 1800 but regained independence in 1964–79. Through all this period the local tongue survived and flourished, though it was not recognised as the national language either by the Knights (who used Latin and Italian) or at first by the British (who worked hard to replace Italian with English). Malta, staunchly Catholic, is now officially bilingual in Maltese and English, while Italian retains a powerful influence.

Maltese is written in the Latin alphabet with four extra letters, *ċ ġ ż ħ*. It has many Italian loanwords: so many that some used to claim it as a dialect of Italian. English loanwords are fewer. Two years of French rule, 1798–1800, bequeathed two essential greetings to Maltese: *bongu* and *bonswa* from *bonjour* and *bonsoir* 'good morning, good evening'.

The first ten numerals in Maltese are: *wieħed, tnejn, tlieta, erbgħa, ħamsa, sitta, sebgħa, tmienja, disgħa, għaxra*.

MANDEKAN

5,000,000 SPEAKERS

Mali, Senegal, Guinea, Ivory Coast, Burkina Faso, Sierra Leone

Mandekan, one of the Mande group of NIGER-CONGO LANGUAGES, is, historically and culturally, among the most important languages of the world. Its extent matches, and sometimes goes beyond, the borders of the medieval Islamic Empire of Mali. Five hundred years ago, as the old empire faded away, Mandekan began to split into dialects, each of which has sometimes been counted as a separate language.

This article deals with them together: for if political disintegration made the dialects grow apart, Mandekan songs and epics, transmitted by itinerant poets, slowed down the process of change, kept archaic forms of language in current use, and aided mutual understanding across this vast area.

Mandekan is now the preferred term among linguists for the group of dialects sometimes called Manding or Mandingo. Local versions of this same term include *Malinke, Manenka, Mandinka*. The variety called *Bambara* is known to its own speakers as *Bamana-koma, Bamananke* being their name for themselves. *Dyula* is also spelt *Jula*.

Mandingo – under these various names – is the national language of Mali, a major language in four other countries, and the vehicle of a great oral literature. Why has almost nobody outside Africa heard of it? It has too many names; its territory has long been fragmented, by the succession of native empires and the now-fossilised colonial frontiers; and the history and literature of Africa is still far too little known.

Several thousand years ago, dialects ancestral to the Mande and Atlantic groups of Niger-Congo languages must have arrived here in inland West Africa. The two did not necessarily arrive at the same time. The Atlantic group is represented notably by FULANI. 'Proto-Mande' perhaps began to divide into the future Mande language group around 2000 BC. The modern Mande languages include MENDE, SUSU, SONINKE and Mandekan.

Much later, with political developments culminating in the Empire of Mali, Mandekan itself spread widely across the region, and began to split into dialects, two of which are now represented by Bambara and Dyula.

Most recently, Bambara and Dyula themselves, originating as regional dialects of Mandekan, have spread with trade and politics.

Language of the Mali Empire

A thousand years ago the Empire of Mali was founded. Its most powerful ruler, Kankan Musa (Mansa Musa: reigned 1312–37), held sway from the upper Senegal across to the middle Niger, and from the Sahara to the rainforest. Like many of his subjects, Kankan Musa made the long pilgrimage to Mecca, and his capital was a centre of Arabic learning and science.

Arabic was the language of high culture, religion and diplomacy, but Mandekan was used throughout the empire in administration and trade. Indeed it travelled further, on trade routes southwards into the forests and northwards across the Sahara. Some Mandekan words are recorded by Arabic authors who had travelled in the Western Sudan in the 12th to 14th centuries.

When Europeans began to visit the West African coast in the 15th century they found that Mandekan was the most useful lingua franca between the River Gambia and the Rio Grande.

The empire fell before the rising power of the SONGHAY under Askia Mohammed. With the end of political unity, the widely spread dialects of Mandekan were no longer linked to a central standard, and since the 16th century they have diverged more and more.

Malinke

Malinke and Mandinka are the most common terms for the regional and local dialects into which Mandekan has divided. Viewed on a map, they still recall the shape of the empire. They form a wide arc that begins from the Atlantic coast of the Gambia, southern Senegal (Casamance), Guiné and northern Guinea. It stretches from there eastwards across south-western Mali (the most populous part of the country) and northern Ivory Coast to north-western Burkina Faso, where the Black Volta roughly marks an eastern boundary.

Most speakers of these dialects are Muslims. Many are businessmen, and Muslim communities of 'Malinke' or 'Maninka' speakers have grown up in various West African cities such as Monrovia.

Bambara

Bambara, a dialect of the older Mandekan, developed as a new standard language in the lands between the upper Niger and its tributary the Bani. Here, in the early 17th century, after the Empire of Mali had disappeared and its eastern successor, the SONGHAY Empire, had declined in turn, the non-Islamic Bamana-nke established an independent state. It developed into the two kingdoms of Bamana Segou (whose capital was at Segou) and Bamana Masa-si, 'the Bamana of the King's clan' (whose capital was at Kaarta). In the 19th century, not long before the French invasion, both kingdoms fell to the FULANI Empire.

With the increase of these kingdoms' power and trade, Bambara became an important second language over a wide region – and it still is, in spite of the political ups and downs of the last century. Some of the local languages are closely related Mandekan (Malinke) dialects; some are quite different, even entirely unrelated, such as Songhay.

Bambara is now an official language, almost the national language, of Mali. Under French rule Bambara speakers were widely employed in the civil service and the army: thus Bambara became an important language in the administration of Mauritania and Niger (as well as Mali, Senegal, Guinea, Ivory Coast and Upper Volta) and was the lingua franca of local troops.

Dyula

Dyula, a second offshoot of the older Mandekan, spread in quite a different way. The Malinke dialects of western Burkina Faso and northern Ivory Coast – especially those of the region of Kong – have, over the centuries, gradually extended their influence in an entirely peaceful way. Alongside their influence, their language spread as well.

Relatively well educated, the Muslim speakers of the Dyula dialect gradually constituted a local elite. They were called on to arbitrate in disputes. Their names became fashionable. In its own region, Dyula turned into a prestige language, one that was used by chieftains and nobility, in lawsuits and other formal contexts. It is still a major local language in Burkina Faso and northern Ivory Coast.

The Dyula were, first and foremost, long distance traders between the upper Niger valley and the southern coast. Thus, far beyond their home region, and in an altered form that is often called Commercial Dyula, their dialect developed into a language of trade and the marketplace – the language of traders whose mother tongue is often one or another dialect of Mandekan. Linguists are not yet committing themselves as to how radically this kind of Dyula differs from the other kind.

This variety of Dyula is widely known as a second language throughout Ivory Coast and into western Ghana, especially in towns and cities and along main roads and railways. Further west, another and more creolised variety of Mandekan known as *Kangbe*, the 'clear language', is used as a lingua franca where Mandekan speakers regularly trade.

Language and literature

Mandekan oral literature is noted especially for its epics. The cycle of Sunjata and the historical legends of the Bambara kingdom of Segu with its 17th-century ruler Da Monzon are retold by professional poets, *griots*, members of a hereditary and much-respected profession. Traditionally, each *griot* family was attached to a noble family and performed at its ceremonies, but *griots* also travelled and transmitted news: their repertoire was extensive and varied, though generally of epic form interwoven with songs. *Griots* are nowadays as likely to be heard on the radio as performing to a live audience. Hunters' songs are a recognised separate genre, including both historical and modern poetry performed by a different kind of specialist, the *dònso-jeli*, 'hunters' *griot*'.

Several versions of the Mandekan epics have been collected, published and translated into English and French.

Mandekan has borrowed heavily from Arabic, language of the Islamic religion and culture that are shared by practically all speakers of Mandekan. Arabic *tabib* 'doctor' is the origin of Bambara *tubabu* 'European'. More recently loanwords of French origin have multiplied: *monperi* 'Catholic priest' from the French way of addressing priests, *mon père* 'my father'; *leglisi* 'church' from French *l'église* 'the church'.

The dialects of Mandekan differ in their tones and sound patterns, in their vocabulary – including the most basic items, such as articles and prepositions – but not in their grammatical structure.

A Mandekan dialect such as Bambara has three tones, low, high and rising, but the tones are not marked in writing (*è* and *ò* are open vowels), and they are not as crucial to the meaning of every word as they are in Chinese or in some of the languages of the West African coast. For all that, it is best to get the tones right: the words for 'yes' and 'no' are written identically – *ònhòn* – and differ only in that 'no' has a low tone on the second syllable.

Mande Tan and Mande Fu

The first ten numerals in Bambara are: *kelen, fila, saba, naani, duuru, wòoro, wolonwula* or *folonfila, segin, kònòntòn, tan*. This identifies Bambara (and Mandekan as a whole) as a member of the Mande *Tan* or northern Mande subgroup, distinguished from Mande *Fu* or southern Mande languages (for example MENDE) by the word used for 'ten'. The classification was introduced by the French linguist Maurice Delafosse in 1901.

Mandekan speech and the Empire of Mali

Mandekan dialects can be classed into Western, Northern and Southern. The last includes two dialects which have become important international languages, Bambara and Dyula. *Bambara* centres in central Mali; it is also spoken in Ivory Coast, east central Senegal, Gambia, and Kénédougou province of Burkina Faso. *Dyula* centres in north-eastern Ivory Coast and western Burkina Faso.

Aberrant Mandekan dialects, which apparently separated from the main group relatively early, include *Khassonke* of far western Mali; *Kuranko* or Koranko in northern Sierra Leone and Guinea.

SONINKE is among the languages spoken by early opponents of the Empire of Mali. It also is a member of the Mande group, and still has about a million speakers on the borders of Mali, Mauritania and Senegal.

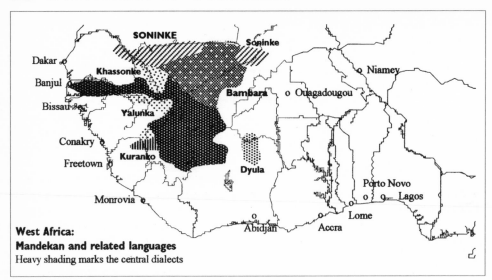

West Africa:
Mandekan and related languages
Heavy shading marks the central dialects

The Mandekan epic

The greatest achievement of Mandekan literature is certainly the epic cycle surrounding the hero Sunjata (or Sundiata or Son-Jara), a ruler of the 13th century: his miraculous birth and boyhood, his exile, his return and victory over the susu. In these societies epic poetry has been the responsibility of hereditary *jelilu*, '*griots*' (this is the French term for West African bards, now used internationally).

Epics of Sunjata have been popular wherever Mandekan dialects are spoken, from Mauretania to Ivory Coast. The epic language differs from everyday speech, blending the features of several dialects. This simple war-song – not epic verse, but sometimes incorporated in epic – may be said to be Sunjata's eulogy:

Minw bè sènè kè	Those who want to go to the farm
i ka sènè kè;	Can go to the farm;
minw bè jago kè	Those who want to go to trade
i ka jago kè;	Can go to trade;
minw bè kèlè kè	Those who want to go to war
i ka kèlè kè.	Can go to war.
Jata ye kèlè kè!	Jata went to war!

Maninka version by Ban Sumana Sisòkò, Mali's foremost *griot*. From *The epic of Son-Jara: a West African tradition* ed. John William Johnson (Bloomington: Indiana University Press, 1986) p. 19

MANIPURI

1,100,000 SPEAKERS

India

Manipuri is (with English) one of the two official languages of the state of Manipur, in the far north-east of India: it is the mother tongue of 60 per cent of the inhabitants of the state. It is closely related to the KUKI-CHIN AND NAGA LANGUAGES (see map there) and is thus one of the SINO-TIBETAN language family.

It is better known to linguists by the local name of the people and their language, *Meithei*. The middle consonant of this is a lateral click – the different-looking form in Assamese, *Mekle*, is another way of writing the same word.

Manipur is the only extensive, relatively level river plain in the area where Kuki-Naga languages are spoken. It is no coincidence that a single kingdom grew up here, and that a single language is spoken, without significant dialect divisions, by a relatively large population group. This is still in origin a strongly rural culture. The name of Imphāl, capital of Manipur, means 'house collection': it grew up less as a town than as a group of villages surrounding the royal enclosure, and as the largest of the many markets of the state.

The Hindu religion of India was introduced to Manipur in the 18th century. A Burmese invasion in 1762 was followed by a long period of instability. British rule came in 1890; within independent India, Manipur gained the position of a state in 1972. Imphāl, once the royal capital, now the state capital, is best known for the British–Japanese battle there in 1944.

As Vaishnavites, Manipuri speakers do not hunt, eat meat or drink alcohol. Their staple is rice, grown in the irrigated fields of the valley.

With Vaishnavism came Indian, specifically Assamese, influence on the Manipuri language, and a continuing cultural interchange between Manipur and Assam. The classic Manipuri tale of Khamba and Thoibi became an Assamese classic as *Khamba Thoibir sadhukatha*, translated by Rajanikanta Bordoloi (1869–1939), author and anthropologist.

The first ten numerals in Manipuri are: *a-mā, a-ni, a-hūm, ma-ri, ma-ngā, ta-rūk, ta-rēt, ni-pān, mā-pan, ta-rā.*

Maori

100,000 SPEAKERS

New Zealand

One of the AUSTRONESIAN LANGUAGES, Maori is spoken where it is as the result of a migration, perhaps rather more than 1,000 years ago, from eastern Polynesia to the previously uninhabited islands now called New Zealand.

When Europeans first came to New Zealand, Maori was spoken, in several dialects, in both North and South Islands. According to oral tradition there was continual travel and contact among speakers of the different dialects, extend-

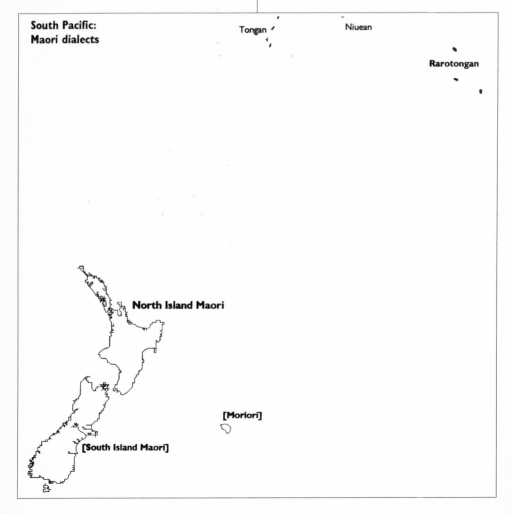

South Pacific: Maori dialects

Tongan

Niuean

Rarotongan

North Island Maori

[Moriori]

[South Island Maori]

ing to both islands, and this certainly helps to explain why dialect differences were rather minor considering the length of time over which they had been able to develop.

The first printed book in Maori was a reader, *E korao no New Zealand* 'Talk from New Zealand' by Thomas Kendall, published in 1815. More than a thousand publications had appeared by 1900, and there is a complete Bible translation in Maori. Much traditional oral literature has been collected and published. The New Zealand government, however, has (at least until recently) worked to suppress Maori in favour of English.

South Island Maori is now extinct; Maoris from North Island conquered South Island in the early 19th century, killing many speakers and absorbing the remainder into their own tribes. Remaining North Island Maori speakers number about 100,000 – all of them bilingual in English – though three times as many people identify themselves as Maoris. Numerous New Zealand place names are of Maori origin.

Maori has ten consonants, *p, t, k, m, n, ng, wh, r, h, w* and five vowels, *a, e, i, o, u: wh* is variously pronounced *f, ph* or *wh*. The first ten numerals (similar to those of SAMOAN) are: *kotahi, rua, toru, whaa, rima, ono, whitu, waru, iwa, tekau*.

Maori dialects

North Island Maori is divided into western and eastern dialects. *South Island Maori* is extinct, as is *Moriori* of the Chatham Islands, which appears to have been closest to the eastern North Island dialect of Maori. *Rarotongan* or *Cook Islands Maori* (40,000 speakers, more than half of them settled in New Zealand) is close enough to Maori for some mutual intelligibility, suggesting a historical link between the two populations.

MARATHI

50,000,000 SPEAKERS

India

Marathi, one of the major INDO-ARYAN LAN-GUAGES in terms of the number of speakers, is one of those that are less known abroad, simply because of the smaller amount of emigration from the Indian state of Maharashtra.

> The region has been called *Mahārāṣṭra* from ancient times. The adjective *Marāṭhī*, now used as the name for the language, is itself as old as the 2nd century AD (in the Sanskrit form *Mahāraṭṭhī*).

Words identifiable as Marathi occur in texts and inscriptions from this region from the 5th century onwards, more especially in those that are in the Prakrit dialect *Mahārāṣṭrī*, which is often considered the ancestor of Marathi – though some linguists doubt the direct link between them.

Inscriptions and texts entirely in Marathi begin in the 11th century but Marathi literature flowers in the 13th, with the remarkable Marathi verse exposition of the Sanskrit *Bhagavadgītā* by the young poet Jñāneśvarī (1271–96). The language as recorded to 1350 is counted as Old Marathi: Middle Marathi, in which there is a major corpus of historical prose, is dated from 1350 to 1800.

It may be that Marathi coexisted with KAN-NADA as a spoken language for an extended period during the first millennium AD, and that heavy influence from both Kannada and Telugu led to its rather rapid differentiation from San-skrit, as compared with the more conservative Hindi.

Some linguists have gone as far as to argue that Marathi is historically a creole. Against this, it is itself conservative in some ways, retaining the three genders of Sanskrit, masculine, feminine and neuter, and the stem alternations known as *guṇa* and *vrddhi* (for example, *pəḍ* 'to fall', *pāḍ* 'to make fall').

From the 14th to the 17th centuries Persian was the language of government in Maharashtra and exerted influence in its turn. There are now many English loanwords.

Marathi and Konkani

Standard *Marathi* is based on the *Deśī* or 'country, hinterland' dialect, specifically on that of the great city of Pune (older English form *Poona*). The *Konkanī* dialect is spoken along the western coastal strip, Konkan. The main eastern dialects are *Varhāḍī* and *Nāgpurī*.

Halbi is often considered a language distinct from Marathi, Oriya and Chhattisgarhi (which all

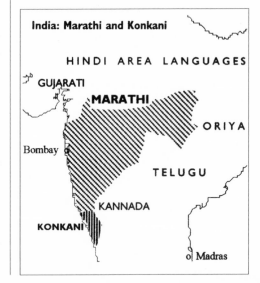

India: Marathi and Konkani

border on it). It has over half a million speakers in Bastar at the southern extremity of Madhya Pradesh, and some features link it to GONDI, the Dravidian language of the jungle tribes of that area. The numerals '1' and '2' are *gotok, duithān*. The numerals '3' and above are like Marathi.

Koṅkaṇī – the language – is spoken from Ratnagiri southwards, notably at Goa, Mangalore and Cochin and in several other scattered coastal enclaves between Goa and Trivandrum.

Marathi in writing

The cursive मोडी *Modi* script was invented for Marathi in the 17th century, but it is now less commonly found even in handwriting: since 1800 it has been officially replaced by a Devanagari alphabet, almost as used for Hindi but with a few different character shapes. It is usually called बालबोध *Balbodh* 'that can be understood by a child'.

Numerals in Marathi		
एक	१	ek
दोन	२	don
तीन	३	tīn
चार	४	cār
पांच	५	pāñc
सहा	६	sahā
सात	७	sāt
आठ	८	āṭh
नऊ	९	na
दहा	१०	dahā

The Devanagari alphabet for Marathi

अ आ इ ई उ ऊ ऋ ए ऐ ओ औ कखगघङ चछजझञ टठडढण तथदधन पफबभम यरलव शषसह
a ā i ī u ū ṛ e ai o au k kh g gh ṅ c ch j jh ñ ṭ ṭh ḍ ḍh ṇ t th d dh n p ph b bh m y r l v ś ṣ s h

MARI

600,000 SPEAKERS

Russia

Mari is one of the URALIC LANGUAGES, spoken in the middle Volga valley in Russia, in the self-governing republic of Mari El. It is rather more distantly related to Finnish than neighbouring Mordvin is.

Mari, the people's own name for themselves, means 'human being' and seems to be a loan from proto-Indo-Iranian. The older term *Cheremis* (German *Tscheremissisch*) is still used by linguists: it was originally the Chuvash name for their Mari neighbours.

To capture the queen

The Mari are renowned beekeepers. This sketch from the notebooks of the 19th-century Mari ethnographer Timofei Yevsevyev shows the reed cage in which the queen bee was traditionally enclosed so that the swarm would settle around her. As she was trapped, the farmer would say this spell:

Müksh-awa, surtetəm saj onyzhə,
yeshetəm pashash kəchkərə
i pashalan tunəktə!
Queen bee, build your palace,
put your family to work and teach them
to make honey!
T. J. Jewsewjew, 'Bienenzucht bei
den Tscheremissen' ed. J. Erdödi in
Journal de la Société Finno-Ougrienne
vol. 73 (1974) pp. 168–204

Present-day Mari country is the remnant of an area that once reached much further to the west. At some time, maybe three thousand years ago, early Mari, early Mordvin and proto-Finnic must have been spoken in adjacent regions, probably stretching all the way from the Volga to the Baltic Sea. The expansion of Russian broke up this hypothetical Finno-Ugric dialect continuum.

Since as long ago as the 8th century, Mari and CHUVASH speakers have lived side by side in their present territories, and there are many Chuvash loanwords in Mari. If the Mari had once been independent, they were so no longer after the Tatar conquest in the 13th century. Tatar domination was replaced by Russian rule in the 16th century.

**Russia:
Mari dialects**

Hill Mari and Meadow Mari

About half the speakers of Mari live in the Mari El Republic. Hill Mari, the western dialect, and Meadow Mari of the central and eastern districts, have developed into separate literary languages, both written in Cyrillic script. The Cheboksary reservoir covers a considerable area of former Hill Mari speech. There are also rather different Eastern and North-western dialects, spoken outside the borders of the republic.

MARSHALLESE

30,000 SPEAKERS

Marshall Islands

Marshallese, one of the Micronesian group of AUSTRONESIAN LANGUAGES, is spoken on the two island chains of the Republic of the Marshall Islands.

Already of interest to American missionaries, the Marshall Islands were briefly a German protectorate and the focus of German trade towards the end of the 19th century. Japanese administration followed after the First World War, and the United States took over in 1945. The Marshall Islands became independent in 1986.

English and Japanese have had the strongest effect on the language.

Linguists have differed astonishingly over the vowels of Marshallese. Byron Bender, in a 1968 paper, argued that there were three vowel phonemes (*a e i*), other vowel sounds being condi-

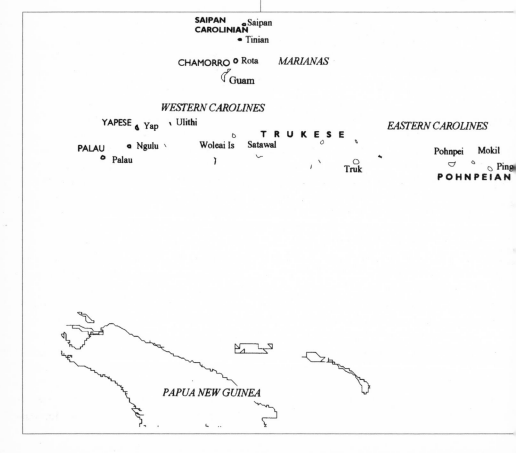

tioned by surrounding consonants. The usual spelling recognises nine. Sheldon Harrison, in 1995, distinguished twelve, and added a distinctive feature of length, giving a total of twenty-four.

Marshallese has lost the complex series of numeral classifiers that are found in the other Micronesian languages (see box at KIRIBATI).

Micronesian languages

KIRIBATI is the language of the Kiribati (Gilbert) island chain, of neighbouring Banaba (or Bwaanaba or Ocean Island), which has a slightly different dialect, and of Niu. It is also spoken in the Line Islands, and there are several migrant communities in the western Pacific. *Northern, Central, Southern* and *Bwaanaba* dialects are distinguished.

Kosraean or Kusaie is the language of 5,000 inhabitants of Kosrae State (Federated States of Micronesia): many inhabitants also speak Ponapean.

Nauruan, with 4,000 speakers, is the traditional language of Nauru. This island, German at the end of the 19th century, was under Australian administration from 1920 until 1968. As a language of trade and later of government, English has been the strongest influence throughout, and there are signs that Nauruan is being abandoned in favour of English.

Pohnpeian or Ponapean has about 22,000 speakers. It is the major language of Pohnpei State (Federated States of Micronesia). *Ngatikese, Pingelapese* and *Mokilese* are counted as dialects of Pohnpeian or as closely related languages. Pohnpeian has a 'high language' with a partly separate vocabulary, used in speaking about people of high rank. Pohnpeian spelling uses *-h* to mark a long vowel, rather like German: *dohl* 'mountain'. German missionaries designed the orthography.

Truk or Ruk or Trukese (22,000 speakers) is the major member of a dialect chain with a total of 40,000 speakers. These languages are spoken in the Caroline Islands. Once nominally Spanish – but plied by American missionaries – they were sold to Germany in 1899, passed to Japan after the First World War and to the United States after the Second World War. They now form states of the Federated States of Micronesia. The languages have numerous English and Japanese loanwords. *Saipan Carolinian*, one of this group, is spoken in the Northern Marianas.

Marshallese has the largest number of speakers (30,000) of any Micronesian language. The western chain of the Marshall Islands is known locally as *Rālik*, 'western islands', the eastern chain as *Ratak*, 'eastern islands'. This is the major dialect division of Marshallese.

The dialects differ in vocabulary – and also in the vowels of words whose first two consonants are identical: Rl. *ipping*, Rt. *piping* 'good at jumping'; Rl. *ellor*, Rt. *lelor* 'shadow'; Rl. *ittil*, Rt. *tūtil* 'burn'; Rl. *ekkot*, Rt. *kōkot* 'strong'.

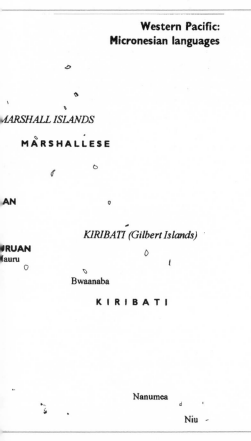

Western Pacific: Micronesian languages

MARSHALL ISLANDS
MÁRSHALLESE

AN

URUAN
Nauru

KIRIBATI *(Gilbert Islands)*

Bwaanaba

KIRIBATI

Nanumea

Niu

See KIRIBATI for a table of numerals in Pohnpeian, Truk and Marshallese.

Examples from Sheldon P. Harrison in *Comparative Austronesian dictionary* ed. Darrell P. Tryon (Berlin: Mouton De Gruyter, 1995-) pt 1 pp. 879–918

	Numerals in Kiribati, Marshallese, Pohnpeian and Truk			
	Kiribati	**Marshallese**	**Pohnpeian**	**Truk**
1	teuana	cuon	ēu	eet
2	uoua	ṛuo	riau	érúúw
3	teniua	cilu	silū	één
4	aua	emæn	pāieu	fáán
5	nimaua	ḷaləm	limau	niim
6	onoua	cilcino	weneu	woon
7	itiua	cilcilimcuon	isu	fúús
8	waniua	ṛuwalitɔk	walū	waan
9	ruaiua	ṛuwatimcuon	tuwau	ttiw
10	tebwina	cɔngɔul	eisek	engoon

In Marshallese, '6' originates as '3 + 3' and '7' as '3 + 3 + 1'.

A series of prefixes is added to the numerals in counting various classes of objects: *féfóch* 'four long objects', *faché* 'four flat objects', *wonossak* 'six pieces of copra', *wonowo* 'six bunches of bananas'. These examples are from Truk. Marshallese, alone among the Micronesian languages, does not have the numeral classifiers.

Comparative Austronesian dictionary ed. Darrell P. Tryon (Berlin: Mouton De Gruyter, 1995–); George L. Campbell, *Compendium of the world's languages* (London: Routledge, 1991)

MASAI

750,000 SPEAKERS

Kenya and Tanzania

One of the Eastern Nilotic group of NILO-SAHARAN LANGUAGES (see map at TURKANA), Masai is a major language of Kenya and Tanzania, spoken by a traditionally pastoral and warlike people who until recently ruled an extensive territory in the East African hinterland.

> *Masai* or *Maasai* is the speakers' own name for themselves. They trace their origin to a migration from the north, led by *Maasinta*, who taught his people how to climb a mountain that lay in their way, and how to brand their cattle.

Masai-speaking country lies across many of the trade routes from the East African coast. The Swahili slave trade route from the Uganda region and Lake Victoria was one of these. The Masai did not take part in the trade but exacted tribute from trade caravans. Thus the language has interacted with Swahili. It has also been influenced by its neighbours: for example, the Kenya dialects of Masai have loanwords from KIKUYU. There has been a long tradition of regular trade in this region in a four-day market system. Women were the traders, and travelled between peoples even when they were (as often) at war.

Europeans began to visit Masai country in 1848. It was divided between British and German colonial governments at the end of the 19th century. German Tanganyika became a British protectorate after the First World War but Masai speakers remained divided between two administrations.

The first ten numerals in Masai are: *obo, aare, okuni, oonguan, imiet, ile, oopishana, isiet, ooudo, tomon.*

> 'The name of a dead child, woman, or warrior is not spoken again, and if the name is an ordinary word, that word is no longer used by the family. Thus, if a Masai man called *Ol-onana*, "the gentle one", died, on his death the word *nana* would be replaced in his family by some such word as *polpol* "smooth".'
>
> G. W. B. Huntingford,
> *The Southern Nilo-Hamites*
> (London: International
> African Institute, 1953) p. 116
>
> The *ol-* in this name is a masculine gender prefix, a form typical of Masai: *ol-arányàni* 'male singer', *enk-arányàni* 'female singer'; *ol-álém* 'sword', *enk-álém* 'knife'.

MAYAN LANGUAGES

The Mayan languages are a long-recognised linguistic family of south-eastern Mexico and Guatemala, one which some would now classify in the wider family of AMERIND LANGUAGES. There are about thirty surviving languages, with perhaps three million speakers in total. Spanish, as national and international language, is now progressively undermining the vitality of all the Mayan languages.

The relationship among the Mayan languages was noted by Lorenzo Hervás y Panduro in *Catalogo delle lingue conosciute e notizia della loro affinità e diversità*, published in Italy in 1784.

Historically these languages are of great importance, for they belonged to the Maya culture that flourished in the Yucatán peninsula in the 4th to 9th centuries, well before the Spanish conquest. Chontal, Chol, Tzeltal, Tzotzil and Yucatec were the main languages of classic Maya civilisation – and they all influenced one another, forming what is sometimes called the 'Lowland Maya linguistic area'.

But the history of Mayan languages is much older than that. Linguists have made solid progress in the reconstruction of 'proto-Maya', ancestral to all the modern languages. Proto-Maya was, it is thought, spoken in the south-eastern, highland parts of modern Maya territory, at least four thousand years ago, and then began to split into dialects and to spread by migration and conquest. Archaeology suggests that Mayans (presumably speaking early forms of Chol, Chontal, Tzeltal and Tzotzil) were to be found in the lowland regions around Tabasco from, at the latest, 800 BC.

Some of the vocabulary of proto-Maya can be recovered: maize (Yucatec *kan*), with some of the technical terminology of maize-growing; marrow, sweet potato, chilli, avocado, maguey, cotton and cacao, among other crops; terms for cooking and weaving, and for religious rites.

The influence of the prehistoric Olmec culture, of central Mexico, was strong in Ma-

yan territory. Olmec itself is not thought to have been a Mayan language, but a member of the Mixe-Zoque group. The hieroglyphic writing system found on lowland Mayan sculptures, and now partly readable (see box at YUCATEC), is clearly a development of the still-undeciphered hieroglyphs used by the Olmecs.

The major Mayan languages

Cakchiquel has 350,000 speakers in Guatemala, where it is used in primary education. Few modern printed texts exist, except school textbooks, yet the 16th-century *Memorial of Tecpán-Atitlán*, a mythological and historical compilation in Cakchiquel, is an important source for later pre-Columbian central America and for the Spanish conquest. The Cakchiquel capital, Iximché, became the first capital of Guatemala.

Chol has 90,000 speakers in Chiapas province, Mexico.

Chontal, with only 40,000 speakers today, was the language of Tabasco.

Huastec has perhaps 70,000 speakers in total. The two main dialects are those of *Veracruz* and *San Luís Potosí* in Mexico.

Central America: Mayan languages

Kekchí or Quecchí has nearly 300,000 speakers in Guatemala and Belize.

Mam is a group of dialects of western Guatemala, with a total of at least 250,000 speakers.

QUICHÉ is the major Mayan language of modern Guatemala, with at least 750,000 speakers.

Tzotzil and *Tzeltal*, neighbouring languages in Chiapas province, Mexico, have 150,000 speakers in total.

YUCATEC or 'Maya', with 500,000 speakers or more, is the modern Mayan language of Yucatán. Yucatec is one of a group of four closely related languages. The other three, *Mopan, Itzá* and *Lacandón*, are spoken by tiny population groups in central Guatemala and Belize. Yucatec itself clearly had a different fate: it moved north into the peninsula of Yucatán, perhaps two thousand years ago – then, as the vehicle of a great civilisation, it spread outwards again, almost swamping its three relatives.

Numerals in Mayan languages			
	Cakchiquel	**Quiché**	**Tzotzil**	**Yucatec**
1	jun	hun	jun	jun
2	ca'i'	cab	chib	ca
3	oxi'	oxib	'oxib	ox
4	caji'	cahib	cahib	can
5	vo'o'	oob	ho'ob	ho
6	vaki'	vacuc	vachib	vac
7	vuku'	vucub	hucub	vuc
8	vakxaki'	vahxac	vaxachib	vaxac
9	beleje	beleheb	valuneb	bolon
10	lajuj	lahuh	lajuneb	lajun

MBUNDU

4,800,000 SPEAKERS OF THE TWO LANGUAGES

Angola

Two important BANTU LANGUAGES of Angola share this name. The first was the language of the *oviMbundu*, a trading people who in the 19th century were second only to the speakers of SWAHILI in the length of their journeys across southern Africa.

> The name is in origin identical with *Bantu*, 'people'. To distinguish it from its neighbour this language has been called *Benguella Mbundu*, *South Mbundu*, and *Umbundu*. OviMbundu traders are called *Mambari* in older historical sources.

South Mbundu is the westernmost of the languages that are historically linked with the expansion of the LUNDA empire in the 16th century. The westbound conquerors were called *Jagas* by contemporary Portuguese sources. They ruled the Benguela highlands of west central Angola. For the next three centuries they dominated the trade that linked coastal Benguela with the upper valleys of the Kasai, Lualaba and Zambezi – the regions now known as Shaba and Zambia. OviMbundu kingdoms such as Bailundu had trading agreements, sometimes amounting to monopolies, with inland states such as the Lunda empire of Mwata Yamvo and the LOZI kingdom ruled by Lewanika. At first slaves were the most valuable commodity in which they dealt: by the end of the 19th century greater profits were coming from ivory, beeswax and rubber.

The South Mbundu language is historically the speech of the Benguela highlands. With trade and slavery it gradually spread along the trade routes of all southern Angola. It came to be particularly widely used in the coastal cities of the south, Lobito, Catambela, Benguela (older Portuguese spelling *Benguella*) and Moçâmedes, where people from many parts of Angola, with different mother tongues, had come to live and work.

South Mbundu is close to Lunda, CHOKWE and LUVALE. However, it is clearly influenced by a different Bantu language which was presumably already spoken on the highlands at the time of the conquests – and this was related to the Bantu languages of sparsely populated Namibia, such as Herero (see map). This influence is seen in the sound pattern of Mbundu, notably its initial vowels. These turn many noun class markers into two-syllable prefixes: *imbo* 'village'; *ovaimbo* 'villages'.

> Early in the twentieth century the Benguela Railway was built, eastwards from Lobito and Benguela to the mining lands of Shaba and Rhodesia (modern Zambia). Its route ran through Ovimbundu territory, and it supplanted the Mbundu trading caravans. Ovimbundu prosperity declined rapidly – yet, with rail transport, Mbundu has spread even further as a common language for inland peoples living near the railway.

Mbundu of the north

Loanda Mbundu (or North Mbundu or Kimbundu or Quimbundu or Ndongo) is in origin the language of the Luanda district, and is related to KONGO. The Portuguese seized the harbour of Luanda (older spelling *Loanda*) from the declining Kingdom of Kongo, in the late 16th century. They made it a metropolis of the slave trade and the capital of their realm of Angola.

Gentio de Angola, 'Gentile of Angola', is one of the very earliest printed books in an African language. It is a series of lessons in Christianity, with Portuguese and Kimbundu texts on facing pages. There are some notes on the grammar and pronunciation of the language. This rare work was published in Lisbon in 1642 or 1643: in the surviving copy in the British Museum the last digit of the date cannot be read.

Luanda Mbundu is still a lingua franca of the trade routes in parts of northern Angola and south-western Congo (Kinshasa).

> *K'ilu lyuti olongila vyakahandangala, p'osi esove lakamwe* – 'There are many little birds at the top of the tree, but the ground beneath is clean'. The answer to this South Mbundu riddle? Stars.
>
> José Francisco Valente, *Gramática Umbundu: a lingua do centro de Angola*. Lisboa: Junta de Investigações do Ultramar, 1964

Benguela Mbundu and Luanda Mbundu

South Mbundu or *Benguela Mbundu*, language of the oviMbundu, has about 3,000,000 speakers. In spite of its extensive territory, which was never politically united, it has only minor dialect divergences, an indication of the ubiquity of travel and trade.

South Mbundu resembles Lunda but shows substrate influence from a relative of the Bantu languages of Namibia. The best known of these are *Herero* (75,000 speakers), *Kwanyama* (150,000) and *Ndonga* (250,000).

North Mbundu or *Luanda Mbundu*, once the dialect of a southern region of the Kingdom of Kongo, has 1,800,000 speakers in Luanda Province, Angola. A close relative is Kongo.

Numerals in South Mbundu and North Mbundu		
South Mbundu		**North Mbundu**
mosi	1	moxi, úmue
vali	2	txiari
tatu	3	tatu
kwāla	4	kuãna
tālo	5	tānu
epandu	6	samanu
epandu vali	7	sambari
echelāla	8	nake
echea	9	txiela
ekwĩ	10	kuĩ

Angola: Mbundu

MENDE

1,000,000 SPEAKERS

Sierra Leone, Liberia

Mende, one of the Mande group of NIGER-CONGO LANGUAGES, is spoken by a people of inland Sierra Leone. Although Mande languages separated from the rest of the Niger-Congo family many thousands of years ago, their history is obscure and it is quite unknown how long Mende has been spoken in its present territory. The Mende were in recent centuries a slave-trading and slave-owning people: this will have helped to spread their language (slavery was abolished in 1928).

In the 19th century Mende speakers for the first time penetrated as far south as the Atlantic coast, which was at that time largely the domain of Bullom (see map at TEMNE). The first Christian school that taught in Mende – a landmark among African languages – was established at Charlotte in 1831 by the Quaker missionary Hannah Kilham.

> The name of *Mende* is native. It is the same in origin as that of several related languages and dialects – MANDEKAN, Mandingo, Malinke – and was the obvious choice by linguists, in the form *Mande*, to denote the whole group with Niger-Congo.

The southward expansion of the Mende came at the right time to open the hinterland of Sierra Leone to British trade and eventually to the British protectorate, proclaimed in 1896. Mende speakers, unaccustomed to any centralised government, were at first outraged by such innovations as taxation, but their rebellion of 1898 was suppressed and they began to work more peacefully alongside the colonial administration. Thus the Mende language spread further. It is now the major language of southern Sierra Leone, used as a lingua franca by many whose first language is Bullom, Banta and Kissi, among others.

The first ten numerals in Mende are: *yera, fele, sawa, nani, lolu, woita, wofera, wayakpa, tau, pu*. Mende is thus one of the Mande Fu languages (see box at MANDEKAN). It is a tonal language, with four tones which are an essential part of the vocabulary and the grammar: *pú* 'put', *pù* 'England', *pû* 'cave', *pǔ* 'ten'. In Mende linguists have identified five separate noun 'plural' categories, each with distinct forms: indefinite plural, definite plural, plural of a person and companions, plural of masses, plural of agents.

Mende and its neighbours

Mende, once called Kosso or Mande, the language of inland southern Sierra Leone, has a northern dialect in an enclave which became separated perhaps a century ago, *Lokko* or Landogo. Port Lokko, in Temne-speaking central Sierra Leone, takes its name from the Lokko slaves who were formerly exported from here.

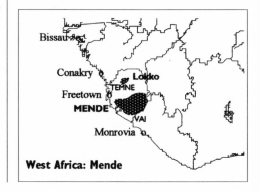

West Africa: Mende

MERU

1,250,000 SPEAKERS

Kenya

Meru is one of the BANTU LANGUAGES: its territory lies in central Kenya, to the north-east of its close relative KIKUYU (see map there), but almost completely surrounded by Oromo-speaking territory. Meru society, like that of the Kikuyu, was traditionally warlike. Among more peaceable occupations, speakers of Meru are well known as beekeepers.

Thagicu is the name of the region from which, long ago, speakers of Kikuyu and related languages may have dispersed, and Thagicu is now the usual name for the language group to which both belong. Local legend tells of the migration of Meru speakers from the coast around 1700; of their old name, *Ngaa*; and their new name, *Meru*, said to mean 'peaceful place'.

Meru serves as a second language for some speakers of smaller neighbouring tongues, Chuka and Tharaka.

Another, quite different, community is also called Meru by outsiders. The Meru of Mount Meru in Tanzania call themselves *Varwa* and speak a Chagga dialect, *Kirwa* or *kiMeru*. Their recurrent conflicts with their German and British rulers helped to discredit the Tanganyikan 'protectorate' and bring about independence in 1961.

MIAO

PERHAPS 5,500,000 SPEAKERS

China and south-east Asian countries

Miao is a group of closely related dialects which, together with YAO (see table of numerals there), make up the Miao-Yao language family. This was once thought to be distantly related to the Sino-Tibetan languages (including Chinese) but the evidence was weak. It has now been argued by Paul Benedict that Miao-Yao is a member of the wider family of AUSTRO-TAI LANGUAGES.

Miao is the official Chinese term for this large linguistic minority; in Vietnamese it is *Meo*, or in full *Man Meo* – *Man* being the Vietnamese and Laotian term for Yao speakers, who were the first of this linguistic family to become known in Vietnam. Miao speakers themselves do not like the term, calling themselves *Hmong*, a name that many linguists also use.

Speakers of Miao were probably known to the Chinese at least two thousand years ago (though Chinese records often include other peoples under the name *Miao*). Their centre, as far back as records go, has been the middle Yangtze valley and what is now the province of Guizhou, where half the five million Miao speakers of China are to be found now. Miao legends tell of an ancient migration from the cold north: historians generally do not believe it.

The history of the language for the last few centuries, so far as it can be reconstructed, has been of retreat under the numerical – and political – pressure of Chinese. Miao is essentially spoken by hill peoples with a record of resistance and rebellion – serious uprisings took place in 1698, 1735, 1795 and 1854. Resulting Chinese campaigns to quell revolt may well have cata-

lysed the gradual Miao migration southwards of recent centuries.

By about 1870 all remaining independent Miao political units had disappeared. But even recent reports tell of traditional epic poetry, recited by skilled performers, narrating Miao heroic deeds in rebellions against the Chinese. As late as 1941–3 the Chinese government was forbidding the use of the language and the wearing of traditional Miao costume.

Once perhaps spoken over a fairly unified territory, Miao now makes up a complex series of speech enclaves – in fact none of the minority languages of China is more widely scattered. Everywhere it is surrounded by Chinese and Tai languages, spoken by wet rice growers in the plains and valleys, while Miao speech remains typical of the hills. Miao speakers, individual families and whole villages, are highly mobile. A migration south-westwards into Vietnam, Laos and Thailand was certainly under way in the 19th century – it may be much older. Miao people in these countries number well over 300,000; in Laos, the Miao of the Xieng Khouang area achieved some political recognition in the 1950s. From Vietnam a sizeable community of Miao speakers has now settled in the United States.

In spite of geographical fragmentation, Miao dialects have not diverged to the point of mutual unintelligibility. It is a predominantly monosyllabic language with around fifty initial consonants, six vowels and seven or eight tones. Miao speakers are frequently bilingual or multilingual; Lao serves as a lingua franca for many southern Miao, while Yunnanese and other dialects of Chinese serve a similar function further north.

Miao has borrowed heavily from Chinese, particularly terms needed in modern life – soap, matches, school, club – and political innovations such as cooperative, industrialisation, commune. Such words are often readily distinguishable: many diphthongs do not occur in native Miao words and identify Chinese loanwords immediately.

Miao was not a written language until Christian missionaries devised a Latin orthography at the beginning of the 20th century. After the Revolution a new romanisation was introduced, closer in style to the pinyin orthography for Chinese.

The Miao-Yao languages

In China, Eastern, Northern and Western Miao dialects are recognised. In Vietnam, Laos and Thailand, dialect distinctions are still traditionally made with the help of dress and customs: here *Hmong Neua* (also spelt *Mong Njua*, Blue or Green Meo) and *Hmong Daw* (White Meo) are the most important groups.

YAO or *Mien* really consists of two languages, *Yao* and *Nu*, each of which has dialect subdivisions. Together they have about 700,000 speakers in China and well over 100,000 in south-east Asian countries.

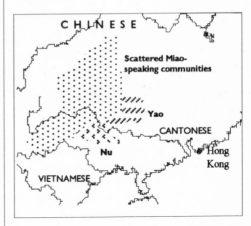

Miao subdivisions

'These communities are so scattered and so broken up into groups and subgroups, there are literally dozens of local names for them, most of which refer to something the Chinese found noteworthy about them, their appearance or location, say, or their dress or their hairstyle. Many of the names are indeed memorable. Here are a few examples: the Shrimp Miao, the Short-skirt Miao, the Long-skirt Miao, the Magpie Miao, the Pointed Miao, the Upside-down Miao, the Steep-slope Miao, the Striped Miao, the Big-board Miao, the Cowrie-shell Miao. Only five such names are widely known, however: the Black Miao, the Red Miao, the White Miao, the Blue Miao (*Qing Miáo*), and the Flowery Miao (*Huá Miáo*).

'The authorities of the People's Republic do not . . . refer to the Miao by those colorful epithets of the past, holding such names to be degrading. Instead . . . they classify the people by the dialect that they speak.'

S. Robert Ramsey, *The languages of China* (Princeton: Princeton University Press, 1987) p. 281

The rice harvest

Lù giế, mblẽ txõu pàng;
Xì giế, mblẽ troa lô;
Poa giế, mblẽ gióa sá;
Chợu giế, hlái mblẽ, nđàu mblẽ.

In the sixth month, the rice flowers;
in the seventh month, the grains form;
in the eighth month, the rice ripens;
in the ninth month, we cut the rice, we thresh the rice.

from a Miao agricultural calendar collected by F. M. Savina

MINANGKABAU

6,500,000 SPEAKERS

Indonesia

One of the AUSTRONESIAN LANGUAGES, and one of the regional languages of Indonesia that are closely related to MALAY (see map and table of numerals there), Minangkabau is spoken in the central part of the western coastal strip of Sumatra: it is the language of the province of Sumatera Barat, 'West Sumatra'. Carried by a busy seaborne trade, it is a well-known lingua franca along the whole of this coast and its offshore islands.

Minangkabau and Kerinci form a single dialect continuum with Malay itself on its native ground. However, the Minangkabau dialects have undergone big phonetic changes, so that they no longer look or sound much like Malay.

Moreover, Minangkabau, as a language of trading communities, has itself spread well beyond its original region. There are colonies of speakers in north-western and south-eastern Sumatra, in the Malay state of Negeri Sembilan, in Bandung and Surabaya on Java, and elsewhere in the archipelago. There are said to be half a million speakers in the Indonesian capital Jakarta.

The story of Anggun Nan Tungga

A traditional cycle of stories is told by oral epic poets, *tukang sijobang*, in western Sumatra. While puppet plays, *randai*, are performed in standard Minangkabau, the epics, *sijobang*, are typically in local dialects. One performer of *sijobang* began his story with this preface:

Lusueh kulindan suto kusuk,	Worn is the thread, the silk is tangled,
sodang tajélo atéh karok,	trailed over the heddles,
lusueh di pétak rang Malako;	worn in the room of the Malaccan;
sunggueh kok bolun tolan tuntuk,	although, my friends, you have not asked me to,
umpamo kojo tukang kakok,	like a workman performing his task,
niat sangajo iko juo aiii . . .	this is just what I want to do . . .

Nigel Phillips, *Sijobang* (Cambridge: Cambridge University Press, 1981) pp. 42–3

MINGRELIAN AND LAZ

POSSIBLY 600,000 SPEAKERS

Georgia, Turkey

A lone in the Kartvelian or South Caucasian family, GEORGIAN (see map there) is an official and literary language with a long written history. In western Georgia – the region closest to the Black Sea coast – the everyday languages are quite distinct from Georgian, though with a family resemblance. In ancient times this was Colchis, from which the Argonauts of Greek legend retrieved the Golden Fleece: later it was Lazica, the western neighbour of early Georgia.

In a compact area of north-western Georgia Mingrelian is spoken. To many it is a mother tongue, though Georgian is the language they learn at school, hear in the media and read in the press. To many speakers of ABKHAZ, in the far north-western extremity of Georgia (and locked in hostility to Georgian rule) Mingrelian functions as an everyday second language, quite unrelated to their own North-west Caucasian speech.

Mingrelian was never listed as a separate ethnic group or language in Soviet statistics: speakers were counted simply as Georgian, and they count themselves as Georgian. Independent Georgia has been too unsettled and too riven with nationalism to allow statistical research on minorities. Some estimates of Mingrelian speakers put them at about half a million. 'Estimates of numbers of Laz speakers in Turkey range from 46,987 (from a 1945 Turkish census) to ten times that number' (Dee Ann Holisky in *The indigenous languages of the Caucasus* vol. 1 ed. Alice C. Harris [Delmar, NY: Caravan Books, 1991] p. 397). Mingrelian and Laz are sometimes grouped together as *Zan* or *Tsan*.

To the south, Georgian dialect areas now reach the sea in the Batumi region; once, it is believed, Mingrelian was spoken here too. Mingrelian dialects would then have shaded gradually into Laz, which is linguistically close to Mingrelian but is generally regarded as sufficiently distinct to count as a third member of the Kartvelian family. Laz is spoken along a strip of the Black Sea shore from Sarpi in Georgia to Pazar in Turkey. Most speakers are bilingual in Turkish. Laz, like Mingrelian, is unwritten and in general ignored by both Turkish and Georgian governments.

Both languages have five vowels and thirty consonants. As in other Caucasian languages, consonant clusters abound. The plural in nouns is marked by a suffix, *-ep* in Mingrelian, *-pe* or *-epe* in Laz.

Denizi görmemiş, Laz'a Kürt denir, 'A Laz who has not seen the sea is called a Kurd' – the Turkish proverb places two Turkish minorities geographically, blurring the linguistic and cultural divide between them.

Numerals in Mingrelian, Laz, Georgian and Svan			
Mingrelian	**Laz**	**Georgian**	**Svan**
1	art'i	art'i	ert'i	eshkhvi
2	zhiri	zhur	ori	ervi
3	sumi	shum	sami	semi
4	'ot'khi	ot'khi	ot'khi	voshdkhv
5	khut'i	khu	khut'i	vokhvishd
6	amshvi	ashi	ek'vsi	mevsgve
7	shk'vit'i	shk'wit'	shvidi	ishgvid
8	ruo	ovro	rva	ara
9	chkhoro	chkhoro	tskhra	chkhara
10	vit'i	vit'	at'i	ieshd

Based on Adolf Dirr, *Einführung in das Studium der kaukasischen Sprachen* (Leipzig: Asia Major, 1928) p. 358

MIXTEC

PERHAPS 250,000 SPEAKERS

Mexico

Mixtec belongs to the Otomanguean family of AMERIND LANGUAGES. It is a language of Mexico, and one of those with a long written tradition, for Mixtec manuscripts are among the major sources on pre-Columbian culture and history.

The name of the speakers and their language identifies them as 'cloud people'. Their historic homeland is Mixteca Alta, Achiutla being the legendary place of origin of the Mixtec people.

Tilantongo is the site of extensive Mixtec ruins and was once their capital. The city is sometimes said to have been founded by non-Mixtec invaders who became assimilated to Mixtec culture. At any rate, at the Spanish conquest, Mixtec commoners would still refer to their rulers in terminology that was not Mixtec but apparently drawn from another Otomanguean language, Cuicatec of Puebla. There was, however, cultural mixing, in later pre-Spanish times, among Mixtec and Puebla peoples.

From Tilantongo Mixtec domination spread eastwards about 900 to Oaxaca, where they displaced their linguistic relatives, the Zapotecs, from Monte Albán. Later they expanded westwards into the Valley of Mexico. Southwards their coastal kingdom centred on Tututepec in the Sierra Madre del Sur.

Some Mixtec manuscripts ('codices') are religious: these have been interpreted by Edward Seler and others. Others are historical, or rather genealogical. They give royal dates of birth and death, ceremonial names of monarchs, lists of their relatives and wives; they record state events, migrations, colonisations, conquests and sacrifices. Some deal with a single place: some, like the Bodley Codex now in Oxford, cover a wider political area.

For a long time it was unclear whether the non-ritual codices were truly historical (as United States researchers thought) or were linked to mythological tales (as German scholars believed). It was not even certain that Mixtec was the language hidden in the pictographs. Alfonso Caso made the breakthrough while studying a map of Teozacoalco made for the Spaniards around 1580. He found that the map included names, dates and genealogies of Mixtec kings – and these matched dates and pictorial versions of names in the codices. From this starting-point, by comparing the codices among themselves, Caso was able to build up a history of Mixtec kings from the 7th to the 17th century, and to show that the sequences of pictographs made sense only when read in Mixtec.

As the Zapotecs were driven eastwards and the Mixtecs took the valley sites, Mixtec borrowed from Zapotec the word for 'turkey' among other luxury items previously unfamiliar to Mixtec speakers. Mixtec also borrowed from Mixe-Zoque such words as proto-Mixe-Zoque *toto* 'paper', *kuku* 'turtle-dove'. The Mixtec medical loanwords in neighbouring Trique suggest some cultural dominance – that Mixtec shamans were called in to cure Trique diseases.

The first ten numerals in Mixtec are: *ĩ´ĩ´, uù, unì, kũũ`, ũ´`ũ, ĩ´nyũ, úshia, unà, ĩ´ĩ, ushì.*

Mixtec, Zapotec and some relatives

The *Mixtec* dialects are spoken in Oaxaca state. Close relatives, with only a few thousand speakers, are *Cuicatec* and *Trique*.

ZAPOTEC is also a language of Oaxaca state. It has about 450,000 speakers.

Other Otomanguean languages, all spoken in Mexico, include *Otomí* (200,000), *Mazahua* (350,000), *Mazatec* (100,000) and *Chinantec* (60,000). There are still others with smaller numbers of speakers.

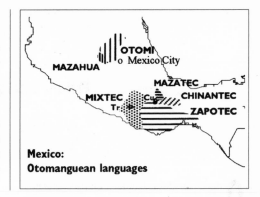

**Mexico:
Otomanguean languages**

MON

PERHAPS 200,000 SPEAKERS

Burma, Thailand

One of the Mon-Khmer group of AUSTROASI-ATIC LANGUAGES, Mon was once the ruling language of a powerful kingdom. Through Mon, Buddhist culture was transmitted to the early speakers of Burmese. By way of Mon script, Burmese and Shan first became written languages. Mon is now a minority language of southern Burma and central Thailand (see map at KHMER), and most of its speakers are bilingual in Burmese or Thai.

Mon is the speakers' own name for themselves and their language. In Burmese they are sometimes *Mun* but traditionally *Talaing*, and that term was used in older English sources, along with *Peguan*, which is now completely obsolete.

There are written sources for Mon history, in the form of stone inscriptions in Mon, from the 7th century onwards. The oldest are from central Thailand, once the Mon kingdom of Dvaravati. The Mon kingdom in Burma, with its old capital at Thaton, is known from the 10th century. It was a centre of Buddhist learning, with close literary and cultural links with Sri Lanka. The Old Mon language of this period had already many loanwords from Pali, and was written in a script of Indic type.

The Burmese monarch Anawrata, in 1057, attacked Thaton and returned to Pagan with manuscripts of the Buddhist scriptures – they would have been in Pali, in Mon script, and perhaps with Mon commentaries.

A Mon kingdom in southern Burma, usually called 'Pegu' in European sources after its chief city, survived until its final conquest by the Burmese in 1757. From that date until 1852 the use of Mon was strongly discouraged: it was forbidden in religious education. The Mon-speaking country then became part of British Burma. In the last two centuries there appears to have been little desire among Mon speakers to emphasise their distinctness as against Burmese.

Although Mon is not an official language in Burma, it is now used again in traditional monastic education, which most boys experience. This has so far ensured the survival of a standard literary form of Mon, which is closest to the dialect spoken in the neighbourhood of Moulmein. Some publications continue to appear in the language.

Mon once influenced Burmese heavily. Recently it has been influenced in its turn – by Burmese and by English. It is not a tonal language but, like Khmer, has a 'clear' and a 'breathy' register, a feature which now forms part of the Burmese sound pattern too.

MONGOLIAN LANGUAGES

PERHAPS 5,000,000 SPEAKERS

China, Mongolia, Russia

A group of closely related languages usually believed to be one of the constituents of the ALTAIC family.

In the 13th century horsemen from Inner Asia, ruled by the Mongol leader Genghis Khan and his son Ögedei, conquered much of the known world, from central Europe to the Pacific coast of Asia. The warriors were, some of them, Mongol speakers; but it is clear that the majority spoke Turkic languages, for it was Turkic languages that spread widely as a result. In due course even the 'Mongol' hordes turned from Mongolian to Turkic as their language of government. Only in China did Mongolian remain for some centuries a court language – to be eventually supplanted by another language of northern invaders, Manchu (see TUNGUSIC LANGUAGES).

However, the great conquests left Mongolian dialects more widespread than they had been before. Their homeland was, and still is, the

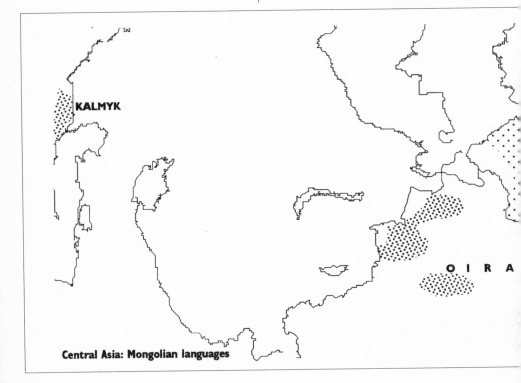

KALMYK

OIRA

Central Asia: Mongolian languages

country we now call Mongolia, with a region of Siberia just to the north and some parts of China to the south and east. Beside this, they can still be heard in Afghanistan, and even, far away to the west, in southern Russia on the conventional borderline between Europe and Asia.

Mongolia itself, once known by reference to China as 'Outer Mongolia', became an independent state – the first true 'Soviet satellite' – in 1924. 'Inner Mongolia' remains an autonomous region of China; about half the speakers of Mongolian live here. Most speakers in Siberia (about 300,000) are in the Russian republic of Buryatia, self-governing since 1992. The Kalmyks occupy the Russian republic of Khalmg Tangch. Its origins go back to the 16th century, when Kalmyk Khan signed a treaty, after the collapse of the Golden Horde, making his people a part of the Russian Empire. The First Kalmyk Regiment, mounted on Bactrian camels, made a great impression on western Europe when they entered Paris in 1814, inspiring Balzac's sketch 'Kalmyks in Paris'.

Mongolia itself, once a theocratic state, re-mains a stronghold of Mahayana Buddhism, a fact with which its Communist governments have had to come to terms. Buddhism came to the Mongols from Tibet, and Tibetan remains a sacred language taught in monasteries, alongside classical Mongolian. Mongolian Buddhists acknowledge the spiritual authority of the Dalai Lama. In Buryatia Buddhist monasticism was almost destroyed in Soviet times, though some young men were able to study in Mongolia. There is now a Buddhist revival. The Kalmyks, too, are Buddhist and traditionally nomadic. Numbering nearly 100,000, the Kalmyks were among Stalin's 'punished peoples', deported en masse to Central Asia in 1944; from 1957 onwards their territory was gradually restored, a process completed only in 1992. There are now 150,000 of them.

The first written records of Mongolian date from the 13th century, under Genghis Khan, when the script was devised (traditionally in 1204). But the first work of Mongolian literature, and one of the greatest, the *Secret History of the Mongols*, was written down in Chinese characters.

Classical Mongolian is the language of the Buddhist scriptures as translated from Tibetan in 1604–34 and printed from wood blocks in Beijing. It is still the literary language for all educated Mongolian speakers. The language displays its cultural history in its numerous loanwords from Sanskrit and Tibetan.

Mongolian and its relatives

The most important language in the group is Mongolian itself, a literary language and group of spoken dialects known under six names in progressively differing varieties. First is *Khalkha*, the national language of modern Mongolia, which is very close to *Menggu*, the main language of 'Inner Mongolia' in China, and also close to *Buryat*, of the Buryat ASSR to the north. Far to their west is the variety called *Kalmyk* in Russia, where it is now spoken to the north of the Caspian – and called *Oirat* in the Xinjiang region of China. The last member is *Moghol* or Mogul, once spoken in Herat, Maimana and Badakshan provinces of

Afghanistan. Having separated from the rest some time ago, Moghol shows archaic features which it shares with old-fashioned literary Mongolian rather than with the other modern forms of Mongolian. Moghol is now almost extinct, but has left traces of its former importance in the form of Moghol loanwords in the Hazaragi dialect of PERSIAN.

There are several other languages in the group, distinct from these partly because they do not share the common inheritance of Mongolian literary culture. Most notable are three local languages of China: *Tu* or Monguor, with about 100,000 speakers in Qinghai, *Dongxiang* or Santa, with 280,000 in Gansu, and *Dagur* or Daur, with 60,000 in Inner Mongolia and Xinjiang.

Numerals in the Mongolian languages				
Classical Mongolian		**Khalkha**	**Buryat**	**Kalmyk**
nigen	1	negen	negen	negn
qoyar	2	khoyor	khoyor	khoyr
ghurban	3	gurav	gurban	hurvn
dürben	4	dürüv	dürben	dörvn
tabun	5	tavan	taban	tavn
jirghughan	6	zurgaan	zurgaan	zurhan
dologhan	7	doloon	doloon	dolan
naiman	8	naiman	naiman	nəəmn
yisün	9	yesön	yühen	yisn
arban	10	arav	arban	arvn

From George L. Campbell, *Compendium of the world's languages* (London: Routledge, 1991) and other sources

Mongolian and Oirat scripts

Mongolian is traditionally written in its own script, derived from the Uighur script that had been borrowed from Sogdian and came ultimately from ARAMAIC. This traditional script is still used in Inner Mongolia, while Oirat in China is written with the related Oirat alphabet devised in 1648. In independent Mongolia the Cyrillic alphabet was introduced for Khalkha and Oirat in 1944, though the traditional script is still used in religious texts. In the Soviet Union a Latin alphabet was assigned to Buryat and Kalmyk in 1931 to be replaced by Cyrillic in 1938.

MÕÕRE

3,000,000 SPEAKERS

Burkina Faso

O ne of the NIGER-CONGO LANGUAGES, Mõõre was the ruling language of the kingdoms of Ouagadougou and Yatenga, founded by conquering horsemen from the Lake Chad area in the 10th century. These two states in the Niger bend survived until the French occupation in the late 1800s, and their influence stretched over most of modern Burkina Faso and northern Ghana.

> *Mossi* is the name of the people (singular *Moagha*) and is sometimes used for the language. The speakers themselves, however, call their language *Mõõre*, 'language of the *Moogho* country'. The usual French spelling is *Moré*.

The populations of these states were of mixed origin and language, including speakers of FULANI and MANDEKAN. Mõõre became the lingua franca, and for many the mother tongue, throughout much of the territory that was to become Haut-Volta under French rule, now the independent state of Burkina Faso. Probably as many as a million people speak it as a second or third language, in addition to the three million for whom it is the mother tongue. Its speakers often migrate to find seasonal and short-term work: thus there are large communities of Mõõre speakers in the southern cities of Ivory Coast, Ghana, Togo and Benin. There are also widely scattered Mõõre settlements in northern Ghana.

Mõõre is a tonal language, with three tones, high, low and falling-rising. A system of long distance drum messages, centred on the royal palace at Ouagadougou, used three-tone drums to match the patterning of normal speech.

There are six noun classes in Mõõre, marked by terminations that are widely different in singular and plural. 'Horse' is *wèefoo*, 'horses' *widi*. There are numerous French loanwords – *livrè* 'book', *àlímétà* 'matches' (French *allumettes*) – and some Songhay loanwords, Songhay being the trading language of this part of the Niger valley. The first ten numerals are: *ié, yí, tá, náasee, nú, ióobee, iópóe, nû, ué, píigá.*

A Mõõre folk tale begins . . .

Em bā sō:āmbā nē ēm bā bá:gá dā kēgà dà:gā
Uncle Hare and uncle Dog went to market –

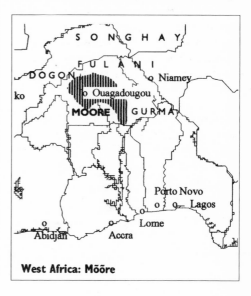

West Africa: Mõõre

MORDVIN

850,000 SPEAKERS

Russia

Mordvin is the official name for two very closely related URALIC LANGUAGES, Erza and Moksha, spoken by a population group to the west of the middle Volga. Only a third of speakers live in Mordovia, now a self-governing republic within Russia: even here they are a minority, outnumbered by Russians. The republic is best known for its former secret city, Sarov (also called Moscow-2, Kremlyovsk, Arzamas-16), the centre of nuclear research which was once conducted largely by prisoners such as Andrei Sakharov.

Morden were among the eleven 'Arctic peoples' who were conquered by the Gothic king Ermanaric in the 4th century, according to a Latin chronicler. Later they submitted to the rulers of Kiev. Russian interest in the Mordvin country had already begun with the capture and refounding of Nizhnii Novgorod, originally a Mordvin town, in 1221. ('Lower Novgorod' is so called to distinguish it from Novgorod the Great, the trading city north-west of Moscow. It was renamed Gorkii between 1932 and 1991.) Russian settlement gathered pace in the 16th century after the Russians smashed the Tatar Khanate of Kazan, and it went hand in hand with Russian influence on the local languages.

Publishing, at first religious and educational, began in the 19th century. Saransk, capital of Mordovia, is the publishing centre. Literary Erza is based on the dialect of Kozlovka, while literary Moksha is based on the dialects of Krasnoslobodsk and Temnikov. Both use Cyrillic script.

Both languages are now heavily loaded with Russian loanwords, particularly Erza; Moksha shows greater Tatar influence. Mordvins have a long history of bilingualism in Russian and of assimilation to Russian society, yet the number of Mordvin speakers tended, at least until quite recently, to remain constant.

Verbs in Erza and Moksha have a complex range of forms, varying for both subject and object, for four tenses and for seven moods: Erza *vanok* 'look!'; *vanikselyiny* 'I wanted to look'; *vaninydyeryavlyiny* 'if I had looked'.

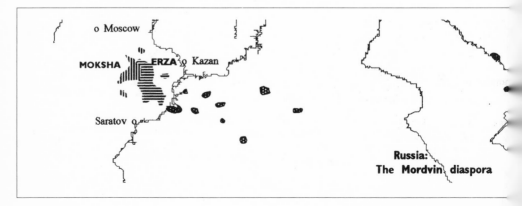

Russia:
The Mordvin diaspora

Better than nothing?

Erχt atiŋǵit babiŋǵit,	There was an old man and old woman
panda pŕasa kudîŋǵist;	In a little house on a hilltop;
ve uš tuma peŋǵiŋǵist,	They had one little log for burning,
ve kraśtima čevîŋǵist,	With one little splinter for kindling,
íûdij śeŕχka śtîŕiŋǵist,	One little girl with legs like reeds,
keńdi peke ćorîŋǵist,	One little boy with a belly like a felt rag,
ksnav śelme atakśkist,	One little hen with eyes like peas,
kańźur śelme avakśkist,	One little chicken with eyes like mustard seeds,
puluftuma parnîŋǵist,	One little foal without a tail,
śuruftuma skalîŋǵist!	One little cow without any horns!

This Moksha folk song is in seven-syllable lines, with a repeated rhyme supplied by the diminutive suffixes (English 'little . . .') on the last word of each line. The text is given in the standard transcription of the Société Finno-Ougrienne, in which an acute accent ´ indicates palatalisation, a very common feature of Moksha.

Proben der mordwinischen Volkslitteratur gesammelt von H. Paasonen. Vol. 1: Erza (Helsinki, 1891. *Journal de la Société Finno-Ougrienne*, 10) pp. 84–5

Erza, Moksha and their neighbours: the map

Mordovskie yazyki, 'the Mordvinian languages', is the official Russian term for this language pair. The Erza and Moksha are viewed by themselves as quite distinct, with independent traditions and no history of close relationships – or even of intermarriage. Moksha is now the language of the Moksha valley, while Erza is spoken in the Sura valley.

Mordvin migrations – often in reaction to Russian invasions and settlement – have made them one of the most scattered peoples of Russia.

Numerals in Erza and Moksha		
Erza		**Moksha**
veyke	1	fkä
kavto	2	kafta
kolmo	3	kolma
nyilye	4	nyilyä
vetye	5	vetyä
koto	6	kota
syisyem	7	syisyəm
kavkso	8	kafksa
veykse	9	veyksa
kemeny	10	keməny

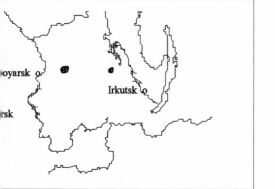

MOZARABIC

Extinct language of Spain

Unique among the ROMANCE LANGUAGES, Mozarabic developed in an Islamic environment, in medieval southern Spain. Although the language of government was Arabic, Romance speech survived among the people of the Kingdom of Granada until eventually, after the Spanish *Reconquista*, it was overwhelmed by the Castilian Spanish of the Christian north.

Arabic *Musta'rib* 'Arabised' is the origin of the term *Mozarabic*.

For a long time it was thought that in Muslim Spain Romance speech had died out completely, to return from the Christian north during the reconquest – although there are local plant names, of Romance origin, in Arabic agricultural and botanical texts from Spain.

But ever since 1851, Mozarabic refrains have been known in Hebrew poetry from Arab Spain.

A hundred years later, S. M. Stern began to find Mozarabic refrains in Arabic poetry too. This is the oldest Romance literature from Spain – some texts are older than the *Poema del Cid* with which Spanish literature begins – and it is evidence of the language that was once spoken across all of central and southern Spain.

It is clear that many of the Arabic loanwords now found in Spanish, Portuguese and Judezmo must have reached those languages by way of Mozarabic. They include Spanish *alcachofa* 'artichoke', *arroz* 'rice', *albérchiga* 'peach' and many other fruits, vegetables and flowers; *aldea* 'village', *alcalde* 'magistrate' and *almirante* 'admiral', which comes from the Arabic word known in English as *emir*.

Examples from W. D. Elcock, *The Romance languages* (London: Faber, 1960)

Mozarabic lyrics: verse and refrain

A typical *muwashshah* verse, in Hebrew or Arabic, gives the atmosphere of a love affair –

'When he is here the city is clothed in his glory,
and she is transported to heaven with pride as long as he remains,
She cries, on the day of his departure – '

In Arabic poetics the rule of the *muwashshah* was that the refrain – the woman's words – should be in colloquial language. In Spain, that meant Mozarabic:

ky fr'yw	– 'Que farayo	– 'What shall I do,
'w ky śyr'd dmyby	o que serad de mibi?	what will become of me?
ḥbyby	Ḥabībī,	Lover,
nwn tytwlgś dmyby	Non te tolgas de mibi!'	do not leave me!'

Thanks to this rule, a forgotten language has been rediscovered. In Arabic script only the consonants are written (left column), and these brief texts pose enormous problems of interpretation.

After S. M. Stern, *Les chansons mozarabes* (Palermo: Manfredi, 1953) pp. 16–17

MUNDARI

850,000 SPEAKERS

India

Mundari is one of the Munda group of languages, spoken by rural peoples of eastern India. These languages are now known to belong, with the Mon-Khmer group of south-east Asia, to the family of AUSTROASIATIC LANGUAGES.

By contrast with the Indo-Aryan and Dravidian groups, Munda languages have traditionally been unwritten and their peoples have little recorded history until they came into the sights of British administrators in India's colonial period. References can be found to forest peoples in classical Sanskrit texts, but their identification with speakers of Munda languages is a matter of faith rather than evidence.

There is now a limited periodical press in Mundari; publications have appeared in all three surrounding scripts, Devanagari (as for Hindi), Bengali and Oriya. The elaborate *Encyclopaedia Mundarica*, of which thirteen volumes were published in the 1930s and 1940s, is a storehouse of the language and its culture. It is in Latin script, as generally preferred by Christian missionaries.

As indicated by the accompanying Mundari song, Mundari are typically hill peoples while the related SANTALI (see table of numerals there) is spoken by lowland farmers.

Mundari and other Munda languages have been spoken alongside Indo-Aryan languages for two millennia. They show the signs of this long coexistence not only in loanwords – in both directions – but also in the structure of typical sentences, which can sometimes be paralleled, word for word, in languages of these quite independent groups.

Major Austroasiatic languages of India: the map

KHASI has numerous dialect divisions. *Synteng* or Jaintia or Pnar, the language of a relatively large kingdom with a distinctive history, has perhaps 80,000 speakers. *Lyngngam* is spoken to the west of other Khasi dialects by a people who show some cultural links with GARO speakers.

Korku has 320,000 speakers in southern Madhya Pradesh and northern Maharashtra.

Kharia has about 150,000 speakers in Bihar.

Mundari has 850,000 speakers, mainly in Bihar.

SANTALI has 4,000,000 speakers, mainly in West Bengal, but including 100,000 in western Bangladesh.

Ho is spoken to the south-east of Mundari, in Singbhum district of Bihar and Mayurbhanj district of Orissa. It has 750,000 speakers.

Bhumij has 100,000 speakers in Mayurbhanj district of Orissa. The number of speakers is declining rapidly.

Sora has 250,000 speakers in Ganjam district of Orissa. 'The British administrator's supreme

Austroasiatic languages of India

ignorance can be exemplified by the report of H. D. Taylor, Agent to the Governor in Ganjam, who in 1900 recommended that Government servants should be encouraged to learn the So:ra: language. He said that "the Sourah language consists, I believe, of only 700 words and is not difficult to acquire; but it is spoken by hill-men" ' (D. P. Pattanayak in *Current trends in linguistics* vol. 5 ed. Thomas A. Sebeok [The Hague: Mouton, 1969] pp. 139–40).

Who planted the mustard?

Búrú re búru ré máni dó,	Millet on every hill,
bérá re béra ré rái;	Mustard in every valley;
límáng lómongá máni dó,	Millet dances,
kídár kódorá rái.	Mustard sways.
Ókoé ge hérléda máni dó,	Who planted the millet?
címaé ge pásiléd rái?	Who sowed the mustard?
límáng lómongá máni dó,	Millet dances,
kídár kódorá rái.	Mustard sways.
Múndakó ge hérléda máni dó,	Mundas planted the millet,
Sántakó ge pásirléd rái;	Santals sowed the mustard;
límáng lómongá máni dó,	Millet dances,
kídár kódorá rái.	Mustard sways.
Síde lége mónéña máni dó,	I want to pick the millet,
ṭóṭa' lége sánañá rái;	I want to nip the mustard.
límáng lómongá máni dó,	Millet dances,
kídár kódorá rái.	Mustard sways.
Álo répe sídeá máni dó,	Don't pick the millet!
álo répe ṭóṭa'éa rái!	Don't nip the mustard!
límáng lómongá máni dó,	Millet dances,
kídár kódorá rái.	Mustard sways.
Tíire múndam gónóngte máni dó,	The millet costs a finger-ring,
Káṭáre póla sátite rái!	The mustard costs a toe-ring:
límáng lómongá máni dó,	Millet dances,
kídár kódorá rái.	Mustard sways.

Ram Dayal Munda, 'Some formal features of traditional Mundari poetry' in *Austroasiatic studies* ed. Philip N. Jenner and others (Honolulu: University Press of Hawaii, 1976) pp. 844–71

An *or jadur* sung as one of a trilogy of songs during the Munda flower festival of February, March or April. In this text the accent ´ marks the strong beat of the verse; the repetition inherent in Mundari style (*buru re buru re* 'on every hill') is offset by the irregular rhythm.

MUONG

800,000 SPEAKERS

Vietnam

Muong is evidently related to VIETNAMESE (see map there); this 'Viet-Muong' group is now generally agreed to belong to the AUSTROASIATIC LANGUAGES.

Muong, the commonly used name for this people and their language, is a mistake – it is the word in Tai languages for a town and its territory. Speakers sometimes call themselves *Mon* or *Mwon*, however, like their distant relatives the MON of Burma. But neither in Muong nor in Vietnamese has there been any comprehensive term for the Muong. Near Vinh the Vietnamese call them *Nha Long*; in Quang Binh the name was *Nguon*. *Ao-ta*, *Sach* and *Tho* are also used – but the last serves also as the name for the Tai language of the northern Vietnamese plains.

Muong is spoken in inland northern Vietnam. Its cultural history has been completely different from that of Vietnamese, the language of a centralised state, penetrated by Chinese culture, in which the arts of writing have been essential to everyday life.

Historically the most likely theory is that the speakers of early Muong and of early Vietnamese, two thousand years ago, lived not far apart. Chinese interest centred on the Vietnamese of the Red River delta: the Muong, in country areas to the south, remained untouched. Theirs is, and has no doubt always been, a rural, agricultural lifestyle, and it was only far later, three or four hundred years ago, that they came gradually to be incorporated in the Vietnamese state. This involved transferring some of the traditional power of the Muong hereditary noble families to Vietnamese-speaking civil servants.

Since this time Vietnamese has influenced Muong pervasively; there are now numerous French loanwords too. Like Vietnamese, Muong is a monosyllabic language. It has five tones.

NA-DENÉ LANGUAGES

The Na-Dené family of languages, apparently unrelated to any other, consists of one clearly identifiable group, Athapaskan, and three minor isolated languages which are much more distantly related, Tlingit, Eyak and Haida. The family grouping was postulated by the linguist Edward Sapir in a seminal paper in the *American anthropologist* in 1915: it remains controversial to this day.

The first element to be recognised, before Sapir's time, was that of the Athapaskan (or Athabaskan) languages, stretching from Alaska to Mexico in four separate geographical zones. NAVAHO, a language of Arizona and New Mexico, has the most speakers today, though its neighbours, the *Apache dialects* with around 15,000 speakers in Texas, New Mexico and Arizona, fill more of the map. The Athapaskan languages of California and those of Oregon are practically extinct ('there are perhaps no speakers under seventy years of age', said Michael Krauss in 1971). The most varied region is western Canada and central Alaska. Canadian languages of the group include *Carrier*, with about 3,600 speakers, Chipewyan with around 5,500, and *Slave* (pronounced, and sometimes spelt, Slavey) with about 2,000. In Alaska the number of speakers of Athapaskan languages is now very small but the variety greatest.

The three distantly related languages are also in Alaska and British Columbia. They are *Tlingit* (about 2,000 speakers in Alaska and British Columbia), Eyak and Haida. *Eyak* was first described by a Russian linguist in 1805. Long forgotten, and overlooked by Sapir himself, the Eyak were rediscovered in Alaska in 1930. By 1990 only one speaker remained alive.

If most specialists now agree that Tlingit and Eyak are somehow linked with the Athabaskan group, that is not true of *Haida*, with its 350 speakers. Here the controversy raised by Sapir has not died down: some, such as Krauss, consider Haida to be a linguistic isolate, with no demonstrated relationship to any other language.

Na-Dené, a relatively small family on the world scale, has not been convincingly linked to any wider grouping. In particular, Joseph Greenberg excludes Na-Dené, along with the Eskimo-Aleut languages, from the Amerind family in which he boldly classes every other language of native America. He suggests that Na-Dené speakers at their first arrival on the American side of the Bering Strait are to be identified with the Paleo-Arctic or Beringian culture of Alaska, dated by archaeologists to 8000 to 5000 BC.

Various proposed affiliations for Na-Dené, for instance with Sino-Tibetan or with Basque, though put forward by respected scholars, have not carried conviction.

Edward Sapir

Sapir (1884–1939) studied under Franz Boas. He was a general linguist whose detailed research was largely in the area of American native languages. As part of a determined attempt to reduce the number of independent families into which American languages were then classified, Sapir renewed the idea, first proposed in 1798 and 1805, of a distant relationship between the Athabaskan languages on the one hand and Tlingit and Haida on the other. In 1929 Sapir published (in an article in the 14th edition of the *Encyclopaedia Britannica*) a classification of all Central and North American languages into six 'super-stocks', one of which was Na-Dené.

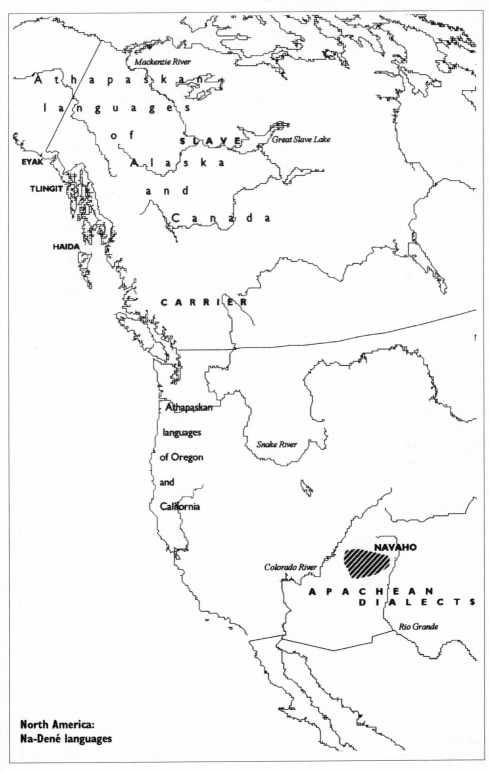

North America:
Na-Dené languages

NAHUATL

PERHAPS 1,250,000 SPEAKERS OF NAHUA DIALECTS

Mexico

Nahuatl is the most important member of the Uto-Aztecan family, now believed by some to belong to a larger family of AMERIND LAN-GUAGES. Nahuatl was the language of the powerful Aztec civilisation so suddenly overwhelmed by the Spanish conquest in the 16th century. Nahuatl is still a major language of Mexico, a country proud of its Aztec inheritance – but Spanish is the only official language of the country.

Among the many languages of central Mexico it can be surprisingly difficult to make links with civilisations of the past. Who exactly were the Toltecs of AD 850 to 1100, masters of the Valley of Mexico in pre-Aztec times? The Aztec rulers, who took power after them, were invaders from the north: but it is unlikely that the Nahuatl language arrived only with the Aztecs. More probably the Toltec civilisation itself had already been Nahua-speaking. The fame of the Toltec capital, Tula, destroyed about AD 1200, seems to survive in the legendary mother-city of *Tollân* known from 15th-century Nahuatl manuscripts.

The Toltecs are known to have sent colonies southwards around AD 900. *Pipil* is the language of this southern migration. Between them, Toltecs and Pipils destroyed much of classical Maya civilisation in their passing.

The Aztec intruders were in the Valley of Mexico in 1256. They founded Tenochtitlán in 1325, and began to expand their empire in the 15th century. Although the valley remained highly fragmented, linguistically and politically, the Aztecs soon dominated it – and were quickly informed of the first Spanish landings, far to the east, in 1517.

Nahuatl, though little known to the mass of speakers of other Mexican languages, had spread widely in the previous two centuries and was by now the most useful long distance language in the region, essential to Spanish conquerors. There was certainly already some bilingualism in Nahuatl. That is why, even after the conquest, Nahuatl loanwords (as well as Spanish loanwords) multiplied in other Mexican languages: loanwords such as Nahuatl *tentzu* 'goat', Totontepec *teents*, Tzotzil *tentsun*. Enjoying Spanish favour, Nahuatl continued to spread while some other languages died away. It even became a kind of official language, recognised as such in a royal ordinance of 1570, though even then it was seen as a stepping-stone to Catholic conversion and eventual Hispanicisation.

From 1770 onwards, education in Mexico officially had to be in Spanish – but, after all, the reach of education was limited, and the position of Nahuatl was still not seriously undermined. The future of the language, two centuries later, is far from clear. In practice, the administration always favours Spanish and, crucially perhaps, Spanish is demanded by the new population mobility of the late 20th century.

Already at the Spanish conquest Nahuatl was being recorded in writing: in sculpted inscriptions, usually brief; and in picture books, which acted as a mnemonic for the reciter of orally remembered texts. The Spaniards destroyed many of these picture books, but the more enlightened among them encouraged the making of others, a record of Nahuatl beliefs and culture, useful (at the very least) to priests who wished to understand the people whom they planned to convert to Christianity.

> Certain manuscripts offer special help in understanding classical Nahuatl pictographic writing. Compiled under Spanish domination, *Codex Mendoza* is 'bilingual'. Pictograms of the ancient type, whose meaning would soon be lost, are here accompanied by interpretations in Spanish. This not only helps to explain the individual symbols and their variations. It also shows that they never corresponded to a precise text (which could have been *translated* into Spanish). Instead, Mexican pictograms stood for a sequence of ideas. Their makers certainly expected them to be read back in Nahuatl or Mixtec. But one who held the key could interpret them in any language. Thus the forgotten maker of *Codex Mendoza* has assisted modern scholars to reconstruct the key.

Bernardino de Sahagún, a Franciscan friar active in 'New Spain' from 1529 to 1590, gathered information from his Mexican students about their own culture and wrote it down in his 'General record of matters of New Spain', which is an encyclopaedia of Aztec religion, astronomy, astrology, economics, daily life, medicine, rhetoric, mineralogy and history. This vast work includes hymns to the Aztec gods, riddles and proverbs, and reproduces selected passages from the old picture books. It survives in two fairly complete versions, in manuscripts at Florence and Madrid.

Some of the pictographic manuscripts are historical, recording – with careful calculation of dates – migrations into the Valley of Mexico, wars between cities, and genealogy. Nahuatl traditional literature included formal speeches of praise and family history, given on public occasions. The manuscripts contain songs and myths: the so-called *Mexican Songs* include lyrics, war songs, mourning songs, burlesque, drama. It was a literature of great complexity, with certain styles specially belonging to different towns and regions. Poetic language involved metaphor, multiple compounds, parallel expres-

sions, and imagery based on jewels, feathers and flowers.

The range of Nahuatl literature shrank with the Spanish ascendancy; but a genre of Catholic religious plays flourished, and they are still performed in Nahuatl-speaking villages.

At a crossroads of Mexican culture, Nahuatl naturally contains loanwords from other American languages, such as Mixe-Zoque (because the early Olmec civilisation spoke a Mixe-Zoque language): from this source comes *nixtamalli* 'maize dough', a staple food; from Mixe-Zoque, too (proto-Mixe-Zoque *kakawa*) comes the Nahuatl word for 'cacao' that was eventually borrowed into European languages (e.g. English *chocolate, cocoa*). Other important loanwords from Nahuatl in European languages include *tomato, avocado*. For things newly introduced after the conquest, Spanish loanwords in Nahuatl have multiplied: from Spanish *naranja* comes Nahuatl *laxa* 'orange'.

Because of its past importance as a lingua franca, loanwords from Nahuatl are to be found in many of the languages of Mexico, including Tepecano, Cora, Huichol, Tequistlatec, Huastec, Yucatec, Quiché and Cakchiquel. A Nahuatl-Spanish pidgin (see also SPANISH) was once widely used in central America. This is how Nahuatl *tequetl* 'work' came to be borrowed into the Lenca language of distant Guatemala, just as Spanish *trabajo* 'work' was borrowed into other Amerindian languages.

Printing in the New World
The first American printed book (1539) was a bilingual catechism in Spanish and Nahuatl. The bishop of Mexico, Francisco de Zumárraga, had imported a printing press to assist the spread of Christianity. The first Nahuatl grammar, by A. de Olmos, *Arte para aprender la lengua mexicana*, appeared in 1547.

Trained in Latin grammar, the Spanish-speaking friars who first codified Nahuatl grammar, in the 16th century, were open-minded enough to realise that they had to devise a new terminology for this utterly different tongue. To classify verb

Kutenai

Northern
Paiute SHOSHONE

HOPI Comanche

Sonoran

languages

Cora
Huichol
NAHUATL
Mexico City o

**North America:
Uto-Aztecan languages**

Pipil

forms they introduced terms such as 'compul-
sive' (causative) and 'applicative' (benefactitive).
The first ten numerals in Nahuatl are *ce, ome, yei,
nahui, macuilli, chicuace, chicome, chicuei, chicunahui,
matlactli*. It can be seen that the numbers '6' to
'9' are formed on the pattern '5 plus 1', '5 plus 2'
and so on.

Uto-Aztecan languages

Nahuatl (or 'Aztec') is the only Uto-Aztecan
language with a large number of speakers –
and the only one which was the vehicle of a
great civilisation. The others are scattered across
the western United States and northern Mexico.

Nahua dialects are classified according to a particular phonetic trait. The lateral affricate or click, *tl*, is typical of the central group of dialects, which are thus properly called *Nahuatl*. Others are known as *Nahual* and *Nahuat*. Central Nahuatl is also known as *México* – language of the Valley of Mexico, after which the great modern city, and the whole nation state of which it is the capital, are both named.

Pipil, once a major language of colonial El Salvador and neighbouring states, is on the verge of extinction: a recent survey gives only twenty elderly speakers, the Pipil ethnic group having adopted Spanish as its mother tongue. Pipil is a Nahua dialect, apparently established as a result of eastward conquests by the Toltecs in the 10th century.

Mayo is the next largest Uto-Aztecan language, spoken by about 50,000 people in Sonora and Sinaloa provinces of Mexico.

Tarahumara also has around 50,000 speakers in Mexico.

Ute, Comanche, Hopi, Shoshone and *Northern Paiute* are among the thirty remaining Uto-Aztecan languages with no more than a few thousand speakers each. Most are on the way to extinction.

The language of human sacrifice

Emphases on war and human sacrifice are well-known features of pre-Columbian Mexican culture. These ideas seem, from archaeology, to have belonged to the conquering Toltecs, around AD 1000, and to have been learnt from them by peoples such as the Aztecs.

In *Codex Magliabechiano*, a second 'bilingual' manuscript, feast days are described. The Spanish text explains: 'This picture shows the unspeakable ritual of the Yndians on the day that they sacrificed men to their idols. Then, before the demon called Mictlantecutl, which means "Lord of the Dead" as explained elsewhere, they placed many cooking pots full of the human flesh, and shared it among the nobles and rulers and those who served in the demon's temple, called *tlamagatl*; and these shared their portions among their friends and families. They say that it tasted as pork tastes now, and this is why they like pork so much.'

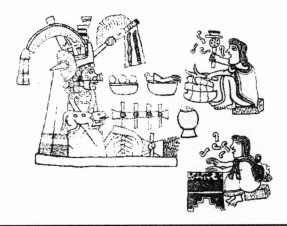

NAVAHO

PERHAPS 120,000 SPEAKERS

United States

Navaho is spoken in Arizona and New Mexico. As one of the NA-DENÉ LANGUAGES (see map there), it is closely related to the various Apache dialects, but – as far as anyone knows – totally unrelated to the majority of its Amerindian neighbours.

An anatomical atlas of Navaho names for parts of the body has over 400 entries. The Navaho and English-speaking compilers realised as they worked that while it is natural in English to start with the head and to work through shoulders, arms, hands, trunk, legs, in Navaho precisely the opposite order comes naturally: you start with the feet and finish with arms, hands and head.

Navaho has a rich oral literature, consisting partly of ceremonial poetry. This belongs to rituals sometimes known (in attempted English renderings) as Blessingway, Beautyway, Windways, Red Antway, Mountainway, Nightway, Shootingway. The Horse Songs that belong to the Blessingway ceremony are especially notable. There are some modern publications in Navaho:

there has been a newspaper in the language, *Adahooniligii*. The *Navajo historical series* has built up into a record of Navaho history and traditions.

Navaho is famous – among linguists – for its resistance to borrowing. Automobile terms, for example, tend to be new coinages in Navaho, not borrowings from English: some of them are formed by extending the meaning of anatomical words, such as 'liver' which now also means 'automobile battery' (according to Basso and Adams in the *American anthropologist* 1967–8). It has also been claimed that most American Indian languages seem to borrow rather little from English – because speakers are bilingual, and simply switch to English when speaking of topics that local languages do not cover.

Navaho once served as a lingua franca for the speakers of the isolated Zuni. When Hopi speakers fled as refugees to the Zuni, Navaho served as the common language between the two peoples.

Navaho distinguishes vowel length, nasality and tone. The first ten numerals in Navaho are: *ła̧ 'i, nāki, tā̀', dī̀', 'acdla', xastā̄⁻'h, tsost'sid, tsēbī̄⁻', náxást 'ēi, nēznā̄⁻'h.*

Invocation

Hayolkál behogán,	House made of dawn,
nahotsoí behogán,	House made of dusk;
kósyildil behogán,	House made of dark cloud,
niltsabaká behogán,	House made of male rain;
a'dilyíl behogán,	House made of dark fog,
niltsabaád behogán,	House made of female rain;
thaditdín behogán,	House made of pollen,
aniltani behogán,	House made of grasshoppers;

Opening invocation of a Navaho prayer. After Washington Matthews in *Navaho myths, prayers and songs* ed. Pliny Earle Goddard (*University of California publications in American archaeology* vol. 5 ii, 1907)

NAXI

250,000 SPEAKERS

China

Naxi is one of the SINO-TIBETAN LANGUAGES. It is sometimes said to be a member of the Burmese-Lolo group, but it may be better regarded as an independent descendant of proto-Tibeto-Burman. It is spoken in northern Yunnan, in and around Lijiang, in a district strongly defended by the encircling Yangtze gorges (for map see BAI).

The forms *Na-khi* and *Nahsi* are also found. It is the native term, and it means 'black man', a reminder of the relatively dark complexion of typical Naxi speakers. In older English writings *Naxi* is sometimes called *Moso*: this is still used as the name of one of the subdivisions of the Naxi people in the neighbourhood of Lugu lake.

The Naxi were apparently independent until their conquest by the Mongols in the 14th century. Thereafter they were subject to China as a tributary people, still with their own rulers, and still prosperous until recent times. The last Naxi prince was killed soon after the communist takeover in 1949. They are still one of the official nationalities of China, and Naxi is used in elementary classes in schools. In Naxi villages, as yet, few people speak Chinese.

Naxi is an essentially monosyllabic language – its open syllables and lack of consonant clusters give it a superficial resemblance to YI and the other Burmese-Lolo languages of China. Its vocabulary and basic structure seem quite different, however. It has been suggested that Naxi speech came from further north, perhaps two thousand years ago, and, in the course of its spread to local speakers in Yunnan, took on the sound patterns of their mother tongues.

Naxi used to be written in its own pictographic script, quite different from that of Chinese. According to legend, the script was invented by King Moubao Azong in the 13th century – yet it seems to preserve some reminiscences of an older time, when Naxi speakers lived in north-western China, with different fauna around them.

The script was used mainly by hereditary poet-priests, *dto-mba*, as an aid in the recitation of texts. 'Anyone can appreciate the graphic beauty of a Naxi text, but only someone well-versed in the mystical lore of Naxi religion can interpret its meaning and translate it into language' (S. R. Ramsey, *The languages of China* (Princeton, 1987) p. 267). The belief system of the Naxi is related to the pre-Buddhist Bon religion of Tibet, and to the Tibetan form of Buddhism itself. Naxi manuscripts can be found in many collections across the world, but its use has now almost died away. A standard romanisation, 'Naxi Pinyin', has been promulgated in China.

The Naxi writing system acts as an aid to the recitation of poetic texts, such as the tragic love story of K'a-mä of which this is the beginning. Not every word needs to be written – just enough to remind the reader what to say.

The poem is in five-syllable lines. A box of characters represents a sentence or sense-unit, usually several lines long. In this illustration the boxes have been numbered so that they can be compared with the translation.

Many of the pictograms are realistic, like the figure with a high headdress which means 'girl' (in the passage above it usually has to be translated 'I', since K'a-mä is talking about herself).

Naxi pictographs

'Ghügh-daw muan ch'ung ho,
muan-daw t'o dgyu ho.' . . .

1. 'Whether I weave gently does not matter;
better not to weave at all.'

2. K'a-mä saw a crow and asked it to carry a message. 'A body is heavy, a message is not; a tree is heavy, its leaves are not; water is heavy, its foam is not.

3–4. To my lover's father Sse-shi, my lover's mother Ch'ung-ch'ung, my lover's friend La-yu, give a message:

5. In the sky above us, three male stars have not yet caught their three female stars; I am one of the three.

6–7. Above the village La-ler-dü the sheep have grazed on all but three tufts of grass; I am one of the three.

8. In my village, a handsome boy has made love to all but three girls; I am one of the three.

9. As you would call your cattle gently home, so call me.'

After J. F. Rock in *Bulletin de l'Ecole Française d'Extrême-Orient* vol. 39 (1939) pp. 25–9

Most characters correspond not to a sound but to an idea. For example, the crescent sign which occurs several times on this page is the negative. Sometimes the word *muan*, 'not', will occur in the corresponding line of verse, but not always; just as, in the English translation above, the negative is usually translated *not* but sometimes by *all but*.

Some characters are used phonetically, in a procedure which may be thought of as punning. For example, in box 4 the monkey-headed character means 'father-in-law', *yü-p'a*, because by coincidence *yü* is the word for 'monkey'. This is one of the methods by which, in the distant past, the Chinese writing system, too, developed its range and flexibility.

NDEBELE

1,600,000 SPEAKERS

Zimbabwe, South Africa

One of the Nguni group of BANTU LANGUAGES, Ndebele is the second language of Zimbabwe (after Shona). Southern Ndebele has an equal number of speakers in the Transvaal, where it is one of the eleven official languages of South Africa (see map at ZULU).

Speakers call their language *isiNdebele* and themselves *amaNdebele*. The word is correctly pronounced with three short *e*s of which the first is stressed, *Ndĕ´bĕlĕ*.

AmaNdebele appears to have been their own version of the name given to them by the Sotho and Tswana speakers in whose land they were settled – *maTebele*. Early English-speaking explorers heard and adopted this Sotho form, calling the people *Matabele* and their northern domain *Matabeleland*.

Southern Ndebele is a language of the Nguni group, close to Zulu. It may represent a gradual spread or a migration northwards of Nguni-language speakers: at any rate it was probably established in the southern and central Transvaal by the 16th century.

The Ndebele language of Zimbabwe arrived there as the result of historical events of the early 19th century. Its origin is in the adventurous story of Mzilikazi, a captive prince who was enrolled as one of the warriors of the Zulu king Shaka. Having offended Shaka, Mzilikazi fled northwards with his followers and at first settled in the Marico valley of Transvaal, in a region inhabited by speakers of Tswana and Southern Ndebele. He ruled there from 1832 to 1837.

After fighting with the advancing Boers, Mzilikazi led a second armed migration, this time probably with larger numbers, and (so legend says) he was advised on what route to take by the missionary Robert Moffat, known to Ndebele speakers as Mshete. The leaders of the expedition were to seek a strangely shaped hill: near modern Bulawayo, on the high Zambezi-Limpopo watershed, in modern Zimbabwe, this hill – *Intaba yezinduna*, the 'hill of the viceroy' – was found. It is at the centre of the present territory of Ndebele speakers.

Originally the language of a military caste, Ndebele spread rapidly among the conquered population of the immediate neighbourhood – most of them probably speakers of Shona dialects. The changeover was speeded by the fact that the captives and the conquered were able to become warriors themselves – for which purpose they had to adopt the Ndebele way of life and the Ndebele language.

Mzilikazi and his successor Lobengula dominated Shona-speaking country and raided far and wide, eventually coming into conflict with the British South Africa Company, which at last drove Lobengula out and annexed his kingdom. Thus, after only fifty-five years of Ndebele supremacy, 'Southern Rhodesia' was under English-speaking rulers from 1893 to 1980. The great city of Bulawayo grew up, and much farming land was seized. Yet, at the end of this period, when Zimbabwe achieved independence, Ndebele remained solidly established as the regional language of the Bulawayo district, just as it had been at the beginning.

Zulu and Ndebele are still to some extent mutually intelligible, though idioms differ and Ndebele has clearly borrowed numerous terms from the languages previously spoken in its territory. It retains the click consonants typical of the Nguni group, written *c, q, x* – the last 'the same as the sound made by a carter to urge on his horse', as one linguist observed.

Most speakers of Ndebele are now bilingual in Shona, the majority language of Zimbabwe. Although the two languages are quite distinct, there is certainly a convergence at work between them. Here, modern political conditions reinforce an earlier tendency, for at the very beginning of its history a large proportion of the speakers of Ndebele had learnt a Shona dialect as their mother tongue.

The first ten numerals in Ndebele are: *nye, bili, tatu, ne, hlanu, tandatu* or *capakanye, capakabili, capakatatu, capakane, itshumi*.

NEPALI

8,000,000 SPEAKERS

Nepal, India

Nepali, one of the Pahari group of INDO-ARYAN LANGUAGES (see map there), is the national language of Nepal, also spoken in the Indian states of West Bengal and Sikkim and in southwest Bhutan.

It is still sometimes called by its old name, *Khas Kurā*, 'Khasa language', a reminder that it first spread across the foothills of Nepal as the everyday language of the Khasa kingdom, which ruled here in the 13th and 14th centuries. Its collapse led to the emergence of numerous petty princedoms using the same mother tongue, including Porbat (whence the language has often been called *Parbatiyā*) and Gorkha. Since Rajput dynasts founded several of these small states, it is often said that the Nepali language itself was brought to Nepal by the Rajputs, but this is definitely untrue.

In 1768–9 Pṛthvīnārāyaṇ Śāh, prince of Gorkha, conquered the NEWARI-speaking Nepal valley, including the city of Kathmandu, which he made his capital. This was the foundation of the modern kingdom of Nepal – and it explains why his own state language, and not the language of Kathmandu itself, became the national language. The term *Nepalese* was first used in a grammar published in Calcutta in 1820 – but *Parbatiyā* remained the official name in Nepal itself until the 1930s.

Since it spread from the state of Gorkha Nepali has also been called *Gorkhali*. This became the special name of the military lingua francas, slightly altered varieties of the language, which came into everyday use in the Nepalese Army (*Gorkhālī bhāṣā*, 'language of Gorkha', in a drill manual of 1874), then the British army (*Gurkhali*) and the modern Indian army (*Gork-*

hali). These soldiers are universally called 'Guerlias'. For Nepali, already widely used in the lower valleys, has continued to spread rapidly, partly as a first language, partly as a lingua franca. The higher valleys of Nepal, Sikkim and Bhutan, where communication is so difficult, speak a bewildering range of *Rāī* and other Sino-Tibetan languages.

Nepali shows the influence of its Sino-Tibetan neighbours. It has an unusual variety of personal pronouns. The second and third person pronouns ('you, he, she') have three alternative forms for degrees of respect. In the second person, for example, an inferior is addressed as *tañ*, an equal as *timi*, a superior as *tapaiñ* or *āphu*. For a table of numerals see KUMAUNI.

जति राई उति कुरा ‖ *Jati Rāī uti kurā*, says the Nepali proverb: 'There are as many languages as there are Rāīs'. The linguistic complexity of the higher valleys, where Rāī and other Sino-Tibetan speakers live, explains the rapid spread of Nepali as a language of communication in the southern Himalaya.

'Gurkhali' and Nepali in writing
The British Army's standard Roman script and the Devanagari equivalents

a ā i ī u ū e ai o au k kh g gh ng ch chh j jh ñ ṭ ṭh ḍ
ḍh ṇ t th d dh n p ph b bh m y r l v sh ṣh s h

प्र प्रा इ ई उ ऊ ए ऐ ओ औ कखगघङ चछजझञ टठडढ
तथदधन पफबभम यरलव शषसह

NEWARI

500,000 SPEAKERS

Nepal, India

One of the SINO-TIBETAN LANGUAGES, Newari is the historic language of the Nepal valley, with its metropolis of Kathmandu. It is only recently that the Indo-Aryan speech of the states of Porbat and Gorkha has come to challenge the position of Newari and has taken the name NEPALI.

By its own speakers Newari is called *Newā: bhāy* or *Nepā: bhāy*, 'Nepal language'. They prefer to call Nepali by an older name, *Khay bhāy* 'Khasa language'.

As one of the row of Sino-Tibetan languages of the southern slopes of the Himalaya, Newari has probably been spoken in its present location for a long time. It is less closely related to Tibetan than are some of its neighbours. Records show that for several centuries at least it was the ruling language of a kingdom at Kathmandu – a kingdom that had participated fully in the Buddhist culture of north India, and retained Buddhism when India lost it.

Newari inscriptions are very numerous from the long reign of Jayayaksa Malla (1428–80) down to the Gorkha conquest of the Nepal valley in 1769. Early inscriptions are often in a mixture of Sanskrit and Newari: the language differs from its relatives to the north precisely in the extent of Sanskrit influence and the great number of Sanskrit and Indo-Aryan loanwords.

Newari was already cultivated as a literary language in the 14th century and perhaps earlier. 'Classical Newari [*le névari de la belle époque*] shows a harmonious balance between the Himalayan dialects, still undeveloped owing to their isolation, impoverished, rough, incapable of expressing advanced thought and abstract ideas,

and the dialects that had become entirely Hinduised through borrowing from the Indo-Aryan languages of the plains. Newari expanded its vocabulary through its native resources, and although it did borrow from the modern Indo-Aryan languages it was able to assimilate these loans and to enrich itself in the process. A considerable number of Newari commentaries on Sanskrit Buddhist texts, and also of Newari translations, survive' (Sylvain Lévi, *Le Népal* (Paris, 1905) vol. 1 pp. 251–2).

The Gorkha conquest marked the end of Newari's role as a state language. It was actually banned from public use between 1846 and 1950, and the number of speakers has probably been in decline for some time.

According to the chronicle *Kirāt mundhum* the goddess Sarasvatī appeared to a 9th-century Limbu king, Sirijanga, took him into a cave, and showed him a series of stone tablets that told the story of the creation – the story with which the chronicle itself begins. Since that time, it is said, the script in which these miraculous tablets were written has been lost and rediscovered several times, the most recent rediscoverer being Imānsiṃha Cemjong, the 20th-century champion of Limbu culture.

Newari was traditionally written in a local script, known in many variants from different periods, related to medieval forms of the Nagari and Bengali scripts of north India. The same script was used locally for Sanskrit texts. When Newari is printed it now appears in the familiar Devanagari alphabet that is used for Nepali. Unlike Nepali, however, Newari has a distinction of vowel length. Long vowels are indicated by : in the script. The first ten numerals in Newari are: *chi, nasi, sõ, pi, ngā, khu, nhaye, cyā, gū, sānha.*

Newari and its neighbours

Newari is the local language of Kathmandu and the Nepal valley. There are some speakers in Bettiah in the Indian state of Bihar.

Limbu or Kirāt has 200,000 speakers in eastern Nepal and Sikkim. It claims an independent literary tradition, but no early texts survive except for a religious chronicle, *Kirāt mundhum*, which has been given the grandiose name 'the Veda of the Kirāts'. The disappearance of old literature is ascribed to an order of the King of Nepal, in

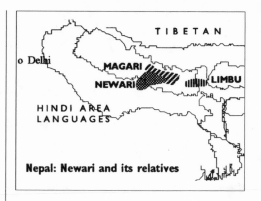

Nepal: Newari and its relatives

1788, that all Limbu books were to be burnt.

Magar or Magari has 500,000 speakers in the central mountains of Nepal.

NIGER-CONGO LANGUAGES

As they studied the languages of Africa south of the Sahara, 19th- and 20th-century scholars noted pervasive similarities that, just as in other parts of the world, led to the identification of families each descended from a single postulated proto-language. Some groupings, the result of more recent migration, were easier to recognise than others: the relationship among the Bantu languages, for example, was clear by the 1850s. Wilhelm Bleek, in 1856, was an early proponent of the wider grouping, covering both southern and western African languages, that is now usually known as Niger-Congo: he called it *Bântu*.

> The Niger-Congo language family, or a similar grouping, has had many names: *Bântu*, *West African*, *Western Sudanic*, *Western Nigritic*, *Niger-Kordofanian*. Names like *Mixed Negro* (and *Semi-Bantu*, see below) were applied as a result of a theory – now seen to be quite unhistorical – that they originated in a mixture between Bantu languages, with their typical noun classes, and AFROASIATIC LANGUAGES which typically have noun gender. The term *Niger-Congo* was invented by Joseph Greenberg, who developed his seminal reclassification of African languages between 1949 and 1963.

Diedrich Westermann had already clearly demonstrated in 1911 and 1927 the relationship of most of the languages now counted in the Niger-Congo family, and later linguistic study of Niger-Congo stems from his work.

Westermann, however, like other scholars of his time, tended to assume two coordinate divisions of the family, Bantu and 'Western Sudanic'. Even Malcolm Guthrie, who worked so fruitfully on Bantu classification in the 1950s and 1960s, could not accept Greenberg's demonstra-

tion that the huge group of Bantu languages was historically an offshoot of a subgroup of a group of one of the main divisions of the Niger-Congo family.

There is a great deal of controversy over the higher levels of classification – which represent population divisions and migrations that took place many thousands of years ago. Greenberg counted West Atlantic, Mande, Gur, Kwa, Benue-Congo and Adamawa-Eastern as six co-ordinate divisions. Kordofanian languages (see below), Greenberg considered, had separated from the family at an earlier date: hence his alternative name for them, Niger-Kordofanian. It is quite widely agreed now that not only Kordofanian, but also the Mande and Atlantic groups and possibly the Ijoid group, split off at a very early stage from the remainder of the family – and the remainder is sometimes called Volta-Congo. Some believe that Niger-Congo and NILO-SAHARAN LANGUAGES, long seen as entirely distinct, will turn out to be distantly related; and that the Mande languages and SONGHAY belong neither to the one family nor to the other, but together form a third family distantly linked to both.

There are hundreds of Niger-Congo languages, though many have only a few thousand speakers each. The lists, here and at BANTU LANGUAGES, show all those with more than 100,000 speakers. The most important of all, typically with over a million speakers, have separate entries in the *Dictionary*, and these are signposted in the following survey.

Kordofanian languages

Isolated and with no close relatives, the Kordofanian languages are spoken by small communities in the Nuba Mountains of Southern

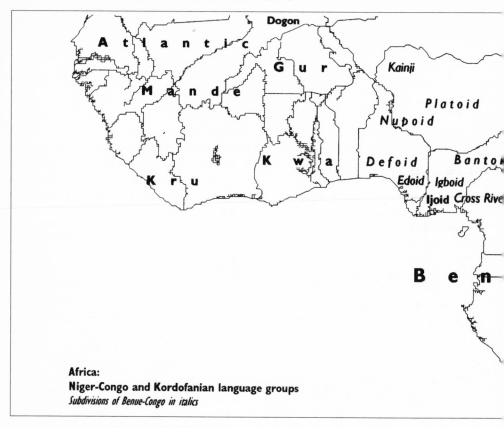

Africa:
Niger-Congo and Kordofanian language groups
Subdivisions of Benue-Congo in italics

Kordofan province, Sudan. Thilo Schadeberg, the linguist who has spent most time on this group, believes that there are about 165,000 speakers. The four dialect groups, centring on the towns of Heiban, Talodi, Rashad and Katla, are quite distantly related: Rashad was the capital of Tegali, a significant kingdom in the 19th century.

Close at hand to the west are the 90,000 speakers of Krongo and other Kadugli languages, spoken to the north-west and south-east of Kadugli in the same province. It is geographically handy to link Kadugli with Kordofanian, but in fact the relationship is quite unproved.

Mande, Atlantic and Ijoid groups

Mande-speaking peoples now live in widely scattered districts of inland West Africa. This group of languages may have been developing separately from the main Niger-Congo family for

twelve thousand years or more, and there must have been many unrecorded migrations in that time. But the large area now covered by MAN-DEKAN, SUSU and SONINKE is certainly the result of fairly recent historical expansion. Although they had probably begun to differentiate from one another by about 2000 BC, the Mande languages (which also include MENDE) were easily seen by 19th-century linguists to be related: Sigismund Koelle's *Polyglotta Africana* (1854), a collection of comparative wordlists, made the relationship obvious.

At least five Mande languages – Mende, Loma, Kpelle, Vai (see below) and Mandekan – have their own scripts, invented by local speakers in the course of the 19th century. There are also indigenous scripts for at least two languages – Fulani and Wolof – in the Atlantic group.

The Atlantic languages (Greenberg's West Atlantic) were probably the next to branch off from Niger-Congo. They are now spoken along

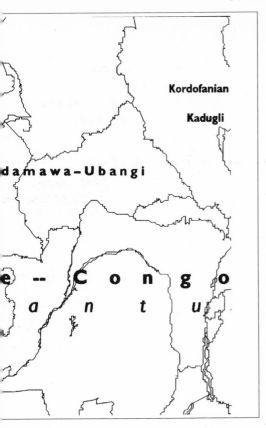

Kordofanian

Kadugli

damawa–Ubangi

e -- C o n g o
a n t u

the Atlantic coast of West Africa, from Mauritania to Liberia, and include Serer, TEMNE and DIOLA. WOLOF, the language of coastal Senegal, was the first African language encountered by Europeans in their seaborne exploration of the Atlantic coasts in the 15th century. The most important of this group is FULANI, whose speakers, traditionally nomadic herdsmen, founded an Islamic empire in eastern Nigeria in the 19th century. Fulani now has the widest geographical range of any single African language.

The IJO language of the Niger Delta seems to be an isolated member of Niger-Congo. It also separated very early, and has sometimes been thought to be an aberrant relative of the Mande group.

Central Niger-Congo

Perhaps ten thousand years ago the proto-Volta-Congo language, from which Kordofanian,

Mande, Atlantic and Ijoid had already separated, began to split into several dialects which are the origin of the remaining divisions of Niger-Congo.

The KRU LANGUAGES (sometimes included in the Kwa group, below) are spoken in the forests of southern Liberia and Ivory Coast. Kru people worked on European ships as early as the 16th century, and there are still Klao, Grebo and Bassa-speaking communities in several West African port cities. Bété, of the Ivory Coast, has the largest number of speakers of any Kru language today.

Senufo, sometimes spoken of as a single language rather than a dialect group, straddles the frontiers of Ivory Coast, Burkina Faso and Mali. It is hard to place in any Niger-Congo subgroup. *Senari* is the dialect with the largest number of speakers. The first ten numerals in the Bamana dialect are: *nene, shyoni, tare, tityere, kaguru, gbani, gbarashyo, shyolake, untu-lake, kantoke* (*gbarashyo* means 'second 6'). These numerals show scarcely any similarity with those of Mõõre.

The Gur or Voltaic languages, spoken in the savanna country of Burkina Faso and the northern parts of Ivory Coast, Ghana, Togo and Benin, form a highly disparate group, difficult to classify. Apart from MÕÕRE, widely used as a second language in Burkina Faso, major members of the group are Dagaari, Gourmantché, Frafra or Gurenne and (some say) the Senufo dialects. Dogon, a language of eastern Mali, used to be counted among the Gur languages, but the relationship is doubtful: it has also been considered a member of the Mande group.

The Adamawa-Ubangi languages (Greenberg's Adamawa-Eastern) are the easternmost of any in the Niger-Congo family except Kordofanian and Bantu. They divide into two subgroups. Historically the most important Adamawa language is Mbum, which used to be a lingua franca of the Tibati-Ngaoundéré region but has now given way to Fulani. Languages of the Ubangi subgroup were carried far to the east by recent migrations of conquering peoples, notably ZANDE. Ngbandi is important as the basis of the creole SANGO, now the national language of the Central African Republic. Two further members of this group are GBAYA and BANDA.

The Kwa languages (merely a subdivision of the much more miscellaneous Kwa group postulated by earlier scholars) include three of the most important Ghanaian languages, AKAN, EWE and GA, and a major Ivory Coast language, BAULE.

Benue-Congo Languages

By far the largest subdivision of the Niger-Congo family is Benue-Congo. Once known as Semi-Bantu or Benue-Cross, the nature of its relationship with the BANTU LANGUAGES was

clarified by Greenberg: the latter are simply an offshoot of the Bantoid group of Benue-Congo. In this *Dictionary* they are given a separate entry because of their large number and their geographical extent. The remaining Bantoid languages are spoken in a much smaller, well-defined region of Nigeria and Cameroun: the best known of them is TIV.

EFIK belongs to the Cross River subgroup. Two of the national languages of Nigeria, YORUBA and IGBO, are Benue-Congo languages, along with EDO, language of the Empire of Benin. Proto-Benue-Congo may have been spoken around the Niger-Benue confluence, from where the existing languages have gradually spread.

The subdivisions of Niger-Congo

Major Niger-Congo languages

AKAN	5,000,000	Ghana, Ivory Coast
Attié	220,000	Ivory Coast
Awutu	100,000	Ghana
Balanta	300,000	Guiné
Bamendjou	100,000	Cameroun
Bamun	220,000	Cameroun
BANDA	1,000,000	Central African Republic
Bassa	300,000	Liberia
BAULE with Anyin	2,000,000	Ivory Coast, Ghana
Bété	700,000	Ivory Coast
Birom	200,000	Nigeria
Bobo Fing	175,000	Burkina Faso, Mali
Boomu and Bwamu, or Bobo Wule	450,000	Mali, Burkina Faso
Borgu or Bariba	250,000	Benin, Nigeria
Buli	150,000	Ghana, Burkina Faso
Bullom or Sherbro	175,000	Sierra Leone
Busa and Boko	100,000	Benin, Nigeria
Dagaari with Birifor and Waali	650,000	Ghana, Burkina Faso
Dan and Toura	500,000	Ivory Coast, Liberia
DIOLA	500,000	Senegal
Ditammari and Tamberma	120,000	Benin, Togo
Dogon	500,000	Mali and Burkina Faso
Ebira or Igbira	500,000	Nigeria
EDO	1,350,000	Nigeria
EFIK and Ibibio	2,750,000	Nigeria
EWE and Fon	3,500,000	Togo, Benin, Ghana
Frafra or Gurenne	500,000	Ghana, Burkina Faso
FULANI	15,000,000	West African countries

GA	1,000,000	Ghana
Gbagyi	250,000	Nigeria
GBAYA	850,000	Central African Republic, Cameroun
Ghomala'	250,000	Cameroun
Gokana and Kana	150,000	Nigeria
Gonja	120,000	central Ghana
Gourmantché or Gurma	400,000	Burkina Faso, Togo, Benin, Niger
Grebo and Krumen	250,000	Ivory Coast, Liberia
Gua	120,000	Ghana
Guéré, Wobe and Krahn	450,000	Ivory Coast, Liberia
Guro and Yaouré	220,000	Ivory Coast
Idoma	300,000	Nigeria
Ife or Ana	100,000	Togo, Benin
Igala	800,000	Nigeria
IGBO	12,000,000	Nigeria
Igede	120,000	Nigeria
IJO	600,000	Nigeria
Isoko	300,000	Nigeria
Itsekiri	500,000	Nigeria
Jarawa	150,000	Nigeria
Jju or Kaje	300,000	Nigeria
Jukun dialects	125,000	Nigeria, Cameroun
Kabiyé or Kabré	400,000	Togo, Benin
Kambari	100,000	Nigeria
Kissi	450,000	Liberia, Sierra Leone, Guinea
Klao	200,000	Liberia and West African port cities
Kom	120,000	Cameroun
Konkomba	350,000	Togo
Kono	120,000	Sierra Leone
Kpelle	600,000	Guinea and Liberia
Kulango or Koulan	175,000	Ivory Coast, Ghana
Kusaal	200,000	Ghana, Burkina Faso
Lamnso'	120,000	Cameroun
Limba	250,000	Sierra Leone
Lobi	200,000	Burkina Faso, Ivory Coast
Loma	120,000	Liberia
Mande of Burkina Faso	400,000	Burkina Faso, Ghana
MANDEKAN	5,000,000	Mali, Senegal, Guinea, Ivory Coast, Burkina Faso, Sierra Leone
Mandyak, Mankanya and Papel	250,000	Guiné
Manja	120,000	Central African Republic
Mano	150,000	Liberia
Mbanza	220,000	Congo (Kinshasa)
Medumba	200,000	Cameroun
MENDE	1,000,000	Sierra Leone, Liberia
Moba and Bimoba	200,000	Togo, Burkina Faso, Ghana
MÕÕRE	3,000,000	Burkina Faso
Nawdm	100,000	Togo

Ngbaka	900,000	Congo (Kinshasa)
Ngbandi	210,000	Congo (Kinshasa), Central African Republic
Ngyemboon	100,000	Cameroun
Northern Samo	125,000	Burkina Faso
NUPE	1,000,000	Nigeria
Nzema and Ahanta	350,000	Ivory Coast, Ghana
Rubassa	100,000	Nigeria
SANGO	5,000,000, mainly as second language	Central African Republic
Senufo of Ivory Coast, or Cebaara or Senadi	450,000	Ivory Coast
Senufo of Mali, or Mamara or Bamana	300,000	Mali
Serer	650,000	Senegal, Gambia
Sisaala	120,000	Ghana, Burkina Faso
SONINKE	1,000,000	Mali, Senegal, Mauritania
SUSU	700,000	Guinea, Sierra Leone
Tarok	140,000	Nigeria
Tem	300,000	Togo, Benin
TEMNE	950,000	Sierra Leone
TIV	1,500,000	Nigeria
Toma	120,000	Guinea
Urhobo	340,000	Nigeria
Vai	75,000	Liberia, Sierra Leone
WOLOF	2,000,000	Senegal, Gambia
Yemba-Nwe	350,000	Cameroun
YORUBA	20,000,000	Nigeria, Benin
ZANDE	1,200,000	Congo (Kinshasa), Central African Republic, Sudan

The Vai syllabary

Vai, a Mande language of about 75,000 speakers in inland Liberia and Sierra Leone, is most notable for its special script, invented by Momolu Duwalu Bukele in the 1830s. It came to him in a dream, or so he told Sigismund Koelle (perhaps the first European to hear of the script, in 1849). Though not taught in schools, the two hundred characters of the Vai syllabary continue to be used in letter-writing, diaries and Bible translations.

Vai was the language of a warrior people of the mid 16th century, known in European writings of the period as *Mani* or *Kquoja*.

Polyglotta Africana

Sigismund Koelle made a great contribution to African linguistics with the publication of *Polyglotta Africana* in 1854. This was a collection of almost 300 words and phrases in well over a hundred languages – all collected from freed slaves settled in Sierra Leone. It was criticised by some 19th-century scholars, but the real test is that Koelle's book was used then and is still used now. For some languages, even now, no better vocabulary exists. Practically all the languages he listed can be identified (though he had never visited the places where they originated).

Koelle's work was published by the Church Missionary Society in London. He also worked on Vai and its syllabary, and on KANURI.

NILO-SAHARAN LANGUAGES

The linguist Joseph Greenberg, in 1963, proposed the recognition of a Nilo-Saharan language family, grouping together numerous languages of Uganda, Ethiopia, Sudan and Chad, for many of which no generally accepted family links had previously been suggested. Greenberg's proposals have partly been confirmed by later research. The languages and language groups do differ quite radically from one another, suggesting that many thousands of years have passed since the postulated proto-Nilo-Saharan language may have been spoken.

Across a belt of north central Africa, all the way from Lake Turkana to the middle Niger, archaeologists have identified a highly specialised way of life that came into existence in the eighth millennium BC, when this area was a good deal wetter than it is today. This 'aquatic tradition', making full use of lake and river resources, has been linked by J. E. G. Sutton and Patrick Munson, in the 1970s, with the initial expansion of Nilo-Saharan languages. Not all linguists agree: some believe that proto-Nilo-Saharan must be dated rather more than ten thousand years ago. But it is a striking fact that the modern languages of the group, from Songhay to Turkana, actually map this 'aquatic tradition' rather accurately.

The isolates of Nilo-Saharan

Far distant from the other members of the group, and long considered quite unrelated to other known languages, SONGHAY is spoken by over two million people in the middle Niger valley. Half a million people in the southern Sudan speak Fur. The little-known Gumuz is spoken at the confluence of the Diddesa and Blue Nile in Ethiopia. Kunama, a language of Eritrea, is usually classified in the Chari-Nile group, but is very different from its claimed relatives.

> Catholic missionaries have competed with Norwegian Lutherans for converts among the Kunama. The result: a good supply of Kunama books in the Latin alphabet – very unusual for former Ethiopia, in which most languages are printed in the Ethiopic script – but with two different sets of spelling rules.

The Saharan languages include KANURI, a major language of northern Nigeria, along with Teda and Zaghawa. The small Maban language group includes MABA, Massalat and Mimi. There is another small, distinct group called Koman, the largest member of which, Kwama, is spoken on the Ethiopia–Sudan border.

The Chari-Nile group

Greenberg's Chari-Nile group of languages, which he made the main constituent of his Nilo-Saharan family, is not accepted by all scholars as a real unity. Its two subgroups and one language isolate (Berta, an Ethiopian language) can instead be regarded as immediate components of Nilo-Saharan.

The Central Sudanic subgroup includes languages of Congo (Kinshasa), Uganda and Chad: Lendu, Logo, Lugbara, Madi, Mangbetu, and SARA.

The East Sudanic subgroup is the most extensive geographically, extending from Sudan to Tanzania. Many of these languages have only small numbers of speakers. There are separate entries in this dictionary for KALENJIN (the major *Nandi* language) and the NUBIAN LANGUAGES; Pökoot and Datoga also belong here. But two subdivisions within East Sudanic are especially important.

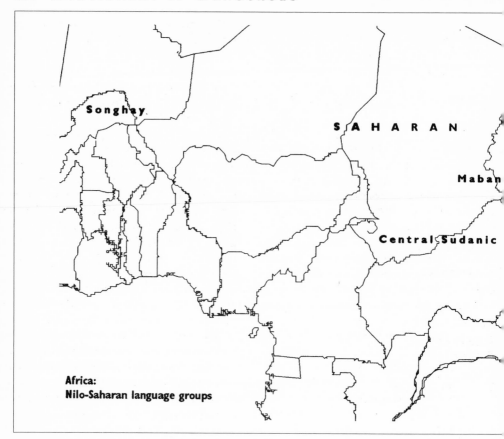

Africa:
Nilo-Saharan language groups

Major Nilo-Saharan languages

Acholi	700,000	Uganda
Adhola	235,000	Uganda
Alur	800,000	Congo (Kinshasa) and Uganda
Bari	340,000	Sudan and Uganda
Berta	60,000	Ethiopia and Sudan
Daju and Sila	150,000	Chad and Sudan
Datoga	400,000	Tanzania
DINKA	1,350,000	Sudan
Fur	500,000	Darfur District, Sudan
Gumuz	90,000	Ethiopia
Kakwa	148,000	Sudan and Congo (Kinshasa)
KALENJIN	1,400,000	Kenya
KANURI	4,000,000	Nigeria, Niger, Chad, Cameroun
Kuman	150,000	Uganda
Kunama	50,000	Eritrea
Kwama	15,000	Ethiopia
Lango of Uganda	800,000	Uganda
Lendu	490,000	Congo (Kinshasa)

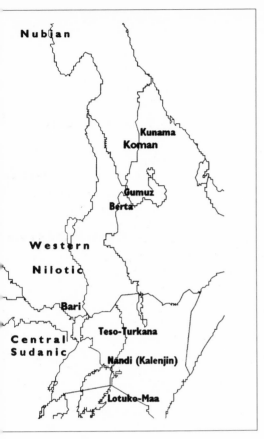

First, the Nilotic or *Western Nilotic* languages include DINKA, Nuer, the LUO languages and others.

Secondly, a subdivision of languages of East Africa was once called *Nilo-Hamitic*. 'Nilo-Hamitic' or even *Half-Hamitic* seemed appropriate for speakers of Teso, Karamojong, Turkana, Masai and others – at a time when many African languages were explained through theories of racial mixture – because Cushitic (i.e. Hamitic or AFROASIATIC) components were seen in them and their culture. The term was in common use till the 1950s. In 1966 a new name, *Paranilotic* 'not quite Nilotic', was suggested for these same languages. *Eastern Nilotic* is now the preferred name. Together they form a continuous geographical sequence, with mainly Afroasiatic languages to their east and mainly Nilotic and Bantu languages to their west.

Eastern Nilotic (see map at TURKANA) is itself divided into three groups: *Bari*, mostly in Sudan, including Bari and Kakwa; *Teso-Turkana*, in Uganda and north-western Kenya, including TESO and the Karamojong group (one of which is Turkana); and *Lotuko-Maa*, including MASAI and Otuho.

Logo	210,000	Congo (Kinshasa)
Lugbara	920,000	Uganda
LUO	3,200,000	Kenya, Tanzania
MABA with Massalat and Mimi	300,000	Chad
Madi	233,000	Uganda
Mangbetu	650,000	Congo (Kinshasa) and Uganda
MASAI with Samburu	750,000	Kenya and Tanzania
NUBIAN LANGUAGES	1,000,000	Sudan, Egypt
Nuer	850,000	Sudan, Ethiopia
Otuho	185,000	Sudan
Pökoot or Suk	170,000	Kenya and Uganda
Sabaot	100,000	Kenya
SARA including Mbai and Ngambai	700,000	Chad
Shilluk	175,000	Sudan
SONGHAY	2,000,000	Niger, Mali, Nigeria, Burkina Faso, Benin
Tama and Sungor	165,000	Chad and Sudan, most speakers bilingual in Arabic

Teda	200,000	Chad and Libya
TESO	1,300,000	Uganda, Kenya
Thuri	154,000	Sudan
Tugen	150,000	Kenya
TURKANA and Karamojong	650,000	Kenya, Uganda, Sudan, Ethiopia
Zaghawa	123,000	Sudan and Chad

Nkore

4,600,000 SPEAKERS OF 'RUTARA' LANGUAGES

Uganda, Tanzania

N kore, one of the major languages of Uganda, belongs to the Rutara or Western Lacustrine group of BANTU LANGUAGES. The languages of this group – which also includes Kiga and Nyoro in Uganda, Haya and Zinza in Tanzania – are so close to one another that speakers of any one can easily understand the others, so they are dealt with together here.

Detailed genealogical histories are important to Nkore and Nyoro speakers, but their relation to movements of population and to linguistic changes is at best indirect. At any rate, these are the dialects of a group of kingdoms to the west and south of Buganda, in a region where Bantu languages have certainly been spoken for about two thousand years.

Their written history begins with J. H. Speke's travels through the region in 1862. At the establishment of the British protectorate, in 1896, buNyoro was a small but historic kingdom. BuToro had become a separate state only around 1830. Under British influence the four kingdoms ruled by the baHima caste (see box), Nkore, Buhweju, Buzimba and Igara, were united into a single district of Ankole, ruled from Nkore, in 1914.

Nyankole or *Nkore* is thus a 20th-century concept, the language of the new district of Ankole. However, the dialects of the four old kingdoms were almost identical.

The term *ruTara* is also a recent invention, named after the early kingdom of Kitara which, according to traditions widespread in the region, once held sway on the western shores of Lake Victoria from its capital at Bwera in Buganda.

In colonial times these kingdoms were given significantly fewer privileges than the favoured kingdom of Buganda. And GANDA's special position lasted into the early years of independence. Together the Rutara group forms the second largest linguistic community in Uganda, amounting to a fifth of the population. Yet by comparison with the slightly larger Ganda language group, Nkore and its relatives are very little seen or heard in press and media.

For a table of numerals see GANDA.

Names with a meaning

In Nkore-Kiga, personal names often take the form of nicknames based on a detail of personal history. For example:

Ke-emerwa, from the saying *akaizire keemerwa* 'you have to take what comes';

Nkagwe-guhira, from *omuriro nkagweguhira gwanyotsya* 'I got some fire and it burnt me', a saying hinting at an unhappy marriage.

After Charles Taylor, *Nkore-Kiga* (London: Croom Helm, 1985)

Farmers and servants

There are traditionally three castes among the speakers of Nkore, Tooro and Nyoro. The *baHima* or *baHuma*, a traditionally cattle-keeping people, have higher status than the *baIru*. A third group of recent arrivals, the *baBito*, formed the royal caste. There is no linguistic difference among the three.

There is a Nyoro myth that explains and validates their stratification of society into rulers or 'people of the drum', *baKama*, cattle-farmers, *baHuma*, and servants, *baIru*. They are said to be the descendants of the youngest, second and eldest sons respectively of the creator god, Ruhanga. BaNyoro go on to say that the baHuma have never ruled the country; in other words, that the three successive royal dynasties of buNyoro, *baTembuzi*, *baCwezi* and *baBito*, were none of them baHuma. The Nkore say, however, that the brief but powerful baCwezi dynasty, which ruled the great kingdom of Kitara, was baHuma in origin. Most people accept that the founders of the third dynasty, baBito, were speakers of a LUO language.

Unlike the Tutsi among speakers of RUNDI and Rwanda, the baHuma in buNyoro and buToro now retain little of their traditional political and economic dominance. The distinction between the two castes is known to everyone – but no longer important in everyday life. The baHima of Ankole are somewhat more powerful; and here there is a middle caste, the *baMbari*, children of baHima men and their baIru concubines.

Based on Brian K. Taylor, *The Western Lacustrine Bantu* (London: International African Institute, 1962) and other sources

Nkore and its relatives: the Rutara group

Nkore or Nyankole or Runyankore (1,500,000 speakers) is the language of the kingdom of Nkore (Ankole), now part of Uganda. Nkore and Kiga are now generally regarded in Uganda as a single language, *Nkore-Kiga*.

Kiga or ruKiga or Chiga or Ciga (1,000,000 speakers) and the closely related *Hororo* or ruHororo are spoken in what is now Kigezi district of Uganda. There was no kingdom and no castes here: traditional power was held by priests of the Nyabingi cult. Under British rule they were regarded as subversive and replaced by Ganda-speaking agents.

Nyoro or Runyoro (1,000,000 speakers) is the language of the kingdom of Bunyoro. It is close

to *Tooro* or Rutooro of the old kingdom of Toro. *Hema-Sud*, 'South Hema' of Congo (Kinshasa), is a continuation of the Tooro dialect continuum. It is so called to distinguish it from its neighbour *Hema-Nord* 'North Hema', a Nilo-Saharan language.

In Tanzania, *Haya* or luHaya or Kihaya (1,100,000 speakers) includes the dialects *Nyambo* (or Karagwe) and *Zinza*. This region was annexed by Germany in 1890 and first occupied by Britain in 1916.

Kerebe has 100,000 speakers on Ukerewe Island in the southern part of Lake Victoria, and in neighbouring Kibara. It is close to Haya linguistically.

BaHima cattle raids and their poetry

The praise poems of the baHima are an outstanding feature of Nkore literature. This is the opening of an 88-line poem describing an incident in 1949. Each line begins with a new praise-name of the hero or another participant.

Rugumyána nkahiga!
rutashoróórwa bakándekura nkabanza;
rutarimbííka ébikoomi nkabyetuuramu . . .
I who give courage to my companions
made a vow!
I who am not rejected was sent out in advance;
I who do not hesitate descended upon
their camps . . .

H. F. Morris, *The heroic recitations of the Bahima of Ankole* (Oxford: Clarendon Press, 1964) pp. 66–7

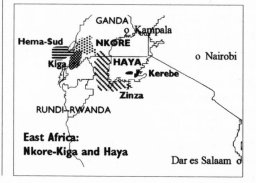

East Africa: Nkore-Kiga and Haya

NORWEGIAN

5,000,000 SPEAKERS

Norway

A descendant of OLD NORSE, Norwegian is the language of the long, narrow western strip of the Scandinavian peninsula. It is now the official language of Norway – but it has only recently acquired this status.

Old Norse was the language of the once-powerful medieval kingdom of Norway, with its successive capitals at Nidaros (Trondheim), Bergen and Oslo. Its heyday lasted from the 9th to the 14th century. The literature of this period, much of it poetry and historical prose inspired by the royal court, is in a language which cannot really be distinguished from early ICELANDIC: some of it, such as the royal 'sagas' or histories collected as *Heimskringla*, is by Icelanders.

Norway then became subject in turn to Sweden and to Denmark. The influence of Danish was strengthened with the Reformation, for no translation of the Bible into Norwegian appeared. There was no printing press in Norway until the 17th century, and no university until the foundation of the University of Christiania (Oslo) in 1811.

Through this period there was heavy influence, too, from German: High German, because of its cultural and educational pre-eminence, but particularly the Low German of the Hansa merchants, who dominated Norwegian trade from their establishments at Oslo, Bergen and Tønsberg.

Thus, for centuries, Norwegian was a series of local dialects of which none formed a standard. Danish was the government language, the literary language, and the language of higher education. The language spoken and written by educated Norwegians was in essence Danish – though with a distinctive Norwegian accent.

Norway separated from Denmark in 1814. Education at first continued in Danish (renamed *Norsk* or *Modersmaal*) but in the 1830s a movement developed to create a national language.

Why? Because the Danish standard was too different from the everyday speech of any Norwegian and thus difficult for schoolchildren to learn; and because, so nationalists thought, every nation should have its own language.

How was this national language to be created? The poet Henrik Wergeland argued for the enriching of the existing standard with elements drawn from colloquial Norwegian and the various regional dialects. Essentially this was the route followed in the great folk tale collection by P. C. Asbjørnsen and Jørgen Moe, *Norske Folke-eventyr* (1842–4). Others, such as Ivar Aasen, wanted to build a new language on the basis of selected dialects, looking back to Old Norse when enrichment was needed and cutting out all possible foreign forms, especially those that had a Danish or German feel. Both points of view have had their supporters – from the 1830s to the present day.

So there are two standard languages in Norway. One, *Landsmål* 'language of the country' (the term was Aasen's invention), is closely and very consciously based on the Norwegian dialects, particularly the country dialects of western Norway. Since 1929 it has been officially called *Nynorsk* 'New Norwegian'. The other, *Riksmål* 'national language', now officially *Bokmål* 'book language', was developed, in sympathy with

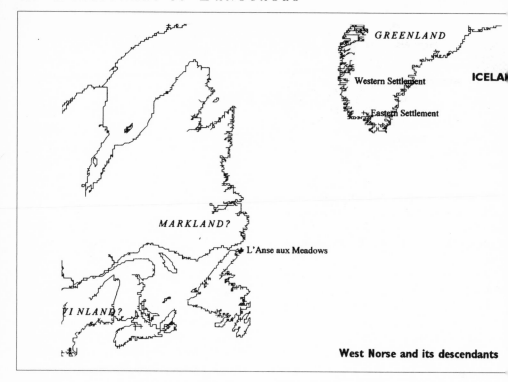

GREENLAND

Western Settlement

ICELA

Eastern Settlement

MARKLAND?

L'Anse aux Meadows

VINLAND?

West Norse and its descendants

Wergeland's ideas, by Knud Knudsen and others. It has a strong Danish flavour – but its resemblance is to written, not to spoken Danish – and a firmer base in the educated speech of 19th-century Oslo and Bergen. The 19th-century playwright Henrik Ibsen, the best-known figure of Norwegian literature internationally, eventually favoured Knudsen's Riksmål. So did the novelists Sigrid Undset and Knut Hamsun.

Schools can choose either, and many civil servants need to be able to handle both forms. Both are subject to occasional change by parliamentary commission, and (not surprisingly) a movement for *Samnorsk*, 'Union Norwegian', has gained some ground.

The pronunciation of Norwegian (of all varieties) seems closer to Swedish than to Danish: hence the most unfair cliché that Norwegian is 'Danish with a Swedish accent'.

Russenorsk, now extinct, was a mixed pidgin language used among Norwegian and Russian fishermen along the coast of the White Sea and northern Norway in the 19th century. Alongside Russian and Norwegian words Russenorsk included a few each from French, English, Dutch, Swedish, Finnish and Lapp. Unusual among pidgins, the speakers were social equals: this no doubt explains why the two main languages contributed almost equally to the vocabulary of Russenorsk. In 1917 the Allied blockade of Russian ports ended the trade, and the pidgin soon disappeared.

Descendants of West Norse

The modern descendants of West Norse are FAROESE, ICELANDIC and NORWEGIAN.

The dialects of Norwegian can be grouped as West Norwegian (including Bergen and Stavanger) and East Norwegian, which stretches inland from Oslo. The Central and North Norwegian dialects of the northern coast are subdivisions of East Norwegian.

East Norwegian, like Swedish, often has pure vowels where West Norwegian has diphthongs, e.g. *sten* for *stein* 'stone'.

Crosses mark former centres of West Norse

speech where the language is now extinct. They include Man, Dublin, the Orkneys (*Orkneyjar*) and Shetland (*Hjaltland*). Greenlanders established a settlement briefly on the coast of New England (*Vinland*), but abandoned it after three years.

As a result of migration in the 19th century there are more than half a million speakers of Norwegian in the United States.

NUBIAN LANGUAGES

PERHAPS 1,000,000 SPEAKERS

Sudan, Egypt

Nubian is a close-knit group of NILO-SAHARAN LANGUAGES, and has a much longer recorded history than any other member of the family.

From 850 BC until AD 300 there was an independent kingdom, south of Egypt, in the middle Nile valley. It was known to the Egyptians, and to its own rulers, as *Kush*; its name in Greek and Latin was *Meroe*. Its stone inscriptions were at first in EGYPTIAN; later ones are in another language, known to scholars as Meroitic, which seems to be unrelated to any of its neighbours. The writing system was deciphered by F. Ll. Griffith – there are twenty-three alphabetic symbols, borrowed from Egyptian scripts – but no one has yet made sense of the language.

With the coming of Christianity to the middle Nile, in the 6th century, the kingdoms of Nobatia (or Meris) and Makouria emerge into history. Their records are in 'Nubian', an early form of modern *Nobiin*. So what happened to Meroitic? When did Nubian begin to be spoken in the Nile valley, and how did this Nilo-Saharan language first reach the middle Nile? The answers are far from clear – but it seems most likely that the early homeland of Nubian is some way to the south-west of the modern Nile Nubians: in Darfur, where one minority Nubian language, *Meidob*, is still to be heard, or in Kordofan, where there are more. From here, perhaps not long before the time of Christ, they spread to the Nile valley itself and gradually displaced Meroitic.

People called *Noubai, Nubae, Noba, Annoubades* and *Nobatai* are named in Greek and Latin sources of the early centuries AD. South of them, in modern southern Sudan, were the *Makoritai*. It seems likely that two modern Nubian languages represent these early medieval peoples. The northern is *Nobiin*: its speakers are called *Mahas* in Sudan, *Fadija* in Egypt. The southern is *Dongolawi* or 'Dongolese Nubian', language of the *Danagla* and their recent northern offshoot the *Kenuz*.

The Christian kingdoms of the Nubians disappeared six centuries ago. Modern Nubian speakers are Muslims, and they are bilingual in Arabic. The traditional habitat of speakers of the Nile Nubian languages has largely disappeared under the waters of the High Dam at Aswan, and they have been resettled – a move which is likely to speed the disappearance of their historic languages.

Nile Nubian languages have five vowels and a distinction of vowel length, which may be used in forming derivatives: *baag* 'divide', *bag* 'distribute'; *aab* 'catch in a net', *ab* 'catch in the hand'.

The first ten numerals in Dongolawi Nubian are: *wer, oww, tosk, kemis, digh, gorigh, kolod, idiw, iskod, dimin*.

Based on papers by William Y. Adams and Robin Thelwall in *The archaeological and linguistic reconstruction of African prehistory* ed. C. Ehret, M. Posnansky (Berkeley: University of California Press, 1982) and other sources

Hill Nubian and Nile Nubian

The Nile Nubian languages are *Dongolawi* (with its offshoot *Kenzi*) and *Nobiin*. On the apparent origin of the Kenzi dialect see BEJA.

The Hill Nubian languages, including *Ghulfan* and *Meidob*, are spoken by small groups in southern Kordofan and Darfur.

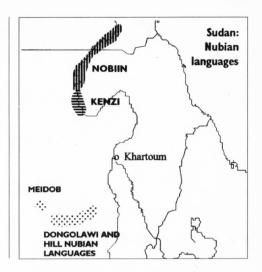

NUPE

1,000,000 SPEAKERS

Nigeria

One of the NIGER-CONGO LANGUAGES of the Benue-Congo group, Nupe is spoken along the Niger and Kaduna rivers in the Emirates of Bida, Agaie, Lapai and Patigi-Lafiagi.

> Nupe speakers call themselves *Nupeci ži*, their language *ezi Nupe* and their country *kin Nupe* 'land of Nupe'. In Hausa they are called *ba Nupe* or *Nufawa*, in Yoruba *Takpa* or *Tapa*. As *Tapa*, Nupe-speaking slaves were to be found in Brazil and Cuba in the 19th century.

Nupe tradition tells of the origin of their ethnic identity in a migration from what is now Igala country to their present location north of the Niger, led by the hero Tsoede or Egedi, five hundred years ago. He is said to have united the indigenous people, till then disorganised. The Nupe kingdom can be found on 18th-century European maps as *Noofy*. It came under Hausa and Fulani domination in the 19th century: after 1870 their ascendancy was followed by that of the Niger Company and the British Government of Nigeria.

Long used in the Niger river trade, Nupe is nowadays a language of radio and television. However, numerous speakers are bilingual in Hausa, the lingua franca of the area and the national language of Northern Nigeria. Yoruba is also known by many. When Christian missionaries began work in Nupe, in 1858, they approached the language by way of Hausa and Yoruba-speaking polyglot interpreters. The majority of Nupe speakers are Muslims: some therefore study Arabic, or are at least able to recite from the Koran.

Nupe is a richly tonal language, with three level tones, a rising tone and a falling tone: *bá* 'be sour', *ba* 'cut', *bà* 'pray', *bǎ* 'not', *bâ* 'slander'. The first ten numerals are: *niní, gúbè, gútá, gúnni, gútsun, gútswànyì, gútwàbà, gútotá, gútwani, gúwo*. '20' is *esi*. Counting in Nupe is by fives and twenties: but for '30', '50' and '70' Yoruba loanwords have been inserted into the system.

> *Ndǎ mi de fitíla niní, a gá lá 'na da u yìzè kpátá le bà yé* – 'My father has only one lamp, but when he lights it the whole world is lit up!' The answer? The moon.

Early Nupe literature

'For a long time it was thought that the Nupes possessed no literature of their own, until the discovery was made a few years ago that there were in existence in the Nupe country a number of songs written in the Aljemi character, and dating back about one hundred years. This bastard Arabic character called Aljemi is in general use in parts of north Africa, and all over the western Sudan; and although it is not at all suited to the Nupe language, still it has been used as the medium of circulating poems and songs intended to be committed to memory, and embodying . . . Mohammedanism . . . with curious allusions and statements which are certainly not to be found in the Koran.'

A. W. Banfield, J. M. Macintyre,
A grammar of the Nupe language
(London: SPCK, 1915) p. 122
This is a couplet from a Muslim song from one of these manuscripts:

Abà Jiyà gǎ, Ye kpe ze ètá Nupe ci èjiṇ yèbó?
Abǔ Bàkǎrì egi Anàsì ci èkóní, ci èjiṇ yèbo.
Aba Jiya says, Do you know those who
speak Nupe and are giving thanks?
Abu Bakari son of Anasi is singing,
he is giving thanks.

Nupe and its dialects: the map

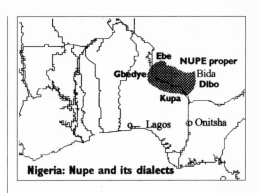

Nigeria: Nupe and its dialects

The major dialects of Nupe are *Nupe* proper, *Ebe*, *Dibo* or Zitako, *Kupa* and *Gbedye*. The river people, *Kyedye*, with colonies as far south as Onitsha, speak Nupe proper. The Nupe spoken in Bida, *'higher* *Nupe'* with its Hausa loanwords, is recognised as the prestige form of the language; it, or at any rate Nupe proper, is known to speakers of other dialects.

NYANJA

4,000,000 OR MORE SPEAKERS

Malawi, Mozambique, Zambia, Zimbabwe

Under its various names, Nyanja is the language of central and southern Malawi and of surrounding districts of Zambia, Mozambique and Tanzania. One of the BANTU LANGUAGES, Nyanja remained the language of local administration when, under the name Nyasaland, the heart of this country became a British protectorate.

> *Nyanja, chiNyanja, ciNyanja, Nyasa* and *Niassa* are all variants of the usual name for the language and its speakers, meaning 'Lake' or 'Lake people'. *Cewa* or *chiChewa* is the western Nyanja dialect. Cewa and Chichewa are sometimes used, in Zambia and Malawi, as names for the language as a whole – or for the true regional language, as opposed to the lingua franca of British administration and of Zambian cities.
>
> The speakers of Nyanja and neighbouring languages were grouped by 19th-century explorers, including David Livingstone, as *Maravi* or *Malawi*; this was revived as the name of the newly independent state.

Nyanja-speaking people have a tradition of origin in the Zaire basin, several hundred years ago. What is certain is that the language has been spoken along the southern shores of Lake Nyasa and the Shire river for some centuries; that it was once the language of an extensive political federation; and that in the last 150 years several successive population movements have redrawn some details of the ethnic map.

At the end of their long march from Zululand several groups of the Ngoni settled in Nyanja-speaking country in the 1830s and 1840s and ruled it as conquerors. Their language is no longer spoken here, but people of some Nyanja-speaking areas regard themselves today as Ngoni rather than Nyanja.

In southern Malawi and neighbouring districts of Mozambique, Nyanja speakers are intermixed in a complex pattern with speakers of Yao, Makua, Lomwe and Chwabo. This is partly the result of recent migrations (in particular, Yao incursions in the late 19th century), but the evidence suggests that such movements have been going on for rather longer than that.

To the north-west, the extensive territory where the Cewa dialect of Nyanja is now spoken results from a migration that began about two hundred years ago.

Language of the police

Missionaries and tea and tobacco planters came to live in the Nyanja-speaking region in the late 19th and early 20th centuries. From working with them, many Nyanja had become useful white-collar workers just at the time when British domination was extending over what is now Zambia and Zimbabwe.

Nyanja, already the language of a large and relatively well-educated population, spread over great distances. It was used in local government offices, in the police and the army, all over the British Central African territories that were briefly united as the Federation of Rhodesia and Nyasaland. Nyanja became one of the four languages of the Zambian Copperbelt (see BEMBA), and it remains the lingua franca of the Zambian capital, Lusaka. But the European tide has receded, and in the long term, as with Fanakalo (see ZULU), the police and government overtones of Nyanja can be seen to have lessened its popularity outside its homeland.

Rival missionaries set up three literary standards for Nyanja. The Blantyre Mission was established on the Shire plateau in 1876 and published in Mang'anja; the Dutch Reformed Church mission worked in Cewa, while the Universities Mission to Central Africa favoured the Lake Nyanja dialect. The artificial 'Union Nyanja' of the Bible translation published in 1922 was not a success.

Cewa or Nyanja is the major African language of Malawi and the second most widely known of the eight official languages of Zambia, spoken by fewer people than Bemba but by more people than English. The first ten numerals are: *-modzi, -wiri, -tatu, -nayi, -sanu, -sanu ndi -modzi, -sanu ndi -wiri, -sanu ndi -tatu, -sanu ndi -nayi, khumi.*

Nyanja, Sena and Tumbuka

The dialects of Nyanja are *Cewa* or Chewa or Ancheya in the west, *Peta* in the south-west, *Nyanja* near Blantyre, *Mang'anja* in the lower Shire valley and *Nyasa* on the eastern shore of Lake Nyasa.

To the south and west, the closely related SENA is the language spoken along the Zambezi in Mozambique. There are 1,200,000 speakers. *Nyungwe* or Tete, a northern variant of Sena, has

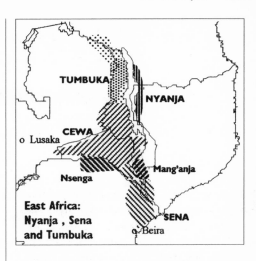

East Africa: Nyanja, Sena and Tumbuka

250,000 speakers. *Kunda* or ciKunda (100,000 speakers) is the language of a trading people, metalworkers who also dealt in slaves and elephants, with old-established settlements along the Zambezi–Luangwa trade route. Their name may be Nyanja in origin: *mcikunda* 'fighter'. Their language is close to Sena and Nyanja, but their ancestry is said to be varied, with links to many of the peoples of central Mozambique.

Outside the group usually regarded as Maravi or Malawi, TUMBUKA is the main member of a group of small dialects spoken in northern Malawi and eastern Zambia.

OCCITAN

SEVERAL MILLION SPEAKERS

France

Provençal, now more often called Occitan, was in medieval times one of the major ROMANCE LANGUAGES, known and cultivated over much of western Europe as the vehicle of beautiful lyric poetry. The survival of Occitan is now threatened by the inexorable spread of French.

The term *Provençal* is often used of the medieval literary language, one of whose main centres was the court of Provence. It is not a suitable term for the modern language, which is actually spoken in a much wider area of France than the region of Provence (whose name comes from Latin *provincia*, 'the province', a by-name dating from the period before Julius Caesar's conquests, when this was still the only part of Gaul that was under Roman rule).

Traditionally the medieval languages of France were distinguished by the word for 'yes': the northern language, French, was called the *langue d'oïl* (but in modern French 'yes' is now *oui*) and the southern was the *langue d'oc*. From this derive the old regional name *Languedoc* and also the modern name for the language and its territory, *Occitan*, *Occitanie*.

Recorded from the 10th century onwards, as learned Latin began to give way to the local spoken tongue in documents and poetry, Provençal is best known as the language of the troubadours. Their poetry of love, satire and war was performed in royal and noble courts in France, in Spain and across Europe. In that multilingual environment Provençal was, from the 12th to the 14th century, the language of lyric: kings were not ashamed to compose and sing in it. Provençal poetry was later imitated in Sicilian and other Italian dialects, in Galician-Portuguese and in German. Some trace the origin of Provençal lyric song to the influence of Arabic culture, spread across Spain and into southern France by the Islamic conquests.

As France became a unified nation state, Provençal rapidly declined in importance after the 15th century. The prophet of the language's revival was Frédéric Mistral (1830–1914), whose long poem *Mireiò* was much admired. Mistral gained the Nobel Prize for Literature in 1904. But no one literary standard was agreed on, and the writing and reading of Occitan literature remains a minority interest in southern France. In schools and in all official and public contexts French is required: fewer and fewer children in each generation have Occitan as their mother tongue.

Like medieval French, Provençal retained two of the six Latin noun cases: for example,

Europe: Catalan and Occitan

nominative *iois* ('joy', subject of a clause) and accusative *ioi* ('joy', direct or indirect object) both appear in lines 1–2 of the poem by the Countess of Die (see box). In other ways, medieval Provençal and modern Occitan are closer to Catalan than to French.

The first ten numerals in Occitan are: *un, dous, tres, quatre, cinq, sièis, sèt, vue, nòu, dès. Shuadit,* the language of Provençal Jews, was a special form of Occitan with borrowings from Hebrew and other Jewish languages. It has been extinct since 1977.

Playing with words

This 12th-century poem shows how word forms could be neatly varied to give the rhyme and parallelism that was at the centre of Occitan poetic style. It is by one of the earliest Occitan poets, the 'Countess of Die'. Scholars have puzzled over her identity, but she remains mysterious.

Ab ioi et ab ioven m'apais	I pleasure myself with joy and youthfulness,
e iois e iovens m'apaia,	And joy and youthfulness pleasure me,
que mos amics es lo plus gais	For my lover is the gayest
per qu'eu sui coindeta e gaia,	Through whom I am happy and gay,
e pois eu li sui veraia	And since I am true to him
be.is taing q'el me sia verais,	It is well that he is true to me,
c'anc de lui amar no m'estrais	And I never escape from loving him
ni ai cor que m'en estraia.	And I have not the heart to escape this.

In lines 3–4 and 5–6 the final adjectives alternate between masculine (*gais, verais*) and feminine (*gaia, veraia*). Lines 1–2 and 7–8, using the same rhymes, end with verbs that alternate between 1st person (*-ais*) and 3rd person (*-aia*).

Text from *Songs of the women troubadours* ed. Matilda Tomaryn Bruckner, Laurie Shepard, Sarah White (New York: Garland, 1995) p. 2

OJIBWA

80,000 SPEAKERS

Canada, United States

One of the Algonquian family of Amerind languages, Ojibwa was once spoken north of Lake Huron and on both sides of Lake Superior, extending as far as what is now North Dakota.

Alternative names are *Chippewa, Chipewyan*.

Ojibwa speakers were traditionally semi-nomadic hunter-gatherers, relying on wild rice gathering, on migratory hunting in winter, and on fishing at settled sites in summer. As with the Cree, their territory was at its greatest extent in the 18th century, when they took land formerly claimed by the Sioux and Fox peoples. They were firm allies of the French through this period. Meanwhile the fur trade with Europeans in the 18th and 19th centuries was destabilising Ojibwa culture, enriching the chieftains and turning their office into a hereditary one.

Ojibwa is still spoken from Ontario westwards to North Dakota in scattered Indian reservations (see map at ALGONQUIAN LANGUAGES).

The language of the Ottawa or Odawa, after whom Canada's national capital is named, is sometimes called *Eastern Ojibwa*. In historical tradition Ojibwa, Ottawa and Potawatomi, speakers of three related Algonquian languages, together made up an alliance known as the 'three fires'.

The first ten numerals in Ojibwa are: *pēshikwan, nīshan, nissan, nīwan, nānan, ninkotwāssan, nīshwāssan, nisshwāssan, shānkassan, mintāssan.*

It was on the myths of the Ojibwa – collected in the *Algic researches* of Henry R. Schoolcraft (1839) – that Longfellow based his epic *Hiawatha*.

Writing Ojibwa

In writing Ojibwa, a syllabary (based on the one used for CREE) has competed with the Roman alphabet. Its inventor, the missionary James Evans, had worked first with Ojibwa, for which he devised a Latin transliteration. By the time he was transferred to Cree territory he had concluded that a newly designed syllabary would work better. Invented in 1840, the Cree syllabary was soon adopted in Ojibwa writing and printing. It is partly inspired by English shorthand.

OLD NORSE

EARLY LANGUAGE OF SCANDINAVIA

Old Norse represents one of the three early branches of the GERMANIC LANGUAGES. It is the oldest recorded form of what are now the five modern Scandinavian languages.

The earliest period of Old Norse, 'proto-Nordic', extends from about AD 300 to 800. The only records of it at this period are Runic inscriptions (see box) along with some Scandinavian words and names in Latin and Anglo-Saxon texts. There is as yet no sign of dialect differences.

Between 800 and 1050 dialects begin to emerge. The principal division is between East and West Norse: the great mountain chain of Scandinavia, the 'Keel', *Kjølen* in Norwegian, *Kölen* in Swedish, marks the dividing line.

West Norse was spoken in Norway and a growing area of Viking settlement in the north Atlantic. About thirty Runic inscriptions survive on the Isle of Man as a reminder that Old Norse, not Manx, was that island's first written language. More Norse inscriptions are to be found in Ireland and in Orkney. But the most important of the Viking colonies was certainly Iceland. West Norse is the immediate ancestor of modern NORWEGIAN (see map there), FAROESE and ICELANDIC.

East Norse was spoken in Denmark, Sweden, coastal Finland and Estonia, and the eastern territories once ruled by Vikings. The Danelaw, the Norse conquests in eastern England, were occupied and settled from Denmark more than from Norway. Had a Norse language survived in East Anglia, Lincolnshire and Yorkshire, it would have been East Norse! As it is, numerous Norse words have been borrowed into English, including *skip, skirt, egg, steak* (Norwegian *steke* 'to roast'). More are to be found in north-eastern English dialects: *laik* 'to play'. Viking trade and conquest in western Russia has left plenty of linguistic evidence, including Christian names

such as *Igor* and *Olga* and the name of *Russia* (*Rus*) itself. East Norse is the ancestor of modern SWEDISH and DANISH (see map there).

The earliest name for what we now call Old Norse was *Dånsk tunga*, 'Danish tongue'. *Norrønt mál* was the term for what is essentially the same language as spoken in Norway and Iceland, 'West Norse'.

The best-known collection of Old Norse poetry is the *Edda*, sometimes called 'Elder' or 'Poetic Edda' to distinguish it from a later prose work on Norse mythology. The *Edda* poems reflect pagan beliefs. Old Norse literature shades imperceptibly into Old Icelandic and Old Norwegian.

The Scandinavian languages as a group have several features that mark them off from other Germanic languages. The standard languages have two genders, common and neuter (though Icelandic and Faroese still have three). In the standard languages and nearly all the dialects the definite article 'the' is suffixed to the noun. Faroese and Icelandic differ from the rest, appearing in many ways more archaic: this is partly the result of the very heavy Low German and High German influence on the 'continental' Scandinavian languages, an influence which the island languages escaped.

'Each of the Scandinavian languages has its own "flavour". Swedish can be very formal and "correct", but also has a surprising amount of grace, and has now shed most of the syntactical heaviness it used to share with German. Norwegian is rugged and salty, and infinitely varied, while Danish has an amazing lightness and a pronunciation which positively lends itself to comedy' (M. O'C. Walshe, *Introduction to the Scandinavian languages* (London: André Deutsch, 1965) p. 13).

Norn, the language of Shetland and Orkney

West Norse was known in Old English as *Norren*. One of its descendants bore the same name – the now-forgotten Norse language, *Norn*, once spoken by the inhabitants of the Shetland Islands (*Hjaltland* in Old Norse). These were a Norwegian possession until about 1400, then Danish, and were only later annexed by Scotland. It was not until the 18th century that English gradually became the majority language of the Shetlands.

Plenty of Norse vocabulary still survives in the Shetland dialect: *rossifaks* 'white-topped waves, white horses', *dala-mist* 'valley mist'.

The Orkneys and Outer Hebrides were also Norse territory. In Orkney, English began to replace Norn as the everyday language around 1700; in the Hebrides Gaelic was replacing Norn as early as 1400.

The Runic script

ᚠᚢᚦᚨᚱᚲᚷᚹᚺᚾᛁᛃᛇᛈᛉᛊᛏᛒᛖᛗᛚᛜᛟᛞ

f u t h a r k g w h n i j ė p z s t b e m l ng d o

Font: *runic.ttf* of Digital Type Foundry

The Runic script was apparently invented, soon after the time of Christ, on the basis of the Greek alphabet. Like Greek, it has 24 letters. Its angular shape was demanded for ease of carving on beech wood. Few early wood inscriptions survive, but there are many Runic inscriptions on stone, in Germany, Scandinavia, Ireland and northern Britain. It was traditionally called *Futhark* after its first six letters.

The Runic letter ᚦ, derived from the Greek δ and used for the fricative sound *th*, was afterwards adopted in the Old English and Old Norse versions of the Latin alphabet for this same sound, which was unknown in Latin. As Þ, this letter is still used in modern Icelandic.

The Eggjum stone

These mysterious runes are among the oldest surviving texts in Old Norse. The stone was discovered by a farmer at Eggjum, near the Sognefjord in south-western Norway, in 1917. The inscription (text below), dated to roughly AD 700, is very difficult to read and interpret. Lines 5–6 are apparently a riddle whose solution would be the dead man's name.

ᚠᛁᚼᚼᛩᚱᛁᚢ ᚼᛩ ᛏᚢᚠ�057ᚼ ᛆᚠᚼᛗᚼᛏᛆᚼᚤᚱᛩᚱᛁᚼᛏ'' ...

Hin warb naseu mar,	A man spattered blood,
made Þaim kaiba i bormoÞa huni.	smearing the rowlocks of the holed boat.
Huwar ob kam harsi a,	Who was he who came this far,
h[i a] lat gotna?	came to the land of men?
Fiskr or f[lai]nauim suemade,	'Fish-from-the-spear-stream,
fokl i frakn[a il] galandi.	bird-shrieking-in-battle.'
Sa [tu] misurki.	He died by crime.
Ni s solu sot,	The sun has not struck this stone,
ut ni sakse stain skorin.	nor has sword scored it.
Ni s[akr] mar nakda,	No outlaw must lay him bare,
ni snar[Þi]r ni wiltir manr lagi.	no vagrants nor wild men.

After Otto Springer, in *Indo-European and Indo-Europeans* ed. Cardona (Philadelphia 1970) pp. 35–48

OLD SLAVONIC

Classical language of Eastern Europe

In the 9th century Christian missionaries from the Byzantine Empire began the large-scale conversion of speakers of SLAVONIC LANGUAGES – which, at that date, had not yet differentiated very widely from the ancestral form of speech that linguists reconstruct as 'proto-Slavonic'.

The court to which the missionaries were first invited, in 862, was that of Prince Rastislav of Great Moravia. The local tongue must have been an early form of Czech. But the first missionaries, Saints Cyril and Methodius, had learnt their Slavonic speech in Macedonia, near Saloniki. Thus the language of the early translations – Bibles and religious manuals – in what we now know as Old Slavonic is closer to modern Macedonian and Bulgarian than to the other Slavonic languages.

Old (Church) Slavonic or *Old Slavic* is sometimes called *Old Bulgarian* to emphasise its geographical origin (the Macedonian language being regarded as a form of Bulgarian). The name *Church Slavonic* is often reserved for the later 'Russianised' form of the language.

Old Slavonic is essentially the language of the 9th- and 10th-century texts. A developed form of Old Slavonic, with some features of spoken Bulgarian, was written in the monasteries of Bulgaria and Macedonia, and notably at the Bulgarian capital of Trnovo and the great monastic centre at Ohrid. Old Slavonic also spread, with Christianity, in Serbia, in the Romanian principalities, in Ukraine and eventually in Russia. But as a result of lengthy warfare ending only with the Turkish conquests and the revival of Russia, the Bulgarian, Serbian, Romanian and Ukrainian-Russian varieties of Old Slavonic tended to develop in isolation, each with an increasing number of local features and with very different pronunciations.

Old Slavonic reigned in Bulgaria and Serbia until the 14th century, when a linguistic reform and literary revival led by the Bulgarian Patriarch Evtimii was closely followed by the Turkish victories, notably the Battle of Kosovo, celebrated in Serbian epic, in 1389 and the fall of Trnovo in 1393. Ukrainian Church Slavonic was for four centuries the principal administrative and literary language of Ukraine, but it lost this role with the partition of Ukraine in 1387.

Evtimii's linguistic reform, then, came as Old Slavonic was about to lose its dominant role in Bulgaria, Serbia and the Ukraine. However, as an official and literary language it long remained in regular use in the Romanian principalities of Wallachia and Moldavia: in modern Romanian a great deal of everyday vocabulary is still of Old Slavonic origin. And the linguistic reform had its fullest effect in Russia, where the Bulgarian scholar Kiprian was appointed Metropolitan of All Russia in 1389. Church Slavonic in its 14th-century Russian rebirth was by now a very different language from the spoken language that surrounded it.

After an abortive revolt at Pec in 1690 Serbian refugees settled in Hungary and were succoured by Russian missionaries. From this time onwards the Russian variety or 'Church Slavonic' was adopted in Serbian churches, while a Serbian-Church Slavonic mixture, *Slavenoserbian*, became the language of education. Russianised Church Slavonic spread to Bulgaria in the 18th century, and it is still to be heard in Orthodox church services in Russia and eastern Europe. Old Slavonic and Church Slavonic loanwords can be identified in all the modern Slavonic languages.

Old Slavonic has three numbers, singular, dual and plural. Verbs have two series of forms for perfective and imperfective aspect. The first ten numerals are: *jedinə, dəva, tr'ye, chetıre, pět', shest', sedm', osm', devět', desět'*.

The alphabets of Old Slavonic

When a previously unwritten language was to be used for religious conversion, it was quite normal to invent a wholly new alphabet for it. The Gothic, Armenian and Georgian alphabets, among others, originated in this way. Thus St Cyril, one of the two missionaries to the Slavs of Great Moravia, invented the *Glagolica* – the Glagolitic alphabet, see the top row of the box – to be used for texts in Slavonic.

Great Moravia soon collapsed and the focus of the mission shifted south, to Bulgaria. Here, probably, it seemed best to use a writing system that was closer to Greek and easier for Greek-educated missionaries to learn. This may have been the origin of the 'Cyrillic' script (see the middle row). This is now used in a modernised form for many of the Slavonic languages. The earliest Cyrillic inscriptions are found in Bulgaria and Romania, and date from the 10th century.

This view of the origin of the Cyrillic alphabet is controversial – but it does explain why Cyrillic letter shapes are like Greek for sounds that exist in Greek, and are like Glagolitic for sounds that are unknown in Greek. Others believe that Cyrillic was in existence before the time of

the mission as a way of writing Slavonic names in Greek documents: but there is no real evidence for this. The traditional story is that St Cyril invented both Glagolitic and Cyrillic (and the latter is, after all, named after him) but it is difficult to see why he would have invented two alphabets to serve essentially the same purpose.

In Catholic Croatia the Glagolitic alphabet continued to be used until the late 19th century. Elsewhere in Eastern Europe it was soon forgotten.

Two manuscripts of the 11th century are thought to preserve Old Slavonic in its purest form. Known as Codex Zographensis and Codex Marianus, they contain Gospel translations from the Greek. They are in Glagolitic script: in later texts the Cyrillic alphabet was adopted.

The Cyrillic and Glagolitic alphabets in Church Slavonic

АБВГ ДЕЖ З Ѕ И І Н Ћ К Л М N О П Р С Т ОУ Ф Х Ѡ
Ц Ч Ш Щ Ъ ЪІ Ь Ѣ Ю ІА К Ѧ Ѫ Х Ѩ Ѯ Ѱ Ѳ Ѵ

Ⰰ Ⰱ Ⰲ Ⰳ Ⰴ Ⰵ Ⰶ Ⰷ Ⰸ Ⰻ Ⰹ Ⰺ Ⰽ Ⰾ Ⰿ Ⱀ Ⱁ Ⱂ Ⱃ Ⱄ Ⱅ Ⱆ Ⱇ Ⱈ Ⱉ
Ⱋ Ⱌ Ⱍ Ⱎ Ⱏ Ⱐ Ⱑ Ⱓ Ⱔ Ⱗ __ Ⱎ Ⱉ Ⱈ __ Ⱚ _

a b v g d e zh dz z i i gy k l m n o p r s t u f kh o ts
ch sh sht ə ı) yɛ yu ya ye ē õ yē yõ x ps f i

OMOTIC LANGUAGES

The Omotic group are AFROASIATIC LANGUAGES spoken in Ethiopia. They differ strongly from the Semitic languages like Amharic and the Cushitic languages such as Somali and Oromo. The researches of Harold Fleming and Lionel Bender in the 1970s first demonstrated that Omotic was a separate division of the Afroasiatic family. It includes some of the languages once grouped under the name *Sidama*.

Omotic is named after the River Omo, along whose tributaries most speakers of Omotic languages live. *Sidama* is an OROMO word: whatever its origin, it came to mean 'foreign, not Oromo'.

Most Omotic languages are little known and spoken by small communities. The two important groups are Gonga, which includes the historic Kefa, and Ometo, whose major representative is WOLAYTTA. For a map see GONGA.

Janjero and its royal language

Janjero is the language of the little-known former kingdom of Janjero, north-east of Kefa. It is first mentioned in Ethiopian records in 1427 and was conquered by the Emperor Menelek in 1894. Its remarkable customs, including human sacrifice, were described by the two Europeans who visited it – in 1613 and Antonio Cecchi in the 1870s.

'The people call themselves *Yamma* or *Yem*. The name by which they are better known is the [Oromo] form of the Amharic *zenjaro*, "baboon" . . . (the Italian spelling is *Giangero*).

'The royal language of Janjero consisted of a special vocabulary for parts of the body, weapons, and verbs of action referring to the king. Thus "eye" in common Janjero is *afa*, but *kema* in the royal language; "eat" is *ma* in common speech, *bos* in the royal language; and "spear", *ebo* in common speech, is *me'a* in the royal language. The language of respect used special words to describe the ordinary actions of notables: "eat" is *ma* in common speech, but *ta* in the language of respect. Improper use of the royal language was punished by death.'

G. W. B. Huntingford, *The Galla of Ethiopia. The kingdoms of Kafa and Janjero* (London: International African Institute, 1955) p. 137

ORIYA

22,000,000 SPEAKERS

India

O riya is the language of the Indian state of Orissa. It is one of the Eastern INDO-ARYAN LANGUAGES, closely related to neighbouring Bengali.

There are a few inscriptions in Oriya from dates as early as the 10th century, though at this date the language is not really distinguishable from Bengali. Longer inscriptions appear in the 13th and literary texts in the 15th. Rule of Orissa by the TELUGU-speaking Telingas and the MARATHI-speaking Nagpur dynasty of Bhonsla were followed by Bengali cultural and political dominance in the 19th and early 20th centuries, for the British paid little direct attention to Orissa and its culture (it became a separate state within British India in 1936). All three of these episodes have left their mark on the language.

In a world context Oriya is one of the least known of major Indian languages. Its poetic literature is extensive but little studied outside the borders of the state. Older texts are almost all inspired by Hindu mythology: there are more than a dozen reworkings of the Sanskrit *Rāmāyana* in Oriya. One of them is due to the founder of modern Oriya literature, Fakirmohan Senapati (1843–1918), who also wrote novels notable for their evocation of real everyday Oriya speech patterns.

Standard Oriya shows relatively little influence from the Austroasiatic languages, such as SANTALI, which are spoken in western Orissa.

The inland dialect Sambalpuri (for map see ASSAMESE) is much more heavily influenced by them.

For a table of numerals see BENGALI.

> Orissa is best known outside India for the great temple of *Jagannātha*, a name of Krishna, at Puri. Thanks to the processions in his honour, this god's name is the origin of the English word *juggernaut*.

Oriya script

The alphabet is historically related to Bengali, but it looks wholly different – because whereas Bengali script is suited to writing with a pen, Oriya is perfectly adapted to writing with a stylus on palm leaves, the traditional material for manuscript texts. There must be no long horizontal strokes – like the 'washing-line' on which Devanagari and Bengali scripts appear to depend – because these would split the leaf. Oriya substitutes the half-circles built into almost every character.

The Oriya consonants

କ ଖ ଗ ଘ ଙ ଚ ଛ ଜ ଝ ଞ ଟ ଠ ଡ ଢ ଣ ତ ଥ ଦ ଧ ନ ପ ଫ ବ ଭ ମ ଯ ର ଲ ଳ ଶ ଷ ସ ହ

k kh g gh ṅ c ch j jh ñ ṭ ṭh ḍ ḍh ṇ t th d dh n p ph b bh m y r l ḷ ś ṣ s h

OROMO

7,500,000 SPEAKERS

Ethiopia, Kenya, Somalia

O ne of the CUSHITIC LANGUAGES of the Afro-asiatic family, Galla is the major regional language of Ethiopia, though the national language is AMHARIC.

The name *Oromo*, now standard among linguists and official in Ethiopia in the form *Orominya*, is what the speakers call their language and themselves (the plural is *Oromota*). In local genealogy, it was Oromo son of Omer who long ago crossed the sea from Arabia and became the founder of the nation. *Galla* is the term found in most older sources. It was used only by Amharic and other foreign speakers.

The historical nucleus of Oromo speech is at the eastern end of its present territory, around and to the south of Harar. It is clear from Ethiopic and foreign records that Oromo speakers conquered much of central and western Ethiopia in the 16th and 17th centuries, including large areas of former GONGA speech. Oromo spread partly through these conquests, partly through slavery, for Oromo societies both kept slaves and sold them to neighbouring peoples. Slavery survived in eastern Ethiopia until the late 1930s.

Until the 19th century Oromo speakers, pastoralists and traders, dominated what is now south-eastern Ethiopia and the hinterland of eastern Kenya: they formed the essential link between the Swahili and Somali speakers of the coast (whom they called *Hamara* or *Abba shuffa*, 'people with clothes') and inland populations such as the KAMBA. 'Galla' is still a lingua franca in eastern Kenya, e.g. for speakers of Pokomo, but more now use Swahili.

Wello, Eastern and Southern Oromo speakers are largely Muslim. In these areas men often know some Arabic, but only those who have studied the religion are able to read and write it well.

Oromo is a language with a rich oral literature, including poetry, songs and historical traditions. Henry Salt's *Voyage to Abyssinia* (1814) contained a word list of Oromo, but the first published work by a native Oromo speaker was *The Galla spelling book* by Onesimus Nesib (see box). Until the 1970s Oromo was not favoured as a written language in Ethiopia. It was scarcely to be heard on the radio and seldom seen in print. The Amharic alphabet is normally used for written and printed Oromo.

Oromo has six vowels, with a long-short distinction, and high and low tones. The first ten numerals are: *tokko, lama, sadii, afur, shan, ja'a, torba, saddeet, sagal, kudan*.

The Galla spelling book

'Of written literature perhaps the most interesting is *The Galla spelling book, by Onesimos Nsib, a native Galla. Printed at the Swedish Mission Press, Moncullo near Massowah, 1894.* This is the English title; it has also a Galla title written in Amharic characters which reads, in English, "The beginning of teaching, that is, a book of words for those who teach the Galla language, to show the people of Galla land the way to God (*Waqa*), collected and printed by Awaj Onesimos and Ganon Aster, made this side of Massawa in the village of Monkullo 1894 years after our Lord Jesus Christ was born." The texts in this book are in the Mača dialect of Limmu, from which Onesimos came. Its purpose seems to have been to discredit the Swedish Mission, for the texts ostensibly intended to "show the Galla the way to God" include songs of love and war, and ritual songs relating to pagan worship and the cult of Atete, the Galla fertility goddess.'

G. W. B. Huntingford, *The Galla of Ethiopia* (London: International African Institute, 1955) p. 18

Onesimos (c. 1855–1931) actually spent many years translating the Bible and other religious texts into Oromo. He also compiled an Oromo–Swedish dictionary. He was a slave, purchased and freed in 1870 and sent by the Swedish Evangelical Mission to study in Sweden 1876–81.

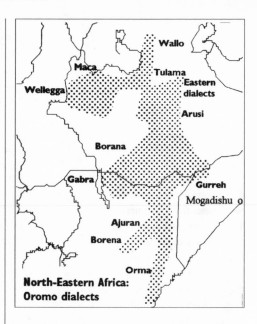

North-Eastern Africa: Oromo dialects

The dialects of Oromo

In Ethiopia the major dialect divisions are *Wellegga*, *Mača*, *Tulama* (the dialect of Shoa, the heartland of modern Ethiopia), *Wallo* (where Oromo speakers are much intermixed with Amharic), *Eastern* (centring on Harar), *Arusi* and – to the south – *Borena*. The city of Harar itself has its own language, *Harari*.

In Kenya, three dialects can be distinguished: that of the Borena, Sakuye and Ajuran (a 'Somali' tribe in which many speakers are bilingual in Somali and Oromo); that of the Orma or Wardai, also spoken in Somalia; and that of the Gabra and Gurreh (who, again, consider themselves Somali). The Gurreh tribe extends into Ethiopia and Somalia.

OSSETE

500,000 SPEAKERS

Russia, Georgia

Speakers of Ossete are separated by hundreds of miles from their nearest linguistic relatives. They are the last remnant of the steppe nomads of eastern Europe and central Asia who were speakers of IRANIAN LANGUAGES – Sarmatians, Scythians, Saka, Alans. They once ranged from the middle Danube valley to the foothills of the Pamir, and were prominent in Greek, Latin and Chinese history.

Politically divided, Ossetia lies across the centre of the northern Caucasus. Southern Ossetia is a district of newly independent Georgia. Political tensions there led to armed conflict in 1989–92. Northern Ossetia is within the borders of Russia, and has been nurtured as a bulwark of Soviet Russian influence among its neighbours.

Many Ossete speakers are bilingual in their national language, either Russian or Georgian. These are now a strong influence on the language. Other neighbouring languages, Turkic and especially Caucasian, have also affected Ossete: the large number of consonants, 33 in the Iron dialect, is a typical Caucasian trait. It has had little contact with other Iranian languages for as long as two thousand years. Like them, Ossete has lost the old noun declensions of Indo-European – but unlike them it has developed a new declension system with nine cases, nominative, genitive, dative, allative, ablative, inessive, adessive, equative and comitative.

The two main dialects of Ossete, Iron and Digor, are so different that they are scarcely mutually intelligible. There is some written literature in Digor, which is spoken on the western edges of North Ossetia. Iron is the basis of standard Ossete, used in literature, education and the press. It is written in Cyrillic script, like Russian, with the addition of the letter Æ æ for a front *a* sound. Until 1954 South Ossetia used the Georgian alphabet: this provided symbols for the ejective or glottalic consonants *k' c' č' t' p'*, which Ossete shares with its neighbours the CAUCASIAN LANGUAGES. In Cyrillic these are written къ цъ чъ тъ пъ.

The first ten numerals in Ossete are: *iu, dyuö, örtö, tsyppar, fondz, ökhsöz, avd, ast, farast, dös.*

The Alans and the Zelenchuk inscription

The language of the Alans was the direct ancestor of Ossete. They first emerge into history as they crossed the Caucasus, in the 1st century AD, to raid Armenia and the Parthian Empire (Josephus, *The Jewish War* 7.7.4).

The only surviving text in the Alan language is an inscription in Greek characters, from the 10th century AD, found beside the River Zelenchuk.

The Caucasus: Ossete

PALAEOSIBERIAN LANGUAGES

The minority languages of Siberia that do not belong to any of the larger language families are grouped, for convenience, under the label *Palaeosiberian*, 'old Siberian', or *Palaeoasiatic*. Some linguists used to call them *Hyperborean*, a word originally used in classical Greek for a mythical people who lived 'beyond the North Wind'.

These labels cover three entirely isolated languages – and one very small family, Chukotko-Kamchatkan, so named after the two Pacific peninsulas of north-eastern Siberia where these languages are spoken. Counting all together, they are spoken by only twenty-five thousand people. As with the SAMOYEDIC LANGUAGES and TUNGUSIC LANGUAGES, and some others of northern Russia, it is unlikely that the number of speakers of any individual language was ever more than a few thousand: Siberia has never been a hospitable environment. Yet, as with some of these others, there are strongly marked dialect distinctions within the languages, and

Scattered KET-speaking communities

**Northern Asia:
Palaeosiberian languages**

there is typically a cultural and linguistic divide between speakers who are nomadic and those who are settled. The facts show that languages can survive, for hundreds or thousands of years, with a tiny, highly scattered and mobile population base. In the past, at least, size did not matter.

The Chukotko-Kamchatkan languages include Chukchi or Luorawetlan, Koryak or Nymylyan, and Itelmen or Kamchadal, this last probably on the way to extinction. Together they occupy the far north-east of Siberian Russia. They are now threatened with extinction, by Russian development and migration.

Chukchi has 11,000 speakers on the far eastern Chukotka peninsula, and is used in primary schools and occasional publications. The small number of speakers belies Chukchi's regional importance. It was once the lingua franca of the north-eastern Siberian coasts: Yupik (see ESKIMO-

ALEUT LANGUAGES) has many Chukchi loanwords. There are Tundra Chukchi, nomadic reindeer-breeders, and Sea Chukchi settled on the coasts of the Bering Strait.

Koryak has about 6,000 speakers, settled on the Kamchatka peninsula. It is less favoured politically: children are taught in Russian.

The remaining three 'Palaeosiberian languages' have little in common with one another, and very little in common with any other known languages: they are true isolates. They are also far apart on the map. In fact the only reason for linking them together under one heading is the very dubious one of linguistic tradition.

Nivkh or Gilyak is spoken – in two very distinct dialects – by about 2,000 people on the banks of the lower Amur and on Sakhalin island. Yukagir has only 300 speakers, with two main dialects. The Tundra Yukagir lead a nomadic life in the valleys of the Alazeya and Chukoch'ya; the Kolyma Yukagir hunt and fish on the banks of the Yasachnaya and Korkodon.

Ket, or Yenisei Ostyak, is unique among the languages of Siberia in having a tone system: in this point, at least, it resembles Chinese, and it has actually been argued that Ket is a Sino-Tibetan language. It also has gender, masculine, feminine and neuter – again an oddity among Siberian languages. Ket is an isolate now, but two hundred years ago it was not: three other languages of 18th-century Siberia, Arin, Assan and Kott, were related to it. All died out long ago.

Nivkh numerals

Nivkh has no close link with Japanese: but it does share one remarkable feature with Japanese, the numeral classifier system. For the numerals '1' to '5' there are twenty-six different forms depending on the class of object that is being counted. If it is a boat, the numerals are *ńim, mim, ťem, nəm, t'om*. If it is a dog-sledge, they are *ńiŗ, miŗ, ťeŗ, nəŗ, t'oŗ*.

Example from Bernard Comrie, *The languages of the Soviet Union* (Cambridge: Cambridge University Press, 1981) p. 269

PALI

Classical language of south and south-east Asia

Pali is one of the Prakrits (see INDO-ARYAN LANGUAGES), the one in which the dialogues of the Buddha, who died in the early 5th century BC, were recorded and recited. For a table of numerals see SANSKRIT.

> *Pāli* meant 'series of texts, canon': *Pālibhāsā* was 'the language of the Canon'. Outsiders later misunderstood this compound word: Simon de la Loubère (*The Kingdom of Siam* (London, 1693)) took *Pali* to be the proper name of the language, and so did some Burmese and Sinhalese writers.

The text of the Buddha's teachings, and the other scriptures of the Theravada tradition, were – according to later sources – fixed at the first, second and third Buddhist Councils, the last of which took place under the Emperor Aśoka, who reigned c. 274–232 BC. But they were transmitted only in the memory and through the mouths of believers until, in Sri Lanka just before the time of Christ, they were at last written down.

If this is true, it may help to explain why Pali, the language of these scriptures, is a mixed dialect, not identical with the speech of any district of northern India, and showing signs of interference both from SANSKRIT and from the Dravidian languages of the south. It is certainly not – as tradition insisted – the *Māgadhī* or colloquial of north-eastern India, some form of which the Buddha himself must have spoken.

Once fixed in writing, Pali became the fairly stable medium in which Buddhists of the southern, Theravada tradition studied and wrote. The religion, and with it the Pali canon, spread successively to speakers of Sinhalese, Mon, Burmese, Thai and various languages of inland south-east Asia. Buddhism eventually disappeared from India proper, but Buddhists from Sri Lanka, Burma, Thailand, Laos and Cambodia still continue to learn and use this now-classical language of ancient India. Later Pali naturally shows the influence of its writers' varied mother tongues.

The dialogues of the Buddha are among the masterpieces of world literature. Another Pali classic is the *Questions of King Milinda*, recording a semi-legendary encounter between the Greek king of Bactria, Menander, and the Buddhist philosopher Nagasena. The stories of the Buddha's former lives, *Jātaka*, make up a far more complex text than these. Each of the 547 stories consists of brief verses (in a form of Pali with some archaic features), a prose retelling, a frame narrative and a detailed commentary on the verses.

Like the *Jātaka*, the corpus of Pali literature in its full form tends to be an interweaving of text, paraphrase, translation, commentary and sub-commentary. Many texts are bilingual. Most later writing comes from Sri Lanka, Burma (which adopted the Pali canon in the 11th century), then also Thailand and Cambodia. In all these countries the texts were normally recorded on palm leaf manuscripts, in local scripts. Local scripts are still used in printing Pali texts. European Buddhists and scholars – following this tradition – use the Latin alphabet.

As Pali became a classical language, one that had to be learned, a tradition of linguistic works developed. The dictionary *Abhidhanappadipika* 'The lamp of nouns' was compiled by Moggallana, in the 12th century, on the model of the Sanskrit dictionary *Amarakoœa*. A Sinhala translation of it was made in the 13th century.

Literary rule

Sahassam api ce pāthā anatthapadasaṃhitā
ekaṃ pāthāpadaṃ seyyo yaṃ sutvā upasammati.
Better than a thousand anthologies of the path of wickedness
Is one single verse whose hearing brings peace.

Dhammapada, verse 101

The *Dhammapada* 'Path of morality' is an ancient collection of verse sayings attributed to the Buddha. Like the verses of the *Jātaka*, the *Dhammapada* gave rise to a later collection of prose tales, intended to explain why each verse was spoken. These stories, known as *Dhammapadaṭṭ-akathā* Dhammapada commentary', have been translated into English as *Buddhist legends*.

PAMPANGAN

1,850,000 SPEAKERS

Philippines

One of the AUSTRONESIAN LANGUAGES, Pampangan is the main language of Pampanga province, in the central Luzon plain and immediately to the north-west of Manila (see map at TAGALOG). Pampangan is one of the eight 'major languages' of the Philippines.

Alternative forms of the name are *Kapampangan* and *Pampango.*

Pampangan was once written in a native script, a descendant of the Brahmi script of ancient India. This remained in use until fairly late in the Spanish period. However, printing in Pampangan – in Latin script – began as early as 1618.

Spelling was at first close to that of Spanish: a new orthography, similar to that adopted for Tagalog, was introduced in 1965.

Outside its heartland, there is a *barrio Kapampangan* 'Pampangan suburb' in Paco in metropolitan Manila. Pampangan is also spoken in four cities of Tarlac province (Bamban, Concepcion, Tarlac itself and Capas) and two cities of Bataan province (Dinalupihan and Hermosa) near the western borders of Pampanga.

The first ten numerals in Pampangan are: *métung, adwá, atlú, ápat, limá, anám, pitú, walú, siám, apúlu.*

PANGASINAN

1,650,000 SPEAKERS

Philippines

One of the AUSTRONESIAN LANGUAGES, Pangasinan is spoken in the central part of Pangasinan province in north central Luzon (see map at TAGALOG). It is particularly the language of the Lingayen gulf region, spoken in San Carlos, Dagupan, Lingayen (the provincial capital) and other nearby market towns. Around this heartland, the closely related Ilocano is the everyday language: Pangasinan speakers are almost equalled by Ilocano speakers in numbers, even in their home province.

Pangalato, the alternative name of Pangasinan, is a derogatory term now little used.

Numerals in Pangasinan

In Pangasinan there are two sets of numerals. The inherited ones are used in traditional contexts: Spanish loan numerals are used in telling the time and, often, in trade.

Pangasinan		Spanish
sakey, isa	1	uno
dua	2	dos
talo	3	tres
apat	4	kuatro
lima	5	singko
anem	6	sais
pito	7	siete
walo	8	ocho
siam	9	nueve
samplo	10	dies

Richard A. Benton, *Pangasinan reference grammar* (Honolulu: University of Hawaii Press, 1971)

PANJABI

PERHAPS 60,000,000 SPEAKERS

Pakistan, India

It is agreed among linguists that there are two Panjabi languages, one (Standard or Eastern or simply Panjabi) spoken in both India and Pakistan, the other (Lahnda or Western or sometimes 'Punjabi') entirely in Pakistan. Panjabi belongs to the INDO-ARYAN LANGUAGES, and to the dialect continuum of northern India and Pakistan: it has no firm frontiers with its neighbours, Hindi, Rajasthani and Sindhi.

Panjab is a place name of Persian origin: it means 'the five rivers', for the region is defined by the five great rivers, Jelam, Chenāb, Rāvī, Biās and Satlaj, which join the lower Indus. *Punjab* is an old-fashioned Anglo-Indian spelling of the word. The term *Lahnda* that was invented by Sir George Grierson, compiler of the *Linguistic Survey of India*, for the western dialects, comes from a Panjabi word for 'western'.

Indo-Aryan languages were spoken in this region from the early first millennium BC if not before. There are records of a language identifiable as Panjabi dating from the 11th century AD, but Panjabi literature really begins in the 15th century, and, from the start, follows two traditions. First came that of the Sufis, Muslim mystics, whose poetry – in Arabic script – was influenced by Persian traditions. The religious writings of the Sikhs, beginning almost at the same time, drew inspiration both from Sufi and from Hindu traditions. The Sikh scriptures, written by Guru Nanak (1469–1539) and his successors, make up the *Guru Granth Sahib*, the 'holy book of the Gurus', which was compiled by the fifth Guru, Arjan, in 1604. These early forms of Panjabi were very similar to the Braj that has now developed into

Hindi: indeed, Panjabi and Hindi are to some extent mutually intelligible even now.

In Pakistan the Sufi and Muslim tradition of Panjabi literature is nowadays weak, supplanted by Urdu, though the language is still pre-eminent in local Sufi contexts. Panjabi is little used in broadcasting and the press: Urdu (and English) take its place. In India, on the other hand, a modern standard of literary Panjabi was established in the 19th century, and Sikh authors write and publish copiously in the language.

In India, Panjabi now has about 15,000,000 speakers. Panjabi language and Gurmukhi script are identified with the Sikh religion; so much so that non-Sikhs are tempted to describe their language as Hindi, and some write in the Devanagari script that is typical of Hindi.

In Pakistan, where its speakers are Muslims, Panjabi or Lahnda is even more seriously under-reported in census figures. These dialects are actually spoken by the majority of the inhabitants of Pakistan, but many prefer to give their language as Urdu, Pakistan's official national language, in which they are for practical purposes bilingual. It is also under-reported because there has been no agreed name to cover the western dialects, differing fairly strongly as they do from the modern standard written language which is based on the dialects of Amritsar and Lahore. Terms like Western Panjabi and Lahnda are for linguists; Jatki, Multani and Hindko belong to individual dialects or dialect groups.

Sikhs are traditionally mobile. As soldiers in the British Army many served in Singapore, Hong Kong and Australia. In the early years of this century considerable numbers went as railway workers to East Africa, as farmers to British

Columbia and California. From about 1950 there was massive migration to Britain. The 400,000 or more Panjabi speakers now in Britain cluster in certain larger cities, including London (the boroughs of Southall and Newham), Birmingham, Wolverhampton, Coventry, Leeds and Bradford.

Texts from the *Guru Granth Sahib*, now some four hundred years old, are used in Sikh religious ritual. The language is still comprehensible without much difficulty to worshippers. Whatever their language of education, Sikhs need to know the Gurmukhi script in order to read and understand the scriptures.

Panjabi is unusual among Indo-Aryan languages in having three tones on stressed syllables: falling, as in ਘੋੜਾ *kòṛa* 'horse'; high rising, as in ਕੋਹੜਾ *kóṛa* 'leprous'; level, as in ਕੋੜਾ *kōṛa* 'whip'. The scripts (like those of south-east Asia) indicate the tones by varying not the vowel signs but the consonant symbols.

Example from G. A. Zograph, *Languages of South Asia* tr. G. L. Campbell (London: Routledge, 1982) pp. 49–50

Panjabi and its dialects

Western Panjabi or *Lahnda* can be divided into Southern, North-western and North-eastern dialects. The Southern dialects (south of the Salt Range) include *Shāhpūrī* and *Mūltānī*. These merge into the SIRAIKI of Sind. The North-western dialects, sometimes called *Hindkō*, include the dialects of Attock, Kohat, Peshawar and Abbottabad. The North-eastern dialects include the *Pōṭhwārī* of Rawalpindi.

Mājhī is the central Panjabi dialect, spoken in the regions of Lahore and Amritsar. This is the dialect that forms the basis of standard Panjabi and the language of literature. There is naturally considerable variation in the standard as spoken by Muslim and by Sikh speakers, the former in Pakistan, the latter in India.

Eastern Panjabi includes *Dōābī*, dialect 'of the two rivers'; *Pōwādhī*, *Rāṭhī*, *Mālwāī*, and *Bhaṭṭiānī*, linguistically close to Rajasthani and spoken in Ferozepore and Ganganagar Districts. Eastern Panjabi dialects shade into Western Hindi.

Also sometimes regarded as a dialect of Panjabi is DOGRI, the language of Jammu, with its dialects *Kāṅgrī*, *Kaṇḍiālī* and *Bhateālī* (the last-named spoken in Chamba District, Himachal Pradesh).

The Gurmukhi alphabet

ਅ ਆ ਇ ਈ ਉ ਊ ਏ ਐ ਓ ਔ ਕਖਗਘਙ ਚਛਜਝਞ ਟਠਡਢਣ ਤਥਦਧਨ ਪਫਬਭਮ ਯਰਲਵੜ ਸਸਹ

a ā i ī u e ai o au k kh g gh ṅ c ch j jh ñ ṭ ṭh ḍ ḍh ṇ t th d dh n p ph b bh m y r l v ś s h

---

The Gurmukhi script

Panjabi is most often written and printed in *Gurmukhi* script, 'from the mouth of the Guru'. This was devised by Angad, the second Sikh guru, in the 16th century. It is a formalised and extended version of the *Landa* script that was and still is used by tradesmen in Panjab and Sind. The usual Roman transliteration, given here, follows the normal style for south Asian romanisation and does not attempt to mark tones. In Pakistan Panjabi is written in the Perso-Arabic script familiar from URDU.

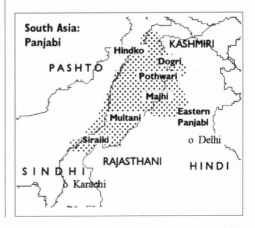

South Asia: Panjabi

Numerals in Panjabi and Romani			
	Standard Panjabi	**Pothwari**	**Multani**	**Romani**
1	ek	hikk	hekk	ek
2	do	do	ḍ ṃ	dui
3	tin	tre	trae	trin
4	car	cār	cār	shtar
5	pañj	pañj	pañj	pañj
6	che	che	che	sho
7	sat	satt	satt	efta
8	aṭh	aṭṭh	aṭṭh	okhto
9	nau	nauṃ	naṃ	enya
10	das	das	ḍāh	desh

In some Romani dialects, as here, the numerals '7' to '9' are borrowed from Greek.

Papiamentu

250,000 SPEAKERS

Curacao, Bonaire, Aruba

Papiamentu is a creole based on PORTUGUESE and SPANISH. Spoken on three of the islands of the Dutch Antilles, it naturally shows Dutch influence on its vocabulary.

Linguists dispute the relative strength of Portuguese and Spanish influences in the make-up of Papiamentu. In early Dutch Curacao, in the late 17th century, the strongest linguistic presence may have been that of Spanish and Portuguese Jews, previously settled in Latin America, refugees from the Inquisition. They became active in the Dutch trade in African slaves, for which Curacao was the main entrepot.

Papiamentu might well help in studying the early history of JUDEZMO.

Developing largely independently of standard Spanish, and spoken by the great majority of inhabitants of the three Dutch islands, Papiamentu is now the essential lingua franca on all three, widely used among all social classes. It was recently made an official language of Curacao and Bonaire, though not of Aruba, where Dutch alone has that status.

Of the three island dialects that of Aruba, which lies close to the Venezuelan coast, shows continuing influence of Spanish.

Papuan Languages

'Papuan' is a catch-all term for the languages of New Guinea (Irian) and nearby islands that do not belong to the family of AUSTRONESIAN LANGUAGES.

New Guinea was so called, in the 16th century, by the Spanish explorer Ortiz de Retes. He likened the dark-skinned, frizzy-haired people of this great unexplored island to those of the Guinea coast in West Africa. Papua, the general term for the inhabitants and their languages, derives from Malay papuah 'frizzy'. The Malay name for the island, however, is Irian.

This is linguistically the most complex region of the world. In mountainous, forested and swampy country, full of obstacles to travel, the languages of New Guinea have been developing and interacting for 40,000 years. It is only relatively recently that languages from the outside world, Austronesian and then Indo-European, have become established on the island. These provide its three best-known lingua francas – MALAY, HIRI MOTU and the English-based pidgin, TOK PISIN.

Communities in New Guinea are typically small: even in the heavily populated Highlands, villages seldom have more than three hundred inhabitants. The language map is an elaborate patchwork, and it will appear still more fragmented when exploration is complete. Languages move as groups migrate; they merge or disappear as one community comes to dominate another; they split as villages lose contact with one another.

Ternate, the island sultanate off Halmahera, once ruled parts of the northern New Guinea coast. In the 19th century the Dutch claimed the west, the British the south-east, and the Germans the north-east of the island. British and German territories, brought together under Australian government, became independent as Papua New Guinea or PNG. Dutch territory was transferred to Indonesia in 1962 and forms the province called Irian Jaya.

The first surviving wordlist of a Papuan language (excluding TERNATE) was made by two passengers on the Dutch ship Triton, when it called at Utanata, where Miriam was spoken, in 1828. Papuan languages were shown to be historically distinct from Austronesian by S. H. Ray in a paper on 'The languages of British New Guinea' presented to the Ninth Orientalist Congress in 1893.

It is a massive challenge to historical linguistics to trace language relationships that may date back 40,000 years or more. Genealogical trees have been drawn that link all the languages of New Guinea into a very few 'phyla', but for the present these all-embracing families are little more than blueprints for further research.

The administrative centre of Irian Jaya, once called Hollandia ('Netherlands' in Modern Latin), is now Jayapura ('Victory City' in Sanskrit), both languages quite alien to the culture of this remarkable island. Port Moresby, capital of PNG, is so called because Captain John Moresby mapped this natural harbour in 1873 and named it, modestly, after his father, Admiral Sir Fairfax Moresby.

Non-Austronesian languages of New Guinea

About 750 Papuan languages are known, some of them very patchily. The great majority have fewer than 2,000 speakers apiece. Only those spoken by relatively large communities are listed here. For the West Papuan family see TERNATE.

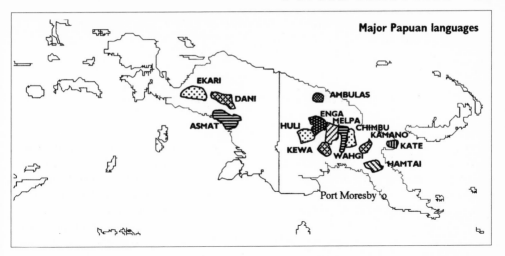

Major Papuan languages

For the Timor-Alor-Pantar family see box at MALAY.

Hamtai, Kamea or Kukukuku (40,000 speakers) belongs to the Angan family of Gulf, Morobe and Eastern Highlands provinces.

Asmat or Yas, with Citak and Kamoro, forms an important group (70,000 speakers) of the Central and South New Guinean family of the south coast of Irian Jaya.

The Dani-Kwerba language family includes as many as 300,000 speakers of the dialects of *Dani*, in inland northern Irian Jaya.

The East New Guinea Highlands family is a very large one. Languages of this family include *Enga* (165,000 speakers) and *Huli* (70,000), both of Southern Highlands and Enga Provinces; *Melpa* or Medlpa (70,000) and Wahgi (45,000), of Western Highlands Province; the *Chimbu* group (70,000), in Chimbu Province; the *Kewa* languages (60,000), in Southern Highlands Province; *Kamano* (50,000), in Eastern Highlands Province.

Kâte, of Morobe Province, is used as a religious language by the Lutheran church, and is known to a total of 80,000 people. It belongs to the Huon-Finisterre family.

The Sepik-Ramu family, a very extensive one, includes *Ambulas*, with 35,000 speakers in East Sepik Province.

Ekari (100,000 speakers) is a language of the Highlands. It belongs to the Wissel Lakes-Kemandoga family.

Language pride in Papua New Guinea

Neighbouring groups in Papua New Guinea had contact through intermarriage, trade and warfare, leading to a certain amount of bilingualism or competence in other dialects. A sizeable minority of New Guinean women have had the experience of being linguistic 'foreigners' in the village into which they have married.

'We might well ask why such contacts did not lead to a *lessening* of linguistic differences. A partial explanation probably lies in the fact that New Guineans often make use of other-language and other-dialect knowledge in rhetoric and verbal art, highlighting the known differences between their own and neighbouring speech varieties. It appears that contacts with and awareness of other languages have led not to levelling but to heightened consciousness of and pride in difference.'

Gillian Sankoff, *The social life of language* (University of Pennsylvania Press, 1980) pp. 9–10, abridged

PASHTO

PERHAPS 14,000,000 SPEAKERS

Afghanistan, Pakistan

Pashto is one of the two official languages of Afghanistan. Among modern IRANIAN LANGUAGES it is second only to Persian in the length of its written history. For the other official language of Afghanistan, see PERSIAN, DARI AND TAJIK.

> The usual name *Pashto* (written *Pushtu* in older English sources) may in origin be identical with *Persian*, originating in a proto-Iranian form **parsawā* 'Persian language'. The speakers are called *Pakhtūn* in northern Afghanistan, *Pashtūn* in the south, and *Pathān* in Pakistan. The name *Afghan* is occasionally used for the language.

Pashto literature is recorded in manuscript form from the 16th century onwards. A 17th-century author, Khushḥāl Khān Khaṭak, is now regarded as Afghanistan's national poet. But Pashto has become a language of education and the press only in the course of the 20th century. The Dari variety of PERSIAN was the language of government in Afghanistan until 1933, when Pashto was given this role. Arabic script is used, in its Persian form, with several added symbols.

> This state belonged to a people called *Patane*, lords of the hill country. Just as those who live on the skirts of the Pyrenees, on both sides, control the passes by which we cross from Spain to France, so these Pathans control the only two land routes into India.
>
> *Décadas da Ásia* (iv.vi.1) by the Portuguese historian João de Barros, 1553

The first ten numerals are *yau, dwa, dre, calor, pinjə, špaž, owə, atə, nəh, las.* Pashto has borrowed heavily from Persian, the former ruling language in this region, and from languages of Pakistan including Western Panjabi and Urdu. It has acquired the retroflex consonants *ṭ ḍ ṛ ṇ* that are typical of the Indian linguistic area.

Pashto in Afghanistan and Pakistan

The Pashto-speaking population is almost equally divided between the two countries. Speakers in Pakistan are known as Pathans or Afghans.

Kandahar belongs to the South-western dialect group, Kabul to the North-western (sometimes called 'Eastern', forgetting the Pakistani speakers). The South-eastern dialects are those of Baluchistan, the North-eastern those of the North West Frontier Province of Pakistan, including Peshawar. The Kandahar and Peshawar dialects are the basis of the two standard written forms of Pashto.

Pashto and its neighbours

Moral

Wagə̀řī wǎřa . kāř na xpə́l kā;	All men work for their own good;
mardān haɣə́ day . če kāř da bə́l kā.	The real man is he who works for others.

Lines 1–2 of a rubā'ī by Khushḥāl Khān. In Pashto, as in Persian, this is a four-line verse form in which lines 1, 2 and 4 rhyme. Each half-line has five or six syllables.

Transliteration and translation: D. N. Mackenzie, 'Pashto verse' in *Bulletin of the School of Oriental and African studies* vol. 21 (1958) pp. 319–33

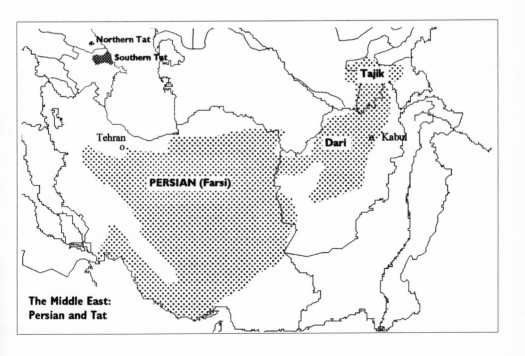

**The Middle East:
Persian and Tat**

PERSIAN, DARI AND TAJIK

PERHAPS 31,000,000 SPEAKERS

Iran, Afghanistan, Tajikistan

Persian has a far longer recorded history than any of the other IRANIAN LANGUAGES – a time-span which almost equals that of a fellow Indo-European language, Greek. It is the national language of Iran; in the form of Tajik, of Tajik-istan; in the form of Dari, one of the national languages of Afghanistan.

Within the wider geographical context of Iran, the region known to Greeks and Romans as *Persis* corresponds to the modern province still called *Fārs*. *Fārsī* or *Pārsī* is the natural name for the language of this region, homeland of the rulers of the ancient Persian and later Sassanian Empires. *Pārsī-yi Darī*, 'Persian of the court', spread as such to Persian-ruled countries such as Afghanistan, particularly to the cities: there it is now called *Darī* or Kabuli.

Tājik was originally (as *Tāzī*) a name given by Iranians to the invading Arabs. Turkic peoples, before their own conversion to Islam, adopted *Tāzīk* as a name for both Arabs and Muslim Persians.

ARAMAIC, not Persian, was the trade and civil service language of the Persian Empire. But its rulers, from Darius I (550–486 BC) onwards, were proud of their Persian origin. Old Persian springs to life as one of the three languages of the Behistun inscription in which Darius announced his achievements (see box).

As the Persian Empire fell to Alexander of Macedon and his Greek successors, Aramaic gave way to Greek: but Greek never spread far in Iran. Soon the Parthian Empire, whose ruling class was Iranian, held sway from Iraq to Afghanistan: the language of its elite, Parthian, gradually replaced Greek in administration.

Parthian, an Iranian language close to Old Persian but not its lineal descendant, was used increasingly for literature – by Zoroas-trians, Christians and Manichaeans. Most Parthian texts that survive today come not from Iran but far off to the east, at the old oases on the Silk Road in Chinese Xinjiang. Texts in Parthian, Middle Persian, Uighur, Khotanese, Tocharian, Sanskrit, Tibetan, Chinese and other languages testify to the multilingual culture of these remarkable cities.

Persis remained independent of the Parthians. From here, eventually, emerged the next ruling dynasty, that of the Sassanian Empire, which ruled the Middle East from the 3rd to the 7th century. Its language is called *Pehlevi* – the traditional name – or *Middle Persian* or (when written in the old Avestan script) *Pāzand*.

Zoroastrianism – in its later form, sometimes described as 'fire worship' – was the state reli-gion of the Sassanians, as it had been of Darius and his successors long before. The holy books of Zarathustra's teachings were now collected and written down. They were in the ancient AVESTAN language, which was becoming difficult for worshippers to understand. Middle Persian literature consists largely of commentaries on the Avestan texts alongside new legends and hymns.

The fact that Parthian, Middle Persian and Avestan were all written in Aramaic script testifies to the transmission of the written culture of the Persian Empire, through the years of Greek domination, to its Parthian and Sassanian successors.

The Islamic conquest of the Sassanian Empire begins a new phase in the history of the Persian language. At first ARABIC was the language of government and culture: in particular, Arabic had to be used in Islamic worship. Persians are outstanding among authors of medieval Arabic poetry and prose.

With political resurgence, literature in *Modern Persian* emerged. Now written in the Arabic script, the language is full of Arabic loanwords, spreading from religious and administrative terminology to many facets of everyday life. Persian poetry has borrowed metres and verse forms from Arabic, and has transmitted them in turn to Turkish and Urdu. But Persian literature is far from imitative. One of the earliest masterpieces of Modern Persian, the 10th-century *Shāh-nāma* of Firdausī, is a literary epic – a form unknown to Arabic literature – that gathers and retells the long, legendary history of Persia. Original to Persian is the four-line *rubā'ī* best known in the verses of Omar Khayyām (1048–1131) that were turned so elegantly into English by Edward Fitzgerald.

Once more a language of government, under Mongolian and Turkish rulers, Persian was brought to Turkey, to central Asia and to India. It was the language of administration in India for hundreds of years – in Kashmir until after 1900.

In the earlier period of British rule, Persian was still the most useful linguistic accomplishment for the British who were involved with the administration of India. Even in the 19th century the British in India learned Persian before, or in addition to, 'Hindustani' or Urdu. The Persian of India was by now a distinct variety, heavily influenced both by the Turkish of the old ruling class and by the Indian culture that surrounded it. Textbooks warned British students that this was not the language of Iran.

Now almost forgotten in India, Persian remains a language of power well beyond the frontiers of Iran. Often called *Dari*, literally the 'court language', it is the second language of Afghanistan and acts as a lingua franca throughout the country. It was the language of government there until 1933. The nomadic Aimaq and the Hazaragi of Afghanistan, culturally distinct, are Persian speakers.

To the north again, Persian speakers were a considerable proportion of the population in central Asia when that region came under Russian rule in the 19th century. The Soviet Union attempted to divide central Asia on linguistic lines: Tajikistan was formed as the national republic for Persian speakers of the north. Now an independent state, its tortuous frontiers are evidence that linguistic boundaries could not be effectively drawn here. Speakers of 'Tajik' and UZBEK lived side by side, and still form sizeable minorities in each other's republics.

Old Persian retained the noun inflexions of proto-Iranian, but Modern Persian has lost them almost completely. The noun suffix *-i*, called *izāfeh*, which derives from the Old Persian *yo* 'who, which', is used so frequently to form noun-noun and noun-adjective phrases that it is a distinguishing mark of Persian – and is often found in loans in Turkish and Urdu.

Persian displays its long history in loanwords from many sources. From Akkadian *pīru* 'elephant' came Old Persian *pīru* 'ivory' (and, from this, Sanskrit *pīlu* and modern Persian *fīl*); other early loanwords from Semitic languages are *mashk*, name of the inflated skins that armies can use to cross rivers; *tandūr* 'clay oven'. Greek *diphthera* 'skin' is the origin of middle Persian *diftar* 'book' and so of modern Persian *diftar* 'exercise book' and of *daftar* 'office'. From Chinese comes *chang* 'harp'. But the majority of the vocabulary of modern written Persian comes from Arabic; other, more recent loans are drawn from Turkish (especially military terminology), French and English.

Persian and its relatives: the map on page 493

Persian, Dari and Tajik are the most-used names for the varieties of Persian that are standard in Iran, Afghanistan and Tajikistan. Although any national state tends gradually to develop its own linguistic standard, the differences between these three are as yet slight. However, 'Colloquial Persian is not everywhere alike. The pronunciation may differ largely. So I found the pronunciation of the priest in the fire-temple at Yazd difficult to follow, after becoming accustomed to the Isfahānī pronunciation. Vocabulary also may differ. In Isfahān I used the word *gurīkht* "he ran away" in vain. They had *varmālīd*. But *gurīkht* was known to the villagers of Taft near Yazd' (H. W. Bailey, 'Western Iranian dialects' in *Transactions of the Philological Society* (1933) pp. 46–64).

Northern Tat or *Jewish Tat* is the language of the Mountain Jews, a population of perhaps 15,000 in Dagestan (Russia) and at Kuba and Vartashen on the northern edge of Azerbaijan. Their cultural centre is Derbent. For these speakers, Tat is a language of education and the press.

Southern Tat is spoken by Muslims in northeastern Azerbaijan. Their official language is AZERI, in which most are bilingual.

Still further to the south, a quite separate group of Iranian languages, spoken in Khalkhal and Qazvin in Iran, is confusingly called *Azari*,

Tati or *Southern Tati*. These belong to the 'Caspian dialects' and are not mapped here (see GILAKI).

Numerals in Persian			
		Middle Persian (Pehlevi)	Modern Persian
1	١	ēvak	yak
2	٢	dō	dō
3	٣	sē	sih
4	٤	chahār	chahār
5	٥	panj	panj
6	٦	shash	shish
7	٧	haft	haft
8	٨	hasht	hasht
9	٩	nō	nuh
10	١٠	dah	dah

Persian in writing

The letters ث ص sound like Persian س ; ط sounds like Persian ت. The three superfluous letters, along with ح ذ ض ظ ع, are hardly ever used except in Arabic loanwords.

In Soviet Tajikistan Latin script was adopted in the 1920s, to be replaced by Cyrillic script around 1940.

The Persian alphabet

ي ه و ن م ل گ ک ک ق ف غ ع ظ ط ض ص ش س ژ ز ر ذ د خ ح چ ج ث ت پ ب ا

a b p t ṣ j č ḥ kh d ẕ r z z s š ṩ ż ṭ ẓ ' gh f q k g l m n v h y

POLISH

40,000,000 SPEAKERS

Poland

Polish is one of the West SLAVONIC LANGUAGES – a close relative of Czech, Slovak and Sorbian.

> *Polak* is the name Poles have traditionally given to themselves, and as *Polack* it is sometimes used in US English for 'Polish immigrant'. It may once have meant 'people of the fields', as does the related word *Poljane*. Several foreign names for the country – Latin *Polonia*, French *Pologne*, German *Polen*, English *Poland* – come directly from this. In other languages a quite different term is used instead of 'Pole' or 'Polish': Hungarian *Lengyel*, Lithuanian *Leñkas*.
>
> An obsolete English word for a three-masted merchant ship, *polacre*, means simply 'Polish'.

The River Vistula, which flows through central Poland from south to north, roughly marked the prehistoric western limit of Slavonic-speaking territory. One of the chain of northern migrations that brought on the collapse of the Roman Empire was a Slavonic expansion westwards, across the Vistula, into what is now western Poland and eastern Germany. In due course the pressure was reversed: throughout medieval times German speakers pushed eastwards again into Poland, conducting what could be described at times as a crusade or a war of extermination. The German defeat at Tannenberg in East Prussia, in 1410, marks the end of this long episode. Even after it, however, German was a language of culture and power in Poland.

Throughout this period Poland remained an independent state and at times a very powerful one, uniting with Lithuania in 1569 to rule the regions now called Belarus and Ukraine. But Polish sovereignty was extinguished in 1795, and its territory was shared out between Prussia, Austria and Russia.

Poland reasserted its independence in 1918 after the Russian Revolution, gaining territory both from Germany in the west and north and from Belorussia and Ukraine in the east. Vilnius, which is now the capital of Lithuania, had a Polish majority and was Polish territory between 1920 and 1939. Poland suffered disastrously in the Second World War. In its aftermath the country's frontiers were drastically redrawn. German speakers were driven westwards across the 'Oder-Neisse line', the new western border, while the Soviet Union also advanced westwards into territory that had formerly been Polish. For some decades Poland itself was a Soviet satellite state – but in the 1980s Polish resistance eventually undermined Russian rule over eastern Europe.

Poland has been a Christian state since AD 966, and remains staunchly Catholic. Christianity was introduced by missionaries from the Czech lands. Polish thus has many early Czech loanwords. Latin loanwords came later, less from religious than from humanist and scholarly influences. Because of the country's later political history there are also loans from German, Belorussian and Ukrainian.

Polish literature begins with a 14th-century collection of sermons, *Kazania świętokrzyskie*, and a hymn, *Bogurodzica*, which may be older. At this early period much writing, both religious and secular, was in Latin. The greatest Polish poets are perhaps the Renaissance humanist Jan Kochanowski (1530–84) and the exiled 'national bard' Adam Mickiewicz (1798–1855), author of the epic *Pan Tadeusz*.

Among a later generation of émigrés from Poland was the English novelist Joseph Conrad (1857–1924; born Konrad Korzeniowski), who began his career as a sailor.

Emigré communities grew further during and after the Second World War, with Poland's continuing political vicissitudes. The three largest communities are in the United States, Canada and Britain. The core of the Polish-speaking community in Britain, numbering 90,000, is formed by the airmen and soldiers who fought with the allies after the German seizure of Poland. At least two-thirds of this exiled group was male, leading to much intermarriage – and so to rapid assimilation. A Polish daily newspaper is still published in London, *Dziennik Polski*.

A strong Polish minority remains in Lithuania and in western Belarus. Until the 18th century Polish had been the language of the elite in these countries, as it was also in the Ukraine. The Belorussian coat of arms once bore the words 'Proletarians of all countries, unite!' in Belorussian, Russian, Polish and Yiddish.

Polish has an oddly complex system of grammatical gender. The singular has masculine, feminine and neuter genders – and, in the accusative case and masculine gender only, a further distinction between animates and inanimates. The plural has only a 'masculine personal' and an unmarked gender, the former used for groups including at least one human male. For a table of numerals see CZECH.

Asserting Polish

A niechaj narodowie wżdy postronni znają	Let other nations always know
Iż Polacy nie gęsi, że swój język mają!	That Poles are not geese, but have their language too!

Mikolaj Rej (1505–69); from R. G. A. de Bray, *Guide to the Slavonic languages* (London: Dent, 1951) p. 591

The Western Slavonic languages

'Literary *Polish* has drawn upon the dialects of the three successive capitals of the land: the Great Polish dialect of Gniezno, the Little Polish dialect of Cracow and the Mazovian dialect of Warsaw. The Silesian dialects served it as a filter for Western borrowings during the Middle Ages and the Renaissance, while the dialects of the eastern borderlands influenced it during the Baroque and Romantic periods . . . This is why the debate on the origin of the Polish literary language, which raged from the beginning of this century until after World War II and pitted the Great Polish hypothesis against the Little Polish one, has predictably ended in a deadlock' (*The Slavic literary languages: formation and development* ed. Alexander M. Schenker, Edward Stankiewicz (New Haven, 1980) p. 209).

The Mazovian dialect of Polish shares some features with *Kashubian* (Cassubian or Pomeranian), the language of about 150,000 speakers in the countryside around Danzig. All are bilingual in Polish: many can claim to be quadrilingual, speaking also the Low German of their former peasant neighbours and the High German they were taught at school. Kashubian is identifiable in documents from the 15th century onwards. There is some local literature in print, though no standard spelling has been fixed.

Europe: Western Slavonic languages

SORBIAN is the only remaining Slavonic language that is spoken west of the rivers Oder and Neisse in what is now Germany. *Lower Sorbian* is the speech of the countryside around Cottbus, south of Berlin. *Upper Sorbian* centres on Bautzen near the Czech border.

Polabian was once spoken to the north and north-west of Berlin. It became extinct around 1700.

There is a continuum of dialects from CZECH south-eastwards through *Moravian* to SLOVAK. Moravian dialects differ from south to north, the northern having much in common with neighbouring varieties of Polish. Slovak divides into Western, Central and Eastern dialects. The Central dialect has similarities with South Slavonic languages such as Slovene, although geographically separated from them.

The look of Polish

The Latin alphabet required drastic adjustment to Polish phonetics. Symbols were required for the nasal vowels *ą* and *ę*, the palatalised consonants *pi bi fi vi mi ki gi*, the alveo-palatal fricatives *cz dż sz ż rz* and the palatal fricatives *ć ci dź dzi ś si ź zi ń ni*. It is the frequent use of *z* (a rare letter in most other European spelling systems) that makes Polish look so unpronounceable.

PORTUGUESE

155,000,000 SPEAKERS

Portugal, Brazil, Mozambique, Angola, Guiné and Cape Verde

One of the ROMANCE LANGUAGES, Portuguese is in origin a twin of GALICIAN (see map there). Through Portuguese discoveries and conquests it has become one of the major languages of the world.

The Iberian peninsula is the western extremity of the area in which Latin had become the everyday language of the Roman Empire. As the empire collapsed, the north-west corner of the peninsula – modern Galicia and northern Portugal – became the territory of a tribe of Germanic invaders, the Suebi. Little is known of the language they spoke, though it is possible that one Portuguese word, *britar* 'break', may come from Suebic. Latin remained the everyday language: this region is the cradle of early Galician-Portuguese, ancestor of the two modern languages.

Most of Portugal, like most of Spain, came under Arabic-speaking rule in 711–18. The Cantabrian mountains, south as far as the River Douro, remained unconquered: here the two fiefs of Galicia and Portugal were established. Portugal – south of the River Minho, and already including some new conquests as far south as the Mondego – became an independent kingdom in 1143. Portugal's dialect spread southwards with continuing conquests, displacing the somewhat different Romance dialect, MOZARABIC, which had been spoken by the subject population in the Islamic period. But that is only half the story: like Spanish, Portuguese has borrowed from Arabic many terms for cultural concepts, government and administration, architecture and the arts, evidence that the high Islamic culture of the south exerted great influence on the conquering Christians of the north.

Galician-Portuguese is first recorded in the late 12th century, in legal documents and in the earliest examples of a lyric poetry which continued to flourish until the 14th (see box). Even in Spain, Portuguese was felt to be the proper language for lyric: the devotional *Cantigas de Santa Maria* are the work of Alfonso the Wise, King of Spain (reigned 1252–84). By the 14th century Galician and Portuguese were beginning to grow apart, Galicia remaining a backwater of Spain while Portugal was self-consciously independent, except for the sixty-year 'captivity' – the union with Philip II's Spain – in 1578–1640. During that period, some Portuguese intellectuals took to writing Spanish.

The growth of the Portuguese kingdom and the progress of its discoveries and conquests were recorded in a series of chronicles, histories and memoirs, including the monumental *Décadas da Asia* of João de Barros (named after the 'Decades', ten-book divisions of the Roman history written fifteen centuries earlier by Livy). The voyage of Vasco da Gama was also immortalised in one of the greatest of literary epics, *Os Lusíadas* by Luís de Camões.

By the 16th century Portuguese must have sounded very much as it does today. Writers and scholars liked to emphasise its differences from Spanish and its historical links with Latin: old-fashioned Portuguese spelling reinforced these, continually reverting to the Latin forms of words in defiance of real pronunciation. A reform (*nova ortografia*, 'new spelling') was adopted in Portugal in 1916: slightly modified, it was accepted in Brazil in 1931. It abandoned these 'etymological' spellings in favour of a relatively phonetic system. However, with nasal vowels, 'whispered' final vowels and frequent final *sh/zh* sounds Portuguese pronunciation is highly distinctive. While Portuguese speakers can understand Spanish relatively easily, Spanish speakers find spoken Portuguese much more difficult.

Besides its Arabic loanwords Portuguese has borrowed from Tupí, from Indian and south-east Asian languages, and from French. There are now many English loanwords. For a table of numerals see CATALAN.

The world-wide range of Portuguese

With the settlement of the Azores in 1439, and later Madeira, Portuguese became one of the first European languages to spread outside Europe by colonisation. Soon afterwards Portuguese speakers began to settle in Brazil. Eventually Brazil came to outweigh by far the tiny mother country, not only in size but in terms of number of Portuguese speakers.

The Portuguese of Portugal and that of Brazil have a relationship comparable to British and American English. To European speakers of the language, Brazilian Portuguese has a distinctive accent, some important differences in vocabulary and some minor differences in spelling. Naturally, a considerable proportion of modern Portuguese literature is in fact Brazilian literature.

However, the range of varieties of Brazilian Portuguese may well be greater than those of American English – for good historical reasons. For a long period the lingua franca of Brazil was not Portuguese at all but Lingua Geral (see TUPI): this gave way to pidgin and creole varieties of Portuguese, as well as to the standard language. Africans brought to Brazil as slaves used a pidgin Portuguese as their language of communication. Even recently, numerous migrants to Brazil from European countries have developed their own community languages: *Fazendeiro* was the creole once spoken in São Paulo by a mixed Italian-African population.

A true Brazilian Creole form of Portuguese still exists in some rural black communities; it is known as *Tabarenho, Matutenho* or *Caipira*.

Portuguese creoles and pidgin languages

On Portugal's Indian Ocean trade routes, pidgin Portuguese must have been in use from the 16th century onwards: arguably its origin goes back even to the earliest West African voyages in the 15th century. For a while, Portuguese pidgin was a lingua franca of trade between Europeans and Indians in India. In the Portuguese territories of Africa and Asia this pidgin must have become a mother tongue, a creole, quite early.

In its original locality it has living and thriving descendants: the CRIOULO of Cape Verde Islands and Guiné, the related creoles of São Tomé and Príncipe (where Portuguese remains the language of education), and (on an island that long ago came under Spanish rule) *Fá d'Ambó* 'Language of Annobón'.

In the larger mainland territories of Angola and Mozambique stable Portuguese creoles have not become established, though pidgin forms of the language have been used. In both of these, now independent states, Portuguese retains its importance as a language of administration and education. The distinctive Portuguese of Angola is used by several novelists.

As a household language and a lingua franca, pidgin Portuguese was already so well established in Sri Lanka, which the Portuguese lost

---

Sri Lanka Portuguese Creole in 1807

'There is still a large body of inhabitants at Columbo and the other settlements in Ceylon, known by the name of Portuguese. They probably number to the amount of five thousand; they are, however, completely degenerated, and exhibit complexions of a blacker hue than any of the original natives . . . The greater part of them were admitted by the Dutch to all the privileges of citizens, under the denomination of burghers. A corruption of their original language is still spoken over all the sea coasts. It is very easily learned, and proves of great utility to a traveller who has not time to study the more difficult dialects of the natives.'

Rev. James Cordiner, *A description of Ceylon* (London, 1807) pp. 88–9

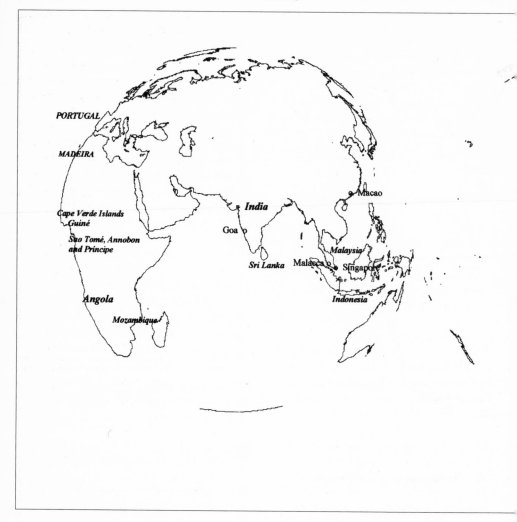

PORTUGAL

MADEIRA

Cape Verde Islands
Guiné

São Tomé, Annobon
and Príncipe

Angola

Mozambique

India

Goa

Sri Lanka   Malacca

Macao

Malaysia

Singapore

Indonesia

to the Dutch between 1632 and 1658, that it not only survived but was adopted in Dutch households too. Portuguese Creole, influenced by both Tamil and Sinhala, is still spoken there by several thousand people of mixed European, Lankan and African origin, who are known as 'Burghers' and 'Kaffirs'. The larger groups are to be found in Colombo, Trincomalee and Batticaloa. There is also a community of Creole speakers in Kandy, though that city was never under Portuguese rule: it was the capital of an independent kingdom in Portuguese and Dutch times.

At Goa, the long-lasting base of Portuguese rule in India, the linguistic history is quite different. Continuing contacts between Portugal and the colony led to gradual changes in the creole, which – by the time of the Indian takeover in 1961 – was better described as a strongly marked regional form of Portuguese.

Further east, in Malaysia, Malaccan Creole or *Papia Kristang* still has some thousands of speakers; Singapore Portuguese is still in religious use in the Catholic community. Several recorded Portuguese pidgins and creoles of coastal towns in south-east Asia and Indonesia are now extinct, including that of Jakarta – but in Macao, a Portuguese possession due to become Chinese in 1999, there are perhaps, 4,000 speakers of the *Macauenho* creole.

The early Portuguese pidgin of the West African coast has more descendants than this.

Portuguese as a world language

There seems to be no doubt that it is part of the ancestry of the Spanish, English and French creoles of the Atlantic and Indian Oceans. Each of them has a different history, and the Portuguese element is most easily recognisable in PAPIAMENTU (usually classed as a Spanish creole) and Saramaccan and Matuwari, which have become ENGLISH CREOLES.

Portuguese has not ceased to spread across the world. There are currently at least 4,000,000 Portuguese-speaking émigrés, including as many as 1,000,000 migrant workers in France. There are strong Portuguese settlements in California, Massachusetts and Toronto and a large community of Madeiran origin in Venezuela.

The influence of Portuguese

The Portuguese discoveries and conquests were crucial in establishing contacts between European cultures and those of other continents. In west and east Africa, southern Asia, the Malay archipelago and south America, the presence of Portuguese mariners, traders, soldiers, missionaries and administrators ensured that Portuguese loanwords would be adopted in many of the languages of the world. In African languages the commonest Portuguese loanwords are *mesa* 'table', *sapata* 'shoe' (originally from Persian by way of Turkish and Italian), *chumbo* 'lead', *igreja* 'church', *ouro* 'gold', *prata* 'silver', *chapeu* 'hat' (originally from French) and *carreta* 'cart'. Portuguese provided names for newly imported American fruits and other foods: *mandioca* 'manioc, cassava', *goiaba* 'guavas', *ananas* 'pineapple', *papaia* 'pawpaw', *milhos* 'maize'.

Examples from J. Knappert in D. Dalby and others, *Language and history in Africa* (London: Cass, 1970) p. 86

The influence of Portuguese pidgin

Words from the 15th-century Portuguese West African Pidgin have become familiar across the world.

Savvy: *Savvy* – from Portuguese *saber* or Lingua Franca *sabir* – means 'know' in many of the creole languages of the world: *sibi* in Crioulo, *sabe* in Krio and Bislama, *save* in Tok Pisin, *sabiam* in Kamtok. By the 18th century, this word had been borrowed from the pidgins or creoles into English, where *savvy* colloquially means 'know-how' or 'skill'.

Piccaninny: Portuguese *pequenino* means 'little one, child'. By 1657 the word was in the pidgin or creole of Barbados. The form in Bislama and Tok Pisin is *pikinini*; in Sranan (the English creole of Suriname) it is *pikië*; in Kamtok it is *pikin*, in Jamaican Creole *pikni*. In the English of colonial America, South Africa and Australasia *piccaninny* became a usual word for a 'black child'.

Examples from Frederic G. Cassidy in *Pidginization and creolization of languages* ed. Dell Hymes (Cambridge: Cambridge University Press, 1971) pp. 207–9

Portuguese lyric

Proençaes soen mui ben trobar	The Provençals can make very good songs
e dizen eles que é con amor,	and they say that they do it with love,
mays os que troban no tempo da frol	but of people who make songs at the time of flowers
e non en outro, sey eu ben que non	and not at other times, I know very well that they
am tam gran coyta no seu coraçon	have no such great care in their hearts
qual m'eu por mia senhor vejo levar.	as I feel in mine for my lord.

In general, medieval Galician-Portuguese lyric poetry owes much to Provençal (OCCITAN) models. But the typical *Cantiga de amigo*, in which the speaker is a woman mourning an absent lover, is not so close to Provençal poetry in its feeling – as King Diniz (1279–1323), author of this example, rightly says. In fact it has more in common with the tone of Mozarabic lyrics, suggesting that it reflects something of the medieval popular songs of the Iberian peninsula.

The early lyric poetry of Portugal was forgotten for centuries. In the 19th century much of it came to light once more in two priceless manuscripts discovered in Italian libraries.

QUECHUA

PERHAPS 9,000,000 SPEAKERS

Bolivia, Peru, Ecuador, Argentina, Colombia

One of the AMERIND LANGUAGES, Quechua was the ruling language of the powerful Inca empire destroyed by Spanish conquerors in the 16th century.

Quechua (Quichua in Ecuador and Argentina) is said to derive from a local term for the temperate Andean valleys and their inhabitants. By Peruvian speakers themselves the language is sometimes called *runa simi*, 'language of men', and some linguists have used that term to distinguish the old Quechua dialects of central Peru. By early Spanish authors it was called *lengua general*, or more fully *lengua general del Inga*, the 'common language of the Incas', or *lengua general del Perú*. Colombian dialects are called *Inga* or *Ingano*, 'Inca'.

The first printed work in Quechua was a dictionary by Domingo de Santo Tomás, published in 1560. Early texts of importance include Jurado Palomino's *Quechua catechism*, the hymns collected by Cristóbal de Molina, and the dramas *El pobre mas rico* (16th century), *Usca paucar* (18th century) and *Ollantay*. In spite of the large number of speakers, Quechua nowadays appears rather little in print and in the media.

The wide geographical range of Quechua reflects the reach of Inca government in its last years. The most distant regions of Quechua speech, in Ecuador, Colombia, southern Peru, Bolivia and northern Argentina, are unexpectedly alike in some dialect details. This suggests that they originate from relatively recent colonisation at a time when a standard form of speech formed a lingua franca throughout the vast empire – an empire that was surprisingly centralised in its administration, with a highly organised army and much movement of population. By contrast, the dialects of central Peru are more strongly differentiated, as if originating from an earlier historical period.

Curiously, Quechua had not been the language of the empire's ruling stratum for very long. Until the Inca themselves came to power, in the 15th century, the rulers had been speakers of *Chimú*. This unrelated language survived among a few speakers until the 19th century, but it is now extinct. For an outline of Chimú see George L. Campbell, *Compendium of the world's languages* (London: Routledge, 1991) pp. 302–5.

Quechua has continued to spread, superseding local languages, under Spanish rule, though at the same time it continually gives way to Spanish. There was once a pidgin language, *Media lengua*, with Spanish grammar but largely Quechua vocabulary. Modern pidgins still exist: *Chaupi lengua* in Ecuador, *Llapui* in Bolivia, the latter with Quechua suffixes but Spanish words.

Nowadays Spanish, as the official language throughout the Andes, threatens the continued vitality of Quechua. In Peru Quechua was declared joint official language in 1975, but lost this status in the constitution of 1979.

Quechua 'documents' were transmitted across the Inca empire by means of quipu strings. The colour of the strings, the shape of the knots and the number of knots all contributed to fix a meaning which could be repeated by the messenger who carried the string, but, it is usually argued, could not be reconstructed by others. Those found by archaeologists could not be

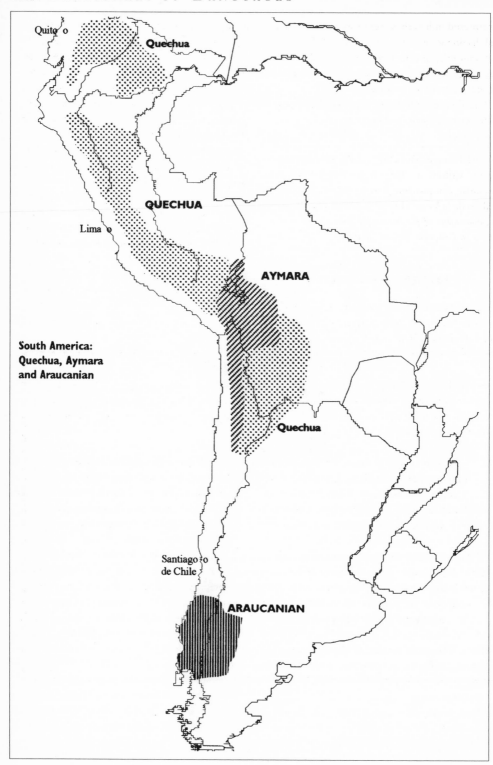

South America:
Quechua, Aymara
and Araucanian

interpreted unless they were essentially numerical, having to do with astronomy and the calendar. However, recent research by W. B. Glynn has suggested that quipu strings were a partly phonetic recording system.

The first ten numerals in Quechua are: *shuj, ishcai, quinsa, tahua, pichica, sucta, canchis, pusaj, iscun, chunja.*

> Crucial for reconstructing Inca civilisation is a work written in Spanish by the son of a Spanish conquistador and an Inca lady. Garcilaso de la Vega 'el Inca' published his *Royal commentaries of the Incas and general history of Peru* in Córdoba, Spain, in 1609.

Languages of the Andes

Quechua extends widely along the Andes chain, an indication of the former extent of Inca power and colonisation. The oldest dialects appear to be those of central Peru (Ancash, Huánuco, Junín, Pasco and part of Lima department).

Quechua country is divided by the Aymara-speaking region in Bolivia. The Quechuan dialects from the Bolivian border north-westwards as far as Ayacucho have been said to show signs of stronger Aymara influence than the rest, as if Aymara had earlier been spoken there.

AYMARA, which itself shows strong Quechua influence, has about 2,000,000 speakers in the neighbourhood of Lake Titicaca.

ARAUCANIAN speakers, who number about 300,000, classify themselves as *Pikunche* 'northerners', *Huilliche* (or Veliche) 'southerners' and *Pehuenche* 'foresters'. Dialect differences among these are said to be considerable.

In early colonial times three *lenguas generales*, 'common languages', of the Andes were recognised: Quechua, Aymara and the now-extinct Puquina. Jesuit missionaries were expected to learn all three.

The traditions of Huarochirí

Inca mythology and ritual are recorded in the *Traditions of Huarochirí*, written in Quechua for the Spanish missionary Francisco de Avila. Avila ordered the record to be made because 'diabolical practices are best combated by those who are fully informed of them'. But what did his Quechua assistant (known only as 'Tomás') think of the task? He begins:

> Runa Yno ñiscap Machoncuna ñaupa pacha quillcacta yachanman carca, chayca hinantin causascancunapas manam canancamapas chincaycuc canman, himanam Viracochapas sinchi cascanpas canancama ricurin, hinatacmi canman. Chayhina captinpas canancama mana quillcasca captinpas caypim churani cay huc yayayuc Guarocherí ñiscap Machoncunap causascanta, yma ffeenioccha carcan, yma yñach canancamapas causan, chay chaycunacta . . .

If the Ancients of the people called Indians (*Yno*) had known writing, then all the traditions of their former life, now doomed to fade away, would have been preserved. They would have shared the fortune of the Spaniards (*Viracocha*) whose traditions and past prowess are on record. Since it is not so, I shall write down the traditions of the Ancients of the land called Guarocherí, into whom one father breathed life: their *faith* and their customs as they are remembered to this day . . .

The 'one father' of the district of Guarocherí is the Inca god Pariacaca – and yet, for the 'faith' of the Ancients, the writer borrows a word from the Spanish missionaries, *fe*.

QUICHÉ

850,000 SPEAKERS

Guatemala

One of the MAYAN LANGUAGES, Quiché was at the time of the Spanish ascendancy the language of an important people whose centre of government was at Utatlán in modern Guatemala. Quiché speakers now form the second largest linguistic community of Guatemala, but the language has no official status.

The masterpiece of traditional Quiché literature, *Popol Vuh* 'Book of Counsel', was written down in the Latin alphabet in the 16th century on the basis of an earlier text in Mayan hieroglyphics. Both versions are now lost, but a 17th-century copy of the alphabetic text survives. It tells the mythical and historical story of the Quiché. A second important work is *Rabinal Achí*, a drama, apparently pre-Columbian in origin but written down only in the 19th century. Its lengthy dialogues take place between a victor and a prisoner of war who is fated to be sacrificed. Quiché poetic literature, like that of NAHUATL, is typified not by metre but by the use of parallel expressions.

Quiché has many loanwords from Nahuatl. They clearly come from a dialect similar to one now spoken on the Pacific coast, and, just as clearly, they result not from Aztec activities (which did not reach this part of central America) but from earlier Toltec influence. The words concerned are mainly religious or military: examples include 'altar', 'incense', 'demon', 'axe', 'palace' – but also 'cradle' and 'fishnet'.

The creation of human beings

In their last, successful attempts to create human beings, the Gods found the necessary ingredients in the Mountain of Nourishment:

'Thus they were pleased with the provisions of the Good Mountain, full of sweets, stiff with yellow maize and white maize, thick with pataxte and cacao, stuffed with zapotes, anonas, jacotes, nances, matasanos and sweetmeats, rich foods filling the stronghold that is called Broken Place, Place of Bitter Water. All edible fruits were there, all cereals large and small, all vegetables large and small' (*Popol Vuh*).

RAJASTHANI

PERHAPS 20,000,000 SPEAKERS

India

Rajasthani is the collective name for the INDO-ARYAN LANGUAGES or dialects of the Indian state of Rajasthan (see map at GUJARATI). Rajasthan was politically highly fragmented, consisting until the end of British rule of numerous small feudal states.

In a wide sense Rajasthan now belongs to the Hindi-speaking area. In censuses, many speakers will say that their language is Hindi. There is no strong literary tradition in any modern Rajasthani dialect: Hindi is the usual written language. However, Rajasthani is linguistically closer to Gujarati than to Hindi, and it makes most sense to regard it as an independent language. Old Gujarati, as recorded in texts of the 12th to 14th centuries, is the common ancestor of both Gujarati and the Rajasthani dialects of today.

Heroic literature, as well as religious poetry, was much cultivated at the courts of old Rajasthan. At most of them, the Braj form of HINDI was the usual medium. At the court of Marwar, however, two literary languages were in use. *Pingal* was a mixture of Apabhramsa and Braj with local Rajasthani elements. *Dingal*, known in manuscripts from the 15th century onwards, was a literary form of Rajasthani itself: it is sometimes described as the caste dialect of the *caṛans* or bards.

Numerals in two Rajasthani dialects		
Mālvī		**Mārwāṛī**
ek	1	ek
do	2	doy
tīn	3	tīn
cār	4	ciyār
pāñc	5	pāñc
che	6	chau
sāt	7	sāt
āṭh	8	āṭh
nau	9	nau
das	10	das

Pābūjī: brigand, local god and epic hero

Heroic and epic song is popular in modern Rajasthan. The story of Pābūjī, a 14th-century brigand or warlord, is performed by singer-priests, *bhopos*. This is the opening of an episode recorded from performance in 1976:

Baiṭā Pābūjī koḷū maṇḍa rai darbār:
baiṭā ṭhākar Pābūjī ek ghoṛāṃ rī vātāṃ kījai cāḷvai.
Cāṃdā sāṃvat phir ryā āṃpe aṇ dhartī rai cārum kījai mer:
Pābū rai caḍāī deval nī miḷai . . .

Pābūjī was seated in his court at Koḷ;
As he sat there lord Pābūjī raised the matter of horses.
'Chāndā my chieftain, we have travelled round the four borders of the earth,
We have not found a horse for Pābūjī to ride . . .'

John D. Smith, *The Epic of Pābūjī* (Cambridge: Cambridge University Press, 1991) pp. 116, 285

REJANG

PERHAPS 1,000,000 SPEAKERS

Indonesia

One of the AUSTRONESIAN LANGUAGES, Rejang is spoken to the south of Minangkabau and to the north-west of its close relative Lampung along the south-western coastal strip of Sumatra.

Contacts with Malay, the trade language of the archipelago, go back hundreds of years. Today there is much bilingualism in Indonesian, now the official form of Malay: massive migration from other parts of Indonesia threatens the stability of Rejang and Lampung culture.

Rejang has a rich literature of love lyrics, tribal histories and epics – which outsiders have traditionally not been allowed to hear. It is largely a literature of group performance, transmitted orally. However, texts are sometimes written down in the old Rejang alphabet ultimately descended from the Brahmi of ancient India. Only a small proportion of the population needs literacy in this alphabet, though it is also used for magical and medical incantations and spells. The local poetic language mixes Rejang words with older Malay.

The Rejang alphabet

'The Rejang writing is so simple, uniform, and perspicuous, both in regard to the form of the characters and disposition of the syllables, that from this evidence alone I should not hesitate to pronounce it the design and execution of one head and hand.'

William Marsden, 'Remarks on the Sumatran languages' in
Philosophical transactions of the Royal Society of London vol. 71 (1781)

ha ga nga ta da na pa ba ma cha ja nya sa ra la ya wa ha mba ngga nda nja a

---

Barat lawut	As the sea
tunggu maring gunung	On a mountain
meteri keilangan	The princess is lost
sumeui maring gunung	To an ancestral tiger on the mountain,
meteri kekasi	The princess my love.
ruma ketunun	A house of weaving;
bulan purnama	A full moon.

Lover's poem of grief, written on a bamboo tile. Translation by Mervyn Jaspan, *Redjang ka-ga-nga texts* (Canberra: Australian National University, 1964) pp. 36–7, 68

RIFIA

PERHAPS 1,500,000 SPEAKERS

Morocco, Algeria

Rifia is one of the BERBER LANGUAGES (see map there). It is spoken along the northern coast of Morocco and eastwards into western Algeria as far as the neighbourhood of Alhucemas. There are scattered groups of Rifia speakers even further east, as far as Arzeu, the result of recent migrations.

The Berber languages of Morocco are sometimes grouped under the name Shilha, and Rifia may be called Northern Shilha. It is also called locally *Tarifit*, 'language of the Riff', the name of the people who speak it. It has no official status in Morocco or Algeria. Male speakers are usually bilingual in Arabic, but women are not.

ROMANCE LANGUAGES

The last Roman Emperor was deposed and the western empire, shaken by Germanic invasions and internal chaos, collapsed in AD 476.

For five centuries LATIN had been the language of government and education, and the everyday language of a growing number of people, throughout the western provinces, from Spain all the way to the Balkans. Easy travel and communications had kept the spoken Latin of the empire surprisingly uniform: there were no big dialect differences.

Latin was far too well established to disappear: but with political fragmentation, there was no longer anything to prevent local accents and dialects emerging. Some became the languages of independent governments. These, overshadowing their rivals, achieved the status of standard languages.

And so, where it has not been displaced by later invasions, Latin still survives – in the form of its descendants, the Romance languages. In fifteen hundred years, they have grown widely apart; yet all can be clearly seen to originate in the language of the Roman Empire.

The Romance languages all differ from Latin in one interesting way. They have a definite article, equivalent of English *the*: French *le, la, les*; Portuguese *o, a, os, as* and so on. How did this feature originate? It has been suggested that the idea is borrowed from Greek. Admittedly such basic features are not usually borrowed from language to language. But Christian texts, in Greek and in literal Latin translation, had a huge influence on the way that later Latin was spoken and written. In these texts Latin *ille* 'that' is frequently used as an equivalent to Greek *ho* 'the'; and this Latin word is indeed the origin of the Romance definite article.

Lingua Franca

Ever since people began to sail the Mediterranean they have had to communicate with speakers of other, multiple languages. Indirectly we know of the resulting language mixtures even in prehistoric times, thanks to the word-borrowing to which early Mediterranean languages such as Latin, Greek and Egyptian offer clues.

In the Middle Ages, for the first time, a few wordlists and phrases of the Mediterranean trade language were written down. It was called *Lingua Franca*, 'Frankish language', after the usual Arab term for West Europeans. It also has the name *Sabir* – which meant 'know' in Lingua Franca – because a common opening gambit was 'Do you know . . . ?' This same word, origin of English *savvy*, turns up in many of the modern pidgins and creoles of the world (see box at PORTUGUESE). The words of Lingua Franca came from Italian, Occitan, Catalan, Spanish, Portuguese and Arabic (*taibo* 'good' is the one Arabic word in Encina's poem, see box).

This trade language or pidgin of Mediterranean seaports had also another use. The Christian slaves acquired in large numbers by the Barbary pirates of Islamic North Africa needed to communicate with one another and with their owners: Lingua Franca served their purpose, gradually shifting in vocabulary depending on the current origins of slaves.

Lingua Franca no longer exists: or does it? In North Africa in the 19th century the slaves' Lingua Franca eventually merged into French. But from its use on the Mediterranean seaways and coasts a form of Lingua Franca came to be spoken among British homosexual groups, especially sailors and theatre people, under the name *Polari* (meaning 'speak', Italian *parlare*). And according to one theory, championed by the linguist Keith Whinnom, the French and Eng-

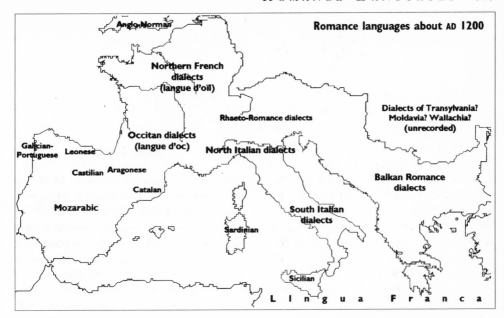

Romance languages about AD 1200

Anglo-Norman

Northern French dialects (langue d'oïl)

Rhaeto-Romance dialects

Dialects of Transylvania? Moldavia? Wallachia? (unrecorded)

Occitan dialects (langue d'oc)

Galician-Portuguese   Leonese

Castilian   Aragonese

Catalan

North Italian dialects

Balkan Romance dialects

Mozarabic

Sardinian

South Italian dialects

Sicilian

L i n g u a   F r a n c a

lish creoles of the world all descend from medieval Lingua Franca because this was the basis of the 16th-century Portuguese traders' pidgin.

Lingua Franca is the oldest recorded trade language or pidgin. So the phrase *lingua franca* has become a standard term for a medium of communication among speakers of multiple languages.

The reach of Rome

The first map shows Latin in retreat. The invasions of the Lombards, Goths and Franks had no long-term impact on the developing Latin/Romance speech of the old empire. Anglo-Saxon, Slavonic, Hungarian and Arabic settlements had a stronger effect. In these regions, by the 12th century, Romance speech had disappeared. MOZARABIC, the Romance language of Islamic Spain, was to be replaced by Spanish in the course of the *Reconquista*. Dalmatian, the language of the Adriatic coast, died out in the 19th century. Throughout the Middle Ages, Lingua Franca aided communication in the multilingual ports of the Mediterranean.

In the second map the Romance languages of modern Europe are shown. The 20th-century Romance languages are PORTUGUESE, GALICIAN, SPANISH, CATALAN, OCCITAN, FRENCH, ITALIAN,

Reconstruction confirmed

A 'proto-Romance' language can be reconstructed from the modern Romance languages, just as with other language groups. There is one difference: a real ancestral language, Latin, is on record. So what do the slight differences between reconstructed proto-Romance and actual Latin mean? In general, they show the difference between the high culture of the educated elite – the writers and audience of classical Latin literature – and the everyday speech of the masses. It was the latter that gave rise to the various Romance languages. Also they remind us that even in a rich corpus of literature some rare words may go unrecorded.

On occasion, scholars reconstruct forms in proto-Romance, and these forms are later discovered in previously unknown documents or inscriptions. Thus on the basis of Romanian *strut*, Italian *struzzo*, Provençal and Catalan *estrus* and Old Spanish *estruç*, 'ostrich', we would reconstruct a proto-Romance form *strūtju*; this form has now been discovered, written *struthius*, in the late Latin translations of the Greek medical writer Oribasius.

Robert A. Hall, Jr., *External history of the Romance languages* (New York: American Elsevier, 1974) p. 74, adapted

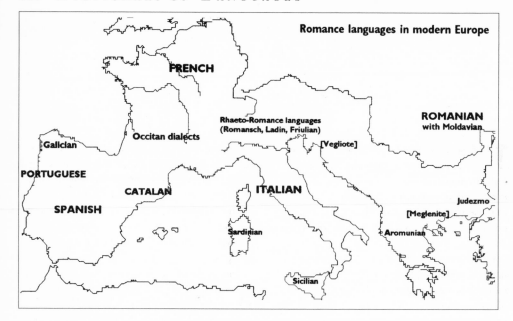

Romance languages in modern Europe

FRENCH

Rhaeto-Romance languages
(Romansch, Ladin, Friulian)

ROMANIAN
with Moldavian

Occitan dialects

Galician

[Vegliote]

PORTUGUESE

CATALAN

ITALIAN

Judezmo

SPANISH

[Meglenite]

Sardinian

Aromunian

Sicilian

The earliest record of Romance speech

In AD 842 an alliance between Charles the Bald and Louis the German was sealed by the taking of mutual oaths by the French and German monarchs and by their armies. So that everyone could understand what was going on, the oaths were taken in the everyday languages of the two countries, and not in Latin. The official chronicler Nithard recorded the proceedings word for word. Louis took the oath in French:

Pro Deo amur et pro christian poblo et nostro commun salvament, dist di in avant, in quant Deus savir et podir me dunat, si salvarai eo cist meon fradre Karlo et in aiudha er in cadhuna cosa, si cum om per dreit son fradra salvar dift, in o quid il mi altre si fazet et ab Ludher nul plaid nunquam prindrai, qui, meon vol, cist meon fradre Karle in damno sit.

For God's love and for the Christian people and our common salvation, from this day onward, so far as God gives me knowledge and power, I will defend this my brother Charles and will be of help in everything, as a man in justice ought to defend his brother, so long as he does the same for me, and I will accept no plea from Lothar which might, by my will, damage this my brother Charles.
For the German text as sworn by Charles, see box at GERMAN.
Nithard, *Histoire des fils de Louis le Pieux* ed. Ph. Lauer (Paris: Les Belles Lettres, 1926) p. 104

SARDINIAN, ROMANSCH, Ladin, Friulian, ROMANIAN and AROMUNIAN. Three of these have been carried far across the world as the languages of colonial empires. They now have descendants of their own. For more details see FRENCH CREOLES, PORTUGUESE and SPANISH.

The Mediterranean pilgrimage

Peregrin taibo cristian,	Good Christian pilgrim,
Si kerer andar Jordan	If you want to reach the Jordan
Pilya per tis jornis pan,	Steal bread for your days of travel,
Ke no trobar pan ne vin.	For you will find neither bread nor wine.

Lingua Franca song of 1521: after L. P. Harvey and others, 'Lingua Franca in a villancico by Encina' in *Revue de littérature comparée* vol. 41 (1967) pp. 572–9

ROMANI

POSSIBLY 3,000,000 OR MORE SPEAKERS

There seem to have been three separate westward emigrations of nomadic peoples from India in medieval times. Through the centuries, the travelling musicians and dancers belonging to these peoples have had a powerful influence on the poetry and art of Europe and western Asia.

From one of these peoples descend the Lomavren, nomadic groups of Azerbaijan and Armenia, who once spoke a quite distinct language. They now speak ARMENIAN in a special dialect that retains many Indo-Aryan words.

From another came the Domari (Nawari or Nuri), the still numerous Gypsies of Syria, Lebanon, Israel, Egypt and other Middle Eastern countries. The Karachi, a related group, live in Iran and central Asia. The Mıtırp are a smaller group living in south-eastern Turkey.

The third migration is that of the Roma, with whose language this article is concerned.

> The *Roma*'s name for themselves dates from the period during which they lived in the Byzantine or 'Roman' Empire. They reached Europe from the East at a time when awareness was growing of the Islamic challenge to European Christendom: hence the tendency to confuse them with Muslims and to call them 'Egyptians' (English *Gypsies*), 'Tatars', 'Saracens'. They have been called 'Bohemians', too, because Bohemia was an important Romani centre from the 15th century to the mid 20th. The oldest recorded Greek name for the Roma is *athinganoi*, 'avoiding the touch', a reminder of their rules of ritual purity.
>
> The term *Vlach*, used for one major Romani dialect group, can cause confusion. It has also been used in the past for the Romanian and Aromunian languages and their speakers.

Like Lomavren and Domari, Romani is one of the INDO-ARYAN LANGUAGES and it seems to be most closely related to PANJABI. It is far from clear when the earliest speakers of Romani left northern India. Dates as early as the 5th century and the 8th century have been suggested. Their westward migration had reached south-eastern Europe by the 13th century, perhaps earlier.

The Balkans and Transylvania are major centres of Romani population, and Romani shared in some of the phenomena of language convergence that characterise Balkan languages (see ALBANIAN). Romani dialects divide easily into Vlach and non-Vlach. The ancestors of the Vlach dialect speakers underwent four hundred years of serfdom in what is now Romania, and after the 1860s spread across the southern Balkans and across the world. Their language is naturally strongly influenced by ROMANIAN and has in turn influenced Romanian. Non-Vlach dialects descend from the Romani who bypassed Romania and reached central Europe by way of Serbia and Croatia from the early 15th century on, spreading from there. In these dialects there are no Hungarian and few Romanian loanwords.

Roma were subject to execution in Britain in the 17th century. Well over a million were killed under German rule between 1933 and 1945, though German satellite states, such as Slovakia, did not take part in this genocide. Later, in communist eastern Europe, many Roma were forcibly settled in villages to obliterate their traditional way of life.

Like the Indian peoples to whom they are related, Roma subdivide into stable castes with differing traditions, trades and dialects. Most of these groups retain a nomadic way of life, though others settle in towns and villages. The Roma population of many countries is thus complicated in its make-up and difficult to map.

Romani as a standard language

The usual external attitudes to Romani language and culture have been lack of comprehension alternating with dangerous hostility. However, in a few countries where Romani speakers are still to be found in quite large numbers, the language is beginning to be recognised as a medium for education and literature.

In Macedonia it has constitutional status and is taught in some schools. Work has been done there on the standardisation of language and spelling, based on the majority Arlija dialect with some modifications to accommodate Džambaz.

In former Czechoslovakia, too, a standard written form was developed after the liberalisation of 1969. This is based on the Carpathian-type dialect of the majority Slovak Roma, and is used (particularly in Slovakia) in poetry, plays and journalism.

Offshoots of Romani

There is a big difference between the dialects that still have a recognisably Romani structure, and those that have adopted the grammar of the surrounding language while still using some Romani words. Linguists call these para-Romani languages.

Roma communities may come to share part of their lifestyle, and thus need to communicate, with other elements: in Britain, for example, they have interacted with local outlaws and 'drop-outs', and with Irish, Scottish and Welsh travellers. An Anglo-Romani pidgin may have first developed, as long ago as the 16th century, to allow communication among these groups while maintaining the privacy associated with the traditional Romani culture, with its long-inherited rules of ritual purity. In Britain Romani itself has now almost died as a mother tongue, but Anglo-Romani, learnt by boys at the age of nine or ten as they begin to work with their fathers, is still much used. There may be 90,000 speakers in Britain and twice that number in the United States and Australia.

In a similar way, para-Romani languages are known that are based on the grammars of German, Catalan, Portuguese, Basque, Spanish, Greek, Swedish and Norwegian.

Anglo-Romani (the linguists' term) is called by its speakers *Pogadi-jib* 'broken language', *Posh 'n' posh* 'half and half' and other similar names, showing clearly its origin as a mixture of Romani and English. The Spanish equivalent, *Caló*, gets its name from the Romani word *kalo* 'black' because of its speakers' typical complexion: it is also called *Romano* (a mixed Romani-Spanish word).

Caló is a mixture of the extinct Romani dialect of Spain (apparently closely related to Balkan and north European Romani) and of the Andalusian dialect of Spanish. All speakers of Caló are bilingual, but even when their Spanish is a quite different dialect, their Caló has the same Andalusian features. Caló has a history of at least two

---

Domari: language of Middle Eastern Gypsies

The little-known language of the Gypsies of the Levant belongs, like Romani, to the Indo-Aryan group. Scholars dispute whether Domari and Romani had the same early history – whether they result from the same migration out of India, or from two migrations at different times. This is the beginning of a fairy tale in Domari:

Asta yikaki tilla-tmalik, potres des u shtar u shtarne. Qolde goresan u minde khalesan u gare.
Laherde eqasri atre ghulaskaki, u dires ghulaski das u shtar u shtarne . . .

There was one king who had eighteen sons. They mounted their horses and went away.
They saw a castle that belonged to a ghoul, and the ghoul had eighteen daughters . . .

R. A. Stewart Macalister, *The language of the Nawar or Zutt, the nomad smiths of Palestine* (London: Bernard Quaritch, 1914)

hundred years, and probably much longer, but most of the half-million Spanish Gypsies now use it less and less. It is also spoken – still with Andalusian Spanish features – in Portugal and in some South American countries.

Various forms of Turkish slang, argot and secret languages incorporate Romani loan-words. Clearly there was once an Anatolian dialect of Romani: it exists no longer, though, as a result of recent migrations, some speakers of Balkan Romani dialects now live in Anatolia. The Gypsy language *Boşa*, spoken in eastern Turkey near Lake Van, is a variety of ARMENIAN.

The secrets of Roma

Romani and para-Romani languages have a special advantage to their speakers: most of those with whom they do business will never learn to understand them. Even when Romani adopts the grammar of neighbouring languages, it maintains a distinct, and thus secret, vocabulary.

Bobaní: Why is La Habana, capital of Cuba, called *Bobaní* in Caló, the language of the Spanish Romani? The cant name comes from a simple pun. In the original name *Haba*, which happens to be the Spanish for 'bean', is followed by -n- and the Spanish feminine ending -a. Look for equivalents in Caló and you will find *bobi* 'bean' + -n- + -í the feminine ending, hence *bobaní*.

After Peter Bakker in Romani in contact: the history, structure and sociology of a language ed. Yaron Matras (Amsterdam: Benjamins, 1995) p. 133

Roma and the wider world

Gorgio: *Gadžó*, feminine *gadží*, is the Romani term for a non-Gypsy. The Roma recognise their own distinctiveness with the saying *Rom Romeha, gadžo, gadžeha* 'Rom goes with Rom, foreigner with foreigner'. This word has become known in several languages. In English it is usually spelt *gorgio*. In Bulgarian *gádže* now means 'boy friend, girl friend, lover'. In colloquial Romanian *gagiu* means 'man, he-man' and the feminine *gagică* means 'girl friend, pretty girl'. In the Romanian translation of the Popeye cartoons, *Gagica* is the name of Popeye's girl friend Olive Oyl. The words also have a pejorative meaning: *gagiu* 'gigolo', *gagică* 'easy lay'.

After Corinna Leschber in Romani in contact: the history, structure and sociology of a language ed. Yaron Matras (Amsterdam: Benjamins, 1995) p. 162

ROMANIAN

24,000,000 SPEAKERS

Romania, Moldova, Ukraine

One of the ROMANCE LANGUAGES descended from Latin, Romanian is the majority language of Romania and of Moldova, and is spoken by minorities in Ukraine, the United States, Australia and other countries. Its closest relatives are AROMUNIAN and Italian.

Romanian is known to its own speakers as *limba română*. Until recently the spellings *Roumanian, Rumanian* were standard. Traditionally, speakers of Romanian were known to their neighbours as Vlachs (Hungarian *Oláh*, Greek *Vlákhos*), hence the name of *Wallachia*: the Romanians themselves call this province *Țara Românească*, 'Romanian land'. For ideological reasons Romanian was called *limba moldovenească*, 'Moldavian', in Soviet Moldova.

Romanian was the last of the major Romance languages to be recorded in writing, in documents and religious texts of the mid 16th century.

Where were the speakers of Romanian in medieval times? Hungarians and Romanians dispute this endlessly. Did Latin speakers maintain their language in the mineral-rich mountains of Transylvania, after the Roman legions retreated from there in AD 271? Or did Latin speakers from further south – modern Yugoslavia and Bulgaria – gradually migrate northwards in medieval times? In that case, might the Hungarians have reached Transylvania before the future Romanians did? Both sides have relied on the thousand-year-old puzzle in their arguments about who should rule modern Transylvania.

Three Romanian-speaking provinces emerge from the mists of medieval Balkan history: Wallachia, the lower Danube plains; Moldavia, reaching north from the Danube delta towards Ukraine and Poland; and, tucked in the fold of the Carpathians, Transylvania (known to Germans as *Siebenbürgen*, the seven castles, and to Hungarians as *Erdély*, the woodland). For centuries these provinces were divided by politics. Moldavia and Wallachia were Christian principalities subject to the Turkish Empire; Transylvania was generally under Hungarian and Austrian rule, and still has large Hungarian and German minorities. Fleetingly united under Michael the Brave in 1599–1601, the three provinces were brought together again in 1918. Eastern Moldavia was seized by the Soviet Union in 1944: as Moldova it is now an independent country.

Romanian and its neighbours

Romanian has in some ways remained especially close to Latin. It is the only Romance language that has a 'case' distinction in nouns, formed with the help of the definite article (Latin *ille*, 'that') which is now suffixed to the noun: *drac*, 'devil' (earlier 'snake'); *dracul*, 'the Devil'; *dracului*, 'of the Devil'.

Romanian also shows very strong structural influence from an early form of Slavonic – as if, at the time of the Slav invasions of the Balkans, large numbers of Slavonic speakers rapidly adopted the then standard language of the region. The numbers '1' to '10' are purely Latin in origin: *unu, doi, trei, patru, cinci, șase, șapte, opt, noi, zece*. Numbers from eleven onwards are made up of Latin roots arranged in the Slavonic way. Hyphens are inserted in these examples to clarify the structure: *un-spre-zece* 'eleven', literally 'one on ten', just like Russian *odin-na-desat'*; *trei-zeci* 'thirty', literally 'three tens', like Russian *tri-desat'*.

Old Slavonic has continued to exert a dominating effect on Romanian as the traditional language of the Orthodox Church. More recently French has had intellectual prestige. The basic vocabulary remains Romance, but with many shifts of meaning: *bărbat* 'man' (earlier 'bearded'); *inimă* 'heart' (earlier 'spirit'); *pămînt* 'world' (earlier 'pavement'). There are numerous loanwords from Old Slavonic, German, modern Greek, Turkish and French: *izvor* 'spring'; *halbă* 'beer mug'; *drum* 'road'; *tutun* 'tobacco'; *bagaj* 'luggage'. Colloquial Romanian borrows liberally from ROMANI, though these loanwords tend to be left out of dictionaries.

A sequence of historical chronicles comes out of the earliest period of Romanian writing. But this was a multilingual culture, and Moldavia's greatest 18th-century writer, Prince Dimitrie Cantemir, wrote in Latin, German and Turkish as well as Romanian. His monumental *History of the Growth and Decline of the Ottoman Empire* was first published (in 1734) in English translation. Folk song in Romania has drawn vigour from its varied origins: Gypsies have been among its chief exponents. The French composer Berlioz was inspired by it, as were native poets such as Vasile Alecsandri.

Romanian was first written in a local variant of the old Cyrillic alphabet, as used for Old Slavonic. The Latin alphabet was adopted in the 19th century. As elsewhere in the Soviet Union, a modern Cyrillic alphabet was used in Moldova between 1944 and 1991. Independent Moldova now refers to its language as 'Romanian' and uses the Latin alphabet.

Romance languages of the Balkans

Romanian and its relatives have interesting features in common with other Balkan languages (see also ALBANIAN).

Romanian is the language of the three contiguous provinces, Wallachia, Moldavia (including Bessarabia, now Moldova) and Transylvania. To the east of Moldavia, a Romanian-speaking minority on the left bank of the Dniester formed the basis of a Moldavian republic, part of Ukraine, in early Soviet times. When the Soviet Union annexed Bessarabia in 1940, the newly created Moldavian Soviet Republic (independent Moldova from 1991) incorporated part of this early Moldavian SSR – the district now known as Transnistria. Romanian speakers are the largest single population group there, but they make up only about 40 per cent of the total population, the remainder being Ukrainian and Russian speakers.

AROMUNIAN is spoken in the neighbourhood of lakes Ohrid and Prespa, in north-western Greece, eastern Albania and south-western Macedonia.

Meglenite is the language of a community of *Vlashi* who have lived in a remote mountainous district of Greece north of Saloniki. They had become Muslims in the 18th century. As such they were liable to expulsion from Greece after 1923, and most of them settled in Turkey, where their language may now be extinct. A few are said to remain in Greece.

Romance languages of the Balkans

ROMANSCH

65,000 SPEAKERS

Switzerland

One of the less known of the ROMANCE LAN-GUAGES, Romansch was recognised in 1938 as the fourth national language of Switzerland, alongside German, French and Italian.

> Romansch is spoken in the canton of *Grisons* or *Graubünden*, 'the Grey League', which preserves the name of a self-defence organisation of Romance speakers set up in the 15th century. It became part of Switzerland in 1803. Germans once called this language *Chur-Wälsch*, ' "Welsh" or foreign speech of Chur', for Chur was the capital of Roman Rhaetia and was once the centre of Romansch. Chur, even its cross-river suburb *Wälschdörfli* ' "Welsh" village', now speaks German: Romansch survives only in the upper valleys of the Rhine and the Inn.

Its origin is as a dialect of the provincial Latin of the central Alps, which were incorporated in the Roman Empire during the reign of Augustus. Before Roman times the area appears to have been Celtic-speaking; by the end of the Roman Empire there must have been an unbroken region of distinctive Romance speech here, gradually driven into the high valleys by the encroachment of German from the north and of Italian from the south.

Romansch itself, with its long history of local linguistic pride and a high rate of literacy, has so far survived and even prospered. The Engadine dialect was first printed as early as 1552 in Jacob Bifrun's *Christiauna fuorma*, a catechism; a translation of the New Testament followed in 1560. Both Romansch and Engadine, in several varieties, are used as school languages and in the local media.

> Two other 'Rhaeto-Romance' languages, Ladin and Friulian, survive in the Italian Alps.
>
> Ladin is spoken in four valleys radiating from the mountain core of the Dolomites: those of the Avisio and Noce, traditionally Venetian territory, and those of the Gadera and Gardena, which were Austrian until 1919. Ladin has some use in primary schools and is locally recognised in the region of Trentino-Alto Adige.
>
> Friulian covers a much larger territory and has as many as 600,000 speakers. Trieste was a Friulian-speaking city in medieval times, but Venetian long ago replaced Friulian as the everyday speech of the head of the Adriatic. In spite of its large number of speakers Friulian has no official status nationally or regionally: it has been historically overshadowed by Venetian and is now in thrall to Italian. Yet it remains an everyday medium of communication, and many local German and Slovene speakers are bilingual in Friulian. It has some literature, too: Pier Paolo Pasolini's first book of poetry was in Friulian, and he founded the now defunct Academiuta di Lenga Furlana 'Academy of the Friulian Language'.

The Rhaeto-Romance languages on the map

Romansch is the language of the upper Rhine valley, spoken by a largely Catholic population. The *Sursevan* 'above the woods' dialect, centring on Disentis, is the standard form. It is divided by the forest of Flims from *Subselvan*.

Rhaeto-Romance numerals		
Surselvan		**Friulian**
in, ina	1	un, une
dus, duas	2	doi, dos
treis	3	tre
quater	4	cuatri
tschun	5	cinc
sis	6	sis
siat	7	siet
otg	8	vot
nov	9	nuv
diesch	10	dis

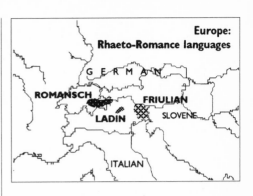

Engadine, close to Romansch, is spoken in the upper Inn by a Protestant population. The chief town here is Samaden.

Ladin is spoken in four valleys of the Dolomites. It may have about 30,000 speakers.

Friulian is the local language of the Italian autonomous region of Friuli-Venezia Giulia. There are over half a million speakers there, and a few in neighbouring districts of Slovenia.

Fair Catine

Indulà vastu, Catine biele?	Where are you going, fair Catine?
O voi a moris de baràz, o missâr pari.	I'm going blackberrying, father.
Mostrimi lis moris di barâz, Catine biele –	Show me the blackberries, fair Catine –
La ciavra lis à mangiadis, o missâr pari.	The goat ate them, father.
Mostrimi la ciavra, Catine biele –	Show me the goat, fair Catine –
Il beciâr la à copade, o missâr pari.	The butcher killed it, father.
Mostrimi il beciâr, Catine biele –	Show me the butcher, fair Catine –
Il beciâr al è sotiara, o missâr pari.	He's under the earth, father.
Mostrimi la tiara, Catine biele –	Show me the earth, fair Catine –
La nêf la à taponada, o missâr pari . . .	The snow has covered it, father . . .

After D. B. Gregor, *Friulan: language and literature*
(New York: Oleander Press, 1975) pp. 284–5

Aràz 'bramble' is one of the local words that seems to descend from an early Celtic language, cf. Irish and Breton *barr* 'branch'.

RUNDI, RWANDA AND HA

12,000,000 SPEAKERS

Burundi, Rwanda, Tanzania, Congo (Kinshasa) and Uganda

These, with two smaller dialect groups, belong to the BANTU LANGUAGES: they make up the Southern Lacustrine group. Speakers of any one of the five can easily understand the others, so it is logical to treat them as one language here.

> The full local names of these languages are *kinyaRwanda* 'language of Rwanda', *kiRundi* and *kiHa* or *giHa*; the traditional states were *Rwanda*, *buRundi* and *buHa*.

Burundi and Rwanda, in spite of fearsome ethnic divisions, have no language problem or linguistic minorities. Like neighbouring peoples to the east (see NKORE), they consist of political units in which two main castes have existed side by side – the tall, cattle-owning Tutsi, historically supreme, and the peasant Hutu. Below these again are the Twa, hunters and gatherers, potters and musicians. It is said that the dialect of the Twa is easily distinguishable from that of the other two castes.

Early Bantu speakers, apparently represented by the modern Hutu, have probably occupied this region for over two thousand years. The arrival of the Tutsi from the north-east is an event of a few hundred years ago, according to oral tradition. They were probably speakers of a NILO-SAHARAN language (not 'Hamites' or Afro-asiatic language speakers, as anthropologists used to think). Whatever they spoke on their arrival, they soon adopted the Bantu language of the ancestors of the Hutu.

The three kingdoms were annexed by Germany at the end of the 19th century and occu-pied by Belgian troops in 1916. Buha was acquired by Britain in 1921 and is now part of Tanzania. Rwanda and Burundi remained under Belgian rule until 1962 when they regained their status as independent states.

Rwanda oral literature was composed partly by the Hutu, whose speciality was court literature: historical prose, dynastic poems, poems in praise of cattle, and warrior poems of self-praise. This literature, carefully transmitted by admired and skilled performers, is in a complex and archaic language – for full understanding of the verse, prose commentaries are said to be needed. Rundi, too, has its poetry in praise of one's ruler, one's cows and oneself. Popular poetry, tales and songs, some traditionally performed by Twa singers and clowns, included songs to console a newly married girl.

Rundi and Rwanda are now the official lan-guages, alongside French, of Burundi and Rwanda. Although knowledge of Rwanda or Rundi by itself ensures communication over a wide area, Swahili, the regional language of East Africa, remains important in trade and everyday life. French, the language of the Belgian pro-tectorate which governed 'Ruanda-Urundi' until 1962, is taught in secondary schools and is still a medium of culture in the two independent countries. There are French loanwords in Rwan-da and Rundi, such as *zuzi* from French *juge* 'judge'.

Rwanda has a distinction of vowel length, four tones and seven distinct sentence-level intona-tion patterns. For a table of numerals see GANDA.

Rundi, Rwanda and their relatives

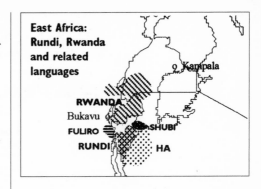

East Africa:
Rundi, Rwanda
and related
languages

Ha, with 725,000 speakers, is a language of Kigoma Province, Tanzania. Here the two castes are Tusi and Ha.

Rundi has about 5,000,000 speakers and is the national language of Burundi. It extends into the district of Bugufi in Tanzania.

Rwanda or Runyarwanda has rather over 6,000,000 speakers. It is spoken by both sides in the Rwandan fighting, and by minorities in Uganda (Bufumbira in the Kigezi district) and Congo (Kinshasa). Recently a huge number of Rwanda-speaking refugees have fled to Congo.

Shubi has 150,000 speakers.

Fuliru, with 275,000 speakers in Congo (Kin-shasa), was classed by Guthrie alongside Rundi, Rwanda and Ha; other linguists separate them.

These languages form a single dialect continuum with NKORE and its relatives.

RUSSIAN

PERHAPS 175,000,000 SPEAKERS

Russia, Ukraine, Kazakhstan, Belarus, Estonia and other Soviet successor states

One of the Eastern SLAVONIC LANGUAGES, Russian was spoken in the northern marches of the expanding Slavonic-speaking territory in the first millennium AD.

> Rus' was once the name of the principality ruled from Kiev – modern Ukraine. In medieval times the cultural and political centre of gravity shifted to Moscow, and thus the language of Moscow came to be called *Russian*.

The crystallisation of Russian as a separate language can be traced to the Mongolian-Tatar conquests of the mid 13th century and their destruction of Kiev in 1242. This was soon followed by Lithuanian and Polish annexation of Ukraine. Kiev, capital of Ukraine, had previously given religious and political leadership. Constantinople, metropolis of Orthodox Christianity, itself faltered and was to fall.

Moscow had once been a northern outpost, and was still to be subject to the Golden Horde of the Mongols and Tatars for another two and a half centuries. For all that, Moscow now came to be seen as the 'Third Rome', inheritor of the spiritual mantle of the Roman and Byzantine empires. Russian missionaries were eventually to spread Christianity to many of the peoples of greater Russia.

The language of this religious flowering was the Ukrainian-Russian variety of OLD SLAVONIC. Spoken Russian of the period – *Middle Russian* – shines through it in the adjustments that writers made, consciously or unconsciously, in the old sacred language, and in the everyday words that were introduced into documents and historical writings in discussing everyday matters.

Spoken Russian became, for the first time, a fully written language with the reforms of Peter the Great (1672–1725). Not only did he introduce a revised alphabet (see box): he encouraged authors to write as they spoke. Mikhail Lomonosov (1711–65) reasserted the suitability of the transitional Moscow dialect as the Russian standard (though the Court was then at St Petersburg). It is this historic Moscow accent that contributes to the spoken Russian of today some of its characteristic sound profile, notably the pronunciation of unstressed *o* as *a*.

The first great period of Russian literature was the 19th century – the period of Tolstoi's and Dostoyevskii's novels, of Pushkin's limpid verse, and of some great collections of folk poetry and folk tales. The Soviet period was both good and bad for Russian language and literature: good because literacy is far more widespread and Russian is extensively known as a second language; bad in that publication was restricted and ideologically steered, more effectively than under the monarchy.

In spite of modern developments, Russian retains – by comparison with Ukrainian – a great number of loanwords from Church Slavonic, inherited from the centuries during which this was the only written language of Russia. Examples of other loanwords are *zhemchug* 'pearl' from Tatar; *rınok* 'market' from Polish; masculine *sportsmen*, feminine *sportsmenka* 'athlete' from English. Russian also forms new words by calquing: *neboskryob* has the same meaning, and the same structure, as English 'skyscraper'.

Russian is generally thought one of the more difficult of Indo-European languages for an English learner. Word stress is heavy and affects the pronunciation of surrounding sounds, but it is not easily predictable and not marked in the script. In noun and adjective declension there are three genders, six cases and two numbers. Verbs generally have two 'aspects', perfective and imperfective (a frequentative aspect is also found). The basic forms of these cannot be predicted from one another by any simple rule, and a range of forms to mark tense, mood, number and person is derived from each.

Russian is the source of some English words, including *samovar* and *cosmonaut*.

The Russian diaspora

After throwing off Tatar domination, Russian expansion from the 15th century first encompassed Kazan and Astrakhan (two of the three khanates once owing allegiance to the Golden Horde), then Siberia, where trading ventures were followed by Russian administration and Christian missionaries. In the north Russian influence moved outwards from the seventeen historic northern cities that were early centres of settled life: Apatiti, Bilibino, Vorkuta, Vuktyl, Dudinka, Igarka, Inta, Kovdor, Murmansk, Nikel, Nadym, Norilsk, Salekhard, Severomorsk, Urengoy, Usinsk, Yakutsk. Even Alaska was in the Russian sphere until 1860, and Russian was becoming a lingua franca for Amerindians there.

Meanwhile there came expansion into Karelia, Belarus and Ukraine, then the Crimea and the Caucasus, which Russia struggled to subjugate in a 'Hundred Years War' from 1760 to 1860. Finally, in the 19th century, central Asia was annexed. All these regions submitted to Russian settlement, Russian-led administration and education, and the increasing dominance of Russian in public life.

In many regions, autonomous armed Cossack settlements (see KAZAKH) marked the front line of Russian expansion. Cossacks are now once again a significant political force, with a measure of self-government. Mass migration and resettlement, including that of minority peoples, spread the use of Russian as the only available lingua franca (see also box at AZERI). Russian political exiles and criminals have, for generations, been dispatched to prisons and labour camps in northern European Russia, Siberia

and central Asia: if they survived incarceration, they sometimes married and settled locally. The social and political outcasts of Russia swelled the numbers of the Russian diaspora, creating fearful problems for the Soviet Union's successor states.

During the 19th century Russia also encompassed Finland, Estonia, Latvia, Lithuania, Bessarabia (Moldova) and a large part of Poland. At the 1918 Revolution these territories were lost. Of the minority language regions of the old Russian Empire that remained, the larger ones became constituent republics of the new Soviet Union. Russians continued to settle in these regions in ever larger numbers. Meanwhile Tuva and Mongolia became Soviet satellites. In the course of the Second World War the Soviet Union annexed Tuva and reconquered Estonia, Latvia, Lithuania and Bessarabia along with the easternmost provinces of Poland, Czechoslovakia and Hungary.

At the end of the war the German population was expelled from East Prussia, which was divided between Poland and the Soviet Union. The Soviet sector, centred on Kaliningrad (formerly Königsberg), was repopulated mostly with Russians, who remain there in a heavily armed enclave now bordered by Poland and independent Lithuania.

Poland, East Germany, Czechoslovakia, Hungary, Bulgaria and Cuba were Soviet satellite states from the end of the war until the collapse under Gorbachev. East Germany was especially heavily garrisoned, and many Russian military families settled there. In the same period Soviet influence over Yugoslavia, Albania, Romania, China, North Vietnam and North Korea was significant though less consistent. Several other countries, including Angola, Mozambique, Libya, Ethiopia and Afghanistan, experienced heavy Russian economic and military activity. Russian soldiers, technical advisers and labourers lived in some of these countries in considerable numbers and for long periods, and their own peoples went to work and study in Russia.

Russian has influenced the language of all these countries, notably the vocabularies of science, warfare, education and politics. For the present, Russian is much used in international communication among former Soviet countries, where it

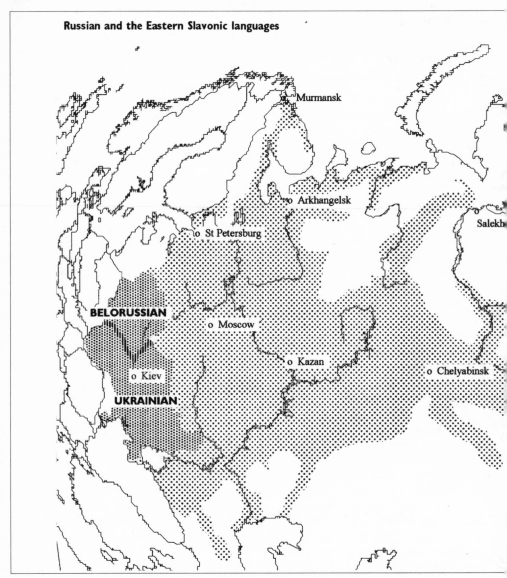

Russian and the Eastern Slavonic languages

Murmansk

Arkhangelsk

Salekh

o St Petersburg

BELORUSSIAN

o Moscow

o Kazan

o Chelyabinsk

o Kiev

UKRAINIAN

is at least a second language for millions of people. But almost everywhere this position is being eroded, generally in favour of English.

For, in the last decade, the Soviet Union has disintegrated. Led by Lithuania, all the Soviet republics have declared their independence. Self-government has been granted to numerous minority peoples that had not had Soviet republic status: even some of these, such as the Tatars and the Chechens, are pushing more or less violently for full independence.

This has left some very large minorities of Russian speakers, once confident of their dominant status, now cut off from power and struggling for equality. Russia's television service still broadcasts to these minorities, and a local Russian press exists in nearly all the former Soviet countries. From some territories, including Chechnya and Tuva, many Russian settlers have fled; in Azerbaijan, Uzbekistan, Tajikistan, Turkmenistan, Kazakhstan and Kyrgyzstan, a decline in the Russian population already noticeable in the

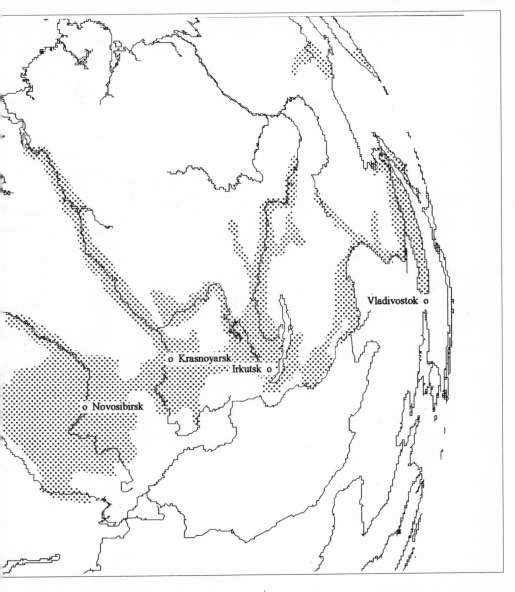

o Novosibirsk

o Krasnoyarsk

Irkutsk o

Vladivostok o

1970s has gradually speeded up as Russian speakers face unpopularity and discrimination. The very large Russian minority settled in northern Kazakhstan is the most secure. In the west there are powerful Russian minorities in Estonia, Latvia, Belarus and Ukraine.

Russian émigré communities, already sizeable in the 19th century, grew markedly after the 1917 Revolution and during the troubled 1930s and 1940s. There has been an important Russian émigré press in Paris, London, New York and other cities. Much of the best Russian literature of the 20th century was published abroad, in a language that was becoming somewhat old-fashioned, to find few Russian readers – because 'subversive' literature could not be imported into the Soviet Union.

Some Northern dialects of Russian have the unusual feature of a suffixed definite article, like Bulgarian and other Balkan languages: *dom* 'house', *domot* 'the house'.

The Eastern Slavonic languages

The three languages form a dialect continuum. In particular, the North-eastern dialects of *Belorussian* resemble neighbouring Russian dialects; the South-western dialects resemble northern Ukrainian.

Standard *Ukrainian* is based on the Eastern or Left-Bank dialects of Kiev and Poltava. The Dnieper makes a clear boundary between these and the Western dialects, which have some resemblance to Polish. Speakers of the dialect of Transcarpathian Ukraine, which until 1944 belonged to Czechoslovakia, sometimes now claim for it the status of a separate language, *Transcarpathian Ruthenian.*

The Northern and Southern dialect groups of *Russian* are separated by a belt of transitional 'Central' dialects. Moscow's own dialect is one of these: its vowels are like those of the South, its consonants like those of the North.

The Russian alphabet

А Б В Г Д Е Ё Ж З И Й К Л М Н О П Р С Т У
Ф Х Ц Ч Ш Щ Ъ Ы Ь Э Ю Я

а б в г е ё ж з и й к л м н о п р с т у ф х ц ш щ ъ ы
ь э ю я

a b v g d ye yo zh z i ĭ k l m n o p r s t u f kh ts ch
sh shch " i ' e yu ya

ы, transliterated *i* in this book, usually appears as *y* when Russian words and names are included in English texts. This *grazhdanka* or secular alphabet was introduced by Peter the Great in 1708 to take the place of the Old Slavonic form of the Cyrillic script. Four more letters initially carried over from Old Slavonic – IѴѢѲ iѵѣө i i ye f – were eliminated in the reform of 1917/18.

The tale of Igor's campaign

Чи ли въспѣти было, вѣщей Бояне,	Or you might have begun your song thus,
Велесовь внуче:	wizard Boyan, grandson of Veles:
'Комони пжуть за Сулою, –	'Horses neigh beyond the Sula,
звенить слава въ Кыеве;	glory rings out in Kiev;
трбы трубять въ Новѣградѣ, –	trumpets sound in Novgorod,
стоять стязи въ Путивлѣ.'	standards are raised in Putivl'!'

From *The tale of Igor's campaign*

Slovo o polku Igoreve is the story of young Igor's disastrous campaign in the year 1185 – undertaken without the permission of his sovereign, the Prince of Kiev – against the wild Polovtsy ('Cumans'). It is the tale of his defeat, captivity and escape. More than that, this medieval narrative in poetic prose is 'a moving record of the last decades of Kievan Russia, on the eve of the Mongol invasion, and of her struggle to survive in an age of chivalry and disaster, of heroism and folly, of civil strife and barbarian invasions' (Dimitri Obolensky, *The Penguin book of Russian verse* (Harmondsworth, 1962) p. xxxiii). The only known manuscript of the tale was discovered around 1790 and was destroyed in the fire of Moscow in 1812, but not before an edition had been printed. Borodin's opera *Prince Igor* is based on the story.

The *byliny*, ballads collected in recent times from peasant singers in the Russian countryside, seem to recreate essentially the same world, though in them the enemy is usually (anachronistically) the Tatars. They centre on Kiev (and 'Prince Vladimir') or on the trading city of Novgorod. One of the Novgorod cycle is the story of Sadko, the minstrel who became a rich merchant.

The first politically correct language?

Official, party-approved Russian was a dull language, spoken with the 'wooden tongue' that Stalin recommended. Concepts and institutions had to be named in such a way as to enjoin a correct point of view. This produced long, boring phrases which (because life is too short) had to be abridged in everyday use.

Official form	Everyday form	Formal translation	Everyday equivalent
Vsesoyuznii Leninskii Kommunisticheskii Soyuz Molodyozhi	Komsomol	Lenin's All-Union Communist League of Young People	Scouts
Soyuz Sovetskikh Sotsiyalisticheskikh Respublik	SSSR; Sovetskii Soyuz	Union of Soviet Socialist Republics	USSR; Soviet Union
Vyssheye Uchebnoye Zavedeniye	Vuz	Higher Education Institution	College

SAMI

PERHAPS 30,000 SPEAKERS

Norway, Sweden, Finland

Sami, often called Lapp, one of the URALIC LANGUAGES, is spoken by gradually shrinking nomadic communities who traditionally lived by reindeer herding and fishing in the inhospitable northern regions of Norway, Sweden, Finland and Karelia.

In early times the Sami were known to outsiders as *Fenni* (Latin), *Finnar* (Old Norse: see box). They were *Finni mitissimi* 'Sami, the mildest of people' to a Latin historian of the Goths. The word possibly derives from proto-Scandinavian *finna* 'to find', because Sami speakers were foragers and hunters. The more usual modern name *Lapp*, applied to them by the Finns, is first recorded in the 13th century. *Sami* or *Saami*, now the preferred term, is based on the speakers' own name for themselves, *sápme* singular, *sámeht* plural. It is the same name as that of one of the historic tribes of the Finns, *Häme*.

Nothing was written in Sami till Nicolaus Andreas, a Swedish priest, printed an ABC and *Missal* in 1619. But the early history of the language can still be traced – through loanwords.

By 1500 BC, speakers of 'Early Proto-Finnic', the proto-language that would eventually split into Sami, Finnish and Estonian, were in contact with speakers of BALTIC and GERMANIC LANGUAGES: thus, from Baltic dialects, Lithuanian *lãšis* 'salmon' reappears as Sami *luossâ*; Latvian *dagla* 'touchwood, tinder' as Sami *duowle*; from proto-Germanic, Anglo-Saxon *hos*, Gothic *hansa* 'troop', German *Hansa* 'guild' reappears as Sami *guosse* 'guest'. They must have been settled around the shores of the southern Baltic at that period. Finnish and Estonian continued to bor-

row from Baltic languages after 1000 BC, but Sami did not. So, by then, early Sami speakers must have been moving north, away from these other groups.

At a later time, perhaps around AD 500, they were interacting with speakers of an early form of OLD NORSE: thus Swedish *sår* 'wound' reappears as Sami *saire, sarje*; Old Norse *fló* 'flea' as Sami *lawkes*; Swedish *ko* 'cow' as Sami *gussâ*. It is probable that by that time Sami was spoken across its present very wide geographical range, from central Norway to Karelia and the White Sea. It began to split into dialects: thus, from about AD 800 onwards, loanwords from early forms of Norwegian, Swedish and Finnish occur in the individual Sami dialects rather than in the language as a whole.

Its close relationship with Estonian and Finnish is only half the story of Sami. Its speakers are very different, in way of life, customs, beliefs, and also physically, from most Finns. It is clear that as Sami spread across the wide north of Scandinavia it also became the language of an already existing, unrelated people, whose way of life was already similar to that of the modern Sami. They, and their now forgotten language, explain the striking differences between Sami and Finnish.

Fewer than half of the people who consider themselves Sami or Lapp still speak the language. Only about 2,500 live in northern Finland (commonly thought of as the Lapp homeland) and all of them are bilingual in Finnish. The largest number of Sami speakers, about 10,000, now live in Norway, and the Northern Sami dialect is most often used in writing. It is also called *Norwegian Lapp*, but is spoken in parts of

Sweden and Finland as well as in Norway.

There has been a succession of spelling rules, from the first Norwegian Lapp publication in 1728 to the common orthography for all three countries adopted in 1978. There are three periodicals in Sami and occasional radio broadcasts, but not much publishing except for schoolbooks and religious books.

Sami is a 'synthetic' or 'agglutinating' lan-guage of long compound words and of compli-cated phonetics. It is notable for its rhythmical stress pattern. Words are stressed on the first syllable, with secondary stresses on odd syl-lables. Even syllables are unstressed. (For the numerals see ESTONIAN.)

Examples from Mikko Korhonen in *The Uralic languages: description, history and foreign influences* ed. Denis Sinor (Leiden: Brill, 1988)

Empty country

An early record of the Sami – and of the Permians (see KOMI) further east – is in King Alfred's Anglo-Saxon version of Orosius' Latin *Histories*. It includes a note about a Norwegian merchant, Ohthere, who had reported to Alfred in person on the voyage eastwards from northern Norway to the White Sea:

Ac him wæs ealne weg weste land on þæt steorbord, butan fiscerum & fuglerum & huntum,
& þæt wæron eall Finnas; & him wæs á widsǽ on ðæt bæcbord. Þa Beormas hæfdon swiþe
wel gebúd hira land; ac hie ne dorston þær on cuman. Ac þara Terfinna land wæs eal weste buton
ðær huntan gewicodon, oþþe fisceras, oþþe fugeleras . . . Þa Finnas, him þuhte, & þa Beormas
spræcon neah an geþeode.

To starboard there was empty country all the way, except for fishers, birdcatchers and hunters.
They were all *Finnas* [Sami]. The *Beormas* [Permians] farmed their land well, but one dare
not land there; the land of the *Terfinnas* was all empty, except where hunters or fishers or birdcatchers
lived . . . The Sami and the Permians, it seemed to him [Ohthere],
spoke nearly the same language.

King Alfred's Orosius ed. H. Sweet (London, 1883)

The power of Sami

The oldest recorded text in Sami is a single word, 'Come to me' – part of a three-word message or spell (the other two words are in Old Norse) scratched in runes on a medieval wooden shovel, which was discovered in a bog at Indriðastaðir in Skorradal, Iceland, hundreds of miles of rough sea from the lands where Sami is spoken. The message – which scholars date to about 1200 – reads:

Boattiatmik Inkialtr kærþi
Come to me, Ingjald, please!

From Magnus Olsen, Knut Bergsland, *Lappisk i en islandsk runeinnskrift* (Oslo: Dybwad, 1943)
(*Avhandlinger utgitt av Det Norske Videnskaps–Akademi I Oslo, hist.-filos. Klasse*, 1943 no. 2)

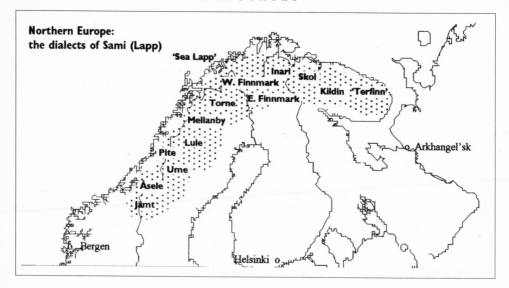

Northern Europe:
the dialects of Sami (Lapp)

Sami and its dialects

The line between Jämt Sami and Åsele Sami is the southern border of ancient *Finnmark*, the Sami territory that paralleled the northern Norwegian coastal realm of Halogaland. Later the Jämt and Åsele Sami were known as 'Mountain Lapps', paying tribute both to Norway, where they spent the summer, and to Sweden where they wintered in the lowland forests. The Ume Sami to their north were 'Forest Lapps', settled entirely in Sweden.

The Sami nomadic lifestyle has had to contend with such interruptions as the delimitation of the Norway–Sweden frontier, in 1751, and the freezing of the Soviet Union's borders in the 20th century.

The dialect of the Sea Lapps, fishers settled on the far northern shores of Norway, has almost died out, replaced by Norwegian.

Based on Pekka Sammallahti, 'Die Definition von Sprachgrenzen in einem Kontinuum von Dialekten: die Lappischen Sprachen und einige Grundfragen der Dialektologie' in *Dialectologia Uralica* ed. Wolfgang Veenker (Wiesbaden: Harrassowitz, 1985) pp. 149–58 and other sources

SAMOAN

200,000 SPEAKERS

Western Samoa, American Samoa

Samoan is a Polynesian language, belonging to the Oceanic branch of AUSTRONESIAN LANGUAGES. It is the language of the politically divided island group of Samoa in the western Pacific (see map at TONGAN). There are migrant communities in Hawaii, New Zealand, Australia and the United States.

Western Samoa has about 160,000 inhabitants, American Samoa about 30,000. In spite of the political frontier Samoan has no important geographical dialects. But the standard language does differ considerably from the colloquial. Colloquial Samoan is called *Tautala leaga*, 'bad language'. *Tautala lelei* 'good language' is used formally – in broadcasting, in church and school,

in writing, in poetry and in talking to Europeans. A polite register, with some hundreds of special words, is used when talking to people of high status.

Tautala lelei has thirteen consonants; *tautala leaga* has only ten, lacking *t n r*. There are no consonant clusters or final consonants, so 'ice cream' becomes *aisakulimi* in Samoan.

The first ten numerals in Samoan are: *tasi, lua, tolu, fā, lima, ono, fitu, valu, iva, sefulu*.

Based on Ulrike Mosel, 'Samoan' in *Comparative Austronesian dictionary* ed. Darrell P. Tryon (Berlin: Mouton De Gruyter, 1995–) pt 1 pp. 943–6 and other sources

SAMOYEDIC LANGUAGES

These form a distinct branch of the URALIC LANGUAGES, spoken by very small numbers of forest and tundra dwellers and traders in western Siberia. The three northern Samoyedic languages are Nenets, Enets and Nganasan. Several southern Samoyedic languages are known from reports by 19th-century travellers, but only one – Selkup – survives.

Nenets, Enets and *Nganasan* are words of the same origin: they mean 'real person' in the respective languages. *Söl'qup*, in the Selkup language, means 'earth man', a reminder, perhaps, that the Selkup used to live in underground houses excavated in steep river banks. *Yurak*, the traditional outsiders' name for Nenets, seems to be a Russian version of the Nenets word for 'friend' – which is how the Nenets would have described themselves when negotiating trading links with the Russians.

In Nenets nouns have seven cases and four declensions, known to linguists as absolute, pos-sessive, predestinate-possessive and predicative. In the two possessive declensions, nouns are inflected for three persons and three numbers (singular, dual and plural) as well as for case. The total number of possible forms for each noun runs into hundreds: *we'* 'dog', *wengkayunyi* 'my two dogs', *wengkayud* 'your two dogs' . . .

Scattered and fragmented as the Samoyedic languages and dialects are, their speakers are linguistically sophisticated. Most are multilingual: they regularly come into contact not only with other Samoyedic languages but also Khanty and Mansi (see HUNGARIAN), YAKUT and Dolgan, TUNGUSIC LANGUAGES such as Evenki, and, ever increasingly, RUSSIAN.

The most widespread language of the group is *Nenets* or Yurak, spoken by 27,000 people. There are two dialects. About 1,000, spread over an area of nearly fifty thousand square kilometres, speak Forest Nenets. They hunt, fish and keep small herds of reindeer. The remainder range the tundra between the White Sea and the Yenisei

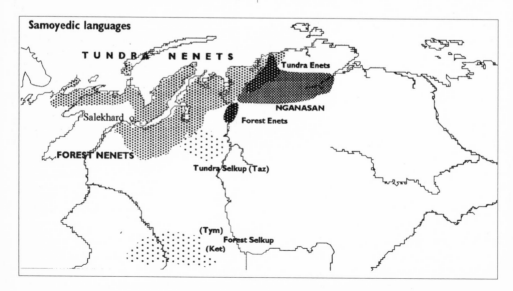

Samoyedic languages

delta, and speak Tundra Nenets. With their huge herds of thousands of reindeer they go north to the Arctic coast in summer, south to the forest edge in winter. The two dialects sound rather different, but most vocabulary is shared. Standard written Nenets, used in local primary schools, is based on the Tundra dialect of Bolshaya Zemlya.

Enets or Yenisei Samoyed, a closely related language, is spoken by an ethnic group of about 300, subdivided into four clans. Two-thirds of them, 'Tundra Enets', live as nomads on the tundra east of the Yenisei estuary. The rest, 'Forest Enets', occupy a taiga region close to the right bank of the Yenisei.

Nganasan or Tavgi has about 900 speakers in the vast Arctic wastes of the Taimyr Peninsula. They are traditionally hunters of wild reindeer. An eastern group, *Aja*' or 'younger brothers', are former Evenki speakers whose language nowadays is a distinct form of Nganasan.

Selkup is properly the name for one localised northern dialect, which is the basis for the written form of Selkup (or Ostyak Samoyed) used in schools. Fishers, hunters and foragers, its speakers live on the banks of the Taz, Turuhan, Baïkha and Yelogui rivers. Northern (Taz), Central (Tym) and Southern (Ket) dialects, each with sub-dialects, are easily distinguished – yet the total number of speakers is only about 2,000.

Founder of Samoyed linguistics

Mathias Alexander Castrén (1813–52) travelled at the request of the Russian Imperial Academy of Sciences. A colleague of Elias Lönnrot (see FINNISH), he made two epic journeys in Arctic Russia, preparing reports, ethnographic studies, grammars and wordlists of many languages. Castrén was appointed Professor of Finnish at Helsinki in 1851, and married in the same year. His health broken by tireless exploration in inhospitable climates and primitive conditions, he died a few months later.

Numerals in two Samoyedic languages (from Castrén's notes)

Forest Nenets		Selkup
ngop	1	oker
shtye	2	sitte
nyahar	3	naagur
tyeat	4	teetta
samblyang	5	somblea
mat'	6	muktet
sheu	7	seeldyu
shenttyeat	8	sitte tyaadin göt
kashem yut	9	oker tyaadin göt
yut	10	kööt

The origin of the numerals '8' and '9' – 'two less than ten', 'one less than ten' – is more obvious in Selkup than in Nenets. The Latin numerals '18' and '19', *duodeviginti, undeviginti*, are built in just the same way.

From *Samojedische Sprachmaterialien gesammelt von M. A. Castrén und T. Lehtisalo* (Helsinki: Suomalais–Ugrilainen Seura, 1960)

SANGO

PERHAPS 5,000,000 SPEAKERS OF SANGO AS A LINGUA FRANCA

Central African Republic

Sango is a creole based on a dialect of Ng-bandi, which is one of the Ubangi group of NIGER-CONGO LANGUAGES, with a very long history in the Ubangi valley. Sango is now the 'national language' of the Central African Republic.

Sango was the dialect of a fishing people living around Mobaye on the River Ubangi. In the 19th century Sango began to be known as a language of trade westwards and downriver among the Gbanziri and Buraka, but it was after 1889, when the French founded their fort Bangui (now capital of the Central African Republic), that the use of Sango (by now a simplified, pidginised off-shoot of the original dialect) grew more rapidly. French traders, soldiers and administrators used the river for communications, and took many of the Gbanziri, Buraka and other river people into their service. Where French was as yet un-known, Sango had to be the common language in which communication took place.

This language of trade and urban employ-ment is known in French as *Sango Commercial*, and its own users call it *Sango tí Salawísi* 'Working Sango' – *salawísi* comes from French *service* 'employment'. It developed by way of *Sango ti tulúgu*, 'Soldiers' Sango'.

When colonial development turned inland, Sango was already the favoured language in local government, the army and trade. It was also easy for most people to learn, deriving as it does from a member of the Ubangi group. Thus it now serves as a second language almost throughout the Central African Republic, for speakers whose mother tongues are Banda, GBAYA, Gubu, Lang-basi, Manja, Mono, Togbo – all of them Ubangi languages – and for speakers of Kare, a Bantu language. Historically, to travel, to trade, to find work outside one's home village, to be sophis-ticated, one had to know Sango.

Christian missionaries found Sango essential to their purposes. It was they who developed a written form of the language for textbooks and Bible translations, which began to appear in the 1920s. However, the Roman Catholics and the Protestants did not work together. The Protes-tants use a standard form of the language, and a spelling, based on the dialect of Bossangoa in the north, while the Roman Catholic standard lan-guage and spelling originate from Mbaiki near Bangui.

The true standard, however, from which re-gional dialects borrow and to which they adapt more or less, is not that of the priests but of the traders and truck drivers, whose Sango is fairly homogeneous all over the country. The Sango spoken by children also tends to be much more uniform than that of their parents. While traders' and children's Sango borrows readily from French, old people's Sango is much more influenced by local languages.

In 1965 Sango officially became the national language of the Central African Republic, though French is the language used for official publications. Sango is still, for most people, a second language rather than a mother tongue, but in the big towns the number who speak only Sango and French, and never learn a regional language, is growing all the time.

The first ten numerals in Sango are: *ókɔ, óse, otá, osió, ukú, omaná, mbásámbárá, miombe, ngom-báya, bale ókɔ.*

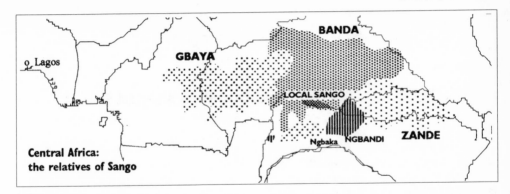

Central Africa:
the relatives of Sango

Banda, Zande, Sango, Ngbandi and Gbaya

Banda, Zande, Ngbandi and Gbaya are four Ubangian languages whose early speakers, at least three thousand years ago, migrated from the west into the area that is now divided between southern Sudan and the Central African Republic.

ZANDE speakers lived mostly in Sudan until, in the 18th century, they invaded the country between the Uele and Mbomu rivers, now in Congo (Kinshasa). Five Zande dialects are usually recognised.

Ngbandi speakers had earlier moved south-westwards to the land between the Ubangi and the Zaire. There are now 200,000 of them, mostly in Congo (Kinshasa). Most are bilingual in LINGALA, the major lingua franca of northern Congo. But meanwhile, through its own use as a lingua franca of the Ubangi fishing people and traders, Ngbandi has given rise to the much more important and widespread *Sango*.

BANDA and GBAYA are the hinterland languages of the Central African Republic. While Zande and Ngbandi speakers migrated in turn eastwards and south-westwards, Banda and Gbaya probably remained roughly where they were throughout the last two millennia, and have gradually split into numerous dialects, now so distinct that some are not mutually intelligible.

SANSKRIT

CLASSICAL LANGUAGE OF INDIA

Sanskrit is the linguistic parent of all the INDO-ARYAN LANGUAGES. It was the inspiration to the remarkable linguistic researches of ancient Indian grammarians – and it catalysed the development of linguistics in Europe in the 19th and 20th centuries.

Saṃskṛta, so named by later Indians, was 'the perfected language', by contrast with *Prākṛta*, 'the common language'.

No contemporary records in Sanskrit survive from before the 2nd century AD (when Indian rulers began to use Sanskrit, instead of everyday Prakrit, for their inscriptions). But the language is far older than that.

Vedic and classical Sanskrit

The oldest form of Sanskrit now known is in the venerable poems of the *Rgveda*, a collection of religious lyrics usually thought to have been composed around 1000 BC. They are the sacred texts of Hindu worship, transmitted orally for many centuries and still recited, word perfect, in modern rituals. The dialects in which they are composed must have been current somewhere in north-western India – not a 'perfected language' but a real spoken language of three thousand years ago.

From that point onwards, the history of Sanskrit diverges from that of the colloquial languages of India. In everyday speech, the early Vedic dialects developed and diverged, by way of the regional Prakrits of the first millennia BC and AD, into the Indo-Aryan languages of today.

Meanwhile, in ritual and in learned memory, around the *Rgveda* poems other texts gathered, in gradually developing forms of 'Vedic Sanskrit'. Successively the later Vedas, the Brahmanas, the Upaniṣads became canonical in their turn. There soon followed a vast scholarly apparatus of commentaries, paraphrases and glossaries whose purpose was to ensure the true pronunciation and correct understanding of the ancient collections.

This apparatus is so comprehensive that the *Rgveda* must certainly have been transmitted accurately from the mid first millennium BC until it was eventually written down. The linguistic work also led – about 400 BC – to the writing of a grammar, not of Vedic but of the somewhat later language of the scholars and commentators, which was evidently itself no longer the speech of every day. This grammar by Pāṇini, so concise and formulaic that commentaries on it have to be many times its length, is often admired (less often read) by modern theoretical linguists.

What Pāṇini fixed, and later authors wrote on his pattern, was 'classical Sanskrit'. It is a beautiful, flexible, musical language, the vehicle of remarkably luxuriant poetry and astonishingly concise prose. It was never anyone's mother tongue.

Classical Sanskrit literature flourished for a whole millennium after Pāṇini's time: in fact it has never ceased to be cultivated. Many of the earlier texts are now lost. Aśvaghoṣa's *Buddhacarita*, the story of the Buddha, written in the 1st century AD and known from later manuscripts, is one of the oldest that survives. Kālidāsa, who wrote plays and poetry in the 5th century, is the acknowledged master. Later writings stretched almost infinitely the flexibility of Pāṇini's linguistic design, with compound words of enormous length and ever more extravagant rhetorical figures.

The volume of classical Sanskrit literature is vast. The language is still used for poetry, technical writing and doctoral dissertations: modern Sanskrit works are regularly published. The readership is limited, but by no means vanishing. In the Indian census of 1971, 200,000 people claimed to speak the language. Sanskrit, and not only the Vedic Sanskrit of the *Rgveda*, can still be heard in the religious rituals of Hindu sects.

Sanskrit as a world language

In the early centuries AD Sanskrit gradually gained a role as the 'official' and learned language of all India – and of the many countries then under Indian political and religious influence. By now it was far removed from the everyday language of north India. It had to be learnt. Once learnt, it evidently served for communication very widely.

As a sign of its wide familiarity, a popular form of Sanskrit was used for oral epic poetry not long after Pāṇini's time. Eventually written down at vast length, the *Mahābhārata* became India's national epic. No less popular, the *Rāmāyaṇa* of Vālmīki, perhaps composed about AD 200, told the story of Rama using the same form. Their language is far simpler than that of contemporary classical Sanskrit poetry. They have inspired translations, imitations and retellings in all the modern languages of India.

There are Sanskrit inscriptions of the first millennium AD not only from India itself but also from Sri Lanka, Burma, Thailand, Cambodia, Vietnam, Malaya, Sumatra, Java and Borneo. While the very oldest Sanskrit inscription comes from India, almost as old is the stele of Vo-canh in Vietnam, about AD 200: by this time Sanskrit had become an elite language of the states of Fu-

nan and Champa in Indochina, as it was soon to be in the Malay archipelago. Sanskrit literature gave both themes and poetic forms to the literature, sculpture and painting of south-east Asia and Indonesia. All the languages of culture in the region have borrowed heavily from Sanskrit.

The holy texts of Buddhism, first composed in PALI, were translated into Sanskrit, fleshed out with extensive new writings and commentaries, and studied in China, Japan and Tibet. At first it was a very strange kind of Sanskrit, Prakrit words put back artificially into Sanskrit shapes, 'Buddhist Hybrid Sanskrit'. Likewise the Jain holy texts, originally in ARDHAMAGADHI, accrued Sanskrit translations and commentaries. Not only inscriptions but versified state histories, such as the Kashmiri Kalhana's *Rājataraṅginī*, show the importance of Sanskrit to Indian royal courts.

The nature of Sanskrit

It was in the 18th century that Europeans began seriously to explore the literary culture of India. From the beginning, those who learnt the classical language, Sanskrit, were impressed by its similarity to the Greek and Latin of their own school and university studies. Some thought it was actually the parent language of Greek and Latin: for the rather different view of Sir William Jones, essentially a view that linguists would still accept, see box at INDO-EUROPEAN LANGUAGES. The 'perfection' of Sanskrit – the complexity of its forms and the impressive way that the tradition of Pāṇini had reduced them to rule – continued to enthrall linguists: 19th-century at-

---

A list of Hindu divinities

बभ्रुरेको विष्णुः सूनरो युवाञ्ज्यङ्क्ते हिरण्ययम्
[Soma]
योनिमक आ ससाद घोतनो sन्तर्दवेषु मेधिरः
[Agni]
वाशीमेको बिभर्ति हस्त आयसीमन्तर्देवेषु निधुविः
[Tvaṣṭr]
वज्रमेको बिभर्ति हस्त आहितं तन वृत्राणि जिघ्नते
[Indra]
तिग्ममेको बिभर्ति हस्त आयधं शुचिरुग्रो जलाषभेषजः
[Rudra]

One – brown, bitextile, cheerful, young –
gilds him with sweet gold.
One, nestling, flames in his furrow,
wise amid the gods.
One's hand holds an adze of iron,
working amid the gods.
One's hand holds a skybolt fast:
with it he kills his foes.
One's hand holds a piercing blade –
bright, angry, drenching, calming . . .
Rgveda 8.29, attributed to Kasyapa or Vaivasvata Manu

Indo-Aryan horse races

Older than the oldest surviving Sanskrit texts, there is indirect evidence that a mysterious Indo-Aryan language was known, far away to the west, in the Hurrite-speaking kingdom of the Mitanni in eastern Anatolia. An émigré or captive Mitannian named Kikkuli wrote a manual of horsemanship in HITTITE – in which he incorporated technical terms, for the length of a race as measured in 'turns' of the course, that are unmistakably Indo-Aryan:

eka-vartanna	one-lap
tera-vartanna	three-lap
panza-vartanna	five-lap
satta-vartanna	seven-lap
navartanna	nine-lap

No Indo-Aryan language texts survive in Near Eastern cuneiform. How did these exotic words get into their author's vocabulary? The Mitanni must have learnt their horsemanship skills from Indo-Aryan teachers, by way of a diplomatic link, a migration or a conquest that is otherwise quite unrecorded.

The words listed above can be compared with the Sanskrit numerals in the next box.

Numerals in Sanskrit and Pali

Sanskrit		Pali
ekas	1	eko
dvau	2	dve
trayas	3	ti
catvāras	4	catu
pañca	5	pañca
ṣaṭ	6	cha
sapta	7	satta
aṣṭau	8	aṭṭha
nava	9	nava
daśa	10	dasa

climate – from any country where proto-Indo-European may have been spoken. Words for plants, animals and products specific to India were borrowed or newly coined. *Tāla* 'palm', *khala* 'threshing-floor' came from DRAVIDIAN LANGUAGES; *marica* 'pepper' came from an Austroasiatic language; *hastin* 'elephant' was an invented word, literally 'the one with a hand [on its trunk]'.

Sanskrit in writing

Sanskrit can be written and printed in almost any of the scripts of south and south-east Asia – and it still is. Most often used nowadays is the Devanagari of north Indian languages. The standard Latin transliteration given in the box was adopted by a congress of Orientalists a century ago and is almost universally accepted among modern scholars.

Additional symbols for ṝ and ḹ scarcely occur in practice.

tempts at reconstructing proto-Indo-European still look too much like Sanskrit and not enough like the European offspring of the family.

Sanskrit is indeed in many ways our closest single source for proto-Indo-European. It was spoken, however, a world away – in geography and in

Sanskrit in Devanagari and Roman

अ आ इ ई उ ऊ ऋ ऌ ए ऐ ओ औ क्ख ग घ ङ च छ ज झ ञ ट ठ ड ढ ण त थ द ध न प फ ब भ म य र ल व श ष स ह

a ā i ī u ū r̥ l̥ e ai o au k kh g gh ṅ c ch j jh ñ ṭ ṭh ḍ ḍh ṇ t th d dh n p ph b bh m y r l v ś ṣ s h

SANTALI

4,000,000 SPEAKERS

India, Bangladesh

Santali is one of the Munda languages of rural eastern India (see map at MUNDARI). These are now known to belong to the family of AUSTROASIATIC LANGUAGES.

Santali is spoken in the western districts of West Bengal; there are about 100,000 speakers in Bangladesh. It is traditionally an unwritten language; speakers who learn to read and write do so in Bengali or Oriya, and on the occasions when Santali is written, Bengali or Oriya scripts are generally used. Christian missionaries and their followers have preferred Latin script.

As with its close relative Mundari, Santali and its speakers have little recorded history before the 19th century. While Mundari are typically hill peoples, many Santali speakers are lowland farmers (see box at MUNDARI): many, too, have migrated to Assam to find work in the tea plantations there.

The most important scholarly work on Santali is the great five-volume dictionary by the missionary P. W. Bodding, published in Oslo in 1929–36. Bodding's Santali grammar remained unfinished at his death.

Numerals in MUNDARI and Santali

Mundari		Santali
mid'	1	mit'
barya	2	bar
apia	3	pɛ
upunia	4	pɔn
mõrea	5	mɔ̃rɛ̃
turwia	6	turui
ēa	7	eae
irylia	8	irɪl
ārea	9	arɛ
gelea	10	gɛl

The traditional counting system continues in twenties up to '400'. '20' in Santali is *mit' isi*. In both Mundari and Santali, however, the native numerals are used less than before: Hindi (or, in the case of Santali, Bengali) numerals are taking their place.

The checked *t'* in Santali *mit'* 'one' was the same sound which 'has received wide publicity in Harry Lauder's pronunciation of *Sat'urday night*', according to the missionary linguist R. M. Macphail.

In search of a tradition

'The Santali *Ol Cemet'* script was devised about fifty years ago by a Santal, Pandit Raghunath Murmu, as part of his extensive program for culturally upgrading the Santali community. As he saw it, every respectable high-culture language in India had its own script and an old (written) literature. He provided Santali with an ingenious, indigenous, and custom made script, and was also responsible for providing a Santali classical epic as the Santali analogue to the [Sanskrit] *Mahābhārata*. The script is not based on Devanagari principles; it is an alphabet with all vowels indicated by separate letters ordered linearly on the Roman model.'

Norman H. Zide in *Current trends in linguistics* vol. 5 (The Hague: Mouton, 1969) pp. 425–6

SARA

900,000 SPEAKERS

Chad

S ara, a group of dialects belonging to the NILO-SAHARAN LANGUAGES, is spoken in the south-western corner of Chad, south of N'Djamena, between the Logone and Chari rivers.

Sara speakers were particularly mobile during the French suzerainty in central Africa. Many of them worked on the Congo–Ocean railway from Brazzaville to Pointe-Noire, others at the port cities of Congo (Brazzaville), Gabon and Camer-oun, others again at desert outposts in Chad and Niger, where they served in the militia. In colonial times, therefore, Sara was heard in many of the larger towns of French central Africa.

Sara has three tones, which are important in verb conjugation. It has the unusual feature of a doubled plural form: *de* 'person', *dege* 'people', *degege* 'parties of people'.

SARDINIAN

PERHAPS 1,500,000 SPEAKERS

Sardinia

The Sardinian dialects are widely recognised as a language separate from ITALIAN (see map there). Of all the ROMANCE LANGUAGES, Sardinian is agreed to be the closest to classical Latin. Why?

The answer is that Sardinia was one of the earliest Roman conquests, in 238 BC. Latin must soon have been widely used there, as a lingua franca of the army, administration and trade. And this was early Latin, pre-classical even, before the rapid changes that were soon to affect the language. The last population upheaval was in 177, when tens of thousands of Sardinians were sold in Italy as slaves. After the vast conquests of the 1st century, when population interchanges and troop movements were spreading the 'vulgar' Latin of the empire, Sardinia, no longer rebellious, had become a backwater.

In medieval times Catalan and Spanish were the languages of government in Sardinia. Italian was little used there until 1714, but since that time it has been the official and literary language of the island. Long despised and rejected by Italian authorities, Sardinian is a language almost without literature, although occasional records of the language go back as far as AD 1080. It has now been recognised as a regional language of Sardinia, in second place to Italian, a change of status which may help to keep Sardinian alive. It is still widely used on the island, though all younger people are bilingual in Italian.

Sardinian was already seen by medieval Italians as quite a different language from their own: Dante, who wrote on the Italian dialects, saw Sardinian as something distinct, 'imitating Latin as apes imitate men'. In a troubadour verse by Raimbaut de Vacqueyras an imagined Genoese lady finds her suitor's Provençal as difficult as the speech of 'a German or Sardinian or Berber': *no t'entend plui d'un Toesco, o Sardo o Barbari*.

While all the other Romance languages developed a seven-vowel system, Sardinian retains the five vowels of classical Latin. There are four dialects. Logudorese, spoken inland, is least affected by Spanish, Catalan and Italian, and gives the strongest impression of closeness to Latin.

Corsican is spoken by about 170,000 inhabitants of the island of Corsica, which has been French territory almost continuously since 1769 – coincidentally the year in which the most famous Corsican, Napoleon Bonaparte, was born. The language shows natural similarities to the Tuscan dialects of Italian, with independent features deriving from the curious history of Corsica, which has seldom accepted external rule without resistance. French has been the language of education and administration for well over a century: Corsican survives, so far, in local and household contexts.

Numerals in Italian, Sardinian and Corsican

	Italian	Sardinian	Corsican
1	uno, una	unu, una	unu
2	due	duos, duas	dui
3	tre	tres	tre
4	quattro	battor	quàtru
5	cinque	kimbe	cinque
6	sei	ses	sei
7	sette	sette	sette
8	otto	otto	ôttu
9	nove	nove	novu
10	dieci	deke	dèce

SASAK

2,100,000 SPEAKERS

Indonesia

Sasak, one of the AUSTRONESIAN LANGUAGES, is spoken on the island of Lombok, east of Bali.

The island was politically and culturally under Balinese influence from the 17th century until recently but, unlike Bali, it is largely Muslim. Sasak has thus been influenced both by Balinese and by Arabic, as well as by Malay and its newer official form, Indonesian. The same *aksara* 'script' used for JAVANESE (see table there) and Balinese has also been used in the past for Sasak, but most of those who write the language now adopt the Latin script familiar from Indonesian.

The first ten numerals in Sasak are: *səkek, duə, təlu, əmpat, limə, nəm, pitu', balu', siwa', sə-pulu.*

Balinese, Sasak and Sumbawa

The three languages are close to one another linguistically.

Sasak, spoken in Lombok, is traditionally divided into five dialect groups: *ngeno-ngene, meno-mene, mriak-mriku, kuto-kute, ngeto-ngete.*

BALINESE is spoken in Bali and Nusa Penida,

Indonesia: Balinese, Sasak and Sumbawa

with an enclave in Lombok. The conservative Mountain dialects are to be distinguished from the Lowland group; within this, the north-eastern dialects form the standard of the press and media, while the dialect of Denpasar, in the south, is quite distinctive. Balinese dominance of Sasak radiated from the area of Mataram and Cakranegara, where there are still about 80,000 speakers of Balinese.

Sumbawa is the language of the western extremity of Sumbawa island. It has about 300,000 speakers.

SEMITIC LANGUAGES

This group of languages of the Near East shares a similar grammatical structure and easily recognised relationships among words: it is clear that they descend from a single, lost, 'proto-Semitic' language, perhaps spoken about four thousand years ago. The Semitic group is more distantly related to several others in a family spanning much of north Africa: together they are usually known as the AFROASIATIC LANGUAGES.

> The *Semitic* group is so called because A. L. Schlözer, in 1781, looking for a term to denote the group including ARABIC, HEBREW and ARAMAIC, saw that the speakers of these languages were descendants of Noah's son Shem or Sem, according to the biblical story in Genesis 10.21–31 and 11.10–26.

Later it was observed that the South Arabian languages, classical ETHIOPIC and many of the modern languages of Ethiopia (see AMHARIC and map there) belong to the Semitic group too. And as cuneiform tablets and inscriptions of the ancient Near East began to be deciphered, in the 19th century, some of these languages, notably AKKADIAN, turned out to be Semitic as well.

In the earliest written records, speakers of Semitic languages – Akkadian, Hebrew, Phoenician and others – lived in what are now Iraq, Syria, Lebanon, Jordan and Israel.

> *Ugaritic* is the name given to the language of the ancient city of Ugarit (modern Rās Šamra). A rich collection of texts in Ugaritic dates from the 14th and 13th centuries BC. It was a North-west Semitic language, with a unique feature – its script is cuneiform (formed of wedge-shaped strokes for impressing on clay tablets) like Akkadian, yet it is a true alphabet, each symbol representing a single consonant as in Hebrew and Arabic.

Phoenician inscriptions come from the cities along the eastern coast of the Mediterranean and are dated between the 10th and 1st centuries BC. They also are in an alphabetic script, and one that was not designed for writing on clay tablets. These early Phoenician scripts are again crucial in the history of the alphabet: they were the source from which the first known Aramaic, Hebrew, Moabite and Samaritan alphabets developed. Inscriptions in Punic, a variety of Phoenician, are known from the neighbourhood of ancient Carthage, the powerful Phoenician colony in what is now Tunisia. An Etruscan–Phoenician bilingual inscription, unfortunately too short to help much with the decipherment of Etruscan, was found at Pyrgi in Italy.

Semitic languages share an important structural peculiarity. Roots, embodying a basic meaning, consist of consonants alone: vowels are inserted, and prefixes and suffixes added, in fixed patterns, to make complete noun and verb forms and other derivatives.

It may well be because of this feature (also true of ancient EGYPTIAN and other Afroasiatic languages) that early alphabets, developed for Egyptian and the early Semitic languages, provide symbols for consonants only: the reader was able to insert vowels in reading based on a knowledge of the general structure of the language. This feature made for quicker writing. However, when applied to languages with quite different structures, such writing conventions were inadequate. The later history of alphabets is partly a history of the solutions to this early design fault.

For maps of the modern Semitic languages see ARABIC, ARAMAIC, AMHARIC.

SENA

1,200,000 SPEAKERS

Mozambique

ena is the name for one of the BANTU LAN-GUAGES, one that is closely related to the now better-known NYANJA (see map there). It is spoken south of the Nyanja-speaking region, in central Mozambique. In Portuguese colonial times Sena was regarded as one of the three major African languages of the country.

Historically it is the language of an ancient town, *Sena* – a nexus of trade on the lower Zambezi – and of the surrounding peoples. When first described in Portuguese sources, in 1571, Sena had probably already been in existence for some centuries, used by Muslim – Arabic- and Swahili-speaking – traders who dealt in the cotton cloth of this region and in the gold that came from the old-established annual fairs of the Manyika goldfields far inland (see SHONA). The Portuguese built a settlement nearby, with a church dedicated to St Catherine of Siena, and until the 1760s Sena was a centre of Portuguese rule in central Mozambique. Tete later took its place.

The first grammar of Sena was written by an anonymous Portuguese around 1680 – a reminder of its early importance in European trade. He called it *Arte da lingua de Cafre*, 'Grammar of the language of Kaffir'. In later sources the language appears as *Cafreal de Sena*, *Chisena* or *Senna*.

SERBIAN, CROATIAN AND BOSNIAN

18,500,000 SPEAKERS

Serbia, Croatia, Bosnia, Montenegro

These are the current names for one of the South SLAVONIC LANGUAGES, best known as Serbo-Croat, the majority language of the former Federal Republic of Yugoslavia.

Illyrian dialects (possibly related to modern Albanian) had been spoken in the western Balkans at the time of the Roman conquest, and had gradually been supplanted by Latin. Romans called the region *Illyria* and *Dalmatia* (both names have occasionally been used for Serbo-Croat). Slavonic speakers probably settled here in the 6th and 7th centuries AD.

The division between Croatians and Serbians is in origin a religious one. After conversion to Christianity, in the 9th century, both groups used the OLD SLAVONIC liturgy. The Croatians, gradually aligning themselves to Rome, retained the Glagolitic alphabet of the earliest Slavonic texts – and eventually adopted Latin script for everyday use. The Serbians maintained their links with Constantinople, and Serbia became one of the main centres of literacy in Old Slavonic in the widely used Cyrillic script. A third religious element entered the scene when, after the Turkish conquest of Serbia and Bosnia, Islam gradually spread in the cities and towns of Bosnia, and there the language was sometimes written in Arabic script.

Croatia remained largely outside the Turkish Empire: here the languages of power until the end of the 19th century were the German of Austria and the Italian of Venice, the latter particularly along the Adriatic coast. Montenegro (*Crnagora*, the 'Black Mountain') maintained an obscure independence.

In spite of political and religious divides and in spite of the different scripts, the language spoken over this whole region was relatively uniform. Until the 18th century the languages of literature, education and government were very varied – German, Hungarian, Italian, Latin, Old Slavonic, Slavenoserbian (a mixture of Russian Church Slavonic and Serbian), Turkish. There had been some writing in the local language, mostly in Croatia, with varying spellings.

Vuk Karadžić (1787–1864), a Serbian who lived for most of his life in Vienna, was inspired by Bosnian–Serbian folk poetry to spread the use of the popular language. He received support from Jernej Kopitar, the Slovene linguistic reformer. Vuk's collections of songs, beginning 1814, his grammar of 1814 and his dictionary of 1818 began the process of formulating a new Serbian national language. It was firmly based on a Hercegovinan dialect: Vuk had family links with the region, and much of the greatest folk poetry came from there. This choice did not please all Serbs – but it happened to place the new Serbian language very close to the dialects of Croatia, and by the Literary Accord of 1850 it was accepted as the literary language of Croatia too, replacing the local standards in which some Croatian literature had already been written.

Serbia and Montenegro continued to use the Cyrillic script. Croatia used Latin: so did Bosnia as the Arabic script fell out of use. Spelling reforms promulgated by Vuk and others made Latin and Cyrillic easily interchangeable.

In 1918, with the formation of Yugoslavia, for the first time nearly all the speakers of Serbo-Croat were under the same government. Their continuing cultural differences were marked by the division into Croatia, Bosnia, Serbia and Montenegro when Yugoslavia became a Federal Republic in 1945 – and were disastrously highlighted when it collapsed into warring states at the end of the 1980s.

The two standards, Croatian and Serbian, have now been joined and will grow further apart. They already differed in some features. Serbian has tended to borrow international terms from other languages, while Croatian has tended to invent words, often 'calques': Serbian *biblioteka*, Croatian *knjižica* 'library'. Besides this, Serbian is richer in Turkish and Greek loans while there are more numerous Latin and German words in Croatian.

Beyond the Balkans

Many Serbians fled northwards to Hungary after a failed revolt against Turkish rule in 1690. The Serbian population of Vojvodina, then in southern Hungary, dates from this migration. Vojvodina was incorporated in Yugoslavia in 1918. Under the Austrian Empire there were important communities of Serbo-Croat speakers in Vienna and Budapest.

Today, émigré Serbo-Croat speakers are numerous. There are at least 250,000 in the United States. Some Muslim speakers of Serbo-Croat have escaped religious persecution by fleeing to Turkey: as many as 100,000 had done so by 1980, and others have followed since the recent warfare in Bosnia.

A Croat community, now numbering 20,000, settled around Oberpullendorf, in Austria, in the 16th century. They were sometimes called Wasserkroaten (water Croats). Until 1921 the official language that surrounded them was Hungarian: now it is the German of Austria. There is some publishing in Croat in this district: the spoken language, however, has changed so much that people from Croatia can no longer understand it without help.

The names of Serbo-Croat

'The term "Serbo-Croatian", including names of both groups, has a very recent origin. In Serbo-Croatian the language is, or has been, called by the following names: *srpskohrvatski* and *hrvatskosrpski* "Serbo-Croatian, Croato-Serbian", *srpski ili hrvatski* and *hrvatski ili srpski* "Serbian or Croatian, Croatian or Serbian", *srpski* "Serbian", *hrvatski* "Croatian", *ilirski* "Illyrian", and occasionally even *naš jezik* or *naški* "our language". In the 18th century, regional terms like *slavonski* "Slavonian" were also common. These terms have been used with a number of meanings and connotations. Their exact significance depends as much on the writer's dialect as on the period involved. One of the striking features of the *Kniževni dogovor* "Literary Accord" of 1850, which established the principle of a unified literary language for the Serbs and Croats, is its failure to name the language. One wonders if this omission was deliberate or simply an oversight on the part of the signers.'

Kenneth E. Naylor, 'Serbo-Croatian' in *The Slavic literary languages: formation and development* ed. Alexander M. Schenker, Edward Stankiewicz (New Haven, 1980) pp. 65–83, abridged

The South Slavonic languages

Literary *Slovene* is based on the Lower Carniola (*Dolenjsko*) dialect with some features from *Gorenjsko*, which includes Ljubljana, to the north. The Slovene-speaking districts of Carinthia (*Korosko*) in Austria have dialect features linking them to Slovak and an archaic stress pattern.

Serbo-Croat dialects are customarily classified by the word used for 'what': *što, kaj* or *ča*. *Štokavian* covers all of Serbia, Montenegro and Bosnia and parts of Croatia. All the dialects are mutually intelligible, though the *Čakavian* of the northern Adriatic coast and islands is difficult for others because of its accentuation, which is more like that of Slovene and Russian. A division into

**The Serbian alphabet and
the Croatian/Bosnian equivalents**

А Б В Г Д Ђ Е Ж З И Ј К Л М Н
Њ О П Р С Т Ћ У Ф Х Ц Ч Џ Ш
а б в г д ђ е ж з и ј к л м н
њ о п р с т ћ у ф х ц ч џ ш
A B V G D Đ E Ž Z I J K L M N
Nj O P R S T Ć U F H C Č Dž Š
a b v g d đ e ž z i j k l m n
nj o p r s t ć u f h c č dž š

South-Eastern Europe:
South Slavonic languages

sub-dialects is made according to a typical vowel or diphthong developing from earlier Slavonic Ѣ. In most of Serbia the sub-dialect is *Ekavian* while in Croatia, Bosnia and Montenegro *Ijeka-vian* is most widespread.

Macedonian dialects can be classified by word stress: on the third syllable from the end in the widespread western dialects, on the second from the end in the Castoria and Florina areas of Greece, and variable in other northern Greek districts and in the Pirin region of Bulgaria.

Standard *Bulgarian* is based on the eastern dialects but with a mixture of western features. In the western dialects, as in Serbia, earlier Ѣ develops into *e*, while in the east it most often becomes *ya*. The western dialect of Sofia and its neighbourhood is known as *Shopski*.

SEYCHELLOIS

75,000 SPEAKERS

Seychelles

One of the FRENCH CREOLES, Seychellois or Seselwa or Seychelles Creole is the mother tongue of 95 per cent of the inhabitants of the Seychelles.

French was the language of the original colonisers. Under English rule, from 1811 to 1976, English was the language of administration, while French remained the language of the educated elite. Through this period the Creole of the majority was not used in writing or in any official context. The first book in Seychelles Creole, a translation of St Mark's Gospel, appeared only in 1974.

Shortly after independence, in 1981–2, Creole was declared the first national language (English and French being the other two) and became the language of primary education. There was a flood of reading books, textbooks and government publications in Creole.

SHAN

PERHAPS 3,000,000 SPEAKERS

Burma, China, Thailand

Shan belongs to the TAI LANGUAGES. Spoken by several million people in inner south-east Asia, Shan was once the ruling language of most of the 'Shan states' that used to maintain a precarious autonomy in the highland valleys between Burma, China and Thailand. The land routes linking Burma with China pass through this region, and Shans have traditionally been prominent in long distance trade.

Shan is a Burmese name. Speakers call themselves *Tai*, distinguishing southerners as *Tai Taü* and northerners as *Tayok* and *Tai Neua*.

Shan chronicles trace the history of some states as far back as the early 13th century: this includes the old principality of Mogaung, now Burmese-speaking, and the AHOM domain in the valley of Assam. In the vacuum left by the collapse of the Pagan kingdom in Burma, Shan-speaking rulers extended their power over much of the Burmese plains, but linguistically they were soon absorbed by the surrounding Burmese. In most of the remaining Shan states, Shan speakers were numerically dominant in the valleys, surrounded by numerous hill peoples, including speakers of WA, Palaung, HANI, LAHU and LISU. In the northern Shan states there is a complex cultural interchange among speakers of Shan and of JINGHPAW.

Shan is the most widely spoken language of two adjacent administrative districts. One is the Shan State in eastern Burma, over which the Burmese Army and local warlords have fought for decades. North of this is the Dehong Dai autonomous region of Yunnan, China. Shan is also the dominant language in the Maehongson district in north-western Thailand.

Shan is a written language with its own alphabet, which, like that of Burmese, is an adaptation of the MON script. The traditional culture is Theravada Buddhist, originally acquired by way of Burma. Buddhist 'birth stories' and other local legends are written in Shan; the scriptures are studied in PALI, which is written not in Shan but in Burmese script.

The best-known dialect has been the Burmese Shan standard of the old city of Möngnai, once a state capital and the seat of a Burmese viceroy. Chinese Shan or Tai Nüa is the dialect of the Shan-speaking districts of Yunnan. Between these two falls the dialect of Hsenwi, a state that used to maintain close relations with the Chinese administration. Northern Burmese Shan is perceptibly different from the southern dialect, with six tones instead of five. For a table of numerals see TAI LANGUAGES.

A Shan city in decay

'From Möngnai a fine view of the whole valley. On the west are abrupt jungle-covered rocks crowned with pagodas. The slope is finely wooded, and for the great part overgrown with jungle. A long road, which might be made into a magnificent drive, leads up to the town. The brick walls are about ten feet high, machicolated and falling to ruins. The town has every sign of having been at one time fine and spacious, now a pitiful wreck. Pitched [camp] in the centre of the town by the side of the road under a pipal tree. Shortly after arrival the Prince sent me four watermelons and two water-jars.'

Sir George Scott: Diary, May 1887 (India Office Library and Archives)

Shan and Ahom

There are three major subdivisions of Shan, in terms both of dialect and of culture. *Southern Burmese Shan* roughly matches the area administered from Möngnai (Burmese *Monè*) before the British conquest, and the western part of the 'Southern Shan States' of British rule. *Northern Burmese Shan* is spoken in the area administered from Hsenwi (Burmese *Theinni*) in the 18th and 19th centuries, the 'Northern Shan States' of British rule. In earlier centuries this area acknowledged Chinese suzerainty. *Chinese Shan* (or Tai Nüa, Tai Mao) is the language of the states to the north and east of these, which have generally been subject to China and are now grouped in the Dehong Dai autonomous region.

There are smaller, more scattered remnants of Shan states in north-western Burma, notably in the valley of Hkamti Long, where there are about 3,000 remaining speakers of Hkamti Shan. Shan rule once stretched as far as the valley of Assam, where until the 18th century AHOM was the ruling language.

South-East Asia: Shan

Shan scripts

The traditional alphabet, shown here, has not enough symbols to express the sounds of Shan fully. There are two standard styles of writing, known traditionally as Burmese Shan (with rounded characters) and Chinese Shan (a cursive script). Based on these different styles, new extended alphabets, with symbols indicating the tones, have now been adopted in printing in Burma and China. The Hkamti script, a third variety, is now almost forgotten.

The Shan alphabet

ka kha nga sa hsa nya ta hta na pa hpa ma ya ra la wa sha ha a

SHONA

8,000,000 SPEAKERS

Zimbabwe, Mozambique

One of the BANTU LANGUAGES, Shona is the overall standard form of the dialects that are spoken by most inhabitants of the country once called Southern Rhodesia. Shona is now the national language and lingua franca of independent Zimbabwe. There are also many speakers of Shona dialects in Mozambique.

No local traditional name is known for the whole Shona group as now defined: people generally used to identify themselves with smaller ethnic groupings. *Shona* is in origin a name applied by NDEBELE speakers to the conquered population, but it is now widely accepted. From it come the older English terms *Mashona* for the people, *Mashonaland* for their territory, and *Chishona* for the Zezuru dialect.

In stark contrast with the Bantu languages that lie to the south, from NDEBELE to XHOSA, Shona comprises a series of distinct, related dialects each of which has a fairly compact territory. This testifies to a long period of relatively peaceful development *in situ*, and makes it almost certain that early Shona speakers were the builders of the 8th- and 9th-century stone *zimbabwe*, the towns and burial places whose ruins are the most striking archaeological feature of the country, and after which it has now been named.

Portuguese reports of the 16th and 17th centuries describe the Empire of Monomotapa and name several peoples who can be identified with still-existing Shona ethnic groups and dialects, notably *Manica* and *Mocaranga* (Manyika and Karanga), the latter being the most powerful.

The first recorded foreign invasion is that of the NDEBELE, in 1838: they conquered some southern Shona districts and established supremacy over the rest. It was not long after this that David Livingstone travelled through 'Mashonaland', visiting and naming the Victoria Falls in 1855. English-speaking settlers, at first under the auspices of Cecil Rhodes's British South Africa Company, held power for a hundred years until independence in 1980.

Shona dialects were first used in writing by Christian missionaries, who began to work among Shona speakers in 1859 and produced religious books and Bible translations in Karanga, Zezuru, Manyika and Ndau.

The dialects were so close to one another that the competition of several written forms within Southern Rhodesia was seen as undesirable by the British colonial administration, both for its own reasons and for the sake of the nascent publishing industry. In 1931 the linguist Clement Doke recommended that Shona and NDEBELE be the two official African languages of the territory, and that the official literary form of Shona be based on the Karanga and Zezuru dialects. These were grammatically very much alike, they were the largest two dialects in terms of number of speakers, and Zezuru was the dialect of the capital (then called Salisbury).

Foreign loanwords in Shona include *mufarinya* 'cassava' from Portuguese *farinha* 'flour'; *mutsara* 'line' from Swahili *mstari* and originally Arabic *mistara* 'ruled line on paper'. Shona also has numerous Afrikaans loanwords.

The first ten numerals are: *poshi, piri, tatu, cina, shanu, tanhatu, cinomnge, rusere, pfumbamnge, gumi.*

Shona literature and music

'Traditional literature is expressed in clan histories, folktales and proverbs. In the folk tales the principal character is the Hare (Sulo, Shulwe, Tsuro), who assumes many qualities, but there are also other important animals – lion, zebra, baboon – and some well-known human [characters]. Stories are told at night by one of the family elders, and while a few of the tales point a moral, the main emphasis is on entertainment.

'There are war songs, hunting songs, love songs, work songs and ritual songs. Most songs among the Shona are associated with musical accompaniment and frequently with action. Karanga of the Victoria District are outstanding composers of the whole country, and many of their musical compositions have spread, with variations, from one tribe to another.

'Dancing is also highly developed, and in association with song and musical accompaniment marks such social events as marriages, funeral ceremonies (at which the women sing) and exorcism.'

Hilda Kuper, 'The Shona' in *Ethnographic survey of Africa. Southern Africa* part 4 (London: International African Institute, 1954) p. 14, abridged

The standardisation of literary Shona

Recommendation 5. That a dictionary of Shona be prepared, to be as inclusive as possible of words from Zezuru, Karanga, Manyika, and Ndau. That for the present Korekore words be admitted sparingly and that the use of colloquial words from the dialects of Budya, Tavara, Karombe, Danda, Teve, Eangwe etc. be discouraged.

Clement C. Doke, *Report on the unification of Shona dialects*, Salisbury, 1931.

Doke's standard Shona has gradually come into being: the *Standard Shona dictionary* appeared at last in 1966. Doke's recommendations on spelling were less successful. Like many English-speaking linguists of his time, he liked the Africa Alphabet of the International Institute for African Languages and Cultures. He recommended a 33-letter version for Shona, with several characters not found on normal typewriters or in normal printing fonts. These were dropped in 1955, but it was only in 1967 that an adequate and generally acceptable orthography was introduced.

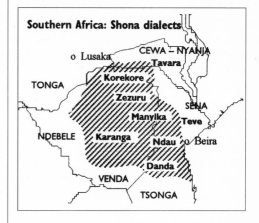

Southern Africa: Shona dialects

Shona lullaby

Rú-u, rú-u, rú-u, rú-u,
Harúrúhwe, wáchema mwaná –
Harúrúhwe, wáchema mwaná:
E, é, é, é, tazvínzwa, babá!
maítweíko, babá, wangu?
matadzírweíko némwana?

Rú-u, rú-u, rú-u, rú-u,
Harúrúhwe, the child is crying,
Harúrúhwe, the child is crying:
E, é, é, é, I heard your complaint, father!
What has been done to you, father?
How has your child offended you?

A. C. Hodza, *Shona praise poetry* (Oxford: Clarendon Press, 1979) p. 19

SINDHI

9,000,000 SPEAKERS

Pakistan, India

O ne of the INDO-ARYAN LANGUAGES, Sindhi is spoken in south-eastern Pakistan, centring on the city of Hyderabad. Within Sindhi territory, Karachi forms an enclave with a majority of Urdu speakers. There are also about a million Sindhi speakers in India – some settled close to the Pakistan border, others in trading communities in many of the big cities.

Sind, the lower Indus region, was the first part of India to be captured by the Muslims, in 712. Its name was already ancient – a variant of the river name, *Indus* in Latin but *Sindhu* in Sanskrit.

At the time of the Muslim conquest Indo-Aryan languages had already been spoken here for over a thousand years. From this point onwards, however, Sind was often to be politically distinct from neighbouring parts of India, and its language, too, gradually became distinct. Arabic and then Persian were the languages of government for a thousand years. Sindhi has, naturally, numerous loanwords from these languages and relatively few from Sanskrit.

There are a few early records of the Indo-Aryan speech of Sind, from the 8th century onwards, and evidence exists that literature in the local language was being written down. It is lost, however: as far as surviving texts are concerned, a native Sindhi literature begins at the end of the 15th century. Its main tradition is of lyric poetry, most often showing Sufi inspiration. The greatest Sindhi poet is perhaps Shah Abdul Latif of Bhit (1689–1752).

Sindhi is usually written in its own script, adapted in 1852, under British influence, from the Perso-Arabic script used for Urdu. Unlike Urdu, printed Sindhi is often typeset rather than calligraphed.

The first ten numerals in Sindhi are *hiku, bba, ṭī, cāre, pañja, cha, sata, aṭha, nava, ḍḍaha*.

Sindhi and Kacchi

Vicolī is the 'standard' dialect of Sindhi, on which the modern literary language is based. *Lāsī* is the dialect of Las Bela, *Lārī* that of the lower Indus. *Tharelī*, spoken in the eastern desert region, is close to Rajasthani. In the desert region of Cutch, in north-western Gujarat state, India, *Kacchī* has about 500,000 speakers. Linguistically it is best regarded as a Sindhi dialect, but its speakers use Gujarati as their literary language. When written, Kacchi uses the Gujarati alphabet.

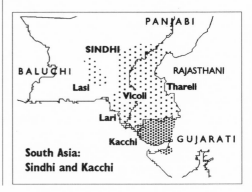

South Asia:
Sindhi and Kacchi

Kacchī balladry

Kumārī kandh namāyā, goṭeṃ ghā kerī:
coṭā jhalyā cosarā, vaḍhy ūṃ kandh vicā . . .

Virgins bowed their necks, bridegrooms struck the blows:
They seized their four-braided hair, and struck them across the neck.

The disastrous aftermath of the battle of Jhārā in 1762, when Ghulām Shāh Kalhorā of Sind conquered Cutch.

Linguistic Survey of India vol. 8 part 1 ed. Sir G. A. Grierson (Calcutta, 1919) pp. 201–6

SINHALA

12,000,000 SPEAKERS

Sri Lanka

Sinhala or Sinhalese is the majority language of Sri Lanka (Ceylon), spoken by at least two-thirds of the population. It is one of the INDO-ARYAN LANGUAGES, separated by hundreds of miles from its relatives, for in south India DRAVIDIAN LANGUAGES are spoken.

> The island figures as *Laṅkā* in classical Sanskrit literature, notably the epic *Rāmāyaṇa*, which tells the story of Rāma's invasion of the island to recover his captive wife Sitā. *Sri Lanka* (the honorific prefix *Śrī* is a modern embellishment) is thus a revival of an ancient name. But the island was better known as *Sinhāladvīpa*, locally *Sihaladipa* (a name already found in a Greek source of the 6th century): this is the origin of the language name *Sinhala* and of the traditional medieval and modern names for the island, Arabic *Sarandīb*, Portuguese *Ceilão*, English *Ceylon*.

How did Sinhala come to be spoken where it is? The Pali history of Sri Lanka, *Mahāvaṃsa*, tells that the language was brought to Sri Lanka by settlers under the leadership of Vijaya in the very year of the *nibbāna* or 'extinguishing' of the Buddha in distant northern India, a date given as 504 BC. Linguists have concluded that this cannot be far from the truth: for Sinhala branched off from the other Indo-Aryan languages at a very early stage, long before dialect divisions among them had hardened into language boundaries. An Indo-Aryan colonisation must indeed have taken place around the 6th century. And by the 3rd century BC inscriptions from Sri Lanka show that the ancestor of Sinhala had already developed some of the special features of modern Sinhala – notably the absence of

an aspirated/unaspirated distinction in consonants, one of the many ways in which Sinhala shows the influence of its Dravidian neighbour TAMIL.

The inscriptions are all that we have to trace the history of the language until the 9th century AD, the date of the earliest surviving Sinhala literature. The older poetic form of Sinhala, the vehicle of medieval poetry, is *Elu*. This was already an archaic tongue, one that had to be formally learnt, in the 13th century, for that was when the grammar *Sidatsaṅgarāva* was compiled, on the model of classical Tamil grammars. This venerable work now serves as a source of information on lost early literature. The dictionary tradition begins with *Piyummala*, a guide to poetic synonyms, dating from the 15th century – and, even earlier, with a Sinhala translation of the Pali dictionary *Abhidhānappadīpikā*.

Sri Lanka was an early stronghold of Buddhism and has remained one of the principal centres of this religion. Thus, throughout its history, Sinhala has coexisted with Pali, the classical language of Theravada Buddhism and the language of religious education. The two languages must at the outset have differed only slightly. Commentaries on Pali texts have been a traditional genre of Sinhala literature, and the language is full of Pali loanwords. For centuries Buddhist monks and scholars have travelled between Sri Lanka, Burma, Thailand and Cambodia.

The island was divided among seven kingdoms when first visited by Portuguese explorers in 1505. The final result of long warfare by Portuguese, Dutch and British invaders was that the whole island came under British rule from

1803 with the conquest of the kingdom of Kandy. Portuguese missionaries had made many converts to Christianity. Although Catholics were persecuted under Dutch rule, which lasted in Colombo from 1656 to 1795, as many as 10 per cent of the population are Catholics today.

A Sinhala–Dutch dictionary, the first involving a European language, appeared in 1759, and a Sinhala–English dictionary in 1821.

English was the medium of education till 1948. In independent Sri Lanka Sinhala was proclaimed the sole official language in 1956. A destructive civil war, concentrated in the north of the country where there is a Tamil-speaking majority, led to the emigration of large numbers of Tamil speakers, but eventually to the recognition in 1987 of official status for English and Tamil; the war, however, continues. English is often used informally in administrative contexts, but Sinhala remains the official national language and civil servants must be prepared and able to use it.

There is a considerable émigré population of Sinhala speakers in Singapore, Thailand, the United Arab Emirates and Canada.

Spoken as it is at a crossroads of international trade and travel, Sinhala has borrowed from many languages. It has been influenced by Dravidian languages, especially Tamil, in phonology, vocabulary and syntax. Portuguese became a powerful influence in the 16th century; Dutch and English followed. Loanwords include *kamise* 'shirt' and *keju* 'cheese' from Portuguese; *kokis* 'cake' and *almariya* 'wardrobe' from Dutch; *telifon* 'telephone', with many other modern terms, from English.

Sinhala has a suffixed definite article in singular nouns: *miniha* 'man', *minihek* 'the man', *minissu* 'men'. The first ten numerals are: *eka, deka, tuna, hatara, paha, haya, hata, aṭa, namaya, dahaya*.

Literary and colloquial Sinhala

What was said above of loanwords leads to the crucial distinction between literary or 'high' and colloquial or 'low' Sinhala: for while colloquial Sinhala adopts modern loanwords freely, the literary variety draws on Sanskrit, Pali and *Eḷu* for its abstract and technical vocabulary. The attraction of English is so powerful that it is noticeable in both varieties. In literary Sinhala one finds Sanskrit-like new compounds that turn out to be modelled ('calqued') on English compounds or expressions, while colloquial Sinhala has numerous pure borrowings from English.

Literary Sinhala is associated with Buddhism and education; it is the language of newspapers, official documents and formal oratory. It is used in media news reports and government forms. It is the language of most printed books, including poetry and novels (though passages of dialogue may be written in the colloquial language).

The difference between the two forms is so great that they may legitimately be regarded as two languages. It involves not only the vocabulary but also the basic structural words of the language and the grammar of noun and verb forms: in literary Sinhala verb forms are marked for person, in spoken they are not. Even the personal pronouns differ.

All speakers learn to understand literary Sinhala to some extent: its everyday uses make this ability almost indispensable. But not all learn it thoroughly. The vocabulary is the greatest barrier to the unpractised hearer or reader. It requires sound education and practised skills to produce literary Sinhala extempore for extended periods: relatively few speakers can do this without difficulty. Since 1947 there have been calls for the use of colloquial Sinhala as the official and literary standard, and this controversy continues. Meanwhile, a formal variety of colloquial Sinhala, with some of the grammatical features of the literary language, is now used in lectures, political speeches, sermons and pop songs.

Among the dialects of Sinhala, Kandyan shows more Tamil influence, partly because it lies nearer to areas of Tamil speech in Sri Lanka and India, partly because Kandy remained independent of European rule until 1803. The low-country dialect has adopted more loans from Portuguese, Dutch and English. The dialect of

Colombo and the south-west is becoming the national standard. Cutting across geographical borders, the dialects of *Rodiyas* or untouchables, and of *Ahikuntakayas* or travellers, are distinctive, with some of the features of a 'secret language' intended to exclude outsiders. Farmers and foragers are said to have a secret vocabulary of auspicious words to counteract the effect of evil spirits and to ward off the dangers of the forest.

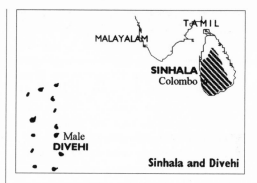

Sinhala and Divehi

Sinhala and Divehi

Sinhala is the majority language everywhere in Sri Lanka except in the north-east, where the majority speaks Tamil. Many Tamil speakers are bilingual in Sinhala.

The distinctive *Vedda* dialect is spoken by a small aboriginal group whose ancestors may be surmised to have spoken an unrelated language, now forgotten.

DIVEHI is the language of the Maldives, also spoken on Minicoy Island, India, where there are about 5,000 speakers.

The Sinhala script

The Sinhala alphabet is one of the descendants of Brahmi (see INDO-ARYAN LANGUAGES). Like other Indic scripts it is written from left to right.

In its development through the centuries the script has gradually become more rounded: it is perfectly adapted for writing on palm-leaves with a stylus. The usual printed fonts have exaggerated heavy and light strokes, which is not a feature of the handwritten script. The tiny loops and circles typical of Sinhala are easily confused in poorly printed text.

SINO-TIBETAN LANGUAGES

The Sino-Tibetan language family includes three main groups: CHINESE, the KAREN LANGUAGES and the Tibeto-Burman languages.

The fact of a relationship among the languages of the Tibeto-Burman branch has been recognised for many years. Karen is very different from these. Chinese differs even more extensively, and must have separated from the rest many thousands of years ago, but the phonetics and some of the vocabulary of proto-Sino-Tibetan have been successfully reconstructed and the ultimate relationship among these languages is not in doubt.

Their prehistory has not been fully worked out. It seems possible that proto-Sino-Tibetan was spoken, perhaps ten thousand years ago or more, in south-eastern China, not far from where the dialects ancestral to the AUSTRO-TAI LANGUAGES were also spoken. From here the speakers of early Karen and Tibeto-Burman dialects will have moved gradually westwards, though there is no evidence for the migration beyond the presence of those languages where they are now on the map of south-east Asia. Meanwhile speakers of early Chinese dialects will have spread generally north-westwards from their evident nucleus near the south-eastern coast.

Pyu, the earliest known written language of Burma, extinct for almost a thousand years, was also a Sino-Tibetan language: its closer relationships are uncertain. The Pyu stone inscriptions were deciphered by C. O. Blagden, in 1917, on the basis of the four-language Myazedi inscription at Pagan in central Burma.

It used to be assumed that the Miao-Yao languages (see MIAO and YAO) and the TAI LANGUAGES would turn out to be related to Sino-Tibetan, but that was a false lead. As monosyl-labic, tonal languages they are superficially very like Chinese; but then Chinese has changed drastically from its proto-Sino-Tibetan ancestor – and the changes may partly have been the result of interaction with early forms of Miao, Yao, Tai and other languages now believed to belong to the Austro-Tai family.

Proto-Sino-Tibetan was not as thoroughly monosyllabic as so many of its descendants are. Nor can proto-Sino-Tibetan tones be reconstructed, and it may not have been tonal at all, though again the great majority of modern Sino-Tibetan languages do make use of tones.

Reconstructing proto-Sino-Tibetan from the 'monosyllabic' languages of today

'If a high-powered racing car is driven at terrific speed into a cement wall, the results on the car will somewhat parallel those on polysyllabic Sino-Tibetan words. The front part will be greatly compressed, parts will have dropped out, and there will be considerable distortion; but the body will probably remain fairly intact.'

Robert Shafer, *Introduction to Sino-Tibetan* (Wiesbaden: Harrassavitzgh 1974) p. 21

The controversial subgrouping of Sino-Tibetan

The CHINESE languages make up one main division of Sino-Tibetan. Clearly related to the rest, they have been developing separately from them for many thousands of years.

The KAREN LANGUAGES are sufficiently distinct for most linguists to agree that they too form a main division, separate from both Chinese and Tibeto-Burman.

The Tibeto-Burman languages, the third division, have spread and divided far more widely than the other two. They pose a difficult problem of subgrouping – a solution to which would help to elucidate the prehistory of south-east Asia and southern China. The most likely subdivisions of Tibeto-Burman seem to be those numbered 1 to 5 below.

1. JINGHPAW or Kachin.

2. Rung. Languages that may belong to this group include Rawang, with 100,000 speakers in Kachin State, Burma, and Qiang or Ch'iang or Dzorgaish, with 130,000 speakers in Sichuan, China. Some scholars think that Tangut (cf. 4 below) belongs here.

3. Kado, a language with 200,000 speakers in Burma, China and Laos.

4. The Burmese-Lolo languages, including AKHA, Burmese, LAHU, LISU, Maru, Tujia and YI or Lolo: for all these see map at BURMESE. The extinct TANGUT or Hsihsia was possibly also a member. BAI and NAXI may be distant relatives of this group, but their status is uncertain.

5. The Bodic languages, so called by linguists from the native name of Tibet, *Bod*. This includes TIBETAN itself and its close relatives Gurung (150,000 speakers in Nepal), Tamang (500,000 speakers) and Jiarong (100,000 speakers in Sichuan); also NEWARI, Limbu and Magar.

6. The Baric group, the most complex of all, which seems to have several subdivisions. The BODO-GARO LANGUAGES include Bodo, Garo and Tripuri. The KUKI-CHIN AND NAGA LANGUAGES include many languages of relatively small communities; they are close to the Mikir-Meithei group, consisting of MANIPURI and Mikir. The Mirish or Abor-Miri-Dafla or North Assam languages include Adi or Miri (500,000 speakers in Assam and Tibet) and Lhoba (200,000 speakers in Arunachal Pradesh and China).

SIRAIKI

PERHAPS 15,000,000 SPEAKERS

Pakistan

One of the INDO-ARYAN LANGUAGES, Siraiki has not until recently been regarded as a separate language. It may be considered a dialect or a continuation of Western PANJABI (see map there), spoken in the lower Indus valley in a region where SINDHI is also spoken.

Siraiki has been the vehicle of religious poetry, collected in manuscripts and occasionally published. But – in a local backlash against an influx of Muslim speakers of 'eastern' Panjabi, religious exiles from India after the 1947 partition – there has in recent years been agitation among local intellectuals and politicians for 'language status' for Siraiki in Pakistan.

The first ten numerals in Siraiki are: *hik, du, trɛ, cār, pañj, chi, sat, aṭh, naõ, dah.*

Aukhā bbaṃdhī rakhaṇ yārīdā
jiveṃ kachā dhāggā.

Friendship is as hard to rebind
as a half-untwisted thread . . .

Opening of a Siraiki poem, from *Linguistic survey of India* vol. 8 part 1

SLAVONIC LANGUAGES

A branch of the family of INDO-EUROPEAN LANGUAGES, the Slavonic languages are spoken in Russia and eastern Europe by a total of 300,000,000 speakers.

As far back as they can be traced historically, Slavonic speakers called themselves by a name like *Slověne*. As *Sklavenoi* they are mentioned by Greek historians in the 6th century AD. For the language family as a whole many linguists now prefer the term *Slavic* to *Slavonic*.

At the battle of the river Lech, in 955, so many Slavonic prisoners were captured by the Germans that their ethnic name developed a new meaning – still seen in English *slave*, French *esclave*, Italian *schiavo*. The Venetian dialect form *ciao* 'goodbye', now popular in Italian and occasionally in fashion in English, is the same word in origin. Thus it means literally 'I am your slave'.

Among the early Indo-European dialects we can discern a group – those that eventually became Baltic, Slavonic, Iranian and Indo-Aryan languages – in which a particular sound change took place, the change from *k* to *s*. In these languages, therefore, the word for 'hundred' begins with *s*. These dialects shared much more than the single sound change. A range of similarities, in sounds, in grammar, in vocabulary, links the Slavonic and Baltic languages. Slavonic languages, and sometimes the Balto-Slavic group as a whole, share a great deal with the Indo-Iranian languages too. For many hundreds of years they must have been spoken in adjacent regions, probably of the southern Ukraine, before the speakers of Indo-Iranian began the long, slow movement south-eastwards that has led their linguistic descendants to Iran and northern India.

Slavonic speakers, meanwhile, in all probability stayed exactly where they were: but their territory must gradually have expanded, reaching the Oder, and even the Elbe, to the west. There was certainly long term interaction between Slavonic and Germanic dialects.

Finally, in the early centuries of the Byzantine Empire, a startling series of migrations and conquests took Slavonic speech south into the Balkans. The Latin dialects of south-eastern Europe were almost engulfed, though ROMANIAN and AROMUNIAN remain, heavily influenced by Slavonic. The language of the Bulgars (see CHUVASH) was soon forgotten. Documents suggest that Slavonic speakers once formed a majority in mainland Greece. The modern languages of Bulgaria and the countries of former Yugoslavia are the legacy of these medieval Slavonic invasions.

The first recorded form of Slavonic speech is in the Christian texts in OLD SLAVONIC, many of them translations from Greek, which began to be written during the mission of Saints Constantine and Methodius to the Principality of Great Moravia in 862–3.

The missionaries had learnt their Slavonic much further to the south, in Macedonia, but at that date the spoken Slavonic languages cannot have differentiated very greatly and the texts they wrote could probably be understood by all Slavs.

Meanwhile about ten modern Slavonic languages have developed a written and literary form. They are still rather closer to one another than (for instance) Germanic or Romance languages. For some examples see the tables of Slavonic numerals at BELORUSSIAN, CZECH and SLOVENE.

Members of the group

SLOVENE, SERBIAN and Croatian, MACEDONIAN and BULGARIAN are grouped as 'South Slavonic'. Geographically cut off from the rest, these languages result from Slavonic incursions into the Byzantine Empire in the 7th to 9th centuries.

CZECH and SLOVAK, POLISH and SORBIAN form the West Slavonic group. There is strong dialect differentiation in Poland: some would count Kashubian as a separate language.

The Eastern Slavonic languages (BELORUSSIAN, UKRAINIAN and RUSSIAN) were the last to differentiate, as the medieval Russian principalities became tributary to Lithuania, Poland and the Golden Horde. Ruthenian, spoken to the southwest of the Carpathians, may be considered a dialect of Ukrainian – but some claim for it the status of a language.

For maps see SERBIAN, POLISH and RUSSIAN.

The trees of central Europe

For the woodland trees that are well known in the Ukraine and southern Russia, the Slavonic languages have inherited names that come from proto-Indo-European or from a very early period of proto-Slavonic. But for trees that are native only to the west of the Vistula and the Dniester, beech, sycamore maple, larch, yew and sorb, they use names borrowed from other languages. This seems to show that the Slavonic dialects developed east of those two rivers – and it confirms that the migrations leading to the differentiation of Western and Southern Slavonic languages, from Sorbian to Bulgarian, came later.

Beech: *buk* in Russian and Polish, *bukva* in Serbian and Croatian: the Slavonic word was borrowed from a Germanic form such as Gothic *boka*. There was a proto-Indo-European word for 'beech': it was **bhāgos*. It survived, with its original meaning, in Celtic Latin as well as in Germanic. Early Greek and Slavonic speakers, long settled in regions where the beech was unknown, used this word to name other trees. Greek *phēgós* means 'Valonia oak, *Quercus macrolepis*', and Russian *buzina* (with dialect forms like *bas, baznyk*) means 'elder'.

Maple, sycamore: *jawor* in Polish, *javor* in Russian and Serbian, are names for certain maple trees (including what the British call 'sycamore'). The word was borrowed from a Germanic form such as German *Ahorn*, related to Latin *acer*.

Sorb: Serbian, Croatian and Slovene *brek*, Czech *břek*, and Slovak *brekyňa* are names for the sorb or serviceberry, the rowan that is native to central Europe. This word seems to be borrowed from a Germanic form like German *Birke* 'birch', adopted as a name for the sorb because the two trees have similar bark.

Based on Zbigniew Golab, *The origin of the Slavs: a linguist's view* (Columbus, Ohio: Slavica, 1992) pp. 273–80

SLOVAK

5,500,000 SPEAKERS

Slovakia

Separated from Poland by an almost continuous mountain range, a continuum of dialects occupies the territory that, for most of this century, was united as Czechoslovakia. They are closely similar to one another and mutually intelligible: however, two standard languages have emerged from them, Czech and Slovak. They are Western SLAVONIC LANGUAGES.

Slovák, plural *Slováci*, the name that Slovak speakers use for themselves, is a variant of the term *Slavonic* that is applied to the whole language group. It is first recorded in a document of 1485. They call their language *Slovenský* (a name easily confused with that of Slovene).

Slovak is spoken in the mountainous region that lies due north of Hungary (see map at POLISH). The territory has no tradition of political independence, having previously existed as a state only briefly under German domination in 1939–45.

In the 9th century the Slovak region belonged to the Kingdom of Great Moravia. But for many hundreds of years after that it was part of Hungary, and Hungarian was its official language. However, documents in Slovak, or in Czech with recognisable Slovak features, are known from the 15th century onwards. The origin of modern standard Slovak may thus be traced to unofficial use, in local administration and by a local intelligentsia, of a language which, though close to Czech, was developing to serve their own needs on the basis of their spoken dialects. Czech and Slovak standards continued to compete: in a religious context Czech may be seen as the Protestant language, Slovak as the Catholic language in early modern Slovakia. It was only in the 19th century that a widely accepted literary standard Slovak emerged. A landmark is the appearance of L'udovit Štur's *Nárečja slovenskuo alebo potreba písaňja v tomto nárečí* 'Slovak speech, or the necessity of writing in this dialect' in Bratislava in 1846.

When the region was at last detached from Hungary to become part of the newly formed Czechoslovakia, in 1918–38, Slovak language and literature were able to flourish, yet their separate status was not fully accepted by the Czech majority. In post-war Czechoslovakia Slovak had a higher status. It is now, almost for the first time, the national language of an independent country, one whose people have in the past been held together by little more than their language. An inherited defensiveness leads to strong discrimination in favour of standard Slovak, against local dialects and against minority languages such as ROMANI.

Although Slovak and Czech are so similar (see the table of numerals at CZECH), Slovak is one of the easiest of languages for other Slavonic speakers to learn, while Czech is one of the more difficult. This is partly because of the *česká přehláska* 'Czech vowel mutation', a comprehensive series of sound changes beginning around the 14th century which affected vowels that followed palatalised consonants. Slovak, on the other hand, geographically central to the Slavonic world, has links with Southern and Eastern Slavonic languages as well as with the adjacent Czech and Polish.

SLOVENE

2,000,000 SPEAKERS

Slovenia

Slovene, one of the South SLAVONIC LANGUAGES, is the national language of the Republic of Slovenia, until recently part of Yugoslavia.

Slovenski is now the local name for the language – in origin the same name as that of the *Slavonic* language family. Owing to its political fragmentation in earlier centuries, dialects of Slovene were sometimes identified as separate languages with their own names: *Kranjski* for the speech of Krajnska or Carniola, *Windisch* (a German word with pejorative overtones, see SORBIAN) for that of Styria and Austrian Carinthia.

Slavonic speakers must have settled in this region soon after the fall of the Roman Empire, perhaps at the same time as in Slovakia. The two languages have some similarities although they have been geographically separated ever since the arrival of the Hungarians in the 9th century.

For a thousand years most Slovene speakers were Austrian subjects. Hungarian, Italian, but most of all German, were the languages of the cities and the elite in this part of the Austrian Empire.

Slovene was often seen as nothing more than a rustic dialect. Yet publishing in Slovene began quite early, with a *Catechism* and an ABC printed by Primož Trubar in 1551. The great Bible translation of 1584 included a glossary explaining the Krajnska and other local words that were used, so that Southern Slavonic speakers in general would also be able to read it. Slovene speakers are largely Roman Catholic, but it was Protestant publishing that contributed most to the early development of written Slovene. From the beginning the Latin alphabet was used.

In the following centuries there was a jostling for position – a 'battle of the forms' – between the local Slovene dialects and a generalised literary language. The latter, which had begun to emerge even in Trubar's books, was based on the Krajnska dialect of Ljubljana more than on any other, but it has features drawn from several dialects. There was also a need to fix the spelling of Slovene: writers in local dialects had based their spelling practice on Italian, German or Hungarian patterns. The influence of German word order and syntax was gradually cut back.

Some writers and theorists went further, planning for a unified future South Slavonic or even 'pan-Slavic' language. But the Vienna Accord of 1850, uniting the SERBIAN AND CROATIAN literary languages, left the remaining South Slavonic languages – including Slovene – to find their own future. Meanwhile, after the short-lived French invasion of 1811, Slovene had been accepted for the first time as a language of education, local administration and the press. It naturally became the official language of Slovenia, first as one of the constituents of federal Yugoslavia, and at last as an independent republic.

There are communities of Slovene speakers in Hungary, Italy and Austria near the Slovene borders (for map see SERBIAN). The Austrian Slovenes live in three valleys, Gailtal, Rosental and Jauntal. By recent counts there are 20,000 of them, but they form a majority only in one or two villages. In Italy, in and around Trieste, there are about 30,000 Slovene speakers. They are a majority in the small towns of San Dorligo della Valle and Sgonico. Trieste itself, once the seaport of the multilingual Austro-Hungarian Empire, has a large Italian majority.

Kar ne pride iz srca, se ne prime srca: What does not come from the heart does not move the heart.

Numerals in South Slavonic languages

In this table Macedonian and Bulgarian are given in Latin transliteration. Slovene appears in its original Latin script, while the Serbo-Croat form is given in both Latin (for Croatian) and Cyrillic (for Serbian).

	Slovene	Croatian	Serbian	Macedonian	Bulgarian
1	en	jedan	један	eden	edin
2	dva	dva	два	dva	dva
3	trije	tri	три	tri	tri
4	štirje	četiri	четири	chetiri	chetiri
5	pet	pet	пет	pet	pet
6	šest	šest	шест	shest	shest
7	sedem	sedam	седам	sedum	sedem
8	osem	osam	осам	osum	osem
9	devet	devet	девет	devet	devet
10	deset	deset	десет	deset	deset

SOGDIAN

EXTINCT LANGUAGE OF CENTRAL ASIA

S ogdiane, as it is called in Greek texts, or *Suguda* in Persian inscriptions, was a region of central Asia between the rivers Amu Darya and Syr Darya. It belonged to the Persian Empire, and afterwards to Alexander and his successors. Little is known of its history in the millennium that elapsed between then and the Islamic conquest in the 8th century: but coins, inscriptions and a few historical references show that it was at times independent and influential.

Among the Middle IRANIAN LANGUAGES, the importance of Sogdian – our name for the language of this little-known region – comes from its geographical position. Sogdiana lay across the Silk Road, and was deeply involved in the trade. Sogdian became a lingua franca: texts in it are now found at oases far to the east, in Chinese Xinjiang, where Sogdian trading communities must have lived and where Sogdian language and literature must have been cultivated.

Chorasmian was the Iranian language spoken west of Sogdiana, on the lower course of the Amu Darya. Chorasmia or Khwarezm was likewise for a long time an independent state, eventually succumbing to the Islamic expansion. There is no Chorasmian literature, but the language is known from inscriptions, documents, and short quotations by Arabic authors. These sources range from the 3rd century BC to the 13th century AD.

Sogdian had a rich literature, long forgotten but now rediscovered in early manuscripts from the Silk Road cities – Buddhist texts, Manichaean texts and Christian texts, all in distinctive scripts. These poems and scriptures, in a once well-known language, helped to spread the beliefs and philosophy of three great religions well beyond Sogdiana itself to the heartlands of Asia.

Most of the surviving manuscripts come from finds at Tunhuang and Turfan in Xinjiang.

Sogdian eventually died away, replaced by the Tajik variety of PERSIAN and by UZBEK. But one community of about two thousand people, settled in northern Tajikistan, still speaks *Yaghnobi*, the direct descendant of medieval Sogdian (see map at IRANIAN LANGUAGES).

The *Bactrian* language, spoken to the south of Sogdiana, is found on coins and a few inscriptions of the early centuries AD in Greek script – a reminder that this region had been the centre of a once-powerful Greek kingdom. The letter þ was added to the script to represent the sound *sh*, unknown in Greek.

Numerals in Sogdian and Chorasmian

Sogdian		Chorasmian
'yw	1	'yw
'ðw	2	'ðw'
'ðry	3	šy
ctf'r	4	cf'r
pnc	5	pnc
xwšw	6	'x̣
'βt	7	'βd
'št	8	'št
nw'	9	š'ð
ðs'	10	ðẙs

Vowels are not fully recorded in the original scripts and cannot be reconstructed with certainty. The transliterations are those conventionally adopted by Iranian scholars.

I. Gershevitch, *A grammar of Manichean Sogdian*. Oxford, 1954; Helmut Humbach, 'Choresmian' in *Compendium linguarum iranicarum* ed. Rüdiger Schmitt (Wiesbaden: Reichert, 1989) pp. 193–203

SOMALI

5,500,000 SPEAKERS

Somalia, Ethiopia, Kenya, Djibouti

Somali is one of the CUSHITIC LANGUAGES of the Afroasiatic family. It is the national language of Somalia, acting as a lingua franca for speakers of minority languages throughout the country.

According to one theory, the 'Horn of Africa' is the region from which the earliest Afroasiatic languages began to spread, many thousands of years ago. From the time of the first historical records, two thousand years ago or more, all available evidence suggests that Somali has been spoken precisely where it is spoken today, in what is now Somalia and by a significant minority in south-eastern Ethiopia. Its speakers are traditionally nomadic pastoralists; their mobility has been only partly arrested by the frontiers that the French, Italians, British and Ethiopians have drawn across the Somali plateau.

People of this region were once known as *Berber*, hence the name of the town of Berbera. They call themselves *Soomaali*'. The word is first found, in an Ethiopic form, in a 15th-century praise poem for an Ethiopian king's victories over his eastern neighbours. It seems to derive from the name of a legendary ancestor, *Soma* or *Samale* – but many other origins have been suggested, including the two Somali words *so* 'go' plus *mal* 'milk' as an indication of a pastoral way of life.

There are no significant early records of the language. Henry Salt's *Voyage to Abyssinia* (1814) contained a wordlist of Somali: the French linguist Antoine d'Abbadie published further work on the language in 1839.

Although unwritten until recently, Somali is the vehicle of a rich oral literature. Poetry is alliterative: verse forms seem to be home-grown, uninfluenced by Arabic or other foreign forms. Both poetry and prose focus on Somali history and legend. Tales of local Sufi saints are also popular. Traditional bards, some of them now specialising in political poems and propaganda, are prominent in the media.

Close contact and migration between the Horn of Africa and the Arabian peninsula dates back at least two thousand years: over all that time Arabic has influenced Somali. As the vehicle of the Islamic religion, in which the Koran must be recited, Arabic is a highly important language of culture in modern Somali towns but it tends to be known by men only. During the early years of British and Italian occupation Arabic acted as the medium of communication between Somalis and invaders.

On independence in 1960 Somali seemed destined to be the natural language of government, yet no national writing system was agreed on until 1972. A foreign-educated elite, literate in English or Italian, retained influence during this early period: Arabic literacy was also prized.

Until 1972 Somali had been written in several ways: in the Latin alphabet, with various spelling rules influenced by English or Italian; in the Arabic alphabet; and in the *Far Soomaali* or *Cusmaaniya* script which was invented specifically for Somali. Orthodox Muslims often saw the Latin alphabet as a vehicle of Western influence, but Arabic script, poor in its marking of vowels, was unsuitable for the vowel-rich sound pattern of Somali.

The Latin orthography finally adopted in 1972 is easy to write and print, having no accents or diacritical marks. At the same time Somali was made the sole official language of Somalia, and most civil servants met the three-month deadline for literacy in their mother tongue.

Somali has naturally many Arabic loanwords. Other borrowings include *miis* 'table' from Portuguese *mesa*.

Somali has an unusual vowel pattern of five 'normal' and five 'fronted' vowels. There is also a long-short distinction, giving twenty vowel phonemes in all. The deep-throat pharyngeal consonants, typical of the language, are written *q x*. There are four tones: tone in Somali has grammatical uses, helping to indicate number, gender and case: *Sōōmáálì* 'a Somali', *Sōōmāālì* 'Somalis'; *'Áràb* 'an Arab', *'Āràb* 'Arabs'.

The first ten numerals are: *ków, lábba, sáddex, áfar, shán, líx, toddobá, siddéed, sagaal, toban.*

Somali dialects

'Common Somali' is the dialect of most Somalians (notably the *Ishaak, Dir, Darod* and *Hawiya* people) and of most Kenyan speakers of Somali. There are two other important dialects: 'Central' or *Rahanweyn* Somali, whose speakers are to be found in Upper Juba province, and *Coastal Somali* of Benadir province and of Mandera district of Kenya. Many speakers of these also know

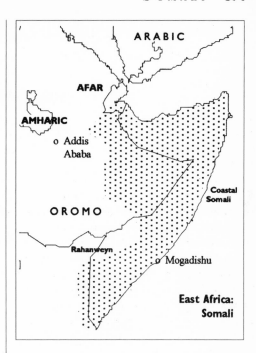

East Africa:
Somali

Common Somali, which is the language of broadcasting in Somalia and in Kenya.

About 900,000 Somali speakers live in Ethiopia, 300,000 in Kenya and 200,000 in Djibouti.

OROMO is the closest linguistic relative of Somali. Also related to Somali are Saho and AFAR (see map there).

SONGHAY

2,000,000 SPEAKERS

Niger, Mali, Nigeria, Burkina Faso, Benin

Songhay, one of the NILO-SAHARAN LANGUAGES though with no close relatives, is a language of trade along the middle Niger, from Mopti in Mali to Gaya on the border of Niger and Nigeria.

The three peoples who speak the language call themselves *Sōngai*, *Zarma* and *Dendi*, or *koyroboro* 'one of the country'; their language is *Sōngai kine* 'language of the Songhay' or *koyra kine* 'language of the country'. In French its name has sometimes been spelt *Sonrhaï*.

The Songhay people had been converted to Islam in the 11th century. Some Songhay words are recorded by Arabic authors who had travelled in the Western Sudan in the 12th to 14th centuries.

The importance of Songhay as a language, however, dates from the brief flowering of the Songhay empire under Sonni Ali and Askia Mohammed I (Mohammed Ture) in the 15th and 16th centuries. From its old capital of Gao, in western Mali, the empire now extended its influence from Senegal all the way to northern Nigeria – until, soon afterwards, a Moroccan invasion destroyed it.

Ever since that collapse, Songhay has remained an important means of communication along the middle Niger. It is still learnt as a second language by some of the peoples living along the river. It is an official regional language in Niger, Mali and Benin; the Djerma dialect has separate official status in Niger.

Songhay has two tones and a distinction of vowel length. A noun is marked as definite or as plural by a change of suffix: *gorgo* 'hen', *gorga* 'the hen'; *haw* 'cow', *hawiyan* 'cows'. Although Arabic and Songhay have coexisted for many centuries,

and although many speakers have learnt Arabic as the language of Islam, Songhay does not have a large number of Arabic loanwords: it has, however, borrowed freely from Hausa.

Songhay and its neighbours

Speakers of *Songhay* as a first language are concentrated in south-western Mali and the modern state of Niger (where the dialect is *Djerma* or Zarma) and in northern Benin (where the dialect is *Dendi* or Dandawa). The third dialect zone, further up the Niger from Tombouctou to Mopti, is that of Songhay proper. The Zabarima, who raided and eventually settled in northern Ghana in the 19th century, speak a Djerma dialect.

... end of the story
ăy-cã-bō kā dánjí!
my mouse's head has fallen in the fire!

The traditional sentence with which the Songhay storyteller ends his tale.

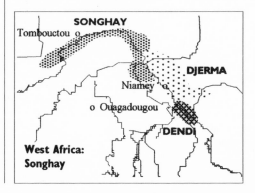

West Africa: Songhay

Numerals in Songhay and Djerma

Songhay		Djerma
afo	1	-a fo
ahinka	2	-ihinka
ahinza	3	-ihinza
atatyi	4	-itaaci
agu	5	-igu
iddu	6	-iddu
iye	7	-iyye
ahaku	8	-ahakku
yagga	9	-egga, yagga
awey	10	-iway

In the newly standard written form of Djerma, numerals are written as suffixes to nouns, linked by the definite suffix -a, -e, -i (the Djerma numerals are from information by Hamidou Ko in M. Malherbe, *Les langues de l'humanité* (Paris, 1995) p. 1662). But the basic numeral forms are practically identical in Songhai proper and Djerma.

SONINKE

1,000,000 SPEAKERS

Mali, Senegal, Mauritania

One of the Mande Tan group of NIGER-CONGO LANGUAGES, Soninke is a language of inland West Africa, at the point where the frontiers of Mali, Mauritania and Senegal meet (for map see MANDEKAN). Soninke is called *Sarakollé* in Wolof, the main language of Senegal: the word means 'light-coloured person' in Soninke. The language is called *Maraka* in Mandekan.

The SUSU and Soninke were among the early enemies of the Empire of Mali in the 13th century. Some Soninke words are recorded by Arabic authors who had travelled in the Western Sudan in the 12th to 14th centuries. European records of the language date back to the 17th century: under the name *Saracole* it figures in a multilingual glossary made for the French Royal Senegal Company in 1690.

Since their territory was acquired by France (and divided among three administrative units, now independent states) many Soninke have emigrated to France: so many that their language serves as a lingua franca in West African communities in French cities.

Soninke has borrowed from Arabic, the language of Islam, and from French. The first ten numerals in Soninke are: *baane, fillo, sikko, naxato, karago, tumũ, ñeru, segu, kabu, tamũ*.

SORBIAN

100,000 SPEAKERS

Germany

Sorbian marks the far north-west of the SLAVONIC LANGUAGES – the only living linguistic reminder that the north German plain was once partly Slavonic-speaking.

> Sorbian speakers call themselves *Serbja*, a name identical with that of the Serbians of former Yugoslavia which perhaps is that of an early Slavonic tribe. The language was traditionally called *Wendisch* in German, a name that goes back two thousand years to the *Venethi* mentioned by the Roman historian, Tacitus, as eastern neighbours of the Germani. *Wendisch* has a pejorative slant and is now less used. In some older books Sorbian is called *Lusatian* after the province where it is spoken.

There are in reality two Sorbian languages, each of which has its own literary form. In the German countryside to the south-east of Berlin the speakers of Lower Sorbian are settled around the city of Cottbus or *Chośebuz*. Further south, in and around the town of Bautzen or *Budyšin*, Upper Sorbian is spoken (for map see POLISH). Although they share a name, the two languages are quite distinct: see, for some examples, the table of numerals at CZECH.

After periods of Polish and Czech rule in the 11th and 12th centuries, Lusatia became part of the German state of Saxony, which traditionally allowed an official role to Sorbian (the Crown Prince was expected to learn the language). The Cottbus region, however, passed to the Kingdom of Prussia in 1815, and Lower Sorbian speakers found themselves under pressure to turn to German. Later, under Nazism, the use of Sorbian was officially forbidden. Communist East Germany recognised Sorbian as an official language, and it is still used in local schools.

The first major text in Sorbian is a manuscript translation of the New Testament into Lower Sorbian, made in 1548 by Miklawuš Jakubica. The first grammar of Upper Sorbian was published in Prague in 1679. There has been a Sorbian newspaper press for over two hundred years.

In the 18th century Sorbian students were found particularly at Leipzig and Breslau and at the Catholic Sorbian Seminary in Prague: the student societies kept in touch with one another and with the increasing momentum of Slavonic nationalism. Strong local organisations, which have helped to keep the language and literature alive in the 19th and 20th centuries, include the cultural academy *Maćica Serbska*.

> Further reminders of the former Slavonic presence in present-day Germany are well-known place names. *Leipzig*, host to international trade fairs ever since medieval times and the second city of former East Germany, was once *Lipsk* from Slavonic *lipa* 'lime tree'. Its neighbour *Dresden*, which suffered so severely in the Second World War, is in origin *Drežďane*, 'people of the marshy woods'.

SOTHO

7,400,000 SPEAKERS

South Africa, Lesotho

Sotho is the name of two related BANTU LAN-GUAGES, both of them now official languages of South Africa. Speakers of the dialects called Northern Sotho form the fifth largest language community there, just ahead of speakers of English as a mother tongue. Southern Sotho is the national language of Lesotho and also has a large number of speakers in South Africa. There is a Sotho-Tswana television channel in South Africa.

In Sotho itself the language is called *seSotho* and the people *baSotho*: hence the older English names – *Sesuto* for the language, and *Basutoland* for the now independent country that is called *Lesotho*, 'country of the Sotho'.

Sotho and TSWANA form one of the two major groups of Bantu languages in South Africa, the other being 'Nguni' (see maps here and at ZULU). The two groups, though related, do not make up a dialect continuum, suggesting that their differences crystallised at a time when they were geographically separate – and perhaps one or both groups of speakers were not yet in precisely their present position.

Overall, in recent centuries, Nguni languages have been in the ascendant and Sotho-Tswana in retreat. The separate history – the resurgence – of Southern Sotho comes from the establishment and steady expansion of a powerful kingdom by Moshoeshoe in the early 19th century. In the following decades, parts of this kingdom were seized by Afrikaans and English speakers, becoming the 'conquered territories' of the Orange Free State. But the remainder, as Basutoland, was governed as a British protectorate from 1884, and Moshoeshoe's descendants retained power.

Swiss and French missionaries of the Paris Evangelical Mission Society assisted Sotho diplomacy at this period; they also helped to spread literacy and education. Basutoland regained independence, as Lesotho, in 1966: Sotho and English are its official languages.

Historically, the Southern Sotho are Moshoeshoe's people. Sotho is their common language – whatever their origins – and they are traditionally cattle farmers. Lesotho is marked by massive mountain plateaus, but it is in the lowlands, to the west of these, that most Southern Sotho speakers live.

The political dominance of Zulu, during the centuries preceding Moshoeshoe, led to extensive Zulu influence on most dialects of the Sotho and Tswana group. The large numbers of Zulu speakers who became subjects of the baSotho kingdom in the 19th century and eventually adopted Sotho as their language, increased this effect on Southern Sotho in particular. Hundreds of Zulu loanwords are to be found in Southern Sotho: *hosasa* 'tomorrow', *haholo* 'a lot', *-kgolophala* 'become fat'. Southern Sotho now has click phonemes such as are typical of Zulu – sounds which Zulu in turn had borrowed from Khoisan languages. However, for the three Zulu clicks *c* (dental) *q* (palatal) *x* (lateral), Southern Sotho has only one, *q*.

Southern Sotho, unlike the rest of the group, has developed an 'avoidance language', *hlonepho*, used by women in the presence of some male relatives. This practice is widespread in the Nguni languages (see box at XHOSA) and is clearly borrowed by Southern Sotho from Zulu.

Written Southern Sotho uses *o* and *e* not only as vowel signs but also for the semivowels *w* and

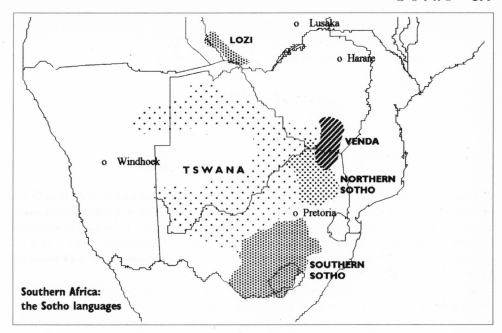

Southern Africa:
the Sotho languages

y, a vestige of the origins of written Sotho in the work of the French-speaking missionaries in the 19th century. Like other Bantu languages, Sotho has a system of noun classes marked by prefixes: see table at LOZI.

Lessons in verse

The 'puberty schools' of the baSotho were traditionally the occasion for the recital of didactic songs, learnt in advance from elder brothers and sisters. In this traditional Sotho literature the rules of daily life were transmitted from each generation to the next.

'The opening of the [boys'] school is marked by a formal party at the local chief's meeting place, *lekhotla*. An ox will be presented to the chief and another slaughtered for the party . . . The following morning, the candidates for instruction are initiated into the school by the performance of the collective ceremony of circumcision.

'After these opening ritual activities, the real work of the school begins. The period of instruction is nowadays some two or three months. The boys are taught obedience to their fathers and mothers. They are introduced to the rules of seniority and respect. Loyalty and obedience to the chieftainship take second place to the importance of correct lineal and family relationship behaviour. The curriculum also includes instruction in sexual morality and the rules of sexual behaviour. All this instruction is conveyed through the medium of songs which the candidates sing all through the night . . .

'Information about the girls' schools is scanty . . . Their instruction concerns itself with matters relating to womanhood, domestic and agricultural activities, sex and behaviour towards men.'

V. G. J. Sheddick, *The Southern Sotho* (London: International African Institute, 1953) pp. 31–2

Northern Sotho

Northern Sotho, formerly 'Transvaal Sotho', now in full *seSotho na Leboa*, is a modern concept: a label for several related dialects, one of which, *Pedi*, is the basis of a standard written language. Pedi speakers, historically forming one of several kingdoms in the Transvaal, migrated southwards as labourers in large numbers and drew the attention of 19th-century missionaries to their language, whose written form was therefore based on the migrants' speech. Speakers of other dialects initially saw no special prestige in it.

For a table of numerals in Northern and Southern Sotho see TSWANA.

The Sotho languages

Northern Sotho has 3,500,000 speakers in Transvaal. *Pedi* is the dialect that gave rise to the first written form of Northern Sotho: its origins are in the Lulu mountains west of Ohrigstad and Lydenburg.

Southern Sotho has 2,700,000 speakers in South Africa and 1,200,000 in Lesotho. Local dialects are said to have been more noticeable in the past than they are now.

TSWANA or Western Sotho, although mutually intelligible with Pedi, is usually treated as a separate language. It has 3,600,000 speakers in South Africa and about 850,000 in Botswana.

LOZI, one of the national languages of Zambia, spoken by 450,000 in the upper Zambezi valley, is in origin the Sotho speech of the Kololo, who conquered this region in the early 19th century.

VENDA, spoken in Zimbabwe and the northern Transvaal, is not closely related to any of its neighbours.

Sotho praise poetry

Preserving the memory of leaders and battles recent or long past, praise poetry is an important part of Sotho oral literature, as already observed by the French missionary Casalis in 1833. This is the opening of a modern praise poem commemorating Moshoeshoe II:

Lona le ratang ho roka baholo,
le roka hampe le siea mohale,
le siea Thesele oa Mokhachane . . .

You who are fond of praising the ancestors,
your praises are poor when you leave out the warrior,
When you leave out Thesele son of Mokhachane . . .

Lithoko: Sotho praise-poems ed. M. Damane, P. B. Sanders (Oxford: Clarendon Press, 1974) pp. 73, 270

SPANISH

225,000,000 SPEAKERS

Spain, Costa Rica, Cuba, Dominican Republic, Mexico, Guatemala, Honduras, El Salvador, Nicaragua, Panama, Colombia, Venezuela, Ecuador, Peru, Bolivia, Chile, Argentina, Paraguay, Uruguay, United States, Puerto Rico

Spanish, one of the ROMANCE LANGUAGES and thus a direct descendant of Latin, is now the major language of the Iberian peninsula, the south-western extremity of Europe. As a result of Spanish discoveries and conquests five hundred years ago, it is also the ruling language of most of America, south of the United States – Mexico border and west of Brazil. In terms of the number of speakers who learn it as a mother tongue, Spanish is the third most popular language in the world after Chinese and English.

> The peninsula south of the Pyrenees was called *Iberia* by the Greeks but *Hispania* by the Romans. *H* was not pronounced in later Latin, and a short *i* regularly became *e*. Thus, in Spanish, the country is called *España* and its language *Español*.
>
> *Latin America*, from Mexico to Argentina, is so called because its two ruling languages, Spanish and Portuguese, are descendants of Latin.

As Latin spread across the western Roman Empire it gradually superseded the local languages of prehistoric western Europe. In Spain, inscriptions (as yet not fully deciphered) show that several languages existed, one of them – BASQUE – still surviving in the Pyrenean foothills. Iberian, apparently spoken over much of central Spain, was probably unrelated to Basque. Spanish *huerga* 'spree' and *huelga* 'industrial strike' both originate from a pre-Roman, perhaps Iberian word *folga*: *huelga* reached Spanish by way of the regional dialect of Andalusia. Spanish *izquierdo* 'left' is also a pre-Roman word, paralleled by Basque *ezkerr*, Gascon *kerr*.

The Vandals and Visigoths, Germanic invaders who successively occupied Spain after the end of the Roman Empire, contributed rather little to Spanish vocabulary. Far more important was the Islamic conquest of 711–18, after which much of Spain was ruled by an Arabic-speaking elite for five hundred years – indeed the Islamic Kingdom of Granada survived until 1492.

As a result of this long Arabic domination many Arabic loanwords are to be found in Spanish, particularly for aspects of high culture – government, science, architecture, dress and jewellery, music, food. Examples include *alcalde* 'mayor', *algodón* 'cotton', *almirante* 'admiral': this last comes from the Arabic *amīr*, which is also the origin of English *emir* and (by way of French) *admiral*.

> It is curious that these Arabic words are nearly always borrowed complete with the definite article, *al-*. Surely, at any period, Spanish speakers could have identified and separated off the Arabic definite article, which is so similar to the Spanish *el*? A possible explanation is that the words were first learnt, in the early days of Islamic rule in Spain, from what was probably a majority of BERBER troops in the Islamic armies. Berber itself has no similar definite article (its nearest approach is the feminine suffix *-t*), so these north African speakers of army Arabic would have learnt the words, complete with article, as if they were indivisible. In this form they will have become part of MOZARABIC, eventually to reach Spanish in the course of the Reconquest.

The Christian reconquest of Spain, *Reconquista*, began from the northern mountains, which the Muslims had never been able to subdue. It was conducted by a row of five small states: Portugal in the west, Catalonia in the east, and between these Leon, Castile and Aragon. A sixth state, Navarre, astride the Pyrenees, took little part. In their historic regions of northern Spain the distinctive dialects of Leon and Aragon can still be heard. But history brought Castile to the fore: thus, as the Mozarabic- and Arabic-speaking people of the south adopted the speech and the way of life of their new Christian rulers, Castilian was the dialect to which they turned.

So medieval Castilian is the main source of modern Spanish, and *Castilian* (Spanish *Castellano*) is an alternative name for the language. The name of the old kingdom derives from Latin *castella*, 'the fortresses'.

The first written records of early Spanish are in glosses, translations written between the lines, in Latin religious manuscripts from 10th-century Navarre and Castile. Law codes (*fueros*, from Latin *forum*) began to be translated into Spanish in the 12th century: the early Spanish epic, *Poema del Cid*, was perhaps first written down about the same date, though the surviving manuscript seems to have been copied in 1307. In real life its hero, the 'Cid', captured Valencia from its Islamic rulers in 1092.

The flowering of Spanish prose in the 13th century was largely the work of King Alfonso 'the Wise' of Castile (reigned 1252–84) and his court. Spanish grammars and dictionaries began to appear in the 15th and 16th centuries.

Because of its importance across the world, particularly in exploration and trade, Spanish is the origin or the transmitter of numerous loanwords that are now part of modern English. Examples are *potato*, which comes via Spanish *patata* from the word *batata* 'sweet potato' in a native language of Haiti; *maize*, which comes by way of Spanish *maiz* from Carib, the main native language of the early Caribbean; *canyon* or *cañon*, a special meaning given in the Spanish dialect of New Mexico to a word originally meaning 'tube, pipe' (*caña* 'cane').

For a table of numerals in Spanish see CATALAN.

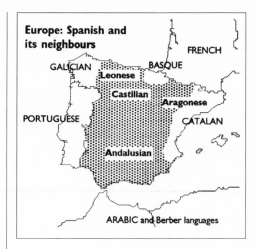

Europe: Spanish and its neighbours

FRENCH
GALICIAN · · · · · BASQUE
Leonese
Castilian
Aragonese
PORTUGUESE
CATALAN
Andalusian

ARABIC and Berber languages

The borrowing of cultural concepts

Spanish *trabajo* 'work' was borrowed into many American Indian languages – and Nahuatl *tequetl* 'work' was borrowed into Lenca of Guatemala, where the Spaniards used Nahuatl as a lingua franca. Yet American Indians laboured hard before the Europeans came. Why, then, did they need the term? William Bright explains by citing Marshall McLuhan: ' "Work" . . . does not exist in a preliterate world. The primitive hunter or fisherman did no work, any more than does the poet, painter, or thinker of today. Where the whole man is involved there is no work.'

William Bright in *Native languages of the Americas* ed. Thomas A. Sebeok (New York: Plenum, 1976)

Spanish in Spain, Latin America and elsewhere

The ascendancy of Spanish in the Iberian peninsula comes from the Reconquest, completed in 1492 – and the marriage of Ferdinand of Aragon with Isabella of Castile, in 1479, which made Castilian the ruling language of both Castile and Catalonia. From this date onwards, Catalan fought to survive as a language of literature

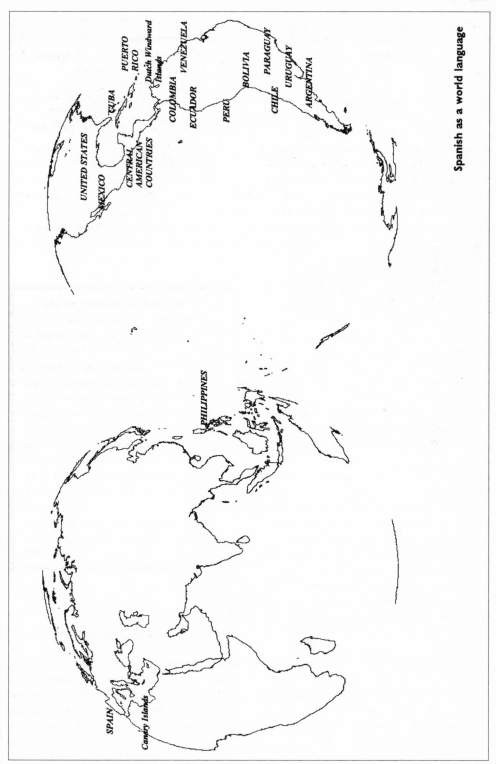

Spanish as a world language

and culture. Galician, in the far north-west, has a far less flourishing status than Catalan; Leonese and Aragonese have not in modern times been considered anything more than dialects of Spanish.

The dialects of southern Spain are dialects of Castilian, not of Leonese or Aragonese. Andalusian is sometimes claimed as the immediate parent of American Spanish varieties, but this is an oversimplification: migration to America came from all regions of Spain, and the Latin American dialects reflect this.

It was also in the 1490s that the Jews of Spain (the *Sephardim*) were expelled. Most of them settled in the Ottoman Empire (the majority of their descendants are now in Israel). Since that time, their language has developed independently of its parent Spanish. It is now known as JUDEZMO.

In the same fateful year of 1492 the Genoese adventurer, Christopher Columbus, under Spanish patronage, discovered America. Spanish conquerors, settlers and missionaries were soon spreading across the Americas from Florida ('country of flowers') and California southwards to Chile and Argentina ('silver country'). Alongside NAHUATL and QUECHUA Spanish immediately became an essential lingua franca throughout this huge territory, with the exception of Portuguese-ruled Brazil. Until around 1800 Spanish America was part of a Spanish empire, ruled from Madrid. By the time that independence came, the status of Spanish was unquestioned, and it is now the official language in all Spain's old American territories, with the exception of those that now form part of the United States.

American Spanish has existed in many varieties. At one end of the spectrum are the regional 'standard languages', which differ from the Castilian of Madrid more as regional accents than as true dialects. It is by 'accent' rather than by special choices of words that Latin Americans can most easily recognise one another's country of origin. Each has its peculiarities: Mexican Spanish, because of its many borrowings from Nahuatl and other local languages, has a consonant cluster *tl-*: *tlaco* 'coin'.

At the other end, there are numerous mixed languages, pidgins and creoles which have grown up and died away in the course of the five centuries of Spanish-speaking rule and settlement: Nahuatl Spanish and Quechua-Spanish mixtures (*Chaupi Lengua* 'half language' and *Media Lengua* 'middle language'); Slave and Caribbean Spanish; the Spanish of Puerto Rico and Cuba with its creole elements. Puerto Rican Spanish is now heavily influenced by American English in its grammar and vocabulary. The local language of the Dutch Antilles, PAPIAMENTU, is generally regarded as a Spanish creole.

Ironically, new mixed forms of European languages are found in Spanish America. *Dialecto Fronterizo* was a mixed Spanish-Portuguese dialect spoken on the Brazil–Uruguay border.

Argentina was for many years a popular destination for Italian emigrants. Around Buenos Aires *Cocoliche*, a pidgin Italian-Spanish, used to be spoken by great numbers of settlers. It was never likely to develop into a stable language or even a creole: after all, true Spanish is relatively easy for Italians to learn. Yet Cocoliche has had a long history, for with each new wave of Italian migrants the pool of Italian speech was refreshed. There were many stages of Cocoliche between good Italian and good Spanish: speakers soon learnt to add a Spanish plural, *-s*, to their words; it took much longer to adopt an unfamiliar sound like the fricative *j* so typical of Spanish.

North of 'Latin America', Spanish is well known to have served as a lingua franca for contacts between Europeans and Indians in what are now the western United States. It was used, perhaps as early as the late 17th century, for communication among the Pueblo Indians themselves, since their own languages were quite different from one another. Spanish loanwords are to be found in many North American Indian languages. Spanish place names (*Nevada*, 'snow-covered'; *Colorado*, 'coloured, red'; *Los Angeles*, 'The Angels'; *San Francisco*, 'Saint Francis') are the most obvious reminder of Spanish exploration and influence here.

Nowadays there are several varieties of Spanish in the United States. *Pachuco* or

Pochismo, which originated as a Spanish-English contact language, is nowadays used as an argot by 'Chicano' young people in Arizona and southern California. *Chicano* – in several variant forms – is spoken in New York and Florida by people from Cuba and Puerto Rico, and in California, Texas, New Mexico and Arizona by people of Mexican descent. Chicano naturally has English loanwords: *flonquear* from American English *flunk* 'fail an examination'; *Quit* from American English *Kid*, often as part of a nickname.

'Tirilones', men of Mexican origin living in El Paso, Texas, use a secret dialect called *Caló* (which is properly the name of the para-ROMANI language of Spanish Gypsies). Originally based on Spanish, the Caló of El Paso contains many words that would be quite unfamiliar to speakers of Mexican Spanish, and many words used in new senses. Caló seems to adopt new words frequently so that it remains difficult for outsiders. Women do not speak it. Other secret and criminal languages based on Spanish are also called Caló.

Philippine Creole Spanish

Spain ruled the Philippine Islands for over 300 years. Yet Spanish was never very widely used there: the Philippines used TAGALOG and other languages in long distance trade and there was little need for another. By the time the United States took power in the Philippines, only about one-tenth of the population knew Spanish.

However, some communities did develop a Spanish creole, known as *Chabacano*, and a quarter of a million people still speak it. On the south side of Manila Bay Chabacano is spoken in Cavite City and in Ternate: this is the point of origin of the creole, for Ternate (named after one of the Moluccas) was founded by migrants from the Moluccas, under Spanish domination, in the 17th century. The original migrants evidently spoke Portuguese pidgin, and its influence can still be traced in Chabacano.

When the Spanish took far-off Zamboanga on the western tip of Mindanao in 1718, it must have been settled by people from Manila Bay and also by HILIGAYNON-speaking troops from the islands of Panay and Negros. The creole called *Zamboangueño*, which is the language of the Christian communities of Zamboanga region and of Basilan island, is still identifiably a variant of Chabacano, but it shows strong influence from Hiligaynon and Tagalog, both spoken far to the north. Zamboangueño, with over 150,000 speakers, is one of the trade languages of the archipelago between Mindanao and Sabah.

The naming of accents

Spanish speakers have a range of terms to identify special features of one another's pronunciation and vocabulary.

Seseo and **ceceo**: Seseo is the pronunciation of *c*, before *e* or *i*, like *s* and not like English *th* (which is the pronunciation in Castilian and the standard Spanish of Madrid). The *s* pronunciation is widespread in Spain and Latin America. Ceceo is what an English speaker would call 'a lisp': the pronunciation of *s* with the *th* sound. In a sense it is the converse of seseo. It is typical of the Spanish of Seville and Cadiz.

Voseo: The use of *vos* instead of *tú* as the singular equivalent of 'you': most Latin American speakers do this, but not those in northern and central Mexico, in northern and central Peru or in northern Uruguay.

Yeísmo versus **lleísmo**: The use of a *y* sound for the written *ll* of Spanish is now much more widespread than the traditional 'palatal *l*' (the nearest English sound to this is *ly*). Yeísmo is gaining ground rapidly in both Spain and Latin America, but it has not reached speakers from the Andean highlands (all the way from Colombia to northern Argentina).

Žeísmo: The use of a *zh* sound instead of standard *y* and sometimes instead of the 'palatal *l*'. This is typical of Central America, southeastern Mexico, Ecuador, Paraguay, Uruguay and part of Argentina.

Value judgments?

In Zamboangueño, the Spanish creole of Christian communities in Mindanao, a scale of moral judgments was once built into the vocabulary: favourable words seem to come from Spanish, unfavourable from Philippine languages.

grande	large	dyutay	small
alto	tall	pandak	short
lihero	fast	mahinay	slow
agudu	sharp	mapurul	dull
liso	smooth	makasap	rough
dulse	sweet	mapa'it	bitter
manso	tame	ma'ilap	wild
bunito	pretty	umalin	ugly
derecho	straight	tiku'	bent
byeho	old person	bata'	child
plores	blossom	putut	bud
soltero	unmarried boy	dalaga	unmarried girl

After Charles O. Frake in *Pidginization and creolization of languages* ed. Dell Hymes (Cambridge: Cambridge University Press, 1971) p. 232

SUKUMA

4,000,000 SPEAKERS

Tanzania

Sukuma is the most important of a closely related group of BANTU LANGUAGES spoken in central and south-western Tanzania. It is in a linguistically varied neighbourhood, with Khoisan, Cushitic, Nilotic and Nilo-Saharan languages in the vicinity.

In the 19th century, when German missionaries and administrators were exploring Tanganyika, Nyamwezi was the first of this group of languages to be noticed. The Nyamwezi themselves were long distance traders, and other traffic passed through their territory. Sukuma, with a far larger number of speakers but in a less explored region, was regarded as a dialect of Nyamwezi, and its name *kiSukuma*, 'language of the north', describes it from the Nyamwezi point of view.

Sukuma now has by far the largest number of speakers of any regional language of Tanzania. But more and more Sukuma speakers are becoming bilingual in Swahili, the national language of Tanzania.

Sukuma has a remarkable tonal pattern. In most words one syllable has, grammatically, a high tone: but this high tone is heard not in its own place but one, two or (most often) three syllables further on in the spoken sentence. Thus the three words *akabóna, babíti, bataale*, have a quite different tone pattern when spoken in a sentence: *akabona bábiti batáale*, 'he saw tall passers-by'. In Nyamwezi, by contrast, 'the intonation is different', as local speakers say: the high tone only shifts one syllable on.

Example from Derek Nurse, *Description of sample Bantu languages of Tanzania (African languages* vol. 5 no. 1, London: International African Institute, 1979) p. 48

People who shit the moon

'The term Nyamwezi is of Swahili origin, and is fairly recent. It arose in the last century during the trade caravans. My grandfather told me that in those days a caravan would leave Tabora at new moon to arrive in Bagamoyo or at the Dar es Salaam coast at the following new moon. Since this was a regular occurrence, the Zalamo started teasing the caravanists, calling them 'the people who excrete the moon', *wanyamwezi* (from the verb *ku-nya*) because their arrival at the coast nearly always coincided with the new moon. Apparently, since there had already developed a joking relationship, *utani*, between the Zalamo and the people from Tabora, the term was not resisted. Since my grandfather did in fact take part in the trade caravans, I have every reason to consider his explanation a viable one.'

C. Maganga in Nurse (1979) p. 57

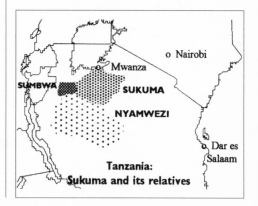

Tanzania:
Sukuma and its relatives

Sukuma and its relatives:
Bantu languages of western Tanzania

Sukuma, Nyamwezi and Sumbwa are best considered dialects of one another. They are locally regarded as separate languages, though they are so close that speakers of any one have little difficulty with the others.

Sukuma itself, with 4,000,000 speakers, is usually divided into four dialects: *kiMunasukuma*, language of the northerners; *kiMunangweli*, of the westerners; *kiMunadakama*, of the southerners, closest to Nyamwezi; *kiMunakiya* or kiMunantuzu, of the easterners.

Sumbwa has 190,000 speakers. It is unlike the other languages of the group in having five rather than seven vowels. It shows signs of influence from Zinza, a Bantu language of the Rutara group, to the north.

SUMERIAN

Extinct language of Iraq

Sumerian is the oldest human language on record, its earliest texts dating from 3100 BC. It is a language with no known relatives, living or extinct.

Once the ruling language of an ancient culture in southern Iraq, Sumerian perhaps ceased to be spoken as early as 2000 BC. But it continued to be written for another two thousand years. The Assyrian king Ashurbanipal, in the 7th century, was proud of his ability to read classical Sumerian. After that it was forgotten, and the very name of Sumer was forgotten.

When AKKADIAN cuneiform texts were gradually deciphered, in the 19th century, scholars realised that an even older language was to be found on some of these tablets. Fortunately, this mysterious language had been difficult for the Akkadian scribes to learn: so they had compiled parallel texts and glossaries, and these have been extremely helpful in the work of decipherment. It was eventually realised that the language belonged to an ancient city state, Sumer, in southern Iraq. It was therefore given the name Sumerian.

The Sumerian language, and the Sumerian cuneiform script, can be seen to have developed gradually over their eleven hundred years of active life. At first used mainly for business and administrative texts, the script came to be used after 2500 BC for royal inscriptions and for religious poetry. Two hundred years later the Akkadians conquered Sumer. From that point onwards the old language was less used in government, while its script was adapted for Akkadian – and eventually for other languages of the Near East. But most Sumerian literature – including the *Epic of Gilgamesh* and other myths and legends – survives to be read today in texts that were written many centuries after this, and long after Sumerian had ceased to be an everyday spoken language.

As the classical language of a highly developed state, Sumerian had a considerable influence on Akkadian. Sumerian words were borrowed into Akkadian, and, even more frequently, Sumerian written word forms ('Sumerograms') were made to stand for the equivalent Akkadian words in cuneiform writing. Sumerograms are found in Hittite and other cuneiform texts too.

It is not surprising that no relatives of Sumerian have been discovered. Nearly all the languages of the world of 3000 BC are now completely unknown. Not long afterwards, at any rate, it is clear that the Near East was linguistically highly fragmented, for Hittite, Urartian, Akkadian and Elamite represent four completely separate language families, and Sumerian simply makes a fifth.

How we read Sumerian script

'Akkadian is a Semitic language, but Sumerian is a language isolate of a very different type, and with a very different phonemic inventory. The values we give to cuneiform signs in Sumerian texts are based on Akkadian values and on ancient glosses. Since most of these glosses date from periods when Sumerian was no longer spoken, i.e. from a milieu speaking Akkadian or other Semitic languages, it is said that we view Sumerian phonology through Akkadian glasses. However, since the signs used to write Akkadian had been adapted from an originally Sumerian system of cuneiform writing, we might also say that our Akkadian glasses were made by Sumerian opticians.'

Jerrold S. Cooper in *The world's writing systems* ed. Peter T. Daniels, William Bright (New York: Oxford University Press, 1996) p. 37

Sumerian was an 'agglutinating' language, one in which a basic word form is given a series of affixes to indicate its function in the sentence. Two main dialects can be recognised in the language written down in the tablets: *eme-gir* is the administrative language, while *eme-sal* is used for hymns and chants. It has been suggested that *eme-sal* originates not as a regional dialect but as the distinctive speech of Sumerian women.

The first ten numerals in Sumerian were *desh, min, pesh, lim, i, i-ash, i-min, i-ush, i-lim, hu.*

Once upon a time

Storytellers in many languages begin with a set phrase or sentence, like English 'Once upon a time', that draws listeners' attention. This stylistic feature can be traced five thousand years back, to the opening of Sumerian tales such as *Ašnan and her seven sons*:

U$_4$ re u$_4$ re na-nam	It happened in those days, in those days,
gi$_6$ re gi$_6$ re na-nam	It happened in those nights, in those nights,
mu re mu re na-nam . . .	It happened in those years, in those years . . .

In standard Sumerian transliteration, subscript numbers (*u*$_4$ and *gi*$_6$ above) are used to mark duplication in the script: the scribe used the fourth alternative form of *u*, the sixth alternative for *gi*.

After Jeremy Black, 'Some structural features of Sumerian narrative poetry'
in *Mesopotamian epic literature: oral or aural?* ed. Marianna E. Vogelzang,
Herman L. J. Vanstiphout (Lewiston: Edwin Mellen Press, 1992) pp. 71–101

SUNDANESE

27,000,000 SPEAKERS

Indonesia

Sundanese belongs to the group of major AUSTRONESIAN LANGUAGES of the Greater Sunda Islands. It is the everyday speech of the western third of the island of Java, and, in terms of numbers, is Indonesia's third language, spoken by nearly one-sixth of the national population. But Indonesian (MALAY), not Sundanese, is the most used language of Jakarta, the capital of Indonesia, which thus forms a large enclave in Sundanese territory.

Sundanese has for many centuries had a history very like that of JAVANESE (see map there), which is spoken in central and eastern Java. Yet there has been much argument among linguists as to whether Sundanese belongs with Javanese, or rather with Malay, in the family groupings within Austronesian.

Like Javanese, Sundanese shows the effects of Sanskrit, Malay and Arabic influence – and also has many loanwords from Javanese itself. Sundanese has the separate 'formal' and 'informal' speech registers typical of neighbouring languages. As with Balinese and Madurese, the formal vocabulary consists very largely of Javanese loanwords.

Numerals in Javanese and Sundanese			
	Javanese Ngoko	Javanese Krama	Sundanese
1	siji	setunggal	hiji
2	loro	kalih	dua
3	telu	tiga	tilu
4	papat	sekawan	opat
5	lima	gangsal	lima
6	enem	enem	gănăp
7	pitu	pitu	tujuh
8	walu	walu	dalapan
9	sanga	sanga	salapan
10	sepuluh	sedasa	sapulu

Sundanese in writing

Sundanese has a long written history. It has been written in three quite different scripts. The *aksara* or alphabet of Indian type is nowadays identical with that of Javanese, though the spelling rules are different. Arabic script is also used. But commonest now is the Latin alphabet, which uses an orthography similar to that of Indonesian.

SUSU

700,000 SPEAKERS

Guinea, Sierra Leone

One of the NIGER-CONGO LANGUAGES of the Mande Fu group, Susu is a coastal lingua franca of Guinea and the main language of the capital, Conakry. It is also spoken on the northwestern borders of Sierra Leone.

The Susu, an inland people who have fairly recently migrated towards the Atlantic, were among the early enemies of the Empire of Mali in the 13th century. In the 18th century Susu had reached the coast, being spoken as far south as the Sierra Leone estuary. Susu speakers came under the British sphere of influence on the establishment of Sierra Leone Colony in 1788, but most Susu territory was acquired by the French in 1889 and is now in Guinea.

Susu speakers are largely Muslim, and the language shows Arabic as well as French influence. The first ten numerals are: *keren, firin, sakhan, nani, suli, seni, solofere, solo masakhan, solo manani, fu*.

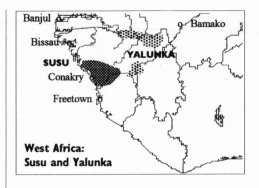

West Africa:
Susu and Yalunka

Susu and Yalunka

Susu (in French *Soussou*) is spoken in Guinea and northern Sierra Leone.

Yalunka, closely related to Susu, has 30,000 speakers further inland on the borders between Guinea and Sierra Leone.

SWAHILI

PERHAPS 4,000,000 SPEAKERS OF SWAHILI AS A MOTHER TONGUE

Tanzania, Kenya, Congo (Kinshasa)

One of the BANTU LANGUAGES, and strongly influenced by Arabic, Swahili is probably the most widely spoken indigenous African language. Swahili is the official language of Tanzania, and it is the most widely spoken language in Kenya and Uganda. Well over 40,000,000 speakers use Swahili either as a first or a second language.

> The name *kiSwahili* means 'coastal language' from Arabic *sawāhil* 'coasts'. Until very recently, this is precisely what Swahili was – a language of the coastal peoples, which, from its geographical position, tended to absorb foreign influences and to be used more and more widely in trade. The language group to which Swahili belongs is sometimes called *Sabaki*, a name suggested by Christopher Ehret, from the Sabaki river of eastern Kenya.
>
> The Swahili-speaking Muslim trading communities considered themselves Arabs and they were often so called by Europeans in colonial times. The Portuguese called them *Moros* and the English *Moors* or *Blackamoors*.
>
> *Zanzibar* was once the name of the whole coast, as well as of the island. It is an Arabic form of Persian *zangī-bār*, 'country of the negroes'. *Zingis* and *Zanj* are recorded as the name for the islands, the coast and their empire from the 2nd century onwards.

From a postulated prehistoric Eastern Bantu centre of dispersal, in the Great Lakes region, early Sabaki dialects were probably beginning to spread into their present locations in the first centuries AD. It was some centuries after that when northern Mozambique and the Comores

were reached, as archaeological evidence confirms.

As that settlement was continuing, the speakers of one Sabaki dialect, 'proto-Swahili', were already becoming ubiquitous in the coastal trade: they, or at any rate their language, began to radiate widely from their original excellent location at Zanzibar and Pemba. Thus the oldest island Swahili dialects are probably just as old as Mwani and Comorian – but they have differentiated less from the parent language, because their communities tended to remain in close touch.

East African seaborne trade has been, for two thousand years, dominated by people of Arabic culture, the actual languages involved in this trade being Persian, Gujarati, Konkani, Swahili itself and, most honoured, Arabic. According to Greek sources, around AD 100 Arabs were already established at the port of Rhapta (Dar es Salaam), where they ruled 'by some ancient right' and were already familiar with the local language, whatever it then was. Islam was introduced very early. The oldest surviving Arabic inscription of this coast dates a mosque at Zanzibar to 1107. By this time the Zanj Empire, centred on Zanzibar, dominated the trade of the western Indian Ocean – and it is said that Swahili influence can be traced in the Arabic dialects of southern Arabia and coastal Iraq.

Until around 1700 Arabic was the only *written* language of this coastal, island and ocean culture – a culture in which literacy was already relatively widespread. The first known manuscript of Swahili poetry, an epic, dates from 1728. It is naturally in Arabic script. The Latin script was introduced and Swahili printing began, under

European influence, in the 19th century: the first newspaper, *Habari ya Mwezi*, a missionary publication, appeared at Magila in 1895. Arabic script is still very widely used.

At first concentrated on coastal islands, Swahili-speaking traders began to found more coastal settlements in the 13th century (Mombasa is one). When the Portuguese arrived, in 1498, Arabic and Swahili were important languages all along the coast. Alongside the spread of everyday Swahili, Koranic schools and the religious use of Arabic spread also. Many Swahili speakers of this heartland are descendants of slaves, including, probably, a large proportion of YAO and NYANJA origin. Immigration of Arabic speakers may have reached a peak in the 18th century: their descendants also now speak Swahili.

Tabora, founded about 1820, was a staging post on the longer inland routes. During the 19th century, and maybe earlier, Swahili-speaking slave traders and other adventurers crossed Lake Tanganyika and ranged beyond as far as the Lualaba valley. The name of Tippu Tip, who made trading expeditions into Congo (Kinshasa) from 1870 to 1884, is rightly linked to the early expansion of Swahili in Congo, though the language was already known there. His Muslim Swahili-speaking warriors, who eventually formed colonies in what became the Congo Free State, were known to the Belgians as *Arabisés*, to themselves and others as *wangwana* 'free men' – hence the modern name *kiNgwana* for Zaire Swahili, 'language of free men'. Here too, Islamic schools were founded and Arabic has its place as the special language of religion.

In Tanganyika, under German occupation from 1884, and in the whole of East Africa as it fell under British and Belgian rule, Swahili was taken up as the most convenient available means of communication with inland peoples, at least some of whom already knew the language. Far fewer learnt German or English. In British times Swahili came to replace the various mother tongues of Tanganyika as the language that the administration prescribed for school use.

Thus when independence came Swahili was the natural choice as the national language of Tanzania.

National varieties and creolised forms of Swahili

Nowadays Swahili is learnt as a first language on the islands of Zanzibar, Lamu, Pate and Pemba and by a fairly small number of people on the Kenya coast. More important, it is the first language for a rapidly growing number of city-dwellers in Tanzania. More important still, it is the language that all Tanzanian schoolchildren need to know. It remains true that most of the speakers of Swahili learn another African language first, but more and more now use Swahili for preference. All over East Africa, the learning in childhood of at least three languages – a local language, Swahili and English – is the usual rule.

Within Tanzania the older, coastal dialects of Swahili, particularly those of the islands, persist. New regional varieties, influenced by various inland languages and reflecting cultural differences, can be seen emerging, but they will remain closer to the prestigious standard language of education and the media.

The colonial British of Kenya took a completely different view of Swahili: they found it a useful tool of domination, but despised it. Linguistic surveys of the early post-colonial period retained this view, evaluating Swahili as a useful language for Kenya, but not one that carried prestige. Later history has shown the emptiness of this inherited viewpoint. Kenya, too, has adopted Swahili as its national language.

A variety of Swahili that spread as a lingua franca in Kenya and Uganda was once characterised as 'Up-Country Swahili', *kiSwahili cha bara*. 'Up-Country Swahili' shaded into a pidgin language, Kenya Pidgin Swahili, once very widely used by speakers who had no opportunity to learn a more standard variety – and into a special pidgin, *kiSettla*, that was used between the European settlers of Kenya and their African employees. *KiVita*, 'war language', was the jargon of the British East African army.

Cutchi-Swahili or *kiHindi* has been used as the name of the speech variety of South Asians in Kenya, its name recalling their predominant origin from the Cutch peninsula. Another pidgin Swahili, *Barracoon*, a mixed language with elements of Arabic, Portuguese and Malagasy, was used in the Mozambique ports in the 19th century. It scarcely survives today. But a form of Swahili nearer to the current standard remains a lingua franca of trade in north-western Madagascar and in northern Mozambique, where the *kiMwani* dialect is influenced by local MAKONDE.

Swahili was briefly a school language of Uganda. Uganda's British rulers once planned to make it the local official language, but abandoned an idea which, to the speakers of Ganda, was unpleasantly reminiscent of the settler ethos of Kenya. Swahili is still the language of the Ugandan army and police force, and an essential lingua franca in Uganda generally.

Swahili is important in trade in Rwanda and Burundi, a position it achieved as a result of the 19th-century expansion of trade from the East African coast. Rather surprisingly, this position has not yet been undermined either by French, which was the language of power here for nearly a century, or by the local languages (see RUNDI) common to almost the whole population.

Zaire Swahili, known locally as *Ngwana* or kiNgwana or Kiungwana, is the most extensive lingua franca of eastern Congo, important in the media and in everyday contact between people of different languages. It is a distinct regional variety of Swahili, heavily influenced by Congolese languages and differing considerably from the standard Swahili of Tanzania.

In Lubumbashi (Elisabethville), the capital of the Shaba region of Congo, because of the early recruitment of mine workers from north-eastern Congo, Rwanda, Burundi and East Africa, a distinct form of Swahili, perhaps a true creole, has become the city's lingua franca. Nowadays more workers come from Luba-speaking districts, but they adopt Lubumbashi Swahili as their second language. It is used in the popular press, in plays, and especially among schoolchildren. The standard Swahili of Tanzania is difficult for Lubumbashi speakers even to understand.

The first ten numerals in Standard Swahili are: *moja, mbili, tatu, nne, tano, sita, saba, nane, tisa, kumi.* It is a sign of Swahili's history as a language of trade that three of these ('6', '7', '9') are borrowed from Arabic, thus abandoning the quinary counting system, more usual in Bantu languages, in which 'six' is formed as 'five plus one' or 'over to the right hand'. The three borrowed numerals are invariable: the smaller numerals, as usual in Bantu languages, must agree in class with the noun that they qualify. Thus *mayai matatu*, 'three eggs'; *vitabu vitano*, 'five books'.

The Swahili word for 'book' in this example is borrowed from Arabic, like many cultural and religious terms: Arabic *kitāb* fitted well with the Swahili 'inanimate' noun class, giving singular *kitabu*, plural *vitabu*. Swahili also has numerous Portuguese loanwords, for example *gereza* 'prison' from Portuguese *igreja* 'church'. English loanwords include *buluu* 'blue', *kilabu* (plural *vilabu*) 'club, nightclub'. Swahili has naturally borrowed heavily from MALAGASY, the language of the southern island of Madagascar with which there has been constant interchange and trade: *divai* 'wine' is from Malagasy, where it derived originally from the French *du vin* 'some wine'.

The rapid spread of Swahili is partly due to slavery and the need for a lingua franca among communities of captured slaves, *watumwa*, home-bred slaves, *wakulia*, freed former slaves, *wahuru*, and their descendants, *wahadimu*. One of the Swahili dialects of Zanzibar takes its name from the *wahadimu*. *Wahuru*, with a different prefix, becomes *uhuru*, 'freedom' or 'land of the freed', a potent political catchword at the end of the colonial period.

Bantu languages of the East African coast

Some *North East Coast Languages* differ from the rest of the Bantu family in their sound pattern: Zalamo and Swahili, for example, have no tones, but instead a stress accent.

Asu or *Pare*, known to its own speakers as Chasu, has 300,000 speakers in Pare district. A northern and a southern dialect can be distinguished.

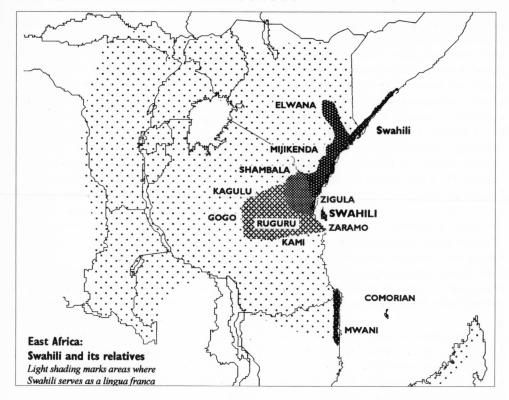

East Africa:
Swahili and its relatives
Light shading marks areas where
Swahili serves as a lingua franca

'God' and 'Gods'

'The Swahili prefer to use the Arabic word for God, *Ilahi* or *Allahu*. There is a word of Bantu origin – *Mungu* – which has been used exclusively by Christian missionaries, who naturally did not feel inclined to use an Islamic term. Mohammedans would point out, however, that *Mungu* has a plural *miungu* "gods, i.e. idols". A plural of Allah is absolutely inconceivable and this may explain the preference of the Swahili Islamic writers for this word.'

Jan Knappert, 'Contribution from the study of loanwords to the cultural history of Africa' in D. Dalby and others, *Language and history in Africa* (London: Cass, 1970) pp. 78–88

The Ruvu group includes Gogo, Kagulu, Kami, Ruguru and Zalamo. *Gogo*, with almost 1,000,000 speakers, is the language of the Dodoma district, with three recognised dialects: *ciNyambwa* to the west, *ciNyaugogo* near Dodoma,

ciTumba to the east. *Kagulu* has 225,000 speakers. *Kami* has 300,000 speakers south of Dar es Salaam. *Ruguru* or Lugulu has 500,000 speakers in the Uluguru mountains. *Zalamo* or Zaramo has 450,000 speakers in the country south, west and north of Dar es Salaam.

The Seuta group includes Ngulu, Shambala and Zigula. *Ngulu* has 130,000 speakers. *Shambala* or Shambaa has 500,000 speakers in the Usambara mountains. Shambala is notable for its complex verb forms. A verb may have around eighty combinations of infixes marking tense and aspect, in addition to negative markers and personal prefixes: *mwadika*, 'you cooked'; *nemudike* 'you will cook'; *titazadika*, 'we will cook (contrary to assumption)'; *watavyadika*, 'these will cook (by contrast with others)'; *hemuzedika*, 'you did not cook'. *Zigula* has over 300,000 speakers north of Dar es Salaam.

The Sabaki group is a chain of languages running roughly north–south, from the Tana river valley of Kenya to the Comores Islands: Elwana, Mijikenda, Swahili, Mwani and Comorian. The larger languages are Mijikenda, Comorian and Swahili itself. *Mijikenda*, comprising *Nyika* (a subgroup including *Giriama* and *Digo*) and *Pokomo*, has nearly 1,000,000 speakers in eastern Kenya and Tanzania. There has long been a tendency for speakers of these languages to shift to Swahili, so statistics are difficult to fix. *Comorian* or Komoro has 450,000 on the Comores archipelago. *Ngazija* or Shingazidja is the dialect of Grande Comore, while *Nzwani* is the dialect of Anjouan. The points of origin of *Swahili* itself are Pemba and Zanzibar islands.

The spread of Swahili

The older Swahili dialects are coastal ones. The language was once spoken at ports and harbours all the way from Mogadishu in Somalia to Sofala (Beira) and Chibwene in middle Mozambique.

Surviving coastal dialects are marked with dark shading on the map.

In the 19th century the language spread rapidly inland, at first with Swahili trade and conquest, afterwards with German and British administration and the migration of workers. Shading indicates the regions where it is regularly used today.

Swahili is the official language of Tanzania, the usual medium of secondary education, government and broadcasting. *Unguja* or kiUnguja, one of the three dialects of Zanzibar island, owing its origin to the highly mobile population of 19th-century Zanzibar, is the basis of Standard Swahili. The other two dialects spoken on Zanzibar, *Hadimu* ('language of the descendants of slaves') and *Tumbatu* ('of Tumbatu Island'), have a more archaic character.

Spelling it out

Swahili, language of a rapidly growing population and for many speakers a second or third language, has far fewer complex verb forms than its relatives. While Shambala uses affixes to show verbal 'mood', Swahili tends to use separate adverbs or auxiliary verbs:

Shambala		Swahili
Tedika inu manga	**Please** cook this cassava	**Hebu** pika huu mhogo
Ziya mbogha taa**za**zidika	We **really did** cook the vegetables	Zile mboga **tulija** zipika
Uja mushi **ne**tidikiye manga	That day we **actually** cooked cassava	Siku ile **tulikuwa** tumepika mhogo

Examples from Ruth M. Besha, 'Mood in Bantu languages: an exemplification from Shambala' in *Studies in Tanzanian languages* (Tokyo: ILCAA, 1989) pp. 205–22

The further simplification typical of pidgin languages can be seen in Kenya Pidgin Swahili in the question words. A pattern already found in Standard Swahili (first two examples) has been extended to the whole range:

Kenya Pidgin Swahili		Standard Swahili
saa gani?	'hour which?' = when?	saa ngapi?
namna gani?	'kind which?' = how?	namna gani?
siku kani?	'day which?' = when?	lini?
kitu gani?	'thing which?' = what?	nini?
sababu gani?	'reason which?' = why?	kwa nini?

Examples from Bernd Heine in *Readings in creole studies* ed. Ian F. Hancock (Gent: Story-Scientia, 1979) p. 95

SWAZI

1,600,000 SPEAKERS

South Africa, Swaziland, Mozambique

One of the Nguni group of BANTU LANGUAGES, Swazi or Swati is the national language of Swaziland, where there are 600,000 speakers. It also has about 900,000 speakers in neighbouring districts of South Africa, where it is one of the eleven official languages (see map at ZULU). Swaziland is a country of rocky highlands, *inkangala*, and of bush-covered lowland plains, *lihlandza*, which are cut off by the Lubombo mountains from the Mozambique coast.

When Afrikaans- and English-speaking invaders first approached the country it was ruled by Mswati II (1839–68). Their Zulu contacts called its people *emaSwazi*, 'people of Mswati'. The modern names for the language and the country derive from this.

Swati and *siSwati* are the forms now preferred by linguistic purists, since *Swazi* with a *z* was of Zulu origin; but, as names for the language, all these are foreign. The speakers have traditionally called themselves *ebantfu bakaNgwane*, 'people of Ngwane', the founder of the monarchy, and their language *siNgwane*.

It is probable that Nguni language speakers have occupied the region of modern Swaziland for about a thousand years. Cattle are their traditional wealth: 'epigrams, symbolism, riddles and praise songs are built around them; the king is honoured as the Bull of the people' (H. Kuper).

The ruling family of Swaziland traces its origin to a migration from the north in the late 15th century, and first occupied a part of Swaziland under Ngwane III, who died c. 1780. His burial site in a cave in a tree-covered hill at Lobamba is a place of pilgrimage. His grandson Sobhuza I

(ruled 1815–39) settled near the modern capital, and established a powerful monarchy which managed to survive the damaging land seizures of the late 19th and early 20th centuries.

About a third of the kingdom escaped incorporation in South Africa and remained a British protectorate until independence in 1968. Here, few speak English, though many know some Zulu. The Swazi-speaking people of the rural Transvaal have tended to retain their language, and their emotional ties with the monarchy, while those more widely spread across South Africa, especially city-dwellers, may be gradually absorbed by majority Sotho, Zulu and Xhosa speakers. In the Swazi-speaking districts of Mozambique Tsonga is the dominant language.

Swazi, like the other Nguni languages, has the click consonants that are otherwise typical of KHOISAN LANGUAGES. Their presence indicates close interaction with speakers of one or other of those languages in the past.

Praise poetry and legendary history

Swazi praise poetry is composed in a special Zuluised literary dialect, while prose myths and legends are typically told in a purer form of Swazi.

'The main literary productions are the praise poems, *tibongo*, developed in each reign round the character and activities of the rulers, and recited, together with those of their predecessors, on national occasions. Praise poems of other personalities have a local circulation. Animals, particularly cattle . . . have also provided suitable subjects. There may be one or more versions, and the individual composer is often not known . . . Official praisers are chosen by the rulers for their memory and dramatic abilities, and are listened to with admiration.

'Swazi prose is in the form of myths, legends, fables and tales, handed down from generation to generation. Swazi myths of origin are few, simple, and generally accepted. Legends dealing with clan and tribal history are often complicated and usually recalled by the old men for specific legal or ritual purposes; fables and tales are reserved for entertainment in the evening, and are told mainly by old women. In the tales, the main characters are often of royal birth; in the fables, the most popular animal is the hare. While tales and fables are told essentially for entertainment, they may also point a moral. For this purpose, however, the Swazi . . . have a wealth of proverb and idiom. Riddles and verbal memory games are popular with children.'

H. Kuper, *The Swazi* (London: International African Institute, 1952) pp. 14–15

Revising Bantu prehistory

'We have come a long way from believing that the Bantu-speaking people crossed the Limpopo river around 1652. This is one of the great myths of twentieth-century South African historiography. Archaeological research has shown that Bantu-speaking people herding livestock and practising cultivation were already established in the Transvaal and Natal before AD 300,' writes R. Bailey in *Language and social history: studies in South African sociolinguistics* ed. Rajend Mesthrie (Cape Town: David Philip, 1995) p. 39.

The revised view may be correct (see also map 1 at BANTU LANGUAGES) but Bailey's brief statement obscures the discontinuity between two types of evidence. Archaeological research cannot really show what language these people spoke. It may be significant that *inkomo*, the word for 'cattle' in Nguni languages, seems to be a KHOISAN loanword.

SWEDISH

9,000,000 SPEAKERS

Sweden, Finland

Swedish is one of the descendants of OLD NORSE. Specifically it derives from the East Norse dialect, like Danish. It is the official language of the Kingdom of Sweden, whose origins go back to the 7th century.

> The Germanic tribe *Sviones* is mentioned by the Roman historian Tacitus in the 1st century AD. *Sverige*, the modern native name of Sweden, comes directly from the medieval *Sveariki*, the 'kingdom of Svea', whose centre was the province still called *Svea*.

The range of modern standard Swedish is very different from its historical extent. This history is still partially reflected in surviving dialect boundaries.

To the west, much of the region that we think of as southern Sweden was part of Denmark until 1658, when the provinces of Skåne, Blekinge and Halland were conquered. Denmark also ruled the Baltic islands of Bornholm (which has remained Danish) and Gotland, acquired by Sweden in 1645.

To the east, Finland was Swedish territory from the 12th century until 1809, and Swedish was for much of this time the only language of government and education. In the 12th, 13th and 14th centuries Swedes had settled in large numbers in the Åland Islands, which lie to the east in the Gulf of Bothnia, and also on the western and southern coasts of Finland and in coastal parts of Estonia.

Two of these areas of Swedish speech still survive, both of them now within the borders of Finland, where there are nowadays 300,000 speakers of Swedish. The Åland islands are almost completely autonomous: Swedish is their only language, and Finnish is not even taught in most schools. Mainland Finland is, by its constitution, bilingual, with equal rights for Swedish and Finnish. In addition there is now a large number of Swedish-speaking immigrants in the United States.

Modern Swedish literature may be said to begin with 'Gustav Vasa's Bible', translated and published under King Gustav Vasa's patronage in 1540–1.

Swedish vocabulary includes Greek and Latin loanwords, particularly religious terms (*biskop* 'bishop'; *brev* 'letter'); Low German, introduced at the period when the Hansa towns controlled Baltic trade (*frukost* 'breakfast', *bädd* 'bed'). More recently, High German influence appears in the way that technical terms are formed.

Descendants of East Norse

The modern descendants of East Norse are DANISH and SWEDISH. There are no firm frontiers between the two: they form a single dialect continuum.

The three principal dialects of Danish are Jutish (of the Jutland peninsula), Island Danish and the *Sydsvenska mål*, 'South Swedish' or Dano-Swedish dialect group, which includes the island of Bornholm. Some linguists count the latter group as Swedish.

Asterisks on the map mark former centres of East Norse speech where the language is now extinct. They include Scarborough (*Skarðaborg*), Grimsby (*Grimsbær*), York, Rouen, Ladoga (*Aldeigjaborg*), Novgorod (*Holmgarðr*) and Kiev (*Kænugarðr*). Norse and Anglo-Saxon warriors formed the Varangian Guard at Constantinople (*Miklagarðr*).

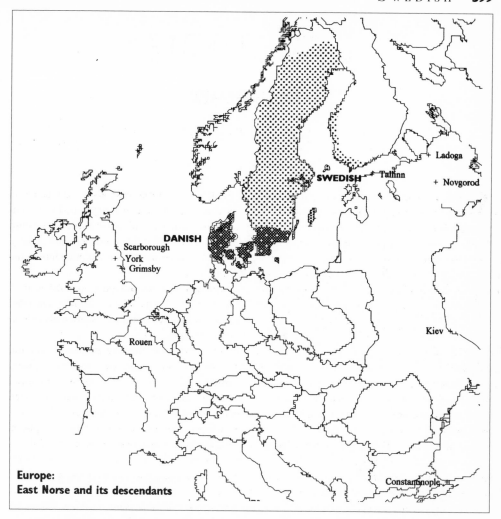

Europe:
East Norse and its descendants

		Numerals in Scandinavian languages			
	Swedish	**Danish**	**Norwegian**	**Faroese**	**Icelandic**
1	en, ett	en, et	en, ei, et	ein	einn, ein, eitt
2	två	to	to	tveir	tveir, tvær, tvö
3	tre	tre	tre	tríggir	þrír, þrjár, þrjú
4	fyra	fire	fire	fýra	fjórir, fjórar, fjögur
5	fem	fem	fem	fimm	fimm
6	sex	seks	seks	seks	sex
7	sju	syv	syv, sju	sjey	sjö
8	åtta	otte	otte	átta	átta
9	nio	ni	ni	níggju	níu
10	tio	ti	ti	tíggju	tíu

TAGALOG

10,500,000 SPEAKERS

Philippines

Among the AUSTRONESIAN LANGUAGES of the Philippines. Tagalog happened to be the one that was spoken in the Manila region of southern Luzon. It was also the language of the early manifestos of the resistance against Spain and the United States. As early as 1897 came the proposal that Tagalog should be the national language of the independent Philippines. When independence was in sight, Tagalog was indeed declared the basis of the new 'national language', and it has been taught as such in schools from 1940 onwards, though in some provinces opposition to it remains. By now nearly three-quarters of the population can use Tagalog – a remarkable advance for what was, a century ago, a regional language with no official recognition at all.

Tagalog is said to mean 'river people', from *taga-* 'place of origin' and *ilog* 'river'. For the national language the name Tagalog has been officially replaced by *Pilipino*. This, incidentally, is a local form of the name of the islands, a name commemorating Philip II, who was King of Spain when the islands came under Spanish rule in 1565. In theory, *Pilipino* is to be replaced in due course by *Filipino* (see box).

The Philippine archipelago was ruled by Spain until 1898. Spanish is not now a major language of the Philippines, but the inheritance of Spanish culture, and of Catholic Christianity spread by Spanish missionaries, is to be traced everywhere. The typical *barrio fiesta* (Spanish loanwords: 'village festival') of the Philippines is celebrated annually in Holland Park, London, by Filipinos in Britain. It has been argued that the complex system of polite address forms in Tagalog is borrowed from or modelled on that of Spanish.

After an abortive declaration of independence American rule followed in 1898–1946 (interrupted by Japanese occupation), and American military bases remain. English is thus a major language of the Philippines still. Education was officially bilingual from 1957, combining Tagalog with a local language. Since 1974 trilingual education is the general practice, in a local language for the first years, in Tagalog and English later. This has influenced Tagalog pervasively. English loanwords occur frequently in everyday speech and in journalism. 'Taglish' is the name given to a mixed jargon fashionable among young people.

Tagalog was already a language of written culture at the Spanish invasion. A 1593 bilingual publication in Spanish and Tagalog, *Doctrina christiana*, prints the Tagalog in an Indic-type script, not unlike that still used for MAKASAR. However, no historical records survive from that period or before. It is only clear that Tagalog, and the other Philippine languages to which it is related, had gradually spread over the islands in the preceding three or four thousand years, having originally been introduced in a migration from Taiwan, the presumed origin of all the Austronesian languages.

The script soon fell out of use. In the Spanish period, publishing in Tagalog and the other regional languages was largely religious in inspiration – yet it can be seen, from the beginning, to incorporate Tagalog poetic forms. Spanish in origin, the *corrido*, metrical romance, *pasyon*, Christian passion play, and *komedya*, theatrical 'comedy' of Christian–Muslim warfare, all three became lively and fully naturalised forms of Tagalog literature. Manila has now a flourishing press both in Tagalog and in English.

In recent decades Tagalog has spread from its original location both as a second language and as the language of migrants, who have settled widely in Luzon and in coastal parts of Mindoro and Palawan. It is much heard in cities all over the Philippines and on the proliferating broadcast media. Large Tagalog-speaking communities exist in the United States, and migrant workers are to be found in many countries of the world.

'National language' and 'regional language of southern Luzon' are simply two ways of looking at the same language, Tagalog. There has been a movement to replace Spanish and English loanwords with native coinages: *salumpuwit* for the Spanish loanword *silya* 'seat'; *banyuhay* for the English loanword *metamorposis*. But it is clear that Tagalog, as a lingua franca, will naturally draw on the vocabulary of Spanish, English and the other regional languages of the Philippines. Some sounds (such as the *f* of *Filipino*) occur only in loanwords.

The linguist Leonard Bloomfield produced a grammar of Tagalog as one of his earliest pieces of research, in 1917. He broke away from the Latin and Spanish tradition of Tagalog grammar, analysing the language afresh and bringing out its contrasts with European languages and their grammar.

For a table of numerals see BIKOL.

Examples from R. David Zorc, 'Tagalog' in *Comparative Austronesian dictionary: an introduction to Austronesian studies*, ed. Darrell T. Tryon (Berlin: Mouton De Gruyter, 1995–) pt 1 pp. 335–41

The Philippines: Tagalog and its rivals

ILOCANO
Pangasinan
LUZON
Kapampangan
BIKOL
TAGALOG
WARAY-WARAY
HILIGAYNON
PALAWAN
CEBUANO
MINDANAO

Filipino: language of the future

In its 1973 constitution the Philippine government looked forward to a new language, *Filipino*, declaring: 'The National Assembly shall take steps towards the development and formal adoption of a common national language to be known as Filipino . . . Until otherwise provided by law, English and Pilipino shall be the official languages' (1973 Constitution of the Philippines, article xv, section 3, paras 2–3).

To forestall regional opposition to Tagalog-Pilipino, the plan was to invent a truly inclusive national language, with a grammar and vocabulary based somehow on all the regional languages. Some work has been done since 1973, but language planning of this kind usually fails. Redesigned Filipino is not likely to progress far: instead, 'Filipino' may gradually replace 'Pilipino' as a name for Tagalog viewed as the national language.

Tagalog and its regional rivals

The eight 'major languages' of the Philippines are Tagalog, Ilocano, Pangasinan, Kapampangan, Bikol, and the three Bisayan languages, Cebuano, Hiligaynon and Waray-Waray: for the last three see map at CEBUANO. Together these eight are the mother tongues of nearly 90 per cent of the population of the Philippines.

Tagalog dominates in Greater Manila, Bataan, Batangas, Bulacan, Cavite, Laguna, Marinduque, Nueva Ecija, Mindoro Occidental, Mindoro Oriental, Quezon and Rizal. It is becoming the lingua franca of many cities and towns throughout the Philippines. Standard Filipino is based on the Tagalog dialect of Manila. Tagalog and Filipino are now used, as lingua franca, throughout the Philippines, even where they are no one's mother tongue.

BIKOL is the major language of southern Luzon: Albay, Camarines Sur, Catanduanas, Sorsogon, and parts of Camarines Norte and Masbate.

ILOCANO, the language of north-western

Luzon, is dominant in the provinces of La Union, Ilocos Sur, Ilocos Norte and Abra. It is also widely spoken further to the south-west in Tarlac, Pangasinan and Zambales, and in parts of Mindoro island. It is also spoken in far-off Cotabato on the island of Mindanao.

PANGASINAN is the language of the central part of Pangasinan province in north central Luzon.

KAPAMPANGAN is spoken in Pampanga province, north-west of Manila, as well as in four cities of Tarlac (Bamban, Concepcion, Tarlac itself and Capas) and two cities of Bataan (Dinalupihan and Hermosa) near the western borders of Pampanga.

TAHITIAN

100,000 SPEAKERS

French Polynesia

Tahitian, one of the Oceanic branch of AUS-TRONESIAN LANGUAGES, is spoken by about two-thirds of the population of French Polynesia. This island group of the central Pacific is known in English as the Society Islands: better known is the name of the largest island, Tahiti.

The first printed book in Tahitian was an ABC, *Te Aebi no Tahiti*, by John Davies, published in 1810. Much literature, mostly religious and educational, has appeared since then.

Since the first European contact Tahitian has been changing rather rapidly and has been considerably influenced by French. Tahitian has some official status locally, since knowledge of the language is required for Polynesians (though not for French speakers) in government service. As the language of local administration, of central health, social and educational services, and of local broadcasting, Tahitian is a lingua

franca in the territory and the local languages of the smaller islands are giving way to it. Mangarevan, Rapan, Tuamotuan and Tubuai-Rurutu (all of them Polynesian languages) are among those that show signs of succumbing to Tahitian in its lingua franca form, *Neo-Tahitian* as it is sometimes called.

Even among Polynesian languages Tahitian is unusual in its sound pattern, having only nine consonant phonemes, *p t ' f v h m n r*. It has five vowels and, since a syllable may contain one or any two vowels, a total of twenty-five diphthongs.

The first ten numerals in Tahitian are: *tahi, piti, toru, maha, pae, ōno, hitu, va'u, iva, hō'ē ahuru*.

Tahitian on the map

Like the West Indies, the Society Islands are divided by mariners into a Leeward and a Wind-

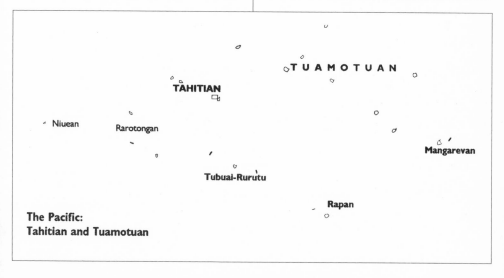

The Pacific:
Tahitian and Tuamotuan

ward group. There are some dialect differences between the two.

Tuamotuan, with 15,000 speakers, is the language of the Low or Dangerous archipelago. Along with the small island languages *Mangarevan*, *Rapan* and *Tubuai-Rurutu*, it is now in decline: Tahitian is taking their place.

TAI LANGUAGES

The major constituent of the KADAI LANGUAGES, one of the groupings that probably belongs to the postulated AUSTRO-TAI family, is Tai – a group of closely related languages usually classified into three roughly geographical divisions.

The South-western division includes the two best known, THAI or Siamese, spoken in central Thailand, and Lao of Laos and north-eastern Thailand. A continuum of dialects in areas to the north of these begins with AHOM, an extinct language of the Indian state of Assam, and SHAN; it continues eastwards with LANNA THAI and ends with the minority languages of Laos and Vietnam usually known as Black Tai, Red Tai and White Tai (see map at LAO).

The Central group includes THO, NUNG and Southern Zhuang. Northern Zhuang and BUYI are classified as the Northern group. These are all minority languages of southern China and the northern borders of Vietnam (see map at ZHUANG).

Because of some obvious similarities with Chinese, and because, like Chinese, they are monosyllabic and tonal languages, it has often been assumed that Tai languages and SINO-TIBETAN LANGUAGES are ultimately related. Most scholars now agree that these similarities are due to borrowing. Instead, evidence has accumulated for a link between Tai and other languages of south-east Asia in a postulated family of AUSTRO-TAI LANGUAGES.

Tai or *Thai*, 'free', is the people's own term for themselves: linguists have chosen the variant *Tai* as the name for the language family, while *Thai* normally means the national language of Thailand.

Many foreigners use another term for Tai peoples. In Assam they were called *Asam*, locally pronounced *Ohom*; in Burmese and Khmer, they are called *Shan*, *Syam*; in Chinese they have been called *Sien*. Assam and *Siam*, as country names, both derive from this term.

Dai, in Chinese, is the name for the South-western members of the family: *Zhuang-Dai* is the Chinese term for the grouping called *Tai* by linguists writing in English.

Tai chronicles trace the history of individual Tai-speaking states back no further than the 12th century, and this really does seem to be the approximate date of the appearance of Tai ruling groups in south-east Asia. The details of Tai history before this time are not known, but

Numerals in Tai languages

	Shan	Thai	Lao	Northern Zhuang
1	nöng, ét	nöng, ɛt	nöng, ɛt	īt, děw
2	sóng	sóng	sóng	sŏng, ngey
3	sám	sám	sám	săm
4	si	si	si	séy
5	hà'	hà'	ha	hā, ngù
6	hók	hok	hok	rèk, gok
7	cét	cet	cet	cāt
8	pɛt	pɛt	pɛt	pét
9	kàw'	kàw'	kàw	kōw
10	síp	sip	sip	cip

The second form for 'one' is used in compounds, e.g. in Shan *síp ét* 'eleven'. Forms in the three south-western Tai languages (Shan, Thai and Lao) differ only in the tones. For Thai numerals in original script see table at THAI.

the ultimate origin of the language group must be in south-eastern China, where many Tai speakers are still to be found: it is from here, several thousand years ago, that early Austronesian language speakers must also have dispersed.

Many Thai historians hold to the theory that the Yunnanese kingdom of Nanchao, once powerful and independent, destroyed by a Mongol invasion in 1253, was Tai-speaking. The fall of Nanchao was thought to explain the apparent rapid spread of Tai speakers towards the south at about this period. It now seems more likely that the languages of Nanchao were BAI and YI, or something like them. It is not unlikely that some Tai states with long histories, including Hsip Hsong Pan Na (see LANNA THAI), were in early times tributary to Nanchao.

TAMASHEQ

PERHAPS 1,000,000 SPEAKERS

Niger, Mali, Burkina Faso, Algeria, Libya

Tamasheq, one of the BERBER LANGUAGES (see map at TAMAZIGHT), is spoken by the *Tuareg* (singular *Targi*) of the Sahara.

The name *Tamasheq* identifies it as the language of the *Amaziɣ* 'Berbers'.

In spite of the unbroken tradition of writing in the *tifinagh* alphabet, no long texts are known from earlier periods of Tamasheq. Interest in the language stemmed from European exploration of the Sahara.

The major dialects of today centre on Timbuktu, Tahoua, Aïr (*Tayart*) and Hoggar. But, as the language of a nomadic people, Tamasheq has surprisingly small dialect differences across the vast area over which it is spoken. There are about 450,000 speakers in Niger, about 300,000 in Mali and 150,000 in Burkina Faso. In all three countries, Tamasheq is recognised as a regional official language and is used in schools and adult education. Numbers in southern Algeria and Libya are much smaller.

Tamasheq has, naturally, fewer Arabic loanwords than the Berber languages of the north, where the long term influence of Islamic culture, radiating from the cities, has been almost overwhelming. By contrast, Tamasheq draws loanwords from African languages such as Hausa.

Like the other Berber languages, Tamasheq has a gender distinction in which feminine forms are typified by a *-t* suffix, as seen in the table of numerals.

Tamasheq (Tayart) numerals		
Masculine		**Feminine**
iyan	1	iyăt
əsshin	2	sənatăt
kərăd	3	kəradăt
əkkoz	4	əkkozăt
səmmos	5	səmmosăt
saeḍis	6	səḍisăt
əssa	7	əssayăt
əttam	8	əttamăt
təẓa	9	təẓayă
məraw	10	mərawăt

M. Malherbe, *Les langages de l'humanité* (Paris: Laffont, 1995) p. 1545

Tifinagh

The *Tifinagh* ('Phoenician') script still used by some Tuareg communities is descended from the alphabet used for the 'Old Libyan' Berber languages in pre-Roman times. It is not taught in schools: it is used for private notes, love letters, and in decoration. It is astonishing that it has survived, with uses that seem to observers so unimportant, for two thousand years – but it may be a crucial factor that women do not learn to read Arabic, the language and script used by most Tuareg for public purposes.

Attempts to use Tifinagh for other purposes, whether in Bible translations or in Berber nationalist movements, have failed.

TAMAZIGHT

3,000,000 SPEAKERS

Morocco, Algeria

Tamazight is one of the BERBER LANGUAGES. Its speakers gave their name to the whole language group, for it is spoken by the people called *Beraber* and is sometimes simply referred to as 'Berber'. But this was originally a derogatory Greek word, 'barbarian', and the speakers' own name for their language, *Tamazight* 'language of the *Amaziɣ* or Berbers', is more often used. The name occurs in Ibn Khaldūn's 13th-century *History of the Berbers*: 'their ancestor was *Mazigh*'.

The Berber languages of Morocco are sometimes grouped under the name Shilha: in these terms Tamazight is 'Central Shilha'. It has about

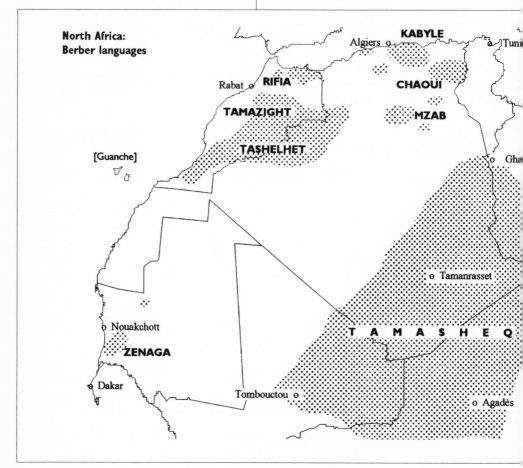

North Africa:
Berber languages

1,800,000 speakers in the Middle Atlas region of northern Morocco, and perhaps another 1,200,000 in western Algeria. It has no official status in either state: in Algeria, a constitutional amendment in 1996 declared Arabic the sole language of business, education and administration. Men of the Tamazight country are usually bilingual in Arabic, but Tamazight remains the language of the household.

Tamazight literature is largely oral. Some manuscript collections of poetry in Arabic script have been collected and published. *The forgotten hill*, the first feature film in Tamazight, shot in Algeria, appeared in 1997.

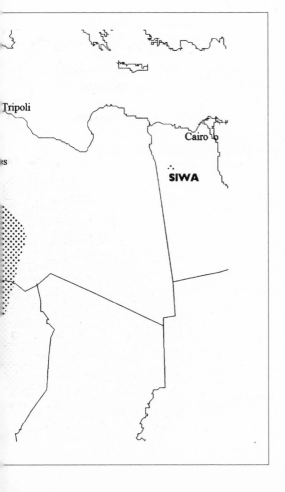

TAMIL

52,000,000 SPEAKERS

India, Sri Lanka, Malaysia, Vietnam, Singapore

Belonging to the family of DRAVIDIAN LAN-
GUAGES, Tamil is the first language of the
Indian state of Tamilnadu and is spoken by a
minority of over 2,000,000 speakers in north-
eastern Sri Lanka.

Tamil or *Tamiz* is a Tamil form of the old
Sanskrit name for the southern Indian kingdom, *Drāviḍa*, and is thus the term that
foreigners have applied to the region and
the language for nearly two thousand years.

For all this time, and even for longer, Tamil
has been spoken in the area of modern Tamilnadu. Cave inscriptions, in a mixture of early
Tamil and Prakrit, date back as far as the 3rd
century BC. The earliest Tamil literature goes
back perhaps to the 1st century AD: partly Bud-
dhist-inspired, it consists of lyric poems, epics –
and a grammar, *Tolkappiyam*.

Medieval Tamil is dated from AD 700 to 1500:
Hindu religious influence now supplanted Buddhism, but Tamil, unlike its twin language MA-
LAYALAM, remained not especially receptive to
Sanskrit loanwords. It is from this period that the
written and spoken forms of the language have
grown apart, for literary Tamil remains close to
the prescriptions of the grammarian PavaNanti-
munivar's *Nannul*, compiled in the 13th century
and itself drawing on the more ancient texts.

The 19th century saw attempts to bring modern spoken Tamil into written form, partly in the
context of Christian missionary activity. The
style of, for instance, school readers and of the
dialogue passages in fiction still differs very
strongly from that of formal prose.

Tamil has a much smaller range of consonant
phonemes than other Indian languages (see
box). Verb forms include suffixes for person,

Southern Asia: Tamil and Malayalam

number, and in the case of the third person also for one of three genders (male, female, non-human). Verbs also have a negative conjugation. There are many differences in noun and verb forms between literary and spoken Tamil.

Beyond India

Tamil speakers have been among the readiest of the inhabitants of India to migrate for work and to settle abroad. The first records of Tamil trading colonies overseas are in Tamil inscriptions from southern Thailand, in the 9th century, and from northern Sumatra, dating from 1088 onwards. Tamil is now spoken in Malaysia, in Vietnam, in Singapore (where it is one of the four national languages), on the island of Zanzibar, and in many other countries.

In nearby Sri Lanka there are two layers of Tamil speech. The 'indigenous' dialects, long established in the country, have over 2,000,000 speakers in the north of the island. The 900,000 speakers of 'Indian Tamil' are the descendants of tea plantation workers brought to the central hills in the mid 19th century. The dialects may begin to converge as speakers of indigenous Tamil become familiar with Indian Tamil through imported films, radio and television.

Sri Lanka has suffered serious linguistic unrest. The Sinhala-Only Bill of 1956, requiring the use of Sinhala in official contexts, eroded the position not only of English (its stated intention) but also of Tamil. Rebellion flared. Over 200,000 Tamil speakers fled abroad in the course of the 1980s. In 1987 Tamil and English nominally regained their old position as official languages, but the dispute, once aroused, has not been easy to calm.

Tamil and Malayalam

Tamil is spoken in the Indian state of Tamilnadu, in Sri Lanka (3,100,000), and by large communities in Malaysia (1,750,000), Vietnam (perhaps 1,000,000), Singapore (200,000) and other countries across the world.

Malayalam, historically an offshoot of Tamil, is the language of the Indian state of Kerala. Malayalam communities abroad tend to be counted with Tamil communities and to assimilate to Tamil as their home language.

The twelve initial vowels of Tamil

அ ஆ இ ஈ உ ஊ எ ஏ ஐ ஒ ஓ ஔ
a ā i ī u ū e ē ai o ō au

The eighteen consonants of Tamil

க ங ச ஞ ட ண த ந ப
ம ய ர ல வ ழ ள ற ன
k ṅ c ñ ṭ ṇ t n p m y r l v ḻ ḷ ṟ ṉ

The Tamil script

As with other scripts descended from Brahmi, consonants are combined with following vowels to make a single character group. Unlike others, Tamil has no compound consonant symbols.

The Tamil script, admirably efficient in plan, is strictly limited to what is necessary to write Tamil phonemically. It works well in writing the literary language and for traditional vocabulary. Speakers from written texts, actors for example,

VIETNAMESE
Saigon
Penang
MALAY
Kuala Lumpur
Malacca
Singapore

learn to make a fairly complex set of conversions, subconsciously, as they speak.

However, Tamil script does not go well with the way that Tamil speakers now use language. Sanskrit words can be inserted in Tamil texts with the help of extra 'grantha' characters; but English and other loanwords have no such traditional help and are difficult to write. So the modern spoken language, now with many international loanwords and an extended range of sounds to accommodate them, cannot be fully written in Tamil script.

TANGUT

Extinct language of western China

Tangut, known in Chinese as *Xixia* (older transliteration *Hsihsia*), was one of the SINO-TIBETAN LANGUAGES and apparently a member of the Burmese-Lolo group.

The kingdom of the Tangut was a major power in north-western China in early medieval times. In AD 1037 a script of about 6,600 characters was devised for their national language, credited to 'the Teacher Iri'. It flourished for only two centuries. Genghis Khan was killed in 1226 at the siege of the Tangut capital. His son Kublai wreaked fierce revenge on the Tangut. Those who remained continued to use their Buddhist texts until about the 16th century, after which time the language clearly ceased to be known.

The Tangut script has been deciphered with the help of a Chinese–Tangut dictionary, the *Sea of characters*, compiled by the Chinese diplomatic service in the 12th century. Like Chinese, it was a pictographic script extended by the phonetic use of rhymes. Character combinations were formed by borrowing the consonant value from one character and the vowel from another. The sounds of Tangut have been only partly recovered. Like Chinese, it was clearly a tonal language.

TASHELHET

PERHAPS 3,000,000 SPEAKERS

Morocco, Algeria, Mauritania

Tashelhet or Tachelhit is one of the BERBER LANGUAGES (see map at TAMAZIGHT).

The Berber languages of Morocco are sometimes grouped under the name Shilha. Tashelhet is the one from which this name derives, for the two words are identical in origin: speakers call themselves *Shlḥi*, sometimes rendered *Chleuh* in French or *Shluh* in English. They call their language *T-ashlḥi-t*, with the *t-* prefix and *-t* suffix typical of a feminine noun.

Tashelhet has no official status in Morocco or Algeria. Male speakers are usually bilingual in Arabic, but women are not.

The first ten numerals in Tashelhet, in their masculine forms, are: *yan, sin, kraḍ, kkuẓ, smmus, sḍis, sa, tam, ttẓa, mraw*. Feminine numerals are formed with a final *-t: yat, snat, kraṭṭ, kkuẓt* and so on up. Arabic tends to be used for counting above '10'.

The twelve months in Tashelhet

The influence of imperial Latin, at the south-western extremity of the Roman Empire, seems to be indicated by the month names in Tashelhet. It has been argued that they are borrowed, not directly from Latin, but, much later, from Spanish, which had inherited these names from Latin.

Latin	Tashelhet	Spanish
januarius	innayr	enero
februarius	xubrayr	febrero
martius	marṣ	marzo
aprilis	ibrir	abril
maius	mayyuh	mayo
junius	yunyu	junio
julius	yulyuz	julio
augustus	ɣušt	agosto
september	šuṭambir	setiembre
october	kṭubṛ	octubre
november	nuwambir	noviembre
december	dujanbir	diciembre

After J. Bynon, 'Linguistics and Berber history' in *Language and history in Africa* ed. D. Dalby (London: Cass, 1970) pp. 64–77

Tatar

6,000,000 SPEAKERS

Russia

Tatar is one of the TURKIC LANGUAGES, spoken in European Russia to the west of the Urals. For a table of numerals see BASHKIR.

Ruled and led by Mongolians, the warriors subject to the Golden Horde were largely Tatar-speaking and Muslim. They overran Rus' in the 13th century, destroying the old capital, Kiev, in 1242. Kiev and Ukraine were soon lost to them, but they dominated Moscow for two hundred and fifty years – and ever after, Muslim peoples encountered by the Russians were usually called by them 'Tatar'. At this period there was inter-marriage and intermixture between Russian and Tatar nobility. The Russian language still shows the influence of Tatar, and such figures as Boris Godunov and the novelist Fyodor Dostoyevskii could claim Tatar descent.

In the 15th century Moscow threw off the Tatar overlordship, and soon afterwards, as its power grew, conquered the Golden Horde's khanates of Kazan and Astrakhan. The khanate of Crimea was annexed by Catherine the Great in 1783.

Turkic and Mongolian speakers had settled in these three neighbourhoods. For the Kalmyks of Astrakhan see MONGOLIAN LANGUAGES; for the 'Tatars' of the Crimea see box. The true Tatars were those of Kazan, and it is south-east of Kazan that most Tatar speakers are to be found today. After submitting to Russia themselves they were active once more in the subsequent spread of Russian power to the Caucasus, Azerbaijan and Central Asia. In all these regions Tatars served as interpreters, administrators and – most signifi-cantly – teachers and missionaries in a 19th-century Muslim renewal.

The Tatar diaspora is numerous, both inside Russia (see map) and beyond its borders. There are Tatar communities in the Bulgarian Dobruja, for example. A World Congress of Tatars as-sembled in Kazan in 1992.

> Tatarstan, now an autonomous republic with-in Russia, has an independent-minded gov-ernment and a powerful Muslim party. One politician, Fauzia Bairamova, said in 1992: 'I would like to be able to say that Russia has contributed more to Tatar civilisation than prostitution and alcoholism. Sadly, I cannot.'

The dispersal of the Crimean Tatars

That ill-fated group of peoples, the Crimean Muslims and Jews, once had six distinct lan-guages. The Muslims of the south coast of the Crimea spoke Crimean Ottoman, a branch of the south-western group of Turkic languages. Those in the centre around Bahçesaray spoke Central Crimean Turkic, and those from the steppe spoke Crimean Tatar, a Kypchak language: both of these were western Turkic. The nomadic Nogai, of the northern Crimea and beyond, spoke a language of their own (see KAZAKH); their history is traced to Amir Noghay in the 13th century.

One Jewish people of the Crimea, the Krym-chaks, had their own language, close to Uzbek, but gradually assimilating to Crimean Tatar. These were orthodox, Talmudic Jews. Another, the Karaim, were 'heretical', owing their reli-gious beliefs to a sect of Judaism that split off in Basra in the 8th century. Imperial Russia recognised the Karaites as a separate religion, centred at Evpatoriya in the Crimea, led by a *ḥakam* (Hebrew: 'sage'). The language of the

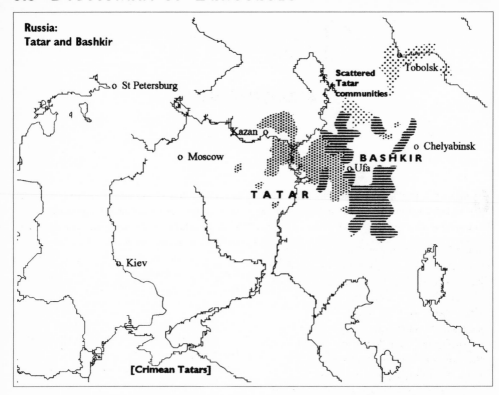

Russia:
Tatar and Bashkir

o St Petersburg

Scattered
Tatar
communities

Tobolsk.

Kazan

o Moscow

BASHKIR

o Chelyabinsk

Ufa

T A T A R

Kiev

[Crimean Tatars]

Karaim is a quite distinct offshoot of Turkic, and the Karaim traced their historical origin to the mysterious Khazar Empire, which had indeed adopted Judaism as its state religion and ruled the south Russian steppe in the 7th to 10th centuries. Both of these Jewish peoples had scriptures in Hebrew, but they used their own Turkic languages – written in Hebrew characters – in everyday life.

There were also Gothic, Greek, Slavonic, Arab and Iranian communities along the Crimean coast. This complex, multilingual society was doomed when Ottoman protection for the once-autonomous Khanate of the Crimea gave way to Russian rule around 1800. Population movements then were intensified by the Crimean War in 1853–6, the German occupation during the Second World War, and the Soviet deportations that followed.

Already in the 1780s many Crimean Tatars and Jews had migrated to the European provinces of the Ottoman Empire – and, as the empire continued to shrink, moved on again to Turkey. A majority of the remaining population fled, following these same routes, in the disastrous 1850s. Crimean Ottoman is so close to Turkish that its speakers soon gave up their language. Karaim had already spread to Lithuania and Poland.

Of the minority that remained in the Crimea, the Krymchaks, as Jews, were killed by the Germans in 1944. The Karaim, accepted by them as Turks whose religion alone was Jewish, were not killed. There are perhaps 20,000 Karaim today, most of them now in Israel – but few still speak their ancestral language. The Tatars, numbering about 190,000, were deported en masse to Central Asia in 1944; well over a quarter of these died in the first five years of exile. They were not officially allowed to return until 1990. Since then as many as 50,000 have found their way back to the eastern Crimea, but over 200,000 remain in Central Asia.

Based on Peter Alford Andrews, *Ethnic groups in the Republic of Turkey* (Wiesbaden: Steiner, 1989) and other sources

TELUGU

45,000,000 SPEAKERS

India

One of the DRAVIDIAN LANGUAGES, Telugu is the language of the Indian state of Andhra Pradesh (for map see KANNADA).

Telugu is a later, local form of the name *Telinga* once given to this region and its people in Sanskrit texts. *Andhra* is an alternative, used officially in the state name (*pradeśa*, 'province') and locally for the people and their language. In some older English writings it is called *Gentoo*, from Portuguese *Gentio*: from the point of view of early European traders, speakers of this language were the 'gentiles' of the Empire of Vijayanagar, in contrast with the *Moros*, the 'Moors' or Muslims, who were more in evidence on the western coast of India.

Within India Telugu perhaps has a larger number of speakers than any other Dravidian language. It is known from inscriptions beginning in the 6th century AD and from literature beginning around 1100. The Middle Telugu period is reckoned from the 11th to 15th centuries. It was in this period that the literary language became fixed in form. Among the early classics are versions of the Sanskrit epics and *purāṇas*, notably the 11th-century *Andhra Mahābhāratam* of Nannaya. Early modern Telugu court poetry was interwoven with music and dance; the mixed verse and prose form of the *prabandha* is a special feature of this literature.

By the beginning of the 20th century literary and spoken Telugu were almost two different languages. After long dispute between classicists and modernists, a modernised literary language, much closer to everyday speech, is now almost universal in current writing and in the media.

Telugu has three genders – but only two distinct gender forms. In the singular of nouns, feminine and non-human genders are combined, so that the distinction is masculine/non-masculine; in the plural, masculine and feminine are combined, and the distinction is human/non-human. The positive/negative opposition is incorporated in some verb forms: *ammutāḍu* 'he sells it', *ammaḍu* 'he does not sell it'.

Telugu has undergone lengthy, pervasive influence from Sanskrit, the traditional learned language of the subcontinent, and also from the Prakrits, the spoken Indo-Aryan languages of medieval northern India. As a result, the vocabulary of traditional literary Telugu is heavily Indo-Aryan, and so is that of the modern spoken language. At least one Telugu scholar argues that Sanskrit, not proto-Dravidian, is the true parent of Telugu.

Polite address in Telugu

Politeness is expressed by the choice of pronouns: *nuwwu* 'you (singular)' is informal, while *mīru* 'you (plural)' also functions as honorific singular. The third person pronouns have a four-way distinction for males and a three-way distinction for females: listed from low to high these are *wāḍu, atanu, āyana, wāru* 'he', and *adi, āme, wāru* 'she'. The choice depends on the age and education of speaker and hearer, the social context and the speaker's intentions.

After Bh. Krishnamurti, 'Telugu' in *International encyclopedia of linguistics* (New York: Oxford University Press, 1992) vol. 4 pp. 137–41

Numerals in Telugu and Kannada		
Telugu		**Kannada**
oṇḍu, oka	1	oṃdu
reṇḍu	2	eradu
mūḍu	3	mūru
nālugu	4	nālku
eidu	5	aidu
āṟu	6	āru
ēḍu	7	ēḷu
enimidi	8	eṃṭu
tommidi	9	oṃbhattu
padi	10	hattu

Telugu script

Telugu script is very similar to that of Kannada. As with other descendants of the Brahmi script, a consonant is combined with a following vowel in each symbol. Compound consonants are usually easy to pick out as they generally involve subsidiary symbols written below the line.

The Telugu consonants

కఖగఘ చఛజఝ టఠడఢణ తథదధన పఫబభమ యరలవ శషసహళ

k kh g gh c ch j jh ṭ ṭh ḍ ḍh ṇ t th d dh n p ph b bh m y r l v ś ṣ s h ḷ

TEMNE

1,000,000 SPEAKERS

Sierra Leone, Guinea

Temne or Themne or Timne, a member of the Atlantic group of NIGER-CONGO LANGUAGES, is the predominant language of north-western Sierra Leone.

The first European notice of Temne came in a wordlist made by an English mariner in 1582; the language was also seen as important by the Jesuit mission to Sierra Leone in 1610. Temne speakers (*aTemne*, as they call themselves) remained significant on a regional scale in the 17th century, when they clearly ruled the coastal hinterland of southern Guinea and northern Sierra Leone, enriched by trading contacts with Europeans. At this period the related Bullom or Sherbro was the dominant language on the coast itself, but it soon gave way to Temne in the north and later to Mende in the south. It was the Temne who ruled at the site of Freetown, which they ceded to the British in 1788. This marks the establishment of Sierra Leone Colony, under which some Temne lived: most remained independent, though at times under Mende domination, until a British Protectorate was proclaimed in the hinterland in 1896.

Christian missionaries began to work among Temne speakers in the 1790s. Many Temne are Muslim, and the language shows Arabic influence. Temne serves as a second language to as many as a quarter of a million speakers of local languages including Bullom, Susu, Lokko and Limba.

Temne and its relatives

Temne has a northern (*Sanda*) and a southern (*Yonni*) dialect. *Baga* and *Landoma* are a series of dialects of southern Guinea that are best counted as belonging to Temne.

Limba or Yimbe has about 250,000 speakers in inland northern Sierra Leone.

Bullom (as the speakers call themselves) or Sherbro, now a relatively minor language with about 175,000 speakers, was once the lingua franca of the coast. There are several early wordlists in Bullom compiled by European mariners and traders. *Northern Bullom* has a small number of remaining speakers in coastal parts of Temne country. *Krim* or Kim is a southern dialect of Bullom.

Northern Kissi or Gizi has nearly 300,000 speakers in Guinea. The *Southern* dialect is spoken by about 150,000 people in north-western Liberia and Sierra Leone.

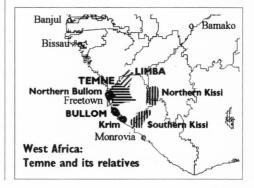

West Africa:
Temne and its relatives

TERNATE

70,000 SPEAKERS

Indonesia

Ternate belongs to the North Halmaheran group of West PAPUAN LANGUAGES. The other groups of this family are spoken on the Bird's Head peninsula of West Irian.

Ternate and its relatives (see map) are the only languages of any of the Papuan families that are spoken outside the immediate vicinity of New Guinea. It is not known whether they came to Halmahera from New Guinea, or whether early speakers of the Bird's Head languages migrated there from Halmahera. At any rate, there are still close contacts between the two regions.

The importance of Ternate, and its twin language Tidore, is that they were spoken on the two small islands off western Halmahera which are known to history and legend as the 'Spice Islands'. Until the 16th century, these were the only places in the world where cloves grew. The prized spice was known to India, China and the Roman Empire by the last centuries BC – though its buyers long believed that it came from Java. Clearly the first stage of its long journey was handled by local traders.

The rulers of Ternate and Tidore grew rich and powerful on the profits from their luxury export. They competed for the overlordship of all of Halmahera and the central Moluccas. Both island states became Islamic sultanates in the 15th century. Ternate and Tidore are recorded in writing – in Arabic script – from this period onwards.

A layer of Ternate loanwords is naturally found in Tobelo and Galela, the related languages of the coastal peoples of north-east Halmahera and Morotai. Tobelo and Galela seamen manned the war canoes with which Ternate raided the north coast of New Guinea. Ternate had an even stronger influence on neighbouring Sahu: Sahu-speaking communities supplied rice and domestic servants to the nobility of Ternate. Ternate loanwords are found in many of the Austronesian languages of the Moluccas.

From its earliest recorded history Ternate was rich in Malay loanwords, an indication of already longstanding trade contacts. Portuguese and Dutch, languages of successive European intruders, have also influenced Ternate.

Besides its use as a mother tongue, Ternate is still spoken today by many of the inhabitants of northern Halmahera. Their own languages (see map) were not written down until the Christian missionaries of the Utrechtse Zendingsvereeniging began studying them, and making Biblical translations, in 1866.

Ternate as language of rhetoric and ritual

Ternate is no longer a major language of trade: this role is taken by the local variety of MALAY. But its prestigious history as the language of the Sultans of Ternate has ensured its place in ceremonial.

'Many Tobelo are anxious to learn words or phrases of Ternatese. Some of this may be due to whatever oratorical tradition makes some Tobelo want to incorporate a few basic words of several languages into their conversation . . . Ternatese predominates, specifically, in the language of traditional chants, of magical formulae, and of the give-and-take of marriage consultations between families of the bride and groom.

'One proper setting for the traditional chants

is the proud festivity of the last step of the marriage process, when the new daughter-in-law arrives at the house of her groom's parents and (traditionally, for three separate nights) she is 'displayed' perfectly motionless in her finest regalia of heirlooms (borrowed for the occasion from as many relatives as possible), constantly waited upon by her new sisters-in-law, while the older generation among her new male in-laws, chewing the slightly narcotic betel nut and drinking the palm-wine that ideally should flow freely on such occasions, sing their chants in Ternatese to the hearty beating of gongs and deer-skin drums.'

Paul Michael Taylor, *The folk biology of the Tobelo people* (Washington: Smithsonian Institution Press, 1990) p. 14

The West Papuan languages

Ternate is spoken on Ternate itself and in several towns on the facing coast of Halmahera. The *Tidore* dialect, likewise, is spoken on Tidore and in three coastal enclaves. Ternate is known throughout northern Halmahera.

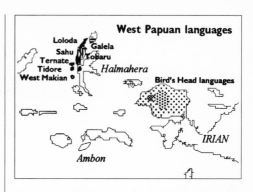

Sahu (10,000 speakers), *Loloda* or Loda (12,000), *Tobaru* or Tabaru (15,000), *Galela* (25,000, also known more widely as a language of love poetry) and *West Makian* (12,000) are all members of the North Halmaheran group. So is *Tobelo* or Tugutil (at least 25,000 speakers), the language of the north-east Halmaheran coast and of the eastern highlands, which is itself known in many parts of the island. It is spoken as far off as Ambon to the west and Raja Ampat to the east.

The Bird's Head group of the West Papuan family includes *Moraid* or Hattam (12,000 speakers), *Mai Brat* (20,000 speakers) and some smaller languages.

TESO

1,300,000 SPEAKERS

Uganda, Kenya

One of the Eastern Nilotic group of NILO-SAHARAN LANGUAGES (see map at TURKANA), Teso is traditionally said to have been brought to eastern Uganda in a migration from further east, led by the culture hero Teso.

> The language was once called *Dum* by outsiders. Speakers call themselves *Iteso* (singular *Etesot*). The form *Ateso* is sometimes found. In Kenya, where a distinct dialect is spoken (see map at TURKANA), the official term is *Itesyo*. Among Ganda speakers, the Teso to their east are known as *bakide*, a word said to mean 'naked people' – but it may derive from Teso *kide* 'east'.

At the end of the 19th century Ganda-speaking agents brought most of Teso territory under the British protectorate of Uganda, and reorganised its political system. From then onwards Teso has adopted an increasing number of Ganda loanwords. Other Bantu languages, such as Luyia, have also influenced Teso.

The first ten numerals in Teso, in their feminine forms, are: *adiope, aarei, auni, aoŋom, akany, akany kape, akany kaarei, akany kauni, akany kaoŋom, atomon.*

The Teso alphabet

a b c d e g i j k l m n ŋ ny o p r s t u w y

Under British rule a Teso alphabet was developed, under missionary influence, by the Teso Orthography Committee. The Christian sects could not agree over spelling, however: Catholic and Protestant orthographies differ.

THAI

PERHAPS 25,000,000 SPEAKERS

Thailand

The best known of the TAI LANGUAGES, Thai is the national language of Thailand, spoken by the great majority of the population in the central and southern parts of the country (see map at LAO).

Historically the Thai kingdom is the largest and most powerful of the many large and small Tai principalities that emerged in south-east Asia in the 12th and 13th centuries. The Chao Phraya valley, the centre of Thailand, was once ruled by the Mon kingdom of Dvaravati, and a small MON-speaking minority remains not far to the west of Bangkok.

From successive capitals – Sukhotai, Ayutthaya, Bangkok – Thai monarchs have achieved suzerainty over distant provinces and subject states, including Nan and Chiangmai (both now part of Thailand) and most of Laos. Bangkok was the only Tai capital that remained entirely independent through the colonial period, though it lost the Laotian states on the left bank of the Mekong, which were surrendered to France.

Thai society is firmly Buddhist. Linguistically, Sanskrit and Khmer were the early vehicles of Indic cultural and religious influence, now largely supplanted by Pali. The linguistic influence of Chinese is also very important. The Thai writing system (see box) is a careful adaptation of that of Khmer to a language with a very different sound pattern.

Thai was from the beginning of its known history the official language of a monarchical state. It has a special vocabulary of respect, used in court ritual and in the addressing of royalty. Thai literature and art, which show Indian and Khmer inspiration, have developed a distinctive flavour. The older literature includes chronicles and histories as well as poetry and religious texts. There is a flourishing modern publishing industry. One distinctive feature is the production of funeral or memorial volumes. These are often the vehicle for publishing a work of literary scholarship or local history, dedicated to the memory of a friend or patron.

Numerals in Thai

Thai numerals	Thai script	Transcription
1	๑	nง̣ng
2	๒	sɔ́ng
3	๓	sám
4	๔	sị̀
5	๕	hà'
6	๖	hǫk
7	๗	cet
8	๘	pɛt
9	๙	kàw'
10	๑๐	sịp

The Thai alphabet

กขฃคฅฆง จฉชซฌญ ฎฏฐฑฒณ ดตถทธน บปผฝพฟภม ยรฤลฦวศษสหฬอฮ

k kh ng c ch s y d t th n d t th n b p ph f m y r l w s h a

กะ กิ กี กุ เกะ แกะ โกะ-เกาะ เกอะ กำ ใก ไก เกา กา กี กี กู เก แก โก กอ กัว เกีย เกือ เกอ

In the top line, of Thai consonants, many symbols appear to duplicate one another: they are used for borrowed Pali and Sanskrit words, and to help in representing tone distinctions. There are 25 vowel signs. To exemplify them, all 25 are shown in the bottom line in conjunction with the consonant ก *k*.

The inscription of Ram Khamhaeng

'Previously these Thai letters did not exist. In 1205, year of the goat [AD 1283], Prince Ram Khamhaeng set all his will and all his heart on inventing the Thai letters, and the letters exist because the Prince invented them.'

The history of the Thai language and of Thai script begins with the inscription of Prince Ram Khamhaeng of Sukhotai, who in 1292 boasted of having established peace, law, trade, monasteries – and a new alphabet – at his capital city. Some Thai scholars believe the inscription (extract above) is 'too good to be true', and is a 19th-century forgery.

Whoever was its inventor, the Thai writing system was designed specifically for Thai (though redundant consonants were retained in order to render Pali and Sanskrit loanwords accurately). Until the present century, not Thai but Khmer script was used in Thailand in the writing and printing of Pali.

THO

1,000,000 SPEAKERS

Vietnam

Tho is one of the TAI LANGUAGES, forming the southern end of the Northern and Central Tai dialect continuum (see map at ZHUANG). It is a major language of northern Vietnam. Tho speakers are a population of the plains and river valleys to the north and north-east of the Red River delta.

The name *Tho*, 'soil' in literary Vietnamese, is exactly comparable with Chinese *T'u-jen*, 'people of the soil', an older name for Zhuang. In Vietnam *Tho* is now considered pejorative and *Tay* is preferred.

In the same way that Zhuang speakers are more Chinese than most other minority groups in China, so Tho speakers are more Vietnamese in their culture than the other Tai peoples of Vietnam. An elite class, *Tho-ti*, is said to descend from the Vietnamese officials who were first sent out to govern the Tho country in the 15th and 16th centuries. The Tho-ti, unlike other Tho speakers, are traditionally Mahayana Buddhists – and they officiate at rituals honouring the spirit of the soil, for, among the Tho, Buddhism is mixed with Confucianism, with ancestor worship like that of the Chinese and Vietnamese, and with the propitiation of spirits.

Tho has traditionally been written in a modified form of Chinese script, apparently based on the method once used for writing Vietnamese. This script was put to use mainly for recording songs. Genealogy has been an important matter to Tho speakers, and families kept a genealogy book which had to be consulted before a marriage could be agreed on in order to ensure that the couple were not related.

TIBETAN

PERHAPS 6,000,000 SPEAKERS

China, Bhutan, India, Nepal

Tibetan is the language of the ancient and unique culture of the highest country in the world, the plateau and mountain chains that lie north of the Himalaya. It is one of the SINO-TIBETAN LANGUAGES.

Tibetan has a long recorded history. It was first written down in the 7th century, when a king in southern Tibet, Sron-btsan sgam-po, dispatched his minister Thon-mi Sambhoṭa to India to bring back information on Buddhism. The minister is said to have invented the script and to have written a grammar of Tibetan – on Sanskrit lines – in thirty stanzas (if only all grammars were as short as that). Translation of Buddhist texts into Tibetan was immediately begun. A Sanskrit–Tibetan dictionary, *Mahā-vyutpatti*, was compiled in the 9th century. Printing from carved wood blocks, a technique introduced from China, began very early and is still practised in some Himalayan monasteries.

Tibetan literature now forms a vast corpus, partly translated from Sanskrit and Chinese, partly original and inspired by the special paths that monastic Buddhism has taken in Tibet. The non-Buddhist Bon religion has its own literature. An unusual genre is that of 'rediscovered' texts, *gter-ma*, claimed as the works of venerated teachers of the distant past which have lain hidden for centuries in mountain caves.

Tibet was for many centuries an autonomous theocratic state, occasionally entirely independent, more usually interdependent in various ways with Mongolia and with China. Tibet is now a province of China, and since 1959 Chinese policy has tended to favour the destruction of Tibetan civilisation. However, many Tibetan speakers fled into exile in the 1950s and 1960s. Tibetan Buddhism and its literature are thus at present maintained by a worldwide diaspora, drawing some strength from Tibetan communities of the southern Himalaya beyond the Chinese border. Classical Tibetan is a literary language for all of these, still in use in Bhutan, Sikkim, Nepal and Ladakh. The Namgyal Institute of Tibetology, in Sikkim, is said to have the largest collection of Tibetan books in the world outside St Petersburg and Beijing.

Tibetan texts may contain Sanskrit proper names, but the language has few direct loanwords. However, written Tibetan is influenced by the word-building and the sentence structure of Sanskrit, which are closely imitated in translations and original texts on Buddhism. Tibetan, in turn, exerts influence: to Mongolians it is the classical language of Buddhism, widely taught in Mongolia till a few decades ago.

Classical Tibetan, as first committed to writing, seems not to have been a tonal language. Ladakhi, even today, has no tones. But the modern Tibetan of Lhasa is very definitely tonal (see box). The script and the various dialects allow linguists to glimpse the kinds of changes through which tones can arise in a language.

Tibetan words and names are very variously spelt in foreign writings. This is because Tibetan spelling, little changed from its 7th-century origins, now has a highly complex – though still regular – relationship with the way the modern language sounds.

How tones originate

'Written Tibetan, Amdo Sherpa, gLo-skad and Central Tibetan all represent different stages of

The centre of the world

 རྒྱ་གར་ཤར་གྱི་རྨ། | Rgya-gar śar-gyi rma-bya | A peacock from eastern India,
ཀོང་ཡུལ་མཐིལ་གྱི་ནེ་ཙོ། | Kong-yul mthil-gyi ne-tso | A parrot from deepest Kong,
འཁྲུངས་ས་འཁྲུངས་ཡུལ་མི་གཅིག | 'khrungs-sa 'khrungs-yul mi gcig | Born and bred far apart,
འཛོམས་ས་ཆོས་འཁོར་ལྷ་ས། | 'dzoms-sa chos-'khor Lha-sa. | Live together in holy Lhasa.

Rgya-gar, said to mean 'white country', is the Tibetan name for India. *Kong-po* in eastern Tibet is a region of deep, thickly forested valleys. This poem by the Sixth Dalai Lama (1683–1706) exemplifies the typical two-syllable rhythm of Tibetan literary writing, both verse and poetic prose. The emphasis falls on the first of each syllable pair.

tonogenesis: 1. Written Tibetan represents the original pre-tonal stage, with its various prefixes and suffixes and its oppositions between voicing, voicelessness and aspiration. 2. Amdo Sherpa represents a second stage. The suffixes remain as in Written Tibetan, but the effect of the prefixes has been lost except for nasal initials; however, as a result tonal distinctions now exist for nasals. 3. gLo-skad represents a third stage. Tones can only be set up for the nasals and the sibilants, but contrasting phonetic pitch patterns are emerging for all initials. 4. Central Tibetan represents a final stage, where syllable structures are extremely simplified and tonal distinctions exist for all series.'

Yasuhiko Nagano in *Linguistics of the Sino-Tibetan area: papers presented to Paul K. Benedict* (Canberra: Australian National University, 1985) p. 462

Tibetan and its dialects

Tibetan is both a standard written language and a group of modern spoken dialects or languages, not all of which are mutually intelligible. Most of them share the culture and the classical literature of Tibetan Buddhism. As yet, too little is known of Tibetan dialects for adequate mapping. Besides 'Central Tibetan', the speech of Lhasa and its region, they include:

Choni, Amdo, Kham and other dialects spoken to the north and east of central Tibet, extending into the Chinese provinces of Qinghai and Yunnan.

Bumthang, Tsangla, Ngalong, the three major regional dialects of Bhutan (all mutually unintelligible), with over 1,000,000 speakers in total. DZONGKHA (see also map there), a lingua franca form of Ngalong, is now the national language of Bhutan.

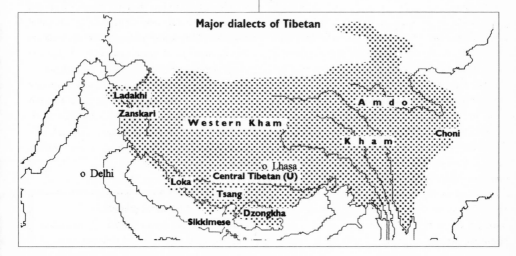

Major dialects of Tibetan

Sikkimese, the Tibetan dialect of Sikkim.

Kagate, gLo-skad or Loka of Mustang, and other Tibetan dialects spoken by the 'Sherpa' and related peoples of Nepal.

Lahuli, Zanskari, Ladakhi, Purik and *Balti*, Tibetan dialects of India and Kashmir, with perhaps 600,000 speakers in total. Many urban Ladakhi speakers are bilingual in Hindi, Urdu or English. The standard form of Ladakhi is the dialect of Leh. Classical Tibetan literature can be read with a Ladakhi rather than a central Tibetan pronunciation.

In Sikkim another Sino-Tibetan language exists alongside Tibetan: *Lepcha* or *Rong*, which has a local literary tradition and a distinctive alphabet. There are about 60,000 speakers.

The numerals in Tibetan

Figures	Written form	Central Tibetan pronunciation	Ladakhi pronunciation	Dzongkha pronunciation
༡	གཅིག	chik	chik	dzong
༢	གཉིས	nyi	nyis	nyi
༣	གསུམ	sum	sum	sum
༤	བཞི	shi	zhi	zhi
༥	ལྔ	nga	shnga	nga
༦	དྲུག	dhuk	druk	ṭuk
༧	བདུན	dün	rdun	duin
༨	བརྒྱད	gyä	rgyat	gye
༩	དགུ	gu	rgu	gu
༡༠	བཅུ	chu-thamba	schu	chu-thamba

The Tibetan alphabet

ཀ་ཁ་ག་ང་ ཅ་ཆ་ཇ་ཉ་ ཏ་ཐ་ད་ན་ པ་ཕ་བ་མ་ ཙ་ཚ་ཛ་ཝ་ ཞ་ཟ་འ་ཡ་ ར་ལ་ཤ་ས་ ཧ་ཨ

k kh g ng c ch j ny t th d n p ph
b m ts tsh dz w sh z ' y r l ś s h a

ཨ་ཨི་ཨུ་ཨེ་ཨོ

a i u e o

The Tibetan script

With its monosyllabic structure and complex initial consonants Old Tibetan was utterly different from Sanskrit and from medieval Indian languages. Thus, although recognisably based on an Indian model, the Tibetan script, devised in the 7th century, was built to a new specification, several separate characters making up a typical single syllable, and each syllable marked off with a dot. There are 30 characters, shown in the top line, and five vowel signs, here shown with the character *a*.

The formal version of the script, shown in the box, is ideally suited to woodblock printing, the traditional method of publication in Tibet. But it is very slow to write. Cursive forms exist for informal texts and for private use.

TIGRINYA

PERHAPS 3,500,000 SPEAKERS

Eritrea, Ethiopia

One of the SEMITIC LANGUAGES, Tigrinya is the major language of Eritrea, and of the neighbouring province of Tigre in Ethiopia (for map see AMHARIC). The majority of Tigrinya speakers are Ethiopian Christians: there is a strong minority of Muslims.

Eritrea was conquered by Italy between 1882 and 1889. It was captured by the British in 1941 and transferred to Ethiopia in 1952, becoming independent, after a long and bitter civil war, in April 1993.

Both Tigrinya and Tigre are very similar to ETHIOPIC in their vocabulary. In its word structure, Tigre is closer to the classical language than is Tigrinya. The two modern languages are not mutually intelligible. Muslim Tigrinya speakers are often bilingual in Arabic.

Tigrinya, like Amharic, has seven vowels. As in other Semitic languages, plurals are normally formed by internal vowel changes: *färäs* 'horse', *'afras* 'horses'.

To Eritreans, *Tigre* means 'the common people' or 'serfs': hence the name of the province Tigre. *Tigrinya* (sometimes written *Tigriña*, or with the Italian spelling *Tigrigna*) is an Amharic form, 'the language of *Tigre* province'. The language is also called *Tigray* or Tigrai in earlier sources, but this is confusingly close to another language name, *Tigre*.

Tigre, with 100,000 speakers (or many more: estimates vary widely), is a quite distinct language of Eritrea. An early wordlist of Tigre was published by Henry Salt in his *Voyage to Abyssinia* in 1814. In Ethiopia people of Eritrea and of Tigre province are alike called 'Tigre': few are aware that Tigre and Tigrinya are different languages.

Numerals in AMHARIC, ETHIOPIC and Tigrinya

	Amharic	Ethiopic: masculine and feminine		Tigrinya
1	and	'ahadū	'ahattī	hadə
2	hulätt	kələ'ētū	kələ'ētī	kəlatte
3	sost	shalastū	shalās	sələste
4	arat	'arba'tū	'rbā'	'arba'te
5	amməst	khaməstū	khams	hammushte
6	səddəst	sədəstū	səssū	shuddushte
7	säbat	sab'atū	sabɛū	shob'atte
8	səmmənt	samantū	samānī	shommonte
9	zäṭäñ	təs'atū	təsɛū	tesh'atte
10	asser	'ashartū	'ashrū	'assərte

TIV

1,500,000 SPEAKERS

Nigeria

One of the NIGER-CONGO LANGUAGES, Tiv is the most important in the Southern Bantoid subgroup of Benue-Congo, and is thus one of the most closely related languages to proto-Bantu, the ancestor of the BANTU LANGUAGES of today. It has five tones, important in verb conjugation, and a system of nine noun classes.

Tiv is the speakers' own name for themselves: it is the name of the ancestor from whom they all claim descent. In the early 20th century most authors called them *Munshi*, the Hausa name for them. 'Hausa, noted for their folk etymologies, say it means "We have eaten them", the answer Tiv are said to have made to Hausa traders seeking brothers who had disappeared in Tivland. Tiv today say that this name was first applied to them by Fulani, and that it was a herd of Fulani cattle which they had eaten. The term *Munshi* was used officially until the 1920s.'

By their neighbours, the speakers of Jukun, Tiv are known as *Mbitse* 'strangers' – possibly a sign that their present location is the result of migration. Certainly Tiv traditions told of a migration from hills in the south-east.

The earliest recorded visit to Tiv country by Europeans is in 1852, though earlier notes on the language had been made in Fernando Po in 1848 and in Freetown, Sierra Leone, in 1850, based on information from freed slaves.

The Tiv were an independent people, not grouped into a centralised state. Traditionally they are subsistence farmers, but many now migrate to work in the cities and towns of Nigeria. Tiv-speaking country was annexed by the British only between 1906 and 1912. It was at this time, too, that Christian missionaries began to work among Tiv speakers, and produced translations and educational literature in the language, which had thus far been unwritten.

'The reputation of the Tiv has undergone several startling reversals. According to Baikie, Hutchinson and [the YORUBA linguist] Crowther they were a fearsome, savage lot of cannibals whose unsavoury reputation spread as far as the Gold Coast. This notion was current until some time after 1880 . . . During the later days of the Niger Company and the early days of the Protectorate, the Tiv became a solid, brave and respectable people defending their homes and preserving their independence against the constantly increasing danger of encroachment by the British. Some reports went so far as to say that the "Munshi" lived in dense forest land and formed an extensive, autocratic kingdom . . .

'In the opinion of the writers of this report, missionary influence has not been very great in Tivland; this, we feel, is attributable much more to the nature of the Tiv than to that of the missions.'

Law, inheritance and genealogy are complex matters in traditional Tiv Society; oratory is a crucial skill. 'An elder should be skilled in discussion (*ɔron kwagh*), that is, as a man of the moot-court (*or jil*) and as arbitrator. Such skill involves a knowledge of the individual and genealogical histories of all the people (and their immediate ancestors) of the lineage group (*nongo*) among whom he has influence.'

The first ten numerals in Tiv are: *mom, uhar,*

utar, unyiyin, uta'an, uteratar, uta'an kar uhar, unyigenyi, uta'an kar unyiyin, puwe.

Quotations throughout this entry are from Laura and Paul Bohannan, *The Tiv of central Nigeria* (London: International African Institute, 1953)

The dialects of Tiv

Tiv is the language of Tiv Division in Benue-Plateau State, and has recently been spreading to Wukari, Lafia and Idoma Divisions. Some speakers live across the Cameroun border in Akwaya subdivision of South West Province.

'There are no dialects within Tivland itself. Tiv boast that they all speak the same language and that they can all understand one another. They tease one another, however, about accents (*liam*), which are roughly coordinated with area. There is the *Utisha* accent of south-eastern Tivland noted for its exaggerated palatalization of vowels. The *Shitire* accent (which includes most Tiv east of the Katsina Ala River) is much slower than other accents and has a tendency to merge all vowels into an indeterminate sound (like *a* in English *along*) . . . *Kparev* (central and south-central) accent is distinguished for rapidity and, according to some Tiv, contains additional sub-accent groups, like *Kunav*'s preference for *dj* sounds where other Kparev use *dz*. Vocabulary,

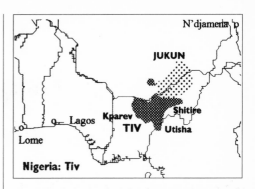

Nigeria: Tiv

particularly the names of plants and of utensils, changes from one part of Tivland to another; this provides Tiv with conversation, however, rather than any major source of misunderstanding.

'Shitire accent has a slight dominance when Tiv is written, for it was here that Dutch Reformed Church missionaries first learned Tiv and reduced it to writing. However, Kparev accent is most widely known, in large part because Kparev trade more widely and hence travel more widely.'

The *Jukun* dialects are not closely related to Tiv but they have interacted with one another significantly. In total Jukun has about 125,000 speakers in the Gongola and Plateau states of Nigeria and in Cameroun; it is spoken by the *Wurku* river people of the middle Benue, and serves locally as a lingua franca.

TOCHARIAN LANGUAGES

EXTINCT LANGUAGES OF CHINA

In the finds of manuscripts at the old oases on the Silk Road, many religions and many languages were represented. There was great excitement when it was realised that two lost languages of about AD 600, first rediscovered in these texts, belonged to a previously unknown branch of the INDO-EUROPEAN LANGUAGES.

Incautiously, scholars named these languages *Tocharian* after a tribe encountered by Greeks in Afghanistan in the 2nd century BC. There is really no reason to link them to this name. They called their speech *Arshi-käntu*, apparently 'Aryan'. The two languages are customarily distinguished as *Tocharian A* and *Tocharian B*.

Tocharian A, or *Turfanian*, was already a dead language when the texts we have were written down. It was used only in Buddhist scriptures and liturgies, and the people of Turfan and Karashahr needed glossaries or translations when they wished to understand it. Tocharian B or *Kuchean* was the ruling language of the Buddhist city-state of Kuqa, where it was soon to be replaced by UIGHUR. Tocharian B contributed loanwords to the Iranian language KHOTANESE, and influenced its script. Influences came in the other direction too: words such as *patsāṅk* 'window' and *sām* 'enemy' are of Iranian origin.

Although the Tocharian A and B manuscripts were found side by side, the two languages had actually been growing apart linguistically for hundreds of years. And it was soon found that Tocharian had quite astonishing relationships with the other Indo-European languages. Its strongest similarities were not with Indo-Aryan or Iranian languages, spoken a thousand miles away to the south-west, but with Celtic, Italic and Hittite, four thousand miles off. Like these, Tocharian belonged to the *centum* group (see box at INDO-EUROPEAN).

To explain this it is not necessary to imagine that the ancestors of the Tocharians once lived in western Europe. The true answer is that when the *satem* sound change occurred in Slavonic, Indo-Iranian, Albanian and Armenian, these were still Indo-European dialects spoken side by side. But by that time Hittite to the south, Celtic and others to the west and Tocharian somewhere to the east were all on the edge of the Indo-European dialect continuum, and none of them was affected by the change. So the Tocharian speakers were already on their way to their far-off destination among the cities of the Silk Road.

The first ten numerals in Tocharian A are: *sas, wu, tre, shtwar, päñ, ṣäk, ṣpäk, okät, ñu, shäk.*

TOK PISIN

2,000,000 SPEAKERS OF TOK PISIN AS A SECOND LANGUAGE

Papua New Guinea

Tok Pisin is a pidgin language, or more correctly a creole, based on ENGLISH. It is the principal lingua franca of Papua New Guinea and one of the three official languages of the country, alongside English and HIRI MOTU.

Tok Pisin is the native form of the English words 'Pidgin Talk': in context this distinguishes it from the local languages, collectively referred to as *Tok Ples* 'language of the place'. It has also been called *Neo-Melanesian, Melanesian Pidgin, New Guinea Pidgin* or simply *Pidgin.*

Tok Pisin originated in the late 19th century as a form of the widespread English pidgin of the South Sea Islands, best known as *Beach-la-Mar* (see also BISLAMA). Once it had been introduced to eastern New Guinea – territories then under German and British influence – the pidgin spread rapidly. It served better as a lingua franca even than Motu, and was certainly more promising than English or German, because the clear structure of a pidgin aids rapid learning by speakers of differing linguistic backgrounds. This was all the more necessary, since, in the newly annexed colonies, people speaking numerous local languages had suddenly to learn to work together as servants, government employees, farm workers and seamen.

It may well be that the pidgin prospered better under German rule, in the north-east, than under the English in the south-east, since Germans, though they disliked using an English-based lingua franca, could not avoid taking the trouble to learn it properly. Australians, who ruled both the former British and the former German territories during most of the 20th century, tended to disapprove of the pidgin equally strongly. The Japanese occupation during the Second World War forced a revision of this view: pidgin, already used by missionaries, now became the principal language of Australian as well as Japanese propaganda.

In independent Papua New Guinea Tok Pisin is the principal language of the media and of town life. It is the mother tongue of well over 100,000 young people, a number that is growing rapidly. Meanwhile, standard English is widely taught and is infiltrating Tok Pisin ever more strongly. Other, older influences can still be traced: it has been suggested that the absence of voiced final stops (so *rot* 'road'; *dok* 'dog') shows the phonetic influence of German. Like Austronesian languages, Tok Pisin has a rich series of personal pronouns: for the first person these are *mi* 'I', *yumitupela* 'we, including person addressed, total two', *yumitripela* 'ditto, total three', *yumi* 'ditto, indefinite total', *mitupela* 'we two, excluding person addressed', *mitripela* 'we three, ditto', *mipela* 'we all, ditto'.

Examples from John Holm, *Pidgins and creoles* (Cambridge: Cambridge University Press, 1989) pp. 529–34

'Rude words' in Tok Pisin

Standard Tok Pisin includes several important words whose English originals are 'improper'. In the 19th-century canefields, plantations and mines, language was used forcefully. The formerly 'rude words' are perfectly polite and proper in Tok Pisin. *As lo bilong gavman* ('arse law', basic law of the Government) means 'constitution'; *mi bagarap* means 'I'm tired'.

TONGA

900,000 SPEAKERS

Zambia, Zimbabwe

Tonga is one of the BANTU LANGUAGES and one of the eight official languages of Zambia. Speakers of Tonga, Ila and Lenje (see map at BEMBA) are together known as *Bantu Botatwe*, the 'three peoples'. It is from this word *bantu* 'people' that the name of the whole language family is derived.

The history of these three peoples, so far as it can be traced, is one of subjection to raids and conquests, culminating in that of the British. The Kololo, who introduced the LOZI language to the Zambezi valley, annexed the Ila and the southern half of Tonga-speaking territory in the 1830s. The southern dialect of Tonga now shows noticeable Lozi influence. Until 1906 slavery was practised locally and Tonga and Ila speakers were often taken as slaves by the Lozi, some to be sold on to MBUNDU traders.

Under British suzerainty, beginning in 1890, Tonga-speaking territory, which lay astride the Zambezi with a majority to the north, was split between Northern Rhodesia (Zambia) and Southern Rhodesia (Zimbabwe). The most productive lands of the Three Peoples were seized by colonial settlers and the slave system was gradually replaced by one of agricultural and migrant labour, many Tonga speakers working in the mines of southern Africa.

The Twa of the Kafue and Lukanga swamps are perhaps of Bushman origin (see KHOISAN LANGUAGES), but they now speak Tonga, Ila and Lenje like their neighbours.

Ka zuba o mwana kulu mwinzhila: If you hide with a child, there'll be a leg sticking out in the road – or, when you go into danger, choose your companions carefully. *Matako aswangene ta budi mutukuta*: When buttocks meet, there's always sweat – or, if you spend your life with someone, you're bound to quarrel.

After Edwin W. Smith, *A handbook of the Ila language* (London: Oxford University Press, 1907)

Numerals in Tonga and Ila

Tonga		Ila
-mwi	1	-mwi
-bili	2	-bili
-tatu	3	-tatwe
-ni	4	-ne
-sanwe	5	-sanwe
-sanwe a -mwi	6	chisambomwi
-sanwe a -bili	7	chiloba
-sanwe a -tatu	8	lusele
-sanwe a -ni	9	ifuka
ikumi	10	ikumi

As with most other Bantu languages, a singular or plural prefix must be added to the numerals '1' to '5' agreeing with the class of the noun that is qualified. In Tonga, the numerals from '6' to '9' require two prefixes.

TONGAN

130,000 SPEAKERS

Tonga

Tongan is a Polynesian language, belonging to the Oceanic branch of AUSTRONESIAN LANGUAGES. It is the official language of the kingdom of Tonga in the western Pacific.

Tonga was an influential place in medieval times, according to oral historical tradition. There was a Tongan Empire that extended to Samoa, Niue, Rotuma, Futuna and East Uvea. Recent linguistic research supports this, identifying Polynesian – most probably Tongan – loanwords in Vanuatu and in languages as distant as Kiribati, Ponapean and Mokilese.

Tonga, the 'Friendly Islands' of European explorers, became a British protectorate in the 19th century but remained self-governing. Wesleyan and French Catholic missionaries competed for converts, and developed different spellings in their grammars and religious texts in Tongan. The current spelling system was laid down by the Privy Council of Tonga in 1943.

Tongan does have loanwords from English, Fijian and Samoan. But all through the colonial period the language has remained in official use in education and government, and loanwords are balanced by new words formed from local roots: *tangata* 'man' gives such new terms as *tangata-tui-su*, 'man who sews shoes, i.e. cobbler', the *su* being a loanward from English.

The first ten numerals in Tongan are: *taha, ua, tolu, fā, nima, ono, fitu, valu, hiva, hongofalu.*

Based on Paul Geraghty, 'Tongan' in *Comparative Austronesian dictionary* ed. Darrell P. Tryon (Berlin: Mouton De Gruyter, 1995–) pt 1 pp. 937–42 and other sources

Tongan, Niuean and Samoan

Tongan is spoken throughout Tonga, though the native language of one northern island, *Niuafo'ou*, is distinct and rather closer to Samoan. In 1616 the Dutch mariner Jacob le Maire made a wordlist of the language of another Tongan island, *Niuatoputapu*. This also was close to Samoan: but Tongan is what is now spoken by the 1,500 modern inhabitants of Niuatoputapu.

Le Maire also made a wordlist of *East Futuna*, a language of the Futuna or Hoorn Islands in the territory of Wallis and Futuna. It now has 3,000 or more speakers.

Niuean has about 10,000 speakers (but only about 2,000 on the island of Niue) and is related to Tongan. Niue is a self-governing territory dependent on New Zealand, where the great majority of speakers live.

SAMOAN is the language of Western Samoa and American Samoa. Linguistic differences between the two jurisdictions are very slight.

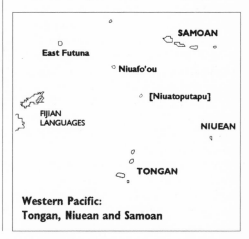

**Western Pacific:
Tongan, Niuean and Samoan**

TSONGA

4,000,000 SPEAKERS OF TSONGA, RONGA AND TSWA

South Africa, Mozambique

Tsonga, Ronga and Tswa are three BANTU LAN-GUAGES so close to one another that speakers of any one can understand the other two with little difficulty.

Thonga, the oldest form of the name, is of Zulu origin and means 'vassal'.

In the early 19th century the Shangana, war-riors of ZULU and Xhosa origin, established the Gaza Empire in this region, with its capital at Mandlakazi on the lower Limpopo. Portuguese rule was established by encouraging civil war between rival sons of the conqueror, Manukosi, who died in 1859.

The Swiss missionaries of the Paris Evangelical Mission Society, who first developed a written form of this language in the 1870s, based their early work on the *Gwamba* variety, a lingua franca spoken by recent migrants from several parts of the Mozambique coast to the Spelonken district of Transvaal, south of the Levubu river. The missionaries learnt the language through Sotho, well known as a second language in northern Transvaal. Their first publication, widely known as 'the *buku*', was a Bible reader, printed in Swit-zerland in 1883. Later missionary writings incor-porated features of the *Djonga* of the coastal plain between the Limpopo and Nkomati.

Partly as a result of rivalry among missions, partly because of local resistance to the despised Gwamba dialect and perhaps to its Sotho colour-ing, a separate religious literature was soon after-wards developed in the *Ronga* spoken south of the Nkomati in the Lourenço Marques (Maputo) re-gion. The first primer in Ronga appeared in 1894.

The special features of *Tswa* are explained by the fact that it was the dialect of the Gaza Empire. All forms of Tsonga came under Zulu influence, and now have Zulu loanwords, but even the phonetics of the language have been affected and in some dialects click consonants, typical of Zulu, can be heard.

The first ten numerals are *-ngwe, -biri, -raru, mune, ntlhanu, ntlhanu na -ngwe, ntlhanu na -biri, ntlhanu na -raru, ntlhanu na mune, khume.*

Tsonga, Ronga and Tswa

Tsonga or Thonga or xiTsonga counts 1,500,000 speakers in Mozambique, where it is known as *Shangaan*, and 1,300,000 in South Africa, where it is one of the eleven official languages. It is a grouping of dialects including Djonga, Khosa and Hlanganou.

Ronga or Landim is spoken north-west of Maputo, while the Maputo and Tembe dialects lie to the south. The three dialects may total 500,000 speakers.

Tswa has 700,000 speakers north of the Limpo-po in Mozambique. Hlengwe is the inland dialect.

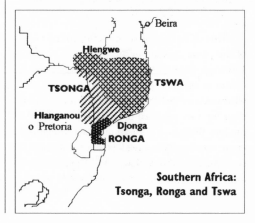

Southern Africa: Tsonga, Ronga and Tswa

TSWANA

4,500,000 SPEAKERS

South Africa, Botswana

One of the BANTU LANGUAGES, Tswana is mutually intelligible with Northern SOTHO (see map there); but as the national language of Botswana, where there are about 850,000 speakers, it has developed a separate identity. Tswana functions as a lingua franca all over Botswana, and is important in South Africa.

The speakers of *seTswana* are *baTswana* in their own language. Some say that the word means 'those who went out' (*-tswa*, 'to go out') or 'the separators' (*-tswaana*, 'to separate') – and certainly the oral traditions of the Tswana peoples tell of repeated fragmentation of political groupings.

Southern dialects of Tswana have a palatal fricative: for example, Rolong dialect *-chwa* 'to go out' instead of standard *-tswa*. Since the southern baTswana were the first to be encountered by English-speaking explorers, the standard form of the ethnic term in British writings became *Bechuana*, with the southern palatal fricative: hence the former English names of colony and protectorate, *Bechuanaland*.

Historically, then, Tswana is the Sotho dialect of the people settled in the upper valley of the Limpopo. That settlement dates from at least four centuries ago, and probably more. They spread westwards in the 18th and 19th centuries until their territory included the south-eastern part of modern Botswana: at the same time Kololo (see LOZI) and Ndebele invaders were encroaching from the east, and Afrikaans and English-speaking colonists had begun to seize much of their southern and eastern lands. When colonial boundaries were drawn Tswana-speaking territory was split between western Transvaal, north-eastern Cape Colony (briefly 'British Bechuanaland') and a third division whose chiefs successfully petitioned the British Government for direct rule. This became the British 'protectorate' of Bechuanaland and is now independent Botswana.

Ironically Tswana had low status in Transvaal, where the majority of its speakers live, yet became the 'national' language in Botswana, where speakers of Tswana as a mother tongue are the – politically dominant – minority. In Botswana many speakers are bilingual in local languages, both Bantu (e.g. Herero) and KHOISAN. The *Kgatla* dialect is the basis of the standard language in South Africa, where Tswana is now one of the eleven official languages.

Christian missions arrived in 1816, and gradually spread the knowledge of writing. The first book on Tswana, *A grammar of the Bechuana language*, was published by the Wesleyan missionary James Archbell in 1838. Tswana is written with frequent word divisions (*ke a e bona* for *keaebona* 'I see it') because of the missionaries' first attempts to grasp the grammar of the language, still enshrined in the orthography that they devised for it. Tswana was the African language learnt by the explorer David Livingstone.

There is now a well-established literature in Tswana, beginning with Bible translations but including a variety of formerly oral literature – legends, proverbs and riddles, praise poetry, songs and traditional history.

Numerals in Sotho and Tswana		
	Southern Sotho	Northern Sotho	Tswana
1	-'ngoē	-tee	-ngwe
2	-beli	-bedi	-bêdi
3	-rarō	-raro	-raro
4	-nè	-nê	-nê
5	-hlanō	-hlano	-tlhano
6	-tshēletsēng	selêla	-rataro
7	-supileng	shupa	shupa
8	-robileng mēnò ēlē 'meli	seswai	fêra mebêdi
9	-robileng mōnò ōlē mōng	senyane	fêra mongwe fêla
10	lēshōmè	lesomê	leshome

TULU

1,200,000 SPEAKERS

India

Tulu is one of the DRAVIDIAN LANGUAGES of India, and a geographical surprise. Sandwiched between the much larger numbers of Kannada speakers to the north and Malayalam speakers to the south, Tulu is spoken in a small district of coastal Karnataka – its traditional boundaries being the Chandragiri and Kalyānapuri rivers (see map at KANNADA). But it is very definitely a dialect neither of Kannada nor of Malayalam. It differs strongly from both, and is even in some ways reminiscent of the Central Dravidian languages of the inland minority peoples further north.

Missionaries at Mangalore published a few books in Tulu using Kannada script: on the few occasions when Tulu continues to be printed, this script is still used. Although there is very little written literature in Tulu, it is a language with a very powerful tradition of oral literature.

The dialect spoken by the Brahman caste is notably different from standard Tulu. Most speakers of the language are bilingual in Kannada, the state language of Karnataka.

The first ten numerals in Tulu are: *onji, raḍḍ, mūji, nāl, ein, āji, ēḷ, eṇma, ormba, patt.*

TUMBUKA

1,500,000 SPEAKERS

Malawi, Zambia

Tumbuka, one of the BANTU LANGUAGES, is spoken in Malawi and a few districts of eastern Zambia (see map at NYANJA).

According to oral tradition, a group of ivory traders from the Indian Ocean coast established a kingdom – the Chikuramayembe dynasty – in the Tumbuka country in the late 18th century, unifying what had until then been separate small chiefdoms. Much of the region was conquered in the 1830s and 1840s by Ngoni warriors from Zululand. Thereafter the Ngoni formed a ruling class. In much of Tumbuka country and around Chipata (Fort Jameson) people nowadays consider themselves to belong to the Ngoni people:

yet their languages are scarcely distinguishable from those of their Tumbuka- and Nsenga-speaking neighbours. They are said still to use the real Ngoni – a variant of 19th-century Zulu – in songs and royal praise poems. It certainly remained in use in lawsuits for nearly a century after the migration.

Tumbuka is not one of the official languages of Malawi or Zambia. Nyanja and English are used for all official purposes. The first ten numerals in Tumbuka are: *-moza, -wiri, -tatu, -nayi, -nkonde* or *-sanu, -sanu na, -moza, -sanu na -wiri, -sanu na -tatu, -sanu na -nayi, kumi.*

Tumbuka praise poetry

Chakatumbu ka usipa,	Slim-bellied as the whitebait,
chituwi wakusonyora,	prickly-spined as the *chituwi* fish,
cha maso nga ndi mere,	red-eyed like the *mere*,
cha mpuno nga ndi ngolo;	long-nosed like the *ngolo*;
sango za pa luji kwawika Nyirenda!	the *sango* of the deep lake are offered to Nyirenda!

Praise formula for Kawunga, a vassal of Chikuramayembe, whose people became known as *nyirenda* 'centipedes'.

T. Cullen Young, *Notes on the speech of the Tumbuka-Kamanga peoples in the Northern province of Nyasaland* (London: Religious Tract Society, 1932) pp. 171–3

TUNGUSIC LANGUAGES

The last Imperial family that reigned in Beijing, the Qing or Manchu dynasty, seized power in 1644 and were driven out in 1912. Manchu was the ancestral language of the Qing court and was once a major language of the north-eastern province of Manchuria, bridgehead of the Japanese invasion of China in the 1930s.

It belongs to the little-known Tungusic group of languages, usually believed to form part of the ALTAIC family. All Tungusic languages are spoken by very small population groups in northern China and eastern Siberia.

Manchu is the only Tungusic language with a written history. In the 17th century the Manchu rulers of China, who had at first ruled through the medium of MONGOLIAN, adapted Mongolian script to their own language, drawing some ideas from the Korean syllabary. However, in the 18th and 19th centuries Chinese – language of an overwhelming majority – gradually replaced Manchu in all official and literary contexts.

The Tungusic languages

Even or *Lamut* has 7,000 speakers in Sakha, the Kamchatka peninsula and the eastern Siberian coast of Russia.

Evenki or *Tungus* is the major Tungusic language of Russia, with 12,000 speakers – widely scattered in the Siberian forests – and perhaps another 10,000 in China.

Manchu has the honourable status of an official nationality of China – but fewer than 1,000 surviving speakers. However, a variety known as *Colloquial Manchu* or *Xibo*, transplanted with a Manchu garrison to fortresses in Xinjiang centuries ago, still numbers about 27,000 speakers.

Nanai or *Goldi* has about 7,000 speakers on the banks of the lower Amur.

Orochen has about 2,000 speakers in northern Manchuria.

Several other Tungusic languages survive, with only a few hundred speakers apiece.

Numerals in Manchu, Evenki and Nanai

	Manchu	Evenki	Nanai
1	emu	umūn	emun
2	juwe	dyūr	dyuer
3	ilan	ilan	ilan
4	duin	digin	duin
5	sunja	tungga	toinga
6	ninggun	nyungun	nyungun
7	nadan	nadan	nadan
8	jakon	dyapkun	dyakpun
9	uyun	ēgin	khuyun
10	juwan	dyān	dyoan

From George L. Campbell, *Compendium of the world's languages* (London: Routledge, 1991)

The mountain forest

Manchu literature now has few readers. There was once a strong tradition of oral poetry, which can still be sensed in the written texts despite their dependence on Chinese genres. This is a rare example of Manchu lyric song, remembered from his childhood by Professor Yadamsürengiin Shariibuu. It reminds us that the Manchu had completely separated themselves from their linguistic relatives, such as the Orochen, who remained hunters and foragers in the Siberian forest.

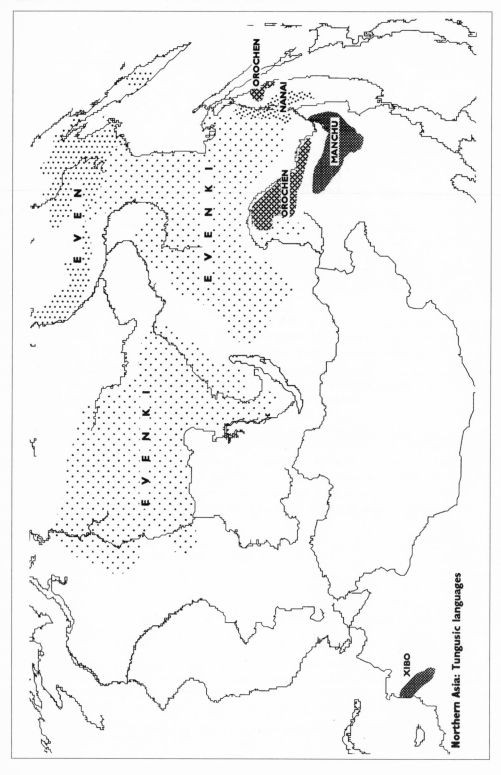

Northern Asia: Tungusic languages

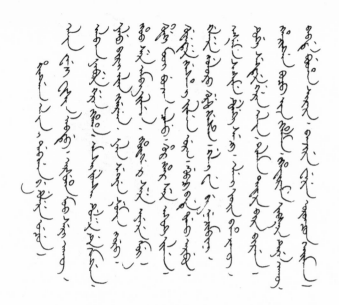

Crossing a pass in the Hinggan Mountains

The mountain forest is dense and wide and full of thorns:
We messengers suffer both coming and going.
The Yalu has three streams, their sources deep and distant,
Their sound as of water flowing, surging, roaring.
Among the leaves of the forest a noise of horses,
An echo of birdsong. Darkness all around.
No one is safe from wild beasts and birds.
We hurry endlessly – we never arrive.
Every mountain is cloud-covered, every stream is hidden in fog,
Gnats and mosquitoes attack us restlessly.
And, all around, the *Orochen* live by their hunting.

After Juha Janhunen, 'A Manchu song from Mongolia' in
Journal de la Société Finno-Ougrienne vol. 77 (1981) pp. 207–18

TUPÍ

3,000 SPEAKERS

Brazil

Tupí, or Tupinambá, was originally the name for a group of dialects spoken along the eastern coast of Brazil when the Portuguese first began to explore the country. Tupí and GUARANÍ (see map there), with some minority languages, together form a group which may belong to the postulated family of AMERIND LANGUAGES.

The Portuguese settlement led to the evolution of a standardised, simplified form of Tupí, often called *Lingua Geral*, 'Common Language' – a development that has been compared to that of the Hellenistic form of GREEK, whose usual name *koinē* also means 'Common'. In the 17th and 18th centuries this standard Tupí was spoken throughout Portuguese Brazil, and religious texts were published in it: Antonio de Araujo's *Catechism* appeared in 1618.

Initially it was probably a second language everywhere: but it soon began to serve as a mother tongue for the children of mixed Portuguese-Tupí households, and for town-dwellers generally. Jesuit missionaries, in an attempt to isolate their Amerindian converts from the demoralising effect of contact with the Portuguese community, in some places preferred not to teach them Portuguese but Lingua Geral.

But the language of the elite was Portuguese. By the 19th century, especially with the establishment of an independent Brazilian court and government, Lingua Geral rapidly lost ground in coastal Brazil.

Meanwhile, however, it had been found useful by explorers, traders and settlers striking inland into the vast Amazon basin. Here, although the inhabitants did not originally speak Tupí dialects, the relatively simple Lingua Geral emerged as a more convenient medium of communication than Portuguese or any local language. Thus, rapidly changing, it was to have a new lease of life in the 19th and early 20th centuries as the lingua franca of the inland regions of Brazil.

Portuguese has now taken its place as first or second language almost throughout Brazil, though along the Rio Negro there are still about 3,000 speakers of modern Tupí, Lingua Geral or Nheengatú.

Many Tupí loanwords are to be found in modern Portuguese. Some have become international words, such as *mandihoca*, Portuguese *mandioca* 'manioc, cassava', which has spread as far as French and English – and all the way to Swahili *mahogo*.

TURKANA

650,000 SPEAKERS OF TURKANA AND KARAMOJONG

Kenya, Uganda, Sudan, Ethiopia

The Karamojong group of NILO-SAHARAN LAN-GUAGES is spoken in East Africa. Turkana, its best-known member, is the language of the hot, dry Rift Valley of Kenya: the massive western escarpment of this, which divides Kenya from Uganda, also divides Turkana from the related karamojong. Seen from the escarpment, Turkana country appears a vast sandy plain far below, where the flat scenery is relieved by isolated mountain blocks, and where dust devils rise in high columns for most of the day. On descending, it seems at first glance impossible for men or animals to live there.

Turkana speakers call themselves *ngiTurkana* (singular *eTurkanait*) and their territory *Turkwen*. Throughout it, they are traditionally divided into two groups, *ngimonia* 'people of the forest' and *ngicuro* 'people of the rough plains'.

Turkana speakers are a pastoral people, keeping goats, sheep and cattle and living off their milk, blood and meat as well as off berries and nuts. They were visited by Swahili traders, in the 19th century and perhaps before. The country was sketchily under Ethiopian administration from the 1880s, but the British Africa Rifles conquered most of it between 1909 and 1926, and these conquests went to Kenya (the majority) and Sudan.

Apart from soldiers, few outsiders have spent long in Turkana country: among early expeditions that ventured in, there were several deaths from starvation. Only the bravest of linguists have been attracted to this part of the Rift Valley.

The first ten numerals in Turkana are: *a-pey`*, *nga-arey`*, *nga-uni`*, *nga-omwɔn`*, *nga-kànį*, *nga-*

kanì-ka-pey, *nga-kanì-ka-arey*, *nga-kanì-ka-uni*, *nga-kanì-ka-omwɔn*, *nga-tɔmɔn*.

How did Turkana come to be the language of the Rift Valley? 'There is a story that a poor Jie woman went down the escarpment looking for food and reached Moru Naiyece in the Tarash valley, where she found plenty of berries. Some Jie searching for a lost bull eventually found it with the woman and, seeing that there was food, some of them moved down and settled there, becoming the ancestors of the Turkana tribe.'

G. W. B. Huntingford, *The Northern Nilo-Hamites* (London: International African Institute, 1953) p. 12

The Eastern Nilotic (Nilo-Hamitic) languages

The *Bari* division of this group consists of Bari itself, *Kakwa* and *Mandari*. Its centre is in southern Sudan.

The *Karamojong* group includes Turkana of Kenya and – on the highlands surrounding the Rift Valley – Karamojong itself, which is spoken in slightly varying dialects by the Karamojong, Jie and Dodos of Uganda and the little-known Toposa and Jiye of Sudan. The form of Turkana spoken in Ethiopia and the south-eastern corner of Sudan is called *Nyangatom*.

TESO or *Itesyo* is the language of a neighbouring, far more accessible region in Uganda. Its speakers share many cultural traits with their immediate neighbours, speakers of Bantu languages. The dialect of Ngora is the usually accepted standard. The *i-* of the alternative language name shows it to be an inappropriate form, for it is the male gender prefix: *ítèsò* 'Teso man', *átèsò* 'Teso woman'.

MASAI, *Otuho* and their relatives form the *Lotuko-Maa* division of Eastern Nilotic. Masai is spoken in an extensive, sparsely populated territory in central Kenya and Tanzania. Masai and *Samburu*, its northern dialect in Kenya, are mutually intelligible but have usually been treated as different languages. *Otuho* or Lotuko is a language of southern Sudan.

KALENJIN is the usual name now for the *Nandi group* of dialects, which includes Nandi itself, *Kipsigis*, *Päkot* and others. The group includes Sebei, pastoralist neighbours of the agricultural Gisu and thus included in the local term *baMasaba*, 'people who live on Mount Elgon' (see also LUYIA).

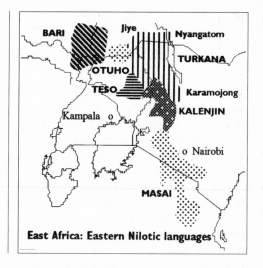

East Africa: Eastern Nilotic languages

Karamojong praise poetry of the Jie

On ritual and other occasions, the praise songs of the grandfathers' generation were recorded, one of which began:

Nyamonia a ngikosowa
awatar angitome –
ioye, nyengori.

The forest of buffaloes:
the elephants were were standing there,
O, the dark grey ones.

and the other:

Toremo, nyetome, i toremo.
Atome ayong.

Spear the elephant, spear it.
I am the elephant.

John Lamphear, *The traditional history of the Jie of Uganda* (Oxford: Clarendon Press, 1976) pp. 41–2

TURKIC LANGUAGES

Like others of the ALTAIC family, Turkic languages originated in central and northern Asia, where, as their recorded history dawns about 1,500 years ago, they were spoken by already widespread communities of nomadic horse-breeders, shepherds and metal-workers.

Their first steppe empire was established, in a revolt against the little-known Juan-Juan, in 552–5. It was centred in western Mongolia, and its diplomatic contacts extended from Byzantium to China. Turkic languages, all quite closely related to one another, are now spoken across a wide swathe of Russia and central Asia, even extending to the Near East and southeastern Europe – as a result of a series of epic migrations and conquests. Turkic speakers did not always initiate these wanderings, but their horsemen were typically the majority among the warriors. Thus their languages remain as evidence of the great empires, while MONGOLIAN LANGUAGES are far less widespread.

Islam had begun to find adherents among Turkic speakers by the 11th century. Thus Turkic languages today are spoken chiefly by Muslims – though this does not apply to Chuvash or Yakut. Most were once written in the Arabic script. However, the Cyrillic alphabet, long used for Chuvash under Russian influence, has also been used for all the other Turkic languages of the old Soviet Union. Turkish, Azeri and Uzbek have adopted the Latin alphabet. Uighur, one of the most significant minority languages of China, is written in its own script, a descendant of the ancient Syriac alphabet which came to western China with the Manichaean religion thirteen hundred years ago.

Even while they were developing along separate lines, the Turkic languages were mostly alike in admitting numerous important loanwords from Arabic and Persian – words so basic to every language that they are seldom borrowed from one to another. Arabic *wa* 'and' is found in Azeri *va*. The Persian subordinating conjunction *ke* re-

appears in Azeri, Turkish and Uzbek *ki*, though the logic of the surrounding sentence is quite different in Persian and in these Turkic languages.

Traditional literature in Turkic languages is notable for epics of heroic adventure, for shorter romantic tales (*hikaye*), and, equally, for brief love poems of haunting beauty. Oral epic poetry has been collected from many Turkic peoples in the 20th century, and it is still to be heard in some places.

> The geography of Turkic conquest is reflected not least in Turkic proverbs. Of a suburb of Istanbul: *Kasimpaşalı, eli maşalı*, 'The men of Kasimpaşa often carry knives'. Of two towns in Xinjiang: *Sayramdın uğrı, Kuçadın güi*, 'Sayram for its thieves, Kuqa for its cuckolds'.
>
> Examples from *Philologiae turcicae fundamenta* vol. 2 ed. Pertev Naili Boratav and others (Wiesbaden: Steiner, 1965) p. 69

The spread of Turkic languages

The oldest Turkic migration that has left linguistic traces is that of the Bulgars, feared in early medieval Europe: their remnant, now peacefully settled near Kazan' (in part of medieval Great Bulgaria), speak CHUVASH. Although unrecorded in history, the original split of early Chuvash from proto-Turkic must have come two thousand years ago or more.

Then proto-Turkic began to divide into dialects. To the north Altai, Khakas and Tuva speakers (see map 2) have probably migrated little, while the related YAKUT spread gradually further north-eastwards into the Siberian forest and tundra. To the south the Uighur settled and ruled the cities of the Silk Road. This is the origin of UIGHUR and UZBEK, the Eastern or Chagatai group of Turkic languages.

With later empires came the spread of nomadic Turkic speakers of the central Asian mountains. Beginning from what are now Kazakhstan and Kyrgyzstan, this Western or Kipchak group spread westwards with the conquering horsemen. Thus the group includes KAZAKH with Karakalpak and Nogai, KYRGYZ, KUMYK with Karachai and Balkar, TATAR and BASHKIR.

South-westwards the Seljuk Turks extended their rule across western Asia and beyond. In their wake, the Southern, Turkmen or Oghuz group of Turkic languages, TURKMEN, AZERI and TURKISH gradually spread across parts of Iran, Azerbaijan, Turkey and the Balkans. Salar, a language of 55,000 speakers in north-western China, also belongs to this group.

The Northern Turkic languages

Altai with 50,000 speakers, Khakas with 60,000 and Tuva with 200,000 – and the minority Shor and Tofa – are all languages of Asiatic Russia. The three peoples were converted to Buddhism through Mongolia and have traditionally been under Mongolian cultural influence. Until recently Mongolian was the written language that they used. These three languages are now written in Cyrillic script.

Tuva or Tuvinian was the language of Tannu Tuva, a state that remained precariously independent between 1921 and 1944 but was then incorporated in the Soviet Union. Buddhism, 'feudalism' and traditional agriculture were gradually undermined, leaving Tuva with severe social problems of youth crime, alcohol and drug abuse. There are also speakers across the border in Mongolia. Tuva's Buddhism came by way of Mongolia, and the language has many Mongolian loanwords. The Mongolians call this people *Tsaatan* 'reindeer herders'.

Khakas is a group of Turkic dialects spoken by disparate minorities in the self-governing republic of Khakassia in Russian Siberia – and also spoken by the 'Yellow Uighurs' in the Chinese province of Gansu. The term Khakas was invented in early Soviet times.

Altai (Oirot) is spoken in the Mountain Altai Region. A small language, it has the distinction of sharing its name with the very diverse linguistic family of which the Turkic languages form one branch. A significant part of the Altai country is contaminated by radiation as a result of the Semipalatinsk nuclear test in 1949: the population here is in decline.

The First Türk Emperors

The 'Orkhon inscriptions', discovered in the Orkhon valley in Mongolia and in the upper Yenisei valley in Siberia, are the oldest full-length texts in a Turkic language. They are major historical sources for the early central Asian empires. They show justifiable pride in the achievements of the ruling family. The rhythmic style displays a haunting parallelism – repetition with variations – which is typical of oral and traditional literature in many languages. The inscriptions are written in a 'Runic' script, so called because it looks rather like the runes of early Scandinavia.

When the blue sky high above and the brown earth down below had been created, between the two were created the sons of men; and above the sons of men stood my ancestors, the Kaghans Bumin and Ishtemi. Having become masters of the Türk people, they established and ruled its empire and fixed the law of the country. Many were their enemies in the four corners of the world, but they campaigned against them. They conquered and pacified many nations in the four corners of the world: they made them bow their heads and bend their knees.

These were wise kaghans, these were brave Kaghans, and all their officers were wise and brave, and all the nobles and all the people were just. Thus it was that they were able to master so great an empire, and to govern it, and to uphold the law.

8th-century Orkhon inscription. Translation after Denis Sinor, *Inner Asia: history, civilization, languages* (Bloomington: Indiana University, 1969) p. 103

Language of the Huns

Little is known of the language spoken by the briefly powerful and destructive Huns, who burst into European and Chinese history in the 4th century AD. The Buddhist monk Fotudeng spoke a few words of oracular advice in Hunnish to the north-eastern Hun monarch in 329. The monk's words were recorded in Chinese script:

秀 支 替 戾 岡、僕 谷 劬 禿 當

On Fotudeng's historic advice the monarch defeated a rival warlord and established himself as Chinese emperor, founder of the Later Zhou dynasty. But what was the advice? In 4th-century Chinese these characters were pronounced: Syog tieg t'iei liəd kāng b'uok kuk g'iw t'uk tāng. (See B. Karlgren, *Grammata Serica*. Stockholm, 1940.)

Louis Bazin was able to interpret this puzzling text as a rhyming couplet in an early form of Turkic, several hundred years older than any other now known:

Süg Tägti idqang,   Send out your army,
boqughigh tutqang.   Capture the warlord!

After L. Bazin, 'Un texte proto-Turc du IVe siècle: le distique Hiong-nou du *Tsin-chou*' in *Oriens* vol. 1 (1948) pp. 208–19

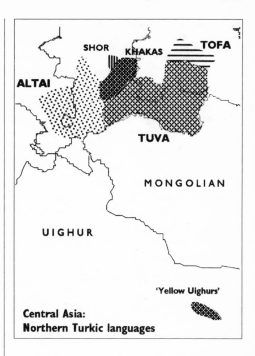

Central Asia:
Northern Turkic languages

Cyrillic for Russian and Cyrillic for Turkic languages

А Б В Г Д Е Ё Ж З И Й К Л М Н О П Р С Т У Ф Х Ц Ч Ш Щ Ъ Ы Ь Э Ю Я

а б в г е ё ж з и й к л м н о п р с т у ф х ц ч ш щ ъ ы ь э ю я

a b v g d ye yo zh z i ĭ k l m n o p r s t u f kh ts ch sh shch " ı ' e yu ya

To the letters of the standard Cyrillic alphabet, shown above in its Russian form, the different Turkic languages make a wide variety of additions:

Ӑ ӑ	*ă* Chuvash
Гъ гъ	*gh* Kumyk, Karachai, Balkar
Гь гь	*h* Kumyk
Ғ ғ	*gh* Khakas, Bashkir, Kazakh, Karakalpak, Uighur
Ҕ ҕ	*gh* Yakut
ДЖ дж	*j* Balkar
Дь дь	*j* Yakut
Ӗ ӗ	*ə* Chuvash
Ж җ	*j* Tatar, Uighur, Turkmen
Ҙ ҙ	*ð* Bashkir
І і	*ə* Khakas, Kazakh
Ј ј	*j* Altai
Къ къ	*q* Kumyk, Karachai, Balkar
Қ қ	*q* Kazakh, Karakalpak, Uighur
Ҡ ҡ	*q* Bashkir
НГ нг	*ng* Kumyk, Balkar, Karakalpak
Нъ нъ	*ng* Khakas, Karachai, Nogai
Нь нь	*ny* Yakut
Ң ң	*ng* Yakut, Tuva, Tatar, Bashkir, Kazakh, Kyrgyz, Uighur, Turkmen
Ҥ ҥ	*ng* Altai
Оь оь	*ö* Kumyk, Nogai
Ӧ ӧ	*ö* Khakas, Altai
Ө ө	*ö* Yakut, Tuva, Tatar, Bashkir, Kazakh, Karakalpak, Kyrgyz, Uighur, Turkmen
Ҫ ҫ	*sy* Chuvash, *th* Bashkir
ў ў	*w* Karachai
Уь уь	*ü* Kumyk, Nogai
Ӱ ӱ	*ü* Chuvash, Khakas, Altai
Ү ү	*ü* Yakut, Tuva, Tatar, Bashkir, Kazakh, Kyrgyz, Uighur, Turkmen
Ұ ұ	*ō* Kazakh
һ һ	*h* Yakut, Tatar, Bashkir, Kazakh, Uighur
Ч ч	*j* Khakas
Ә ә	*ä* Tatar, Bashkir, Kazakh, Uighur, Turkmen

Based on Nicholas Poppe, *Introduction to Altaic linguistics* (Wiesbaden: Harrassowitz, 1965) pp. 53–5

TURKISH

PERHAPS 50,000,000 SPEAKERS

Turkey, Northern Cyprus

One of the TURKIC LANGUAGES, national language of Turkey and of Northern Cyprus, Turkish is also spoken by shrinking communities in other countries that were once part of the Ottoman Empire.

Turkish is most closely related to Azeri and Turkmen (for a table of numerals see AZERI). All three languages were established as the result of a series of conquests and migrations of nomadic Turkic peoples, principally the Oghuz, from northern central Asia, beginning in the 6th century and largely completed by the 13th. The main languages of what is now Turkey had until then been Greek, Armenian and Kurdish. The long political and cultural dominance of Turkish, established by the 13th century, meant that it gradually became the language of the vast majority in the country; for all that, the other three languages were still spoken by millions at the beginning of the 20th century. Massacres and mass migrations have now transformed the picture: only the Kurdish minority is still numerically significant.

> The name *Turkish* is used both for the language of Turkey itself (sometimes called *Osmanli Turkish*) and for the whole group (for which *Turkic* is preferred in this book). *Osmanli* is the name of the Ottoman dynasty established by 'Osmān I, who died in 1324.

The first Anatolian dynasty of Turkic origin was that of the Seljuks. They had previously ruled in Iran and absorbed the Islamic religion and Persian culture – which were inherited from them by the Turkish-speaking Ottomans, who succeeded to power in the 13th century. Thus Turkish is more pervasively influenced by Persian (and through Persian by Arabic) than are the other Turkic languages. The language of older poetry can be so heavily laden with Arabic and Persian that it may not appear at first sight to be Turkish at all. The genres and the rhetoric of this literature are all Persian-derived.

Older in origin than this rich classical Turkish literature of the Ottoman period, the traditional tales of *Dede Korkut* are known from two manuscripts of the 16th century in a dialect close to Turkish or Azeri. Related tales in other Turkic languages have been collected by scholars of oral literature. Although superficially set in Anatolia at the time of the Turkish conquests, many features of the manuscript tales belong to the pre-Islamic legendary history of the Oghuz. They are 'in prose interspersed with rhythmic, alliterative, and assonant or rhyming passages of *soylama*, "declamation". The level of the language fluctuates, now highly poetic and dignified, now racy and colloquial' (G. Lewis, *The book of Dede Korkut* (Harmondsworth, 1974) p. 14).

In the 19th century Turkish literature began to look to France for its inspiration. The Revolution of 1908 and the reforms of Atatürk (see box) furthered the change to a secular, western-influenced, nationalist culture. Research on the early history of Turkic peoples and their languages led to attempts to 'purify' Turkish, eliminating Ottoman words borrowed from Arabic and Persian and replacing them with rediscovered ancient Turkic words. Some of these had actually survived in peripheral dialects, such as Cypriot, but the main effect of the reform was to put a distance between the new written language and the speech of every day.

The geography of Turkish

Turkey is by no means homogeneous ethnically or linguistically, but the extreme nationalism of Turkish political life makes research on minorities difficult. The Yörük and Türkmen of western and central Anatolia are traditionally nomadic pastoralists. The Tahtacı are foresters, the Abdal are musicians and tinkers. *Abdal düğünden, çocuk oyundan usanmaz* is the proverb: 'A child never tires of playing, nor an Abdal of weddings.' All four groups speak dialects of Turkish, though the Abdal also have a secret language of their own. The Alevi (Kızılbaş) religion of the Türkmen, with their tribe and clan organisation and their traditions of migration from central Asia long ago, distinguishes them from the sedentary populations of Anatolia who have gradually adopted their language.

Until the early years of this century there was a large population of Christian Turkish speakers of Armenian origin in parts of Asia Minor. Their literature, in a form of Turkish with Armenian loanwords, was written and printed in the Armenian alphabet. Armenian oral poets of this region were often skilled both in Armenian and in Turkish. This population was largely killed in the genocide of 1913. There were also Turkish-speaking Christians of Greek origin, *Karamanlı-lar*, and thus a Turkish literature in the Greek alphabet. Most of these were moved to Greece in the population exchange of 1924, and their special form of Turkish is now almost extinct.

Also just outside the borders of 20th-century Turkey, a significant Turkish minority population (120,000 in 1974) had long been settled in Cyprus, where the majority was Greek. Since 1974 there has been an enforced division of the

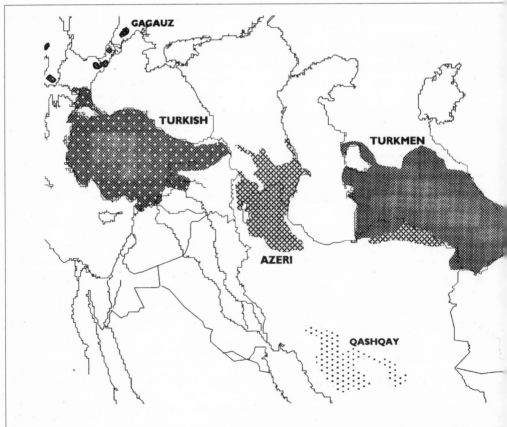

island on religious and linguistic lines. In Turkish Northern Cyprus the government has attempted to impose standard Turkish as the national language: this has met with some resistance from the inhabitants, who are, however, now almost outnumbered by new immigrants from Turkey.

Over a hundred thousand 'Meskhetian' Turks, from the Turkish border region of Georgia, were exiled to Uzbekistan during the Second World War, apparently owing to Stalin's personal distrust of Caucasian Muslims. Their numbers have doubled in exile and their perceived prosperity has excited ethnic violence in which many have died. They remain unwelcome in independent Georgia, but some have resettled near their former home, in Azerbaijan, in lands from which LEZGHIANS have been uprooted.

**Central Asia:
Turkish, Azeri and Turkmen**

Under the Ottoman Empire, Turkish, the language of government and culture, spread widely in south-eastern Europe, particularly among town-dwellers. In the 20th century as many as 1,100,000 'Rumelian' Turkish speakers have been expelled from Greece, Bulgaria and the former Yugoslavia, most of these fleeing to Turkey. A minority still remains in Europe.

Gagauz is the name of the Turkic language – with many Slavonic words in its vocabulary – spoken by communities of Greek Orthodox Christians of Turkic descent who live in several Balkan countries. The largest group, numbering well over a hundred thousand, is in south-western Moldova, where they recently claimed the position of a self-governing republic. Others live near Varna in Bulgaria.

There are some more or less stable Turkish-speaking minority populations elsewhere, including perhaps 90,000 Turkish Cypriots in Britain. They cluster in the Green Lanes and Islington districts of London, and are large enough to be a political force, regularly canvassed for support for the shaky international status of Northern Cyprus. In Germany the number of Turkish speakers is much greater but many are short-term migrant workers.

Türkiyede altmışaltı buçuk millet var: 'There are sixty-six and a half nations in Turkey', some Turks say. The half-nation is the Gypsies (a half more than the status allowed them in many clichés elsewhere).

A Turkish proverb claims to characterise the two minorities seen as most dangerous to the comfortable order of things, *Çingene çalar, Kürt oynar*: 'If the Gypsy plays, the Kurd will dance.' The *Mıtırp*, a Gypsy caste of musicians, actually do live in close contact with the Kurds of Turkey and Iraq and are bilingual in Kurdish.

Examples from Peter Alford Andrews and others, *Ethnic groups in the Republic of Turkey* (Wiesbaden: Steiner, 1989)

Vowel harmony

A highly distinctive feature of practically all the Turkic languages is vowel harmony. In Turkish, for example, vowels can be classified according to three features:

	Unrounded		Rounded	
	High	Low	High	Low
Back	ı	a	u	o
Front	i	e	ü	ö

1. If the first vowel of a word is a back vowel, the others will also be back vowels.
2. If the first vowel is a front vowel, the others will also be front vowels.
3. Unrounded vowels are followed by unrounded.
4. Rounded vowels are followed by low unrounded or high rounded.

Frequently the principle is applied even to loanwords. The football term 'penalty' appears in Turkish not as *penalti* but as *penaltı*, the front *i* changing to back *ı* under the influence of the preceding back *a*. The French *épaulette* becomes *apolet*. The standard Turkish for 'bus' is *otobüs*, a phonetic spelling of the French *autobus*, but in uneducated speech the pronunciations *otobus* and even *otobos* are heard, as the front *ü* does not come naturally after two back *o*s. Similarly, the French *vapeur*, 'steamship', has become *vapur*, though the Turkish phonetic spelling would be *vapör*.

G. L. Lewis, *Teach yourself Turkish* (London: English Universities Press, 1953) p. 20

The Turkish alphabet

By a 1928 decree of Mustafa Kemal Atatürk, Turkish exchanged its old Arabic script for a new Latin alphabet of 29 letters.

A B C Ç D E F G Ğ H I İ J K L
M N O Ö P R S Ş T U Ü V Y Z
a b c ç d e f g ğ h ı i j k l
m n o ö p r s ş t u ü v y z

Turkmen, Azeri and Turkish

Owing to continuing migration, speakers of these three very similar languages are intermixed.

TURKMEN is the national language of Turkmenistan.

AZERI is spoken in northern Iran and in the independent republic of Azerbaijan. There are also minorities in Georgia and Turkey. Azeri is an important lingua franca in the Russian republic of Dagestan.

Qāshqāy has perhaps 100,000 speakers in the Persian province of Fars.

Turkish, the national language of Turkey and of Northern Cyprus, is spoken by significant minorities in Bulgaria, Macedonia, Serbia and Bosnia.

Gagauz has over 100,000 speakers in south-western Moldova.

TURKMEN

4,000,000 SPEAKERS

Turkmenistan, Uzbekistan, Iran, Iraq, Afghanistan

O ne of the TURKIC LANGUAGES, Turkmen is the national language of the formerly Soviet republic of Turkmenistan.

The majority language of the region was probably formerly Iranian. Turkic speakers began to migrate here from the north in the 6th to 10th centuries. Oghuz Turks, from Mongolia, may have formed the majority, but by the 11th century the new name *Turkmen* was being used by Arabic authors. Islam became the majority religion here in the 11th century. The continuing movement south-westwards of Oghuz and Seljuk Turks resulted eventually in the settlement not only of modern Turkmenistan but also, much further to the west, of Azerbaijan and Turkey, whose languages are closely related to Turkmen (see map at TURKISH and table of numerals at AZERI).

Political power in the region was long disputed between the Golden Horde, established to the north, and Persia to the south. Russia conquered Turkmenistan in the 1880s.

Until the 20th century Turkmen was not a written language, but there is a corpus of Turkmen oral epic poetry, including versions of the *Story of Dede Korkut* also known from a Turkish manuscript. Other stories dealt with the medieval wars of the Turks as reflected in popular tradition. In Soviet times Turkmen was written successively in Arabic, Latin and Cyrillic scripts. A new Latin alphabet, based on that used for Turkish, has been adopted since independence in 1991.

Bardı ärän qonuq bulup qutqá saqár,

qaldí **alıǧ oyuq** körüp ävní yıqár.

Gone are the fine men who think
it lucky to welcome a guest;
Still around are the bad ones who strike
camp when they see you in the distance.

Two pessimistic lines mark the traditional beginning of Turkmen literature. Taken from the collected poems of the 11th-century author Maḥmūd Kāşġarī, they include words specific to the dialect that would later split into Turkmen, Azeri and Turkish.

After Johannes Benzing, 'Die türkmenische Literatur' in *Philologiae turcicae fundamenta* vol. 2 ed. Pertev Naili Boratav and others (Wiesbaden: Steiner, 1965) p. 724

UDMURT

550,000 SPEAKERS

Russia

One of the URALIC LANGUAGES, Udmurt is spoken in Udmurtia, in eastern European Russia, south of the related KOMI, in the valleys of the rivers Vyatka and Kama (see map at KOMI).

Udmurt is the speakers' own name for themselves and their language, and is officially used in Russian too. By most other outsiders they are called Votyak *(German* Wotjak).

Of all the Uralic languages Udmurt may be the one that has migrated least. The Bronze Age Turbino culture (second millennium BC) and the Iron Age Ananino culture (first millennium BC), as archaeologists call them, may mark the location of a proto-Permian language, ancestor of Udmurt and Komi. Both centre on the valley of the Kama, a middle Volga tributary. Udmurt speakers simply stayed put, sometimes dominated by external powers such as the Tatars and the Russians.

The language was first recorded in the 18th century. Udmurt religious books multiplied in the 19th, though Christian Russia never entirely succeeded in eradicating the pagan religion of the Udmurt. However, the area over which Udmurt is spoken has gradually shrunk under the pressure of Russian expansion and Russian-led development.

'The Votyaks have attracted the attention of ethnologists because of their extensive sexual promiscuity' is probably the most interesting sentence in Björn Collinder's *An introduction to the Uralic languages* (Berkeley: University of California Press, 1965).

A nation of poets

'Folklore collectors remarked that every Votyak was able to improvise. There were occasions that simply obliged a Votyak man or woman to improvise a song: a young man joining the army, a young woman going to marry, a housewife receiving guests or seeing them out of her home, all alike practised the art of improvisation.'

Péter Domokos, 'Finno-Ugrian folk poetry' in *Ancient cultures of the Uralian peoples* (Budapest: Corvina, 1976) p. 295

The first Udmurt textbook

Odyk, kyk, kvin', nil', vit',
kuat', sizim, kiamys, ukmys, das

The first ten numerals in Udmurt – from the above double-page spread in *Sochineniya prinadlezhashcheniya k grammatike Votskago* (Writings on Udmurt grammar), published in St Petersburg in 1775 and probably compiled under the supervision of Archbishop Venyamin Putsek-Grigorovich of Kazan', an accomplished linguist. In this textbook Udmurt is in the left column, Russian in the right, both in Cyrillic script.

UIGHUR

6,750,000 SPEAKERS

China

O ne of the TURKIC LANGUAGES, Uighur is spoken by one of the most important national minorities of China, occupying the Xinjiang ('New Frontier') Autonomous Region. There is a minority of Uighur speakers in three former Soviet republics of central Asia.

The Uighur Empire was established by this nomadic Turkic people in western Mongolia in 745 AD, in succession to the earliest Türk empire whose history is recorded in the Orkhon runic inscriptions (see box at TURKIC LANGUAGES). In 762 it adopted the syncretistic religion of the prophet Mani, brought by SOGDIAN missionaries, and thus became the world's only known Manichaean state.

The Uighurs were driven from power by the Kyrgyz (whose territory then lay to their north) and fled to the lands that lie on either side of the Silk Road as it crosses the heights of central Asia on its way from China to the West. Here speakers of Uighur, and its offshoot UZBEK, settled and prospered, as they ruled the valleys and oases through which the inland trade in silk and other luxuries had to pass. Buddhism and Nestorian Christianity competed with Manichaeism; eventually the Uighurs were converted to Sunni Islam in the 11th century.

In 1755 the Uighurs came under Chinese rule. They were the major participants in the 'Mohammedan uprising' in western China in 1862–77. In spite of further rebellions, leading to Soviet interest in the region in the 1930s, it remained part of China. As recently as the 1950s Uighur adopted numerous Russian loanwords; since then, naturally enough, Chinese has been the major influence.

Earlier forms of the language of the Uighurs,

mostly written in a script similar to that of Mongolian, are conventionally called Ancient Turkic (9th and 10th centuries), Karakhanid (11th to 13th centuries) and post-Karakhanid (13th and 14th centuries). Buddhist texts survive from the earlier period, translated from Sanskrit via Tocharian or Sogdian; there are also Manichaean and Nestorian texts, and translations from Chinese such as an adaptation of the fortune-telling *I Ching*.

Uighur script

The traditional Uighur form of writing was based on an early medieval Sogdian script, ultimately derived from Aramaic. Its transmission to central Asia followed the route of the Silk Road – and accompanied the texts and teachings of Manichaeism. In turn, the Mongolians borrowed Uighur script and applied it to their own language. Uighur script differed from Sogdian in one essential way: like Chinese it is written from top to bottom, not from right to left.

Uighur is now normally written in Arabic script. In the 1950s and 1960s the Chinese government attempted to effect a change to the Latin alphabet. For a while this was taught in all schools. It now appears to have been abandoned, and Arabic script is used again in the local press.

Uighur and Uzbek

First recorded from western Mongolia, Uighur has for many centuries been the major language of the central Asian region now known as Xinjiang (Sinkiang) in China. The modern literary language is based on the dialect of the regional capital, Urumchi. Uighur dialects of Xinjiang can be divided into three groups: Central, Lobnor and Khotan.

The Uighur spoken by about 200,000 people in Kazakhstan, Kyrgyzstan and Uzbekistan is written in Cyrillic script, and is sometimes classed as the *Ili* dialect.

In Soviet times standard written Uzbek was at first based on the dialect of the city of Turkestan – in Kazakhstan, north of the Uzbek border. This had undergone relatively little Persian influence. Now, however, the more cosmopolitan dialect of Tashkent is paramount.

Numerals in Uighur and Uzbek

Uighur		Uzbek
bir	1	bir
ikki	2	ikki
üch	3	uch
töt	4	tŭrt
bäsh	5	besh
altä	6	olti
yättä	7	yetti
säkkiz	8	sakkiz
toqquz	9	tŭqqiz
on	10	ŭn

from Kurtulus Öztupçu and others, *Dictionary of the Turkic languages* (London: Routledge, 1996)

He knew all the languages and scripts

'A Persian historian recorded a legend of the origin of the Uighur empire. At the confluence of two rivers, Selenge and Tughla, stood a mound. A light which descended from heaven made this mound pregnant. Day by day the mound grew bigger: finally, "as with pregnant women at the time of their delivery", a door opened and inside were five cells, "like tents", in each of which sat a baby boy. The Uighurs chose as their leader, from among the five boys, Buku Khan, for he was superior to the others in beauty, strength of mind and judgment – and he knew all the tongues and writings of the different peoples.'

From 'Ala al-Din 'Ata-Malik Juvaini, *The history of the world conqueror* translated from the text of Mirza Muhammad Qazvini by J.A. Boyle (Manchester: Manchester University Press, 1958) vol. 1 pp. 55–6

UKRAINIAN

45,000,000 SPEAKERS

Ukraine

One of the Eastern SLAVONIC LANGUAGES, Ukrainian has a longer history than Russian. Formerly the second largest language of the Soviet Union, it is now the national language of a major independent state in eastern Europe, with its capital at Kiev (for map see RUSSIAN).

> In Russian *Ukraina* means 'borderland' and referred to the eastern Ukraine, settled by the Cossack borderers. Until the 20th century Ukrainian speakers generally called themselves *Rusyny*, meaning 'Russians' (the translation often used abroad was 'Ruthenians'). Historically Kiev was indeed the centre of the land of *Rus'*.

Ukrainian is probably spoken on the territory where, in prehistoric times, the proto-Slavonic dialects first developed and began to spread. Its recorded history begins in the century after the official conversion of the principality of Kiev to Christianity in 988.

The Bible translations and religious texts that Byzantine missionaries brought to Kiev were in OLD SLAVONIC, the written language that had already been used to take the Christian religion to other Slavonic-speaking peoples. Old Slavonic continued to be the single significant written language of Ukraine for several centuries: it is the language of the *Russian Primary Chronicle* and other major early texts. However, Ukrainian is to be seen in many of these texts. It is there both in the 'mistakes' made by religious writers while writing or copying Old Slavonic, and in the vernacular words that were necessarily introduced into chronicles and other documents when discussing local matters for which no Biblical word could be found. At this stage 'Old Ukrainian' is not to be distinguished from *Old Russian*, which is the name often given to the vernacular element in these manuscripts.

Mongolian and Tatar warriors of the Golden Horde destroyed Kiev in 1240. Moscow, too, was to be subject to the Horde, while most of Ukraine passed to the Lithuanians (whose written language at this time was an early form of BELORUSSIAN). From this point onwards the histories of Ukrainian and Russian diverge.

Poland, already ruler of Galicia, annexed the remainder of Ukraine in the 16th century. Latin (the old official language of Poland) and Polish itself now had an official role in Ukraine. The deciding factor in the country's subsequent history was the arrival of the Cossacks, armed adventurers and vagabonds of miscellaneous origins who settled the empty lands of eastern Ukraine. Their 18th-century leader, Bohdan Khmelnytsky, invited Russian help against Polish domination. Under Catherine the Great the Cossacks eventually moved on, to settle the Russian frontiers further east, but Ukraine remained in Russian hands (except for its westernmost region, eastern Galicia, which belonged to Austria-Hungary).

In the 17th century the Belorussian language of former Lithuanian rule had continued to be used, even by the Cossacks, and had gradually adopted Ukrainian features: it was called *prostaya mova*, 'common tongue'. Under Russian rule, however, Ukrainian came to be considered no more than a local dialect of Russian (often called *Little Russian*). While authors such as Tarash Shevchenko and Pan'ko Kulish, inspired by European Romanticism, were developing a language and a literature based on popular speech and folklore, the cultivation of Ukrainian was officially frowned on. An 1876 decree forbade the printing or importing of Ukrainian books. The 19th-century revival of Ukrainian poetry and historiography was thus conducted partly underground, or from neighbouring Galicia where Ukrainian nationalism was able to flourish. The Galician dialect thus became a major influence on standard Ukrainian.

Briefly independent in 1918–19, Ukraine was reconquered and declared a Soviet Republic. Its western and southern provinces were divided among Poland, Czechoslovakia and Romania – Galicia, formerly Austrian, going to Poland – but were repossessed in 1944. The old linguistic attitudes were not wholly abandoned under Soviet rule. Russian had priority in education and employment. Ukrainian began to lose its status as the official language of Soviet Ukraine. Many Ukrainians speak Russian fluently: there is also a very large Russian minority in eastern Ukraine and in the major cities.

To the surprise of many Russians, Ukraine asserted its independence in 1991. Its traditional links with central Europe, broken under Soviet rule, are now being cultivated once more. Priority is given to relations with the United States and Canada, where there are strong Ukrainian minorities. Canada numbers 600,000 of a total of four million Ukrainian émigrés worldwide. The descendants of the million Ukrainians who migrated to central Asia and Siberia under Soviet rule are, in many cases, now returning.

In many ways still close to Russian, Ukrainian is a language with its own character – a language in which one can speak of Сокира така тупа що як за мамою кинути би не був гріх, 'an axe so dull that it would not be a sin to throw it at your mother'.

In Britain there are about 20,000 Ukrainians. Most of them, young men arriving at the end of the Second World War, married women of other immigrant communities with strong religious beliefs (especially Italian, Austrian and Irish). The Ukrainian community clusters in Lancashire, Yorkshire and the Midlands. While modern Ukrainian of the Ukraine has been increasingly influenced by Russian, the Ukrainian of the emigrants and their children incorporates more and more English words and English turns of phrase.

Ukrainian is written in the Cyrillic alphabet. It can be distinguished at a glance from Russian (see table there) by its use of three additional vowel symbols, Є є for *ye*, I i for *i*, and Ï ï for *yi*. An additional consonant, Г г for *g*, also occurs. For a table of Ukrainian numerals see BELORUSSIAN.

URALIC LANGUAGES

A family of languages of northern Europe and western Siberia. There are in total only 24,000,000 speakers of Uralic languages, but the family includes three national languages, ESTONIAN, FINNISH and HUNGARIAN, as well as several important minorities of European Russia (KOMI, MARI, MORDVIN, UDMURT) and the language of the SAMI or Lapps of northern Scandinavia.

The first written records of Uralic languages date back only to the 13th century. Their earlier history can be traced through notes in historical writings of other nations (especially Romans, Greeks and Chinese) and before that by linguistic reconstruction, which includes the tracing of loanwords between Uralic and other languages. Alongside this goes archaeological exploration of the prehistoric cultures of north-eastern Europe.

Proto-Uralic dialects ancestral to all the modern languages may have been spoken on both sides of the central and northern Ural Mountains – the traditional dividing line between Europe and Asia – in the sixth millennium BC or even before. From this linguistic community the SAMOYEDIC LANGUAGES must have separated first, for these are most different from the rest. Their speakers have perhaps always been foragers and hunters in the forests and tundra of Siberia.

Before the Ugric dialects (with later Hungarian) had separated from the Finno-Permian dialects (with later Finnish), proto-Finno-Ugric borrowed some significant words from proto-Indo-Iranian: the two early languages must, at this time, have been close enough for regular contact. Examples include proto-Indo-Iranian *septa* 'seven', modern Hungarian *hét*; *shata* 'hundred', Finnish *sata*, Hungarian *száz*; *sharva* 'horn', Finnish *sarvi*, Hungarian *szarv*; *orbho* 'orphan', Finnish *orpo*, Hungarian *árva*.

The Ural Mountains themselves may have formed the dividing line between the proto-Ugric and proto-Finno-Permian dialects, a division which perhaps became established in the third millennium BC. Ugric languages now consist of Khanty and Mansi, still spoken east of the Urals, and Hungarian, whose speakers finally settled in central Europe after centuries of migration.

The Finno-Permian peoples, perhaps always settled on the European side of the Urals, may be tentatively identified with a series of Neolithic, Bronze Age and Iron Age cultures of the upper Volga and its tributary the Kama – and soon spreading to the neighbourhood of the eastern shores of the Baltic. Linguistically, the first to become separated were the most eastern group, the Permian dialects that were to become modern Udmurt and Komi. The remainder (Mari, Mordvin, Sami and the proto-Finnic group that gave rise to modern Estonian and Finnish) began to separate into distinct languages in the course of the first millennium BC.

Proto-Uralic trees

Tree names shared among the modern Uralic languages help to locate the habitat of the speakers of proto-Uralic about eight thousand years ago, and of proto-Finno-Ugric in the next two millennia.

Picea obovata, spruce	proto-Uralic *kowese*	Finnish *kuusi*
Pinus sibirica, cembra pine	proto-Uralic *sıkse*	Komi *sus-*
Abies sibirica, Siberian fir	proto-Uralic *nyulka*	Mari *nulgo*
Betula spp., birch	proto-Uralic *kojwa*	Finnish *koivu*
Populus spp., poplar	proto-Uralic *poje*	Mordvin *poj*
Salix spp., willow	proto-Uralic *paje*	Hungarian *fagyal*
Pinus silvestris, fir	proto-Uralic *juwe*;	Mansi *jiw*
	proto-Finno-Ugric *penye*	Hungarian *fenyo*

Larix sibirica, larch	proto-Finno-Ugric *nyänge*	Komi *nyia*
Ulmus spp., elm	proto-Finno-Ugric *syala*	Hungarian *szil*

Three trees are crucial. Cembra pine and Siberian fir were slowly spreading across the Urals westwards in proto-Uralic times; elm was meanwhile spreading eastwards from central Europe, and reached the north-western Ural foothills. The region where proto-Uralic dialects were spoken most probably included the relatively narrow zone, west of the Ural watershed, where the two trees met.

URDU

40,000,000 SPEAKERS

India, Pakistan

One of the INDO-ARYAN LANGUAGES, Urdu is the twin of HINDI. It has the same origin in the regional language of the country around Delhi. Culturally, the two languages are a world apart.

Urdū is in full *Zabān-i-urdū*, 'language of the camp' – a Persian phrase that incorporates the Turkish word *ordu*. Thus 'Urdu' is the same in origin as *horde*, see box at UZBEK. The spoken Urdu of the 19th century, one of the major languages of British India, was then called *Hindustani* – the lingua franca of the subcontinent whose Persian name is *Hindūstān*, 'country of the Hindus'.

Urdu, in origin the speech of the northern Indian Muslim courts and cities, spread as a lingua franca in India wherever Mughal influence was felt. Evidently well known and serviceable in both north and south, it was much favoured during the early expansion of British rule.

The earliest Urdu poetry, of the 16th and 17th centuries, comes from the Muslim courts of the south of India, particularly Hyderabad. At the beginning of the 19th century, the British Fort William College encouraged the development of a new literary standard on the basis of the Urdu of Delhi, a literary language intended to supplant the Braj form of Hindi. But this policy overlooked the fact that Islam was a minority religion in India, and Urdu vocabulary and style, under Persian influence, had drifted away from its popular base. Its script, too, was not ideal for an Indo-Aryan language and unsuitable for typesetting.

When, at independence, India split on religious lines, Urdu, which had the best-developed cultural tradition among languages of Indian Muslims, took its place as the sole official language of Pakistan. It is thus widely spoken there as a second language, but it is the mother tongue of only a minority, numbering about 8,000,000 – and many of these are emigrants or children of emigrants from North India. Their main centre is Karachi. Urdu functions as the literary language of the numerically dominant PANJABI and Lahnda speakers of Pakistan.

In India, *Dakhinī Urdū* (Urdu 'of the Deccan, of the south') still centres on Hyderabad, Bijapur, Gulbarga and other mainly Muslim towns of the Deccan plateau. Urdu is still widely spoken in the big northern Indian cities. The total number of speakers in India may be as many as 32,000,000 – a figure is difficult to give, since they may well be competent in Urdu and Hindi equally.

The history of Urdu as a lingua franca lives on in its use in pidginised form as a trading language in great cities such as Calcutta and Bombay – both of which owe their early growth to their status as centres of British rule. Naturally influenced by the majority languages (Bengali and Marathi respectively), *Bazār Hindustānī* in these cities serves for communication among those who do not themselves speak Bengali or Marathi.

Outside the subcontinent, Urdu is the cultural language of many emigrant communities of Indian Muslims, particularly Panjabi and Gujarati speakers.

Urdu is written in a script based on Arabic, with added letters as used for Persian, and some variants specific to Urdu. It is usually printed from calligraphy. Its typical sloping style cannot be satisfactorily imitated with movable type. One or two specially designed word-processing programs are now able to generate good written Urdu.

Numerals in Hindi and Urdu

	Hindi	Urdu
1	ek	एक
2	do	दो
3	tīn	तीन
4	cār	चार
5	pāñc	पाच
6	cha	छ्
7	sāt	सात
8	āṭh	आठ
9	nau	नौ
10	das	दस

Urdu in print

بیابان عاشقان کو ملك اسكندر برابر ہی

ہر اك گوهر انچهو کا بخت کی اختر برابر ہی

To a lover, the desert equals Alexander's kingdom,
And each pearl of a tear is a lucky star.

Lines 1–2 of a ghazal by Wali Dakhani (1668–1743): after John A. Haywood, 'Wali Dakhani and the development of Dakhini Urdu Sufi Poetry' in *Acta orientalia* vol. 28 (1964–5) pp. 153–74

UZBEK

16,000,000 SPEAKERS

Uzbekistan, Afghanistan

In terms of number of speakers, Uzbek is the second largest of the TURKIC LANGUAGES, after Turkish itself, and it was the third largest language of the old Soviet Union after Russian and Ukrainian. The Uzbek capital, Tashkent, is the greatest metropolis of central Asia (see map at UIGHUR).

Uzbak Khān (1312–40), of the Golden Horde, became a Muslim, and his name was applied to the Muslim Turks who owed allegiance to the Horde. Their descendants moved eastwards, towards central Asia, in the fifteenth century, and established khanates in Kokand, Khiva and Bokhara. The city-dwellers, their subjects, were partly PERSIAN-speaking Tajiks: others spoke a Turkic language, a variant of early Uighur. There has been centuries-long interchange and intermarriage between the two. The modern form of this Turkic language is called *Özbäk* (*Uzbek* in most foreign languages) after the far-ranging conqueror and his nomadic followers.

Chagatai was the older written language of the Uzbek khanates and the Golden Horde. It takes its name from one of the sons of Genghis Khan, who ruled in central Asia in the 13th century.

Used by Timur (ruled 1369–1407) and his descendants, notably Sultan Husain Baykara (ruled 1469–1506), it was at Husain's court that Chagatai emerged as a literary medium – a Turkic language competing for the very first time with Arabic and Persian – in the hands of the poet Alisher Navoi (1440–1501). Chagatai is now sometimes called 'Old Uzbek', though Uzbek is only one of the several modern Turkic languages spoken where Chagatai once held sway.

The three Uzbek khanates were incorporated in the Russian Empire between 1865 and 1876. Russian influence on the language – alongside that of the Islamic missionary TATARS – now began to overlay that of Arabic and Persian. The 'local customary tongues' (essentially Uzbek and KYRGYZ) were declared equal with Russian in 1918, but until the 1920s Uzbek was scarcely identified or named as a separate language.

Its status was assured with the creation of the Uzbek Republic, within the Soviet Union, in 1924. There was a movement to 'cleanse' Uzbek of Arabic and Persian loanwords – but Russian loanwords multiplied meanwhile.

The first wholly Uzbek newspaper, *Turkiston Viloyatining Gazeti*, had appeared in 1893. Supplanting the Arabic script inherited from Chagatai writing, a Latin alphabet was used from 1927, to be replaced in turn by Cyrillic in 1940. In the last few years the Latin alphabet has been officially readopted in independent Uzbekistan, but its widespread use lies somewhere in the future. Everywhere, indeed, one sees the catch-phrase in Cyrillic script, Узбекистан – келажачи буюк давлам, 'Uzbekistan, a state with a great future'.

The region once ruled by the Uzbek is now divided between Uzbekistan, Afghanistan and Kazakhstan. There are at least a million Uzbek speakers in Afghanistan, where it is recognised as a national language and used in broadcasting. Numbers there grew as a result of emigration from Uzbekistan in Soviet times.

Central Asia: Uighur and Uzbek

One of the main areas where Persian (Tajik) influence is felt is the tendency for the vowel system to shift from the typical ten-vowel system of most Turkic languages, with distinctive front-rounded and back-unrounded vowels (*ö ü, ə ɪ*), to a six-vowel system practically identical to that of Tajik. The process is not complete, and it has not occurred in all the dialects, but it is far advanced in the city dialects of Tashkent and Samarkand.

For a table of numerals see UIGHUR.

> The Golden Horde was not a band of nomadic warriors. It was the camp – Russian *orda*, Turkish *ordu* – which was their mobile capital. The language name URDU has the same origin.

A riddle

Ol ne dur kim şahddin tatlıq erür hammārǧa,
Ihtiyār etsäm satarnı kirmägäy bāzārǧa?

What is sweeter than honey to the eyes,
Yet much as I wanted to sell it
I could not get it to market?

The answer? Sleep.

Uvaysi (18th-century woman poet)

The Chagatai alphabet

ي و ه ن م ل ك ك ق ف غ ع ظ ط ض ص ش س ز ز ز ذ د ج ج ح ج خ ث ت ب ب ا

a b p t ş j ḥ kh č d z̧ r z ž s š ş z̧ ṭ z̧ ' gh f q k g l m n h v y

In the Arabic script as used for Chagatai, the two semivowel signs (the last two letters of the alphabet) were also used for vowels: و *v* served for *o u ö ü*; ی *y* served for *i ɪ*.

VENDA

750,000 SPEAKERS

South Africa

Venda or *tshiVenda* is one of the BANTU LAN-GUAGES and one of the eleven official languages of South Africa. It is rather isolated linguistically, having no close links either with the Nguni group (Zulu and others) or the Sotho group or the Shona group of Bantu languages, which surround it (see map at SOTHO).

In the 18th century, groups from north of the Limpopo – the *Singo* lineage – are said to have crossed to the south and established their overlordship in the Venda country, where they remain powerful. This explains why Venda has quite numerous Shona loanwords. Unlike its neighbours, it has never undergone Zulu influence.

Venda has a special *Musanda* vocabulary which must be used at court, avoiding taboo expressions: thus, if a chief is the subject of the sentence, one does not say – *vhulaha* 'kill' but instead – *ponda*. This is a Shona loanword: in the Zezuru dialect of Shona it means 'execute, murder'.

In the 19th century Venda speakers attracted the attention of the Berlin Missionary Society. The written form of Venda (at first called *Ba-suetla*) was thus the creation of German-speaking missionaries. That resulted in some unexpected spelling conventions, such as *dzh* for the sound that in neighbouring languages is written *j*.

The first ten numerals in Venda are: *-thithi, -vhili, -raru, -na, -tanu, -tanu na -thili, -tanu na -vhili, -tanu na -raru, -tanu na -na, fumi.*

VIETNAMESE

55,000,000 SPEAKERS

Vietnam

Now generally agreed to be one of the AUS-
TROASIATIC LANGUAGES, Vietnamese is so different from its relatives that quite contradictory
views on its origin have been expressed. It is the
official language of Vietnam.

> In recent centuries the cultural centre had been
> the old royal city of Hue, capital of Annam. The
> language has therefore sometimes been called
> *Annamese* or *Annamite*. Vietnam, the 'Viet coun-
> try', is an inclusive term covering also the
> southern region of Cochinchina and the north-
> ern region of Tonkin. Vietnamese is the ma-
> jority language in all three.

For over two thousand years Chinese culture
has exerted a pervasive influence on that of
Vietnam. According to traditional history, China
ruled the kingdom of Annam, which included
Tonkin, from the 2nd century BC until 968, when
Dinh Bo Lanh established himself as an independent monarch. Over the following centuries
Vietnamese rule extended southwards, where
the kingdoms of Champa (see CHAM) and Funan
had once held sway.

Roman Catholic missionaries were involved in
Vietnam from the 17th century, in competition
with Buddhism, Confucianism and the still-pro-
minent survivals of local religion. Their great
contribution to its culture was the *quoc ngu* script,
a special version of the Latin alphabet suited to
the sounds and especially the tones of Vietnamese. Until the early 20th century this coexisted
with *nom*, the Vietnamese adaptation of Chinese
script: but it was encouraged by the French
administration, it promoted the spread of literacy
and thus of new political ideas, and it is now
universally used.

Of Vietnamese literature before the 19th century a great deal is 'Sino-Vietnamese' – not only
dependent on Chinese models but written in
more or less pure Chinese. This includes the
history *Dai Viet su ky* 'Records of Great Viet',
compiled in the 13th century and revised later.
Here the succession of Vietnamese emperors is
traced back to 2879 BC. Literature in true Vietnamese, still full of Chinese words but closer to
its real time and place, is rich in poetry and
legend. The greatest work of Vietnamese literature is *Kim Van Kieu*, the 'Tale of Kieu', a verse
romance by Nguyen-Du (1765–1820).

Until the French conquest, which began in
1862, printing in Vietnam was by means of
woodblocks. Western-style printing in *quoc ngu*
was introduced at once and a newspaper press
developed in the next decades. French, Japanese and American domination ended in thirty
years of war, culminating in the reunification of
independent Vietnam in 1975.

The standard dialect of Vietnamese, represented in the script, is that of Hanoi. This has
six tones: thus the script, too, differentiates
between six tones, though speakers in most of
Vietnam recognise only five. As can be seen from
the box, tones are essential in Vietnamese in
distinguishing the meaning of otherwise identical words.

Chinese words now make up as much as 60
per cent of the vocabulary of written Vietnamese. Many of these loans arrived before the
10th century, as is evident when their Vietnamese pronunciation is compared with modern
Chinese – though the logic is obscured by the
fact that Chinese in Vietnam has, in any case,
continued to be pronounced in the medieval

way. This local form of medieval Chinese, known as *Han*, is traditionally the language of learning of Vietnam.

The six tones of Vietnamese

Name	Sound	Example
bằng	mid falling	ma *'ghost'*
sắc	high rising	má *'mother'*
huyền	low falling	mà *'but'*
hỏi	falling-rising	mỏ *'tomb'*
ngã	high rising glottalised	mã *'horse'*
nặng	low glottalised	mạ *'rice seedling'*

Example from Nguyen Dinh-Hoa, 'Vietnamese' in *International encyclopedia of linguistics* (New York: Oxford University Press, 1992)

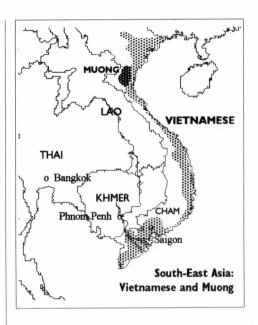

South-East Asia: Vietnamese and Muong

Nom and quoc-ngu

Han was naturally written in Chinese script. *Nom* is the name for Chinese script as applied to Vietnamese, with added characters and character compounds to denote native Vietnamese words. For several centuries, since 1285 at the latest, this was the usual way of writing the language.

The romanisation of Vietnamese was devised by French Catholic missionaries in the 17th century. This specially developed Latin script or *quoc ngu*, with its double diacritics, existed in parallel with *nom* for three centuries, and even-

tually, under French colonial rule, triumphed. It is now the only standard orthography for Vietnamese. In 1993 Ho Chi Minh City University closed its only course in *Han* and the *nom* script: teachers, examiners and interested students had become impossible to find.

The Vietnamese alphabet is shown in the box. Tone marks are not included because they are ignored in the alphabetical order.

The Vietnamese alphabet

a ă â b c ch d đ e ê g gh gi h i k kh l m n ng nh o ô ơ p ph qu r s t th tr u ư v x y

WA

PROBABLY WELL OVER 1,000,000 SPEAKERS

Burma, China

Wa consists of a group of related AUSTRO-ASIATIC LANGUAGES, the main body of whose speakers live on the mountainous borderland between Burma and China. In Burma the region is part of Shan State, but has always been difficult country for the Burmese authorities and a traditional centre of Communist insurgence. Speakers in China belong to the Va and Bulang national minorities.

The legendary centre of the Wa country is Lake Nawngkhio, high in the mountains on the China–Burma frontier. The older history of the language and its speakers is unknown, but Austroasiatic speech may well have a history of several millennia in this region. The population of the Wa country is high and cultivation of the mountain slopes is intense. Their most saleable product is opium, of which this is one of the world's main sources.

> Facts on the Wa country, including its population, are still hard to assemble. Outsiders have not found it easy to get to grips with Wa political philosophy. The British, for example, who annexed the region in the 1890s, could not understand why the village rulers (often given the Shan title *Sawbwa*) would not identify themselves to strangers. Sometimes they disappeared; sometimes they were actually there among the villagers, but unidentifiable. This explains why the first entry in the Wa wordlist published by Lieutenant Daly in 1891 is 'Where is the Sawbwa?'

A further problem has been the prevalence of headhunting (see box). During a China–Burma border delineation in 1900 Wa warriors captured two British heads in a daring raid near a Chinese market town. These two heads were still objects of worship sixty years later.

Apart from their mountain heartland, Wa speakers are to be found in scattered communities in mountainous parts of Xishuangbanna, of the southern Shan State (especially the former state of Kengtung) and of north-western Thailand. For those who have adopted Buddhism and valley agriculture, Shan and Lanna Thai become the adopted languages: it is likely enough that Wa was once the main language of Kengtung and other neighbouring states before the spread of Tai speech.

> *Wa* is the Shan name for this people and is the most widely familiar: *Va* is the Chinese form. *Lawa* is the usual name for the Wa languages of Thailand and their speakers.
>
> The term *La* is also used, specifically for Wa speakers who have adopted Buddhism and other cultural features associated with Tai populations: those who had not were traditionally called *Wa hai* by Shans, *Wild Wa* in English.

The first serious notes on Wa languages were made by French and British explorers in the early 1890s. Wa languages are largely monosyllabic, like their Tai and Tibeto-Burman neighbours, but unlike some other Austroasiatic languages. They have no tones, but they tend to have rich and complicated vowel systems: Chinese researchers have counted fifty 'vocalic nuclei' (vowels and diphthongs) in the Paraok dialect. In the numerals table, the accents ´ and ` make the distinction between 'tense' and 'lax' vowels, one that is paralleled (though with different details and different names) in Mon, Khmer and other Austroasiatic languages.

Wa shows the influence of neighbouring Tai languages, in which some speakers are bilingual. Loans from Shan are found in central Wa dialects such as Paraok; Lawa dialects have borrowed from Lanna Thai; Bulang dialects have borrowed from Lü, the Yunnanese variant of Lanna Thai.

There has been little writing or publishing in Wa languages, and no generally accepted orthography. But the American Baptist Mission Press, in Rangoon, brought out translations of the Gospels of Matthew and John in 1934–5, and some books in Wa have appeared in China at intervals since the 1950s.

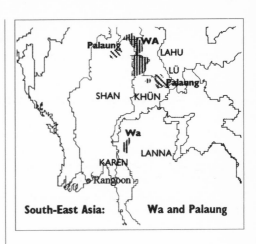

South-East Asia: Wa and Palaung

Exploring the Wa country

'The country is described as very difficult and almost pathless; it is never entered by caravans; fear of the Wa Hai and Muhsö Hai ['Wild LAHU'] is so deep and general that guides could not have been obtained ... No Shans, except those living in the immediate vicinity and who supply the Was with salt and other necessaries, would dare to pass through this region.'

H. Daly, *The Northern Trans-Salween States and the Chinese Border* (Rangoon, 1891)

'[We] passed another avenue of posts, about fifty of them, under big trees, about a third of which contained heads. Any number of small spirit shrines under archways of greenery. Then came upon evidence without question that the head-hunting was in full swing: a human body right across the path, beheaded and with the hands and feet cut off ... Endless bother with guides. Had no sooner started than the guide refused to go beyond the upper villages. He solemnly unfastened a piece of rag, and taking out the two-anna bits that had been given him, handed them back, and then just legged it.'

Sir George Scott's Diary, February 1893 (India Office Library and Archives)

Wa and Palaung

Wa and Palaung form two groups that make up a single branch, 'Palaungic' or Palaung-Wa, of the Austroasiatic language family. Geographically it is centred in the Shan State and western Yunnan. Speakers of these languages are the modern representatives of a population that has an older history in the mountains of inner south-east Asia than the speakers of Tai or Sino-Tibetan languages.

The Wa or 'Waic' languages include *Central Wa* dialects, Paraok, Avüa', La and others; *Phalok*, formerly called Khalo or Mae Rim Lawa; *Lawa* and its dialects; and the dialects of *Bulang* (or Blang or Samtao), counted as a separate Chinese national minority.

The Palaung or Palaung-Rumai group, with perhaps 500,000 speakers in total, includes several languages of Burma and China. Speakers in China belong to the *De'ang* (formerly Běnglóng) national minority. The major language of the group is *Ta-ang* or Palaung, spoken in the former 'Shan State' of Tawngpeng and by minorities in Hsipaw, Hsenwi and Möngmit states, all now part of Shan State, Burma. Minor Palaung languages include *Rumai*; *Riang* and *Yinchia* (also called Black Karen, Striped Karen); *Palê*, including Da-ang and Na-ang; *Ka-ang*, *Ra-ang*.

Numerals in Wa languages and Palaung			
	Kawa	**Lawa**	**Bulang**	**Ta-ang (Palaung)**
1	tì'	thi'	ktì'	ū, hlɛ̄h
2	rá	la	lə'ál	ār
3	lóy	la'ua	lə'ɔ́y	u-āī
4	pón	paun	pún	phōn
5	phúan	phɔn	phɔ́n	phən
6	lìah	lɛs	lɛ̀h	tɔ̄r
7	'alìah	'a-lɛs	harrɛ́h	pūr
8	ntái'	sate'	sətí'	tā
9	ntím	sataim	sətím	thīm
10	káɔ	kau	kul	kör

G. Diffloth, 'The Wa languages' in *Linguistics of the Tibeto-Burman area* vol. 5 no. 2 (1980) pp. 1–182 and other sources

WARAY-WARAY

2,400,000 SPEAKERS

Philippines

One of the Bisayan languages, like CEBUANO (see map there), and thus a member of the larger family of AUSTRONESIAN LANGUAGES, Waray-waray forms a dialect group including *Samar-Leyte, Northern Samar*, and *Gubat* or *Southern Sorsogon*. They are spoken in the islands of Samar and eastern Leyte and part of the Sorsogon district at the southern extremity of Luzon.

The first ten numerals in Waray-waray are: *'usa, duha, tulu, 'upat, lima, 'unum, pitu, walu, siyam, napulu'*.

This dialect group of the two eastern islands of the Visayas chain has no generally agreed name. Speakers often call their language *Binisayaq*, 'Visayan', or else adopt the regional nickname *Waray-waray*, which comes from their local word *waray* 'there isn't any'. The names *Samareño* and *Samar-Leyte* are also used.

WELSH

PERHAPS 500,000 SPEAKERS

United Kingdom

Welsh is one of the two surviving CELTIC LANGUAGES (see map there) that descend from the speech of southern Britain at the time of the Roman conquest: the other is Breton. Although Latin is seen in Wales on stone inscriptions of all kinds that date from the four centuries of Roman rule, Celtic probably remained the everyday language for a large proportion of the population. So it is that after the Anglo-Saxon conquests had spread over what is now England in the 5th and 6th centuries, no trace remained of any native Latin-speaking communities. Celtic speech, alongside religious and literary Latin, lived on and flourished beyond the bounds of the initial Anglo-Saxon expansion in the western part of Britain, the country now known to us as Wales.

Wealas, modern *Welsh*, is in origin simply the Anglo-Saxon term for 'foreigner'. The Welsh name for themselves – equally unspecific – is *Cymry*, 'fellow-countrymen': the language is known as *Cymraeg*.

Britain, Latin *Brittania, Britannia*, is itself a Celtic word in origin, as seen in Welsh *Ynys Prydein* 'the island of Britain'.

Taliesin's poetry tells of a 6th-century king Urien of Rheged in southern Scotland; *Y Gododdin* of Aneirin describes a disastrous battle between Celts and Northumbrians at Catterick in about 600. These two heroic poems, wherever they were composed and at whatever later time they were written down, mark the beginning of recorded Welsh literature. Welsh became the language of great poetry of many kinds. The prose tales usually called the 'Mabinogion' include the earliest known versions of the tales of King Arthur, the 'once and future king', legendary hero of Celtic resistance against the Saxons.

Welsh was the official language of the independent principality of Wales, but that succumbed to the English in 1282. Over the next centuries Wales became increasingly integrated with England, administratively at least, and English gained ground. Ironically it was under a Welsh dynasty – the Tudor Kings of England, in the 16th century – that this development was first enforced by law. The Act of Union of 1536 disqualified Welsh speakers from official employment and established English as the language of the courts. In the 19th and early 20th centuries, while schoolteachers punished and humiliated children who spoke Welsh, the Baptists and other Nonconformist Christian sects helped to keep Welsh literacy alive. Determined resistance led to the gradual easing of official discrimination between 1944, when the first publicly funded Welsh-language schools were established, and 1973, when the first court case was heard entirely in Welsh.

At the beginning of the 20th century half the population of Wales (about 1,000,000 people) could speak Welsh; in 1981 only about 20 per cent knew the language, though in numerical terms that still meant 500,000 people. Few if any speakers are now monolingual – nearly all use English as well as Welsh. There may be 60 per cent or more of Welsh speakers in most of rural western and northern Wales, but in the capital, Cardiff, and its neighbourhood, there are fewer than 10 per cent.

Welsh literature goes back to the 8th century. In the Middle Welsh period, 1150–1400, the language of the court poets formed a standard.

The translation of the Bible in 1588 (into a form of speech which was influenced by this medieval poetry) and the use of biblical language by preachers meant that a standard language became familiar to more people than ever before. Nowadays there are local weekly newspapers, radio, television, and some literary and educational publishing. Education in Welsh is available up to university level.

There is a considerable Welsh-speaking community in London. In the 19th century a Welsh colony was established at Chubut and Puerto Madryn in Argentina. Here Welsh was recognised for official use until the 1930s, but was then replaced with Spanish. Only older people now speak Welsh.

Modern standard literary Welsh is a conservative form of the language: this makes it more difficult to learn, but those who can read it can also read the early classics. *Cymraeg Byw* or 'Living Welsh', a new standard forming a compromise between literary Welsh and the colloquial dialects, was introduced into schools in 1964.

Northern dialects of Welsh are relatively conservative; the south-eastern dialects are structurally furthest from standard literary Welsh. There are some differences in vocabulary between north and south: 'road', northern *ffordd*, *lôn*, southern *heol*; 'oven', northern *popty*, southern *ffwrn*; 'milk', northern *llefrith*, southern *llaeth*; 'cake', northern *teisen*, southern *cacen*.

Cacen 'cake' is one of the many English loanwords in Welsh, like *sir* 'shire, county', *taten* 'potato', *sosban* 'saucepan', *sŵ* 'zoo'. But much of the vocabulary goes back to the Celtic and Indo-European roots of the language: *dant* 'tooth', *môr* 'sea'.

English shares much with Welsh, in its sound pattern, its idioms and its vocabulary. Phrases such as *Sut rydych chi?* 'How are you?' are exactly mirrored in the two languages. Welsh loanwords in English include *pert*, which means 'pretty' in Welsh. Few English linguists know Welsh, so the similarities tend to be overlooked or played down.

Welsh looks difficult to the unfamiliar eye because of some unusual spelling conventions: *w* and *y* are common vowels; *ll* is an unvoiced *l*; *dd* is a voiced *th* sound. To use a Welsh dictionary, one must allow for the so-called mutations of initial consonants in normal speech and writing. The dictionary form *Cymru* 'Wales' can be found in ordinary text, in various surroundings, as *Cymru, Chymru, Gymru, Nghymru*: thus *yng Nghymru* 'in Wales'. For a table of numerals see BRETON.

Latin loanwords in Welsh

Welsh naturally has many Latin loanwords, dating from the time of the Roman Empire, when early Welsh and Latin coexisted for four hundred years: *lleidr* 'thief'; *sebon* 'soap'; *meddyg* 'physician'; *gwin* 'wine'. No wonder that the names of the days of the week are very like those in the Romance languages. In both sets, five of the names commemorate ancient Roman gods.

Welsh	French	
Dydd Llun	lundi	Latin *Dies lunae* 'Moon's day'
Dydd Mawrth	mardi	Latin *Dies Martis* 'Mars's day'
Dydd Mercher	mercredi	Latin *Dies Mercurii* 'Mercury's day'
Dydd Iau	jeudi	Latin *Dies Jovis* 'Jupiter's day'
Dydd Gwener	vendredi	Latin *Dies Veneris* 'Venus's day'
Dydd Sadwrn	samedi	Latin *Dies Saturni* 'Saturn's day'
Dydd Sul	Dimanche	The French originates as *Dies dominica*, 'Lord's day';
		the Welsh, like English, as 'Sun's day', Latin *Dies Solis*

6th-century Wales: Christian hymns in competition with bardic poetry

Arrecto aurium auscultantur captu non Dei laudes canora Christi tironum voce suaviter modulante neumaque ecclesiasticae melodiae, sed propriae, quae nihil sunt, furciferorum referto mendaciis simulque spumanti flegmate proximos quosque roscidaturo praeconum ore ritu bacchantium con-crepante.

With ears pricked up, you attend not to the praises of God, as the tuneful voice of the apprentices of Christ rings sweetly, nor to the breath of religious melody, but to praises of yourself, which are nothing, from the mouth of convicts, stuffed with lies and sure to bedew bystanders with foaming spittle, yelling like priests of Bacchus.

Gildas, *The Ruin of Britain* 34

This Latin lament by a 6th-century abbot is addressed to the Welsh prince Maelgwn.

WOLAYTTA

PERHAPS 1,000,000 SPEAKERS OF OMETO DIALECTS

Ethiopia

Wolaytta is the most important representative of a close-knit group of dialects of southern Ethiopia – to some or all of which names such as *Ometo* and *Welamo* have been given. They belong to the OMOTIC LANGUAGES. Wolaytta is now one of the official literary languages of Ethiopia.

Speakers call themselves *Welamo*. This word, which may be spelt *Walamo*, is often used as a name for the language, but the local name is *Wolaytta*. Variant forms include *Welaita, Waratta*; the official term in Amharic is *Wolaminya*. *Ometo* means 'people of the Omo river' – thus it is identical in origin with the modern name of the larger language group, *Omotic*.

Wolaytta and the Ometo dialects (see map at GONGA) are the speech of small once-independent kingdoms which were conquered by Menelek of Ethiopia in 1894. The first brief wordlist of an Ometo dialect was published by the explorer Charles Tilstone Beke in 1846.

In these dialects – unlike the Gonga languages – neither vowel length nor tone appears to be a significant feature of the sound pattern. The first ten numerals in the Kullo dialect of the town of Jimma are: *ita, naa* (or *laa*), *hezu, oyda, icesh, osuphuna, laphuna, hosphuna, uduphuna, tamma*.

WOLOF

2,000,000 SPEAKERS

Senegal, Gambia

One of the Atlantic group of NIGER-CONGO LANGUAGES (see map at FULANI), Wolof has reached the status of de facto national language of Senegal, more widely broadcast on radio and television than any other except French.

Wolof is the speakers' own name for their language. The French spelling Ouolof is often found. Speakers call their region Dyolof: hence Jolof, occasionally used in English and French as a name for the language.

Wolof is the first language of most of northwestern Senegal, including the capital, Dakar, itself, and the Atlantic coast: as such it is one of the six official regional languages of the country, with two million speakers. To the east and south it is a second language, known to perhaps another four million people – to the great majority of townspeople a rapidly growing number of villagers.

As a coastal people, the Wolof ethnic group, the largest in Senegal, were the first to make significant contact with Europeans. Already in the 16th century Portuguese traders found Wolof interpreters almost as useful to them in this whole region as MANDEKAN speakers. In modern Senegal it became the most widespread language of trade. It is now essential for those looking for work outside their own districts and for all who migrate to a city. Wolof is more and more the language that children learn first, especially those whose parents are from different ethnic backgrounds.

In the Gambia Wolof is spoken by about 100,000 people along the north bank of the river and in the capital, Bathurst. On the south bank KRIO is still used, though it is giving way to Wolof.

Numerals in Wolof, DIOLA **and** FULANI			
	Wolof	**Diola**	**Fulani**
1	bèn	-əkon	go'o
2	ñār	-gaba	dïdï
3	ñèt	-fēgir	tati
4	ñènt	-bākir	nayi
5	jūrom	futɔk	jowi
6	jūrom-bèn	futɔk di -əkon	jeego'o
7	jūrom-ñār	futɔk di -gaba	jeedïdï
8	jūrom-ñèt	futɔk di -fègir	jeetati
9	jūrom-ñènt	futɔk di -bākir	jeenay
10	fuk	unyɛn	sappo

In all three languages the numerals '6' to '9' are formed as '5+1', '5+2' etc. In Diola, the basic four numerals take a prefix matching that of the noun: for example, *si-jamɛn futɔk di si-gaba* 'seven goats'.

XHOSA

6,900,000 SPEAKERS

South Africa

One of the BANTU LANGUAGES, Xhosa is spoken by the second largest language community of South Africa, after Zulu and ahead of Afrikaans. With Swazi, Ndebele and ZULU (see map there) it is a member of the Nguni language group. Long-standing Xhosa interaction with Khoe and other KHOISAN LANGUAGES is signposted by the fact that most Xhosa place names and many personal names are of Khoe origin.

Xhosa used to be called *Kaffir* or *Kaffrarian* (*Caffre* in Portuguese) – a term that equally covered Zulu and several other Bantu languages.

Xhosa shares its older history with ZULU, but – lying at the western end of the 'Nguni' dialect spectrum – Xhosa dialects were most exposed to influence from Khoisan languages, from Afrikaans and from English.

Linguists believe that it was as late as the 18th century that Xhosa completed the development of its unusual sound pattern. This was when Khoe and Xhosa speakers began to merge their social structures, the Khoekhoe becoming members of Xhosa lineages and the Xhosa merging into Khoe chiefdoms. There had probably been interaction between the two groups for much longer than this; now, at any rate, great numbers of Khoe loanwords were adopted into Xhosa, such as *irhamba* 'puff-adder', and with them came the click consonants so typical of the so-called Bushman languages of southern Africa and so rare elsewhere. An astonishing total of twenty-one (some say twenty-five) consonants, including fifteen clicks, were added to the Xhosa sound system at this period.

The bitter and damaging 'Kaffir Wars' of the late 18th and early 19th centuries were sparked by competition for land between Xhosa speakers and Europeans. European interest in the Xhosa language is first evident late in this period. It was only in 1826 that John Bennie, of the Glasgow Missionary Society, produced the first serious dictionary, *A systematic vocabulary of the Kaffrarian language*. John W. Appleyard, a Wesleyan missionary, published an important grammar in 1850.

A second social upheaval has been the labour migration of Xhosa-speaking men within South Africa, focused on Johannesburg and the neighbouring settlements, and intensifying in the 1960s. 'The Transkei', one of the homelands of the late apartheid period in South Africa, was intended as a Xhosa reservation.

As a majority language in its region, Xhosa now functions as a lingua franca for speakers of several smaller languages. There is a good deal of multilingualism between Xhosa on the one hand and Zulu, southern Sotho and English on the other. Nowadays Xhosa naturally incorporates English loanwords: *ibhasi* 'bus', *ititshala* 'teacher'.

Isikhwetha, a secret language, is still used by young men undergoing traditional Xhosa initiation rituals. *Hlonipha* is the women's language of 'respect' or 'avoidance'.

Hlonipha, the avoidance language

Hlonipha means 'respectful avoidance' of certain expressions and forms of behaviour, an avoidance that is particularly expected of women who are married or engaged to be married. To linguists, *hlonipha* is particularly the form of language that is used to avoid taboo expressions.

Numerals in Xhosa and Zulu

Xhosa		Zulu
-nye	1	-nye
-bini	2	-bili
-thathu	3	-tatu
-ne	4	-ne
-hlanu	5	-hlanu
-thandathu	6	isitupa
isixhenxe	7	isikhombisa
isibozo	8	isishiyagalombili
ilithoba	9	isishiyagalolunye
ilishumi	10	ishumi

Expressing high numbers in standard Xhosa and Zulu requires many syllables. For '29 trees' the Xhosa is *imithi engamashumi amabini anethoba*; the Zulu equivalent is *imithi engamashumi amabili nesishiyagalolunye*. In the modern colloquial languages, English loanwords are usually used for high numbers.

In the traditional rules as they have existed among Xhosa and Zulu speakers, women must not pronounce the names of their fathers-in-law, their mothers-in-law nor some other male in-laws. They must not even use syllables from those names:

'Thus, a woman whose father-in-law is named Bongani must avoid the name itself and the syllables *bo* and *nga* – wherever they occur in speech ... the effect on each individual woman's speech may be dramatic.

'A variety of linguistic mechanisms is used to achieve avoidance, including consonant substitution (e.g. *ulunya* 'cruelty' becoming *uluchya*), ellipsis (e.g. *umkhono* 'foreleg' becoming *um'ono*), synonymy (if *kufa* 'die' is to be avoided, *kushona* 'set, die' used in its place), derivation (if *imbuti* 'goat' is to be avoided, *inkhuleko* 'thing for tethering' invented in its place) as well as neologism, archaicism and borrowing' (R. K. Herbert).

Nowadays borrowing is often from English. In the past, frequent intermarriage between Xhosa and Khoisan speakers would have led to the borrowing of sounds and words from Khoisan languages into *hlonipha* speech. This is probably how the rich range of Khoisan consonants, including clicks, came to be adopted into Xhosa and the other Nguni languages. In turn, Southern SOTHO shows heavy borrowing from Zulu (and has adopted one of the Khoisan clicks), and this can be attributed to Zulu-Sotho intermarriage in the 19th century.

Hlonipha does not fit well with modern lifestyles. It can make it impossible to fill in forms correctly. Women often have to abandon it at their place of work. 'Many schoolchildren consider the whole concept a joke' (R. Finlayson). It seems likely that the practice will not last through many more generations.

Based on papers by Robert K. Herbert and R. Finlayson in *Language and social history: studies in South African sociolinguistics* ed. Rajend Mesthrie (Cape Town: David Philip, 1995)

YAKUT

300,000 SPEAKERS

Russia

One of the TURKIC LANGUAGES, Yakut (or Sakha) has been geographically separated from its relatives for many centuries. The Yakut, in their vast Siberian heartland, have a very different environment from that of other Turkic language speakers, and have developed a different way of life, very like that of neighbours who are speakers of TUNGUSIC and PALAEOSIBERIAN LANGUAGES.

To themselves, Yakut are *Sakha*, 'people of the edge'. They did indeed occupy the very edge of the habitable world as known to early Turkic speakers. In Buryat Mongol this same word appears as *Yakhuud*, from which Russians learnt to call the people and their language *Yakut*.

It may have been the Mongolian expansion of the 13th century that separated Yakut speakers from the Turkic regions to the south-east. Their legends tell of an original home on the shores of Lake Baikal. Their territory, formerly Yakutia, is now called Sakha. Fourteen times the size of Britain, Sakha has a population of around 500,000, just over half of whom are Yakut speakers. Russian speakers account for nearly all the rest. The region was already being explored by Russian traders in the 17th century: its modern capital, Yakutsk, was founded by them as a fort and trading post in 1632.

The first alphabet for Yakut, an adaptation of the older Cyrillic alphabet, was devised by Russian missionaries in the early 19th century. A Latin alphabet with a great many additional let-

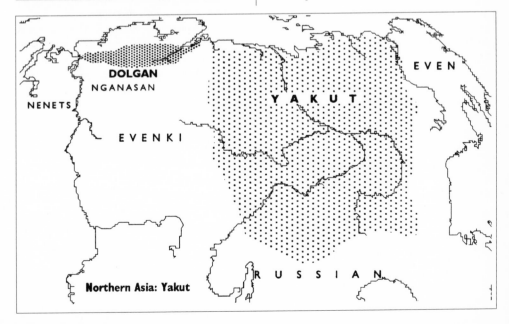

Northern Asia: Yakut

ters was used 1922–39, when the modern Cyrillic alphabet – again with extra letters – was introduced. It is only in the 20th century that Yakut has been regularly used in education and the press.

Yakut is close enough to its relatives to be easy for Turkish speakers to learn, though they have to cope with consonant assimilation that multiplies the possible forms of suffixes. The plural suffix, which may be -*ler* or -*lar* in Turkish, has sixteen forms in Yakut: -*lar* -*ler* -*lor* -*lör* -*nar* -*ner* -*nor* -*nör* -*tar* -*ter* -*tor* -*tör* -*dar* -*der* -*dor* -*dör*.

The first ten numerals are: *biit, ikki, üs, tört, bies, alta, sette, aγis, toγus, uon.*

Yakut and its neighbours

The basin of the great River Lena forms most of Sakha, a self-governing republic of Russia. Per-

mafrost makes it impractical to build railways, metalled roads or heavy buildings. Rivers, ice-covered most of the year, are navigable only for a short summer season. Traditionally Yakuts are herders of cattle, horses and (in the further north) reindeer. They are also prominent in the fur trade. The Russian speakers who once threatened to overwhelm Yakutia are now fewer and less well paid.

In the far north-west are 3,000 speakers of the Dolgan language. They are ethnically distinct from the Yakut, but their speech is clearly a divergent dialect of Yakut which appears to have a strong admixture of some Tungusic language. These reinder herders may be descendants of Tungusic speakers who, at some time in the past, took to speaking Yakut.

Epic hero of the north

Yakut oral literature is rich, varied and rooted in the Siberian way of life. Prose tales, short poems and epics have been recorded. In poetry, consonant alliteration is added to the vowel assonance that is built into the structure of all Turkic languages. An epic hero introduces himself:

Хардарыылаах айаннаах,	Khardarılaakh aiannaakh,	Facing a desolate road,
халыан сырыылаах,	khalıan sırılaakh,	Riding a wild-stepping
хара тыа	khara tıa	Forest-black
хайдан түспүтүн курдук	khaidan tüspütün kurduk	Mountain-offspring
хаҥыл хара аттаах	khangil khara attaakh	Untamed raven-black horse,
хаан айыы сизнз	khaan aiıı siene	Inheriting blood-sin,
Халыадьымар Бзргзн – дизн киһибин.	Khalyajimar Bergen dien kihibin.	I am the man called Khalyajımar Bergen.

From John R. Krueger, *Yakut manual* (Bloomington: Indiana University, 1962) p. 225

YAO (AFRICA)

1,200,000 SPEAKERS

Malawi, Tanzania, Mozambique

Yao, one of the BANTU LANGUAGES, is spoken in northern Mozambique and in neighbouring districts of Tanzania and Malawi (for map see MAKUA).

Its speakers traditionally give their ancestral home as a hill called Yao, near Muembe, in north-eastern Mozambique. In Nyanja, Yao speakers are called *Achawa*, a word derived from *Chao*, the singular form of *Yao*.

Traditionally a farming and cattle-keeping people, Yao speakers controlled trade routes between the Lake Nyasa region and the Indian Ocean. For many centuries they dealt with Swahili-speaking traders at the coast, and travelled far inland. In the 19th century they were still prominent in the slave trade. At that time they were expanding their territory in what is now southern Malawi, where Yao speakers formed a ruling class and raided for slaves. The trade was outlawed in 1896, but the language had spread rapidly over the area that they ruled.

By the later 19th century many of the Yao had adopted Islam under Swahili influence. Swahili was the written language of the religious schools.

Unlike its coastal relatives, Makua and Makonde, Yao is unmistakably a tonal language. Linguists have distinguished up to five tones, although, after allowing for variation due to phonetic context, these can be reduced to two. The tones of Yao seem to have no relation to the reconstructed tones of proto-Bantu, and may have originated quite recently.

There are no great dialect differences in Yao, in spite of its wide extent. Since the Yao-speaking country has never been politically united, this geographical uniformity must be a sign of frequent travel and good communications among Yao speakers in the recent past.

The first ten numerals in Yao are *-mo, -wili, -tatu, mcheche, msano, msano na -mo, msano na -wili, msano na -tatu, msano na mcheche, likumi.*

'A man who is going to tell a story says *Tele!* "Full!" and the people answer *Lokote, lokote, kaselo ndi! Lakata!* "Pick it up, the basket is full, heaped up to overflowing!" When he has finished the audience says *Ajokole chitolo, chitakununga!* "Take the rat off the fire or it will smell!" '

Meredith Sanderson, *A Yao grammar*
(London: SPCK, 1922) pp. 118–19

Yao traditions

'The yearly initiation ceremonies, *unyago*, are the principal cultural institution of the Yao. That for the boys, *lupanda*, is the most important. It is held at the end of the dry season, before the bush is burned. Each initiate is accompanied by a sponsor, *nkamusi*, who may be a brother, uncle or friend. Before they set out for the place appointed to be *lupanda*, they all assemble before the chief to be anointed with millet-flour specially prepared by his head wife. The word *lupanda* refers to a forked stick over which the sacrificial flour is poured. This stick is planted at the place of assembly, the *masakasa*. The next day the initiates go to a spot in the bush, where the circumcision is performed, and remain in the bush school, *ndagala*, for about two months, until the wounds are completely healed.

'During these weeks the boys are subjected to rigorous discipline and instructed in various skills and tribal lore. On the last night before the return to the village the initiates undergo a ceremonial bathing, each boy being carried to the stream by a woman, who thereafter is addressed as "elder sister". Finally, with new names, they march to the chief's village to be redeemed by him from the master of ceremonies, *m'micira*, with gifts of cloth. After initiation it is a deadly insult to call a boy by his child-name.

'Most Yao men and women act as sponsors of initiates at least once, and all participate yearly in the great initiation festival for boys and girls. Consequently as they repeat each year the lessons of their own initiation, the ceremonies are the main vehicle of Yao culture.'

Mary Tew, *Peoples of the Lake Nyasa region*
(London: Oxford University Press, 1950)
pp. 19–21, abridged

YAO LANGUAGES

PERHAPS 900,000 SPEAKERS

China and south-east Asian countries

Yao and Nu, with MIAO (see map there), belong to the small Miao-Yao language family, which some linguists consider to be a component of the wider grouping of AUSTRO-TAI LANGUAGES.

Yao is the official term for both languages in China. Speakers call themselves Mien; Man is the term used in Vietnam.

Speakers of the two Yao languages live in the hills of 'Lingnan', southern China. Little is known of their history, as with many other peoples of this region of mountains and valleys, but they are said to have moved southwards from Hunan, under pressure from expanding Chinese rule, in the 12th and 13th centuries. This was possibly the first move in a gradual spread southwards which certainly had reached northern Vietnam by the 17th century. The migration trend may have speeded up in this century, so that some groups are now living as far south as Thailand. The majority remains, however, in the Chinese provinces of Guangxi and Guangdong. Here Yao speakers tend to be hill farmers, while most valley rice-growers speak Chinese or Tai languages.

Though quite distinct from Chinese in their origin, Yao and Nu show very heavy Chinese influence from the centuries of symbiosis between the two languages. Many Yao speakers in China are now bilingual in Chinese. Yao and Cantonese, the Chinese language that is most widely spoken in Yao areas, show interesting similarities in their sound pattern. Both have a similar range of syllable-final consonants, *-m, -n, -ng, -p, -t, -k,* and a distinction of vowel length.

Numerals in Yao, Nu and Miao

	Yao (Mien)	Nu	Miao
1	yat	i^{1a}	i
2	yi^1	aw^1	i^1
3	po^1	pe^1	pu^1
4	$pyey^1$	pla^1	$prey^1$
5	pya^1	pru^1	pra^1
6	$\check{c}u^7$	taw^5	to^5
7	sye^6	$syong^6$	$\check{c}iong^6$
8	cet^8	yu^8	ji^8
9	do^2	caw^2	$\check{c}io^2$
10	$tsyop^8$	caw^8	ku^8

The Yao languages are highly tonal: one analysis of Nu recognises 11 tones, numbered 1 to 8 and (the highest) 1a to 3a. In Nu the numerals '9' and '10' differ only in their tone: the same is true of '1' and '2' in Miao.

Y I

SEVERAL MILLION SPEAKERS

China

With Burmese, which has had a very different history, Yi is one of the two major members of the Burmese-Lolo group of SINO-TIBETAN LANGUAGES.

Lolo is a derogatory term in Chinese, used for speakers of Yi and related languages of Yunnan: westerners used it too, often including the AKHA under this name. The less loaded, but equally unspecific, Chinese term *Yi*, 'hill people', is now preferred by Yi speakers themselves. The group of dialects to which Yi belongs has been called 'Northern Loloish' and 'Nasoid' by linguists, *Nosu* and *Mosu* being among the most common of Yi speakers' traditional names for their own people.

Yi speakers are historically a fiercely independent people. They are found in Chinese records over nearly two thousand years, and sources differ over the extent to which, even now, the 'Independent Yi' of the Cool Mountain, Liangshan in southern Sichuan, have submitted to Chinese control. Yi speakers are traditionally raiders and farmers, producing buckwheat for subsistence and opium for profit.

They distinguished, within their stratified society, 'Black Lolo' – rulers and conquerors, who belonged to the true clan structure – from 'White Lolo', serfs and the descendants of slaves, of varied origin. These again were distinct from slaves. Many slaves and White Lolo had certainly been Chinese speakers; Miao were also enslaved. Thus, in the past, the Yi language spread widely through the practice of conquest and enslavement.

Not all 'White Lolo' are of local origin. The British adventurer Donald Brooke was foolish enough to lead a party into Liangshan in 1909. He was killed, and the rest of his party was enslaved.

Nowadays, with the political and social ascendancy of Chinese, the position is probably reversed. The slaves have been freed, and Yi itself may be a shrinking language as former Yi speakers become Chinese and adopt Chinese speech. Estimates of current speakers of Yi vary from 2,000,000 to 5,500,000.

Most Yi dialects have ten vowels, three tones and a distinction of vowel register, which may be 'laryngealised' or clear. The language has borrowings from Chinese, from Pali (by way of Burmese and Shan) and a few from European languages: the word for 'soap' is Portuguese.

The numerals in Yi or Lolo script

The Yi pictographic writing system (or syllabary, as some would describe it) was used by priests, *pimu*, to record rituals and magical and medical prescriptions. It is 'the same regardless of dialect and thus predates dialect differentiation', according to David Bradley's argument: at any rate its history goes back several hundred years. Although some characters look like Chinese, it is in reality completely independent of the Chinese script. Its application varied: in some districts it was written horizontally, in some vertically like Chinese. Its range of characters varied from place to place, up to around 8,000.

Yi numerals in script

After some decades of discouragement, China's minority policy eventually permitted the adaptation of Yi script for modern uses. It has been reborn as a carefully designed true syllabary of 819 characters – but few learn it.

For the pronunciation of the numerals, see table at LAHU.

YIDDISH

PERHAPS 2,000,000 SPEAKERS

United States, Israel, Russia, Ukraine and many other countries

Yiddish is one of the GERMANIC LANGUAGES – a language closely related to GERMAN, spoken by Jews. The Yiddish language and its culture have suffered more than any other from 20th-century barbarism. About three-quarters of its speakers, well over five million people, were killed in German-occupied Europe between about 1940 and 1945.

How do we explain Yiddish as a separate, German-like language spoken over the same territory where German is spoken?

The origin of Yiddish can be traced to the Rhineland cities of Germany in the early Middle Ages – for Yiddish shows clear links to the old German dialects of the middle Rhine. From their ancient settlements here, German-speaking Jews gradually spread eastwards and south-eastwards, beginning as early as the 10th century, across a vast area of central Europe.

It has been supposed that Jews in medieval Germany initially spoke German no different from that of other inhabitants, and that Yiddish gradually became a distinct language because of the separateness, partly compulsory, of Jewish communities in medieval German cities; because of their independent culture and religion, rooted in their religious languages, Hebrew and Aramaic; and also because, as they spread eastwards across central Europe and into Russia, and as they began to leave Germany itself, Yiddish speakers were eventually no longer surrounded by German speakers.

It is not entirely a false picture: but the origins of Yiddish are more complex, and older, than this. The Jewish communities of the Rhineland were, in the 10th-century context, part of a culture region extending not eastwards into Germany but westwards across most of France; thus medieval French, as well as Aramaic, Hebrew and medieval German, had its part in earliest Yiddish, which has been aptly described (by Max Weinreich, *History of the Yiddish language*, 1980) as a 'fusion language'.

> *Yidish* is the regular equivalent, in Yiddish, of the German word *Jüdisch* 'Jewish'. The term is first found in print in 1597. Among Jews the language has, just as appropriately, been called *Taytsch*, the Yiddish equivalent of *Deutsch* 'German'. In Hebrew terms it may be regarded as the language of the *Ashkenazim*, the 'people of Ashkenazi', which is the medieval Hebrew name for Germany.

Some German words in Hebrew script are found in 12th-century Jewish manuscripts, but the first real texts in a language that can be identified as Yiddish date from the 14th century.

By the 18th century Yiddish-speaking Jewish settlements, most of them in cities, existed from eastern France and north Italy eastwards as far as the Baltic states, Ukraine, Moldavia and the Crimea. The majority, probably, was in the largely German-speaking Holy Roman Empire and Austrian Empire, but a considerable minority was to be found living under various governments to the east. Major cities of Yiddish-speaking settlement included Krakow, Wroclaw, Warsaw, Vilnius, Lvov, Chernovtsy, Odessa and Kiev.

Jews had not been allowed to settle in the old Russian Empire: however, as Russia annexed Ukraine, Belorussia, Lithuania, eastern Poland and the Khanate of the Crimea, mostly in the

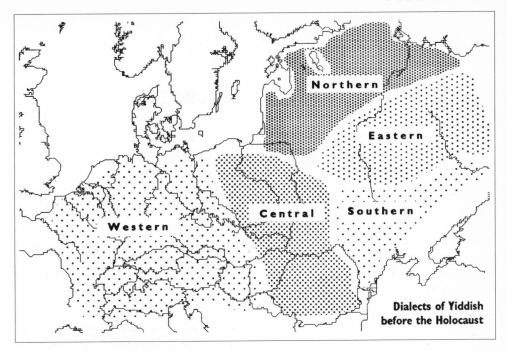

**Dialects of Yiddish
before the Holocaust**

18th century, it also annexed a large number of Jewish citizens. By the beginning of the 20th century they numbered over five million. Nearly all of these were speakers of Yiddish, and most of them lived in separate communities, in urban ghettos and rural shtetls. The Yiddish-speaking population of Belorussia was particularly large: later, in Soviet times, the Belorussian coat of arms would bear the words 'Proletarians of all countries, unite!' in Belorussian, Russian, Polish and Yiddish. Even in the 1990s there are Yiddish radio broadcasts in independent Belarus.

Yiddish literature has been of world importance only since the 18th century, when there were written the most lively and readable of all the texts that have ever been called 'mystical', the tales of Rabbi Nachman of Bratslav.

The diaspora of the 19th and 20th centuries

In the 19th century a westward migration gathered pace, speeded by increases in anti-Jewish activity. Preferred destinations were western Europe, the United States, Argentina and other Latin American countries. Already by 1900 the United States could be regarded as the centre of

Yiddish and its culture. There was, and still is, a very large Yiddish-speaking population in New York. The East End of London – Aldgate, Whitechapel, Spitalfields – was another major Yiddish-speaking community. In the early 20th century migration to Israel became an option, one that has continued to attract large numbers of Yiddish speakers.

Meanwhile, towards the end of the 19th century there was a growing awareness of Yiddish as a language. The first World Congress of Yiddish was held in Czernowitz in 1908.

Most of the German and central European speakers of Yiddish who had not emigrated were killed in the early 1940s. Very few indeed are now to be found in Germany, Poland, the Czech Republic, Slovakia or Hungary.

Most remaining Belorussian, Ukrainian and Lithuanian Jews were also killed during the German occupation of eastern Europe. Of the surviving Jews of the Soviet Union, whose numbers gradually declined through emigration and assimilation, only about a sixth declared their first language as Yiddish in the 1979 census. There are now perhaps 80,000 speakers in Russia, 80,000 in Ukraine and 10,000 in Belarus. The

'Jewish Autonomous Region' of Birobijan, established in eastern Siberia in 1934, has only about 7,000 Jewish inhabitants – though much higher estimates have been published.

Since the Second World War, the general role of Yiddish has been as the mother tongue of refugees from Jewish communities all over eastern Europe. But in this role it will not survive long. Yiddish is generally heavily discouraged in Jewish education, which favours linguistic and cultural assimilation – to Hebrew in Israel, to national languages elsewhere.

But Yiddish has a special importance as the language of fundamentalist communities of Ashkenazi Jews of eastern European origin, concentrated in New York and Israel. Their children are still brought up with Yiddish as their mother tongue, and modern Hebrew is avoided. For this community, Hebrew is the language of religious texts but Yiddish is the language of exposition and of festivity. For them, the old-established Yiddish newspapers – the weeklies *Forverts* and *Der Yid* in New York, the daily *Letste Nayes* in Israel – retain their importance.

Yiddish is almost purely German in its structure. Its vocabulary comes largely from German but also from the other languages spoken by Jews. From Hebrew come numerous terms for religious concepts and tradition. Other loans are drawn from Aramaic, from medieval French, Provençal and Italian, and from the Slavonic languages. Modern Yiddish is rich in English and Russian loanwords. In return, colloquial English borrows freely from Yiddish: *kosher, schmaltz*.

Yiddish is traditionally written in Hebrew script – the feature that most obviously distinguishes it from its close relative German. A new standardised orthography was agreed in 1937. The vowels are written fully in native German words, while loanwords from Hebrew are written with their usual Hebrew spelling in which most vowels are unmarked. A now-standard transliteration into the Latin alphabet, based on the Lithuanian pronunciation of Yiddish, is quite often used.

Yiddish must be seen now as a threatened language. It retains official status in Russia and Belarus, but has none in Israel. As linguistic assimilation proceeds it is likely to give way to Hebrew there, to Spanish in Argentina, and to English in the United States.

Yiddish happens to share with English the alternate forms *a, an* for the indefinite article: *a boym* (German *ein Baum*) 'a tree'; *an oyg* (German *ein Auge*) 'an eye'.

The pre-1945 dialects of Yiddish

After the destruction of central European Jewry in the early 1940s, the former regional dialects of Yiddish scarcely exist in their original locations. The old dialect boundaries can be linked to late medieval and early modern political and cultural frontiers; but they remained fluid and relatively insignificant in the Yiddish context, owing to continuing frequent migration, travel and intermarriage among Jewish communities.

Numerals in Yiddish		
eyns	1	אײנס
zvay	2	צװײ
drey	3	דרײַ
fir	4	פֿיר
finf	5	פֿינף
zcks	6	זעקס
zibn	7	זיבן
akht	8	אַכט
neyn	9	נײַן
tsen	10	צען

Was that a party

Oy, iz dos geven a simkhe!	Oh, was that a party!
Fish un fleysh gebrotn,	Baked fish and roast meat,
gut gefefert, feyn gezaltsn,	Well spiced, finely salted,
Punkt vi s'iz gerotn . . .	Just at its best . . .
	Refrain of a popular song

Mayrev-Yidish 'Western Yiddish' or *Oyberlendish* 'upland language', the dialect of German-speaking lands, Bohemia, northern Italy and Hungary, was already in decline by the early 20th century, because Jews in these areas – especially in Germany itself – were becoming rapidly less isolated, and preferred to adopt local standard languages.

Mizrakh-Yidish or 'Eastern Yiddish' can be regarded as a grouping of three dialects: *Polnish*, *Litvak* and *Galitzianish-Ukraynishe* Yiddish, the latter also called *Interlendish* 'lowland language'.

Yiddish alphabet: Hebrew and Latin

ו‍י ‍ײ‍ ‍ײ‍ ‍ט‍ש‍ ‍ש‍ז‍ש‍ ‍ו‍ו‍ ‍ת‍ ‍ש‍ר‍ק‍צ‍ ‍פ‍ ‍פ‍פ‍ ‍ע‍ס‍נ‍מ‍ל‍כ‍י‍י‍ח‍ז‍ו‍ה‍ד‍ג‍ב‍א‍ ‍א

a o b g d h u z t i y kh l m n s e p f ts k r sh t v zh tsh ey ay oy

---

YORUBA

20,000,000 SPEAKERS

Nigeria, Benin

Yoruba is one of the four national languages of Nigeria, alongside Hausa, Igbo and English. It belongs to the family of NIGER-CONGO LANGUAGES.

Yoruba was originally an outsiders' name for the language and people, but it has long been widely accepted. Early reports refer to *Hio*, *Eyo* and *Oyo*. *Aku* was the name given to their language by the once-influential community of speakers at Freetown, Sierra Leone. Speakers of Yoruba dialects in Benin are called *Nago* (a name used by the Fon or Ewe) or Anago or Nagot; in Togo they are called *Ana*.

The 'Defoid' languages, the immediate group to which Yoruba belongs, are spoken in adjacent parts of south-western Nigeria and Benin, and are probably long established there. Yoruba itself extends into Benin and Togo, and Yoruba traders took the language northwards and eastwards into north-eastern Ghana and the middle Niger valley.

European knowledge of Yoruba speakers and their language came late – not before the early 19th century. At that period, however, many Yoruba were already being sent to the Americas as slaves. Missionary activity began soon afterwards, with the help of freed Yoruba-speaking slaves who had resettled in Freetown. The first publications in Yoruba – brief teaching booklets – were produced by John Raban in 1830–2, but the main figure in early Yoruba literacy was the linguist Samuel Crowther, whose *Yoruba vocabulary* appeared in 1843. The centre of activity moved from Freetown to the Yoruba country around 1850; it was also about then that the

orthography of Yoruba was fixed in its modern form. *Iwe Irohin*, the first vernacular periodical printed in West Africa, appeared at Abeokuta in 1859–67.

Yoruba now has a substantial press and publishing industry. As the local language of Lagos and its hinterland its importance is likely to remain high. Standard Yoruba, much used in the media, is now known and used by speakers of many neighbouring languages, including its relatives Itsekiri and Igala.

Islam is an important religion in the Yoruba country: it came from the north, under Hausa influence, and Yoruba has borrowed many cultural words from Hausa (some originally Arabic: *fitila* 'lamp'). Modern Yoruba includes numerous English loanwords. Yoruba language and culture, shared by a high proportion of slaves of the late 18th and early 19th centuries, have been important in Brazil, Cuba and other American countries.

Yoruba origins

'All Yoruba regard the town of Ife as their place of origin and the *Oni* of Ife has been generally accepted as their ritual leader. The present royal lineages of the various Yoruba chiefdoms trace their descent from *Oduduwa* or *Odua*, the deified culture hero whom Ife mythology credits with the creation of the earth, and from whose seven grandsons the various branches of the Yoruba-speaking peoples claim descent.'

Daryll Forde, *The Yoruba-speaking peoples of southwestern Nigeria* (London: International African Institute, 1951) p. 4

Samuel Crowther

Born around 1806, brought up in Yoruba country, sold as a slave, Samuel (Ajai) Crowther was freed and settled in Freetown, Sierra Leone, where he studied at the Christian Institution in 1827. A natural linguist, he took part in the Niger Expedition of 1841–2: his *Journal of an expedition up the Niger and Tshadda rivers* was published in 1855. He studied Igbo, Tiv, Yoruba and other languages of Nigeria, wrote and translated in several of them, and was the first Christian bishop of West African origin. He died in 1891.

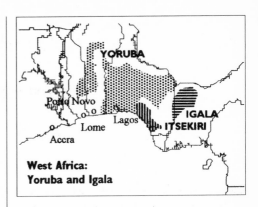

West Africa:
Yoruba and Igala

Yoruba has three level tones, high, mid and low. There are no falling or rising tones. The first twenty numerals are *òkàn, méjì, mẹ́tà, mẹ́rìn, màrún, mẹ̀fà, mèje, mejo, mẹ̀sán, mẹ̀wá; mọ̀kànlá, mejìlá, mẹ́tàlá, mẹ́rinlá, màrúnlá, mẹ́rindílógún, mẹ́tàdílógún, méjìdílógún, mọ̀kàndílógún, ogún*. The numerals from sixteen to twenty are 'counted down' – 'four less than twenty', 'three less than twenty', and so on.

Dialects of Yoruba

Standard Yoruba, close but not identical to the dialect of Oyo, is used in schools, in literature and in contacts between speakers of different dialects. Yoruba dialects extend into Benin and Togo. In Benin the language is called *Nago*, in Togo *Ana*.

Itsekiri or Isekiri or Jekri, with half a million speakers around Warri and Sapele, is sometimes considered a dialect of Yoruba. It is heavily influenced by EDO.

Igala, another member of the Defoid group, has 800,000 speakers.

It is dark

Ailẹ́lẹ́, igi oko parere;	It is dark: the trees in the farm are silent;
akọpẹ ẹruju ko ma kiyesi igba . . .	One who taps palm-wine must look to his climbing rope.

Two oracular lines from *Sixteen cowries: Yoruba divination from Africa to the New World*
ed. William Bascom (Bloomington: Indiana University Press, 1980) pp. 116–17

YUCATEC

500,000 SPEAKERS

Mexico, Belize

One of the MAYAN LANGUAGES (see map and table of numerals there), Yucatec is sometimes called *Maya*, for this is the language of Yucatán, and thus one of the languages directly associated with the monuments of Maya civilisation.

> The first Spanish expedition to this region, in 1517, took two Indians prisoner and renamed them Melchior and Julian. The Governor of New Spain understood the Indians to be saying that their country was called 'Yucatán'. In fact they were saying that they grew *yuca*, 'cassava', to make bread.

Maya culture was in fact multilingual. Over more than two thousand years, Mayan speech had spread northwards and north-westwards from the Guatemalan highlands into the lowlands of south-eastern Mexico. It had already diverged into languages: Tzeltal, Tzotzil, Chontal, Chol and – rather different from these – Yucatec. As lowland Maya culture flowered, between 100 BC and AD 950, these languages were influenced more and more by one another.

> Melchior and Julian, Yucatec speakers, were easily able to make themselves understood in the Tabasco district, where the local language was Chontal but Yucatec was well known. They were the Spaniards' first interpreters on the mainland of Mexico – along with a Carib woman from Jamaica who had been shipwrecked off Yucatan and had learnt the language of her new home.

The Lowland Maya languages were also heavily influenced by the language of the Olmecs, bearers of an older civilisation in central Mexico.

The Olmec language has not been deciphered, but it is clear that it belonged to the Mixe-Zoque group: one reason for believing this is that so many Mixe-Zoque loanwords of all kinds are to be found in Yucatec and other Mayan languages. The word for 'rabbit' was borrowed into Yucatec from Olmec (proto-Mixe-Zoque *kaya* 'rabbit') not because of the everyday importance of rabbits, but because it was a calendrical term: the Mexican calendar was shared and adopted among many cultures, remaining generally the responsibility of a priestly caste. Other Yucatec borrowings from Mixe-Zoque include pMZ *pom* 'incense', *cima* 'calabash', *kakawa* 'cacao' (see box), *kuku* 'turtle-dove'.

Yucatec also borrowed terms from other Mexican languages, including Zapotec (*pi'kku* 'dog' and *mani* 'deer') and Nahuatl. In its turn, Yucatec or another Mayan language has transmitted culture terms to languages of further south: for example, Mayan *cjenek'* 'bean' is to be found in Xinca, Lenca and Jicaque.

Yucatec is first recorded – in short texts of historical and religious significance – in hieroglyphic stone inscriptions on Maya sculptures and buildings from the pre-Columbian period. The same hieroglyphic script was later used to write book texts, on long strips of bark paper, folded concertina fashion. Three, *Codex Dresden*, *Codex Madrid* and *Codex Paris*, written in the 14th or 15th centuries, survive to this day.

More traditional Yucatec literature was written down, in the three centuries that followed the Spanish conquest of Mexico, in the Latin alphabet that the Spaniards had introduced. The so-called *Books of Chilam Balam* are the greatest Yucatec texts. Chilam Balam was said to have lived in the city of Mani before the Spaniards came, and to have prophesied a new religion. Copies of the *Book* – whatever its original form – appear to have been taken to various priestly centres, and in each place local additions were made. The *Books* that now survive include Spanish texts translated into Yucatec, as well as the history of Maya migrations and conquests, time charts and calendars, prophecy, ritual, astrology and medicine. Equally compelling is the *Book of the Songs of Dzitbalché*, an 18th-century manuscript, containing lyric poetry and prayers: notable are two long poems or liturgies narrating the sacrifice of a captive.

Maya hieroglyphs

Central American hieroglyphic writing reached its highest elaboration among the Maya. Recent research, following a breakthrough in the 1950s by Yuri V. Knorosov, has shown that the language could be fully written in a partly phonetic, partly ideographic system. Earlier specialists, such as Eric Thompson, had believed that many short Maya inscriptions on dishes and bowls were meaningless decoration. They are now known to include dedications, artistic information, and even 'recipes'. The first recipe to be deciphered was that for cacao – drinking chocolate.

David Stuart showed that this consists of a drawing of a fish, preceded by a comb-like sign, the syllable *ka-*, and followed by *-w*. The fish symbol turned out to be another version of the comb (the comb is really a fish's fin) so that he was able to read the whole word as *ka-ka-w* 'cacao'.

After Sophie and Michael Coe,
The true history of chocolate (New York:
Thames and Hudson, 1996)

ZANDE

1,200,000 SPEAKERS

Congo (Kinshasa), Central African Republic, Sudan

Zande is one of the most easterly of the Ubangi group of NIGER-CONGO LANGUAGES.

Zande is the name of the language. *Azande*, with the plural *a-* prefix, is the name of the people.

Zande, BANDA, GBAYA and Ngbandi (ancestor of SANGO) are believed to have come to the southwestern Sudan and Central African Republic as a result of a migration from the west, over three thousand years ago. The early speakers of Zande, the Avongura, were to be found mostly in Sudan until the 18th century.

The warlike Avongura then moved southeastwards and invaded the country between the Uele and Mbomu rivers around 1800, eventually conquering all the land from Bangassou (now in the Central African Republic) eastwards to Maridi (Sudan). Although they cannot have been more than a small minority over this huge area, their language, now called Zande, soon became dominant. Succeeding generations of conquered peoples began to consider it their mother tongue and to consider themselves to be Azande.

The Azande attracted 19th-century Arabic-speaking slave traders but retained some political unity until eventually conquered by the French, Egyptians and British after 1899. Their lands were carved up by the colonial powers. The language remains widely spoken, though over a sparsely populated country (see map at SANGO).

Zande is a tonal language – the two tone levels can also be heard on the slit drum, *gugu*, traditionally used for signalling. In its many verb tenses, formed by infixes between the personal prefix and the verb root, Zande resembles Bantu languages. There are four noun genders: masculine, feminine, animal and inanimate.

Arabic influence is demonstrated in loanwords – including *babur* 'steamboat', itself an Arabic loan from French *vapeur*.

The first ten numerals in Zande are: *sa, ue, biata, biama, bisue, bisue bati sa, bisue bati ue, bisue bati biata, bisue bati biama, bawe*.

Two proverbs

Kperende na kpari tiru na sueru

The cricket could cry for itself with its wings
[I can manage by myself]

Badia gbuku na dika ko ku gira rago

It was the owl's friend who kept him back till sunrise
[Choose your companions carefully]

E. C. Gore, *A Zande grammar* (London: Sheldon Press, 1926)

ZAPOTEC

PERHAPS 450,000 SPEAKERS

Mexico

Zapotec is one of the Otomanguean family of AMERIND LANGUAGES, like MIXTEC (see map there). It is many centuries since Zapotec was the speech of a single political entity – if it ever was – and Zapotec is now a group of dialects, some of which are so different that they are not mutually intelligible.

The historic centre of Zapotec culture and language was the hilltop site of Monte Albán, above Oaxaca. Its heyday was AD 600 to 900, but the culture can be traced back with no significant break to 1200 BC. In the later pre-Spanish period, Mixtec speakers expanded eastwards, driving the Zapotec from Monte Albán and its neighbourhood.

The Zapotec, in turn, spread eastwards: for example, it is clear that the speakers of 'Isthmus Zapotec' migrated, not long before the Spanish arrival, from the Zaachila district (south-west of Oaxaca) to the Isthmus of Tehuantepec. According to glottochronology, the controversial statistical technique that attempts to measure the chronological distance between languages, the split between Zaachila Zapotec and Isthmus Zapotec took place 560 years ago.

Earlier Monte Albán inscriptions already show the existence of a writing system. The ritual calendar, of 260 days, stands out as clearly identifiable: the day signs in the script can be identified from their shapes. There are many short inscriptions on various subjects, not yet fully identified: signs include human and animal heads and hands. Details of dress, in the figures depicted in the pictographs, seem to be important.

Among later inscriptions, the typical ones consist of four phrases: an upside-down human head with death-eyes and with detailed, varying head-dress; a 'mountain' with details on it; dates, which can be fully deciphered; and a fourth phrase, seemingly more miscellaneous. Alfonso Caso, who has worked on these texts, suggests that they are reports of conquests.

By contrast with Nahuatl and Mixtec, there are no early Zapotec manuscripts using the pictographs. So no direct help is available for those who try to decipher the Monte Albán pictographic inscriptions. The first Zapotec grammar, written in Latin script, was by J. de Córdova: entitled *Arte de la lengua zapoteca*, it appeared in 1578.

The importance of Zapotec civilisation in the Mexican context is demonstrated by the existence of Zapotec loanwords in Yucatec (Zapotec *pi'kku'* 'dog' and *mani'* 'horse, originally deer') and Huastec (Zapotec *pi'kku'* 'dog', *piçjinja* 'deer, large animal', *taa* 'woven mat', *pisjiicju* 'coatimundi'.

ZHUANG

PERHAPS 11,000,000 SPEAKERS

China, Vietnam

Zhuang is the name for two neighbouring TAI LANGUAGES. The Zhuang count as China's largest minority group, with a population of 13,300,000 (but many of them, probably, speak Chinese rather than Zhuang). Zhuang is officially considered one of the 'major minority' languages of China, alongside Tibetan, Mongolian, Uighur and Korean. Why has hardly anyone outside China heard of it?

The answer is that Zhuang have not, historically, been anxious to project a distinct ethnic identity. They wanted to be Chinese – and Chinese they have largely become.

The older transliteration of the name is *Chuang*. I have also seen *Juang*. The language and its speakers have in the past been called *T'u-jen*, 'people of the soil'.

Southern China is the region from which, it is now supposed, Thai languages originally spread. Thus it is likely that dialects ancestral to Zhuang have been spoken here for over a thousand years, and probably for much longer than that.

Most Zhuang speakers have been bilingual in Chinese for two generations or more. Many have family names which could be argued to be Chinese, and have developed Chinese family histories to go with them. They have continued to speak Zhuang at home and in their own rural communities. Under the Nationalist government this inconveniently large linguistic minority was studiously ignored. Communist China has followed precisely the opposite policy. The large Guangxi Zhuang Autonomous Region was created in 1958, and a Latin orthography was devised in which

books and magazines are regularly published (most of them translations from Chinese). Local radio stations broadcast in Zhuang, and films are dubbed in the language. What was once a little-known language is now widely seen in print, and much studied by Chinese linguists.

Until these recent changes the only way of writing Zhuang was in a local modified form of the Chinese script. This is at least as old as the 18th century, the date of the earliest preserved specimen: how much further it may go back is unknown, but it did spread widely, a similar system being known in THO. It was not used in print, but only for personal notes, trade accounts and letters. There was no standardisation, and it would be difficult to read a text by an unknown writer: 'Zhuang texts are often a farrago of nonce creations and individual and regional variations' (Ramsey). If Zhuang speakers wrote for general information, they wrote in Chinese. The most widespread use of this older Zhuang script was, however, to record the texts of Zhuang songs – here the exact sounds had to be transmitted, so simply writing in Chinese would not do.

The northern and southern dialect groups of Zhuang are so different from one another that they are considered to be two separate languages. Northern Zhuang has six tones in open syllables, two in closed syllables (those ending in -p, -t, -k). Like Chinese, Zhuang is essentially a monosyllabic language. For a table of numerals see TAI LANGUAGES.

Based on S. Robert Ramsey, *The languages of China* (Princeton: Princeton University Press, 1987) pp. 234–43 and other sources

Central and Northern Tai languages

In one accepted classification, Buyi and Northern Zhuang are Northern Tai languages; Southern Zhuang and Tho, with some minor languages, are Central Tai.

BUYI is spoken by a minority population of over 2,000,000 in south-western Guizhou province and around the city of Guiyang. There are a few Buyi-speaking communities in Yunnan, and similar dialects (*Dioi, Giay, Yay*) have been found in Vietnam and Laos.

Northern Zhuang, with perhaps 7,000,000 speakers, includes the dialect of *Wuming*, in central Guangxi, on which standard written and broadcast Zhuang is now based.

Southern Zhuang, with perhaps 4,000,000 speakers, consists of the Tai dialects of south-western Guangxi, close to the Vietnamese border. *Nung, Nung-an* and *Lungchow* are names that linguists have given in the past to varieties of southern Zhuang: 'Nung' is parti-

South-East Asia: Central and Northern Tai languages

cularly used of the language as spoken in northern Vietnam, where its speakers form an official nationality.

THO is the major Tai language of the northern border regions of Vietnam, where there are about 1,000,000 speakers, forming an official nationality of Vietnam.

ZULU

8,800,000 SPEAKERS

South Africa, Lesotho

One of the BANTU LANGUAGES, Zulu is spoken by the largest language community of South Africa. There are also 200,000 speakers in Lesotho.

> Some linguists prefer the prefixed form *isi-Zulu*, literally 'Zulu in language or culture'.
>
> The language group that includes Zulu, Xhosa, Ndebele and Swazi was once called *Kaffir*, Portuguese *Caffre*, a vague word that sometimes denoted all the Bantu languages of southern Africa (it is the Arabic word for 'pagan'). Zulu itself was sometimes called *Zulu-Kaffir*. The group is now usually named *Nguni*, a modern reapplication of a term that once denoted a single constituent element within the Zulu-speaking population. Customarily the variant form *Ngoni* is used for the people who migrated northwards (see map) in the mid 19th century.

It is likely that speakers of languages ancestral to these modern ones were already in Natal in the 9th century, the likely date of the earliest settlements found by archaeologists that are typical of modern 'Nguni' peoples – a central cattle byre surrounded by a row of huts. This marks the beginning of the Later Iron Age in southern Africa.

By the 19th century Nguni language speakers were politically dominant over much of modern South Africa, and at times well beyond its modern borders. Sotho, Pedi (Northern Sotho) and Kgatla (Tswana) speakers had come to share the typical cattle-keeping culture of the Nguni. Parallel with this development, Nguni influence can be traced on their languages.

Zulu had previously been influenced in its turn. Its click consonants originate in loanwords from Khoe or some other KHOISAN language, evidently the result of deep and long-lasting interaction with its speakers. Pastoralism and an associated cattle cult were clearly shared between the two language groups: Zulu words for 'cow', 'sheep' and 'milk' are Khoisan in origin. Seventeen consonants were added to Zulu in the course of this interaction. Zulu (like Xhosa) now has a sound pattern that is most unusual for a Bantu language. In Zulu spelling the three clicks borrowed from Khoisan languages appear as *c* (dental), *q* (palatal), *x* (lateral).

The Zulu empire of Shaka, and the great upheavals of that time, mark a break between earlier and later identifications of peoples – and therefore of languages – in what is now South Africa. Before Shaka's time, the 'Zulu' were simply one clan among many. After the *difaqane* 'forced migrations' of the 1820s and 1830s, the rebellions and famines and population movements in what is now eastern South Africa, a new linguistic map begins to emerge.

Two contemporaries, the Wesleyan John Appleyard and the American missionary Lewis Grout, were the first to make linguistic comparisons of the languages now called Nguni. Grout's work appeared in a paper in volume 1 of the *Journal of the Oriental Society* in 1849: he was also the author of a detailed grammar of Zulu published in 1859.

Both Zulu and Xhosa are official languages in South Africa, and there is television and radio broadcasting in these languages. For the *hlonipha*, the women's 'avoidance language' of Zulu, and for Zulu numerals, see boxes at XHOSA.

Southern Africa:
the Nguni languages

Language of white rule

In the late 19th century a pidgin form of Zulu developed in which Europeans and Indians were able to communicate with Africans. Originating along the Natal coast, 'Fanakalo' spread as far as Rhodesia (modern Zambia and Zimbabwe) with the pioneers who founded Salisbury (Harare) in 1890.

As the mines of the Witwatersrand developed and drew labour from as far away as Malawi and Tanzania, Fanakalo became the lingua franca among migrant workers of different mother tongues, as well as the language of communication between bosses and workers. Employers held classes to teach it formally to new arrivals; but its use is now in steep decline. In the early 20th century it played the same role in the mines of

Zambia and Shaba. There it has now been replaced as an informal lingua franca by Town BEMBA or has given way to SWAHILI, languages which have now no overtones of African subjection.

Enza fana-ga-lo, 'do it like this', was how a master began his instructions to a servant. But this language had many forms and names: *Kitchen Kafir*, as used between mistress and cook; *Garden Kafir; Mine Kafir* as the working language in the gold and diamond mines; *Pidgin Bantu; Basic Bantu*. Africans often called it *silungu-boi*, from Zulu *isilungu* 'white language' and English *boy* 'servant', or else *isilololo*, the 'lo-lo-lo language' because *lo* 'the, this, that' is heard so often in it. In Zambia, it has been called *cikabanga*.

About three-quarters of the words of Fanakalo are Zulu, and about a fifth are English.

Some linguists once thought that Fanakalo would grow into a creole and become the majority language of the black population of South Africa. With hindsight, this was never likely. It was too closely identified with a set of social circumstances: it was the servant-to-master, employee-to-employer language. It was the whites who stuck to Fanakalo so tenaciously: some of them thought it insolent for blacks to use English. Despised by the Africans who used it, Fanakalo never became anybody's mother tongue.

The Nguni languages

Zulu, XHOSA, SWAZI and Southern NDEBELE form a dialect continuum and a close-knit subgroup within the South-eastern group of Bantu. The subgroup is usually known as *Nguni*. *Southern* or *Transvaal Ndebele* has 800,000 speakers. *Swazi* has 1,500,000 speakers in South Africa and Swaziland. *Xhosa* has 6,900,000 speakers in South Africa.

The peoples called *Ngoni*, now to be found in Mozambique, Malawi, Zambia and Tanzania, originate from a series of epic migrations northwards in the 1820s by Zulu and other Nguni warriors looking for freedom from the rule of Shaka. As they travelled they found young men to incorporate in their 'army', and many married local women: thus, even as they settled and (by 1850) founded petty kingdoms, their language was usually on the way to obsolescence – though it lasted long enough to help European explorers, such as David Livingstone, to make themselves understood in the course of very long journeys in south-eastern Africa. In these regions the spoken languages now are TSONGA, TUMBUKA, Nsenga, NYANJA, Nyakyusa, Ngonde and YAO. The true Ngoni or Zulu language does not survive there (except, it is said, in ritual use among Tumbuka- and Nsenga-speaking Ngoni).

The exception is *Northern Ndebele*. This language survived and spread, now numbering 750,000 speakers around Bulawayo in Zimbabwe.

The overtones of Fanakalo

'The "blacks" have to learn it from the "whites" or from their servants – often a somewhat painful process. It is not surprising, therefore, that amongst Africans it is now regarded as a slave-driving jargon, while to many Europeans it is a means of "keeping the Kafir in his place". It denies Africans their tribal status while refusing to admit that they are fit to speak English or Afrikaans.'

Irvine Richardson, 'Some observations on the status of Town Bemba' in *African language studies* vol. 2 (1961) pp. 25–36

English loanwords and Zulu noun prefixes

The TSONGA word *xitimela* looks a Bantu word, with a class 7 prefix, yet it is a loan from English *steamer* via Zulu. English and Afrikaans words with initial *s* + consonant are invariably remorphologized and assigned to the seventh class in Zulu, e.g. *isitolo* 'store', *isipunu* 'spoon', *isipinashi* 'spinach', *isipanji* 'sponge'. When travelling northwards into other Bantu languages, these words retained their allegiance to the seventh noun class, and changed the prefix according to the prevailing sound laws, so that the SHONA word for 'store' became *chitoro*, no longer recognizable as an English word.

Jan Knappert, 'Contribution from the study of loanwords to the cultural history of Africa' in D. Dalby and others, *Language and history in Africa* (London: Cass, 1970) pp. 78–88, abridged

---

Iscamtho

Zulu Yini u-zonda izi-nsizwa na?
Iscamtho Why u-zunda ama-jents?

'Why do you hate young men?'
Jents is borrowed from English *gents*.

Iscamtho, language of rebellion

A jargon of urban youth in the black communities of the Johannesburg region, Iscamtho has grown out of *Shalambombo*, the criminal argot of two gang networks, the mainly Zulu amaLaita and the Sotho amaRussia, both of which operated in Johannesburg between 1890 and the 1930s. There are both Zulu-based and Sotho-based versions of the language. It first became established in the largely Zulu squatter communities of Orlando and Pimville, and the Sotho-speaking Eastern Native Township, Newclare and Moroka Emergency Camp.

Iscamtho is a mixture of Zulu and Sotho, in varying proportions, with English and other languages. In comparison with its Bantu originals it is characterised by vowel loss: *iskule* for Zulu *isikule* 'school'; *Iscamtho*, the language name, for what in Zulu would have been *isiqamtho*, derived from the verb *ukuqamunda* 'talk volubly'.

Among some groups Iscamtho has become an essential marker of status and of masculinity. Fewer women than men use it: those women who do, risk being seen as *isfebe* 'prostitutes' or *i-tiye* 'tea, i.e. shared refreshment'. Iscamtho tends to carry greater prestige than the AFRIKAANS-based Tsotsitaal.

Based on papers by D. K. Ntshangase and others in *Language and social history: studies in South African sociolinguistics* ed. Rajend Mesthrie (Cape Town: David Philip, 1995) with other sources

Glossary

The facts of language are hard to pin into definitions. The words 'typically', 'usually' should be read into many of the definitions below. Examples in this glossary, unless otherwise stated, are English words or sounds.

accent: may be used to denote a *dialect* that only differs from one's own in its sound pattern (a 'British accent', a 'West Country accent'). May also be used for symbols that modify letters of the alphabet (thus *é* may be called 'e with an acute accent'): the technical term for these symbols is *diacritical mark*

accusative: in languages in which nouns have alternative forms (*cases*) depending on their function in the sentence, this is a name for the form that serves as the *object*

affix: a *prefix* or *suffix*

agglutinative: a type of language in which verbs and nouns have a sequence of separately identifiable affixes marking their relationship to one another within a sentence. See *typology* and, for more information, ALTAIC LANGUAGES

alphabet: a form of writing based on the principle of a single sign for each successive distinct sound or *phoneme* of a language. Some people define the scripts of AMHARIC, HINDI and KOREAN (and their relatives) as *syllabaries*, because in them each syllable forms a block. They are more often classed as alphabets, because symbols for each phoneme can be identified within the block

alveolar: a consonant formed by the alveolar ridge and the tip of the tongue (for example, *t, d*)

augmentative: a word with an affix indicating largeness, importance

back vowels: formed at the back of the mouth (for example, *o, u*)

bilingual: a bilingual person can communicate in two languages with equal facility; a bilingual text is written in two languages to be read by speakers of either

calque: a word or phrase built on the model of one in another language (for example, French *gratte-ciel* for skyscraper)

case: a series of alternative forms of a noun serving to mark its function within a sentence. Different names have been chosen by grammarians working on different languages, but *nominative*, *accusative* and *possessive* often occur

compound: a word formed from two or more separately identifiable words (*birdsong*)

concord: marking of more than one word in a sentence, in a pattern that depends on their relationship with one another. See KONGO for more information

consonant: in spoken language, *vowels* alternate with consonants or consonant groups. Consonants are the sounds formed by the momentary narrowing or stopping of the air stream

creole: a language of mixed origins (such as a *pidgin*) which has begun to be used as a *mother tongue*

dental: a consonant formed by the teeth and the tip of the tongue (for example, the sound *th*)

diacritical mark: a symbol (or 'accent') used to modify the letters of an alphabet

dialect: local, relatively uniform, varieties of speech. 'A group of dialects that are mutually comprehensible' is one definition of a *language*

diminutive: a word with an affix indicating smallness, unimportance

diphthong: a vowel whose pronunciation begins at one position in the mouth and ends at another (*eye, oh, I* are among English words that consist of single diphthongs)

family: a grouping of languages descended from a single earlier language. In this book, *family* is used for the largest such groupings that can be demonstrated; *branch*, *group*, *sub-group* are used for subdivisions of these. For very large groupings the terms *stock* and *phylum* have been adopted by some linguists

feminine: see *gender*

fricative: a consonant creating turbulence but not stopping the air stream (for example, *f, v, th, sh*)

front vowels: formed at the front of the mouth (*e, i*)

fusional: a type of language in which words mark their relationship to one another within a sentence by regular modifications which cannot be identified as units separate from the word root. See *typology* and, for more information, ALTAIC LANGUAGES

future: a verb *tense* marking the action as taking place in the future

gender: in many languages, nouns are grouped into two or more *noun classes* which show some parallelism with the male/female classification that we apply to human beings and to animals. This kind of grammatical classification is called 'gender': the most commonly named classes are *masculine, feminine, neuter*

genetic relationship: languages which can be shown to have differentiated from the same earlier language are said to be *related*. In linguistic terms this is often called a genetic relationship, though it has nothing to do with genes and human relationships

glottochronology: calculation of the elapsed time since two languages diverged, by counting the number of words in a standard list that are still in use in both. The technique has not been shown to work accurately

grammar: the set of rules, adopted more or less unconsciously by any speaker, that produces sentences in a particular language

guṇa: in *fusional* languages, a modification made to the vowel of a word root, in order to form a derived word, may be called by the Sanskrit grammarians' name 'guṇa'. The name for a second modification of the same vowel is *vṛddhi*. An example from Sanskrit: root *vid-* 'know', guṇa form *veda* 'knowledge, lore',

vṛddhi form *vaidya* 'one who knows, doctor'. See also MARATHI

ideographic script: a writing system based on the principle of a single sign ('ideogram') for each successive idea – this may mean, roughly but not exactly, one sign per word

infinitive: a verb form which is undefined as to *person* and *number*

intransitive: a verb which, when it forms part of a sentence, has no specified *object*

isolate: a language which cannot be shown to belong to any *family*

isolating: a type of language in which words do not have alternate forms marking their relationship within a sentence. Typically, such relationships are indicated instead by the order of words in the sentence. See *typology*

labial: a consonant formed at the lips (for example, *p, b, f, v, w*)

language: may be defined as a group of *dialects* that are mutually comprehensible; may also mean a *standard language* that is more widely understood and accepted than any local dialect

lingua franca: a language used for communication among speakers of several different mother tongues, often in the course of long distance travel and trade. The original Lingua Franca was used in the harbours and seaways of the medieval Mediterranean (see ROMANCE LANGUAGES)

living language: a language which is still used for everyday communication, or which some people still living learnt as their *mother tongue*

loanword: a word borrowed from another language

logogram: a written word borrowed as a whole into the writing system of another language. Some SUMERIAN logograms were borrowed into AKKADIAN and HITTITE writing: the result is that decipherers do not know the Akkadian and Hittite pronunciation for those words. The curly E is a logogram in English: it is the initial letter of Latin *libra*, but it is read as *pound*

masculine: see *gender*

monolingual: able to communicate in one language only

mood: marking of a verb to indicate the certainty or otherwise of the activity that it denotes. In English, words such as *may*, *might*, *would* are used for this purpose

mother *tongue*: the dialect or language that a child learns first

multilingual: able to communicate in many languages

national *language*: a language that is widely used for communication within a nation state. Its status may be defined legally as 'national language' or '*official language*'. Some governments draw a distinction between these two concepts, but this book does not

neuter: neither masculine nor feminine. See *gender*

nominative: in languages in which nouns have alternative forms (*cases*) depending on their function in the sentence, this is the usual name for the form that serves as the *subject*

noun: a word denoting an object or concept; see *part of speech*

noun *classes*: groupings that regulate the forms of nouns and the forms taken by other words to which these nouns are attached in a sentence. *Gender* is one type of noun classification. Bantu languages (for examples see LOZI and LUBA) have elaborate noun class systems

number: marking, typically of verbs and nouns, to indicate the number of items to which they refer. See *singular* and *plural*

object: in *syntax*, the recipient of the activity that is denoted by a *transitive* verb. For an example see box at OCCITAN

official *language*: a language which may be used in official contexts, such as parliaments, courts, schools and government offices. Its status is usually defined legally as 'official language' or '*national language*'. Some governments draw a distinction between these two concepts, but this book does not

parts *of speech*: a classification of words according to their potential functions in any sentence. The classification may vary from language to language but will include *verbs* and *nouns*

past: a verb *tense* marking the action as having already taken place

person: marking, typically of a verb, to indicate the speaker's relationship to it. In the grammar of most European languages, distinctions are made that identify at least *first person singular* ('I', the speaker is the subject), *first person plural* ('we', the speaker belongs to the group that is the subject), *second person* ('you', the speaker is addressing the subject), *third person* ('he, she, it, they', the subject is neither speaking nor being addressed)

phonemes: the distinctive sounds of which the sound pattern of any language is made up

phylum: see *family*

pidgin: a simplified language developed in regular limited contact between people of different mother tongues, and combining elements from these

plural: in languages in which a grammatical distinction of *number* is marked, the usual distinction is between *singular* (one) and plural (more than one). English makes this distinction: *dog* (singular); *dogs* (plural)

possessive: in languages in which nouns have alternative forms (*cases*) depending on their function in the sentence, this is the usual name for the form that denotes a possessor or owner. In English, nouns have possessive cases, singular and plural; they sound identical but the distinction is marked by the position of an apostrophe: *the dog's bowl* (the bowl belongs to one dog); *the dogs' bowl* (the bowl belongs to more than one dog)

prefix: an addition to the *root* or stem, at the beginning of a word

present: a verb *tense* marking the action as taking place at the moment of speech

proto-*language*: a language postulated as the ancestor of one or more groups of later languages: thus proto-Indo-European is defined as the early language from which all the modern INDO-EUROPEAN LANGUAGES have descended. Often there is no other evidence for a proto-language than the modern languages themselves; it can be reconstructed, up to a point, by comparing the modern forms

reconstruction: words and forms of an earlier language can be reconstructed by comparing the later languages that descend from it. In linguists' jargon, such reconstructions are called 'starred forms' because they are marked with an asterisk to indicate that there is no textual evidence for them

related: see *genetic relationship*

retroflex: a consonant formed by turning the tip of the tongue upwards

root: the basic form of a word from which other forms derive. The concept applies to word forms in *agglutinative* and *fusional* languages but not in *isolating* languages. See AFROASIATIC LANGUAGES for more information

rounded: a sound formed by rounding the lips (for example, *o*, *u*, and German *ö*, *ü*)

rule: the elements that make up the grammar of a language

script: a writing system – an *alphabet*, *syllabary* or *ideographic script*

sign languages: of all the languages not dealt with in this book, sign languages are perhaps the most significant culturally. Their principal use is for communication among those unable to speak or to hear speech. Their grammar has a complexity similar to that of spoken languages, and they change historically in similar ways

singular: in languages in which a grammatical distinction of *number* is marked, the usual distinction is between singular (one) and plural (more than one). See example at *plural*

sociolect: a variety of a language that is typical not of a geographical region (see *dialect*) but of a social class or group

standard *language*: the variety or *dialect* of a language that is generally accepted in formal speech and in the media, and is usually taught in schools

stock: see *family*

stop: a consonant formed by blocking the air stream momentarily (for example, *p*, *b*, *t*, *d*, *ch*, *k*, *g*)

subject: in *syntax*, the performer of the activity that is denoted by the *verb*. For an example see box at OCCITAN

suffix: an addition to the *root* or stem, at the end of a word

syllabary: a form of writing based on the principle of a sign for each successive syllable of a language

syllable: the unit of sound formed by a vowel,

any preceding consonants, and sometimes following consonants

syntax: study and description of the structure of sentences

tense: the traditional grammatical term for verb markings to indicate the time, relative to the moment of speech, at which the activity takes place. In many languages, *past*, *present* and *future* tenses are distinguished, but the detailed use of tenses varies a great deal from one language to another

tonal: a language in which *tones* are essential constituents of the sound pattern of each word

tone: the relative pitch and sound quality of vowels

transitive: a verb which, when it forms part of a grammatical sentence, has a specified *object*

typology: a classification of languages depending on whether alternate forms of words are used to mark relationships within a sentence. The three classes are *isolating*, *fusional* and *agglutinative*. For more information see ALTAIC LANGUAGES

unrounded: a sound formed without rounding the lips (for example, *a*, *e*, *i*)

unvoiced: a sound spoken without vibration of the vocal cords. In English, *p t k f sh ch h* are unvoiced

velar: a consonant formed between the velum and the back of the tongue (for example, *k*, *g*)

verb: in *syntax* and as a *part of speech*, a verb denotes an activity, and may define the relation of other words in the sentence to that activity

voiced: a sound spoken with vibration of the vocal cords. In English, *b d g v z r w y* and all vowels are voiced

vowel: in spoken language, vowels alternate with *consonants* or consonant groups. Vowels are the continuous sounds formed when the air stream is open; they are differentiated by the shaping of the mouth and lips

vowel *harmony*: a rule existing in many languages by which vowels within a word must resemble one another, for example being all *front* or all *back* vowels, all *rounded* or all *unrounded*

vṛddhi: see *guṇa*

Index

Acknowledgements

First of all, I am grateful to the authors whose explanations and examples have been quoted throughout, either because they help to demonstrate a special feature of the language under discussion, or because they relate to themes which emerge from the book as a whole – the multiple social uses of language and oral literature, and the complex ways in which languages have interacted with one another. I am also grateful to Gamma Productions, Vijay K. Patel and other makers of TrueType fonts used in the alphabet tables. The maps are based on outline maps produced by a shareware program, Clpmap, developed by W. W. Mayfield, 23219 Audrey Avenue, Torrance, California 90505.

The London Goodenough Trust for Overseas Graduates and the Institute of Linguists gave me the impulse to begin the *Dictionary of Languages*. Maureen, Elizabeth and Rachel excused me many hours of neglect as I worked on from Abkhaz to Zulu. It was a struggle to mould a shapeless text into a shapely reference book: somehow, Sarah Prest and others at Bloomsbury Publishing managed it.